SOCIAL PROCESSES

Social Processes

An Introduction to Sociology

TAMOTSU SHIBUTANI

University of California Press
BERKELEY LOS ANGELES LONDON

University of California Press
Berkeley and Los Angeles, California

University of California Press, Ltd.
London, England

© 1986 by
The Regents of the University of California

Library of Congress Cataloging-in-Publication Data

Shibutani, Tamotsu, 1920–
   Social processes.

   Includes bibliography and index.
   1. Sociology. I. Title.
HM51.S519   1986   301   85–20846
ISBN 0–520–05050–9 (alk. paper)
ISBN 0–520–05056–8 (pbk. : alk. paper)

Printed in the United States of America

1   2   3   4   5   6   7   8   9

Contents

PART THREE.   TRANSITIONAL PROCESSES

Preface

Those who turn to the study of sociology for the first time, whether they are college students or general readers, do so to develop a better understanding of their society. They expect to form some kind of working orientation toward the events in which they become involved as well as those reported daily in the news. Such expectations are not unreasonable. After all, if they cannot derive that much from their inquiry, what is the point of studying the subject? After three decades of teaching undergraduate sociology courses, I have concluded that the types of structural analysis that prevailed in mid-twentieth-century sociology are simply not adequate for this purpose. Although they are useful for studying organized groups, serious deficiencies become apparent when one attempts to study social change and intergroup conflict.

But we live in a world marked by rapid and continuous change — one filled with uncertainty, confusion, and turmoil. Why are decent young men transformed into beasts when they become involved in mob violence? Why do bureaucracies perpetuate ineffectual programs in callous disregard for their clients? Why do revolutionaries squabble so viciously among themselves after they have succeeded in deposing a hated ruler? Why are human beings unable to correct glaring and acknowledged defects until after some catastrophe has occurred? Such questions are difficult to answer, even tentatively, from the standpoint of structural sociology. I have therefore tried to organize selected findings in sociology and some related disciplines in terms of another conceptual framework — one that views human society as an ongoing process. This approach makes possible the study of stable patterns, transformations, and conflicts from a single, consistent perspective and thereby makes sociology a more effective tool for comprehending modern mass societies.

The term "social process" is ubiquitous in sociological discourse. Like "social control" and "social institution," however, it is used in such diverse ways that it designates nothing in particular. Furthermore, few sociologists have attempted to follow through the implications of process philosophy, a comprehensive perspective for ordering all human experiences (Browning, 1965). Perhaps one reason is that its principles clash with some key assumptions underlying commonsense discourse. We tend to think of the world as being made up of innumerable ready-made things, which in turn are composed of ready-made parts. Research is thus directed toward finding out about various things by breaking them down to their component parts and showing how these parts are related to one another. Thus, empirical knowledge becomes what some philosophers have called an inventory of the "furniture of the universe." Even physicists, who do research in terms of process models, often revert to an emphasis on substance and structure once they leave their laboratories. But there is no fixed world, and there are no definite things except as the human mind contributes to their definition. The universe is in perpetual flux—reality is a continuous process—and thinking, which is a way of doing something, is itself a process that emerges and operates amid other processes. Furthermore, social structures need not be ignored; they are viewed as the manner in which various activities are organized. As in modern physics, statics may be viewed as a special case of dynamics—the study of motion. It may take time to become accustomed to a mode of thought that differs somewhat from our commonsense thinking, but the resulting comprehension makes the effort worthwhile.

In recent decades sociology has become a vast enterprise, involving thousands of dedicated practitioners throughout the world. There are numerous research institutes, large graduate departments, and flourishing professional societies. It would be a serious mistake, however, to regard sociology as an established science, producing knowledge comparable to what is being produced in the physical and biological sciences. Although an extensive body of research literature has developed, some of it highly specialized and requiring considerable technical virtuosity, there are few generalizations that can be regarded as firmly established on the basis of adequate evidence. Although serious efforts at verification have been made, the results have been inconclusive. What is disdainfully dismissed as "anecdotal evidence" is in fact not evidence at all—only illustrations to clarify some point. Thus, any work done in the field today must be viewed as that of pioneers facing a vast wilderness, much like the work of naturalists in the nineteenth century. There is still need for examining specimens, experimenting by trial and error, and improvising ad hoc explanations; such problems are but part of the growing pains of a young discipline.

Although I have stated many of the key ideas in this book explicitly, their tentative character must be clearly understood. They are little more than plausible generalizations not contradicted by widely known facts. With their publication many exceptions and contradictions will be found, and they should be welcomed. Any generalization that holds for a large number of known cases is worth stating, but each exception provides the occasion for further inquiry, which should lead to qualifications and eventually to the formulation of more accurate principles. The aim of this book is to describe how human society works, and any attempt to account for anything so vast, complex, and diversified as social life in the twentieth century is bound to be simplistic. At this point in the history of sociology any statement of this kind can be, at best, only programmatic. What is presented here is obviously just one of several possible ways of ordering the available material.

Even if sociologists have yet to produce a scientific theory of society, our work is not useless. We face all kinds of pressing social problems, and we must do our best to make sense of what is happening in the world. Consistent findings from a long succession of investigations — comparative analyses of historical data, results of sample surveys, case studies of various groups, experiments of all kinds — provide a more reliable basis for judgments than commonsense knowledge. Detailed observations by specialists have produced a better understanding of areas of life unfamiliar to all but those directly involved — interactions among institutionalized patients, unconventional life-styles, social pressures faced by families of executives, the coping strategies of slum dwellers. In societies as diversified as ours such findings have helped dispel many popular superstitions. Large bodies of factual data are being collected and placed in repositories. Generalizations, once formulated, are subjected to critical review; as errors are corrected, our comprehension is improved. Through specialization and focused observation sociologists are becoming informed observers of the contemporary scene. Educators, social workers, reformers, as well as executives in unions, corporations, and governments — all have found some of these materials helpful in planning their work.

The theoretical and research literature in sociology has become so extensive that no single person can possibly cover it. So much material is being published that even specialists have difficulty keeping up with the latest developments in their areas of expertise. Coverage of the literature in this book is therefore highly selective. Those accustomed to reading scientific publications may be surprised that no effort has been made to cite the latest research on the various topics considered. The practice of citing the most recent work is justified only in fields in which knowledge is cumulative, as it is in the natural sciences. Although recent sociological investigations are generally superior to earlier ones, there is no consistent relationship between the accuracy of observations or the validity of generalizations and their date of publication. For the most part I have cited sources that are pertinent, well known, and readily accessible. The documentation is somewhat heavier in areas over which there is less agreement among sociologists, such as the study of emotional behavior. Additional sources have been included as suggested readings at the end of each chapter; most of them are more technical than the text itself, and many have been written from standpoints that differ from the position taken in this book.

Some teachers may also be surprised that there is no treatment of research methods. This does not mean that I regard research procedures as unimportant. Many beginning students, however, find such discussions tedious, especially when the reason for mastering complicated techniques is not clear. Some beginners are so repelled by such presentations that they abandon the study of sociology before they have developed any appreciation of its potential relevance to their lives. Once students have developed an interest in the subject, they will have no difficulty appreciating the importance of mastering techniques for the collection and analysis of reliable data to be used in developing and testing hypotheses.

Although this book differs markedly from other works on general sociology, it is nonetheless an outgrowth of a venerable intellectual tradition—Pragmatism and what has at times been called the "Chicago school" in the social sciences (Bulmer, 1984). During the period preceding World War II a group of scholars in the Midwest, most of them at the University of Chicago, developed a point of view at once both behavioristic and processual. This group included anthropologists (Robert Redfield and Edward Sapir), political scientists (Arthur Bentley, Harold D. Lasswell, Charles Merriam, and Quincy Wright), and sociologists (Albion Small, W. I. Thomas, Robert E. Park, Ernest W. Burgess, Ellsworth Faris, Herbert Blumer, E. Franklin Frazier, Everett C. Hughes, Edwin Sutherland, and Louis Wirth). Although they disagreed among themselves on various matters, for the most part their work rested on a set of similar presuppositions—most of them stated explicitly by two philosophers (John Dewey and George H. Mead). Although many of the key ideas developed by these men and their countless students have been incorporated into the main body of the various social sciences, the conceptual framework per se has passed out of favor. It has become attenuated through disuse, misunderstanding, and misrepresentation in some secondary sources. Only the social psychology has survived as Symbolic Interactionism. Furthermore, the potential of this approach has never been explored. Although I started with this conceptual scheme, I have not felt constrained to confine myself to the views developed by these scholars. My aim is not to resurrect an old school of thought but to use the approach as a point of departure for investigating problems of current interest.

My greatest debt in formulating the approach used in this book is to Robert E. Park; his work, in turn, was strongly influenced by his mentors — John Dewey and Georg Simmel. I wish to acknowledge my enduring debt to Professor Louis Wirth, who first suggested to me that a careful study of Park's writings might point the way to a more satisfactory sociological theory. Those who are familiar with their work will also recognize the influence of three other great teachers with whom I had the privilege of studying—Herbert Blumer, Everett C. Hughes, and W. I. Thomas. Jonathan Turner reviewed the entire manuscript in great detail; since he does his own work from a quite different standpoint, I found his critical comments especially helpful. David Gold was also kind enough to review the manuscript. Although I did not always accept their suggestions, I learned much from their appraisals, and the book has benefited from this added understanding. My wife, Sandy, contributed to this project in many ways in addition to providing encouragement and support—looking up references, criticizing the content, and checking proofs. I also wish to thank Muriel Siry for the extraordinary care and accuracy with which she prepared successive drafts of the manuscript. The overall readability of the text has been enhanced by the editorial staff of the University of California Press, and I am especially grateful to Amy Einsohn and Mary Renaud.

INTRODUCTION

I

SOCIAL TRANSACTIONS

Francis Bacon articulated his grand vision of science early in the seventeenth century. He saw knowledge as the key instrument for manipulating natural processes to improve the lot of human beings, for he was convinced that to control nature one first had to understand how things work. In *Novum Organum* he wrote that "we cannot command nature except by obeying her." He argued that scientific knowledge should be empirically grounded rather than speculative, that scientists should be organized to facilitate their collaboration, and that the entire enterprise should be conducted to enhance the human condition. Although Bacon attained high positions in the government of King James I, he was unable to persuade the crown to follow his suggestions. Not long after his death, however, his writings provided inspiration for others. The Royal Society was founded in London in 1662; not long thereafter several scientific academies were established on the Continent. For more than three hundred years scientists throughout the world have struggled to live up to the ideals Bacon enunciated, dedicating their lives to contributing to the reservoir of reliable knowledge, taking it for granted that the fruits of their work would be used for the benefit of humanity. Only in recent times, especially after some physicists became appalled by the destructiveness of weapons developed on the basis of their research, have serious questions been raised about this ideology.

We live in troubled times. Remarkable advances in medical research have reduced infant mortality and prolonged life but have also led to the possibility of overpopulation. Although some of the dire warnings of demographers may be exaggerated, many natural resources are likely to be exhausted in the not-too-distant future. The distribution of existing resources is so uneven that societies for gourmets flourish at a time when people are starving. As we attempt a more equitable distribution, we shall probably become embroiled in civil and international wars. The immense achievements of the physical sciences have improved the material lot of millions, but they have also enabled us to develop deadly weapons. With the proliferation of nuclear arms the extinction of the human species is for the first time a distinct possibility. In desperate efforts to increase production, most of the world is becoming more industrialized. With increasing production comes greater pollution. Even if we are not incinerated in a nuclear holocaust, many of us may well die of suffocation. As such problems mount, social scientists are asked to help alleviate them. But the different disciplines have not developed at an even pace, and to date findings in the social sciences are not as reliable as those in the other sciences.

Sociology is one of the social sciences. Although not all sociologists are concerned with humanitarian goals, Bacon's ideals have always attracted students to the discipline. Auguste Comte, whom many regard as the founder of sociology, was interested primarily in social progress. During the past century sociology has become a vast enterprise. Research is being conducted in most countries, and the subject is taught in most universities. As we begin our study of the field, several questions arise: What is the subject matter of sociology? What is the state of knowledge in the field? Can an understanding of sociology help us deal more effectively with the pressing problems that confront us?

THE SUBJECT MATTER OF SOCIOLOGY

The Study of Concerted Action.   So far as we know, human beings have always lived in association with one another. Even misanthropes and recluses who have renounced their fellows were once members of families or inhabitants of orphanages. Sociologists have focused their attention on the fact of joint existence, but locating the boundaries of the discipline, which must be done at a high level of abstraction, is not easy. Although many formal definitions of sociology have been proposed, the most comprehensive approach commits sociologists to analyzing various forms of common endeavor — things that people do together in units of two or more. Those who happen to be on the scene of an accident render first aid and send for the police; juvenile gangs become embroiled in fights over territorial prerogatives; lovers of chamber music gather periodically to play together; thousands of people in interrelated corporations work together to produce automobiles; from time to time millions of men and women become mobilized to wage war. Sociology is the study of *social transactions* of all kinds, joint enterprises involving the coordinated efforts of two or more participants.

Thousands of human activities require some measure of teamwork. People work together in pursuit of a wide variety of objectives — struggling across a frontier in covered wagons, constructing skyscrapers, lynching someone accused of a heinous offense, sending spaceships to other planets. The size of transactions also varies — two friends enjoying dinner in a quiet corner of a restaurant, thousands mobilizing for a religious revival, millions of sports fans the world over watching the Olympic Games on television. The participants may be in direct physical contact, or they may be scattered geographically, as are the employees of the postal service of a large country. The required degree of technical skill and refinement in coordination also varies; a symphony orchestra is made up of highly trained musicians, but even small children learn fairly quickly to play jacks. Similar transactions may be performed to varying standards; sandlot baseball games barely resemble the World Series. Transactions also differ in complexity and in the time needed for completion. One may ask a stranger for directions; this involves only two people and is over in a moment or two. But sending astronauts to the moon involves transactions within transactions within transactions. Thus, *cooperation* — the collaboration of two or more people to accomplish some objective that brings satisfaction of some sort to most of the participants — is a pervasive social process. Participation may be voluntary or involuntary, direct or indirect, formal or informal. In many different contexts people with common or complementary interests pool their resources to achieve some end they consider worthwhile.

But there are also many transactions in which the interests of the participants are not compatible. There are many kinds of contests — large or small, mild or vicious, bloody or merely argumentative — ranging from family quarrels over how a child is to be disciplined to chess tournaments to adversary proceedings in courtrooms to total war. Bakers contend with one another to provide the most wholesome and tasty bread, and morticians vie to give peaceful rest to the dead. Even though the participants' interests are incompatible, one side gaining at the expense of the other, such people are still involved in common transactions. Though opposed, each party must still take account of the other. Each side's moves depend on what it expects the foe to do, and the line of action develops in the give-and-take between adversaries.

Social transactions also vary in the extent to which they are organized. Many of them, especially those that are lengthy and complicated, are carried out in groups — people in sustained association who are related to one another in understood ways. Thus, sociologists are interested in the countless groups into which human beings are assembled — families and clans, merchant and craft guilds, church congregations, factories, yacht clubs, motorcycle gangs, legislative bodies. Although groups vary considerably in size, composition, and stability, they are relatively easy to identify. They usually have names, and their boundaries are defined; individuals are either members or they are not. Although sociologists have devoted much time to analyzing organized groups, many transactions involve people who are not members of the same group — such as total strangers who drive daily in the rush hour traffic. Furthermore, many transactions have very little organization. A popular singer's fans sometimes share little more than a common focus of attention. Yet such people can be mobilized for joint action, especially if they are aroused in similar ways by what they regard as unfair treatment of their idol. The disgruntled may join forces in a protest demonstration; if their efforts are not effective, they may organize to enforce their demands.

Virtually all human life consists of participation in a vast array of social transactions. From birth to death each person is involved with other human beings. We cannot survive at birth without the cooperation of others; as we grow older, we partake in an extensive body of transactions — at home, in our neighborhood, at school, at work. Much of what one does in the course of a day one does as a *participant* in a succession of transactions. Thus, much of human behavior consists of *contributions* being made to some larger unit of joint activity. To understand any person's conduct, we must examine the social context in which it occurs. The central task of sociology is to develop and verify *hypotheses* (testable generalizations) concerning the execution of social transactions of all kinds.

The Differentiation of Tasks. Since social transactions vary so extensively, one cannot help but wonder if a limited set of generalizations could account for all of them. This would be a formidable undertaking, to be sure, but virtually all transactions share certain features. One is a division of labor. The various participants do somewhat different things, and each person's contributions are aligned with those of others to make up the total enterprise. For example, a customer in a restaurant need not go into the kitchen to prepare the meal, any more than a clarinetist in an orchestra has to jump up to play the drums. The differentiation of tasks becomes much more specialized and complicated in large organizations with bureaucracies. When a student files a petition, for example, the clerk with whom it is left sends it through channels to several officials, who render a decision; eventually it reaches another clerk, who notifies the student of the action taken. Thus, all social transactions involve a line of action that begins with one person's behavior, is carried on by others, and is finally terminated by the contributions of still others. No one carries out the entire transaction alone, although some participants play more important parts than others. Some only lend moral support; but even interested spectators are participants, for their mere presence often affects the conduct of the more active performers.

These commonplace observations have some important implications that may account for the inadequacy of many popular explanations of human conduct. Since none of the participants in a transaction can accomplish the task alone, they are interdependent. In a sense everyone is temporarily on a team and needs the other members' cooperation. If the transaction is to be successfully completed, the participants cannot do as they please. If a person does not make an adequate contribution, others may refuse to do their part. One cannot even fight effectively if opponents do not respond to hostility in the expected manner. Thus, what happens cannot be explained solely in terms of the attitudes, motives, and personality traits of the individuals involved, although each participant's orientation is certainly important. The study of individual behavior tells us only what a given participant contributes; it does not account for the overall pattern of concerted action.

Development in Social Interaction. Each social transaction has a second characteristic: It is constructed over time in a succession of reciprocating adjustments and readjustments of the participating individuals to one another. Each transaction has a career; it has a beginning and an end, although many transactions are truncated (that is, something happens to prevent their being completed as originally intended). Most transactions are goal oriented, and what is anticipated in the future, when the task has been accomplished, affects decisions that are made in the present. In some instances, as in the production of an automobile, the objective is clearly stated and understood; in many others, as in a flirtation, goals develop and change as the activity proceeds. The conclusion of a social transaction usually brings gratifications of some sort, though not necessarily alike, to each participant. Some transactions are completed quickly; others develop over a long period, sometimes involving many years. Lengthy transactions, such as winning a war, are likely to be complicated, involving many component transactions; if so, the larger transaction is not likely to succeed unless many of the component ones are executed appropriately.

Human beings are not the only creatures living in groups. But one of the distinctive characteristics of human society — compared with insect, bird, or other primate societies — is the extraordinary degree of flexibility found in various forms of joint endeavor. Human beings are better able to take fortuitous circumstances in stride. No two transactions occur in exactly the same way, for each historical situation is unique. But even in very familiar situations, such as purchasing something in a store, unexpected things occur. How people cope with changing circumstances is illustrated by the numerous adjustments members of both football teams make when a pass is intercepted. The defensive players are suddenly converted into blockers as they try to clear a path for the teammate with the ball. Offensive players are immediately transformed into tacklers. Each is on his own, for there are no set plays to follow. Offensive plays are preprogrammed and rehearsed, but an intercepted pass is an accident. The disposition of the various athletes on the field when the mistake occurs cannot be anticipated. Each player must make his own decisions and do his part in furthering his team's cause. Each adjusts somewhat independently to the situation as it develops around him and does whatever he regards as necessary to coordinate his contribution with those of his teammates. Human beings partaking in joint enterprises are not robots; each acts with some measure of autonomy; each can see his or her part in relation to the transaction as a whole. By thinking independently, each decides among several options. This type of flexible coordination rests on the *self-regulation* exercised by each participant. Concerted action usually takes place in a context marked by some fluidity. Uncertainties must be faced, and each participant adjusts somewhat independently to the exigencies of the situation.

Basic Units of Analysis. Sociology attempts to ascertain how human society works. Human existence consists of a complex maze of events; many interrelated activities go on simultaneously. For purposes of study sociologists must cut out abstract units in order to simplify and examine complex occurrences one at a time. The basic unit of analysis is the *social transaction*. Sociologists will ignore some aspects of transactions and emphasize other features that are more likely to provide a fruitful explanation of the course of action. Our central concern is to study how human beings are mobilized to carry out various types of transactions.

Since so many transactions are carried out by people who are in sustained association, sociologists also focus on the social *group*. Whenever the same people come together repeatedly to accomplish common tasks, they tend to develop relatively stable relationships. Sociologists are interested not only in these relationships but also in how members of groups become organized to act. If certain tasks are executed over and over in a similar manner, a pattern of concerted action becomes discernible. This pattern is called the *structure* of the group. We shall be concerned with the formation, maintenance, and dissolution of such patterns.

Many transactions involving members of several different groups are also recurrent and patterned, especially among people who live together in the same *community*. There are many patterns of community life, found in locations ranging from tribal villages to huge metropolitan areas. People generally identify with the place where they live and establish ties with others with whom they share a common habitat and life-style. How people come to be organized into communities, the various arrangements that arise among them, and how community participation affects their lives also interest sociologists. Although the boundaries of communities are becoming increasingly difficult to ascertain in modern mass societies, the community remains an important unit of study.

INSTRUMENTAL COMPONENTS OF TRANSACTIONS

Adaptability is one of the basic characteristics of all living creatures. Even the simplest organism will move away from excessive heat, and a flower turns toward the sun for better exposure, following its movement from dawn to dusk. Like all other organisms, human beings have this capacity to deal with continuously changing environmental conditions by making movements that will maximize the chances of survival and reproduction. What gives the adaptive capacities of our species their distinctive character is the development of language and culture. Other social animals communicate, but human language is far more flexible and extensive than the methods used by other creatures to coordinate their efforts. Indeed, the development of language has transformed the manner in which we are related to our surroundings. The term "culture" refers to the thousands of complex behavior patterns people transmit to succeeding generations through instruction; these acquired patterns supplement and regulate our various inherited instinctive reactions. Because of language and culture, human beings are able to imagine and to think; being able to plan ahead of time facilitates adaptation. Human beings strive not only for survival and reproduction but also for a great many other interests — such as deference from others, desirable places to live, and self-respect. No other creature expends so much effort to collect such objects as diamonds or to keep up with the latest fad. Culture makes possible the extraordinary degree of flexibility and complexity that marks action patterns in human society.

The Formation of Consensus.   The central task of sociology is to account for how various forms of concerted action are carried out as people who find themselves involved in the same situation try to cope with it. How is concerted action possible? Since the individual participants in social transactions differ so much from one another, the problem is more complicated than it first appears to be. Each person is a separate organism and is capable of some measure of autonomy. Each individual has a distinct personality as well as interests that differ somewhat from those of the other participants. A glance at any classroom reveals, for example, a variety of orientations toward school. For some going to school is a means to upward social mobility; for others it is a way of expanding experience and enjoyment of the world; for others it is a way to kill time while looking for something more enjoyable to do; for still others it is a place to search for a suitable mate. Furthermore, each person's contribution to a given transaction is but a fragment of a busy career. The time each student spends in a classroom is but a transitory episode in a lifetime of partaking in thousands of transactions. In addition, each person comes to a given transaction at a somewhat different phase of his or her career; the career lines of the various participants intersect in the transaction. It is not surprising, then, that different students participate in varying ways. Although each enters with a somewhat different orientation, the diverse contributions must fit together in a reciprocating manner or the enterprise will fail. Yet human beings do manage to get a great many things done through teamwork. This is a remarkable accomplishment. How is it done? We shall begin our analysis by looking at some familiar scenes — attending classes, shopping in stores, eating in restaurants, maneuvering a car in traffic. Such well-established transactions constitute only one type of concerted action, but their analysis enables us to introduce some key concepts and hypotheses.

One of the basic postulates of sociology is that each person acts on the basis of his or her *definition of the situation*. Human beings are not passive creatures who simply respond to environmental stimuli; we are constantly interpreting what we perceive. The way people define a situation is reality for them, even if others regard them as mistaken and scientists could prove that they are wrong. A father who is convinced that the devil is scheming against his family would consider himself fortunate to obtain the services of an exorcist; some of his neighbors may raise questions about his sanity. Some police officers dislike youthful radicals, members of some ethnic minorities, and adolescents in slum areas and may treat them unfairly. Members of these groups may regard police officers as "pigs," hypocrites who have no sense of justice and who are deliberately harassing them, even though these officers' spouses would testify to their mates' decency. When the two parties confront each other in some incident, each side is defensive and hypersensitive, frequently misinterpreting each other's gestures and becoming embroiled in needless clashes. In the same way, a professional woman who regards her work as a heavy responsibility may perform effectively but tire quickly, periodically become despondent, and develop ulcers. Since she defines what she does as an obligation, she feels resentful, even though she would not care to pursue any other line of work. Her colleague, who defines her work as enjoyable, may not perform any more effectively but is less likely to develop psychosomatic disorders. One important implication of this simple principle is that people, especially if they are drawn from dissimilar backgrounds of experience, may define the identical situation quite differently.

One essential condition for mounting any kind of joint endeavor is the sharing of a common definition of the situation — the formation of some measure of consensus. *Consensus* is a term that is used in several ways in the social sciences; here it designates coorientation. Each person defines the situation in a particular way and assumes that the other participants have adopted a similar definition. When people (students) define a familiar situation (classroom) in the same manner, they share common understandings of what each is supposed to do. When people share understandings, they also have common expectations of each other. Thus, students expect one another to appear on time and to be reasonably orderly while an instructor directs the exercises for the day. As long as the participants are able to anticipate what the others are likely to do, they can effectively prepare their respective contributions, allowing for the coordination of diverse lines of action. Consensus does not mean that participants necessarily agree on what to do, only that they share a common definition of the situation (Scheff, 1967). Without such coorientation one cannot even argue effectively, and fighting is impossible. Thus, only if the participants are able to develop some measure of consensus can social transactions be carried out. Without it people flounder about and jockey for position. Concerted action cannot be undertaken, for no one can be sure of just what to expect of the others.

Normative Frameworks. The common understandings shared in familiar situations are called *norms.* Social norms are the standards of desired conduct in a transaction that enjoy a high degree of consensus within a group or community. They define the range of acceptable behavior, providing a framework within which participants are expected to make their choices, regardless of personal feelings or preferences. Norms arise in any type of recurrent transaction. Rules of etiquette are found everywhere: how to address other people, how to show interest in them, how to minimize chances of offending them. The range of acceptable conduct is especially narrow in ritualistic observances. When the bride and groom are asked in a wedding ceremony whether they accept each other, for example, their views are not actually being solicited. Anything other than the expected response would bring the transaction to a sudden halt. There are even countless norms outside of organized groups. Goffman (1963) calls these norms "situational properties" (common expectations that are shared within a community). Everyone, including total strangers, is expected to meet minimum standards of conduct. For example, one does not stare at a stranger; as people approach one another, they turn away their eyes — a mutual dimming of headlights. Another example of a conventional norm in our society is the pressure people feel not to disclose their undergarments. This does not arise from a reluctance to display any part of the body; both men and women comfortably appear on beaches in swim trunks or bikinis. Yet it is considered in poor taste to appear in public with any part of one's underwear visible. Thus, norms are standards in terms of which behavior is judged, by both the actor and the observers.

The division of labor in well-established transactions is often worked out to the point where each participant's expected contributions are clearly defined. This specialization suggests that the constituent parts of social transactions are not the individuals involved, but the contributions expected from each of them. These parts are called conventional roles, another key concept in sociology. A *role* is a component part of an organized transaction, a model of what a person enacting that part is expected to contribute. Thus, at the end of each semester, students face a familiar transaction: an examination. The instructor assumes the role of the examiner—formulating the questions, specifying how they are to be answered, perhaps maintaining surveillance to make cheating difficult, collecting the papers, and subsequently evaluating them. Thus, a role is an expected pattern of behavior. In familiar transactions each participant assumes a role and feels constrained to live up to such expectations. Since roles are segments of transactions, they are always related to other roles in understood ways; it makes no sense to speak of an examiner apart from students being tested. Since each person partakes in a succession of transactions each day, one is seldom involved in a single role throughout the day. As people move from one transaction to the next, they enact different roles in each. From time to time a person is called upon to enact more than one role at the same time—such as preparing for an examination while sitting as a passenger on a train.

The role that a person enacts in such familiar transactions usually depends on his or her status. Status is another key concept in sociology. Members of communities and groups that persist tend to develop a network of social relationships, and social *status* refers to the position that one occupies in such organized contexts. Each position is part of a network of positions; therefore, each status is related to other statuses. The incumbents have rights and duties toward those in related positions. Thus, a doctor in a hospital is related in understood ways to those who occupy other positions: nurse, laboratory technician, social worker, orderly, administrator, patient. Regular participants in organized transactions are bound to each other by reciprocating claims and obligations. A claim is what a person in one position can reasonably expect of those in complementary positions. Patients have several claims on a hospital staff—cleanliness, courteous treatment, attention to medical needs. The patients' claims constitute the staff's obligations. Patients also have obligations: to cooperate, to accept professional advice, to be reasonable and considerate of fellow patients. These are claims that hospital workers have on their clients. Each person occupies several statuses—one in the community and one in each of the groups to which he or she belongs.

The concepts of status and role are often confused, for in common parlance the same words are frequently used to refer to both. "Busboy" both designates the status of a restaurant employee and describes the role he enacts whenever customers are through eating (Linton, 1936:113–31). But the incumbents of each status participate in several types of transactions, and the roles they enact may differ in each (Merton, 1957:368–86). An example from American football illustrates this distinction. The position of right guard on the offensive team constitutes a player's status on the team. Although a guard spends most of his time blocking, his role differs from one play to the next. Each play is a separate transaction. When a running back is to plunge into the line, the guard's role consists of joining the center in pushing a defensive player out of the way. If the next play calls for a forward pass, the guard's role consists of backing up to protect the passer. If the next play is an end run, his role may consist of pulling out of the line to lead the interference. Both the status and the roles are impersonal; no matter who the incumbent of the position may be — the starter or a substitute — what is expected in a given play remains the same.

Few activities are as planned and rehearsed as offensive plays in football, but this is precisely what makes it easy to distinguish between status as a position in an organized group and role as the expected contribution to each type of transaction. Similar distinctions are also discernible in less structured contexts. For example, a woman who occupies the status of wife and mother in a middle-class family partakes in many different transactions in that capacity. In each transaction her role is different — companion to her husband, concerned parent at school, astute shopper, good neighbor. She plays several other roles in her position as president of the local tennis club.

Norms are standards of acceptable conduct. They are only rules, however, and may be broken. Norms do not determine behavior. Although people usually comply with the expectations of others, dissent is always possible. A participant may refuse to do a fair share, may contribute reluctantly in a token fashion, may raise questions about the propriety of the demands, may try to develop a new way of doing things, or may just rebel. Similarly, roles are only models, and people do not always live up to their obligations. Since participants in transactions are interdependent, however, the failure of others to meet their obligations can lead to costly failures. Hence, special procedures exist in well-established situations to encourage conformity and to discourage deviation. These are called social *sanctions*. Sanctions imposed by a community or group may be positive or negative. A positive sanction is a way of showing approval to those who comply — bestowing praise, recognition, special considerations, or other rewards. A negative sanction is a way of showing disapproval — a frown, punishment, refusal to reciprocate, or even ostracism. Among people who know one another sanctions tend to be informal — a friendly embrace or a word of caution. Among strangers sanctions tend to be more formal — ceremonies of recognition or arrest and incarceration (Radcliffe-Brown, 1934). Sanctions need rarely be invoked in most familiar situations since each person knows what is anticipated and tries to meet these expectations.

Consensus and Concerted Action. If consensus is established, each participant is able to anticipate what the others are likely to do and can contribute by *role-playing.* In familiar situations transactions are executed largely through the enactment of roles by the participants. Once they share a common definition of the situation, people can locate themselves in their respective positions and prepare to do their part. This does not mean that one is necessarily pleased with a role; on the contrary, people frequently feel trapped by what they regard as unreasonable duties. But much of life consists of carrying out roles in a succession of familiar contexts. People experience the model of appropriate conduct as a set of obligations, many of which become habitual. One feels intuitively what constitutes an appropriate tip for service, and automobile drivers learn to perform with little awareness of what they are doing, except in emergencies. In such familiar contexts, self-regulation consists largely of enacting roles. By recognizing the expectations of others and trying to live up to them, large numbers of people, even total strangers, can carry out countless transactions. For example, students frequently become bored and sleepy in classrooms. Despite their inclinations, they usually struggle to stay awake, even when they realize that the instructor is too preoccupied with other matters to notice a catnapper. Most of us act in ways that we regard as proper, and we often do things we would prefer not to do. We have become so accustomed to role-playing that we usually act in customary ways even when we are alone. Thus, whenever consensus is well established, social transactions usually proceed with the participants enacting their respective roles, making the necessary adjustments required by the exigencies of the situation. This is not the only way people execute concerted action, but it is one of the most common.

The extent to which consensus is established varies considerably, even in familiar situations, and the ease with which a transaction can be executed varies with the extent to which consensus is achieved and maintained. In a religious ceremony, for example, there is near unanimity in defining the situation; except for outsiders who may have wandered in, everyone has a clear understanding of what is happening. Thus, the transaction is carried out even if many of the participants are not strictly attentive. But there are many situations in which such coorientation is not achieved. Glaser and Strauss (1964) suggest several possible "awareness contexts." There are some situations in which all parties share one definition of the situation, others in which some of the participants do not quite understand what the others are taking for granted, others in which some parties are suspicious of what their associates are trying to do, and still others in which all participants realize that those enacting roles are only pretending but do nothing to acknowledge or object to the deception. When consensus is more apparent than real, neither the appropriate norms to be applied nor the roles to be enacted are clear, and some exploration must precede joint endeavor. People become hesitant; their moves become tentative; they may attempt to clarify misunderstandings by asking questions or arguing. A number of studies reveal how disruptions arise from the inability of participants to develop sufficient consensus. Gross et al. (1958) show how divergent conceptions of administrators' roles can reduce the effectiveness and morale of a school system, and several studies show how domestic strife arises when a husband and wife have different conceptions of their respective roles (R. Turner, 1970:135–63).

These observations suggest that social transactions vary considerably in their *degree of institutionalization.* The kinds of transactions discussed thus far have become familiar through repetition; the patterns of coordinated activity have been enacted over and over in much the same manner, so much so that all participants clearly understand the norms, roles, and sanctions to be expected for noncompliance. In each community, networks of interrelated norms provide widely accepted and well-known frameworks within which complex activities can be carried out— economic activities, law enforcement, interactions between total strangers, formal education, the formation and dissolution of families. These networks of well-established norms are called *social institutions.*

Some transactions are so highly institutionalized that the norms are just taken for granted; it does not even occur to anyone that things could be done differently. Everything is preprogrammed, and the only distinctive contribution an individual can make is in the skill and style of performance. In such contexts one's contribution is somewhat like giving a performance on the stage. For example, in an account of her former life as a nun, Baldwin (1957:79–83) notes that virtually everything she did was prescribed; her roles were so clearly defined that there was no room for individuality. Similarly, symphony orchestra conductors may introduce some variations in their interpretation of the score, but the musicians must perform within very narrow limits.

In restaurants, classrooms, stores, and other familiar situations norms are also clearly established, but there is more room for choice. Several acceptable alternatives are available, and the participants can exercise some options within specified boundaries. Although a polite, properly attired, and well-mannered customer is more likely to receive courteous service in a restaurant, others are served as well. On less formal occasions, such as birthday parties or victory celebrations, the participants enjoy even more freedom. Nonetheless, some norms are still enforced. As the guests become inebriated, conversations become less inhibited than usual and some unconventional acts are tolerated. But there are limits beyond which one cannot go; violence, for example, is restrained. Meeting people in bars occurs in a similar atmosphere of informality (Cavan, 1966). In emergencies—earthquakes, floods, bombings in time of war—even fewer prescribed norms apply, and individuals must improvise ways of coping with the situation. Should they disagree on what to do, there are no prescribed ways of settling their differences, and the disgruntled parties may have to go separate ways.

Society as Collective Adaptation. In *The Origin of Species* Charles Darwin shows how various organisms develop their bodily forms and find a niche in the web of life in their efforts to survive, grow, and reproduce. Some species manage by forming cooperative arrangements with others —as in parasitism or symbiosis. Whenever necessary resources are in short supply, however, competition arises among those that need them. Organisms with inherited characteristics that enable them to cope most effectively in that particular situation have competitive advantages and survive; the losers become extinct. Thus, the fauna and flora of any area are the products of natural selection. Human beings are organisms that are implicated in the same biotic processes.

When biologists, on the one hand, speak of adaptation, they are referring to the development of anatomical structures and instinctual patterns that are inherited genetically. Sociologists, on the other hand, are concerned with the development of various patterns of coordinated action. Social transactions of all kinds are joint efforts to come to terms with extant life conditions. If a situation is recurrent, previously successful tactics tend to be used again. When transactions have been repeated frequently enough, the pattern of common endeavor becomes fixed, and the participants can approach one another confidently with set expectations. Thus, social structures of all kinds—in groups and in communities —are products of collective adaptation. But patterns of concerted action, for the most part, do not depend on changes in the genetic makeup of the individual participants. Human beings are constantly striving to come to terms with ever-changing circumstances but do so by developing new ways of acting—by forming new culture patterns—rather than by waiting for the inheritance of traits that happen to be useful. Sociologists are trying to discover regularities in the way such collective adaptations are accomplished.

EXPRESSIVE COMPONENTS OF TRANSACTIONS

Qualitative Differences in Performance. Even when transactions are institutionalized, the line of action may develop in several different ways. The norms of a university classroom are clearly understood; yet no two classes are alike, and each session in the same class is different. One hypothesis that merits consideration is that the manner in which a given transaction is carried out depends on how the individual participants are oriented toward it. Emotional reactions are especially important; each person becomes involved in a transaction in his or her distinctive way. Much depends on one's personality, experience, and specific interests in the situation. Thus, some people look forward to a cocktail party because they enjoy sociability; others attend reluctantly to pursue their political ambitions; others see it as an occasion for showing off their knowledge of esoteric topics in current vogue; some seek out interesting people who may turn out to be entertaining; some always welcome free alcohol; others appear only because they could think of no polite excuse. Another important consideration is the reaction of the participants to one another. Some participants like each other; others feel uneasy in the company of so many people they detest; still others are so concerned with the impression they are making that they hardly notice anything else. University alumni may recruit the finest athletes and hire a coach who is a tactical genius, but the team may never realize its potential if the stars are thoroughly disliked by their teammates. Even when we enact familiar roles —customer, student, guest—our performances may vary perceptibly. Some do the very best they can, going far beyond customary expectations; others may be apathetic, meeting their obligations in a desultory manner.

How much individuals may depart from customary routines varies considerably. When participating in a religious ritual, even an archbishop cannot wander from what tradition and canon law prescribe. Any deviation is viewed as an error. Officials in bureaucratic organizations are hemmed in by formal regulations, public demands, and political considerations. Regardless of their personal preferences, they must choose from among a limited set of options. However, people are left more on their own in informal contexts. The success of a small party depends on who attends and how well the guests get along with one another. These observations may be summarized in a hypothesis: The extent to which any individual can influence the course of events in a transaction varies inversely with its degree of institutionalization. Thus, leadership is of decisive importance in emergencies, when expectations are not fixed;

what happens depends on the imagination and diligence of the individuals who happen to be present.

When transactions are highly institutionalized, variations occur primarily in style of performance. There is a difference between the structure of a transaction (the agreed-on procedures for getting things done) and the style of execution (the manner in which they are done). For example, in their study of U.S. Army Air Force units in World War II, Grinker and Spiegel (1945:25–26) note that, after a crew had been in combat for some time, it took on a definite color, making it distinct from similarly organized groups. The men themselves differentiated among the "hot outfit" with its impressive record of achievement; the "snafu outfit" with its discontent, bickering, and chronically poor performance; the "carefree outfit" with its exuberance, dash, and recklessness; and the colorless unit marked by sober dependability. Such commonly recognized differences cannot be explained in terms of formal norms, for U.S. Army regulations were identical for all units. Similarly, within the same factory, productivity rates vary from one section to another, and in large prisons, riots erupt more frequently in some cellblocks than in others. Style of performance refers to the quality of the coordination and integration of the contributions made by various participants.

The Formation of Emotional Climates. If the emotional reactions of the people involved differ, a social transaction is likely to be performed in the expected manner, with most participants complying with group norms. If the emotional reactions of a substantial portion of the participants converge, however, a diffuse social excitement tends to develop. A common mood emerges that envelops the transaction like an atmosphere, experienced as something that is "in the air." Thus, an unfavorable decision by the referee at a crucial point in a closely contested championship game arouses sudden and widespread indignation among the fans and the prevailing mood becomes "heavy" as hostile gestures and insulting yells fill the air. This contrasts sharply with the gay banter, chatter, and mild flirtations at a picnic or wedding. There is no place for levity at a funeral; even those who do not feel dejected feel constrained to put on a somber mien. Such *emotional climates* vary in both direction and intensity (Park, 1930). Style of performance is most readily discernible in transactions in which the emotional reactions of the participants converge.

Emotional climates arise as much from the participants' responses to one another as from their reactions to the situation. Whenever people come together, their mere awareness of one another's presence sets up a lively interchange of gestures. Human beings are delicately attuned to one another's emotional reactions; they are especially sensitive to indications of suppressed feelings. When people are upset, various bodily changes take place. The color and moisture of the skin may be affected, as in blanching, blushing, or sweating; bodily tension is revealed in strained posture, forced motion, trembling, or twitching; respiration may be affected, as in sighing or rapid and shallow breathing. Most of us have learned to read these externally visible components of bodily changes in emotion as indicators of inner experiences. Each person contributes to the formation of an emotional climate by revealing his or her feelings. People disclose personal feelings not only by what they say and do, but also by how they perform—the intonation of the voice, facial expressions, the rhythm of breathing, movements of the hands. What makes such communication so easy is that emotionally aroused people are especially sensitive to indications of the feelings of those around them. Frightened people seek confirmation of their own fears in the eyes of those around them, just as angry people are responsive to support for their own hostile tendencies. When people perceive expressive movements, they make inferences about the inner experiences of others, and participants are affected by the emotional climate to the extent that they detect the prevailing mood and respond to it by modifying their own conduct.

Emotional climates are important in that they facilitate acts that are consistent with them and inhibit those that are inconsistent. When the prevailing mood is one of great anger, for example, insulting remarks and destructive acts can be executed with ease and impunity. If the prevailing mood is one of awe and reverence, however, anyone shouting an obscenity would become the immediate target of hostility. When the prevailing mood is one of gaiety, anyone who does not pretend to be happy may be accused of being a "party pooper." Thus, a common mood gives direction to the interests and attitudes of the participants. Those who do not feel enthusiastic at the beginning of a transaction may soon become so caught up in the emotional atmosphere that they find themselves doing things they had never imagined doing.

Variations in Group Morale. If the emotional reactions of the participants are intense and positive, transactions are likely to be performed with a high degree of effectiveness. As collective enthusiasm develops, the division of labor arises almost spontaneously, for each person contributes whatever needs to be done. The participants help one another without even being asked. Mutual encouragement is commonplace, and those whose zeal is exemplary are singled out for praise. Those who get behind are urged on good-naturedly. The few who do not share the prevailing mood feel pressured to comply; those who fail repeatedly to live up to expectations are scorned as slackers. If an organized group performs consistently in this manner, it is characterized as having high morale. Members of such groups usually feel positive about themselves. They often develop a strong sense of mutual identification; they develop pride in their group, become conscious of its reputation, and take pleasure in displaying emblems of belonging to it. This type of performance becomes especially important in any kind of contest, and military personnel and professional athletes have long sought ways of attaining it.

If emotional reactions are intense and negative, transactions are likely to be executed sluggishly. Factionalism and bickering arise, and compliance with norms becomes reluctant, resulting more from fear of punishment than from a sense of duty. Doubts are expressed about the avowed goals of the enterprise, and those who remain conscientious are dismissed cynically as "suckers." If a group performs consistently in this manner, it is characterized as being demoralized. Members of such groups usually place a low estimate on themselves; there is no group pride; and some try to leave. As the emotional climate becomes one of futility and despair, some participants become preoccupied with hedonistic pursuits or lose themselves in alcohol and other drugs. When confronted by adverse conditions, such groups are likely to disintegrate, for the members become preoccupied only with saving themselves.

The performance of those occupying key positions may be decisive, for they have much to do with deciding how things are to be accomplished. In a pioneering study White and Lippitt (1960) show how the emotional climate that develops in small groups depends on whether the person in charge organizes the activities in an authoritarian or permissive manner. Wilson (1954) describes how emotional climates develop in operating rooms during surgery. Although the routine for each type of surgery is fairly standard in each hospital, each operation is different. He notes that the prevailing mood depends largely on the personality and attitude of the chief surgeon, who is the unquestioned leader of the team. The surgeon's relationships with all other participants — assistant surgeon, anesthetist, nurses — are clearly defined. Cutting open a human body involves immense responsibility; with the patient's life at stake the situation is fraught with anxieties, awe, and excitement. In many instances an effort is made to relieve the tension and to create an atmosphere that is as casual and mundane as possible. Some doctors are jovial, commenting on their good fortune in having the most competent members of the hospital staff assigned to their team. When the chief surgeon is friendly, witty exchanges and small talk accompany the operation. Some doctors are friendly but serious and allow no unnecessary talking at all, and the emotional climate remains tense. Other doctors allow their tempers to flare, aggravating an already difficult situation. Grinker and Spiegel (1945) also point to the remarkable similarities between the style of performance of each air force unit and its commanding officer's personality traits.

The Regulation of Tension. The emotional reactions of participants usually remain within acceptable bounds; occasions arise, however, when they become so intense that the transaction breaks down, sometimes with tragic consequences. The intense anger of fans in soccer and hockey matches has sometimes gotten out of hand, resulting in destructive riots. Jovial celebrations sometimes develop into orgies, and mourners at funerals for martyrs are sometimes so overwhelmed by grief that they join a stampede toward the coffin. When tensions become unmanageable, the normative framework breaks down, and role-playing ceases to be an effective way of contributing to a transaction. Therefore, in well-established groups procedures generally develop for tension management. In recurrent situations in which there are reasonable expectations that feelings may get out of hand, such as funerals, precautionary measures are instituted. Common understandings arise as to how the participants are supposed to feel and how they are to express their feelings. One need only compare funerals in China and in Ireland to appreciate the extent to which such norms differ from one society to another. Many rituals, such as the decorum and solemnity of courtrooms, help keep participants' emotional reactions in check even in the midst of heated litigation. Indeed, in contests of all kinds, where excessive anger is likely to invite defeat, deliberate efforts are made to keep anger under control. The aim in such situations is to raise the tension level just enough to elicit the contenders' maximum effort, but not enough for them to "lose their heads."

SOCIOLOGY AS AN EMERGING DISCIPLINE

Sociology as Scientific Endeavor. Although there are many forms of knowledge — folk wisdom and common sense, religious beliefs, political ideologies, technical know-how — in recent times scientific knowledge has enjoyed the greatest prestige. Indeed, the esteem accorded to science is so great that most people accept scientists' views even when they do not understand them. Such preeminence rests largely on demonstrated utility; of the diverse forms of knowledge, science has proved most useful as the basis for adaptation, primarily because of its greater accuracy. Thus, modern medicine is replacing folk healing methods throughout the world, for its effectiveness has been demonstrated. Scientific knowledge consists largely of *generalizations* (hypotheses). The aim of science is to discover and verify hypotheses about regularities in nature—including the manner in which human beings think and act, individually or in collaboration with others. Scientific knowledge is never complete and absolute; with each discovery hypotheses are reformulated to make them more trustworthy. But generalizations are useful even when they are not entirely accurate. In a world filled with uncertainties we are fortunate to have statements that provide reasonable approximations over a substantial range of situations. Scientific method is a procedure that maximizes the chances of accuracy. The generalizations are based on observations of what happens in the world, and they are tested by evidence—further observations. Whenever possible, experiments are conducted; experimentation is a form of reality-testing—checking the accuracy of hypotheses by seeing whether or not they actually work under certain specified conditions.

Since science enjoys so much prestige, sociologists have been anxious to be included among scientists. Some have become so impatient with the slow progress of their discipline that they have tried to imitate the procedures that have been successful elsewhere, such as measurement and experimentation, whether or not they are appropriate. Unfortunately, merely posing as scientists does not lead these imitators to the production of scientific knowledge. Sociologists, like other scientists, are trying to formulate and test hypotheses. As we observe in diverse historical contexts such events as the crises that ensnare bureaucracies, the failure of different generations in the same family to communicate effectively, the development of revolutionary movements, or the career lines of criminals, we cannot help but note that many things happen over and over in much the same manner. Such events can be classified and described in abstract terms. But sociology is still a very young discipline, barely a century old. Sociologists still must develop the kind of verified knowledge found in the natural sciences. Most generalizations in sociology are plausible but inadequately tested; when sociologists have attempted to verify them, the results have often been inconclusive. This does not mean that sociologists' hypotheses are necessarily wrong, only that they are tentative, for the observed exceptions cannot be ignored. What can be said is that most sociologists are committed to scientific method. They accept empirical evidence as the ultimate criterion in the evaluation of generalizations; neither divine revelation nor the pontification of wise men is regarded as sufficient. The unity of science lies in method, not in subject matter. All scientists work on the assumption that events occur with a regularity sufficient to permit their description in general terms, and sociologists make this assumption about human society.

In analyzing the development of the various sciences, Kuhn (1962:10–22) notes that during the early history of any field practical needs and prevailing values determine the problems on which the practitioners concentrate. This is certainly true of sociology; we are very much concerned with the difficulties that confront humanity. Kuhn also notes that disciplines that are not well established are marked by doctrinal quarrels, and there are indeed several different theoretical orientations in sociology (J. Turner, 1977). Sociologists disagree over how to approach their subject matter—the kinds of assumptions to make about human beings and society, the manner in which questions are to be posed, the kinds of hypotheses to be examined, and the appropriate procedures to use in gathering data to test and revise them. No single approach is generally accepted.

Much of contemporary sociology consists of the study of social structures of all kinds—the organization of groups and communities. Structural analysis consists of breaking down a social unit (a university, for example) into its parts (faculty, students, administrators, clerical and custodial staff) and examining how these components fit together. Such analysis thus places emphasis on the arrangement of constituent elements and the manner in which the participants are related to one another. Indeed, some sociologists have defined their field as the study of social relationships. Serious questions have arisen concerning the adequacy of this approach: It has been criticized as static, as providing political justification for the status quo (Gouldner, 1970; O'Neill, 1972), and as inadequate for the study of social change and intergroup conflict. Nevertheless, researchers who favor this approach have made many important contributions, and their work will be cited throughout this volume.

As noted, what makes a social group something more than a mere aggregation of individuals is its capacity for common endeavor. Thus, it might be more fruitful to emphasize the study of action rather than organization. In recent years this has been called the behavioral approach to the social sciences—the study of human beings in terms of what they do. This is the approach adopted in this book.

The Study of Social Processes. In this book human society will be viewed as an ongoing process, as something that is *becoming* rather than *being*. This way of thinking, based on a distinction borrowed from Greek philosophy, differs somewhat from our commonsense orientation, and it may take some time to become accustomed to it; but it is a more fruitful approach. The entire universe is in a constant state of flux, a continuous stream of events. Life conditions are always changing, and human beings—individually and collectively—must adapt to the developing circumstances. Human society consists of a succession of adjustments and readjustments among associated people through which various patterns of concerted action are formed, maintained, dissolved, and reshaped. Change is continuous, but it may be slow or rapid. Sometimes it occurs so slowly that a community achieves the appearance of stability. A *social process* is a pattern of joint activity that occurs regularly over time, and the task of sociologists is to identify and describe such processes. The basic unit of study is not so much a *thing* and its organization as it is an *event*. We shall focus on the development of various types of events over time, characteristic phases of development, conditions under which identifiable changes take place, and the relationships among various attributes of transactions. The perspective that views society as a process is thus very comprehensive; it enables us to study stability and instability, harmony and disharmony, construction and destruction. Furthermore, most of the results of structural analysis can be easily incorporated into this approach.

Social processes may be classified in many ways, and at this point in the development of sociology it is not possible to say which way is likely to be most productive. We can begin with a breakdown that most easily enables us to order the results of current research.

The study of *agonistic processes* focuses on transactions in which the interests of the participants are in some way opposed. Human beings crave all kinds of objects—gainful employment, attractive mates, prestige, security. Whenever there is not enough of any coveted object to go around, the interests of those who want it become opposed, and competition results. In *competition* each party strives independently for desired objects that are in short supply, as in an essay contest. It is parallel striving; competitors do the best they can, and those who perform most effectively win. Competition thus tends to be impersonal, for competitors are often not conscious of the opposition of interests. Even when there is some awareness, those who lose do not necessarily view the victor with malice; the most deserving party won. Transactions of this type are pervasive and important, and it is through *natural selection* that many groups and communities become what they are. One product of competition is the ordering of people into a common economic system. But countless other arrangements emerge from competition. The distribution of people in space, the mating of couples, the development of fashion movements, the formation of rumors and ideologies, the adoption of innovations—all are to some extent the products of competition and natural selection. As Dewey (1898) indicated, the difference between human beings and other creatures is not that natural selection ceases but that conscious foresight introduces additional alternatives from which choices might be made. Since competition, like cooperation, is so pervasive, it will be discussed in all sections of this book.

But competition is often transformed into rivalry and conflict. If competitors become conscious of each other, if a person is able to identify an opponent and realize that the opponent's success means some kind of loss for oneself, the contest takes on a different character. Thus, politicians vying for an office become conscious of their incompatible interests, and competition is then transformed into *rivalry.* Instead of parallel striving, opponents attempt to manipulate the situation; this is what is commonly called politics. Each party makes moves that maximize its chances of success, even at the expense of its opponent. Although such contests are usually carried on within a normative framework, political tactics are used in a deliberate effort to outdo an opponent. Rivalries sometimes get out of hand, especially when the participants become convinced that success for their opponent means disaster for themselves. Rivalry is then transformed into *conflict,* where the immobilization or destruction of the adversary becomes a major objective. Although enemies are polarized into at least two opposing parties, they are nonetheless interdependent, for the moves of each side are oriented to the tactics of the other. Thus, all agonistic transactions are constructed in a succession of reciprocating adjustments by opponents to each other, each trying to maximize gains while minimizing losses. Some of the most effective cooperation among human beings occurs in conflicts between groups. Such transactions—struggles between unions and corporations, interethnic tension and riots, religious conflict, revolutions, wars—are obviously important. Most of the discussion of rivalry and conflict appears in Part Four.

Both competition and cooperation lead to the establishment of various patterns of concerted action. Since coping behavior that succeeds tends to be repeated, all living creatures create/forms—recurrent patterns of endeavor. This is certainly true of human beings. Once some mode of collaboration proves to be successful, transactions tend to become increasingly institutionalized. Some conventional norms last for centuries. Once such patterns of coordinated activity have been formed, they become frameworks within which subsequent activities tend to be channeled (Simmel, 1971:351–74; Spykman, 1925:20). Customs or laws in a community become the habits and expectations of individuals. Since human beings are creatures of habit, we often continue to do things in a given way long after the circumstances under which such norms originally developed have changed. Although the universe is in constant flux, some changes occur in such small increments that for all practical purposes the patterns appear quite stable (Whitehead, 1929:242–43). In the study of *sustaining processes* we are interested in social transactions that are repeated over and over in a similar manner, where the division of labor persists even when the personnel has been replaced. The study of such processes centers on an interesting question: Since nothing ever happens twice in the same manner, how is such stability possible? What regularities are there in the execution of transactions in which the normative framework does not appear to change? How and under what conditions are fairly enduring patterns of coordinated activity maintained? Part Two of this book is devoted to these questions.

Although some patterns of concerted action endure for a long time, many are transitory, for life conditions continue to change. When normative frameworks that had once been so successful as guides to joint action become inadequate, they are superseded by other patterns that are better suited to the new circumstances. Although such changes are sometimes made through a careful analysis of the new situation and deliberate planning, in most instances the old patterns just fade away. Much dislocation and turmoil characterize periods of rapid and extensive transformation. Whether or not changes are planned, the dissolution of once established patterns and their replacement occurs in regularized ways. Thus, in the study of *transitional processes* we are interested in what some philosophers have called the "unchanging laws of change." How do institutionalized patterns break down? When once established norms are no longer adequate guides to conduct, what do people do? Life must go on. What are the characteristic reactions of people who are caught in situations in which there are no generally accepted norms of conduct? How do people cope in such situations? How do they get together to mobilize their resources in the face of uncertainty? How do new patterns of coordination arise? How do the new patterns become institutionalized? These important questions are addressed in Part Three.

In the study of sustaining and transitional processes a distinction is *not* being made between relatively stable and rapidly changing societies. All these processes are found in all societies. Even in communities that are changing as rapidly as the modern urban centers of developing nations there are many enduring patterns; most activities are carried out within a fairly stable institutional framework. Similarly, even the relatively stable, isolated folk societies once studied by anthropologists undergo some transformations. Competition, rivalry, and conflict are found everywhere. Furthermore, although the processes can be distinguished analytically, in real life they blend, overlap, and coexist even in the same transaction.

Explanations of Social Phenomena. One additional word of caution needs to be added. Social phenomena can be explained in several different ways (MacIver, 1942; Brown, 1963), and the generalizations in this book differ considerably from most popular explanations. In daily discourse various events, including the things that people do, are explained by citing a "cause" — some antecedent event or condition that is regarded as responsible for its occurrence. Many respiratory ailments, for example, are explained by a single prior event — the entrance of some virus into the body. If a person commits a robbery, the police account for it by citing some preceding event: A parolee was unable to find work and was without funds. If an airplane crashes and no mechanical failure is discovered, the "cause" of the accident is said to be "human error." But logicians whose views differ as greatly as those of John Dewey (1938:442 – 62) and Bertrand Russell (1957:174 – 210) have raised serious doubts about the adequacy of such explanations. If one person shoots another, what antecedent event can be singled out as the "cause" of the death? Is it the collapse of vital organs, the cessation of the pumping of the heart, the piercing of the heart by the bullet, the explosion of powder that propelled the bullet, the pulling of the trigger, the anger of the person who fired the gun, the insult that provoked the anger, or other preceding events in the lives of the two that led to this confrontation? Any event that is explained in this manner is being lifted out of a very complicated context. If all the antecedent events are provided in sufficient fullness to make possible some kind of calculation of consequences, they become so numerous that they are unlikely ever to recur in that combination. The principle of causality, as it is used by most logicians and scientists, is *not* the same as the simplistic "cause" and "effect" mode of explanation used in commonsense discourse. To account for the way social transactions develop requires much more than citing "causes."

It should be kept in mind, however, that the manner in which events are customarily explained is an important part of any society. Explaining things in terms of "causes" is a form of behavior that facilitates the execution of social transactions, and it will be studied as part of our subject matter (chapter 3).

SUMMARY AND DISCUSSION

The first task of life is to live, and human society is shaped by the efforts of people to come to terms with the circumstances into which they have been cast. As implausible as it may seem, society as we know it—its skyscrapers and slums, its brutal massacres and beautiful love affairs, its scientific achievements and inability to feed its poor, its museum holdings and child pornography—is a product of people's efforts to live as best they can. Sociology is the study of social transactions. There is a wide variety of transactions, but in all of them the line of action develops through the coordination of the contributions of two or more people. Highly institutionalized transactions are executed largely through the role-playing of the participants, but in situations that are not so well established improvisation becomes necessary. The personal orientation of the participants, especially their emotional reactions, affects the manner in which the transactions are carried out. Although sociologists are striving to meet scientific standards, they have not yet succeeded in the analysis of various transactions, and many disagreements have arisen over how this goal is to be achieved. The perspective adopted in this book is to view human society as a complex network of social processes.

Can sociology help solve the pressing difficulties that confront us? Given the importance of the subject matter, it is indeed distressing that the state of knowledge in the field is still so inadequate. But however tentative its hypotheses, sociology can provide better explanations of how society works than can commonsense knowledge. Knowledge is an instrument that enables us to live more effectively; the more accurate it is, the better it is as a tool for adaptation. Those who are concerned with improving their lot—be they revolutionaries, corporation executives, or legislators—will find that they can act more intelligently with a better appreciation of their situation. Even those whose aspirations are not so lofty may profit from a better understanding of society. One not only can make wiser decisions in problematic situations but also can enhance the chances of getting more enjoyment and fulfillment in life.

It is frustrating that the state of knowledge in the field is so primitive, but this creates a challenge—especially for those considering becoming professional sociologists. Unlike the better-established disciplines, in which research is limited largely to the few areas that are still problematic, sociologists have a vast wilderness to explore. No matter what they elect to study, they will find that they are pioneers making their way through unmapped territory. Thus, those who elect to devote themselves to the systematic study of human society may find themselves immersed in an exciting adventure.

SUGGESTED READINGS

Brown, Robert. 1963. *Explanation in Social Science.* Chicago: Aldine.
  An examination of the various modes of description and explanation used in the social sciences.
Kress, Paul F. 1970. *Social Science and the Idea of Process.* Urbana: University of Illinois Press.
  A critical appraisal of Arthur Bentley's attempt to construct a process approach to the study of human society.
Kurtz, Lester R. 1984. *Evaluating Chicago Sociology: A Guide to the Literature, with an Annotated Bibliography.* Chicago: University of Chicago Press.
  A review of the development of empirically grounded sociology at the University of Chicago from 1892 to 1950.
Mills, C. Wright. 1959. *The Sociological Imagination.* New York: Oxford University Press.
  A scathing account of academic sociology in the mid-twentieth century and its inability to address the problems confronting humanity.
Turner, Jonathan H., and Leonard Beeghley. 1981. *The Emergence of Sociological Theory.* Homewood, Ill.: Dorsey Press.
  Presentation in propositional form of the basic ideas of eight major theorists whose work provided the foundations of modern sociology.

Part One

COMMUNICATIVE PROCESSES

II

SYMBOLIC RECONSTRUCTION

Fascinated by independent reports of people dying upon being hexed in Haiti, Africa, Australia, and elsewhere, Walter Cannon, an eminent physiologist, carefully examined available medical records, whenever possible even interviewing the attending physician. Some victims had died after eating forbidden food, even though scientists agreed the food contained nothing toxic. Others had died after violating some other sacred taboo; still others had died after a medicine man had pointed a bone at them. Cannon eliminated all cases of possible poisoning and concentrated on those in which a competent doctor had examined the body and confirmed that there was no adequate medical explanation for the death. The scattered accounts reveal a number of similarities. Upon learning that a spell has been cast on them, the victims become convinced that they are going to die. Friends and relatives are helpless, for the victims decline all offers of assistance and will not eat, drink, or make any other effort to sustain themselves. If the hex is removed by magical means, they suddenly recover. Otherwise the victim gradually weakens and dies. The records also disclose similar symptoms—rapid pulse, clammy skin, low blood pressure—all indices of intense, sustained emotion. Low blood pressure damages the heart, for there is insufficient oxygen; lack of food and water leads to dehydration, which worsens the condition. After reviewing the evidence, Cannon (1942) concluded that such accounts are not hoaxes and suggested that the victims may have died of intense fear.

People who do not believe in voodoo or a similar religion cannot be killed in this manner. Records show that within the community of believers the victims are treated as if they are already dead. As preparations are made to perform the ceremony to send them on to the next world, the victims become obsessed by the knowledge that everyone else knows of their misfortune (Warner, 1937:242). The phenomenon of voodoo death suggests that human beings are constantly striving to come to terms with the world as they believe it to be, even when scientific evidence fails to support their beliefs. Devout believers in voodoo are not alone in their adherence to scientifically unverifiable beliefs. Toward the end of each year children become preoccupied with a jovial, bearded gentleman who will descend their chimney with gifts; a week later their parents feel obliged to imbibe alcohol to celebrate a midnight that is much like all other midnights. Human beings are constantly adapting to their environment, but such observations raise questions as to the nature of the environment in which people live.

One of the most pervasive beliefs among people the world over is that reality is whatever they experience, that perceptual experience is a mirror image of the world as it actually is. Should anyone seriously disagree with something that any of us sees and hears, we assume that someone must be hallucinating. Yet research in physics, physiology, psychology, and anthropology all confirm that each person's experience of the world is constructed through selective perception, and some philosophers have dismissed the popular view as "the naive realism of common sense." But if reality is not an exact copy of what we believe it to be, what is the character of the environment to which human beings adapt? Furthermore, how is it possible for different people to reach any kind of consensus in defining situations?

MAPPING THE ENVIRONMENT: OBJECTS

The Construction of Objects. The effective environment in which human beings live and act is made up of objects. The term "object," a central concept in sociology, does not necessarily refer to material things. An *object* consists of anything that becomes involved in a social transaction, including material things as well as the goals of the enterprise, other people who are involved, their roles, leadership, beliefs, ideals, and other relevant items. Among the most important objects in most transactions are those the participants form of themselves. As we define the various situations in which we are involved, we usually locate ourselves in the context and recognize our relationship to each of the other participants.

Only when we can place ourselves in the situation can we recognize our responsibilities. Each of our contributions to the transaction may then be affected by considerations such as pride, ambition, or shame.

The physical environment is what it is, but different parts of it enter into our lives as we try to cope with it. We do not respond to all the sensory cues that bombard us; we are selectively responsive to those features of the environment that are relevant to our interests. As we become involved in a social transaction, we become selectively sensitized to whatever has to be taken into account to bring the transaction to satisfactory completion. Even when everyone agrees about the physical attributes of some material object, people with different interests experience it differently. Most French people, for example, regard escargots as one of the most desirable of appetizers, but many other people would never consider eating snails. Similarly, people living in the Pacific Northwest are so accustomed to rain that they hardly notice it; for farmers in the arid Southwest, however, the coming of rain is a major event. Most urban Americans regard the excreta of animals as odious and disgusting, but to peasants throughout the world fertilizer is valuable, and serious quarrels sometimes erupt about proprietory rights over dung left on their land by the animals of others.

Furthermore, many objects do not have a precise physical counterpart. When disgruntled employees condemn "the company," for example, they are referring to some entity that serves as a useful scapegoat, much as the term "establishment" did in the 1960s. Although a corporation can be identified in terms of its assets, its personnel, and its procedures, these are not what is being designated. Often "the company" is used to vaguely personify its more conspicuous officers or to refer to whatever aspects of a corporation the speaker dislikes. Finally, many objects, such as ideas, may have no physical counterpart at all. Thus, the effective environment with which human beings are coping may be quite different from the actual material surroundings.

Objects are units of experience that enable people to carry out their activities. People who live in the same community but are involved in different activities perceive their surroundings somewhat differently. Varying perspectives are most apparent between those with specialized interests, but they occur to some extent among all people. Dog fanciers, for example, are sensitive to all kinds of distinctions among canines that others barely notice. Different breeds are important to them, and they know the key attributes of each. For most people, however, dogs are dogs, some more attractive or more vicious than others. In the same way, a physician notices all kinds of symptoms that escape the attention of the untrained—dilated pupils, swelling, sweating, slight tremors, strained stances—external marks that indicate what is happening within the body. Similarly, geologists or botanists at a picnic see much that others do not; in a real sense they are enjoying a different world. How we organize experiences into objects depends on the activities in which we are involved, and people in various groups often perceive the identical material environment in quite different ways. People who do not speak the same language and have dissimilar cultural backgrounds develop even more divergent perspectives.

A Behavioral Approach to Meaning.   What we do or refuse to do with reference to an object depends on what it means to us. We use the term "meaning" frequently, but we usually find it hard to define. Meaning is often thought to be an attribute of words, or it may be regarded as the inherent characteristic of an object; sometimes we view it as an idea mysteriously floating about in the mind. A number of scholars, including Dewey (1926:179–80), propose a more effective way of approaching the subject. The *meaning* of any object is the manner in which we are organized to act toward it. Thus, the meaning of a utensil is the manner in which we use it. The meaning of an event is the manner in which we are prepared to participate in it—a dance, a political demonstration, a job interview. To a farmer, rain is a welcome gift. To an infantryman, however, the meaning of rain is quite different, for it may be more deadly than some of the enemy's weapons. Thus, meaning is primarily an attribute of behavior and only secondarily the property of the thing itself. The meaning of anything is what one is predisposed to do with it; the object's physical characteristics merely limit what can be done with it. At first this may sound like an unusual way of using the term, but it is actually quite close to common usage and helps us develop a better understanding of human life.

Once we define meaning as a form of behavior, we must consider the behavior patterns in terms of which we can specify the meaning of various objects. But we cannot identify the meaning of most objects by any single pattern of activity. How we handle an object varies from one transaction to another and from one situation to another. A cigarette is something that a smoker lights before inhaling, but it is also something that other people avoid as an obnoxious object, even staying clear of the smoke. Yet both smokers and nonsmokers avoid touching the lighted end. What people do with any object depends on the exigencies of the specific context in which they encounter it. Thus, everyone does a wide variety of things with any familiar object. What unifies these diverse acts is the fact that they are all based on a set of beliefs — often presuppositions that are taken for granted — about the object's characteristics. Some of these beliefs may be mistaken, but we act as if they were true. Thus, the meaning of an object is a fairly stable relationship between it and a living organism. The nature of the relationship depends on the assumptions with which we approach the object. If we assume it has certain attributes — such as being very hot on one end — we are prepared to avoid the part that is likely to burn our skin. As Mead (1938:103–39) puts it, we perceive our world in terms of hypotheses, although they are seldom formulated with the precision required in science. We project expectations onto our world and then become selectively responsive to those cues that will confirm our expectations. A number of psychological experiments support this view (Postman, 1951; Kilpatrick, 1961). Thus, the meaning of an object is the way in which we are oriented toward it — a predisposition or state of readiness to act. Just what we actually do varies with the specific circumstances.

The significance of any object consequently varies from person to person and from group to group, for it depends on how we are prepared to use it. Although this statement sounds complicated at first, all of us intuitively recognize such relationships, especially in detecting differences in the meaning of some common object for different people. We detect the differences precisely by noticing variations in response. If one of our neighbors is constantly washing and polishing his car, gets upset easily when a fender is slightly dented, and speaks proudly and frequently of his car's performance, we infer that the automobile is for him a showpiece and status symbol. If another neighbor pays little attention to the appearance of her car and does not even notice new dents, we infer that her car is only a means of transportation. A television set may be a source of entertainment, a status symbol, an educational device, or just a "boob tube." Some people hate books, considering them a source of drudgery to be read only as a class assignment. Others see books as sources of useful knowledge to be consulted when help is needed to solve problems. Still others enjoy reading and love books as sources of great pleasure. Thus, the meaning of anything is the relatively enduring organization of beliefs that predispose us to respond in one way rather than another. As Peirce (1923:44) puts it, there is no distinction of meaning so fine as to consist of anything more than a possible difference in practice.

The Classification of Objects. No two objects are exactly alike, but the world in which we live is much too complicated for us to treat each unit in terms of its unique features. If we had to consider the distinctive characteristics of each object, adjustments would be slow and difficult. For example, we could encounter rabid animals anywhere, but if we had to stop to ascertain the health of each dog we met, we would soon become immobilized. Since the world is too complex for us to handle each item in terms of its distinctive attributes, we classify objects into categories. Once we do so, we can ignore differences that are irrelevant to what we are doing and act toward all items in each category as if they were alike. Thus, each automobile driver is unique, and each drives in a different manner. But we work on the assumption that all drivers are sufficiently sane not to be bent on running down pedestrians for "kicks." If we did not accept this belief on faith, we could not venture out in traffic. Placing objects into categories helps us cope with a complex and ever-changing world.

Classifications always involve an arbitrary element. The world is filled with things that share some common quality while differing in other respects. Since everything is unique, most objects are classifiable in several ways. We may categorize material things in terms of size, shape, color, or weight. Depending on our interests, we may classify the same thing differently. A fancy wristwatch, for example, may be placed with sundials and hourglasses into the category of timepieces or with brooches and necklaces as jewelry. Just as the meaning of a particular object is a way of acting toward it, the meaning of a category is also an orientation. Once we have classified objects, we can ignore many unique features and become organized to act toward any item in terms of its generic features. Most people maintain a safe distance from snakes without bothering to ascertain whether a particular reptile is dangerous. Popular categories are notoriously inexact, vague, and overlapping. But even scientific concepts, categories that seem so elegantly and precisely defined, are to some extent arbitrary. In spite of such difficulties, however, our ability to classify our experiences into types of objects makes it easier for us to cope with the world—by giving us some notion of what to anticipate upon encountering specific objects for the first time.

Among the most important of the objects we classify are human beings. We realize that no two people in the world are alike, that our categories contain an arbitrary element, but that they nonetheless facilitate concerted action. Human beings may be classified in terms of several criteria: among others, sex, age, height, weight, nationality, occupation, religion, political commitment, income, ethnic identity. Among the most important bases for classification in the United States today are age, sex, occupation, and ethnic identity. We think that younger people know less about the world and are thus likely to be more impulsive and irresponsible. We assume that older people are more mature, even though there is considerable evidence to the contrary. Participants in the women's liberation movement have called attention to the many false assumptions commonly made about women. We classify most adult Americans in terms of what they do to earn a living and address them with a deference commensurate with the estimate placed on the importance of their work. Ethnic identity is also important, and since World War II, considerable effort has been made to expose the falseness of ethnic stereotypes. Because such categories are often inaccurate and sometimes unfair, some have proposed eliminating them. While we cannot quarrel with the ideal that each human being should be addressed in terms of his or her individual characteristics, it is impractical to try to eliminate the categorization of people. As Lippmann (1922:79–156) points out, people simply do not have the time to acquire accurate, detailed knowledge about each of the objects with which they become involved. They have to act in terms of generalities.

Many sexist, racist, and other stereotypes are inaccurate to the point of being unjust. Yet since each of us knows personally only a handful of people, we approach everyone else we encounter as an instance of one or more categories. Sociologists have found it useful to distinguish between *categorical* and *personal* contacts in designating varying degrees of social distance among people. *Social distance* refers to the sense of closeness and mutual identification that human beings feel toward one another, and it varies on a continuum from an enemy whom one hates and wants to destroy to one's most intimate friends. Simmel (1950:307–29) suggests that social distance may be measured roughly in terms of the kind of knowledge that people have of one another. Social distance is smallest when we know the other person as a distinct human being; we are familiar with his or her idiosyncrasies and values, hopes and anxieties, strengths and weaknesses. Social distance is minimized in personal contacts with close friends, members of the family, and co-workers of some duration. Our contacts with all others are likely to be categorical.

Our knowledge of other people is specialized. We know very little about the mail carrier or the clerks in stores we patronize regularly other than in terms of their ability to perform their roles. Such limitations are unavoidable. How can we possibly find out about the personal characteristics of each individual we encounter? We can distinguish one clerk from another, but we make similar assumptions about them all. We neglect their differences; it does not matter how tall they are, what kind of music they like, or what color their skin is. Our relations with such comparative strangers and acquaintances are not necessarily unfriendly or unpleasant. If we are served by the same mail carrier for several years, we may get to like him because of his efficiency and pleasantness. But what do we know of his family life or his aspirations for his children? We know virtually nothing about him as a distinct human being, but all our transactions with him go smoothly. Indeed, there are many transactions we can carry out more effectively when we leave out personal feelings, especially in providing professional services—relationships between teacher and student, social worker and client, nurse and patient, police officer and offender. Precisely because we can treat strangers more objectively, we can accomplish technical tasks more easily.

Meanings as Conventional Norms. The meanings of some objects are idiosyncratic. A person may be nauseated by prunes, excited by white hair, or frightened by green eyes. But the meanings of most objects are orientations that we have learned by participating in social life. Each person learns how to recognize and handle objects while participating in group activities. We are instructed on the proper way to approach and use them and are punished for using them improperly. Objects are constructed in social interaction. We learn to organize our experiences into units similar to those others use. We approach one another with shared expectations concerning the units into which we have organized our experiences; we recognize and define objects in similar ways. The meanings of most objects are social not only because we have learned them from others but also because other people are taken into account as we prepare to act toward them. This suggests that all well-established meanings are conventional norms. We share common understandings as to what we should or should not do with various categories of objects.

EVALUATIONS AND EMOTIONAL REACTIONS

Emotion as an Attribute of Behavior. Although few would discount the importance of emotions in human life, in daily discourse we tend to think and speak vaguely of emotional reactions as something we feel, some inner sensation such as anger, fear, joy, revulsion, or sadness. Sometimes we regard emotion as a condition that "causes" irrational conduct. Much more exploration is needed before we will understand human nature. Considerable research has been done, and while there is no consensus among the experts, several helpful hypotheses have been formulated. Emotion is an attribute of behavior, a characteristic that behavior assumes under certain conditions. We do not do and feel things as separate operations; much of what we do is to some extent emotional. To be sure, there are some objects, such as doorknobs, that we can approach in a purely neutral manner; where activity is not emotional, it appears to be cold and mechanical and is often called "lifeless."

Behavior becomes emotional when the autonomic nervous system (ANS) is activated. Apparently the brain stimulates certain endocrine glands, and hormones such as the adrenocorticotrophic (ACTH) are released; their release activates other hormones, and various chemical changes occur in the body. Pioneering research was done by Cannon (1929), who discovered that whenever ongoing behavior is thwarted, certain changes take place automatically within the body. Such changes include increased secretion of adrenaline, acceleration of the heartbeat, constriction of blood vessels that channel blood to muscles and to the brain, inhibition of stomach contractions, liberation of sugar from the liver, dilation of bronchioles, increase in the metabolism rate, and widening of the pupils of the eyes. As we know from experience, such changes are virtually impossible to control voluntarily; they simply happen. The term "gut reaction" is accurate in that emotional arousal is a biotic pattern in which the stomach is conspicuously involved.

Cannon notes that all these changes render an organism more efficient for physical struggle, for they supply all the essential conditions for continuing action by laboring muscles. Since the changes occur when we encounter frustrations or unusual demands, Cannon declared that emotional arousal is an emergency reaction that facilitates the mobilization of our resources for the extra effort necessary to overcome an obstacle. Selye (1956) calls the changes a "general adaptation syndrome" — what enables one to make extraordinary efforts to meet unusual demands. If the reaction does not become too intense, perception becomes focused, cognition and imagination are sharper, and motor coordination is better. Thus, an organism is able to cope more effectively with emergencies.

But ANS arousal is not confined to situations in which one is thwarted. It may occur after an emergency is over, as when a driver feels palpitating heartbeat and sweats profusely after stopping a car just short of striking a child who has darted in front of it. The kind of exhilaration and joy we feel after completing some arduous task or reaching a goal after a long period of striving can hardly be regarded as an emergency reaction. Paulhan (1930:13–34) suggests that intense lust is aroused when desire cannot be consummated immediately because the necessary object is not at hand. On the basis of such observations, Duffy (1941) proposes the hypothesis that the inner sensations we perceive and label as emotional arise whenever there is some discrepancy between organic mobilization to act and what is actually being done. Thus, in the case of joy, a person is overmobilized; since the task has been completed, there is nothing more to do. Once a desired object is at hand, the act is consummated and lust disappears. We feel anger most intensely when preparing for aggression; when the attack is actually in progress, we feel it less strongly. Anger is experienced more during the sparring than when blows are being struck.

The Direction of Emotional Behavior. When ANS arousal occurs, we cannot always classify our emotional reaction. Sometimes we realize that we are upset, but we cannot label our subjective experience as any particular emotion. But often there is no doubt about how we feel — as in anger or fear. Not only can we recognize the difference between fear and anger, but our behavior takes on a definite direction. An angry person is disposed to approach the environment in a particular manner; perception, cognition, and conation take on a definite bearing. Perception becomes very selective. When we become angry, our attention is focused on the source of frustration, attributes of the object that make us angry, and weaknesses that will enable us to get back at it. Our thinking and imagination are similarly directed. When we are fuming with anger, we imagine beating our adversaries to a pulp or imagine some accident or embarrassment that might befall them, perhaps even their demise. Appropriate neuromuscular sets are activated: We become physically mobilized to attack, even though we may not actually follow through. Similarly, when we are frightened, we take on a definite stance. We become sensitized to cues of danger and try to avoid the source of danger. If we cannot avoid it, we want to escape. If we cannot escape, we turn to defensive measures. If trapped, we lash out in desperation, like a cornered animal. Our thinking and imagination become full of possibilities for getting out of the situation; we may become obsessed with it. This stance is easy to recognize, both in ourselves and in others. Dewey (1934:58–78) labels behavior as expressive when an individual's emotional orientation provides the selective basis for sensitivities to cues and the formation of objects. Emotional orientations thus constitute ways of relating to our environment.

Since we generally have little difficulty differentiating subjectively among fear, anger, and other common emotional reactions, physiologists have searched for organic differences underlying these orientations. But more than a half century of careful research has led to the conclusion that ANS arousal is nonspecific; it is the same in all linguistically distinguishable emotions. Viewed in this light, an experiment performed by Schachter and Singer (1962) is particularly significant, as the following simplified and selective account illustrates. The psychologists informed their subjects that they were participating in a study of the effects of certain vitamins on vision; then they injected one group with epinephrine—a substance also known as adrenaline—and injected another group with a placebo. They warned some of those given epinephrine that they might experience palpitations, tremors, and a flushing of the face as side effects of the "vitamins." They did not tell the others what to anticipate. Thus, the subjects were divided into three categories: epinephrine and warned of possible consequences, epinephrine and not warned, and the placebo.

Each subject then spent some time in a cubicle with a person who appeared to be a fellow experimental subject but who in fact was a trained confederate of the experimenters. In half the cases the confederate pretended to be happy; he was pleasant, played games with scrap paper in the room, and created a congenial atmosphere. In the rest of the cases the confederate pretended to be angry; he complained about the experiment, was sullen, and created a generally unpleasant atmosphere. The subjects who had received a placebo and whose ANS was not aroused were only slightly responsive to the confederate's antics and showed little emotional reaction. Those who received epinephrine but had been warned of possible sensations were for the most part also unresponsive. However, most of those who had been aroused but had not been warned became quite gay or angry—in the direction suggested by the confederate. The experimenters concluded that the direction of emotion does not depend on ANS arousal alone but on cognitive factors, in particular the social context in which the arousal occurs. This is consistent with Becker's (1967) findings that reactions to sensations induced by drugs such a marijuana and LSD depend on how the feelings are interpreted by the subject with the aid of people in whose company the drug is taken.

In the absence of a satisfactory explanation of the direction of emotional reactions, a hypothesis may be proposed, one that enables us to make sense out of many commonplace observations: The direction of emotional behavior depends on a person's definition of the situation, especially on the manner in which one, or any object with which one identifies, is located within the situation. If a woman considers herself in grave danger, for example, her instinctive reaction is to defend herself. A similar reaction is elicited if she views the situation as one in which a close friend, a pet, or some other object of value is imperiled. Some drivers become enraged on being caught in a traffic jam, even when they are in no particular hurry; they define the frustrating circumstance as a personal affront. Others are annoyed at the inconvenience but do not become angry; they define the situation as one of the inevitable nuisances of life. Nor do we react only to our physical surroundings. Much depends on the manner in which we characterize ourselves. If a man views himself as having failed to meet an obligation, his reaction is one of shame; if he defines himself as having failed to live up to his own moral standards, he feels guilt (Piers and Singer, 1953). Many students have had their memory suddenly go blank during an examination. Whether or not they panic depends not only on the importance of the test but also on their estimate of their own ability. The few who regard themselves as geniuses may well be humiliated and become very upset; others may just dismiss the examination as unfairly difficult and curse the teacher. Human beings also react to abstract objects. We may develop intense excitement over the possibility that some political ideology that we dislike will prevail in an election. This hypothesis goes far beyond Schachter and Singer's findings. It suggests that the directing of our emotional reactions is essentially a social process.

The Social Framework of Emotions. Arnold (1960: 177–82) suggests that the direction of emotional reactions depends on our appraisal of objects, but the matter is actually somewhat more complicated. In each community or group, familiar objects are evaluated in customary ways, and these appraisals consistently underlie definitions of situations. But the circumstance under which we encounter the objects is crucial. In our society a bear is regarded as a dangerous object. Our general reaction is avoidance; even imagining an encounter with a bear can be frightening. Yet our reaction differs from one context to another. Should we encounter one on a picnic, most of us would react with fear. Upon seeing a bear in a zoo, however, our reaction may well be one of curiosity. If a ranger on the picnic grounds locks up the animal, we are grateful to the ranger. If someone else then turns it loose again, we feel anger toward the person who has been so careless with a source of danger. Similarly, in every group certain objects are hated, generally because they are believed to be sources of frustration. If we hate something, its mere presence is likely to elicit anger. If a hated object is lost or injured, we experience joy. If it is attacked by a third party, we cheer the assailant; if we feel it necessary, we may even join in the assault. Thus, we generally evaluate objects in conventional ways, and our emotional reactions depend on the particular circumstances in which we have to deal with them.

Our emotional reactions to objects that are evaluated unambiguously are so regular that we can make inferences about such appraisals by observing configurations of responses. How can we tell that people regard an object as base or inferior? They generally avoid it. They are embarrassed if it is present, relieved if it is absent, happy if it is lost. If we inadvertently come into contact with something dirty, we feel revulsion. We may even feel revulsion on observing other people touching a base object, such as a small child playing with excreta. In rural India a person of high caste who accidentally touches a pariah or eats food prepared by a cook of the wrong caste feels contaminated and will be uncomfortable until purification rituals have been performed. The same is true of an object that is evaluated as very desirable — such as a man's fiancee. If she is present, he feels pleasure; if she is absent, he feels anxiety; if she is lost or unaccounted for, he feels deep grief; if she is attacked, he becomes enraged at the assailant (Shand, 1896; Mayeroff, 1971). Such reactions are more apparent when the appraisal enjoys a high degree of consensus, as with a sacred object. The destruction of religious objects or the desecration of graves is likely to elicit spontaneous reactions of outrage. Thus, regular patterns are discernible. The evaluation of an object is a part of its meaning, and the appraisal of that object can be inferred from sets of emotional reactions.

Thus, in every community or group, conventional norms arise concerning the evaluation of objects and the appropriate reaction to various situations. Every society also has a lexicon of emotions, words that describe what the proper reactions should be. We learn to expect certain emotions from a person who is related to some object in an understood way — such as grief over the loss of a family heirloom or elation over a friend's good fortune. We learn to avow such reactions; even if we are not grateful upon receiving a gift, we try to feel that way and sometimes become guilt stricken for not responding as we should (Hochschild, 1979). Furthermore, we become sensitized to expressive movements on the part of others that indicate the anticipated affect. Whenever we perceive another's emotional reaction, we try to understand it by placing that person in a situation in which the response appears appropriate. Sometimes we make judgments about whether the situation warrants the reaction. Perhaps someone is overreacting by becoming unduly angry over economic conditions about which nothing can be done. If we feel that the antagonism is not justified, we may accuse the person of pretense. Anyone who handles an object in a manner that is incongruent with its customary appraisal may be defined as eccentric or even dangerous. Indeed, what psychiatrists call "inappropriate affect" consists precisely of violating such conventional norms. Serious questions are raised about the sanity of people who cry when nothing seems sad or laugh when nothing seems funny. We feel uncomfortable in the presence of someone who apparently enjoys seeing the suffering of others.

Individual Differences in Emotions. What makes the study of emotional behavior so difficult is that the reactions are both global and idiosyncratic. Emotions apparently have an instinctive base; dogs and other animals show the basic patterns of fear, anger, and lust. Once emotions are directed, the patterns — posture, facial expression, motor tendency — are so similar that they are readily recognizable in many contexts. When emotional arousal becomes intense, impression management becomes difficult and people act more impulsively. Such reactions are apparently identical for human beings the world over, even though there are vast differences in the evaluation of particular objects. Indeed, it is the similarity of emotional reactions that sometimes makes possible an initial understanding of those from very different cultural backgrounds. Strangers who do not share a common language may be baffled by many of the things they see, but the detection of familiar emotional reactions often helps them identify with one another as human beings.

There are also differences among individuals who share the same cultural background. Physiologists have detected differences among people in their tendency to react aggressively or to withdraw from stressful situations (Funkenstein, 1955). Even when people share evaluations of objects, each individual has personal experiences that lead to different reactions. Parents, for example, are supposed to be desirable objects, and most people profess to have favorable orientations toward them. In fact, however, many individuals have had painful experiences with their parents and may have developed strongly negative appraisals. They may even hate their parents, feeling guilty that they are not responding appropriately. Thus, even when a high degree of consensus arises, the emotional reactions of various individuals may differ. Sometimes such variations are even exploited. A snake dancer who has little fear of reptiles takes advantage of the fact that most members of the audience fear them. This brings an element of excitement into what might otherwise be a drab performance. Most important, each person has a unique style of reacting, a distinctive mode of expression. Thus, in some contexts only our most intimate associates can tell how we actually feel.

SYMBOLIC REPRESENTATION OF OBJECTS

Characteristics of Symbols. Human life gets many of its distinctive characteristics from the fact that people are able to substitute symbols for meanings of all kinds. A *symbol* stands for something else; it is something to which one responds as if it were an object. Examples include words that stand for categories of objects, the thumbing of a hitchhiker, a handshake of greeting, a flag as an emblem for a nation, a beard as an indication of protest in the early 1960s, a police officer's uniform as an indicator of status, or compulsive hand washing as a way of expiating a sense of guilt.

There is no necessary connection between a symbol and the meaning for which it stands. There is no necessary tie between words—articulated sounds or marks on paper—and the objects they designate. The connection is customary; within each universe of discourse there are norms that certain combinations of sounds or marks stand for certain meanings. Notations in mathematics or in music have no meaning in themselves and have no significance for those who have not been trained to interpret them. On seeing a wink, persons from some cultural backgrounds may assume the winker is having trouble dislodging something from his or her eye. There is nothing intrinsic in a piece of colored cloth that would point to a nation; the proverbial creature from Mars would be baffled on seeing soldiers die for a flag on the battlefield, for even the most careful examination of the cloth would not reveal the importance the soldiers attach to it. Thus, all symbolism implies meanings that cannot be derived directly by examining the symbols themselves. Although the derivation of words is important to students of linguistics concerned with how languages develop, those who seek the real meaning of words by examining their derivations are wasting their time.

Symbolic behavior also involves a reduction in the use of energy. A symbol is usually something that is trivial in itself, but the meaning for which it stands is of considerable significance. Traffic signals are not important in themselves, but they designate meanings of great consequence. The slight difference in sound between "guilty" and "not guilty" has consequences that alter drastically the lives of many people. Before the 1960s many white Americans in the South refused to eat at the same table with Afro-Americans. This was not from fear of contamination; rather, dining together was regarded as an acknowledgment of social equality. Close contact in itself was not seen as objectionable, but what it symbolized was a distinction that many regarded as the basis of their way of life. Anything can become a symbol if it is relatively simple, not too interesting, and not distracting. If it is too interesting in its own right, it may distract attention from the object it represents (Sapir, 1949:564–68).

Referential Symbolism. *Referential symbols* consist of widely accepted means used to designate various objects and categories. In each community there are common understandings that devices such as spoken and written language, mathematical notations, the telegraphic code, uniforms of all sorts, and emblems such as the swastika or the cross stand for various meanings. Just what meanings are being referred to is a matter of custom. For example, speech consists of utterances that are governed by conventional norms. The manner in which various sounds are articulated as well as the order in which the articulation is to occur are not dictated by physical necessity; in each community there are norms of proper usage (grammar), and those who violate them are subject to social sanctions, usually ridicule. The use of symbols to represent objects greatly expands our capacity to cope with our environment and enables us to act toward objects that are not physically present, indeed, even toward objects that have no physical existence at all.

Language is the symbol system par excellence. The various combinations of sounds are easy to produce. The vocal musculature can articulate an infinitely large number of configurations. A limited set of sounds can designate thousands of meanings. When writing is substituted for spoken words, the specifications can become more precise, complex, and lasting. Language is of fundamental importance because it facilitates the manipulation and combination of complex meanings. If the meanings of objects remain organized predispositions to act, as they are with most animals, the extent to which they can be manipulated is limited. If symbols can be used to represent appropriate ways of handling various objects, however, the meanings can be lifted out of the contexts in which they originally took shape and can be combined with other meanings.

Language facilitates interpersonal communication. As long as people share common norms concerning the articulation of sounds and what the combinations represent, they can make all kinds of indications to one another. Thus linguistic norms make possible the sharing of meanings as well as emotional reactions and facilitate the formation of mutual orientations. Without a common language establishing and maintaining consensus becomes very difficult, as becomes obvious whenever we try to coordinate our activities with strangers who do not understand our language. Through linguistic communication we learn about all kinds of objects we have never encountered directly — such as historical events, popular heroes, and places we have never visited. All such objects are an important part of our perspective; even if we have never experienced them directly, we take them into account in making decisions. Some of the things we fear and hate most intensely are objects we have never encountered; they are abstract objects, such as enemies in time of war, that have been constructed through communication. From written sources we can even learn from the experiences of people who have been dead for centuries. Thus, referential symbolism extends our environment enormously.

But language is not the only form of referential symbolism; many other substitutes are used for convenient and easy reference to complex meanings. Bodily gestures of all kinds — gritting one's teeth, caressing someone, placing an arm on someone's shoulder — are also symbols. The firmness of a handshake sometimes indicates the quality of the relationship between two people. Although some bodily gestures are spontaneous expressive movements, many are conventional (Birdwhistell, 1970). For example, if we compare the manner in which people in different cultures express approval, we find that Americans make a circle with thumb and forefinger; the French kiss their fingers; Sicilians pinch their cheeks; and Brazilians pinch their earlobes. Our clothing as well as our coiffure can be symbolic. Short hair was an indication of servitude among the ancient Celts, Germans, and Greeks; when the Manchus conquered China in 1644, they required all male Chinese to wear pigtails as an indication of their loyalty to the regime. Uniforms of all kinds indicate status, and in some communities skin color is an important symbol of rank. Many prostitutes deliberately adorn themselves in line with popular stereotypes to facilitate establishing contact with potential clients. The possession of objects may be symbolic. In some circles owning the latest model of an expensive automobile is an important indicator of rank. Some rituals, such as the exchange of gifts, are performed just to indicate proper respect. Even the arrangement of objects in space may be indicative of other meanings. The show windows of exclusive stores are seldom cluttered; the sparse display is a way of discouraging the poor from bothering to come in. The seating arrangement of guests in formal dinners is sometimes by rank; some guests may be dejected at being placed too far from the hostess, even though they detest her as a person. These examples demonstrate how referential symbols organize the way we experience our environment.

Expressive Symbolism. An *expressive symbol* is a substitute for the direct execution of emotional behavior. The direct expression of emotions such as anger can be costly, and symbolic acts enable us to release emotional tension less disruptively. The apparently meaningless handwashing ritual in some obsessive-compulsive neuroses permits unconscious fulfillment of an inhibited tendency; guilt-ridden persons who define themselves as filthy keep washing their hands in symbolic atonement —

sometimes until their flesh is raw. The symbolic act temporarily dissipates intense emotional reactions through behavior patterns that are far removed from the original context in which the meaning developed. Expressive symbolism is a highly condensed form of substitute behavior for direct expression, allowing for the ready release of emotional tension in conscious or unconscious form.

Expressive symbolism may be found in many different contexts, such as art, ritual, and even politics. All kinds of symbolic acts provide gratifications that may otherwise be difficult to attain. Some scholars regard art as the representation of an emotional state in the language of some artistic mode — pictorial depiction, musical statement, or material fabrication (Dewey, 1934; Langer, 1942). Thus, the songs of Elvis Presley channeled the values of millions. Listening to his songs, and thus vicariously participating in them, gave symbolic expression to the hopes, aspirations, and anxieties of a whole generation of people. Rituals are symbolic acts that reaffirm emotional climates, thus facilitating appropriate conduct — as in funerals or weddings. Courtroom rituals make for solemnity and assure proper decorum. The same is certainly true of many religious ceremonies. Expressive symbolism also plays an important part in politics. Many political events are essentially symbolic acts. The assassination of a hated official may not actually change an unpopular government policy, but it does enable activists and those who feel oppressed to discharge some of their hostility. Similarly, the appointment of an investigative committee may not change a condition that calls for remedial action, but it does help reassure those who feel that something should be done (Edelman, 1964). In 1944, when the Nazi armies were driven out of France, the French shaved the heads of women who had fraternized with the Germans and forced the women to parade nude through their communities. The enraged populace could thus express its disapproval without actually killing the collaborators.

Although it is useful to distinguish analytically between referential and expressive symbolism, the two often blend in daily life. Swearing involves using words of reference but is clearly a form of expression; it permits us to discharge anger without actually assaulting the frustrating object. For many people the national flag is a symbol of reference; it is also associated with emotional reactions that underlie their self-esteem. Thus, the two forms of symbolism merge. Sapir (1927) suggests that referential symbolism may have developed out of expressive symbolism. He points to the possibility that striking out at a dangerous foe gradually took on a referential character; it was first reduced to the gesture of shaking the fist and then further reduced to insulting words. The more dissociated a symbol from its original context, the less emotional it becomes and the more it takes on the character of pure reference.

As referential symbolism becomes highly developed, as in language, it becomes subject to independent usage; hence, poetry and musical forms designate complex meanings completely unrelated to their original contexts. Thus language may have had its roots in dissociated and emotionally denuded cries that originally dissipated emotional tension. Once referential symbolism was established as a by-product of behavior, more conscious symbols of reference were developed by copying in abbreviated or simplified form the thing being designated. But when intense emotional reactions are elicited, the conventional norms fall away, and people once again produce involuntary sounds that are highly expressive—sobbing hysterically, yelling, or even barking. In the same manner, in religious rituals what was once a direct expression of euphoria becomes institutionalized into symbols of membership in a congregation.

Thinking as Inner Communication. What is commonly called "thinking" consists of imagery and subvocal linguistic communication. We talk to ourselves, thus facilitating our making adjustments. Linguistic symbols enable us to contemplate meanings long after the objects are gone; we can organize and reorganize previously learned meanings in new situations. Numerous studies demonstrate that much of thinking is linguistic communication, but one of the most ingenious is Max's (1937) experiment. Since the finger and arm muscles are the locus of gestural communication for the deaf, to detect whether contractions occur when deaf people are thinking the experiment called for electrodes to be placed on those muscles. The control group consisted of persons with normal hearing. Abstract thought problems elicited manual action currents in 84 percent of the deaf but only 31 percent of the control group; no overt movements were visible in either. When deaf subjects were asleep, the onset of dreams could be detected in many instances by the appearance of large action currents in the arm and finger muscles, although such responses were usually not accompanied by overt movements. Thus, cognition consists for the most part of information processing. Reasoning, planning, and foresight are all forms of symbolic communication. Thinking enables us to anticipate what is likely to happen and to get ready prior to commitment in overt behavior.

How any individual defines a situation depends both on referential and expressive symbolism. Since thinking is largely inner speech, people define the situation in which they are involved by telling themselves what is happening. One's reaction to this definition often involves some evaluation and subsequent emotional reaction, which may be expressed directly, may merely affect the style of one's behavior, or may be discharged in symbolic form. Misunderstandings frequently arise when we see unconscious meanings, full of intense emotion, as mere references. As complex as this sounds, we are so accustomed to it that most of us are able to detect fine nuances of meaning in the conduct of others.

HUMAN KNOWLEDGE AS A SOCIAL PROCESS

Symbolic Environments. The effective environment in which human beings live and act is largely symbolic, one that is organized for the most part in terms of linguistic symbols. Through words we develop orientations toward all kinds of objects, including many with which we have never had direct contact. We live in an environment that we construct while participating in social transactions with people with whom we are in sustained association. Each situation, as the participants define it, includes many objects that are not actually present but must nonetheless be taken into account — memories of similar occurrences in the past and aspirations in contexts that are yet to come. At the same time countless features of the natural environment that are actually present — viruses, cosmic rays, objects that are irrelevant to what we are doing, to say nothing of biotic and social processes that are not well understood — are ignored, even though some of them may eventually prove important. Furthermore, since perspectives are constructed with symbols, they may include objects that have no physical existence. People concern themselves with ghosts and witches as well as with objections that others might raise that in fact never materialize. For centuries mathematicians have worked with negative numbers, which refer to entities that cannot possibly exist. To a religious person what is imputed to God certainly makes a difference; whether God's existence can be demonstrated by scientific standards does not matter. Similarly, for those who believe that after death they will join their long-departed ancestors, the reactions imputed to such personifications enter significantly into current decisions. Thus, what makes human beings so different from most other creatures is the fact that we have an imagination.

Our ability to construct objects, to classify them, and to designate them by symbols enables us to experience our ever-changing universe as if it were orderly and predictable. In fact, each historical event is unique; nothing ever occurs twice in exactly the same manner. Our sensory experiences are elusive and never repeat themselves. Every object we encounter is distinctive, even though some precision-made objects are so similar that we cannot tell them apart. We cannot forecast exactly what will happen in any given historical context, not even in a controlled scientific experiment. If we perceived our surroundings as they actually are, coping would be difficult. But we assume that all objects in a given category are alike and that familiar classes of events will take place much as they have before. As long as everyone in a community or group works with the same presuppositions, they are able to understand one another and to act together in the expected manner. Unusual things do occur from time to time, but they are generally discounted as accidents.

Our conception of reality, then, is a reconstruction of the natural environment in terms of the meanings and symbols we have learned. That symbolic environments are learned can be tested easily by talking to a child who has not yet mastered the adult perspective. A youngster who accompanies his parents on a tour of Athens or Rome may refer to the magnificent ruins as "broken-down old buildings." Since he knows nothing of their historical significance, he sees them as mere wreckage. Senden's (1960) report of the initial reactions of people who had been born blind and then acquired vision through surgery is especially revealing. He discovered that the patients at first had difficulty seeing and recognizing in terms of conventional categories items with which they were quite familiar by touch. Indeed, we have become so accustomed to perceiving our surroundings in terms of such symbolic frameworks that most of us can free ourselves from them only under unusual circumstances. Anyone who has attempted any form of Zen or Yoga meditation — where the objective is to cleanse the mind of thinking (linguistic communication) and become totally immersed in the here and now — knows how much training and discipline this practice requires. Anyone who has experimented with LSD, peyote, or other hallucinogens knows how differently one experiences the environment as conventional categories fall away; one has difficulty recognizing many familiar objects, even though his or her perception may be quite accurate (Huxley, 1954). Once we become habituated to our symbolic environment, it is very difficult to escape from it.

In daily life we often distinguish among different forms of knowledge — religion, political ideology, science — each limited to a segment of a community. Although there is some overlap in categories, each form of knowledge constitutes a separate symbolic environment. In each, human experiences are cut into different units and organized in different ways. Each religion is a particular way of locating human beings in the universe; each has its own special objects and presuppositions. Similarly, each political ideology is a distinctive orientation toward the secular world; a confirmed Marxist tends to perceive every difficulty in terms of clashing class interests, even in communities in which others are oblivious to such status differences. Scientific knowledge is made up of a number of symbolic environments — one for each field of specialization. Science is more accurate than other forms of knowledge, largely because the categories of objects are more clearly specified and labeled. Scientific concepts are defined with more precision than the words used in daily discourse. Unlike popular beliefs, scientific hypotheses are stated explicitly. Furthermore, testing the statements for accuracy is an integral part of the procedure for developing such knowledge; experimentation is a form of reality testing. Because it is more accurate, scientific knowledge has proved to be more effective as an instrument for guiding action.

The Social Framework of Knowledge. Since words are so important in organizing symbolic environments, two eminent figures in linguistics — Edward Sapir and Benjamin Whorf — advanced the hypothesis that the knowledge that people develop is shaped and limited by the language used in their community. Each language has its own vocabulary; experiences are organized into different units; and some languages have categories that are totally absent in others. Furthermore, the customary relationships among words (syntax) differs from one language to the next. Sapir (1949) argues that any language, once formed, becomes a self-contained symbolic system that is perpetuated in terms of its own rules. As a group encounters new experiences, it adds new words to the vocabulary, but the additions are manipulated in terms of established rules of grammar. Thus, the manner in which experiences can be defined is circumscribed by such formal limitations, and the language itself becomes a program and guide for mental activity. Whorf (1956) emphasizes differences in syntax. Since there are differences in the order in which things are said, each language develops a habitual way of reporting experiences, a distinctive way of arranging the data of daily life. He characterizes the language of the Hopi Indians as atemporal. Among the Hopi, time varies with each observer; there is no conception of simultaneous occurrence; and there is no plural form for nouns that measure units of time — no such form as "days." A Hopi has to say "I left on the fifth day" rather than "I stayed five days." A Navaho Indian would have difficulty talking about "his" horses, for the language has no possessive pronouns or plural forms.

Several attempts have been made to test the Whorf-Sapir hypothesis, but the results have thus far been inconclusive. If human experiences are in fact organized in terms of linguistic categories, it would follow that people who speak different languages would perceive their surroundings somewhat differently. Semantic diversity is important, for what cannot be stated linguistically is difficult to conceive. Experiences can be classified in many different ways, and in each community nature is dissected along the lines laid down by the native tongue. Words do not determine experience, but they do channel it along certain lines, as a careful study by Carroll and Casagrande (1958) illustrates. In the Navaho language verbs that designate manipulation require an indication of the shape of the object being handled. Thus, a Navaho-speaking person would be expected to be more sensitive to the shape of objects. Ten pairs of objects of varying shape, size, and color were prepared, and it was expected that Navaho-speaking subjects would be more likely to classify them by shape than by color or size. This proved to be true of Navaho-speaking children, when they were compared with English-speaking Navaho children. But another group, some American children in Boston, resembled the Navaho-speaking group. When corrections were made for age, the younger Navaho children were much more sensitive to shape, but the differences diminished with age.

Handicapped people sometimes are not able to learn or use a language in the same manner as others; the Whorf-Sapir hypothesis would suggest that their subjective experiences would be different, and there is some evidence that they are. Helen Keller (1915), who was a blind deaf-mute, indicates in a moving passage in her autobiography that her experiences were unstructured and vague until she learned words. Studies of aphasia, a disorder in which there is an impairment in the use of words, reveal that patients are unable to imagine objects that are not immediately present and are unable to solve simple problems (Head, 1926, 1:349–80). Unfortunately, so many different disorders are labeled aphasic that generalizations are difficult. Evidence has also been sought in studies of schizophrenia. Some patients who are so labeled use words in an idiosyncratic manner and apparently perceive their world quite differently from all others (Sechehaye, 1951; Wolcott, 1970). Here again patients with so many different disorders are labeled schizophrenic that it is difficult to test such generalizations.

If people learn a new language, the organization of their experiences should undergo some change. Some immigrants who have mastered a new language have attested that this is true. Even more dramatic changes are noticeable among converts to different religious or political ideologies, although in these instances some overlapping with their old perspective remains. People who undergo psychoanalysis learn a new vocabulary, and in some cases this leads to new conceptions of human nature as well as new self-definitions. Perhaps the most dramatic change of this kind can be found in the experience of students who master the concepts of a new discipline, such as chemistry, and subsequently discover that they view material objects anew. Several studies have also been made of people who are bilingual to see whether they experience their world differently. Although many interesting results have come out of these studies, none subject the Whorf-Sapir hypothesis to a critical test. Thus, a review of the evidence suggests that the hypothesis is not unfounded; the weight of the evidence supports it, but there are too many unexplained exceptions. The major difficulty is that neither Sapir nor Whorf states his position explicitly in propositional form, and there is considerable disagreement over just what is being tested. Although their position is plausible, considerable refinement and restatement is needed before more conclusive tests can be conducted (Saporta and Bastian, 1961; Fishman, 1971).

Specialists in the sociology of knowledge contend that the manner in which people think is related to their status in the community (Mannheim, 1936). Marx contends that the economic organization of a community provides a framework that limits the range of ideas that will prove effective. All kinds of ideas may be proposed, but they will be forgotten unless they turn out to have some kind of utility. For example, the notion of getting ahead by hard work is likely to be meaningless in a rigidly stratified society in which mobility is almost impossible. Along a similar vein, Veblen (1961) argues that styles of thought are mostly reverberations of the individual's scheme of life, which depends largely on the type of occupation in which one is involved. These hypotheses are also worthy of consideration but have proved difficult to test.

Every society has specialists in the production, storage, and dissemination of knowledge—scholars, shamans, theologians, scientists, dramatists, novelists, artists, teachers, journalists. Since public policy in many communities is made with the advice of such men and women of learning, they often exercise disproportionate influence over the course of events. Such symbol specialists are called *intellectuals*. The definition of their roles varies from one community to another, but they usually perform certain tasks: They interpret and explain new events, especially those that are harmful; they define the responsibilities of rulers; they interpret past experiences and instruct youth in group traditions and skills; they facilitate and guide aesthetic and religious experiences; they assist in the control of nature in engineering projects, military operations, and administrative tasks. As transactions become more complicated, the role of intellectuals is likely to become more specialized; in recent times many intellectuals have been employed as bureaucrats in large organizations.

Although intellectuals are not always readily identifiable as a group, they usually have much in common. Most of them pass through a common educational system where they are exposed to similar subject matter organized in well-established ways. Thus, the prevailing values of a society serve as the framework for all their work. Even innovative work is done within an existing tradition; creative work by a genius is an addition to already existing trends. Since intellectuals have played key roles in advising rulers as well as in starting revolutions, much interest has developed concerning the manner in which they think (Shils, 1968). But even the most innovative thinking does not occur in a vacuum. Most intellectuals are responsive to the expectations of their peers.

Reality Testing as a Social Process. The commonsense view of people throughout the world is that the symbolic environment of their group *is* reality. We take for granted the conventional meanings of objects. But reality is not made up in the human mind. The natural environment is there, and it is what it is; material objects in particular have stubborn characteristics. Anyone who defines a wall as a gossamer substance and tries to walk through it will quickly discern its recalcitrant features. Each act is an instance of reality testing, and activities based on false assumptions usually result in failure. Since our approach to familiar objects is the product of accumulated experience, most meanings are reasonably accurate. Nonetheless all meanings are hypothetical; they may turn out to be mistaken. If activity based on accepted meanings fails, a redefinition becomes necessary. Indeed, intellectuals frequently challenge commonsense knowledge on the grounds that it is inexact and inconsistent. Many popular beliefs are dismissed as superstitions. They are less accurate than scientific knowledge, to be sure; yet such views constitute the basis of most social transactions. Scientists remain within their specialized world only when doing their work; otherwise they share their neighbors' commonsense perspective. Of course, there are beliefs that are not tested in terms of utility. Magical beliefs stand outside the system, and religious knowledge rests on faith. Many beliefs are inconsistent or incompatible, but they remain unquestioned unless something happens that forces a decisive test. Thus, in the long run all symbolic environments are likely to become progressively more accurate approximations of reality. Where reality testing occurs often, as in the sciences, the corrections occur more quickly.

One commonplace assumption with which most people approach

one another is that their perception of reality is just like that of everyone else. When a child or stranger raises questions about some basic assumption, people become amused and condescendingly provide explanations. Thus, popular knowledge assumes an objective and anonymous character, independent of any individual's personal biographical circumstances (Schutz, 1962:74–76). Reality testing is thus a social process. Most of our activities occur in social contexts. Each time we handle an object in the appropriate manner, others act as if nothing unusual has happened, and we assume that they understand what we are doing. If someone approaches a bear as if it were a dog, others will scream a warning. As long as others do not respond in dismay, we continue with confidence. Whenever we are uncertain about something, we check with those around us. For example, if a chair talks to us as we walk by, we pinch ourselves in astonishment. If it talks again, we seek confirmation by asking others if they too heard it. If they are equally surprised, we realize that something has gone awry and investigate. But if everyone else maintains a straight face, we become very upset. Even if we are absolutely certain that we heard a voice come from the chair, we are likely to conclude that we have had a hallucination and may arrange to visit a psychiatrist. Reality testing is not always accurate or conclusive, and many beliefs are sustained through coincidences or inconclusive tests. Nonetheless the criteria of the adequacy of knowledge are social. What is called reality actually consists of meanings that enjoy a high degree of consensus.

Thus, what we assume to be reality is a social process. Human beings are constantly bolstering and supporting one another's perspectives—simply by living up to one another's expectations. Our conception of our environment and our places within it is sustained and reaffirmed from day to day in social interaction. Our conception of reality is as much a product of our responses to one another as it is the product of our reactions to environmental cues. Those who do not partake in our commonly accepted symbolic environment are usually set aside as strange; they are often labeled psychotic. The formation and maintenance of consensus in any given transaction is relatively easy for participants who already share a common symbolic environment.

SUMMARY AND DISCUSSION

Like all other living creatures, human beings are continuously adapting to their ever-changing environment. But the development of symbolic communication, especially language, has transformed the basic character of our surroundings. Although subjective experience is continuous—what William James calls the "stream of consciousness"—people divide it into units that have proved useful in previous social transactions. Those within the same universe of discourse use the same units of experience; they make the same assumptions about these objects; and they refer to these objects with the same symbols. Hence, they are more likely to achieve consensus when confronted by the same situation.

Using symbols to stand for meanings not only facilitates their manipulation, communication with others, but also the construction of an ordered conception of the world—one that includes many objects that are not physically present and some that have no material existence at all. Thus, most human beings strive for considerably more than mere survival and reproduction; they seek happiness, honor, and self-respect. Even after a long, honorable, and successful career and many healthy grandchildren, some are not sure that their lives have been worthwhile. Such considerations apparently do not arise in other animals. Furthermore, the meanings of most objects include evaluations, and all kinds of emotional reactions are elicited. Other animals respond with fear to danger and are aggressive toward sources of frustration. But human beings react emotionally to abstract objects, such as political ideologies. Thus, human beings are constantly striving to come to terms with extant life conditions, but they react in terms of their interpretations. Their definitions are the product of selective responsiveness and may in fact be different from what is objectively present.

Sociology is itself a specialized symbolic environment. Its concepts—such as role-playing, objects, and expressive symbolism—are not entirely unfamiliar to the uninitiated. Yet they do slice experiences into somewhat different units than those commonly used in daily discourse. Thus, we develop a picture of the world that is slightly different from what is taken for granted in common sense. Since sociology is a young discipline, many of its claims still require further testing. Nonetheless an effort is being made to build a more effective way of making sense out of the things people do. By constructing a different way of characterizing the world, we hope to facilitate concerted action that is desired and to minimize the pains and dislocations that are a part of life. Were we unable to do this, there would be little point in building a special vocabulary with which to construct generalizations that differ from popular beliefs.

SUGGESTED READINGS

Berger, Peter L., and Thomas Luckmann. 1966. *The Social Construction of Reality.* New York: Doubleday.

A treatise on how our conception of reality is shaped and reaffirmed in social interaction.

Brown, Roger. 1958. *Words and Things.* Glencoe, Ill.: Free Press.
The organization of linguistic behavior and its relation to perception and knowledge.

Klapp, Orrin E. 1962. *Heroes, Villains, and Fools.* Englewood Cliffs, N.J.: Prentice-Hall.
The manner in which human beings are classified into social types and the significance of such categories in daily life.

Mandler, George. 1975. *Mind and Emotion.* New York: Wiley.
A critical review of physiological and psychological research on emotion from the standpoint of cognitive psychology.

Riezler, Kurt. 1951. *Man: Mutable and Immutable.* Chicago: Henry Regnery.
A treatise on human nature, with emphasis on the importance of symbolization and of sentiments.

Segall, Marshall H., et al. 1966. *The Influence of Culture on Visual Perception.* Indianapolis: Bobbs-Merrill.
A critical examination of anthropological and psychological research on cross-cultural differences in perception.

III

COMMUNICATION AND CULTURE

The Spanish conquistadors first entered Mexico City on 8 November 1519. Although they were astonished at the splendors they beheld, they looked upon the Aztecs as barbarians and were concerned only with seizing their treasures and forcing them to become Christians. Cortez had only four hundred soldiers, sixteen horses, and three cannons. He had formed an alliance with the Tlaxcaltecas, whom the Aztecs had long been capturing for human sacrifices in their religious rites. The Aztecs had superior military power; had there been an open confrontation, Cortez and his allies would probably have been massacred. But the Aztecs defined the Europeans as Quetzalcoatl and other gods returning from over the seas. Moctezuma, their ruler, had been upset by a succession of bad omens. On learning of the arrival of strangers in Vera Cruz, he sent emissaries bearing gifts. Cortez chained the messengers and intimidated them by firing a cannon, confirming the ruler's fears. When Cortez and his troops entered the city, they were welcomed as guests (Leon-Portilla, 1962). Thus began the fateful encounter that led to the destruction of Aztec civilization and the subjugation of the people of Mexico.

Few misunderstandings are so decisive. This one affected the lives of millions of people for centuries to come and underscores an important question: How can persons involved in a common transaction define the identical situation in such sharply contrasting manners? Answering this question will help us understand many of the difficulties that arise in modern mass societies.

COMMUNICATION AS A SERIAL PROCESS

Many persons, including some social scientists, view communication in a mechanical fashion. They think that ideas in one person's head are encoded into linguistic symbols, transmitted through speech, and then decoded by the listener. The result is some kind of mutual understanding, that is, both speaker and listener come to share the same ideas. Something of this sort undoubtedly does take place, but this approach can be misleading. One of its implications, that the speaker and listener are independent entities who stimulate each other through words, is a gross oversimplification.

Communication as Reciprocal Role-taking. We may view communication more profitably as a continuous interchange through which participants in a social transaction coordinate their respective contributions. Occurring among people who are engaging in some kind of common endeavor, communication facilitates their cooperation. It begins when the transaction gets under way and continues until it is over. For example, the social interaction in surgery begins when orderlies and aides wheel in the table bearing sterile equipment. It continues as the personnel chat and joke as they scrub and don sterile gowns and gloves. It goes on while the anesthetist, nurses, and interns test the equipment. The emotional climate becomes more serious when the patient is wheeled into the room. The surgeon may review his or her plans with members of the surgical team, especially if some departure from the standard routine might become necessary. Once the incision has been made, the surgeon issues commands orally or through conventional hand signals, the meanings of which are clearly understood. The surgeon calls for various instruments and orders nurses and assistants to use sponges, hold retractors and clamps, staunch the flow of blood, and maintain clear visibility in the area. The surgeon may periodically consult the anesthetist. Should something unusual occur, should the patient not respond as the team had anticipated from the diagnostic tests, they may have to institute emergency actions. If so, the surgeon makes the decisions, and the lines of authority are clear. When the remedial work is over, the assistants close the wound; the nurses count the sponges to be sure that no foreign matter is left in the body; and the anesthetist takes charge. The atmosphere becomes more relaxed, and more joking and small talk may occur as the participants have their first opportunity to unbend after a tense ordeal. Such interchanges continue until the orderlies and nurses take the patient out and the cleanup begins (Wilson, 1954). Thus, communication is a serial process that facilitates the succession of adjustments and readjustments that are needed in order to accomplish a transaction; flexible coordination requires continuous feedback and correction. People begin communicating as they enter the scene; they say and do what is necessary to coordinate their efforts throughout the enterprise; and they break off their interchanges when they have accomplished the task (Dewey, 1926:166–207).

The participants in any social transaction are interdependent; they need one another's cooperation to complete their common task. The speaker and listener are not separate entities; they are members of a team for the duration of the transaction. This is true even in a fight. Since each individual exercises some measure of self-regulation, however, each can act independently. A person may contribute to a transaction in several different ways. Thus, unless each is able to anticipate just what the others are likely to do, difficulties may arise in coordinating their respective contributions. To anticipate with reasonable accuracy what other people are likely to do requires appreciating how they define the situation, and human beings do this by *role-taking* — the imaginative projection of oneself into the roles being enacted by others to get some appreciation of the situation from their standpoint. (This concept should not be confused with *role-playing*, the enactment of conventional expectations.) Role-taking is a bit like mind reading, and it generally involves some guesswork.

But mind reading is impossible, and people do the next best thing: they make inferences concerning the inner experiences of others by reading external manifestations that serve as indicators. Thus, participants in a common transaction are constantly indicating their views and intentions to one another, especially through speech and bodily gestures. Referential symbolism, especially language, is obviously most important. Participants in joint enterprises usually talk to one another and pay attention to what their associates are saying. They give directions; they raise questions; they protest what they regard as unfair or improper; they provide signals for temporal coordination. Communication is continuous; it seldom ceases when people lapse into silence, for they use other indicators. Any act may be communicative. Each observes what the others are doing. If a man wipes sweat from his brow, he is indicating something, even though he may not utter a word. Even failure or refusal to act in the expected manner is an important indication of the actor's orientation. Not speaking or turning away one's face discloses how one is oriented toward the situation. Thus, communication takes place through several channels — by sound, sight, and even chemical indicators. Strong body odor may be indicative of intense stress.

Speech is generally compounded with expressive movements of all kinds. Since the face is usually exposed to view, those involved in joint undertakings often examine one another's faces in search of fine nuances of shifting emotional reactions. The look in a person's eyes, the changing position of the lips, jaw, or eyebrows, as well as the color and moistness of the skin all serve as the basis for qualifying judgments that rest on speech alone (Ekman et al., 1972). The quality of one's voice is also important. Many regard a high-pitched, shrill, loud, or tremulous voice as indicative of anxiety. Sudden spurts or outbursts of words, lack of pauses, snapping of words, overtalkativeness, forced or inappropriate laughter, and rapid and shallow breathing are also regarded as symptoms of tension. Other features of speech to which people respond intuitively include rhythmic alteration between high and low pitch, sudden variations of speed, sighs, and constant interruption of others (Ruesch and Prestwood, 1949). We also observe the manner in which people do things; strained posture, forced motions, twitches, tremors, as well as the overall rhythm and vigor of muscle movements also provide clues to inner experiences. A desultory and obviously reluctant performance also reveals something of the actor's commitment. Since we are all aware that our acts are being observed, we sometimes exaggerate spontaneous expressive movements to create the appropriate impression; we may even deliberately produce diversionary gestures. Such interchanges are a crucial part of communication, for they disclose something of the personal orientation of the participants. Expressive gestures thus make possible a more refined coordination of efforts.

Role-taking involves perceiving another person, vicariously identifying with that person, and projecting one's own behavioral dispositions to that person (Mead, 1934:253). Thus, it involves imagining oneself to be in another's place and making inferences concerning his or her definition of the situation. Intersubjectivity also involves the expression and recognition of emotional reactions. Among those who share a common symbolic environment, developing mutual understanding is relatively easy. If some misunderstanding should arise, corrections can usually be made in a few sentences. If some participants are less enthusiastic than others, for example, concessions may be made to make the enterprise more palatable to them. Thus, effective communication may be regarded as reciprocal role-taking. Each person imagines the inner experiences of his or her associates. If these inferences are sufficiently accurate, the people can act together, for their respective contributions will fit together in a reciprocating manner.

Social Distance and Communication. The type of mutual understanding that develops through communication varies with the social distance between the participants in a transaction. Most of our contacts with other people are categorical, and communication among strangers and slight acquaintances is largely impersonal. Buber (1958) suggests a useful way of approaching this matter by making a distinction, somewhat exaggerated for effect, between an "I-It" relationship and an "I-Thou" relationship. In an I-It relationship we approach the other person as an instance of a category, for all practical purposes as a "thing." An extreme instance would be the actors in pornographic movies. They are supposedly engaging in one of the most intimate of human transactions, but they often appear uninvolved, mere appendages to genital organs performing a mechanical act. This is not to suggest that impersonal communication is ineffective. As long as people speak the same language, they have little difficulty in forming a reasonable understanding of one another's orientations. Even when we are involved with total strangers, we can place one another into familiar statuses — clerks, pedestrians, ushers, receptionists, guards — and can communicate with sufficient clarity to accomplish countless transactions. Regardless of our personal reactions to such individuals, we are able to develop sufficient consensus. Indeed, the communication of abstract principles may occur more effectively among total strangers with no sentimental ties — as between scholars who read one another's books. Most financial exchanges require only minimal role-taking; even tourists who do not know the local language are able to make purchases.

However, as social distance is reduced, as people come to know one another more intimately, role-taking assumes a different character, becoming what Buber calls an I-Thou relationship. When we recognize someone as a distinct person, we are likely to identify more closely with him or her as a human being. We then assume that the other person's inner experiences are much like our own and become more responsive to his or her feelings. When we have established such sympathetic ties, we develop the capacity to appreciate the other person's pain, suffering, and joys. Such recognition and response is usually immediate and intuitive. Once this happens, it becomes difficult for most people to do anything that would injure the feelings of the other without feeling pangs of guilt, just as we derive great pleasure from observing the good fortune of those whom we like. We often become responsive to slight nuances of meanings, even those that the other is trying to conceal. As Adam Smith once put it, by changing places with another person, we come to conceive of and be affected by what he or she feels. Thus, communication tends to become highly personalized, and mutual understanding becomes both deeper and more extensive. Thus, as social distance is reduced, role-taking becomes more personalized, and those who identify become more responsive to one another's feelings. However, individuals differ considerably in their capacity to identify with others and to relax their personal reserve.

Consensus as a Developing Process. Consensus is never static. Since all situations are in continuous flux, the participants must constantly reconstruct their coorientation in a succession of communicative interchanges. As each transaction develops, they keep redefining the changing situation. The successful execution of any part of the task is a change in the situation; each contribution alters the situation somewhat, and each participant must realize what has happened to make the necessary readjustments. Thus, all participants are continuously redefining the situation in which they are involved. Since they are interdependent, however, they must watch one another to be sure that their redefinitions of the evolving context are sufficiently similar to make further collaboration possible. Thus, coorientation is maintained by a constant reading of one another's words and gestures. Each must keep watching the others to keep pace and to maintain coordination by correct timing. As each transaction is constructed, the consensus that is essential is formed and reformed in constant communication.

When communication breaks down, consensus can no longer be maintained, and transactions become temporarily disorganized or may break down altogether. In his analysis of ground combat during World War II, Marshall (1947:129) notes that whenever members of an infantry squad advancing toward a target are no longer able to see one another, their organizational unity vanishes. What had been a well-disciplined group becomes a scattering of individuals, each protecting himself against enemy fire. When they reestablish contact, they are once again able to proceed as a team. Transactions may be similarly interrupted in many less stressful situations. Participants then get together to ask one another what has happened, to check one another's definitions, and to straighten out misunderstandings. If the participants persist in redefining the developing context in disparate ways, they begin to work at cross-purposes; the misunderstandings are intensified. This happened frequently in the 1960s during confrontations between political demonstrators and the police. If police officers define curious spectators as dangerous objects, they become not only more vigilant but also more pugnacious. The demonstrators in turn become aware of the change in the officers' stance and respond with greater aggressiveness. In many instances serious clashes erupted that neither side desired or intended. Thus even when most participants have the best of intentions, transactions become truncated or redirected if consensus cannot be maintained by effective communication.

FORMATION OF CULTURE PATTERNS

Culture as Collective Adaptation. In common parlance the word "culture" is generally used to refer to enlightenment, sophisticated taste acquired through aesthetic training, and an elegant life-style. In the social sciences, however, the concept is used in a more comprehensive way. To paraphrase Redfield (1941:132), *culture* consists of those conventional understandings, manifested in acts and artifacts, that characterize particular social units — a community or any of its constituent groups. Culture consists of norms. When Redfield speaks of norms manifested in acts, he is referring to models of appropriate ways of doing things. By norms manifested in artifacts, he is referring to appropriate ways of constructing and handling material objects, not to the things themselves. Norms vary considerably from one community to another; in modern mass societies they vary from one group to another within the same community. Just as people in privileged classes operate with rules of etiquette that differ from those of their subordinates, many other customs vary. What is perfectly acceptable in one context may be condemned in another. Indeed, some norms differ so much that what is regarded as natural in one society evokes shock and revulsion in another — practicing infanticide or cannibalism, craving whale blubber, or setting adrift at sea old people who can no longer be fed. When people live in sustained association, they carry out many transactions over and over in much the same manner. The patterns of concerted action that characterize a particular group constitute its culture. Thus, to understand what people are doing, we must apprehend *their* perspective and appreciate *their* definition of the situation.

Each group's culture is the product of the collective adaptations made to the particular circumstances it has faced. The people in each group have learned to cope somewhat successfully with the life conditions they have encountered, and they have accumulated the ways of doing things that have sufficed in the past. Hence, each group has a distinctive culture. Each group has its own language and symbolic environment; its members perceive their world in a particular way. Furthermore, culture refers to behavior patterns that are learned, not to those that are inherited genetically. Sometimes it is difficult to tell the difference, and we may underestimate the extent to which behavior patterns are acquired socially. Some acts — such as reactions to pain — are so spontaneous that they appear to be instinctive; in fact they are learned, for they differ somewhat from one group to another (Zborowski, 1952). Culture refers to norms that are handed down from one generation to the next and taught to other newcomers. To paraphrase Warner (1959:4), culture is a symbolic organization of the remembered experiences of the past as they are newly felt and understood by the living; the human condition of individual mortality and the comparative immortality of our species make most of our communication and collective activities a vast exchange of understandings between the living and the dead. Although some patterns remain fairly stable for a time, cultures are not static; they are undergoing constant change, usually in small increments, as each group is confronted by new circumstances.

Values as Standards. Along with the established procedures for carrying out various activities, *values* — standards of desirability that are independent of specific situations — are among the most important elements of any culture. Common understandings arise in each group concerning what goals people ought to seek, what is required or forbidden, what is honorable and shameful, and what is beautiful and ugly. Values thus provide criteria for selecting among different lines of action and for measuring success or failure; they are the standards for judging what is worthwhile (Williams, 1968). Values thus provide the basis for emotional reactions. Although some values are clearly articulated and taught, many others are only intuitively felt. They are unquestioned, self-justifying premises that account for much of the consistency in responses to recurrent situations among those who share a culture.

Values vary considerably from one culture to another. For example, members of Christian communities value the sanctity of human life; in some other societies human life, especially that of low-ranking members, is cheap. Americans do many things that others regard as wasteful and perhaps stupid. If firefighters and police officers did not risk their own lives trying to force a would-be suicide to back off the top of a building, many citizens would accuse them of being derelict in their duty. If the U.S. Navy did not go to considerable effort and expense to save the life of an ordinary seaman who had contracted an unusual disease, some members of Congress would call for an investigation. People in some other cultures would be able to understand making such an effort to save an admiral, but they may find it odd that anyone would go to so much trouble for an easily replaceable enlisted man.

In capitalist societies a high value is placed on personal property. During the reconstruction period following the Civil War, when the Southern states passed the "black codes" that virtually reduced the emancipated slaves to their previous condition of servitude, the one right left unchallenged was property ownership (Davis, 1945). The property rights of enemy aliens in the United States have been protected even in time of war, although such precautions would be dismissed as ridiculous in many other societies. Klapp (1962) suggests that the spontaneously acclaimed heroes in a group are excellent indicators of its values, for they personify its values. Any listing of those who have won acclaim in this country discloses the diversity of standards in the various groups that make up our nation.

Cultural Axioms. How conscious people are of the norms by which they organize much of their lives varies. Some norms, such as the rules of etiquette, are usually stated explicitly and can be described and explained to children and to strangers. In each culture, however, there are countless norms that are so well established that they are simply taken for granted and regarded as self-evident. Questions of proof or justification seldom arise, for most people are not even aware of these presuppositions. Some of these assumptions are of decisive importance, for they constitute the premises underlying just about everything else that is done in the group, giving it its characteristic style. We may refer to these basic presuppositions as *cultural axioms.*

Examples of cultural axioms include assumptions concerning the place of human beings in the universe. In each culture there is some prevailing view about the relationship of people to their natural environment. In some it is taken for granted that human beings are but playthings of nature (or of God); what will be will be, and it is pointless for anyone to attempt to alter what is inevitable. Sheepherders in some Spanish-American groups in New Mexico, as recently as the 1930s, believed they could do little or nothing to save either their land or flocks from devastating storms. They therefore made little effort to protect their interests. They often accepted illness and death with the same fatalism, some even refusing the services of a doctor on the grounds that their condition was God's will. This type of fatalism can be found among people in many other parts of the world, especially among the impoverished. The orientation commonly found in most industrial societies, especially the United States, provides a sharp contrast. Most Americans look on nature as something to be mastered and used through human effort. Rivers are to be spanned with bridges; mountains are to be crossed by building roads around or through them. If there is not enough water, dams are built, canals are dug, and rivers are diverted. Controlling illness and prolonging life through medical care are taken for granted. Even those who are religious contend that "the Lord helps those who help themselves." Some even believe that it is one's duty to overcome obstacles by ingenuity and hard work (Kluckhohn and Strodtbeck, 1961:13).

Assumptions about time provide another example. We are so much a part of the industrial world that we think of astronomical time — continuous, homogeneous, inexorable — as the natural and only way to measure the duration of events. Sorokin and Merton (1937) point out, however, that this is only one of many ways to reckon the tempo of life. Since time is important for synchronizing and coordinating joint enterprises, the units in terms of which it is viewed vary with the rounds of occupational and religious life. Agricultural people, for example, have a rhythm that is different from those who are employed in factories, and they view time in terms that are connected with their pursuits — the thawing of winter snow, planting, and harvesting. Even in our society we realize that for some purposes time as measured by calendars and clocks is inadequate; in measuring the development of children educators speak of "mental age" as compared with "chronological age." Since the way we experience time is related to our activities, those in occupations in which punctuality is crucial place unusual emphasis on it; Cottrell (1939) writes of railroaders and their expensive watches, their irritation with people who are careless about being on time, and their reluctance to enter transactions that do not fit their temporal requirements.

Some people live in the present, trying to get as much enjoyment as they can now rather than ruminating over past events that cannot be changed or planning for an unpredictable future. Before the Communist revolution, the Chinese were oriented to the past. The future was viewed as unknown and hence something that could not be examined, but a record of the past was available for careful study. One's position was like that of a person sitting on a riverbank, looking downstream at what had passed and thereby benefiting from that knowledge (Peck, 1950). Americans, in contrast, tend to be future oriented. We seldom venerate the old ways simply because of their age, and most of us react sharply to being regarded as old-fashioned. Most Americans are not content with the present and are constantly striving for better things in the future, for their children if not for themselves.

Communication Channels and Culture.   Since culture is the product of collective adaptations, it is constructed and maintained in social interaction. Therefore, people in sustained contact are likely to develop similar perspectives. When people are in regular association, communication channels develop, and every community is crisscrossed with avenues of contact that are regarded as trustworthy sources of information. Although all human beings are capable of communicating in some manner with all others, they usually do not. Except in very unusual instances, such as the assassination of a national leader or the outbreak of war, we address strangers only under prescribed circumstances. Members of the opposite sex in particular find that their intentions may be misinterpreted, should they speak to strangers. Although children are less constrained by such conventional norms, their testimony is seldom accepted with the same confidence as that of adults. *Communication channels,* then, consist of common understandings concerning who may speak to whom, about what subject, with what degree of assurance. Differential association is found in even the simplest of communities.

All communities and organized groups have formal communication channels, clearly defined avenues through which information of various sorts reaches its intended audience. All governing bodies have formal channels to notify the populace of regulations and policy decisions. Every bureaucracy has its communication network, and what is often denounced as red tape consists of difficulties and delays that arise from the necessity of going through prescribed channels. In modern industrial societies the media of mass communication are generally accepted as reliable sources of information. But such formal channels are usually supplemented by auxiliary channels based on personal contacts. Friendship circles arise, and from them sources develop that are reliable for certain kinds of information. During a strike, for example, a union member whose sister-in-law happens to be the manager's secretary may be sought out as a source of vital information. The confidence people have in such auxiliary channels depends on the reputation for personal integrity of the sources. Clandestine channels can also arise to disseminate forbidden information, as among black marketeers, drug addicts, or revolutionaries.

This brings us to a key hypothesis: To the extent that people participate regularly in the same communication channel, they are likely to develop a common culture. Those in sustained contact are likely to share a common symbolic environment. Hence, they are likely not only to define a succession of situations in a similar manner, but also to reinforce one another's perspectives by responding to one another in expected ways. Since they can anticipate one another's reactions fairly accurately, they can cooperate more easily and feel more at ease in each other's company. This hypothesis implies that the boundaries of any culture are set by the limits of effective communication.

Although the proof cannot be regarded as conclusive, evidence in support of this hypothesis comes from several sources, and it is consistent. Any barrier to effective communication leads to the formation of different cultures, even among people who live in the same community. Social isolation—whether from geographical insulation, segregation, or conflict—leads to the formation of distinct cultures. Some mountain communities in the American South have remained so isolated that the people have until recently retained the language and culture of the days of the Revolutionary War (Sherman and Henry, 1933). Members of religious orders to which visitors are rarely admitted and where newspapers and secular literature are prohibited are oblivious to the outside world and develop a unique outlook. People who remain confined in ethnic colonies, especially one in which a different language is spoken, develop a perspective that differs markedly from that of outsiders. They not only find strangers mysterious but are apprehensive even when they encounter one who is obviously friendly. Although such total isolation is rare in modern mass societies, the basic cleavages of any community coincide with the established lines of communication.

If people participate in two or more communication channels, some overlapping of perspectives will occur, and nowadays this is quite common. Children participate in many activities with adults, but they also have a social world of their own. When playing games without adult supervision, they make up many of their own norms. They develop a culture that differs from that of their parents (Opie and Opie, 1959). The partial separation continues as youngsters move into adolescence, when their range of contacts remains different from that of adults. Things they are exposed to in school, occurrences in local teenage hangouts, the popular songs they enjoy, the fads that adults scoff, and their selective response to television and movies — all lead to the formation of an outlook that differs from that of their parents. At the same time they are not oblivious to the demands of the adult world.

If people participate in new communication channels, their perspective will change. Redfield (1941) compared four communities in Yucatán, Mexico — a city, a town, a peasant village, and an isolated Indian settlement. The larger the community, the more contact there was with European culture. The more the Yucatecans were exposed to the communication channels of the modern world, the more their lives resembled those of people in industrial societies. The same change can be seen more dramatically as immigrants develop greater contact with their adopted communities or in upward social mobility in a class society. Similar changes can be noted when someone becomes converted to a religious or political cult.

NORMS OF SOCIAL INTERACTION

Cultures are made up of many kinds of norms, but the shared expectations underlying social interaction are of particular interest to sociologists. Encounters between people are always predicated on a number of assumptions—about the characteristics of human beings generally, about various categories of people, and about the personality of particular individuals. Some types of norms can be found in virtually all societies. One is the norm of reciprocity; those who have been favored by another person are expected to repay the benefactor in some manner or at least to express gratitude (Gouldner, 1960). The same is true of norms of involvement. If a transaction is regarded as important, key participants are expected to pay strict attention and to do their best, although this does not always happen. But many basic norms differ, sometimes in very subtle ways, from one culture to another, and such differences often lead to serious misunderstandings.

The Group and the Individual. In all societies most individuals are members of various groups, although the extent to which a person is expected to subordinate his or her interests to collective goals differs. In some cultures individuals exist only as part of a group and are expected to dedicate themselves to carrying out its interests. An extreme example of this is Japanese culture, especially during the period preceding World War II. Japanese were taught from childhood to conceive of themselves as representatives of groups, most important of all, the family. Filial piety was stressed, and each person took his or her proper station within the family by generation, age, and sex. From birth one was indebted to one's family and was expected to honor this debt to the best of one's ability. All were bound by a network of obligations and were expected to subordinate personal desires to collective requirements. Thus, filial piety was more than mere deference or obedience to parents; people repaid their debt to forebears by passing on to their children the care they had received. Those who exercised authority acted as trustees; father and eldest brother always acted to uphold the honor of the house. Elders who in their youth had had to submit to decisions of the family council demanded the same of their juniors. Love, although desirable, was not necessary; even if one were resentful, one still had to meet familial obligations. Individualism was discouraged from childhood, and rebels were punished at home and scorned by their neighbors. Thus, righteousness consisted of recognizing one's place in a network of mutual indebtedness that embraced forebears, contemporaries, and future generations. If one failed, the entire family was shamed. Most Japanese were bound by a deep sense of obligation to family, community, and nation (Benedict, 1946). This was, of course, an ideal pattern, and deviations were commonplace; but it was the standard by which people judged themselves and one another. Although this illustration is drawn from a single culture, similar collectivistic orientations can be found throughout the world.

In contrast, in much of the United States and northern Europe emphasis has been placed on the rights of individuals. In our society each person is viewed as an autonomous agent and is held responsible for his or her own destiny. Although limitations are placed on the extent to which one may exploit others, it is regarded as natural that each should pursue his or her own interests. This is not to suggest that family and community do not matter. We acknowledge our debts to those who are close to us and respond to their expectations. Nonetheless, our society is individualistic in that few people see themselves as existing primarily to perpetuate and enhance the standing of the group to which they belong. Loyalty to one's group is prized, especially when people become involved in some kind of contest; but individuals rarely conceive of themselves as mere tools for the advancement of their group — except possibly in time of war. Individualism is especially important in the selection of a marriage partner, where personal preference becomes the paramount consideration. Thus, achievement is an individual matter; those who fail to attain their goals hold themselves accountable and often develop feelings of guilt or shame. Defenders of civil liberties demand that the rights of individuals be protected, even at considerable cost to the rest of the community. Most Americans, for example, accept the principle that it is better to allow a few hundred guilty people to escape punishment than to incarcerate unjustly a single innocent person. This type of orientation toward the individual is more commonly found in highly industrialized societies, especially in cities.

Explanations of Human Conduct. Among the most important cultural axioms are presuppositions about human nature; we are constantly making adjustments in terms of our interpretations of one another's conduct. In some cultures it is taken for granted that all human beings are by nature good. If so, deviant behavior is accounted for in terms of evil influences, unfortunate circumstances, or misunderstandings. Such people believe that if human beings could only communicate effectively, all problems would be solved, for everyone acts with the best of intentions. Many Americans believe that human nature is basically egoistical but perfectible through self-discipline and effort, a view that developed during the Protestant Reformation. The dangers of regression are ever present and must be guarded against; goodness can be achieved only by a lifetime of diligent effort (Kluckhohn and Strodtbeck, 1961:11–12). In some cultures it is assumed that human beings must indulge inconvenient impulses from time to time to avoid suffering serious disabilities; in other cultures people believe they can contain even the most powerful impulses by meditation, detachment, or self-sacrifice. A number of religious and political movements have included among their objectives the transformation of human nature. Thus, both in China and in the Soviet Union deliberate attempts have been made to create the kind of person who can live happily and meet civic responsibilities in a socialist state (Bauer, 1952). Such programs imply dissatisfaction with people as they are presumed to be.

The successful execution of social transactions of all kinds requires effective role-taking. All participants must understand what they and the others are doing. The most common way to explain anything in daily discourse is to find a "cause." Thus, we search for some antecedent event or condition that is responsible for the "effect," and most popular efforts to explain human behavior are cast in this mold. Human conduct is most commonly explained through the avowal and imputation of motives (Mills, 1963:439–52). In daily discourse we account for the deeds of others by citing reasons: The clerk was rude because he felt offended by the customer's condescending attitude. We also explain our own conduct by avowing motives: I failed to act honorably because I was jealous and wanted to strike back. Motives are often thought to be the inner "springs" that set off action; in common parlance a motive is regarded as the "cause" of a behavior pattern. Since we make inferences easily and often without much conscious awareness, the procedure appears to be simple and instinctive. Actually what is involved is quite complicated. We may explain a given act—one person's striking another, for example—in several ways, depending on the intentions that are avowed and imputed. We may interpret a blow as a deliberate, malicious act on the part of an angry person or as an accident by someone who was not paying sufficient attention. Indeed, arguments often arise over such imputations.

Even casual observation and reflection disclose that both avowed and imputed motives are for the most part simplistic and often quite inaccurate. Psychoanalysts point out that many motives that people avow are rationalizations, justifications constructed after the deed. The reasons people give sometimes have little to do with their actual conduct. Thus, the popular way in which conduct is explained throughout the world is not to be confused with the more sophisticated analyses developed by psychologists and psychiatrists. In fact, psychologists have begun to investigate how people attribute motives to one another (Harvey and Smith, 1977:36–155). What is important, however, is that people who share a common culture use the same sets of reasons for explaining recurrent activities. They share similar conceptions of human nature and avow and impute similar reasons to account for what people do. If people avow and impute similar motives, they can engage in successful role-taking. Even if all the explanations are inaccurate from a scientific standpoint, the people can understand one another. Using the same motives, by facilitating role-taking, makes consensus and concerted action possible.

Mills points out that each culture has its own vocabulary of motives —plausible reasons for doing things in given types of situations. He notes that in American society the most commonly cited grounds for doing things are largely individualistic, hedonistic, sexual, and pecuniary. Thus, a man who dislikes his neighbors but does not want to admit it can say he sold his house simply because he needed the money. A young and beautiful woman who marries an older and successful man is frequently assumed to have done so for the security and conveniences that money can bring. We also emphasize achievement through personal effort. In a classic study Weber (1958) contends that this ideology developed during the Protestant Reformation and thereby contributed to the rapid industrialization of northern Europe. Since Martin Luther and his fellow reformers objected to the purchase of indulgences to atone for sins, each Protestant had to earn his or her own salvation by renouncing pleasures of the moment and through diligent, sustained effort. Studies by McClelland (1961) disclose that the emphasis on accomplishment through personal endeavor can also be found in many other cultures; it certainly provides meaningful explanations to most Americans. If a man is fiercely dedicated to his work, neglects his wife and children, and eventually rises to a position of eminence, his conduct makes sense even to those who denounce him as driven. People who work with a different vocabulary of motives tend to question such explanations. Thus, Mills notes that if a medieval monk contended that he gave food to a poor but attractive woman "for the glory of God and eternal salvation of his soul," we tend to question him. We suspect that he had sublimated his sexual desires. Similarly, if a Japanese executive who ignored his wife and children for success insists that he had to sacrifice himself in order to advance the standing of his family, other Japanese, even those who disapprove of what he did, would understand him. Outsiders, however, might wonder if his intentions were so lofty. Indeed, we all tend to suspect people who avow motives that are not part of our lexicon.

Norms Concerning Distance.   Cultures differ considerably in the extent and manner in which social distance is maintained. Americans are notorious the world over for informality and the ease with which we lower our personal reserve. We form friendships quickly, although many of them do not last long. Soon after we are introduced to new co-workers, for example, we address them on a first-name basis, visit one another's homes, and speak candidly about our personal preferences. We consider people who do not act in this manner "stuffy." In most other societies, however, such informality is regarded as scandalous. Even when there is no reason to be suspicious or unfriendly, people maintain a polite distance until they have gotten to know and trust one another; the small number of friendships formed often persist for a lifetime. The kind of intimacy that is commonplace for most Americans is reserved for relatives and personal friends of long standing. The institutionalization of interpersonal contacts is carried to extremes in cultures in which people are taught to feel intense shame for any shortcoming. The Japanese, for example, are noted for their politeness, which is a means of maintaining social distance. Even people who have been neighbors for decades greet one another and exchange pleasantries in prescribed sentences; leave-taking is also a prescribed ritual. Male college students who have known each other for years seldom address one another by their first names. Sentimental ties do develop, but personal feelings are disclosed more in the manner in which the rituals of courtesy are performed, in the style of execution. Etiquette is formal.

There are also cultural differences in what is regarded as the appropriate physical space between persons carrying on a conversation. In each culture people learn and get accustomed to what is regarded as the normal interval between two people who are talking. If one person gets too close, the other spontaneously backs up. Hall (1959:160–64) notes that in Latin America the proper space to be maintained in social interaction is less than that in the United States. Latin Americans feel that they cannot talk comfortably unless they are physically quite close. He reports seeing two conversationalists traverse a forty-foot hall; as his Latin friend spoke to him, the American kept retreating, searching for what was for him a more comfortable distance. Each time he backed away, his friend attempted to reestablish his own accustomed distance, until the two finally reached the other end of the room. If one person keeps backing away, the other may be hurt, wondering what he or she has done to justify such an unfriendly reaction. Indeed, many Latin Americans conclude that visitors from the north are cold, withdrawn, and unfriendly. Many Americans who travel south of the Rio Grande complain that friendly natives breathe down their necks, crowd them, and spray their faces with saliva. Even when there are no linguistic problems, misunderstandings may still arise.

Ethnocentrism as Social Isolation. Anthropologists have long pointed out that people who share a culture regard their own norms as the natural way of doing things. The concept to describe this orientation is *ethnocentrism.* Although some psychologists have used the term as synonymous with prejudice, in most of the social sciences it is used in much the same manner as Sumner (1906:13) originally defined it: the tendency of people to use the standards of their own culture to evaluate everything they see. Thus, everyone else is bound to appear inferior, silly, wrong, and sometimes even perverted. We are all ethnocentric to some degree. How can it be avoided? We share an organized perspective with those with whom we have been in sustained association, and it is difficult to see things from any other standpoint. American tourists are often called ethnocentric for scoffing at the inefficient plumbing they find elsewhere, but the people who condemn Americans for their materialism are also ethnocentric. Intellectuals sometimes claim to be cosmopolitan since they can appreciate the values stressed in other cultures. While intellectuals are generally more tolerant of foreigners, they often scoff at others in their own society who cannot meet their special standards. American intellectuals, for example, make little effort to conceal their contempt for those whose outlook toward the world is shaped largely by television.

Many difficulties arise because the differences between cultures are often subtle and hard to describe. Many of the norms of social interaction are cultural axioms. Precisely because these axioms are taken for granted, they are seldom articulated and rarely taught explicitly. Since everything done within a group is predicated on these assumptions, they become the source of serious misunderstandings in transcultural contacts. Cultural axioms enable people who share a common culture to feel at home with one another and leave outsiders wondering what is happening. If someone with a different cultural background does something we cannot explain through our vocabulary of motives, we are baffled. Role-taking is impossible. Seeing someone doing something we regard as sacrilegious without showing the slightest trace of guilt is a shocking experience; the deed appears unnatural, depraved. Thus, people who live by different values are genuinely puzzled by one another's deeds. Many of the problems that confront us arise more from such misunderstandings than from malice.

THE MEDIA OF MASS COMMUNICATION

The mass society in which we live differs from all those that have preceded it largely because of the development of the media of mass communication—books, newspapers, magazines, radio, motion pictures, and television. Technological advances in communication have enabled us to overcome barriers of space, diversity of languages, and even time. McLuhan (1964) notes that the mass media now bind the entire world into a web of instant awareness; communities the world over are becoming contracted into a single "global village." But the size and dispersal of population do not alone give mass societies their distinctive features. The ancient empires of China and Rome were huge, but they were essentially large populations under military administration controlled from a single center. Mass societies are more integrated, and their inhabitants become involved in gigantic transactions, often involving millions of people—supporting their team in the World Series, following scandals such as Watergate, participating in fashion movements, or mobilizing for war. Such massive transactions draw participants from all walks of life. Each participant has some kind of status in local groups and in the community in which he or she resides, but an individual's occupation, religion, educational background, class, sex, and ethnic identity are usually irrelevant as far as participation in mass behavior is concerned. Thus, mass audiences are often regarded as a heterogeneous aggregate of anonymous individuals; the only thing they have in common is a single focus of attention. Yet the convergence of their reactions can be of enormous consequence.

Except for what we experience personally in our own local communities, virtually everything we learn about our environment comes through one or more of these formal communication channels. Indeed, surveillance of our changing world, the collection and dissemination of news, has become a highly institutionalized activity carried on by teams of specialists in formal organizations. Exposure to the mass media is widespread. Television audiences are huge; events of national interest, such as championship games or state funerals, may reach virtually the entire population of a country. Studies indicate that many American children spend more time watching television than they spend in school, and the number of comic books sold each month exceeds the number of children in the country.

Since people act on the basis of definitions that rest on the information they possess, many observers have expressed concern over the potential for domination by those who control the mass media. There is widespread fear in some circles that those who control these sources may manipulate a population by determining its beliefs. The pattern and extent of political control varies considerably with the ideology of each government. In most dictatorial regimes the mass media are either a branch of the government or are closely supervised. In the Soviet Union, for example, the announced policy is to educate the masses and to organize them to achieve the goals of socialism. In nations like ours, in which freedom of expression is guaranteed by law, considerably more variety can be found in the offerings; even here, however, some measure of control is exercised by licensing regulations; censorship in time of war is taken for granted. Hundreds of studies have been made on the "effects" of the mass media, but the findings have been inconsistent and inconclusive (Larsen, 1964; Weiss, 1969). Since access to news can be restricted, we should not underestimate the influence of those who control the mass media. Research discloses, however, that what is presented through the mass media does not determine directly what people believe. Were they able to control public opinion, dictators would not encounter the embarrassing problems that so many of them have to face.

Perception of Mass Media Content. All human perception is selective. Thus, what is perceived from mass media offerings depends on the interests and feelings of the individuals who make up the audience. Different readers concentrate on different parts of the same newspaper, depending on their concerns. What we perceive and how we interpret it depends also on our sensitivities. Some see a given movie as a beautiful love story; others notice only the sensual attributes of the heroine; still others see a message in the plot, in some cases a thesis that would astonish the producer. We are constantly selecting television programs, movies, books, and magazine articles. The media of mass communication are like a huge supermarket from which customers select the offerings they believe will be enjoyable or edifying and avoid whatever they dislike or believe will be boring. If an offering is unfamiliar, we approach it with caution to see what it is like, ready to turn away as soon as it becomes displeasing.

One of the significant findings of audience research is that most people perceive mass media offerings as if they were interacting with the performers; their subjective experience is often one of participating vicariously in the plot. Thus, people who read a novel or are absorbed in a motion picture are not just responding to words and visual images; the developing plot organizes their imagination. Human interest stories in newspapers are much like episodes in a novel, and the generous response of those who read of the plight of some family caught in difficult circumstances reveals the extent to which personal identification is established (H. Hughes, 1940). In an early study of daytime radio serials Warner and Henry (1948) discovered that many fans in the audience regarded the programs as educational. The listeners, although they realized that the stories of attractive, middle-aged people encountering a succession of crises were fictional, thought that the depiction was realistic and felt that they learned from these sources how to handle their own problems more effectively. Whenever a major character in a radio or television serial faces a crisis, thousands of letters pour into the stations suggesting suitable solutions, revealing the extent of the identification and concern of many members of the audience.

The more effective the dramatization, the easier is the vicarious participation in the plot. Even comic strip characters are experienced as people with whom we are in sustained contact. Students who leave home to attend school in another community have to become acquainted with a different combination of comic strips. When they go home for a vacation and see the old, familiar newspapers again, they are delighted to reencounter old friends. Actors who play "tough guy" roles have been challenged to fights in bars, and those who portray doctors have been embarrassed when people consult them for medical advice. Even news of political events, national and international, is often seen as consisting of contests between politicians, generals, and other leaders, who are subsequently held personally accountable for mistakes and credited with victories over which they actually had little control. Thus, communication through the mass media is not basically different from what happens in interpersonal contacts. Although the social interaction is one-sided, the audience identifies with the performers; role-taking occurs. Of course, the extent of the identification established varies considerably from person to person and from one context to another.

Another finding of audience research is that what we notice and learn depends in part on the social setting in which the perception takes place and especially on the views of those in whose company we observe the material. We often see television and motion pictures with friends and discuss what we have read with others. Katz and Lazarsfeld (1955) found that people are influenced by the opinions of friends whom they respect as having some knowledge in the relevant areas. Whose views count most depends on our perception of their expertise. If new recipes or food products are involved, it is the judgment of persons who are regarded as knowledgeable cooks that matters; similarly, the opinions of those who are respected as well informed and reasonable are most important on political matters. This has been called the two-step flow of communication (Katz, 1957).

Mere presentation of materials over the mass media does not guarantee their acceptance. Few people are so stupid as to believe anything they are told simply because it comes from a formal communication channel.

No message is likely to be accepted by anyone who regards it as implausible — inconsistent with what is already taken for granted. We do not accept items that contradict widely held beliefs (Klapper, 1960). For example, studies of audience reactions to motion pictures with antiracist themes disclose that in many cases people are not even conscious of having been the targets of special appeals. They neither accept nor reject the message; those who dislike some ethnic group often fail to understand the point. Thus, the appeal of *Gentlemen's Agreement,* one of the first movies to expose popular misconceptions about Jews, was blunted by the inability of anti-Semitic people to perceive the theme (Cooper and Jahoda, 1947). Katz and Feldman (1962) report that viewers of the Nixon-Kennedy debates during the 1960 presidential campaign recalled statements with which they disagreed but attributed them to the candidate they opposed, regardless of who had actually made them.

In his study of children's reactions to television dramas, Freidson (1953) found that standards of judgment change as the children grow older and develop special interests. Young boys who still accept ghosts as real and become frightened react negatively when the hero with a six-shooter fires ten rounds without reloading. To them, this is obviously contrived. Thus, different segments of a large audience react in diverse ways to the same message. Those from unlike cultural backgrounds have dissimilar standards of judgment; what seems perfectly reasonable to some will strike others as ludicrous. A glance at the letters to the editors of newspapers and magazines, even when the extreme and unprintable ones have been eliminated, reveals the diversity of audience reactions to identical presentations.

Production of Mass Media Content. The power of those who control the media of mass communication is considerable, but it is not unlimited. Information that is withheld from the mass media is not likely to become widely known, and the selective withholding of information can have considerable impact in the long run. To this day very few Russians and Chinese know about the testing of nuclear devices that has occurred in their respective countries. However, popular tastes and public opinion cannot necessarily be dictated from above. During the twentieth century, for example, more than two-thirds of the American newspapers that endorse presidential candidates have supported Republicans; Democrats have not only won more often, but the Republican party keeps getting smaller and smaller.

What is presented over the mass media is prepared by intellectuals — authors, artists, script writers, editors, directors, actors and actresses, technicians, and executives at all levels — who are human beings pursuing careers in the bureaucracies of formal organizations. Rosten (1937), Breed (1955), and Tuchman (1978) show how owners' and managers' interests are reflected in the performance of their employees, even when policy is not explicitly stated. Advertisers and the government also influence content. But there are also pressures toward accuracy and aesthetic standards. Where work is highly technical, the people involved strive to maintain professional standards, and even though such values do not always prevail, many of the workers have a sense of responsibility to their public. Furthermore, writers and other professional personnel judge one another in terms of standards that are different from those of the owners, the government, or the audience. When they compromise their own values to keep their jobs or to advance their careers, they feel ashamed of what they do, realizing that they do not command the respect of their peers. Thus, the efforts of intellectuals to maintain their self-respect limit somewhat the blatancy with which they can serve masters with ulterior motives.

Whether the mass media are a branch of the government or commercial enterprises, they need mass patronage. In commercial enterprises the objective is to make profits; this requires gaining and holding a huge audience — either for direct sales or for what advertisers are willing to pay to sponsor programs. People will not pay attention for long to what does not interest them. Audiences are difficult to hold unless the material is plausible or entertaining. If a dictator orders people to pay attention to some program, they will comply, but they will not take seriously messages that they regard as nonsense. Most people become bored with the constant reiteration of a party line; when propaganda is too blatant, the audience becomes cynical, and the communication channel itself loses its credibility.

Where censorship is known to exist, the audience takes it into account. Bauer and Gleicher (1953) show that many Russians in full sympathy with the regime rely on rumors for information on such matters as policy failures, adverse domestic conditions, opposition to the regime, or the unsavory habits of prominent figures. They take it for granted that news of this sort would not appear in formal communication channels. Those who are in positions of privilege and are better informed are more inclined to rely on rumors for such items, using this information to supplement and correct what they learn in the official media. This happens in any society in which censorship is even suspected and is one reason so many rumors arise everywhere in time of war. Thus, the audience is not defenseless. It can always withhold patronage and does not have to accept messages that do not make sense.

The content of the mass media reinforces preexisting beliefs and values; what is presented may modify the intensity of feelings, but not the direction (Lazarsfeld et al., 1948; Klapper, 1960). Most direct attempts to change widely held views by promotional campaigns have failed. But when changes in deeply rooted beliefs do occur, it appears that the mass media play an important part in channeling them. Following the disclosure of Nazi atrocities against Jews during World War II, American mass media producers made an organized effort to combat unfavorable beliefs about various ethnic groups. Members of ethnic minorities were no longer cast in such stereotyped ways; they came to be depicted in middle-class settings in positions that call for respect both in stories and in advertisements. Scripts were prepared so that the hero or heroine addressed the underprivileged sympathetically and courteously, and stereotyped beliefs were either ridiculed by the hero or heroine or defended by the villain. At first many Americans found the presentations implausible, but over several decades a whole generation has grown up that is no longer dismayed to see members of any ethnic group in positions of high rank. Although ethnic tensions persist in the United States, open ridicule of minorities has virtually ended, and there has been a noticeable reduction in blatant discrimination. Public opinion polls also disclose substantial changes in attitudes toward Afro-Americans. Ironically, this integration accelerated just when the "melting pot" philosophy was being attacked by those seeking their ancestral roots and advocating separatism.

Drastic transformations are also taking place in other areas. Since the 1960s, popular music, movies, and television programs have presented conceptions of love and sex that differ markedly from previous mores. These new views not only reflect actual changes, but also provide new models of conduct for those who are uncertain. Wolfenstein and Leites (1950), in their analysis of major American movies in 1945 and 1946, contend that the themes both reflect and channel the mores. Their finding suggests that the relationship between mass media content and prevailing beliefs is reciprocal. Producers work with a conception of what the audience takes for granted and try to develop acceptable offerings; a satisfied audience is in turn influenced by the media. The audience selects what is meaningful and entertaining and rejects or ignores messages that rest on doubtful premises. Dissatisfied people simply turn to other sources. But those who are curious do learn new lessons.

Characteristics of Mass Societies. One of the distinctive features of a mass society is the breadth of outlook of most of its members. The symbolic environment of most people today, even those without special intellectual interests, extends far beyond the local community in which they live and includes all kinds of objects they have never experienced directly. For example, Americans are concerned with what happens in the Middle East, Southeast Asia, and other places they have never visited, for they realize that their lives might be affected by events in these distant places. Even those who were not overly diligent about studying history are aware of many relevant events of the past. Thus, people in mass societies tend to be more sophisticated. We live in a world that is further extended in space and time than the world of most people in previous periods of history. At the same time, as McLuhan (1964) suggests, most people are spectators of events that may have an impact on their lives. Participation in these events is vicarious; people can only watch what is going on, and they are seldom in a position to do much to alter the course of history.

Since the mass media audience is so large and heterogeneous, accounts must be presented in oversimplified and stereotyped terms. Thus, outside our respective areas of specialization much of our knowledge is superficial, consisting in many instances of cliches and slogans. Only specialists understand each topic. Just as only a mechanic can evaluate critically the claims made about some feature of new automobiles, only an economist can make reasoned judgments about complex problems involving monetary issues. Most people simply do not have the time to learn about all the complex affairs that affect their lives. Ideally citizens in a democratic nation should be sufficiently informed to make rational decisions about all matters on which they are called to vote. In fact, people who work full time, spend a few hours with their family, meet other local commitments, and take some breaks to relax have little time left over to study in detail the problems of water supply in their community or other such issues. It is unreasonable to expect people to be competent in all areas in which they have the legal right to make decisions.

Some critics of mass societies contend that the people in them have been atomized into impotent and undifferentiated masses and that the social bonds that arise in local communities have been totally displaced. This is not true. Those who participate in various forms of mass behavior are anonymous individuals *only* while participating in such large transactions; otherwise they are members of various groups in their local communities. But these people depend less for support from local groups than residents of an isolated village in which everyone knows about everyone else and where everyone receives considerable pressure to comply with local norms. Fear of gossip usually keeps such people in line. In mass societies, however, where local norms are recognized as constituting but one of many possible ways of doing things, people tend to be more emancipated from strict community control. Even allegiance to class, ethnic, or religious groups becomes attenuated, for many individuals derive their values, their sense of personal identity, and their lifestyle from sources beyond — from the mass media. Young people in particular who are dissatisfied with local customs can turn elsewhere for standards of conduct. Thus, distinctions of rank that are important locally become attenuated. All members of mass societies are valued equally as voters, buyers, and spectators. Mere numerical superiority may thus become a criterion of success; those who can mobilize large numbers in support of their interests attain definite advantages (Kornhauser, 1968).

SUMMARY AND DISCUSSION

Communication is the touchstone of society. The mark of any society is the capacity of its members to engage in concerted action. But unless they can communicate, they cannot coordinate their respective contributions to joint undertakings. Thus, all creatures that live in groups — social insects as well as mammals — have techniques of communication, but none has developed a procedure as effective as the symbolic interchanges that occur among human beings. The kind of reciprocal role-taking that is commonplace among people makes possible flexible coordination in complex transactions. Since knowledge is constructed and maintained in social interaction, those who participate regularly in the same communication channels develop a similar symbolic environment; they order their experiences around similar units and make the same assumptions about the various objects that they utilize. In short, they come to share a common culture. This greatly facilitates their joint participation in a wide range of social transactions. In the twentieth century, technological advances have so enhanced communicative procedures that the basic character of human society has been transformed; it is now possible for people to develop common cultures even if they do not live in the same community.

Ethnocentrism is an old problem, but it is taking on a somewhat different character in mass societies. How did the Aztecs mistake Cortez for one of their gods? The Spaniards and the Indians approached each other with perspectives that had developed in total isolation from one another; their symbolic environments were so different that each side had no understanding of the views of the other. It was an accident, an unfortunate one for the Aztecs, that the two parties' definitions dovetailed as well as they did. Although culture shocks still take place, blunders of that magnitude are less likely in modern societies. Indeed, experienced travelers nowadays move about with only the minimum of difficulties. Although misunderstandings still occur in transcultural contacts, they also arise often among people who live in the same community. Difficulties in role-taking among those who live side by side present new problems, which will be pursued in the next chapter.

SUGGESTED READINGS

Berelson, Bernard, and Morris Janowitz (eds.). 1966. *Reader in Public Opinion and Communication.* New York: Free Press.
An anthology containing many classic articles and excerpts on the organization and impact of the media of mass communication.
Cicourel, Aaron. 1974. *Cognitive Sociology.* New York: Free Press.
An examination of some basic presuppositions underlying people's efforts to interpret and communicate their experiences.
Hall, Edward T. 1959. *The Silent Language.* Greenwich, Conn.: Fawcett.
An account of some of the more subtle features of culture that frequently lead to misunderstandings in transcultural contacts.
Hughes, Helen M. 1940. *News and the Human Interest Story.* Chicago: University of Chicago Press.
The disclosure of sentiments in newspaper accounts and typical audience reactions to them.
Kluckhohn, Florence R., and Fred L. Strodtbeck. 1961. *Variations in Value Orientations.* Evanston, Ill.: Row, Peterson.
A comparative study of the cultural axioms in five communities in the American Southwest.
Sapir, Edward. 1949. *Selected Writings of Edward Sapir in Language, Culture, and Personality.* David G. Mandelbaum (ed.). Berkeley and Los Angeles: University of California Press.
An anthology of pioneering studies on language, symbolism, culture, and social psychiatry.

IV

HUMAN COMMUNITIES

In 1803 Robert Malthus presented a thesis about population growth that launched a controversy that has still not ended. He argued that human population, if unchecked, tends to increase in a geometrical ratio, while food supply increases at best in an arithmetical ratio. Therefore, population tends to grow to the limits of the means of subsistence unless the death rate is raised by war, famine, and pestilence or unless the birth rate is lowered by abortion, infanticide, birth control, or moral restraint. Since his contention stood in sharp contrast to the prevailing optimism of the philosophers of the Enlightenment, who saw humanity marching inexorably toward perfection, his views were subjected to severe criticism. The nineteenth century turned out to be a period of phenomenal growth in Europe — with colonization, a period of sustained economic growth, and a marked rise in the standard of living. Thus, disparagement of the Malthusian doctrine became commonplace. Many felt that he had underestimated the potentialities of technical progress and of family limitation by birth control. Some even argued that with increasing knowledge there would be no limits to human capacity to alter the natural environment and use it for our own purposes. Now that the specter of overpopulation haunts us once again, the controversy has been reopened, albeit along more sophisticated lines.

Although technological advances have altered drastically the surroundings in which human beings live, we are still organisms living in a physical world. We live in a natural environment as well as a symbolic environment. But we can use knowledge to manipulate some features of the natural environment, and our central concern in this chapter is to examine the manner in which various patterns of settlement have developed as the inhabitants learned to harness physical and biotic processes. Some technological improvements have led to the formation of communities that no longer have a territorial base. Nonetheless, there appear to be definite limitations to what can be done, and we shall see what happened when regularities in nature have been disregarded, either through ignorance or because of political considerations.

FORMATION OF COMMUNITY PATTERNS

Most people live in settlements of some kind, and the concept of *community* is still useful in sociology. There are many kinds of communities — nomadic tribes, villages, towns, cities, and huge metropolitan areas. Until recently it was relatively easy to identify communities, for most of them had a territorial base. A community is a social unit that is largely self-contained. It has a relatively stable population, and several generations of the same families live there. People who live together for a long time are likely to develop a common language and form a common symbolic environment; they share a culture that facilitates concerted action. Most communities have well-established procedures for maintaining order. Even communities that include some self-governing enclaves, such as ghettos, usually have one ultimate authority. Perhaps most important, where several generations have lived together, a sense of continuity, of mutual identification, and of attachment to the land develops. The people have a sense of belonging there; it is the place where they were born and reared, where their family and friends are, where they feel at home. Even when the inhabitants are conquered by outsiders and are reduced in rank, they continue to view their rulers as intruders, for they feel that the land really belongs to them. Anderson (1938:21–24) refers to such oppressed peoples as "charter member minorities." To be sure, community boundaries are becoming increasingly difficult to ascertain in modern mass societies, but demographers estimate that about 80 percent of the world's population still lives in villages, whose territorial bases are clearly defined.

A Community as an Ecological Unit. All living creatures, plant and animal, occupying a common habitat become implicated with one another in a common web of life. All organisms strive to grow, survive, and reproduce; and each has a niche in an ecosystem that is the product of natural selection. Different species become related in ways that facilitate their effective utilization of available resources. As an example of such cooperation Darwin mentioned a species of purple clover in England. Its supply depends on the number and diligence of humble-bees, which are the only creatures capable of reaching purple clover nectar. The supply of humble-bees depends on the number and diligence of field mice, which destroy their nests. The number of field mice depends in turn on the number of cats that stalk them. If needed resources are in short supply, competition arises, and those that happen to have the characteristics that make them best suited to cope with the circumstances—*competitive advantages*—are most likely to survive and reproduce. Thus, in each habitat a delicate balance is maintained through cooperation and competition. Any disturbance of any part of this intricate balance necessitates adjustments on the part of all organisms in the area. Human beings are part of the web of life in the community in which they live. The organization of any community is the product of the collective adaptations of *all* organisms in the area. (We should not confuse the notion of competitive advantages that arise in particular contexts with the concept of *power*, an attribute of social relationships.)

Community structure depends largely on how energy is converted for human use, which in turn depends on available resources and the culture. Technology, the means of harnessing and using energy in the pursuit of whatever people value, is decisively important, for it limits the type of economic system that develops. All communities—whatever the size, technology, or political ideology—rest on some kind of economic system, a set of organized arrangements for providing livelihood. We live in a complex industrial economy, but we have developed a wide variety of procedures for acquiring, producing, and using available resources. In all economies some kind of division of labor arises; status and role differentiations, at least by age and sex, are found even in the simplest economies. But there are variations in the degree of specialization. In some societies women do all the heavy work; in others people in special categories, sometimes slaves captured for that purpose, do such work. As the specialization of tasks becomes more complicated and few individuals can be self-sufficient, goods must be distributed. Some kind of distribution system, often involving some medium of exchange such as money, develops. The basic problem everywhere is to provide for essential material needs; to do this people enter into enduring relationships to produce and distribute needed objects.

Until quite recently most communities relied on organic energy; food-gathering and food-raising communities depend on plants and animals as energy converters (Duncan, 1964). People have lived in communities based on collectional economies — hunting and gathering food — throughout much of recorded human history. Only a few such communities are left in the world today — the Mbuti pygmies in the rain forest of central Africa, the Bushmen of Kalahari, some Eskimos, the Siriono of Bolivia, and some aborigines of Australia. Even for these people isolation is breaking down, and they are beginning to trade with some of their agricultural neighbors. Since such communities depend so directly on their environment, many of them are nomadic. Whenever game is hunted out or moves on and the desired vegetation is exhausted, the people have to move. Nomadic life limits their material culture, for everything has to be portable. Their technology may be simple, but nomads may develop complex social institutions, for they are interdependent in their day-to-day existence and tend to develop a strong sense of group identity.

Horticultural and pastoral economies require more permanent settlement. Evidence has been found of grain cultivation and the domestication of sheep and goats in the Middle East about ten thousand years ago. Most of the people in the world today — especially in Asia, Africa, and Latin America — live in agricultural communities, in which people attempt to shape the environment rather than simply adjust to it. Villages and towns become focal points in areas that are predominantly agricultural. Most farming is done for subsistence. Woytinsky and Woytinsky (1953) estimate that not more than one farmer in five produces for a market economy; most are concerned primarily with feeding themselves and their families. Most peasants have small holdings; they utilize family labor, work animals, and their own implements. They are not concerned with the least expensive way to produce, as in large-scale agriculture. Particularly noteworthy is their attachment to their land; land is the source of life and everything else that is important to them. It has a special meaning that city dwellers often find difficult to understand. Twentieth-century revolutionaries have discovered that they must take into account the peasants' attachment to land and their lack of concern about producing for large profits.

Industrialization as a Social Process. Industrialization is a system of production based on complex procedures for converting energy from various sources, exploiting scientific knowledge, and creating an intense division of labor to benefit from specialization and standardization. The aim is to reduce the cost per unit of goods and services, and the productive capacity of industrial economies is indeed enormous. The per capita income of people in industrialized nations is incomparably greater than that of people elsewhere. The industrial revolution began in the British Isles between 1750 and 1825, when steam power was first harnessed effectively for manufacturing. Since that time, petroleum, electricity, internal combustion engines, and now atomic power have provided sources of energy. As the effectiveness of this mode of production was demonstrated, it spread quickly to the rest of Europe, to the United States, and later to Japan. Now most countries are striving to raise their standard of living by industrializing, and the globe has been divided into "developed" and "developing" nations by the extent to which they have succeeded. Among the conditions of industrialization are a trained labor force, money as a medium of exchange, markets for products, availability of raw materials, sources of investment funds, and access to technical and scientific knowledge. Thus, industrialization creates a demand for new goods and services, a demand for resources, and a demand for educated workers. Mass education is quickly recognized as essential, and the importance of intellectuals is enhanced. In industrial societies intellectuals are becoming more clearly differentiated from the rest of the population, more highly specialized, and increasingly professionalized.

In his provocative study of the industrial revolution in Europe, Polanyi (1944) contends that effective participation in a market economy requires the formation of a way of thinking that differs from what is taken for granted elsewhere. People must learn to engage in productive activities for remuneration rather than for subsistence alone. Although all other economic systems emphasize reciprocity in exchange, in an industrial economy people must learn to choose among alternatives for the purpose of maximizing output and minimizing cost — thus getting the greatest profit in exchange. For people from many cultural backgrounds such exchanges involve a drastic transformation in their vocabulary of motives. Since money becomes the medium of exchange in so many transactions, various objects come to be evaluated in terms of money. All income is derived from the sale of something, and those who do not produce something must sell their services; thus, a monetary value is placed on people's productive performance — their labor.

The standardization of products and an intense division of labor in which each group of workers carries out a highly specialized task in which they have developed expert skills cuts cost per unit. Thus, industrialization depends on mass production, a pattern of social organization alien to many past cultures. Mass production requires large productive units, a huge factory or a network of plants. Although individuals and families still own some such units, most large enterprises today are owned by stockholders (in capitalist economies) or by the government (in socialist economies). Executives and technicians, who are usually not the owners, manage the plants. Thus, executives, technicians, and clerical workers in corporate bureaucracies have similar training, face similar problems, and often develop similar aspirations—regardless of who owns the unit in which they are employed. The labor force consists of thousands of people who are also separated from ownership. One consequence of this type of organization is the separation of workers from both the product and the means of production. The product—be it an automobile or a can of pineapple—is a collective one; no single worker can produce it alone. Each worker is just a replaceable cog in a large machine. Each person does only a few highly technical tasks, contributing but a small part to the final product. Status in a community thus depends not so much on one's work as on one's job; it depends more on the appraisal of the organization in which one is employed. Pride in work can still be found among artists, artisans, and some professional workers, but others derive their sense of identity more from their jobs (Drucker, 1949).

Another change that has accompanied industrialization is urbanization. Cities existed long before the industrial revolution; they first developed in the Middle East, India, China, Mexico, and Peru as soon as agricultural arts had advanced sufficiently to provide surpluses for those who did not grow their own food. But these cities were trade, financial, administrative, and ceremonial centers as well as fortresses (Sjoberg, 1960). A concentration of people facilitates industrial production, for urbanization provides ready access to both a large labor force and concentrated markets for products. Wherever transportation could bring raw materials together with a labor force and a market, new cities developed, and old ones grew. The economies of proximity bring factories together, and the availability of work in factories brings people together. As changes in agricultural techniques lead to less demand for farm workers, the surplus agricultural workers move to cities to seek jobs in factories, in many instances spawning huge slum areas. The number of large cities in the world remained fairly stable until industrialization; since then, they have increased in both number and size. Between 1900 and 1970, the number of cities with over a million residents increased from 10 to 174.

People brought together in cities for production are not necessarily drawn from the same cultural background. Thus, huge metropolitan centers are characterized by both heterogeneity and density of population. Unlike villagers, urban dwellers cannot know everyone else in the community on a personal basis; thus categorical contacts become commonplace. Everyone comes into contact daily with large numbers of strangers and slight acquaintances but knows personally only a small proportion of the people he or she encounters. All others are placed into various categories in terms of their appearance — dress, skin color, manners, or other indicators of status. Outside of one's immediate neighborhood, social contacts center largely on the exchange of goods and services rather than on personal ties. Thus, most people are in relationships of reciprocal utility; each has something that the other wants. Wirth (1956:110–32) contends that this orientation places a utilitarian accent on urban life. People tend to become more individualistic and rational. They feel no personal obligations to strangers, tend to pursue their own interests, assume that others will do likewise, and usually respect their right to do so. Increasing emphasis must be placed on legal norms since the frequent association of people not restrained by sentimental ties could lead to mutual exploitation in the absence of formal control. Thus, in urban centers the police and courts play a more important part in maintaining order than they do in smaller communities. Wirth is not suggesting that all cities are wild jungles; he is simply noting that the neighborliness that characterizes village life is limited in cities to small friendship circles and relatives (Fischer, 1981). The other contacts are not necessarily unpleasant or hostile — only impersonal.

Adaptation as a Continuous Process. Industrialization and the media of mass communication are converting the entire world into a single socioeconomic order. The only territorial units with political sovereignty are nations, but even they are among the many types of organizational units within a global system (Wallerstein, 1974).

The entire world is now a single ecosystem, but any ecosystem is only in temporary equilibrium. Its persistence is contingent on relative stability in the relationship between the population and its environment. The various relationships among human beings and other creatures are formed initially by natural selection. Once a previously established system is disturbed by changes in life conditions, the selective processes become apparent again. Thus, the introduction of industrial production has resulted in severe dislocations everywhere. The upheavals in England in the early nineteenth century (Osborne, 1970) are much like those in Japan in the early twentieth century (Smith, 1972), and both resemble the problems facing the developing nations of the world today. Now that the demands of population on available resources appear to be approaching their limits, we can reasonably anticipate further transformations with concomitant disruptions.

COMPOSITION OF THE POPULATION

Age and Sex Distribution. The composition of the population of any community is important in that it limits the kinds of social transactions that are likely to occur and creates pressures and selective demands for certain kinds of resources, goods, and services. Communities vary considerably in their population makeup. Age and sex structures of nations differ according to the extent of industrialization. Both fertility and mortality rates in developing nations are higher than in industrialized nations. In most developing nations about 40 percent of the population consists of children under 15; a bit over half the people are between 15 and 64 — the most productive years; the proportion of people over 65 is small. In industrialized nations children make up only about 20 to 25 percent of the population; about two-thirds of the people are between 15 and 64, and the rest are over 65. There are thus three people in their productive years to take care of every two dependents — the children and the retired.

What is happening in the United States today demonstrates the pressures that arise when the composition of a population changes. Low fertility and mortality rates are combining to create a population that will become increasingly older. Women of childbearing age are having fewer children, and improved medical care is increasing life expectancy. Whereas in 1800 the median age of Americans was 16, by 1977 it had risen to 28.9. Although projection is an uncertain art, demographers estimate that if current trends do not change, the median will be 37.3 by the year 2030. Such an aging of the population will affect many aspects of American life — the economy, education, land use, recreation, medical care, housing, and retirement practices. In a country dominated by the old there will be less demand for baby foods, toys, teachers, and maternity wards; but demand will increase for retirement homes, medical care, and recreational facilities suitable for those who are less active. Many American communities have already experienced difficulties in passing school bonds for lack of support by elderly people on fixed incomes whose children are grown. The Social Security system is likely to become more costly. So many retired people are drawing pensions that the system can no longer pay its way. There are now slightly more than five active workers for each Social Security beneficiary, and the time may come when there will not be enough young people working to support the swollen ranks of the retired. The question of the appropriate age at which workers should enter and leave the labor market thus becomes a political issue. Many of the elderly cannot afford to retire, but their continued employment makes it more difficult for the young to find jobs. With the elderly constituting almost one-third of the voters, transformations may be expected in American politics.

Similar variations can be found in sex ratios. The U.S. Census Bureau computes sex ratio in terms of the number of males per 100 females. A high sex ratio (more men than women) is found in developing nations (Ceylon, Pakistan, Libya, Tunisia, India), where women of childbearing age suffer a high mortality rate. High sex ratios are also found in nations into which there has been large-scale immigration from long distances (Israel, Malaya, Argentina, Australia, Canada, New Zealand), for men are more frequently involved in long-distance migrations. A low sex ratio (more women than men) is found in areas marked by severe losses in a succession of wars (France, Germany, Austria) and in areas from which there has been large-scale emigration. Cities tend to have a low sex ratio, and rural areas a high sex ratio. In most industrialized countries the pattern has become fairly stable. There are about 105 males born for every 100 females, but the mortality rate is higher for males of all ages. Thus, as cohorts age the sex ratio declines, reaching 100:100 among 40-to 50-year-olds; after that, the sex ratio becomes progressively lower. Any imbalance in the sex ratio creates problems. One common occurrence is delayed marriages and fewer legitimate births. In frontier communities, where men generally outnumber women by a substantial proportion, prostitution as well as the idealization of "good" women is commonplace. Some demographers are anticipating serious problems in the United States, where an increase in the number of widowed women is expected. Unless the death rate for men is cut drastically, the difference in life expectancy between men and women is likely to widen. Some have jokingly suggested bigamy for elderly men, but this may cease to be a laughing matter.

Categories of Human Beings. Whenever noticeable changes occur in the relative numbers of various categories of people, political issues arise and at times lead to vicious conflicts. People everywhere are placed into categories in terms of conventional norms. In each community human beings are classified and evaluated. One's status in a community and the roles one enacts in various transactions depend on the category in which one is located, but the criteria by which people are classified and the categories themselves vary from one culture to another. Sex differences are generally unambiguous, but classification by age groups varies. How many years people have to live before they are no longer regarded as children and are expected to assume full adult responsibilities differs from culture to culture, as do the norms of what constitutes an elderly person who is no longer expected to perform productive labor. Other categories that play such an important part in the modern world — ethnic identity, class position, and religion — are not biotic units.

One of the most pernicious superstitions of our time is the prevalent belief that human beings are divided into different "races." Race is a popular concept that rests on false assumptions. Anthropologists and geneticists agree that the units they study — people who share a common genetic makeup — do not coincide at all with what are commonly called the "races" of humanity. The term "ethnic group" is preferable to refer to this commonsense category. An *ethnic group* consists of people who conceive of themselves as being alike by virtue of common ancestry, real or fictitious, and who are so regarded by others (Wirth, 1956:237–38).

Even a casual knowledge of anthropology and history reveals that there is no such thing as a pure race, but there are people who conceive of themselves as replicas of distant ancestors in the dawn of history. Belief in common ancestry is usually fictitious, but people act in terms of their definitions. The boundaries of each ethnic group are set by custom. In the United States, for example, people are usually classified as black if they have a single African ancestor. A person with seven greatgrandparents from Africa and one from Europe and a person with seven forebears from Europe and one from Africa have both been classified as black. This ethnic category cannot possibly be homogeneous genetically. Most Americans assume that the distinctions we usually make — black, white, and yellow — represent the natural divisions of humanity. But south of the Rio Grande the important categories are Ladino, Mestizo, and Indio. Africans make all kinds of distinctions among people Americans would classify as black. Many Chinese, Japanese, and Koreans — after centuries of fighting among themselves — would be offended to learn they are regarded as being alike because of their common ancestry, just as many people in Ireland would be infuriated about being lumped with the English. Ethnic categories form the basis of invidious distinctions in many communities, but definitions of these categories vary to an astonishing extent from one part of the world to another.

Although biologists agree that all human beings are of the same genus and species, members of different ethnic groups sometimes act as if they constitute separate species. Arguing that "blood is thicker than water," some feel that their obligations to others with whom they identify on an ethnic basis should supersede all other loyalties. Actually, if there are any significant differences between ethnic groups, they are cultural. What is really important about human beings is the manner in which they think and act, and one's orientation toward the world depends more on what one learns after birth rather than on genetic constitution. Especially where ethnic groups are segregated, those within each enclave develop their own communication channels and thereby come to share a distinctive culture. What are often called "racial traits" are actually habits — ways of thinking and acting that have been acquired in the course of sustained association with others of the same culture. Genetic differences do exist, but they do not coincide with the boundaries of "races." Since people act in terms of definitions, however, those who believe that they are biotically different will act as if they were.

Other important categories include class, religion, and political ideology. Karl Marx defines a class as consisting of people who make similar contributions to a system of production and thereby occupy the same position within an economy. Given this definition, the potential for identifying people on a class basis is always present, for even the simplest economies have some division of labor. However, Marx stresses that people of the same class are unable to act together as a unit unless they develop class consciousness. Thus, as with ethnic groups, a *class* consists of people who conceive of themselves as being alike and sharing common interests by virtue of similarities in the kind of work they do. Religious differences have long played a significant part in history — the spread of Islam, the Crusades of the Middle Ages, the wars in Europe during the Protestant Reformation. In more recent times we have witnessed the struggles between India and Pakistan and the strife in Lebanon and Ireland. As we approach the end of the twentieth century, people may be classifying themselves in terms of another type of commitment — political ideology. In Communist nations — where the existence of class differences is denied, ethnic differences tend to be underplayed or ignored, and religion becomes less important — struggles have broken out among factions professing different degrees of ideological purity.

Population as a Political Issue. By the time the classification of people — whether by class, ethnic identity, or religion — becomes well established, the members of each category identify with one another. They develop consciousness of kind and come to believe they are fundamentally alike and share the same interests. If the cultural differences are conspicuous, they may even come to believe that they are members of different species. When community resources — be they arable land, mineral rights, or access to water — are limited, some kind of competition is likely to develop between categories, and those who happen to have competitive advantages are likely to gain a disproportionate share of what is desired. Many systems of social stratification, in which categories of people are ranked, have their beginnings in such competition (Shibutani and Kwan, 1965:139–250). Unlike other creatures, among human beings most competitive advantages are cultural rather than inherited. Thus, Europeans were able to establish colonies throughout the world and subjugate millions of natives because of their culture — superior military technology and specialized knowledge that enabled them to exploit their environment more effectively.

Once a system of social stratification has been established, those in privileged positions strive to retain their advantages, not only for themselves but for their progeny. As long as their political power remains unchallenged, rulers are not particularly concerned about being outnumbered by their subjects. If the disparity of power is reduced, however, they may come to believe that maintaining their position depends on the relative numbers of people in each category. If this occurs, population control becomes a political issue. Relative numbers may change, either from differential reproduction rates or through migration, and contention often arises on these very points. Those who feel threatened often accuse their adversaries of having too many children — of breeding like "wild animals." English-Canadians in Quebec have long accused French-Canadians, most of whom are Catholic, of reproducing rapidly so they could eventually take over the area (E. C. Hughes, 1943). Much American antagonism on the Pacific Coast during the early twentieth century against Chinese and Japanese immigrants was based on a fear that these ethnic groups reproduced so quickly that they would soon outnumber the white population. They came to be regarded as the "yellow peril" — the vanguard of Asian hordes who would soon inundate the Western Hemisphere (Sabagh and Thomas, 1945). Those who have been concerned with maintaining a privileged class position have similarly accused working-class people of breeding too rapidly. Since the poor can least afford to have so many children, their fecundity has also been cited as evidence of their allegedly inferior mentality. Thus, population becomes a political issue when categories of people struggle for status. Issues of this kind could not arise were it not for the invidious distinctions that people make among themselves.

If opportunities for free migration exist, those who feel persecuted can leave. Thus, countries like the United States and Israel have developed heterogeneous populations by becoming havens for those fleeing persecution or poverty. Where such opportunities are not available, a variety of policies have been adopted to obtain the desired composition.

It is not uncommon for countries to encourage the immigration of the type of people they want by making attractive offers while restricting the immigration of others. Thus, for a time Australia, Canada, and South Africa advertised openly for immigrants of desired ethnic identity (Petersen, 1955). Many governments have limited the immigration of unpopular categories of people while encouraging the assimilation of those already present. Until recently, U.S. immigration policy encouraged immigration of northern Europeans and discouraged everyone else. If a nation's political situation seems critical, forced mass population transfers may be arranged. Soon after World War I, for example, Greeks in Turkey, except those living in Constantinople, were deported in exchange for Moslems in Greece, except those in western Thrace; in all, over a half million people were uprooted (Ladas, 1932). When such measures fail, unpopular minorities have even been massacred, as in the virtual extermination of Indians on the American frontier, the Armenians in Turkey, and the Jews in Nazi Germany. If population becomes an issue, the matter is usually settled by political means.

Drastic changes in the composition of a community's population, whether forced or voluntary, often result in unanticipated dislocations. Among the most dramatic cases of mass expulsion was that of the Moors from Spain in 1610. Attempts to enforce religious conformity had resulted in a century of civil strife. Spaniards became convinced that the presence of such a large alien group was dangerous, for the Moors could align themselves with any enemy that might invade Spain. Since the Moors were the best artisans and agricultural workers, some Spanish leaders argued for retaining a selected number, at least until enough Spaniards had been trained to take their places. But their pleas were overruled, and an estimated half million Moors were expelled. The sudden departure of such a large segment of the population so disrupted the economy that Spain never recovered (Lea, 1901). When Indonesia became an independent nation after World War II, hatred of the Dutch remained, and in time most of the colonists were expelled. This compounded the new nation's difficulties, for the Europeans had provided much of the badly needed technical and skilled personnel. Similar problems on a smaller scale are emerging in large American cities. Although federal intervention temporarily resolved New York's 1975 insolvency, the basic problem still remains: Middle-class urbanites are fleeing in increasing numbers to the suburbs, leaving the cities to impoverished and disadvantaged minorities (Schnore and Sharp, 1964). Such urban flight reduces the tax revenues of the cities but does not proportionately reduce the cost of municipal services. If our cities continue to house larger numbers of the unemployed, the poor, and the elderly, they will have to find new ways to pay for services.

Genetic Transformations. If one of the categories of people — class, ethnic, or religious — remains clearly dominant for some time, its culture tends to prevail. In the United States, for example, the values of northern European cultures hold sway. Mate selection is often based on criteria used by those who hold high rank and are admired and emulated. Among various ethnic minorities, women with light skin, especially those with Caucasoid features, are much in demand. The most successful men in each group are likely to marry women who are considered most attractive by these standards, and their offspring are likely to approximate more closely the desired appearance. Afro-Americans have long made distinctions among themselves on the basis of skin color and have been far more sensitive than others to slight shades of difference. Although the matter is still controversial (Kephart, 1948), it appears that successive generations of Afro-Americans have been getting lighter through intermarriage and preferential mating. The growth of ethnic pride since World War II may alter this tendency, but comparing the skin colors of Afro-Americans and that of Africans south of the Sahara will reveal a clear difference.

The development of the media of mass communication has led to increasing acceptance throughout the world of European standards of what constitutes a desirable human being. A glance at film stars everywhere reveals the extent to which they approximate Western standards. Widespread acceptance of another culture's ideals works considerable hardship on those who happen to diverge from them, for their physical attributes are limited by inheritance. If preferential mating on this basis continues for several generations, the appearances as well as other characteristics of the population are likely to change. Thus, if cultural definitions provide competitive advantages to those who happen to have the desired traits, a population's genetic structure may be transformed through the disproportionate reproduction of those traits. Darwin referred to this process as sexual selection.

SEGREGATION IN URBAN COMMUNITIES

Patterns of Segregation. Urbanization is a key trend today, and increasing industrialization will probably keep it so for decades to come. A community of any size is likely to be segregated to some extent, with members of different categories occupying different sectors; in large cities, however, the patterns of spatial distribution are more readily discernible. All cities have some kind of central place, although what is done there varies considerably. The center — whether it be a marketplace; a commercial district with office buildings, small factories, and stores; a place for administrative buildings; or a place for worship — is usually located at the original site where the community began. Around it each city spreads out like a patchwork quilt, each sector characterized by a particular type of land use, certain kinds of people, and distinctive life-styles. These patterns vary along several dimensions: the number of sections, the size of the units, the degree of homogeneity of the people in each, and the clarity and rigidity of their boundaries. The patterns also depend on how the populace is classified and ranked.

The elite in each community — the wealthy, a traditional aristocracy, members of a ruling ethnic group, or the leaders and more affluent members of a religious or political group — tend to reside together, congregating in what is regarded as the most desired area. Their social contacts are largely restricted to one another, and they tend to cultivate an elegant life-style; sometimes they even speak a language or dialect different from that spoken elsewhere. In North America and in some European cities the privileged usually live in suburban communities far removed from the noise, congestion, and pollution at the center; in most cities elsewhere, however, those of highest rank generally live somewhere near the center. Another common pattern of segregation is the occupation of street-front units by the privileged and alley-front units by others. Even though people of different ranks live in physical proximity, social distance is maintained, and little contact occurs. In many old cities the segregation patterns are so well established that they have become traditional; such cities may be divided into clearly delineated quarters in which each category occupies a sector that extends from the center to the outskirts of the community. In some cases special categories of people — members of a despised religious group or those who have some unpopular occupation, such as slaughtering animals — are isolated into colonies, cultural islands. American cities are divided into neighborhoods. In most instances the boundaries between them are blurred; most American cities have been growing so rapidly that the location of segregated areas has changed from decade to decade.

People of middle rank, who in most instances make up the majority of the population, are distributed throughout the next most desired areas. Within their sector their distribution is seldom random; their area is further segregated, with each subcategory having its own section. In

American cities the residences of blue-collar workers are usually located within easy access to the factories in which they are employed; such areas generally have small, single-family dwellings and less-expensive apartments. White-collar workers tend to live in neighborhoods with somewhat more expensive apartments and fancier homes. Until recently the suburbs were reserved for the wealthy, but the extensive development of moderately priced tracts has made possible the movement of people of middle rank into areas farther from the center.

Slum Areas. In every community the underprivileged — the poverty-stricken, the derelicts, the petty criminals, the despised ethnic and religious minorities — tend to congregate in the least desirable areas. Socialist nations have placed a high priority on clearing slums, and many of them have succeeded; elsewhere in the world, however, slums and shantytowns may be found in all large cities — New York, Mexico City, Rio de Janeiro, Johannesburg, Calcutta. In most countries shantytowns tend to be located at the outskirts of cities. In the United States, however, slums are generally found adjacent to the central business district. These are zones of transition; they were once residential areas but have deteriorated and are being rented as roominghouses until businesses eventually take over. Certain kinds of establishments are characteristically found in "skid row" — bars, pool halls, brothels, pawn shops, and cheap hotels. Tenements draw the poor not only because of low rents but also because of their proximity, often within walking distance, to places of work. Such neighborhoods also attract those who have difficulty finding housing. The most recently arrived immigrants, from rural communities as well as from abroad, often encounter opposition elsewhere and are forced to join those regarded as the dregs of society. Other inhabitants include the "Bohemians." Districts such as Greenwich Village in New York and the Left Bank of Paris have long been centers for aspiring artists, writers, and musicians. Young people seeking excitement or those who cannot afford to live elsewhere also settle there temporarily. The population density in such areas is generally quite high, and the facilities deteriorate rapidly.

When people with such contrasting values and life-styles live side by side, many come to view each other with contempt. Anonymity tends to be exaggerated; sometimes people who have lived in the same tenement for decades do not know one another's names. The utilitarian view of life is also accentuated; since the inhabitants are not tied by personal obligations to neighbors they barely know, they tend to pursue their private interests. The denizens of slums protect themselves against exploitation by assuming a defensive stance, and the prevailing philosophy is to "live and let live." The juxtaposition of so many life-styles thus leads to a relativistic perspective. All kinds of activities are tolerated that would not be permitted elsewhere. But toleration does not arise from mutual understanding, rather more from indifference. Most people just want to avoid trouble, and indifference is a way of immunizing oneself from the personal claims of others. Given the kinds of people who congregate in slums, it is not surprising that the incidence of crime, disease, and dependency is higher in these areas than in any other part of the city. Much of the police and welfare budgets of major cities is allocated to maintaining some semblance of order and sanitation among the underprivileged. Perhaps this is one reason sociologists have shown more interest in these areas than in other parts of urban communities.

Although outsiders often view slums as totally disorganized, studies reveal fairly stable patterns of accommodation. Spatial propinquity forces many residents to participate in common transactions — financial exchanges or mutual defense, if nothing else — and a modus vivendi develops in each locality. Although adults of separate categories tend to maintain social distance, the younger people come to know one another, for they attend the same schools and use the same playgrounds. For their own protection they often form gangs on a territorial, ethnic, or religious basis. Juvenile gangs are tightly knit; the members frequent the same favorite street corners and develop a common language and culture. Informal norms arise concerning territorial prerogatives, who constitutes fair game for robbery or assault, standards of sexual conduct, rules for fighting, and codes of decency and honor among themselves (Whyte, 1943). Miller (1958) contends that the informal norms that often develop in such neighborhoods provide a congenial setting for behavior that is likely to be condemned elsewhere. The key values often include virility, skill in exploiting situations, ability to get one's share of excitement, autonomy, and acceptance of one's fate. Gang members evaluate themselves and one another in terms of such standards. Slum dwellers are aware of the condescension and hostility of outsiders, and this tends to reinforce their animosity toward them. Police officers and social workers come in for special condemnation. Thus, many slum dwellers develop some close personal ties, not unlike the neighborliness found in villages. But the boundaries within which such obligations hold are narrow and are defined by the range of personal contacts (Thrasher, 1936; Sherif and Sherif, 1964; Suttles, 1968).

Ethnic Enclaves. In the United States, especially during the period of large-scale immigration between the Civil War and World War II, a number of ethnic colonies were located in slum areas. These esoteric settlements — bearing such names as Chinatown, Dago Hill, Finntown, Little Bohemia, Little Tokyo, Polonia, and Wop Roost — were the sub-communities in which successive waves of immigrants started their lives in this country. Similar enclaves can now be found in many industrial cities throughout the world. The residents were initially viewed with disdain, and they concentrated in the slums because of cheap rents and absence of organized opposition from neighbors. Then, as the settlements took shape, subsequent immigrants also gathered there. It was the only place where the newcomers did not face a language barrier; it was where their friends and relatives lived; it was the one place where they could continue many familiar cultural patterns of the old country. Thus, much of the segregation was voluntary. People preferred to live in enclaves where they could speak their native language, obtain familiar foods, and attend traditional religious services. Many of these enclaves, at least while the first generation of immigrants was active, became villages within a city. Although surrounded by others who were rejected in American society, the immigrants' sense of ethnic pride enabled many of them to continue living by their own cultural standards. But frequently sharp confrontations arose between the unassimilated immigrants and their American-born children, who attended neighborhood schools and quickly acquired a different culture. For many immigrants the sojourn in slum areas turned out to be temporary. The more successful moved out to secondary areas of settlement, and many of their American-educated children became assimilated into the general population. As one ethnic group departed, it was replaced by the next wave of immigrants; the inner cities are now inhabited by ethnic groups that have arrived most recently — for the most part Afro-Americans, Mexicans, and Puerto Ricans.

But ethnic enclaves are not necessarily located in slum areas; such segregated communities have a long history in many parts of the world. In the Roman Empire, for example, veterans of Roman legions set up their own settlements and enjoyed many privileges not granted to others in the city. In old cities, such as Timbuctoo, where several ethnic groups have been living side by side for centuries, each has its own quarters. Many Jewish ghettos, especially in Eastern Europe, as well as Christian millets (segregated communities) in Moslem cities, were often permitted a considerable measure of self-government. During the period of European colonization the conquerors sometimes set aside the most desirable part of various cities for themselves, as in the International Settlement in Shanghai. In the larger enclaves class differences within the ethnic group were reflected in further segregation inside the colony. What is significant about segregation is that it reinforces cultural differences. Most inhabitants of ethnic colonies seldom contact outsiders, and such differential association tends to perpetuate diverse perspectives. Thus, some ethnic groups have maintained their identity and culture for several centuries even though they were surrounded by others.

The Formation of Segregated Areas. Some kind of segregation is found in all large cities. How is the distribution of people and life-styles to be accounted for? In a pioneering study conducted in Chicago in the 1920s, Burgess (1974:95 – 106) proposed the hypothesis that the spatial distribution of people in a community is initially the product of competition and natural selection rather than of deliberate planning and design. Business enterprises tend to settle where they can operate most effectively — given such considerations as rent, taxes, labor supply, access to raw materials, and markets. The people who settle in cities try to obtain the most desirable housing they can afford; their criteria for desirability include rent and the cost of transportation to work. Thus, American slums are often located in transition zones near the center. Once certain categories of people become concentrated in a given area, businesses that cater to them are also attracted there, giving each district a distinctive appearance. Thus, the distribution of population first develops through self-selection, with people going where they can best afford to live.

Burgess's study has been criticized severely, often for the wrong reasons. It has been called the "concentric circle" theory, and many critics note that cities other than Chicago have not developed in a circular pattern — something that Burgess recognized from the very beginning. But his hypothesis applies only to a growing community in a capitalist economy — marked by little or no planning of housing, greater distinctions of rank, and the freedom of people to live wherever they can afford. His contention that the initial distribution of people in such a community depends on natural selection and that the key competitive advantage is cultural (in this case, money) may well hold.

However, Burgess did not emphasize sufficiently that whenever a pattern of segregation persists for a time, the boundaries tend to become institutionalized, and certain parts of the city come to be regarded as the natural habitat of the category of people who live there. If people always obtained the best housing they could afford, slum dwellers would depart as soon as they could afford to do so, but this does not always happen. Firey (1945) discovered that many Italian immigrants in Boston refused to move out of slum neighborhoods even when they could easily afford better housing. They had lived most of their lives there, and they considered it their home. Ethnic colonies in which a distinctive culture persists are often the only places where the inhabitants feel comfortable. Since the immigrants felt that they were living where they belonged, they saw no reason for moving to live among strangers. Thus, sentiment and symbolism may outweigh such considerations as dirty streets, a high crime rate, and prestige. It is not surprising, then, that in old cities separate quarters are so well established; most of the inhabitants would not dream of living anywhere else, even if somewhat better housing facilities became available. Once any pattern of activity becomes well established, people come to regard it as the proper thing, and it persists long after the conditions that originally brought it into existence have passed.

Segregation is part of the ecosystem of a community. If the equilibrium is disturbed, readjustments must be made, and the process of competition and natural selection may well begin once more. Neighborhoods do not retain their characteristics indefinitely. As housing and other resources begin to wear out, the declining prices make them available for poorer people. As those defined as undesirable invade an area, others begin to leave in ever-increasing numbers. Or parts of a city may be renovated; the adjacent areas may become too expensive because of rising tax rates, and the old inhabitants may be forced to move. Another type of change occurs when the population of a segregated area increases — through a high reproductive rate or through migration — to the point that there is simply not enough room. Then the pressure of population on the available resources becomes too great, and adjustments of some kind are required. The ecosystem is also upset when an old city is industrialized. Factories are built, and the pattern of demand for housing changes. Schnore (1965) has discovered, for example, that many Latin American cities were once divided into quarters around a central plaza. As they become increasingly industrialized, however, they seem to approach the type of growth pattern that Burgess describes for Chicago. The reopening of competition for space is undercutting the traditional boundaries between quarters. Thus, when the equilibrium of an ecosystem is upset, competition is renewed. This sometimes leads to political confrontations and even to bloody conflicts. In the long run, ecological processes will prevail over custom.

A well-documented case of these processes is the formation and collapse of the Black Belt in Chicago. The Black Belt, like most other ethnic colonies, was initially formed through natural selection; it developed in a low-rent area that was close to places of work. Once the enclave was established, it became widely accepted as the proper place for Afro-Americans to live. Special institutions arose to meet the needs of the people there; indeed, it became a city within a metropolis (Drake and Cayton, 1945).

But the pressure of population on available resources mounted during the interwar years. In 1920 there were 109,000 Afro-Americans in Chicago; by 1930 the number had grown to 236,000; and by 1940 it was 271,000. Part of the growth was from a somewhat higher birth rate, but most of it resulted from the large-scale immigration of Afro-American people from the South seeking better opportunities. Although the boundaries of the Black Belt did expand a bit, most of the increase was absorbed by a higher density of population. As the pressures mounted, the boundaries were reinforced by housing covenants, by the differential lending practices of banks, and by the violence of juvenile gangs in surrounding neighborhoods. Furthermore, most Afro-Americans had no particular desire to live outside the area, certainly not in the face of all the hostility they faced. During World War II, immigration from the South increased drastically as war industries welcomed much-needed workers.

By 1950 the Afro-American population in Chicago had risen to 492,000 (Duncan and Duncan, 1957). Although there had been some further expansion of the Black Belt and the creation of a few new enclaves, there simply was not enough room for that many people within the segregated zone. It was impossible to continue the customary patterns, and competition for housing reopened. The boundaries of the Black Belt crumbled, for this time Afro-Americans had acquired new competitive advantages: They were on the whole far better educated and had more income than their predecessors, and many could easily outbid white families for homes in the adjacent areas. Furthermore, the climate of opinion among other Chicagoans had changed, and resistance was weakened by the breakdown of consensus. Many white liberals sided openly with the Afro-Americans, launched political campaigns against continued segregation, and provided money to help finance home purchases. Thus, the redistribution of competitive advantages led to a redistribution of people once the barriers to direct competition broke down.

What happened in Chicago suggests that measures such as gang violence and laws against change may slow down ecological processes but cannot hold them back indefinitely. Attempts to confine a group that is becoming too powerful lead to serious conflicts. The differential treatment of minorities has not yet ended, and recent studies show middle-class Afro-American families occupying tracts with poorer facilities than those of lower-class white families (Erbe, 1975). But there is no longer a readily identifiable Black Belt in Chicago.

CULTURAL DIVERSITY IN MASS SOCIETIES

The Emergence of Social Worlds. One characteristic of modern mass societies is that people who occupy a common habitat do not necessarily share a common culture, and this has led to many serious problems. In their studies of relatively isolated communities anthropologists were once able to speak meaningfully of "culture areas." Where communication is limited largely to face-to-face interaction, only those who live together can communicate effectively; each culture thus has a territorial base, and such regional homogeneity is to be expected. Since people come to share a common culture by partaking in the same communication channels, however, modern developments in mass communication and transportation enable the geographically dispersed to communicate easily and effectively and thus share a similar outlook. Indeed, we live in a society in which next-door neighbors see relatively little of one another, and people in the same occupation are in constant touch with colleagues hundreds of miles away. Most communication channels no longer coincide with geographical boundaries, and most cultures are no longer confined to contiguous areas.

Thus, modern mass societies are made up of a bewildering variety of social worlds—the world of the theater, of high finance, of women's fashions, of race car fans, of heroin addicts, of used car dealers. A *social world* is in many respects a community without a territorial base. The participants in each can understand each other, for they share a common symbolic environment. Increasing numbers of people are participating in such symbolic communities, in which they are bound by common interests rather than a common habitat. Each social world is the product of a distinct set of communication channels, and its boundaries are set by neither physical proximity nor formal group membership, but by the limits of effective communication.

Segregated subcommunities—of social elites, ethnic minorities, religious cults, slum dwellers—still persist, and the people in them sometimes develop a strong sense of mutual identification. But physical proximity alone does not give them their provincial outlook. Indeed, most slum areas contain many social worlds—aspiring radicals, petty thieves, prostitutes and their pimps, small shopkeepers, alcoholics, young Bohemians, recent immigrants—held together by their respective communication networks. Some members of elite groups spend virtually all their time in activities centered around their country club, but others are devoted to activities about which their neighbors know nothing, such as complex corporate finances. Thus, even those who live together share a distinctive culture only to the extent that they remain isolated from outsiders.

Networks of interrelated voluntary associations also become social worlds; since they have their own communication channels, each tends to develop a distinctive culture. Examples of such worlds include those of organized labor, of medicine, of the ballet, of the steel industry, of crime syndicates, of various religious denominations, and of fraternal organizations. Active participants in each established occupation, legal or illegal, tend to develop a common outlook, and many vocations are rapidly becoming professionalized. Although some residents of each locality may well be acquainted with one another, they are also participants in other social units that are geographically dispersed. Each associational network is served by periodicals, such as *Variety, Wall Street Journal, American Legion Magazine, Harvester World,* the publications of alumni associations, and a number of highly specialized journals. Each publication provides access to an arena that is strange to outsiders. Churches such as the Jehovah's Witnesses have not only their own magazines and mimeographed bulletins but radio and television stations as well; and what they present over their channels sometimes flatly contradicts the regular mass media. For most people involvement in occupational, fraternal, or religious organizations tends to be a part-time affair, and total commitment is usually reserved for paid officials. However, in the world of corporation executives and in many professions the participants must devote so much of their time to their work that everything else becomes auxiliary.

There are also a number of loosely organized universes of special interest — such as the worlds of ice hockey, of stamp collectors, of popular music, of chess players, of the followers of each radio or television serial, and of the fans of an author of detective stories. These worlds are held together by selective responsiveness to the mass media. Since the participants are drawn together only by the limited interest they share, there are many degrees of involvement, ranging from the fanatically devoted to the casually interested. Some follow the latest developments closely and subscribe to special publications — such as *Field and Stream, Sports Illustrated, Hotrods, Popular Photography, Seventeen.* Many become interested only when special events take place, such as the World Series or the Super Bowl. Because participants in these social worlds often number in the millions, the latest news in sports, fashions, and the various entertainment fields is carried in the mass media, readily available for anyone sufficiently interested to pay attention. Although these arenas are only loosely organized, the participants develop a common outlook; they share similar values and maintain appropriate standards of conduct, especially if their interests are strong and sustained. The more knowledgeable usually enjoy greater prestige. Thus, fashion-conscious dressers are able to identify one another easily, and their reciprocating appraisals often rest on criteria they do not apply to others. Fishing enthusiasts also have definite standards — to give the game a fighting chance, to use relatively light tackle, to get enjoyment from the skill required in landing the quarry. They are often contemptuous of people who merely want to catch something to eat, especially of those who use worms when fishing for mountain trout. The world of sports fishing is sufficiently organized that total strangers who meet at some resort have no difficulty in discussing their technical problems, just as anonymous customers waiting their turn in a barber shop can discuss knowingly the chances of their favorite athletic team.

Characteristics of Social Worlds. Each social world is made up of people who are sufficiently interested in some central activity to participate to some degree and who through participation come to share a common culture. How a social world is organized depends on the central activity, where and how it is carried out, and the size and spatial distribution of the personnel. Some kinds of core personnel are generally necessary — people who are deeply involved, perform specialized roles, and participate on a regular basis. Thus, in the world of horse racing, track owners, stable boys, jockeys, addicted gamblers, and police officers become associated in ways that keep the transactions moving regularly. Where special equipment is needed, manufacturers and distributors also play an important part.

Beyond such similarities, social worlds vary considerably. Some, like local cults, are small and concentrated; others, like the world of professional journalists, have participants dispersed throughout the globe. Some, like many ethnic minorities, have a relatively homogeneous population; others, like the Democratic party, are made up of so many kinds of people that one wonders what they have in common. Social worlds also differ in the extent and clarity of their boundaries; each is circumscribed, but the border may be wide or narrow, clear or vague. Social worlds also differ in their exclusiveness and in the extent to which they demand the loyalty of their participants. Some require special qualifications for initiation; one cannot become a regular member of a crime syndicate, a nurse in a hospital, or an opera singer simply by announcing one's intentions, but anyone can become a fan of a movie idol. Some worlds are open only to those who dedicate themselves; priests, nuns, and soldiers have one supreme loyalty. In general if the activity is successful enough to persist, its organization is likely to become more complex, and the communication channels become more stable and reliable. Professional baseball began more than a century ago on the basis of informal agreements among some interested people; today it is a vast enterprise based on a network of formal organizations with large bureaucracies.

Each social world develops its own universe of discourse; experiences are categorized in particular ways, and a special vocabulary develops to refer to such meanings. The argot of soldiers, prostitutes, and drug addicts and the dialects used by ethnic minorities differ from the standard tongue. Among automobile dealers an "iron" is a used car that is more than four years old, and a "hook artist" is a dealer who attracts poor credit risks in the hope of repossessing the car when they miss their payments; they may sell some cars as many as ten times. Baseball fans know that a "rhubarb" is not a vegetable, and gamblers realize that "soft play" refers to a stupid bet. Any group's vocabulary, to the extent that it differs from standard speech, is an index of its preoccupations; the special symbols designate the distinctions necessary to carry out group activities. The development of special languages creates further barriers from outsiders, who are often baffled by what is being said.

Each social world also develops its own view of history by a selective emphasis on past events of particular interest. Tennis enthusiasts recall the great performances at Wimbledon and in Davis Cup matches, and they compare the styles of play of current stars with those of the past. In the lore of mountain climbers throughout the world tales abound of the extraordinary courage and skills of certain mountaineers, of daring rescues, and of great achievements against incredible odds. The grim determination of those assaulting the various peaks in the Himalayas can be understood only against this backdrop. Some admirals look with nostalgia to the glorious days of the battleship, and their reluctance to accept the realities of the atomic age must be seen in this light. The dreams of people are epitomized in their heroes and heroines, and there are different ones in each arena. Scientists who have international reputations among their fellow specialists are unknown to outsiders. Baseball fans who have never heard of Albert Einstein can recall the details of the great performances of such idols as Babe Ruth and Carl Hubbell. Thus, active participants in each social world develop a perspective — a way of thinking, acting, and talking about objects of common concern.

Each social world has its own cultural axioms, values, and vocabulary of motives; thus each social world has a different prestige ladder and

typical career lines. Lawyers, circus performers, holdup artists, balle-
rinas, and gossip columnists serve their apprenticeships after some kind
of training. Advancing along an ordered career line, they can measure
their progress against others pursuing the same objectives. Many specialists in the underworld receive some of their most important training in
prisons. Upward mobility and success in each case is measured in terms
of the values shared within the given arena, and outsiders are not likely to
understand why a person undergoes such sacrifices to succeed at something they may regard as trivial or even senseless. What is highly esteemed in one social world is of no consequence in another, and in a
diversified society it is difficult to appreciate someone's aspirations without knowing something about the social world in which he or she seeks to
carve out a career. Among the best organized of social worlds are the
professions. Since a long training period is usually required for admis-
sion, people rarely leave a profession and usually develop a sense of pride
in their calling. Professional groups often develop standards of conduct
that are more stringent than what is required by law, and they have
procedures for punishing their own violators. A special system of control
— professional ethics — upholds their common values. Each profession
is much like a community (Goode, 1957).

Thus, each social world, especially for those who are deeply involved,
becomes much like any other community in which people share a common culture. People organize their lives in terms of its norms. In real life,
as on the stage, each person performs for an audience, and we cannot
understand what people are doing unless we know something about the
audience for whom they are acting. People identify with those who make
up their social world — those included as "we." Those who belong assume obligations for maintaining group traditions and hold themselves
responsible. They have expectations of one another that they do not have
of outsiders, and they are acutely aware of the special claims that others
within the circle have on them. In a class society, for example, aristocrats
answer the distress call of their peers, even though their own servants
may suffer thereby. Znaniecki (1940) notes that most intellectuals perform primarily for other intellectuals; they do not address their work to
society as a whole. A scholar is part of a social world that sets standards
and expectations and accords recognition and support for meeting them.

Since there are so many audiences in a mass society, sociologists have
found it convenient to develop a concept to denote them. A *reference
group* is that social unit whose culture is used as a frame of reference in
defining a succession of situations. It could be a community, a social
world, an organized group, or a small circle of personal friends. Since

reference groups are products of communication channels, some persons may perform for an audience that does not exist at all. A scholar of Greek literature, for example, may live by standards that historians believe to have existed in ancient Greece, glorifying them and seeing everything else with bemused contempt. Some people perform for posterity—an audience about which no one can be certain of anything.

Misunderstandings in Mass Societies. In modern mass societies there is a ceaseless proliferation of new social worlds and constant changes in those that exist. Social worlds are not static; shared perspectives are continually being reconstituted. Well-established social worlds tend to maintain themselves largely through differential sensitivity to news. What is of vital concern to members of one arena may not even be noticed by others. A decision to wage war is of concern to almost everyone, but the outbreak of rivalry between two fashion designers is of no concern to those outside a few social worlds. Those who are not fashion conscious cannot possibly keep up with all the latest developments in the field. Those who participate only intermittently may encounter strange new norms and additions to the vocabulary. New social worlds come into existence with the formation of new communication channels. As life conditions change, social relationships are revised, and once-esteemed social worlds may disappear or become transformed drastically. Thus, people who are not deeply involved and are not paying constant attention to what is happening in a given sector of life may discover that something they had taken for granted no longer exists.

The multiplicity of social worlds is one common source of misunderstandings in our society. If people who are performing for different reference groups participate in the same transaction, difficulties in coordination are likely to arise. When people with different cultural backgrounds live side by side, they are continually thrown into all kinds of social transactions in which they become temporarily interdependent. When they begin with different assumptions, role-taking becomes difficult. Each may define the situation somewhat differently and have different conceptions of the various roles to be enacted. The difficulties are compounded when the participants work with somewhat different vocabularies of motives; if they impute and avow different motives, they are bound to be puzzled by one another's attitudes and deeds. They will have trouble interpreting an unexpected response. In a study of the faculty of a small college Gouldner (1957) noted that some professors were profession-oriented (their reference group consisting of specialists in their field) and others were campus-oriented (their reference group consisting of people in the local community). The former insisted that faculty members should have more time for research and writing and were dissatisfied that only a few others shared their interests. Since they had published more, they could easily find employment elsewhere, and they felt few local attachments. They knew fewer local professors than their campus-oriented colleagues, and they felt that they received more intellectual stimulation from outside the campus. Dedicated teachers attached to the local campus often could not understand these professors' complaints. To comprehend what people do we must know what they take for granted and what they impute to their audience. Thus, the coming together of persons oriented toward different reference groups is one of the major sources of tension in modern societies.

Other difficulties in mass societies arise from simultaneous participation in several social worlds. We participate in as many social worlds as the communication channels in which we regularly partake, and most of us are multicultural. But we all participate in a different combination of communication channels. As Simmel (1955:127–95) puts it, each individual stands at the intersection of the various social worlds in which he or she participates. Some measure of compartmentalization in the lives of inhabitants in mass societies appears inevitable. Each occupies some status in each of the social worlds in which he or she participates. Moving from one transaction to another, a person often has to shift gears. As one's reference group changes, the demands and obligations one feels also change. Each person develops well-integrated behavior patterns that are appropriate in one social world but not in another; one must learn to switch them on and off as the need arises. Although most of the norms of the various social worlds in which one participates are mutually reinforcing or consistent, sometimes one becomes involved in transactions in which two or more reference groups simultaneously make conflicting demands. A supervisor of a factory unit faces both co-workers' and managers' standards; a teaching assistant in a university appreciates both fellow students' and faculty members' viewpoints; a military chaplain is part of a group organized for mass homicide and a member of an organization devoted to peace. To the extent that a person performs for inconsistent reference groups, he or she is likely to develop inner conflicts. Such conflicts complicate life and result in misunderstandings and bouts with one's conscience. The inner conflicts and guilt feelings may become especially severe in periods of rapid social change.

Americans today live by an amazing variety of standards. The inconsistencies and contradictions that characterize modern mass societies are largely products of the multitude of communication channels available and the ease with which individuals may participate in so many of them. People with diverse perspectives come into direct contact, and misunderstandings cannot be avoided. Furthermore, it may be difficult to correct errors when the people involved in a disagreement begin with different presuppositions. Since our assumptions are frequently unstated, we may not even be aware of what we take for granted. What constitutes inappropriate conduct in one social world constitutes conformity to the norms of another. Thus, many of the difficulties that arise are more from ethnocentrism than from deliberate malice.

SUMMARY AND DISCUSSION

How are physical and biotic processes affected by the fact that human beings have sufficient knowledge to manipulate some of the conditions under which they occur? What difference does culture make in human life? Most adaptations are collective, but what constitutes a group is a matter of cultural definition. People band together on the basis of several different criteria and then act as if they constituted separate species. As well as simply striving to survive and reproduce, human beings strive for all kinds of objects that are defined as valuable in their culture. Values are so decisive that if certain traits come to be regarded as desirable, the frequency of certain genetic traits in a population may be changed through preferential mating and selective reproduction.

Throughout most of human history people have been directly dependent on the resources available in the particular habitat they occupied. But changes in culture, especially the development of technology, have transformed the basic patterns of settlement that had lasted for several millennia. Complex technology to convert energy for human use has made possible the construction of huge communities in which millions are able to live in relative comfort and security. But these changes in turn have altered the ways in which people think and relate to one another. Easy communication has created communities of people who are spatially dispersed; those who share a common interest have been able to form all kinds of social worlds. But the basic character of society has not been altered. Human beings are still responsive to the expectations of those with whom they identify, and they pursue careers in terms of the norms of the audience for whom they enact their roles.

Although culture has enhanced considerably the adaptive capacity of human beings, we are still animals involved in a common web of life with all the other organisms with which we share our habitat. Our capacity to use linguistic symbols, to think, and to plan enables us to alter some features of our environment, but we still cannot alter natural processes. Physical and biotic processes operate as they do, whether or not we are aware of them and whether or not we approve of them. We can use natural laws to our benefit only if we have an adequate comprehension of how things work. Thus, to the extent that we learn about the regularities in nature we can use that knowledge to facilitate adaptation. But there are many processes that we do not understand adequately and countless others that we cannot even imagine. Furthermore, instances arise in which people elect to ignore the natural laws that are known, hoping that somehow some miracle will save us, as in the current world population crisis. If the pressure of population on available resources becomes too great, however, even the most firmly established social institutions will crumble, and further adaptations will become necessary for survival. Thus, although modern demographers have pointed to serious deficiencies in Malthus's theory, the basic question that he raised is still with us.

SUGGESTED READINGS

Duncan, Otis D., and Beverly Duncan. 1957. *The Negro Population of Chicago: A Study of Residential Succession.* Chicago: University of Chicago Press.
A detailed study of the formation of an ethnic enclave in a metropolitan area.
Hauser, Philip M., and Leo F. Schnore (eds.). 1965. *The Study of Urbanization.* New York: Wiley.
An interdisciplinary approach to the study of urbanization, with contributions by historians and specialists in the various social sciences.
Redfield, Robert. 1941. *The Folk Culture of Yucatán.* Chicago: University of Chicago Press.
A comparative study of four communities in southern Mexico, disclosing the differential impact of industrialization and urbanization.
Suttles, Gerald D. 1968. *The Social Order of the Slum.* Chicago: University of Chicago Press.
A field study of the Addams area in Chicago, describing the life-styles of various ethnic minorities and the manner in which they have accommodated one another.
Theodorson, George A. (ed.). 1961. *Studies in Human Ecology.* New York: Harper & Row.
An anthology containing standard references from early studies of human ecology in Chicago, critiques of these studies, and more recent developments in theory and research.
Wagner, Philip L. 1960. *The Human Use of the Earth.* Glencoe, Ill.: Free Press.
A geographer's statement of how topography, climate, and technology have altered the place of human beings on this planet.

V

INTERACTION PATTERNS

Since the end of World War II, electronic computers and automated machines have accelerated the rate of technological change. Automation is not the mere mechanization of what had previously been done by human labor, such as a motor-driven cotton picker; automated machines correct their own errors and are thus self-regulating. They work with a speed and precision human labor cannot match, and their use has led to a dramatic decline in cost per unit of production. Such machines are now used to make and roll steel, to mine coal, to weave cloth, and to sort and grade all kinds of things from oranges to bank checks. Computers are used to calculate the best combination of crops and livestock for given farm conditions, to design and test planes before they are built, to diagram the appropriate angles and grades in traffic interchanges, to keep up-to-date inventory records and print orders as the stock of any item approaches depletion. Petroleum refineries, among the first factories to be automated, are now operated by a handful of workers at the central control panel; they are built to carry on productive processes that are too complicated, too rapid, and too dangerous to be controlled by human judgment alone.

The enhancement of production techniques has been so dramatic that some observers have hailed automation as the beginning of a second industrial revolution. These machines will probably continue to be improved and will be applied to more and more sectors of life. People will be relieved of unhealthy, unpleasant, and undignified work, but the machines will create a number of problems, including technological unemployment.

The key to automation is cybernetics—the principles of self-regulation through information processing. Since cybernetics is a way of describing and analyzing the operation of complex systems over time, taking the exigencies of specific situations into account, Buckley (1967) suggests that the conceptual scheme is especially suited for analyzing social transactions. This may well turn out to be the case as both cybernetics and sociology develop further. In the meantime we may borrow some key ideas. One central concept in cybernetics is a simple notion that engineers call *feedback*—the process by which a machine or system monitors its own performance and uses that information to regulate its continued performance. A thermostat measures heat output and feeds back to the furnace signals that regulate fuel input. The heating system is thus self-regulating; when room temperature reaches the point indicated on the thermostat, the supply of fuel is cut off. A scanning device on an antiaircraft gun notes where the shells are going and the distance between their destination and the moving target; this mismatch is progressively corrected with each shot until the target is finally struck.

As these examples illustrate, the detection of error is essential for correction. *Negative feedback* refers to information on deviations from the desired condition—the discrepancy between actual performance and the goal—that is fed back into the machine or system so that corrections can be made. But all cybernated systems are susceptible to a particular type of breakdown. If the corrective action is greater than the error, the original disturbance is amplified with each step, leading to oscillation. Instead of counteracting deviations and settling down, the system is maintained by self-excitation. For example, a malfunctioning thermostat set at 68° may allow a room to heat up to 75°, at which point the air conditioning unit will come on at maximum power and soon plunge the temperature to a chilly 60°, which will activate the heater to come on full blast, and so on. Self-excitation is also found in interpersonal relations—the angrier people become, the more sensitized they are to cues that are infuriating; brooding often leads to an explosion. This pattern of development has been designated as *positive feedback* (Maruyama, 1963).

The focal ideas in cybernetics are old; after all, much of life is a self-regulating process. But our comprehension of the universality of some of the principles is new. The central concern in this chapter is to describe some of the more important ways in which human beings interact as they execute social transactions. Transactions are units of joint activity that develop over time, and the individual participants are self-regulating beings. Hence, some of the concepts of cybernetics are useful in making analyses of human transactions. Two cautions should be added: (1) The reference to cybernetics is not to suggest that human beings are inferior machines; and (2) Only four out of many patterns of social interaction are presented. Many of the distinctions are analytic; in real life several patterns of interaction may coexist in the same transaction. Thus, rivalries among individuals arise in transactions that are basically collaborative, but oversimplifications of this sort facilitate the initial presentation of ideas.

ACCOMMODATION IN ROUTINE SITUATIONS

Many transactions occur in institutionalized settings—playing tennis, voting in an election, being treated by a doctor, or dining in a restaurant. In such routine situations the formation and maintenance of consensus is seldom a problem, for virtually all adults in the community define the situation in much the same manner and the interests of the participants are usually compatible and reciprocal. We do not ordinarily walk into a restaurant unless we want to eat there, and restauranteurs would not be open for business unless they wanted to serve food. Since the situation is so commonplace, the tasks to be performed are familiar to all participants, and except for a few neophytes each has a working conception of what is likely to happen once the transaction gets under way. The activity is already organized in that what each participant is expected to contribute is largely specified. In such standardized contexts social transactions develop through the role-playing of the participants, who adjust to one another through mutual accommodation. Thus, concerted action is largely preprogrammed in that the activity occurs within a framework of well-established norms.

The Casting of Personnel. Virtually all transactions involve a division of labor, and the initial question facing those who are involved is the allocation of tasks. Who is to contribute what to the transaction? The participants must be able to position themselves within the transaction in relation to one another. Institutionalized transactions are somewhat like dramas. To be sure, theatrical presentations are avowedly make-believe while real-life performances are not, but the terminology of the theater is useful in making analyses. We locate ourselves on the scene by casting ourselves into familiar positions. On walking into a restaurant, we assume the status of customer and prepare to enact the conventional role (model of what one is expected to contribute to a transaction) of being served a dinner. Thus, the participants let one another know just where they stand; each engages in impression management. Customers appear in what is regarded as the proper attire for that type of restaurant and stand where the hostess can see them. When approached, they indicate their preferences through appropriate remarks and gestures. Self-casting also involves an avowal of motives, and diners assume that they have come to eat in a pleasant setting. Those who have clear conceptions of the various roles involved know what is expected of customers and exercise sufficient self-discipline to contribute their respective parts. Self-casting also involves accepting the obligations that are comprised in one's role. One forgoes claims to things that are irrelevant or inappropriate to the role and suppresses impulses and feelings that are inconsistent with it. In enacting a role each person is prepared to behave in certain ways and becomes selectively responsive to cues of being treated in understood ways. A conventional role is the accepted way of participating in a recurrent transaction, and we sometimes decide in advance how to stage our performance. If we are inexperienced, we may even prepare for it by rehearsing (Goffman, 1959:1–76).

We must also define the other participants and their interrelationships by casting them into positions: hostess, waiter, cook, cashier, other customers. We must be able to locate the others or we cannot anticipate what they are likely to do. Once we have cast the personnel, we can approach other participants with familiar expectations. Role-taking, which is an essential part of role-playing, is greatly facilitated. We can impute appropriate motives to others and anticipate their behavior, and we can infer their probable intentions. Thus, we can interpret and judge their contributions and prepare to act appropriately on cues. For example, waiters are supposed to provide efficient and courteous service in the hopes of receiving a generous tip. Each customer assumes that the restaurant personnel want to provide the kind of service that will bring customers back again, thereby maximizing profits. However, our inferences may be mistaken. A waiter may conclude that a customer is uncouth but continue to treat the person with appropriate deference. A customer may think a waiter is pretentious to the point of being comical but avoid laughing openly. People usually approach one another within the range of their respective obligations.

The Process of Self-Regulation. For most adults, dining in a restaurant is a familiar drama in which the plot is well known; there is no written script, however, and one cannot get through merely by reading lines.

Furthermore, each customer comes in with a different set of interests. One may be entranced by the decor; another may be attracted by one of the other diners; others may be disappointed at the limited menu; still others may be so famished that they do not care about anything but eating. Each person is preoccupied in different ways. How, then, can concerted action be carried out? Mead (1934:173–78) contends that self-regulation is possible because human beings are able to form objects of themselves. In any situation people become selectively sensitized to any object that is relevant to the successful completion of their act. Since participants in a social transaction are interdependent, they become concerned with the impression they are making on one another. After all, the others may withhold essential cooperation. Thus, we become self-conscious through role-taking. We impute motives to other people; we imagine how the situation appears from their perspective; then in our imagination we look at ourselves from that standpoint. Coordination is facilitated when the participants are able to form objects of themselves from the standpoint they share with the others in the transaction.

Human beings construct their behavior as they go along, adjusting successively to the developing situation as they define it. In self-regulation each person adjusts in advance to the situation in which he or she is involved. By previewing what we are about to do from the standpoint of the others involved, we can anticipate their reactions, engage in self-appraisal, and redirect our behavior if that seems desirable. If what we want to do is likely to please the others, our inclination to do it is facilitated. If what we are about to do is likely to elicit some negative reactions, however, we are likely to inhibit the impulse and consider some alternatives. In important situations we are constantly monitoring our own conduct —past, present, and future. We pretest what we are about to do in our imagination, which enables us to correct errors before they occur, thereby creating the desired impression and avoiding difficulties. Thus, the initial negative feedback is from self-appraisal through role-taking; the anticipated reactions of others constitute the first basis for correction. For example, a young man with intellectual pretentions is anxious to impress his friends at the salad bar. He likes Thousand Island dressing, but since it is so popular, he may fear that his associates would regard him as too common. He next considers blue cheese dressing, but he decides against it because he dislikes cheese in salads. He finally settles for oil and vinegar; he believes that his associates will approve and he finds the taste unobjectionable. This man, like all of us, performs for an audience; his reference group consists of aspiring intellectuals. Thus, human conduct is constructed step by step in a succession of self-correcting adjustments to the changing situation as the individual defines it. Most important, we adjust to the anticipated reactions of others, what we imagine through role-taking, before the responses actually take place, thereby keeping our conduct within the bounds of our role.

Participants are also sensitized to the overt reactions of others, which confirm their expectations. Thus, role-playing is a provisional process. As the line of concerted action unfolds, we test our conception of the role and its execution by checking the actual responses of our companions. As long as they react in the expected manner, we can continue with assurance that our performance is satisfactory. There may even be nods of approval and other indications that we are doing well. Since individuals differ widely in their skill in enacting various roles, however, some mistakes are bound to occur. If the mistakes are important enough to interfere with the orderly continuation of the transaction—such as the waiter's inadvertently bringing food that the diner cannot stand—corrections must be made. These corrections are usually made unoffensively, even if one is quite disgusted; otherwise a crisis may arise, and the transaction may be disrupted. We usually ignore or gloss over minor errors. If someone should make a mistake—belch, use the wrong implement, spill food—others frequently pretend not to notice. A close friend may inform the bungler of the error, but usually in a manner that minimizes embarrassment. We accept any lame excuse to help hapless performers extricate themselves from a difficult situation; indeed, we often go to some length to avoid discrediting impression management. Of course, those who are sufficiently displeased may object openly, challenging the actor's conception of the role.

Thus, a group of diners and the restaurant personnel can coordinate their respective acts in a manner that is flexible enough to take care of the exigencies that arise in most situations. Such coordination is possible because each participant contributes independently to the transaction but is sufficiently sensitive to the views of associates so as to regulate his or her contribution in a manner that will reciprocate the contributions of others. Each person is autonomous, and autonomy depends on feedback. Without feedback a person becomes a creature of impulse, subject to drift, or a victim of external control. The negative feedback that provides the basis for self-regulation comes both from the anticipated reactions of others—which inhibit potentially disruptive impulses before they are carried out—and from their actual responses. Noticing others' reactions is thus a second source of negative feedback. The continuous surveillance by all parties keeps the transaction moving in the expected direction. If all participants engage in such self-regulation, their respective efforts will fit together and result in the smooth execution of the transaction. As long as all participants share a similar perspective, each can preview from the shared standpoint what is intended, and each can direct his or her efforts to facilitate completion of the transaction.

Negotiation of Residual Differences. Even in institutionalized contexts each transaction is unique, and some improvisation is necessary. Incompatible interests may arise; participants may disagree concerning the obligations that make up a role. Some customers may be more demanding than a waiter regards as fair; they may feel that a waiter is too lazy or insulting; they may demand deference that the waiter feels is unjustified. A customer posing as a gourmet may so irk a waiter that he resorts to ostentatious deference, to the point of sarcasm. He may ask questions requiring highly specialized knowledge of the cuisine, knowing full well that the customer does not know the difference. Some individuals may want more than their share; some are constantly seeking "role bargains" (Goode, 1960). Sometimes people with a low level of self-esteem get pleasure from discrediting someone else's impression management by showing off their own superiority; there are some who find they must constantly play games that will bolster their sagging egos (Berne, 1964). At times in the course of a transaction people may come to dislike each other and lose their enthusiasm. They may conclude that what they are getting out of the transaction is not worth taking the trouble to meet the minimum obligations; indeed, they may become so disgusted that they do not care what the others think. All such reactions interfere with effective role-taking and are likely to be disruptive.

If the participants disclose incompatible interests, the situation becomes problematic. Confusion arises, for things that are done with the best of intentions elicit unexpected responses. In such situations participants usually make efforts to modify their contributions, to correct the discrepancies between what is happening and what is regarded as appropriate (Stokes and Hewitt, 1976). Remedial interchanges become necessary to restore consensus, and the question of how norms should apply in the particular situation becomes subject to negotiation. If someone tells a joke that may be in questionable taste, for example, others may become so offended that it becomes necessary to discredit it; the appropriateness may have to be negotiated (Emerson, 1969). Students and teachers sometimes become embroiled in disagreements over grades, especially if the student regards a grade as a reward for the amount of work done but the teacher sees it as an evaluation of the quality of performance. The matter has to be discussed until a mutual understanding is reached. Difficulties may also arise from too much generosity. Someone may do a special favor for another that the latter considers too elaborate. As Blau (1964) points out, a person who gives a gift or renders a valuable service places the recipient under obligation. If the beneficiary cannot reciprocate, the donor develops a claim that may become a source of power. A recipient who wants to reduce the extent of such obligations may resist favors. Such negotiations are essential; neither party wants to go to the point where tempers flare, for the transaction is then truncated, and everyone loses.

Spontaneity and Social Constraints. Goffman (1959:167–207) uses analogies from the theater to reveal the extent to which people are performing for an audience when engaged in role-playing. He proposes comparing how we act when we are on stage with what happens when we retire backstage, among people we know intimately. This comparison suggests that much is concealed, even when there is little conscious effort to deceive. When we are backstage—before or after dining or in the absence of restaurant personnel—we may drop our pose. Talk becomes very candid, and we feel free to derogate the audience. Diners may laugh among themselves about the waiter's pretentiousness, and the waiter can joke with the cook about their deliberately serving the wrong sauce to the phony gourmet. Furthermore, when we are backstage, we can discuss staging problems. Small groups of men or women often review ways of making a good impression on the opposite sex and compare views on particular individuals in whom they are interested. Insecure neophytes may rehearse the difficult parts of their role and arrange for surreptitious cues to facilitate coordination. If a hostess is irked by the liberties taken by a waiter, she does not scold him until the customers are gone; arguments within a team are confined to the rear area. That everyone feels so much more relaxed among intimate associates indicates the extent to which we feel constrained to put on an adequate performance before others.

Most of us recognize intuitively the difference between on-stage and off-stage performances. Members of the audience do not intrude backstage. If it becomes necessary to enter, one knocks to put the people on guard so that they can resume their role-playing. A waiter who accidentally overhears negative remarks pretends that he did not. If he has to bring food within hearing range, he coughs or clears his throat so that the customers will have time to change the subject. Those who accidentally stumble in backstage often withdraw quietly and then reenter noisily to give everyone an opportunity to readjust.

Thus, in standardized transactions, if the participants' interests are compatible, the course of action develops through role-playing and mutual accommodation. Minor difficulties that arise are corrected unobtrusively so that everyone can proceed; the successful termination of the transaction brings gratifications of some sort to everyone. People who share a common culture, even total strangers, impute and avow similar motives and have similar conceptions of conventional roles. Thus, a network of common understandings provides a framework within which to carry out joint action. If people comply with the obligations that constitute their respective roles, the transactions are completed. However, the execution of transactions seldom involves blind conformity to norms, as one would expect of skillfully programmed robots. There are constraints to spontaneity, but they are not necessarily external. Compliance is mostly a matter of self-regulation: Individuals preview their own intentions and direct their own activities. Should anyone go beyond the limits of what is regarded as suitable, others may impose sanctions. But social regulation consists for the most part of people simply acting in ways that they themselves regard as appropriate.

CONFLUENT EXPRESSION AND SUGGESTIBILITY

In some transactions the excitement of the participants becomes so intense that well-established norms are disregarded, and the line of action proceeds in an unconventional manner. When Puccini's *Madama Butterfly* was first performed in Milan in 1904, for example, members of the audience were amused by the esoteric setting and costumes. As their laughter became contagious, some began to complain that the music was a mere repetition of the already familiar *La Bohème.* The hoots, catcalls, and laughter increased until the performers could no longer hear one another, and the composer stalked off angrily with the score. Subsequent audiences have responded differently, and *Madama Butterfly* has become one of the world's best-loved operas.

Many types of gatherings — religious revivals, football rallies, political demonstrations, celebrations, rock concerts, political funerals, and closely contested athletic events — are marked by intense emotional reactions. Excitement sometimes gets out of hand, and on occasion violence erupts. In this section we take as an illustration the riot that occurred on 17 March 1955 during and after a hockey match in Montreal (Katz, 1955). By examining such an extreme instance we are able to see more clearly processes that transpire with less intensity in a great many other contexts.

Formation of a Common Mood. The routine of daily life is often broken by the occurrence of some unusual event that attracts attention and invites uneasy comment. In some instances, such as religious revivals or political demonstrations, some of the participants may attend in the hope of finding excitement. In Montreal tension developed when Clarence Campbell, president of the National Hockey League, suspended for the season Maurice "Rocket" Richard, star of the Montreal Canadiens, for assaulting an opposing player and an intervening official. Fans throughout the city denounced the suspension, which came at a critical point in the hockey season — when the Canadiens were leading the Detroit Red Wings by a scant two points. On the day when the Canadiens were to play against Detroit, demonstrators with placards hailing Richard and condemning Campbell appeared around the Montreal Forum before noon. The number of irate protesters increased throughout the afternoon. In such contexts people who are upset mill about. As increasing numbers become aroused emotionally in the same direction, in this case anger, they become highly responsive to one another. As their reactions converge, an emotional climate emerges. As the tension level rises, communication is facilitated by the reduction of social distance among those who are upset. The customary reserve that people maintain among strangers breaks down; each feels free to address anyone who is similarly aroused; and new communication channels develop on the spot. As they talk over the events, an initial definition of the situation arises. In Montreal, Mr. Campbell came to be identified as the frustrating object, not only as an obstacle to the Canadiens' success but as an affront to the dignity of French-Canadians as well. When it was announced over the loudspeaker that no more seats were available, the demonstrators shouted back, "We don't want seats; we want Campbell."

What happens in such transactions depends on the intensification of the participants' emotional reactions, and the problem is to account for how this happens. One widely entertained hypothesis is that the augmentation of emotional reactions is the product of mutual reinforcement through selective communication. People who are very angry disclose their stance through words and expressive movements. Thus, each participant, in responding to the irate feelings of others by disclosing his or her own anger, reinforces the mood of the others who are already incensed. The mere convergence of people who are similarly aroused leads to the amplification of the feelings of each. Such a closed circuit constitutes positive feedback; each individual's emotional reaction is intensified with each exchange, and the aggregate as a whole becomes marked by increasingly heightened tension. Such mutual reinforcement sometimes augments emotional reactions to a point that individuals rarely achieve in isolation (Park and Burgess, 1924:788–92). Although this type of explanation of crowd phenomena has been criticized (Berk, 1974), evidence indicates that such social facilitation takes place in many contexts among both human beings and other animals (E. Simmel et al., 1968).

As the prevailing mood takes on definite direction—in this case intense anger—an initial self-selection of personnel occurs. Those who are not in sympathy with the developing mood may protest briefly, but they find that their efforts are in vain. Thus, in every sport there are fans who enjoy watching gifted athletes in action, regardless of who wins the game. In Montreal such fans soon realized that they were out of place. Those who did not share the mood felt uncomfortable, even threatened; some departed. Many who went to the stadium to watch hockey, including Richard himself, were aghast at what they observed. In such cases, as the dissidents depart, those who remain consist largely of people who share similar definitions and feelings, and they continue to reinforce one another's orientations. Such self-selection of personnel continues throughout the transaction and results in the assembling of people with similar cognitive and affective orientations.

The Emergence of Consensus. As a common mood crystallizes, the prevailing emotion becomes the basis for selective perception. Cannon (1929) describes emotion as an emergency reaction that facilitates adaptation in challenging situations, but it does so only if the reaction does not become too extreme. Both Stratton (1928) and Selye (1956) show that when emotional reactions pass a certain threshold of intensity behavior becomes focused to the point where it is stereotyped and ineffectual. Perception narrows and attention focuses on a single object (Postman and Bruner, 1948). Easterbrook (1959) shows how the performance of those who are vehemently aroused becomes impaired as their perception narrows and they do not notice cues that for the moment seem irrelevant. We know from daily experience that those who are "up tight" do not hear or see much that is obvious to others. Thus, irate people perceive only what is consistent with their feelings—in our example, the negative attributes of Mr. Campbell, his decision against the Canadiens, and his alleged insult to French-Canadians. Cognition and imagination also become flooded to the point where people become obsessed with a single object—Campbell the ogre. Memory also becomes selective—Mr. Campbell's past decisions in favor of Montreal were forgotten; other unfavorable actions were recalled as further evidence of his perfidy. Although everyone has a different breaking point, there is a level of intensity for each person at which even motor coordination becomes impaired. Thus, beyond a certain level of intensity emotional reactions cease to facilitate adaptation.

As collective excitement intensifies, communication becomes increasingly more selective. As the spontaneous talk goes on, remarks that are inconsistent with the developing mood pass unnoticed or are howled down. A common definition of the situation emerges, but this definition represents the consensus of people whose perspective is constricted. Consensus here develops through one-sided information processing; of the many ideas presented only those that reinforce the developing mood survive. As the tension level rises, people tend to act more impulsively, and conventional norms recede into the background. As the transaction becomes less institutionalized, individual contributions become more important, and agitators play an increasingly important part. Although agitators are often blamed as the "cause" of such disturbances, they are usually people who are just deeply involved, are more affected by the event, and feel more strongly about it than the others. For the most part agitators are pacesetters. They contribute disproportionately to the developing mood, but only those who say things consistent with the mood get a hearing. (Those who condemned Campbell were cheered loudly; others were ignored.) Thus, the leaders are chosen by the led; they are the individuals who express most appropriately and eloquently what the listeners already feel. The emergence of leaders is therefore a reflexive process. Since the definition of the situation is constructed by those who are intensely excited, it tends to be simplistic and stereotyped. In many cases it can be stated in a slogan: "Kill Campbell!" Consensus develops as much from the reactions of the participants to one another as it does from their reactions to the events.

As collective excitement is augmented, the self-selection of personnel continues. Those who disagree find it increasingly difficult to be heard. If their remarks are not ignored, they face open hostility. Some are taunted, and a few may even be assaulted. As they feel threatened, they leave or move to the periphery. Thus, dissidents are silenced or expelled. The product is a homogeneous group, united in its definition of the situation and poised to act in a way consistent with its mood. This creates the appearance of unanimity, the mark of a crowd (Turner and Killian, 1972:12–29). Disagreement is not tolerated; popular despotism is one of the characteristics of crowd behavior.

Mobilization for Action. As the tension level rises, those who are excited experience an urgent craving to act—to do something, anything. They become impatient. Those who are deeply involved can no longer restrain themselves, and some begin to take action. Thus, when Campbell was escorted to his box in the Forum, he was greeted by boos and catcalls. Angry fans began to throw things at him. Before long Campbell, rather than the game, became the center of attention. Each time Detroit scored, the enraged fans vented their anger on him. Campbell was further pelted with programs, bottles, rubber boots, eggs, and tomatoes.

Total preoccupation with a common object, such as Campbell, leads to a temporary loss of self-consciousness by those who are most aroused. As in an audience totally absorbed in an exciting movie, participants in crowds become so preoccupied with the common object of attention that they forget themselves. Without awareness of oneself as an object, there can be no negative feedback. To the extent that a person ceases to monitor his or her own conduct, the person's capacity for self-regulation is reduced. Those who are most excited lose it altogether, and others find it increasingly difficult to fight off urges to act impulsively. As critical judgments become more difficult, increasing numbers of people become more suggestible. If people already feel a strong urge to do something— to attack, to run away, to seize something—merely hearing a proposal to act in that manner or perceiving someone else doing what they want to do is often enough to touch off already organized dispositions. People do not totally lose their ability to regulate themselves; they are suggestible only along lines that are consistent with their already aroused inclinations. Precisely because so many become suggestible at the same time, their activities appear contagious. Those who come only to look and perhaps to scoff sometimes find themselves going along with the others. Some participants in mobs have subsequently reported depersonalization—observing themselves doing things as if they were spectators while knowing full well that they themselves were acting.

A high degree of consensus develops, and, when dissidents are immobilized, the crowd appears to be unanimous. The common understandings that arise in such contexts are not to be confused with conventional norms; Turner and Killian (1972) refer to them as *emergent norms.* They arise through social interaction in a particular situation. As a common goal develops, activity is carried out enthusiastically. One man stepped up to Campbell and struck him, to the cheers of onlookers; another squashed some tomatoes against his shirt. If a division of labor is necessary, it develops spontaneously. Since everyone is committed to the same objective, each contributes selflessly whatever needs to be done. Thus, when the first period ended, the enraged fans began to leave their seats, and a menacing crowd closed in on Campbell's box. At this point someone threw a tear-gas bomb. Everyone was startled. Electric fans were turned on to disperse the fumes, and police officers, who had heretofore been lax in enforcing regulations, intervened decisively and evacuated the stadium. In the confusion Campbell and his party escaped.

The fire department stopped the game, and Campbell ruled it forfeited to Detroit.

Once action gets under way, it tends to escalate through mutual encouragement and support. Participants are emboldened by the support that they feel. Activists believe they have the complete support of those about them, not only because so many are acting in a similar manner but because every contribution arouses cheers and encouragement. At times people who find themselves amid others with similar inclinations experience a sense of invincibility. When everyone appears to be supporting them, nothing can stand in their way. As the frightened and excited fans poured out of the Forum, they mingled with the demonstrators outside. Together they began hurling overshoes, chunks of brick, and whatever else they could find. They tore doors off their hinges. The crowd, estimated at more than ten thousand, besieged the stadium. Before long the enraged mob attacked stores on the ground floor of the Forum. Rioters threw rocks through windows. Then the crowd moved toward Montreal's main shopping district, and some fifty stores were damaged and looted before order was finally restored at about 3 A.M.

The Dissipation of Tension. Crowd behavior is transitory. Once the accumulated tension has been dissipated, people recover their composure, and their usual perspective is restored. As their temporary audience is replaced by one with a more conventional outlook, many in retrospect are surprised at what they had done. Some are shocked and embarrassed. Crowd behavior may appear bizarre, but it emerges in social interaction that differs only slightly from what is found in other forms of concerted action. A high degree of consensus develops through selective perception and communication. As emotional reactions intensify through the convergence of similarly excited people, perception and communication become even more selective — as in a vicious circle. As dissidents are immobilized or expelled, a homogeneous group is left to act on the basis of a transitory definition of the situation. If the participants in a transaction become too excited, their perspective becomes constricted, and a common mood supersedes conventional norms as the basis for concerted action. The riot in Montreal was a case of collective aggression (other forms of crowd behavior will be considered in chapter 10).

STRATEGIC INTERACTION IN RIVALRIES

Rivalry and Politics. If the participants in a transaction come to regard one another as having conflicting interests, the line of action develops through a third pattern of interaction — in the give-and-take of political

tactics. Agonistic processes arise when valued objects are in short supply
—when there is not enough of something that is desired to go around.
Even when there is enough for everyone, if one party wants more than its
share, others must defend themselves against unfair encroachment. At
first there is competition; each side does the best it can to get a share.
When those who are involved in such parallel striving realize that each
party can gain only at the expense of the others, however, they become
acutely aware of their opposition and define one another as rivals. Consciousness of the opposition of interests transforms competition into
rivalry. All sides continue to pursue their interests as they perceive them,
even at the expense of the others, but the pattern of social interaction
changes. Political moves against one another replace independent striving. Each party anticipates opposition and prepares to deal with it. Thus,
in strategic interaction each rival selects the moves likely to bring maximum gain at minimum cost. Human beings seek many nonmaterial
gains; we are often more concerned with enhancing our reputation or
maintaining our self-respect. And we cannot measure cost only in terms
of pain or expenditure of energy; in the long run social disapproval can be
much more costly. Furthermore, loss of self-respect may lead to serious
difficulties in other social contexts. Thus, when opponents square off in
this manner, the line of action takes shape in political interchanges, as
each rival tries to outmaneuver the others.

In most situations the opponents remain in some way interdependent. If they live in the same community or are members of the same
group, they must continue to deal with one another in other transactions
even if their interests in this one are incompatible. In many instances the
participants need one another's support for everything except the point
at issue. Members of a family may disagree on one point, but they have a
great deal in common. Thus, their interests are both complementary and
antagonistic, and most contests are carried on in terms of established
norms. Rivals are constrained by rules. Aside from norms limiting what
opponents may do to one another, there are common understandings
about decency and fair play that one cannot ignore without risking condemnation. While suitors who are rivals may come to dislike one another
intensely, curbs are placed on what each may do. In a moment of anger
one may be disposed to assault the other or to seize an unfair advantage
that may arise. But this may prove costly in the long run. People who are
interdependent want to avoid fighting, and political tactics are ways of
pursuing interests short of open conflict. Recurrent contests are usually
carried on in institutionalized contexts. Many, such as chess or athletic
events, are well organized. The kind of bargaining that occurs in flea

markets is constrained by definite rules, just as the adversary proceedings in courtrooms are carried on in terms of formal norms.

Ordinarily we think of politics on a grand scale, usually in the national and international arena. We think of struggles between nations for resources and markets, propaganda offensives, and diplomatic maneuvers. On the national scene we think of pressure groups, mobilization of public support for legislation, or struggles between management and labor. But the same kinds of tactics are used in countless other contexts. Most organizations are split into factions, if not into formal departments. A clique of deacons in a church, leaders of opposing factions in a union, segments of a college faculty — all use political tactics to advance their interests. Corporation executives sometimes play golf or go yachting with influential associates, even when they derive no pleasure from such activities. Such local maneuvers, often called "peanut politics," may be found in many informal contexts. Sibling rivalries arise in families; the youngest boy may desire a favored position in relation to his brothers and sisters, and his tactics — ingratiating, snitching, or conspiring — are all political moves. Intellectuals at cocktail parties often engage in point making to impress one another and to create an impression that may benefit them in some subsequent transaction. Almost any transaction may be transformed into a rivalry. Although sexual intercourse is basically a collaborative transaction, it may be defined as a contest in which each partner gives up as little as possible for maximum gain (Bengis, 1973).

Many kinds of tactics are used in politics: negotiation, persuasion, coercion. In this section we shall focus on negotiations between individuals involved in a social transaction; negotiations between groups and other tactics will be taken up in chapter 14.

Negotiation as a Social Process. The most common form of political maneuvering is *negotiation* — social interaction in which individuals or groups who recognize their incompatible interests try to arrange a mutually acceptable accommodation through maneuvering and consulting. Such tactics are most likely to be used when the interests of the parties involved are both complementary and antagonistic. The aim of negotiation is to arrive at some jointly acceptable agreement despite differences in interests. Neither party gets everything it wants, but this is better than getting nothing or fighting. If conflict can be avoided, all other activities that are mutually advantageous can continue while the contest goes on. Thus, negotiation occurs when each party is able to see at least one set of terms that is preferable to no agreement at all.

The process of negotiation proceeds through a succession of moves and countermoves that lead eventually to the resolution of differences. Every move depends on each side's conjectures about its opponent's moves and responses; thus, once negotiation gets under way, the participants become interdependent. Negotiations often occur in clearly defined situations — such as the purchase of a used car — and both sides usually understand their respective roles. An experienced negotiator frequently plans out strategy in advance but remains sufficiently flexible to alter the course of action if necessary. Both parties work with a conception of their own interests, including an understanding of the line beyond which they cannot retreat. But they also need a working conception of their adversary's position. What does the other side consider most important — money, saving face, safety? Just what is the opposition willing to give up? What is the line beyond which the opposition cannot back down? Pride is generally recognized as being more important than material considerations, and those experienced in such interchanges go out of their way to enable all parties involved to retain their dignity. Each move that is made is part of a series, and if the offers and counteroffers are successful, the exchange will lead eventually to a mutually acceptable solution. People negotiate for many different things in a wide variety of contexts (Strauss, 1978); we shall consider only a few of the more frequently found patterns.

Bargaining is one of the most common types of negotiation. A good example is the purchase of a used car, one of the few economic arenas today in which something like a free market is still operating. The price paid for a given vehicle may vary considerably, depending on the negotiating skills of the parties involved (Browne, 1973). Plea bargaining is another example. Where court schedules are overcrowded, those charged with minor offenses who are unable to raise bail may find it advantageous to plead guilty to some lesser charge instead of waiting in jail for their trial. The accused may actually spend less time in jail, and the district attorney's office can concentrate on what it considers the more important cases. Out-of-court settlements of insurance claims are achieved through negotiations between the injured party and an adjuster representing the insurance company. Both parties often prefer not to go to court, for the insurance company knows that juries sometimes grant very large awards, and the victim knows that court proceedings could delay any award for years. If neither side is too obstinate, a deal can be worked out that is beneficial to both (Ross, 1970). Many similar exchanges occur in daily life, although the bargaining is not so obvious; all kinds of agreements are reached, but the obligations incurred are not so clearly specified.

Information control is critical in bargaining of this type. To negotiate successfully each party needs to know something of the adversary's intentions — just what the other side is willing to settle for and what it is willing to give up. At the same time each party tries to camouflage its own intentions and create an impression that is likely to further its interests — not disclosing for as long as possible just how far it is willing to retreat (Rubin and Brown, 1975:14–18). Thus, in the beginning neither the used car seller nor the buyer has sufficient information, and they spend some time sparring for position. Many of the early moves are made for impression management. Initial demands are usually higher than what each side wants; each expects to back down a bit. Each side may send up trial balloons to seek more information about the opponent's actual position. With each exchange each side gets a better appreciation of the other's position until they recognize the line beyond which the rival will not retreat. One of the advantages of negotiation, as compared to overt conflict, is that each side learns to appreciate its adversary's difficulties, which enables it to make counteroffers that fall within an acceptable range and are likely to elicit some concessions. Some negotiators may even call their opponents' attention to interests that the latter had forgotten or overlooked in the heat of the contest.

Information control is crucial to successful bargaining, and thus bargainers tend to be self-conscious and deliberate. Since each move discloses something of one's stance, the bargainer's predicament is to make the point while revealing as little as possible about other issues. With each party watching the other carefully for any hint that may turn out to be advantageous, each side must be deliberate and careful. Impression management is important, for how much each opponent is willing to give up depends on his or her estimate of the other. The social interaction that occurs in such contests is almost the opposite of that found under intense collective excitement. The participants are more acutely self-conscious than usual; each side continuously monitors its own moves, often considering in advance the impression they are likely to create. Negative feedback plays an exaggerated part in negotiations of all kinds, and participants take special care not to lose their tempers. Emotional reactions may prove very costly; those who become upset may do something foolish. In politics keeping emotional reactions under control is vital, for they tend to cut off essential negative feedback.

Another common type of negotiation consists of developing working arrangements among people with diverse interests. Illegal arrangements between corrupt politicians and building contractors is a notorious example. The politicians pave the way for licenses and permits, and contractors who cannot quite meet government standards make campaign contributions that will help keep the politicians in office or otherwise further their careers. Strauss et al. (1963) describe the negotiation of an acceptable division of labor by those who work together in hospitals. Because of staff turnovers, few workers actually know all the rules; many rules that are known are not enforced consistently; and many situations fall in the interstices between rules. Thus, the personnel in each ward must work out accommodations. Clashes may arise over the most effective way to run a ward. A physician may prescribe treatment for a patient that creates unnecessary inconveniences for the nurses and aides. If so, they may negotiate some kind of compromise that enables them to give proper care to that patient without having to ignore the others. Physicians who have been at a hospital for some time often develop standing arrangements with the head nurses of various wards and try to get their patients assigned to familiar wards to avoid misunderstandings and further negotiations.

In exchanges of this kind information control is less important than it is in bargaining; tactics such as trade-offs and the juggling of commitments are more common. Relative power—such as the status of the doctor in relation to the nurse—can be of crucial importance. However, tactics such as ingratiation tend to blunt the capacity of those who have advantages. By enhancing one's value to another, one can mitigate and reduce the rival's power (Jones, 1965).

Outcomes of Negotiation. Social transactions that develop through negotiation are built up in fluid situations, and the outcome of each instance depends on many conditions. One important consideration is the political skill of those involved, their ability to perceive and press advantages that arise. People differ considerably in such skills as well as in their desire to engage in such interaction. Some are proud of their ability to "wheel and deal"; others are contemptuous of those who do so, but even they may find themselves in situations requiring them to push for the best bargain. Knowledge and experience often make a difference. Most used car sellers have considerable advantage over their customers, but a buyer can neutralize this by bringing along a friend who is a mechanic. In his study of insurance adjusters Ross (1970:193–94) reveals that claimants with lawyers received settlements from five to twenty times higher than the unrepresented; indeed, when attorneys who specialize in handling accident claims entered the case, the settlements were very high.

A party with a rigid commitment weakens its position. A customer who has already decided to buy a car of a particular color, for example, may have to pass up opportunities for a bargain. The obstinacy of a relative who insists on a high insurance settlement or of an insurance company supervisor who refuses to approve such settlements can lead to the breakdown of negotiations; this necessitates a court case, which may prove costly to both parties. If difficulties arise in negotiations, the outcome may depend on relative power. In plea bargaining in courts, for example, the accused are at a definite disadvantage, for the undesirable option is more costly to them. The prosecutor does not have to make concessions as readily as someone who faces the possibility of spending several months in jail.

The product of such successful maneuvering is a negotiated order. Accommodations of this kind are at best compromises, for neither party gets what it really wants; each has settled for the best possible arrangement for the moment. For this reason the arrangements tend to be unstable. Some agreements are soon forgotten, especially by a party that finds them more costly than anticipated. There may be a change of personnel. Power relationships may change. When conditions are altered, negotiations must be reopened. Many relationships, including some marriages, develop in a continuous succession of interchanges of this kind. Each party is constantly alert for possibilities of bettering its position. As soon as an opportunity arises, negotiations are renewed.

Thus, when the participants in a transaction define one another as rivals, the course of action develops in the give-and-take of political tactics. If a mutually satisfactory solution cannot be reached through politics, the rivalry may intensify. As the parties become more indignant and resentful toward one another, the chances of reaching some kind of agreement decrease. As clashes continue, mutual distrust mounts through positive feedback. If a rivalry gets out of hand, it may be transformed into conflict, where destroying or neutralizing the opponent becomes a primary consideration. If this happens, the pattern of interaction changes once more.

DEVELOPMENT OF MASS BEHAVIOR

Characteristics of Mass Behavior. In modern mass societies large-scale transactions involving in some cases millions of people drawn from all walks of life are constantly developing. They depend on the temporary focusing of popular attention on a common object and the subsequent formation of appropriate behavior patterns. Examples include the development of popular music, fashions in personal adornment (clothing, coiffure, or accessories), popular heroes or heroines in various arenas (sports, politics, or entertainment), best-sellers in books, popular art and entertainment (dances, games, dining practices, movies, or television serials), and booming sales of various consumer goods (cigarettes, household goods, or home decorations). Blumer (1935) contends that mass behavior may arise in any area in which the choices made among behavior patterns cannot be tested decisively in terms of their utility.

Thus, fashion movements may be found even where they are regarded as undesirable. They are found in those sciences in which hypotheses cannot be tested rigorously and especially in fields that are not well established. They are found in medicine, especially when the effectiveness of new drugs or of novel treatments is still subject to debate. They are found even in something as important as child-rearing practices (Vincent, 1951). Intellectuals who sometimes scorn the "sheeplike" behavior of the masses themselves follow slavishly the latest plays, books, and esoteric foods currently in vogue in their social world. Mass behavior is not necessarily confined to any particular type of society. The adoration of popular heroes or heroines may be found in any type of community; fashions in clothing were important long before the development of the mass media. Even dictatorships have difficulty suppressing mass behavior. The current youth culture in Eastern Europe and the Soviet Union has developed in the face of government opposition.

Of special interest is the successive displacement of objects and behavior patterns that appeal simultaneously to geographically dispersed participants. Two key questions, illustrated in terms of fashions in women's clothing, may be raised. Why does a woman purchase a particular dress? Most women are not concerned with contributing their share to the development of some style; each buys clothing that she believes will enhance her attractiveness. But why does she find the dress so appealing now, when ten years before or ten years hence she would not care to be seen in it? Another question arises: Why do millions of women simultaneously now regard a particular style as becoming, only to later all begin to reject it at about the same time? The same questions may be raised about popular songs: Why do some songs simultaneously appeal to so many people and subsequently seem so trivial and boring? To be sure, some objects that burst forth in mass behavior become institutionalized after the initial flurry, such as wristwatches and low-cut shoes. The utility of such objects is obvious. Some popular songs survive to become standards. For the most part, however, objects of mass behavior enjoy meteoric success and then disappear. Thus, fashion provides a contrast to custom. There are similarities in the behavior of large numbers of people, but there is a successive displacement of patterns. The behavior patterns keep changing, and they change together.

Another characteristic of mass behavior is the indirect social interaction among those involved. Most of the millions of people who make up the audience of a television serial, for example, could not possibly communicate directly with one another, nor can all who purchase a new record or dentifrice. For most participants there are no clearly defined roles; they are just interested. To be sure, the participants do not act in a vacuum. People in small groups in each local community who share similar interests often get together to discuss informally the latest objects made available to them through the media of mass communication. But this happens in hundreds of different communities. Thus there is a simultaneous development of similar sensitivities among widely dispersed people who have no opportunity to interact with one another. The media of mass communication provide a common source, but most objects presented on the mass media pass without attracting much attention. When there are profitable sales, advertising by manufacturers may become involved. Specialists in influential positions, such as disc jockeys, may play an important role. But mass behavior cannot be explained in terms of promotion alone. So, how can we account for similarities in the behavior of millions of people, most of whom are not in direct contact with one another?

The Initiation of Patterns. One widespread belief, especially among people who disapprove of various forms of mass behavior, is that fashion movements of all kinds are planned and staged in a conspiracy among business interests who stand to profit from them. Those who dislike the latest fashions often make such charges, and a congressional committee in 1960 gave considerable publicity to "payola" to disc jockeys. Many such promotions have been attempted, but attracting and holding a mass audience is extremely difficult. Garment manufacturers have tried to dictate fashions, but most such efforts have led to huge losses and sometimes to bankruptcy (Nystrom, 1928:10–13). Attempts to push the "midi" skirt in 1970 failed miserably; young women simply looked at them in stores and refused to buy.

A test of sorts was provided in 1948, when the American Federation of Musicians (AFM) banned new recording sessions after a quarrel over paying royalties to musicians for records played over the radio. During the final months of 1947 all popular artists were kept busy cutting enough records to last for some time—including new songs from unreleased movies and upcoming Broadway musicals. Music publishers and recording companies got together on "plug schedules" to ration out the hits, a few at a time. By June 1948 sales had dropped to the point that Columbia Records closed one of its plants; by August the record industry was in doldrums; soon thereafter negotiations between the AFM and the major companies were reopened. They reached an agreement in November. The industry effort to dictate taste in popular music had been a dismal failure.

Totalitarian regimes have attempted to regulate consumer purchases through production control and propaganda. Such attempts have led to grumbling and consumer resistance and at times have resulted in protests bordering on mutiny. In capitalist economies most business executives in fields that depend on popular taste have stopped trying to tell people what to buy. Instead they try to anticipate what is likely to become popular and cautiously prepare some alternatives that seem likely to succeed. They would be happier if feedback were more direct and arrived more quickly. Executives in such industries can prevent some object from ever reaching a mass audience, but they have not been able to dictate popular taste. If government and industry cannot determine the behavior patterns that become popular, how does mass behavior acquire its initial direction?

Most patterns of mass behavior apparently begin among specialists in different social worlds, such as women's fashions or popular music. Various innovations are introduced by intellectuals — artists, composers, writers, dress designers — who are constantly trying to create things that are consistent with the latest trends, objects that give symbolic expression to the latest concerns of the people. Such innovators are familiar with the latest developments — objects that have aroused popular interest — and try to capture the developing spirit of the times; what they aim for is timeliness. A sanctioning elite within that social world selects from these innovations. Thus, in his study of women's fashions in Paris, Blumer (1969) notes that professional buyers select about a half dozen dresses from about thirty new designs. Books are initially selected by editors, and popular tunes are chosen by professional musicians, executives of record companies, and disc jockeys. Of hundreds of creations only a few basic patterns are chosen each year. In the selections made by this sanctioning elite, personal taste plays an important part; fashions are chosen because the buyers regard them as "stunning." However, other considerations enter their judgment. They must choose designs that they believe will be sufficiently appealing to sell; to keep their jobs, they must be able to sense public taste. Members of such elites are also concerned with their reputation within their own reference group. Editors who turn down manuscripts that subsequently become best-sellers lose prestige among fellow editors. Of course, concessions are made to conceptions of popular taste. Many editors disdain popular books, and professional musicians do not necessarily share the taste of the audience for whom they perform (Becker, 1951). But their task is to choose items that are likely to succeed commercially, and mistaken judgments on their part may turn out to be very costly.

Thus, the initial phase in the development of mass behavior is the selection of some innovative pattern by a sanctioning elite—the avant garde within each social world. Although there are some exceptions, an innovation that is not first approved by a sanctioning elite is unlikely to reach the attention of a larger audience. Once a trend is so started, the objects are presented through the mass media. Disc jockeys plug new songs and manufacturers advertise. Although members of such elites do make the popularization of some behavior patterns possible, they cannot dictate mass behavior. Many items that they choose are discarded and soon forgotten, for no one else pays much attention to them. Furthermore, objects occasionally win popularity without the support of such elites. Anything that appeals simultaneously to large numbers of people can become involved in mass behavior, and sometimes objects catch the popular eye by accident. For example, Rudy Vallee introduced the song "As Time Goes By" in 1931, at the height of his popularity. It had only moderate success and was soon forgotten. In 1943 it was used in the popular movie *Casablanca,* and to the surprise of people in the music industry it became a smash hit. Apparently the sensitivities of Americans during World War II differed from their concerns during the Depression.

In his classic study of women's apparel Simmel (1957) declares that fashions develop through differentiation and emulation. Fashions are found only in stratified societies in which upward mobility is possible. Those in the highest rank distinguish themselves from others by various status symbols, such as a new style of clothing. Then, those immediately below copy them. Thus, each new pattern makes a vertical descent as those in each rank emulate the people immediately above them. By the time a pattern has been widely adopted, it no longer serves as a distinguishing emblem, and those on top adopt a new symbol, which in turn begins its downward course. Thus, Simmel contends that any fashion, once launched, marches on inevitably to its doom.

Simmel was writing about the class society in nineteenth-century Europe, and his observations no longer hold in modern mass societies. But each reference group has its own prestige ladder, and within many social worlds fashion movements do develop much as Simmel suggests.

Thus, the style of wearing patched and worn-out jeans in the 1970s began with some popular rock musicians. Although the singers were in the spotlight for their music, their "far out" costumes took hold. Among young people involved in popular music the new pattern became an indication of being up to date. At first such matters are of concern only to those who want to be "in." Within each community women who are fashion conscious or young people preoccupied with the latest song hits get together; they examine the latest offerings with care, discuss them among themselves, and then make choices after mutual consultation (Johnstone and Katz, 1957). Behind the pacesetters are those who wait apprehensively to see what will be "in" and then adopt the practices of those they hope to join. They discard valuable wardrobes, change haircuts, dine in strange restaurants, read books they do not enjoy, and listen to music they may not actually like in order to be up with the latest thing. Thus, the second phase in the development of mass behavior is the adoption of the latest pattern by those who are concerned with their status within a specialized social world.

The Popularization of Patterns. Many innovations remain confined to particular social worlds. If new behavior patterns are not reported by the media of mass communication, most outsiders never learn about them. But mere reporting is not enough; most publicized items pass unnoticed. From time to time, however, a practice adopted in some social world catches the popular eye and arouses widespread interest outside the circle in which it began. Once the direction of popular interest becomes discernible, it is mentioned more frequently in the mass media, and industry steps in. As manufacturers begin their publicity campaigns, increasing numbers of people become involved. Most people in a mass audience are not so concerned with being "in" with the latest practice. They choose songs they enjoy hearing or singing; they read books they consider timely and entertaining; and they buy clothing they believe enhances their appearance. To be sure, they want to be recognized as not being out of touch with the world, but they are not preoccupied with status. This phenomenon suggests that the third phase of mass behavior develops from the convergence of the selections made by individuals who are acting on their own or in consultation with friends whose judgments they respect. These people choose from the various competing patterns, each choosing what he or she likes, and it is the cumulative effect of their individual decisions that constitutes mass behavior. Thus, this phase of mass behavior takes shape through competition and natural selection.

Once some behavior pattern becomes popular, volume manufacturers enter the scene. The clothing industry stops producing old styles, thus limiting selections; only the latest fashions are available in stores. Until the "nostalgia" craze of the 1970s, records of previously popular songs were simply not accessible. Once some pattern becomes well established, conformity is enforced by public opinion. Dissidents are passed by; their protests go unnoticed. Even the uninterested are forced to go along, for those who do not comply appear ridiculous in their own eyes. They are out of date. If those who violate a law or conventional norm are punished for it, they can resist or challenge their tormentor's right to punish. Some may even become martyrs. But the violator of fashions is regarded with amusement and pity. As Sumner (1906:194–95) says, dissenters from fashion are made to feel ludicrous. By resistance they only hurt themselves, not the fashion movement. Once a pattern is well established, dissidents are compelled to conform; in this sense fashions are tyrannical. In the fourth phase of mass behavior, then, widespread conformity arises from satirical sanctions against those who fail to comply.

Mass behavior is often dismissed as trivial. Some of its forms, such as dance crazes or games that capture the popular imagination, develop at a spectacular rate and then disappear, never to be revived. Since they touch only the auxiliary side of life, perhaps they are unimportant. But some instances of mass behavior have had an enormous impact on the course of history. The economic impact may be extensive; the rise and fall of huge corporations may be involved. The popularity of certain political leaders and the emergence of various social movements may rest on mass behavior, and some patterns become institutionalized and become part of the cultural heritage of the people.

Blumer (1969) contends that fashions are to mass societies what customs are to small communities. Both result in uniformity in the behavior of large numbers of people, but fashions do not rest on conventional norms. They are more like emergent norms, and they are usually transitory. Both Blumer and Sapir (1949:373–81) contend that fashions are forms of expressive symbolism; the various forms of mass behavior provide channels for expressing impulses and preferences that are widely held at a given time and place. Expressive symbolism is often difficult to understand, for we do not know the unconscious meanings of various forms, colors, textures, or postures; furthermore, the significance of such items may vary among different social worlds.

Blumer (1935) also notes that mass behavior may enable people to satisfy needs they cannot meet in local communities. Making choices from available patterns provides an opportunity to express dispositions that are vague; they make it possible for people to enjoy and express what they feel. As Spaeth (1934) points out, the lyrics of popular songs enable people to say things they experience but are not eloquent enough to articulate. When large numbers of people simultaneously feel the same way about some object, their collective selection results in mass behavior. The very adoption of a fashion in turn gives form and direction to popular tastes. In giving expression and direction to the spirit of the times fashions embody developing sensitivities. Acceptance then crystallizes new values and provides the foundation for subsequent interests. Thus, popular music and literature affect the outlook of whole generations. The protest songs of the 1960s appear to have shaped and crystallized the resentments of the young and led to rebellions throughout the world. Thus, mass behavior is not concerted action based on consensus; it is more like a phase of developing mass culture. Large numbers of people who are geographically dispersed can develop similar interests and change together; this enables them to keep in touch and to continue to understand one another.

SUMMARY AND DISCUSSION

Social transactions arise in the efforts of human beings to adapt to extant life conditions. As people do their best to cope, those who find themselves cast together interact. In the course of their social interaction a line of activity develops. We have been concerned with four common developmental patterns. In institutionalized contexts social transactions among people with compatible interests arise largely through role-playing and mutual accommodation. With the establishment of consensus those who share common norms live up to one another's expectations. If the participants in a transaction become too excited, their perspectives become constricted through mutual reinforcement, and a common mood supersedes conventional norms as the basis of concerted action. Emergent norms that arise in that context serve as the basis for action. The transformation is temporary, however, and the participants snap back to their conventional perspectives once their emotional reactions have been dissipated. If the participants define one another as rivals, transactions develop in the give-and-take of political tactics. This often results in the formation of an unstable negotiated order. Once the balance of power changes, politics begins again. Mass behavior is a more complex type of social transaction that develops in several stages and involves different forms of sanctions. Trends are shaped largely through natural selection from among the various behavior patterns that attract attention.

John Dewey held that society exists in and through communication, that society *is* a communicative process. Now we are able to appreciate what he had in mind. Every day human beings are involved in all kinds of transactions in which coordination is achieved through various forms of discourse. Collective patterns of all sorts are shaped, dismantled, and reformed in such interchanges. If a transaction is completed successfully, the participants tend to repeat the same patterns when they encounter similar conditions. When a transaction is repeated successfully, the participants come to share common expectations. They can then approach the next transaction in a similar context with greater confidence. In this way, a normative framework is developed.

SUGGESTED READINGS

Buckley, Walter, 1967. *Sociology and Modern Systems Theory.* Englewood Cliffs, N.J.: Prentice-Hall.
> Since social transactions develop over time, the general systems approach is proposed as a fruitful scheme for analyzing them.

Goffman, Erving, 1959. *The Presentation of Self in Everyday Life.* New York: Doubleday.
> A classic statement on how various transactions are accomplished through impression management.

Kerckhoff, Alan C., and Kurt W. Back. 1968. *The June Bug: A Study of Hysterical Contagion.* New York: Appleton-Century-Crofts.
> A detailed analysis of the dissemination of hysterical symptoms in a Southern factory in 1962.

Klapp, Orrin E. 1964. *Symbolic Leaders.* Chicago: Aldine.
> The formation and preservation of beliefs concerning persons who become the objects of mass attention and adoration.

Strauss, Anselm. 1978. *Negotiations.* San Francisco: Jossey-Bass.
> A critical evaluation of theories and empirical studies of various forms of bargaining and negotiation.

Turner, Ralph II., and Lewis M. Killian. 1972. *Collective Behavior.* Englewood Cliffs, N.J.: Prentice-Hall.
> An account of the manner in which people become mobilized to engage in various forms of crowd behavior (chapters 1–9).

Part Two

SUSTAINING PROCESSES

VI

NORMATIVE FRAMEWORKS

People age. Our favorite tree sheds its leaves in the autumn, and the branches we burn turn into ashes. With the coming of spring ice melts and turns into water. The world as we know it is in perpetual flux. Yet, in spite of these ceaseless transformations many features of the world retain sufficient continuity to enable us to recognize them as specific objects. Although we notice such changes, we take it for granted that the tree is the same one that had green leaves in the spring. We recognize an adult friend as the same person we knew as a child, even though biologists assure us that every single cell in a human body is replaced in less than a decade. Observations of this sort caught the attention of philosophers in ancient Greece. Heraclitus contended that nothing in reality remains constant; Zeno and Parmenides insisted that what is real cannot change and that whatever appears to be changing is unreal and illusory. Since that time, these contradictory orientations toward reality have developed into two major streams in Western philosophy. Although most scientists today agree with Heraclitus, in our commonsense orientation most of us tend to regard the world as being stable. Although we realize that nothing happens twice in exactly the same manner, for all practical purposes most objects appear to be sufficiently durable to enable us to treat them as if they were unchanging. Thus, we tend to think of permanence as the natural state of affairs and to regard change as something that needs special explanation.

Although no two transactions are ever carried out in exactly the same way, there are marked similarities in the manner in which concerted action takes place in many situations. In stores, in traffic, and in classrooms things happen over and over in a familiar manner — so much so that the participants can anticipate what they are likely to encounter long before the transaction gets under way. In every community — even in those involved in a war or in those adjusting to technological innovations — many transactions are carried out in established ways. Indeed, without such repetition we could never recognize patterns of concerted action. If we do not assume, as most people do in daily discourse, that permanence is natural, we must explain what appears to be stable in a world that is in continuous flux. The central problem in the study of sustaining processes becomes how we can account for the endurance of various patterns of common endeavor, even in the face of constant changes in life conditions. Our focus in the study of sustaining processes, then, is on the persistent features of social transactions — what sociologists refer to as *social structure*. This includes the study of how communities and their component groups are organized and how these patterns of common endeavor are maintained even when circumstances are never twice the same.

CHARACTERISTICS OF SOCIAL NORMS

Frameworks of Social Norms. In most historical contexts human society takes on the appearance of order. The social structure of any community consists of the countless patterns of coordinated activity that occur over and over in much the same manner. Our daily lives consist for the most part of partaking in familiar routines. Since we execute recurrent transactions in similar ways, our expectations of one another become fixed in habit. We can plan our moves and make decisions with some measure of confidence, for we can anticipate many of the things that are likely to happen. Often the same people are involved repeatedly in similar transactions. As they come to know one another, they become involved in enduring social relationships. Most sociologists have been preoccupied with the study of such organized patterns, their component parts, and the manner in which these parts are related to one another.

Most of the transactions in which we participate in the course of each day occur in institutionalized contexts. In such situations concerted action rests on well-established norms. Although each transaction is unique, the participants approach one another on the basis of standardized expectations. Thus, the network of common understandings shared by the participants provides a framework within which their respective activities are carried out. Human behavior in such well-organized contexts has frequently been explained in terms of compliance with extant norms. However, the norms do not determine behavior; they only define the range of appropriate conduct — what the incumbents of various roles are supposed to do. What actually happens may of course deviate from such standards.

Patterns of concerted action, once they have become institutionalized, tend to persist even after the conditions under which they initially developed have disappeared. Some culture patterns — such as the caste system in rural India, certain rituals of the Catholic church, or the sentence structure of Indo-European languages — have persisted for many centuries. Most norms are less hardy. But the established ways are the comfortable ways. Since human beings are basically creatures of habit, we tend to approach familiar situations with fixed expectations. Habitual patterns, once established, become automatic and tend to resist pressures to change. Thus, wherever the same people have lived together for a time, traditions are likely to develop. People form an intuitive sense of what is appropriate. Traditional practices provide a sense of security, giving us something to cling to, even in unstable contexts. Noticeable changes are often sources of discomfort. We become filled with anxiety whenever we cannot anticipate what is likely to happen. Thus, innovations tend to make many people uncomfortable, and new ideas are frequently resisted even by those who stand to gain from them. Thus, many obsolete practices persist in all communities, a fact that has led many to complain of the inflexibility of human society; Bagehot (1948) contends that the "cake of custom" is the major obstacle to intelligent reform. Indeed, many patterns of concerted action persist until something unusual happens, something that compels a reassessment of the situation.

Range of Applicability. There are many kinds of social norms. They vary along several dimensions, including the boundaries within which they are enforced, the explicitness with which they are stated, and the degree of acceptance and sense of moral obligation that they evoke. Norms differ considerably in their range of applicability. Many are enforced throughout a given community. Thus, most communities have a standard language, and, even when other tongues are spoken, it is understood that all official communication will be in the standard idiom. Those who do not know that language cannot hold others responsible for not being able to understand them. The norms of the marketplace — property rights, techniques of production, procedures for distribution, mediums of exchange — are known throughout a community. Similarly, systems of social stratification — norms on the classification and ranking of people — are communitywide. Most communities have a single source of ultimate authority, and government regulations presumably apply to everyone in designated ways. Such well-established networks of interrelated norms that provide the frameworks within which many essential transactions are executed regularly are often called *social institutions.*

However, many norms hold only within the boundaries of specific groupings within a community. Some apply only to members of a social world. Unwritten rules against unfair practices and the fleecing of unwary customers are well known to members of a given industry; they are usually enforced without attracting undue attention, for unfavorable publicity may lead to government regulation. Conduct that may result in one's expulsion from a country club is of concern only to those who live in affluent suburbs, just as norms against reporting offenses to the police are found only in some working-class neighborhoods and in some ethnic enclaves. Other norms hold only within specific organizations, such as the regulations of a department store. Rituals, passwords, and special ways of approaching a sacred object are known only to members of a religious order; members usually overlook outsiders' transgressions, taking it for granted that others do not understand the order's norms. Still other norms are limited to small groups whose members know one another personally — special arrangements within a family, a clique of coworkers, or a juvenile gang.

Clarity of Statement. One of several useful ways of classifying social norms is in terms of the extent to which they are made explicit and the manner in which they are enforced. *Formal norms,* which are spelled out clearly, usually in writing, include the laws of modern communities and the regulations of various organizations. Where norms are unambiguously stated, the sanctions are also likely to be specified clearly. Thus, formal norms are usually backed by regular procedures for penalizing those who fail to comply, such as being arrested and imprisoned or being dismissed from a job. Those who excel in their compliance receive regular promotions and may even be awarded prizes in formal ceremonies. As communities become increasingly diversified, pressures grow for stating norms more explicitly. Otherwise people with different backgrounds of experience encounter difficulties in understanding one another, and many transactions break down unnecessarily. Thus, in modern mass societies increasing reliance is placed on formal norms.

Although one might guess that the best-established norms are those that are clearly stated, this is not the case. When norms are so firmly grounded that they are taken for granted, no one need say anything about them, except to instruct neophytes. *Conventional norms* are customs. Thus, customary procedures for dressing, eating, and greeting others are clearly understood from regular usage. Although most adults in a community are able to describe the appropriate procedures, most customs are intuitively felt as personal obligations. People feel uncomfortable when things are done in unfamiliar ways. Except in rapidly changing societies marked by considerable social mobility, customs are seldom set down explicitly in writing, as in books on etiquette. Precisely because such norms are not spelled out, disagreements may arise over what constitutes proper usage in a given situation. Specific punishment for obvious violations is frequently not prescribed; therefore, people's reactions to deviations vary considerably, from mild ridicule to vengeful condemnation or even brutal violence. For example, in the South before World War II a male Afro-American who stared at a young white woman risked punishment for "leering." The penalty sometimes consisted of verbal intimidation of the offender, but on some occasions retribution was directed against all Afro-Americans in the community. At times it even resulted in a lynching. Well-established customs are seldom violated. But should customary proscriptions prove ineffective, formal sanctions may be created. The passage of laws against intermarriage, for example, indicates that custom alone is no longer sufficient to enforce the norm (T. V. Smith, 1937).

The common understandings that develop among people who know one another personally are *informal norms.* They may or may not be stated explicitly, and they are usually known only to those within the circle. Examples include a family rule that rock music is not to be played after 8 P.M. or special greetings used by co-workers in an office. Whether a given deed violates informal norms may be subject to negotiation. Even when there is consensus that such norms have been violated, the sanctions imposed vary considerably, depending on the personal relationships among those who happen to be present. The show of displeasure may consist of derogation, scolding, threats, or physical punishment. The offender may be ridiculed or become the subject of unsavory gossip. If the transgression is considered sufficiently serious, the person may even be ostracized. Although such sanctions are informal, the impact can be quite severe. The cutting off of reciprocating responses by those with whom one identifies is very painful; it may leave one isolated from all meaningful contacts.

Emergent norms are transitory and situational. They develop in specific contexts and are enforced by the spontaneous reactions of the people who happen to be present. Despite their ad hoc nature, emergent norms are stringently enforced; in many instances violating emergent norms can be extremely dangerous.

Degree of Acceptance. Norms vary considerably in the extent to which they are accepted by people. When norms are imposed on a community and do not enjoy popular support, violations are commonplace. People comply only when they have to — from fear of punishment. An extreme case consists of the regulations imposed by a conquering army of occupation. The laws are clear, and everyone learns them quickly, for it might be hazardous not to know them. But they are enforceable only when troops are present, and the people take delight in flouting them whenever they can get away with it. When a violation may be detected, even strangers help one another in covering up and maintaining a solid front against the authorities. Many ghetto residents feel as if they were living in a colony governed by foreigners; they often address the police as if they constituted an army of occupation, and they are contemptuous of many laws accepted elsewhere in the city. In rapidly changing societies many norms are challenged. Many customs are rejected as outmoded, and some laws are condemned as unjust. In such contexts those who violate well-known norms feel no guilt. Thus, many young Americans in the 1960s were well aware that smoking marijuana was illegal and took precautions against detection. Although some may have felt badly because their parents disapproved of their smoking, they did not feel guilty about the smoking itself. If they were caught, their reaction was one of resentment rather than contrition. If they were convicted, they were likely to define themselves as martyrs. Thus, if norms are imposed on a community and do not enjoy popular support, they can be enforced only by continuous surveillance. Clearly, the norms would collapse were it not for fear of retribution.

Many norms, however, are so widely accepted that they become a deeply ingrained part of the personal orientations of most individuals. Conformity with such norms is largely routine. We are all presented with ample opportunities to steal, but most of us do not even notice them. Unlike professional thieves, we are simply not sensitized to such contingencies. Except in moments of desperation, the feasibility of theft does not even occur to most of us. Thus, if a norm is generally accepted, most people do not even notice the possibilities for violation. Even if we do notice a chance to steal something, most of us do not feel tempted. Those who are tempted are likely to feel guilty about it, even if no one else knows of their inner thoughts. It is simply not the proper thing to do.

Similarly, why do so many customers leave tips in restaurants they never expect to enter again? In most instances tipping is habitual. Even when we are dissatisfied with the service, we feel cheap if we walk out without leaving something. In the company of friends we may also experience a sense of shame. Thus, people who are tempted to violate a well-established norm are inhibited by a sense of guilt or shame. In Judeo-Christian culture norms against homicide are so deeply ingrained that draftees undergoing infantry training are plagued by doubts over whether they will be able to perform their duties in a combat zone. Studies made in battlefields reveal that many riflemen, even seasoned veterans, do not fire their weapons unless they receive direct orders to do so (Marshall, 1947).

Some norms, such as cultural axioms, are so well established and so widely accepted that they are taken for granted, and people who comply with them are not even aware of their existence. If a stranger should ask for an explanation, many would have difficulty explaining the very rules that they observe. A good example is grammar, which consists of the norms of linguistic behavior, norms that persist only because most people abide by them, albeit with some mistakes. Most children speak the idiomatically correct language of their community, but many of them have difficulty learning grammar — the very rules that they are following and reinforcing whenever they speak or write. Should one notice a violation of norms that are taken for granted — such as the desecration of a sacred object, matricide, or a tree talking to a dog — one's response would be a mixture of shock and bewilderment. Many examples of people's reactions to the violation of cultural axioms have been presented for several decades on the popular television program "Candid Camera." The people are stunned. They feel that something unnatural has happened, and they usually do not know what to do.

ACQUISITION OF SOCIAL NORMS

To get along in any community, social world, or specific group, newcomers — be they infants, immigrants, or other neophytes — must learn the basic norms that make up the culture of those with whom they become involved. Very few of our behavior patterns are innate; we learn norms of all kinds — the meanings of various objects, the manner in which they are evaluated, as well as the appropriate ways of using them in various transactions. *Socialization* refers to the acquisition of those norms that enable a newcomer to act in concert with others. The meanings of various objects are conventional norms; we learn to approach objects as if they had certain attributes. Most studies of socialization have focused on learning by infants, which is in a sense justified. We probably learn more during our early years than at any other time, and what we learn as children becomes the selective base for all subsequent learning. We begin learning at birth, and we probably acquire many meanings—such as those involving gender, the assumptions concerning what is proper for men and women—even before we have learned to use language effectively. We are subsequently able to designate some of these meanings with words, but many key assumptions about sex roles remain little more than an intuitive sense of what is proper. After we master a language, we learn at a much faster pace, for we can learn through symbolic communication as well as through direct experiences. Childhood socialization is certainly important, but most of us continue to learn throughout our lives. Each time we migrate to a new community, get a new job, or join a new group we undergo renewed socialization, and we must learn to perform adequately in each new context.

Socialization Through Participation. We learn things from many sources and in several different ways. Much of the most important socialization, however, occurs through active participation in already organized transactions. The activities are already broken up into roles, and we generally start by learning to enact the simpler ones, those involving little responsibility. How do most Americans learn to play baseball? How do we learn to behave in classrooms? How do we learn about sex? In most instances we learn by becoming involved with people who are more experienced. Performance is at first inexpert and clumsy, but with increasing participation each newcomer acquires more competence and self-confidence. There is much trial and error, and some of the failures may be humiliating. In time, however, we learn the routines and are able to contribute our share so easily that role-playing becomes largely habitual. Thus, each newcomer learns to define situations in roughly the same manner as the seasoned performers and acquires the key values the participants share—what is prized and what is disdained.

Of decisive importance in this process are the reactions of the various people with whom we are associated. They serve as models, as instructors, and as reinforcers. We develop our initial appreciation of most norms by watching others perform. In this way we gain some appreciation of standards of performance. Others also tell us what to do and demonstrate the proper demeanor while doing it. They explain the rationale, especially for inconvenient or painful tasks, and coach us on the proper stance to assume. They not only continue to provide guidance as we begin to participate more actively but also correct our mistakes until our performance becomes acceptable. Others are especially important as reinforcers. By rewarding proper contributions, they buttress the newly developing patterns. Their praise supports successive approximations of satisfactory standards. Our partners thus provide the negative feedback that encourages some behavior patterns and discourages others. Those who are too slow in learning or who rebel face severe sanctions. They may find themselves put off by the coolness of the others, or in some instances they may even be expelled until they are able and willing to act in the expected manner. Seasoned participants thus provide the audience for whom the neophytes perform, an audience that already has fixed expectations. Thus, most socialization consists of learning how to contribute appropriately to already organized transactions.

Since so much socialization goes on in this manner, many meanings are acquired as incidental by-products in transactions in which attention is focused elsewhere. Many meanings are learned without explicit, intentional instruction. Many ethnic stereotypes, for example, are learned and reinforced in contexts that have nothing to do with ethnic identity. Until recently American children frequently decided priority in games by counting: "Eeny, meeny, miny, mo; catch a nigger by the toe." This device was used by countless children who had never seen an Afro-American and did not even understand what they were saying. Similarly, in discussing financial negotiations children sometimes use an expression overheard in adult talk: "to Jew someone down." Many do not realize that the verb refers to an ethnic group. In both cases attention is focused on something other than ethnic identity; the children are merely using an orderly way of deciding who is to enjoy the temporary advantage of being first in a game or describing a transaction in which one is pushing for a better bargain. Although ethnic identity is irrelevant in such learning contexts, the meaning may become fixed; Afro-Americans are represented as inferior objects, and Jews are seen as adroit in handling money (Shibutani and Kwan, 1965:271–80).

Similarly, many mistaken beliefs about women have been transmitted inadvertently in numerous contexts in which attention is not focused on gender. A content analysis of children's books discloses that most of them are about boys, men, and male animals involved in exciting adventures. When women appear, they usually enact insignificant roles, remaining inconspicuous and often even nameless. Boys are presented in adventuresome roles, and they engage in pursuits that demand independence; but girls are usually passive and immobile. Good little girls succeed by looking pretty and serving others, and motherhood is presented as the ideal lifetime status. Mothers who appear in the stories are usually confined to the house (Weitzman et al., 1972). Through continued exposure to such materials during our most formative years all of us, male and female, come to assume that women are creatures with certain "natural" attributes. We often act on the basis of presuppositions acquired in contexts in which no deliberate effort was being made to downgrade women. A great many conventional norms are passed on in this manner.

Learning to Enact Roles. Learning to participate effectively in social transactions is a very complex process (Thornton and Nardi, 1975). First, we must learn just what the incumbent of any status is expected to contribute to each transaction. Then we must become familiar with all the component roles within each transaction. Since each role is but one segment of already organized teamwork, merely learning the role one is to enact is not enough. Thus, those who want to play the position (status) of shortstop on a baseball team must not only learn how to field grounders, to cover bases, to execute double-plays, to back up players taking long throws from the outfield; they must also learn something of all the other defensive positions, as well as how to bat and run bases. Unless each player has some appreciation of what is involved in playing the other positions, effective role-taking is not possible; without some knowledge of all the roles one cannot participate vicariously in the experiences of the other players nor anticipate what each of them is likely to do as the transaction develops. Roles are defined in terms of reciprocal claims and obligations, and each player must have some understanding of what can be expected of the others.

Those who aspire to participate in a transaction begin by observing others, especially those who perform well. Children often imitate their elders as they are forming their initial working conception of various roles, and newcomers in organizations often emulate those who appear to command respect. In many instances novices may engage in fantasy as well. Thus, recruits in the armed forces often find themselves vicariously issuing the commands of close order drill, just as those who aspire to proficiency in athletics daydream of making the key play that wins a crucial game. Those who are just learning often begin with stereotyped conceptions of each role, idealized expectations of what appropriate enactment should involve. By watching, neophytes learn something about each role and gain an overview of the entire transaction. Only by seeing how the various roles are related to one another can we see how any one of them fits into the total pattern. Observers also learn both the rules of the game and the values shared by seasoned performers.

In most instances such anticipatory socialization is followed by some direct instruction. One has to learn a minimum set of "must" behavior patterns, which may be codified into job descriptions and rule books. Most important in acquiring a new role is learning the obligations of the incumbent. One must learn not only the expected behavior patterns but also the various attitudes to be assumed: Never argue with the umpire. One must also learn the appropriate motives to be avowed. As newcomers become more involved, their perspective shifts from that of spectator to that of participant. They become sensitized to the reactions of those who are enacting reciprocating roles, who help them correct errors. Sometimes misinformation acquired as an observer must be unlearned. The most thorough conformity with norms usually occurs at the neophyte level, when those who are still uncertain feel that they must prove their competence, sincerity, and awareness of place.

As they learn the formal and conventional norms on which concerted action is based, newcomers also become familiar with the informal norms that hold among the specific individuals with whom they are involved. Each person has strong preferences and a distinctive style of performance. While participating in new activities each neophyte must take the roles of specific individuals. Some informal norms may be in direct violation of formal norms; so modifications are introduced to suit the preferences of those who are already established in their positions, who are able to define the range of deviation to be permitted. Thus, on a new job we learn which rules we can bend and how much time to take for coffee breaks. In a factory we learn not to cater to people of higher rank nor to engage in "rate busting"—largely from watching how co-workers react to those who are obsequious or who work too hard. Thus, how newcomers learn a role depends to a considerable extent on the personal preferences of those with whom they happen to be in direct contact. Since the inexperienced often imitate and identify with people who control their most important resources, incumbents of reciprocal roles are very important. Each beginner inadvertently picks up or reacts to their distinctive styles. The manner in which instructors influence their students' style of performance is often revealed in the arts and crafts; for example, musicians often reflect the proclivities and prejudices of their teachers.

Each person who has mastered the basic requirements of a role develops a characteristic way of enacting it. Once we are familiar with the range of alternatives, we can begin shaping the role to suit ourselves; much depends on our past experiences and our objectives for the future. Once we know the standard expectations, we can formulate them for ourselves and develop a style of performance that suits our unique abilities, skills, and values. Even roles that are as explicitly defined as the duties of a soldier can be enacted in several ways; most other roles permit even more variation. Since we can usually influence the expectations that others have of us, we can develop a distinctive way of enacting a role and still be accepted. Thus, socialization is more than the mere passive internalization of already established norms. Newcomers are active human beings with peculiar interests and traits. As they make their way through life, they find that some behavior patterns are more advantageous and satisfying than others. Thus, roles are shaped to some extent by the individuals who enact them regularly, for each performs in an idiosyncratic manner (R. Turner, 1962). If the demands of a role are incongruent with one's personal preferences, performances tend to be perfunctory. But if they are congruent, performances are planned and enacted with great care. Once we are thoroughly familiar with the requirements and have developed some experience, we can modify and qualify the rules around our own needs and the demands of others and thus achieve some acceptable balance.

Mastery of most roles requires considerable practice. Sometimes it is necessary to acquire special skills, even to develop certain muscles by sustained exercise. Initially, when we are still learning, we tend to be self-conscious about the role. We act more deliberately. We are sometimes acutely aware of our shortcomings and make considerable effort to overcome them. In time performance becomes largely habitual. By the time we master a role we become aware of the standard expectations of all people who are interested — for example, all baseball fans. Then we learn to evaluate our own performance from this generalized standpoint. Once we know the standard procedures, we can depart from the context in which we received our initial training and can perform anywhere. Thus, skilled baseball players can join total strangers and make adjustments to one another with minimum difficulties. Similarly, experienced schoolteachers or clerical workers are able to move from one job to another, just as soldiers can fill in for casualties in line units and do roughly the same work as the men replaced.

The Emergence of Personal Outlooks. Modern mass societies have become so complex that all citizens must receive considerable training to cope with the demands of daily life. Social transactions have become very complicated, and the component roles are becoming more specialized; people must, therefore, learn a number of technical skills just to get along. Furthermore, people socialized in quite different contexts are brought together in urban communities; hence, some standardization of what is taught becomes necessary. Thus, a number of formal organizations have developed to carry an increasing share of the task of socialization. Most modern communities have established schools, and some compulsory education is the rule. Schools must pass on to coming generations the community's cultural heritage and minimum skills in reading, writing, and counting. In modern societies most people spend virtually all their childhood and early adult years in school, preparing for what lies ahead.

Most large organizations have their own training programs. Just as members of the clergy are required to attend seminaries, doctors and lawyers are required to undergo many years of training in special schools with curricula prescribed by those already in the profession. In such settings students not only learn to meet the standards expected in their occupations but often acquire much of the lore and key values of their social worlds. Thus, training in medical schools consists of more than instruction on therapeutic techniques. In constant encounters with doctors the students learn the ideology of the profession and its informal norms. Nuances of meaning, values, and unspoken assumptions are passed on to succeeding generations of doctors (Becker et al., 1961).

We also learn much from exposure to the media of mass communication, especially from television. According to a 1977 Nielsen survey, American children under five years of age spent an average of 23.5 hours per week before a television set; the average for adults was 44 hours. Although programs such as "Sesame Street" are educational in intent, viewers learn much more from programs designed primarily for entertainment, which depict an exciting world that contrasts sharply with their daily existence—gambling at Monte Carlo, a heroin bust in Harlem, tracking game along the Amazon, power struggles among top executives. By identifying with various characters and participating vicariously in their lives, viewers acquire many values and norms that become part of their outlook. Television programs provide many models of conduct. Thus, a child who has never attended a ballet in person may decide very early that he or she wishes to become a dancer. Quarreling youngsters may attack one another with karate chops. With the advent of telecasting popular sports, overall standards of athletic performance have risen noticeably.

The manner in which anyone becomes oriented toward his or her surroundings depends largely on the combination of communication channels to which the person is exposed. Each has a somewhat different combination. We learn at home, in our neighborhood, in schools, through chance encounters, on the job, and from the mass media. Each person develops a distinctive outlook, for each person is selectively sensitized to different things. As personal interests take shape, they provide the basis for selection. Sooner or later most people learn to do things in a manner that is acceptable to those with whom they are in frequent contact. Activities that elicit desired reactions from others tend to become established as habitual patterns; many other possibilities, including those that may be much desired, are discouraged and may eventually be forgotten. Once people have acquired the perspectives shared in the various reference groups for which they perform, each person becomes a society in miniature, defining situations and enacting roles in appropriate ways.

PERSONAL IDENTITY AND MORAL CONDUCT

All human beings, with the possible exception of very young infants and a few who are psychotic, develop some kind of working orientation toward themselves. The personal world of every individual is centered around him or herself; in making judgments and decisions, in speaking of space and time, each uses him or herself as the central point of reference. This is true not only of egoists but also of the most considerate of people. Each of us is able to recognize our own aspirations, disappointments, and fears, and can distinguish between these and similar experiences on the part of others. Each can identify him or herself as a particular human being, characterized by a distinctive set of attributes. Each human being is unique. We assume that there is no one else exactly like us — who looks, thinks, and acts in the same manner. We take it for granted that there never has been anyone else like any of us in the past and that there never will be an exact duplicate in the future. The fact that human beings regard themselves as such distinct and independent entities makes possible the pinpointing of moral responsibility.

Bases of Personal Identity. Each person comes to regard him or herself as a separate entity, and the formation of this belief is facilitated by the fact that each body is a separate organism. All our experiences are organic processes within the body, beginning with birth and ending with death. Each body has a consistent appearance over time, and we identify ourselves in terms of that appearance. We also use the same name as the symbol for that unit. Most of us are sensitive about our appearance. Noticeable deformities or exceptional attractiveness become the basis for distinctions. Skin color is often an important symbol, for it may limit the status one may attain. Other physical attributes also provide important foundations for self-concepts. Actually the boundaries of an organism are not as clearly demarcated as we usually believe. Is the air in our lungs a part of us or not? Furthermore, we identify with various objects outside the body—our possessions, for example—and experience them as if they were a part of ourselves. People also become concerned with events that occurred before their birth and with those that may occur after their death. Many identify with their ancestors and react sharply to insults to their forebears as if the remarks were addressed to themselves. Concern over descendents, even those yet unborn, also affects our decisions.

A person's sense of identity also rests on the continuity of experiences in time. There are memories of the past that cannot be escaped as well as reasonable aspirations for the future. Since human beings live in a temporal perspective and can survey their deeds both prospectively and retrospectively, they can organize and plan activities that cover considerable periods of time. Many pursue long-range goals. Each person makes sacrifices in the present to achieve something in the future. Various subsidiary movements are preparatory for or subordinated to a pattern as a whole. Each life has the character of a succession of episodes and adventures, and these are integrated into a general scheme—a career.

The feeling of being a distinct human being also arises from a sense of personal autonomy. One feels able to exercise some measure of control over one's own conduct and thus affect one's own destiny. Each is capable of making decisions and of selecting among alternative lines of action. Hence, we assume that all others are also able to exercise similar self-regulation, and this constitutes the basis of morality. Since we assume that we are capable of making choices, we hold ourselves accountable for our own deeds. At the same time we often refuse to accept responsibility for conduct that occurred when we were "not ourselves"—when under great strain, in a state of shock, in a hypnotic trance, or controlled by evil spirits. Whether a person should be held accountable for compulsive behavior, as in kleptomania, is still subject to dispute. We feel it unfair for people to blame us for acts over which we did not have full control, and we apply similar standards to others.

The Self-Concept as an Object.   Each human being develops a sense of personal identity, a working conception of the kind of object he or she is. Each person forms a *self-concept.* We place ourselves into various categories recognized in our community—such as age, sex, religion, class, or ethnic group—and then assume the obligations of the incumbents of each category. We define ourselves in terms of status—within the stratification system of the community and in each of the social worlds and groups in which we participate. We claim the rights, privileges, and immunities of that position; we also accept the special responsibilities that fall on us by virtue of our status. One who is identified as a member of a clan must locate oneself in the genealogy and thereby define one's relationships to the other members. Each of us has some recognition of our more conspicuous personality traits—whether we are bright or dull, clumsy or agile, beautiful or ugly, reclusive or sociable. We also locate ourselves in the various networks of interpersonal relations in which we are implicated; we are related in understood ways to specific individuals and have reciprocal expectations of lovers, friends, relatives, co-workers, and authority figures. Thus, each person locates himself or herself as an object in the symbolic environment.

Although at first glance we might assume that each person's self-concept is nothing more than a reflection of what he or she actually is, this is not the case. The meaning of an object is the manner in which one is predisposed to act toward it; a self-concept is what one means to oneself. Each of us is organized to act with reference to ourself in particular ways—to seek challenging situations, to avoid close contact with members of the opposite sex, to shun the limelight, to be preoccupied with matters of status. Such inclinations to act rest on presuppositions and beliefs about the object. How we are disposed to treat ourselves depends on the kind of human being we believe we are—whether or not these beliefs are accurate. Thus, a self-concept consists of a set of beliefs and presuppositions. Furthermore, we are not born with self-concepts; meanings are constructed in social interaction. Each person's self-concept is the product of participation in a long succession of social transactions—both real and vicarious. Like other meanings, self-concepts are products of socialization, and the anticipated reactions of other people are built into them. We approach others with the expectation of being treated in given ways. Just as the meanings of most other objects are conventional norms—acceptable ways of handling them—so self-concepts contain conventional features in that all socialized persons set accepted standards of conduct for themselves. A self-concept is an abstract object, consisting of everything one believes or takes for granted about oneself. Which of these countless presuppositions is activated depends on what is pertinent in the particular transaction in which one is involved.

All objects are shaped through role-taking in social interaction. If self-concepts are also formed through role-taking while participating in transactions, then their content should depend on the kinds of expectations that are characteristically projected to others with whom we are in sustained association. Thus, Cooley (1922:183–85) writes of the "looking-glass self"—that our idea of ourselves is a reflection of how we think others view us. One widely entertained hypothesis in sociology is that the manner in which people come to conceive of themselves depends on how they believe others view them. Hundreds of commonsense observations indicate that this is frequently the case. If a person is treated consistently with great deference, as would be the case with the daughter of a monarch, she comes to see herself as an important object. If a youngster is told constantly that he is a bad boy, he may become convinced that there is something wrong with him and that he is basically wicked and unlikeable. Experimental studies reveal a positive relationship between perceived judgments of others and self-definitions (Quarantelli and Cooper, 1966), but the findings are not conclusive. In his study of Afro-American families in an urban ghetto Rainwater (1966) describes the manner in which so many of the residents come to regard themselves as inferior objects. When families are disorganized, arguments often become vicious; pretenses to being a competent individual are openly disparaged. People call attention to one another's shortcomings. This situation leads some to conclude that they are unable to find a satisfactory way to live because something is wrong with them. Dark skin color still gets a negative evaluation within many Afro-American communities; a young man with lofty aspirations is reminded repeatedly that he is "nothing but a nigger like everybody else." Thus, many youngsters grow up believing that they are debased objects. Such observations suggest that the hypothesis concerning the formation of self-concepts is basically correct, although it may need some qualification.

Yet, as any psychiatrist can testify, some well-liked and successful people remain convinced that they are undeserving and unlovable. Although popular, they are certain that others would not like them if they only knew the truth about them. This phenomenon suggests that our understanding of how objects are formed is oversimplified. The self-concept, like other objects, is the product of our experiences, but the influence of the various individuals we have encountered is uneven. Some individuals—perhaps parents, older siblings, teachers, or gang leaders—have far greater impact on us than others. Many assumptions about our own attributes—that we are clumsy, troublesome, stupid, or worthless—may be formed early in life. Once such assumptions are established, we take them for granted and form many persistent ways of addressing ourselves on the basis of them. Once dispositions to act toward ourselves become habitual, they are difficult to revise, especially when we take the traits for granted. Most of us are not aware of many of the assumptions we make about ourselves. Once important elements of a self-concept are established, one may develop a trained incapacity to notice contrary evidence. Even when a man with a low level of self-esteem rises in rank and is treated consistently with respect, he is unable to revise his original evaluation of himself. Only when something unusual happens does a person become conscious of such assumptions and realize how ridiculous some of them are. These insights sometimes occur in psychotherapy, but it usually takes considerable time and effort to alter behavior patterns that have persisted for a lifetime. It is clear, then, that the hypothesis must be revised to take account of such observations (Shrauger and Schoeneman, 1979).

Moral Conduct.   Once one's self-concept is formed, one tends to act in ways regarded as being consistent with it, inhibiting impulses that contradict it and facilitating those that are congruent. When one becomes established in a given status — within a community, a social world, or a group — one assumes the duties of that position as personal responsibilities. Thus, a wealthy dowager feels a private obligation to look after the interests of her servants and aides, just as an unemployed husband feels ashamed of being unable to help provide for his family. Once we have defined ourselves and our responsibilities, we try to live up to the standards that we have set for ourselves. We do not always do what we would like; we often fight off temptations, suppressing inclinations to do things we consider beneath our dignity. Similarly, what one regards as the appropriate way to be treated by various parties depends on one's self-concept. We resent being denied what we regard as rightfully ours by virtue of position. Although individuals differ considerably in their capacity for self-regulation, personal pride plays an important part in the lives of most people. Although we are sensitive to the views of others and make sacrifices to form an acceptable impression, most of all we struggle to maintain some measure of self-respect in our own eyes. Those who are unable to meet their own standards are sometimes immobilized by embarrassment; those who fail consistently often denounce themselves and place a low estimate on their worth as a human being. Thus, much of what we do is moral; *moral conduct* is behavior that has no sanction other than the actor's own sense of right and wrong. Each person develops characteristic ways of dealing with various types of situations; the consistency in anyone's behavior—one's personal style—rests to a large extent on the self-concept.

This hypothesis concerning self-definitions and behavior may be tested in a very rough way by examining instances in which people with different self-concepts confront similar situations. A mechanic who is unable to diagnose what is wrong with a stalled car becomes embarrassed; others in the same context are annoyed at the inconvenience but do not condemn themselves. At cocktail parties a man who conceives of himself as handsome does not hesitate to initiate conversations with women he has never met before. His roommate, who is convinced that he is unattractive to women, holds back, not wishing to risk a rebuff that would reinforce his low level of self-esteem. He may be so preoccupied with maintaining his immaculate appearance that he has little awareness of other people. He remains highly self-conscious and apprehensive and avoids transactions that may prove too challenging.

Another rough test of the hypothesis is provided by instances in which someone's self-concept has undergone noticeable change. We would anticipate a corresponding change in some behavior patterns. All of us redefine ourselves somewhat each time our status changes—in moving, for example, from childhood to puberty to marriage to parenthood to old age. On the Andaman Islands people change their names as they move from one status to the next (Radcliffe-Brown, 1964:119–20); this practice eliminates ambiguous periods of transition, for the expectations of the incumbents of each position are well known. Similar name changes are sometimes found in religious conversions; converts enter a different symbolic environment, redefine themselves, and begin acting in ways that baffle their former friends and relatives. People who undergo plastic surgery sometimes redefine themselves, and some of them develop markedly different life-styles (MacGregor, 1974). Some people act differently when they find themselves in situations in which they are anonymous—in a mob, in darkness, at a masquerade party, or in a metropolis where no one can recognize them.

Thus, human beings are not robots who conform blindly to social norms; each person engages in self-regulation. Most people comply with the expectations they impute to others, but they do so in their own way. Those who are heartily in favor of what is expected of them act with enthusiasm; those who find the norms tedious or inconvenient may comply begrudgingly. Sometimes people disclose their inner feelings through negative comments or betray their lack of enthusiasm in expressive movements that are unintentional but readily visible. Those who feel ambivalent may hold back as long as they can or raise questions about the fairness of the demands. From time to time someone rebels and simply refuses to participate. Thus, even when transactions are being carried out, the way in which each person complies with norms depends on how he or she personally feels about the matter.

The Study of Self-Concepts. Many social psychologists agree that self-concepts are important in the organization of behavior, and an extensive body of research literature has developed (Wylie et al., 1979). The systematic investigation of this phenomenon, however, is just getting under way, and many of the findings are inconsistent. Some of these studies are cited where pertinent.

REAFFIRMATION OF SOCIAL NORMS

The Persistence of Perspectives. Life conditions are always changing. From time to time various individuals develop new interests, making some of them dissatisfied with existing norms. A few may refuse to comply; others may do so reluctantly, making only the minimum contributions necessary by going through the motions. In the face of constant pressures toward change, how can we account for the persistence of recognizable patterns of concerted action?

People who share a symbolic environment approach one another with similar expectations. All of us have learned to perceive our surroundings as if the various objects that make up our environment had relatively stable characteristics. We characterize familiar objects of all kinds — things, events, specific people we know, ourselves — in terms of sets of assumptions and beliefs that are shared within our universe of discourse. Most material objects are in fact sufficiently stable to confirm our expectations, but there are also regularities in the responses of people. As long as most people approach one another and other objects with similar assumptions, they are likely to define particular situations in a similar manner. Thus, coorientation is relatively easy to establish and maintain.

Some Reactions to Infractions. Well-established norms are constantly reaffirmed because most people do what is expected of them most of the time. Appropriate behavior patterns are so securely grounded in habit that the possibility of violation does not even occur to most people. When we consider all the possible things that could be done at a dinner party, for example, and compare them to what is actually done, we get some appreciation of the importance of social norms. Only when things go awry, when conformity becomes costly or painful, do questions arise concerning the necessity or desirability of doing things in the prescribed way. Even then only a few norms are questioned; the rest remain taken for granted. In a pioneering study of the presuppositions underlying our definitions of familiar scenes Garfinkel (1967:35–75) uses a series of ingenious exercises to demonstrate the extent to which people in daily contact take similar things for granted. In one class assignment he asked his students to spend from fifteen minutes to an hour viewing activities at home from the standpoint of a boarder rather than as a member of the family. Thus, the students were to suspend their usual assumptions and adopt the perspective of a stranger who was unfamiliar with the family's informal norms. The students were astonished at the extent to which the idiosyncrasies of particular individuals were implicated in their transactions. When a student asked permission to get a snack from the refrigerator or spoke only when spoken to, other family members were stunned. Many of them became angry and accused the students of being inconsiderate and selfish. Thus, the temporary suspension of familiar assumptions disrupts the smooth flow of concerted action, and even people who know one another intimately are not able to carry on as usual.

In another exercise Garfinkel engaged various acquaintances in conversation; after the discussion was well under way, he disclosed that he had hidden a tape recorder under his coat. Many took this as a clear violation of a situational propriety; we assume that what we say in a friendly conversation is intended only for those to whom the remarks are addressed. Most of the people were astonished and asked him what he intended to do with the tape. Several became indignant at what they regarded as a breach of privacy. Although Garfinkel was condemned and perhaps redefined as an odd professor, none of the people who were outraged questioned the norm itself. Thus, someone's failure to comply with group expectations often leads to the breakdown of the transaction and to the condemnation of the offender; the norm, however, remains unquestioned and intact. Indeed, if the violator of the norm is penalized, the act of punishment itself reinforces the norm.

In another exercise Garfinkel asked his students to play tic-tac-toe with their acquaintances; each time the opponent made a move, the student was to erase the mark and put it elsewhere. In about half of some two hundred fifty trials the opponents did not take the gesture at face value. They apparently felt that the unexpected maneuver had some hidden significance; they assumed that the student was after something that had nothing to do with the game. Some even thought that a sexual pass was being made. Thus, when a clear and flagrant violation of a well-established norm occurs, observers frequently try to explain it away in terms of extenuating circumstances. When friends fail to give a civil answer to a question, for example, we often assume that they did not hear it or that they are not feeling well. Thus, people who do the unexpected are judged and corrected in terms of standards that are taken for granted. The variation is accounted for in terms of other widely accepted assumptions (Stokes and Hewitt, 1976). Infractions of deeply ingrained norms are usually explained away in a manner that does not challenge the norm itself. The violations are regarded as exceptions, and exceptions always presuppose a rule.

In still another exercise Garfinkel gave a class assignment in which students were required to haggle over the price of various goods in Los Angeles stores. In the United States it is taken for granted that the merchant fixes the prices of goods; they are not subject to bargaining as they are in flea markets throughout the world. Almost a fourth of the students refused even to try or reported that their efforts were aborted before they reached the test. Those who did the assignment reported experiencing anxieties even when anticipating a trial and especially as they approached a salesperson for the first time. Were it not a class assignment, they would not have gone ahead. Some of the students who did carry out the assignment were astonished to discover that in some stores prices were in fact subject to negotiation! Nonetheless, most of us will probably go through life assuming that this is not the case, for few of us have the courage to make the test. Thus, where norms are well established, people refuse to test them, even when an opportunity to do so arises.

Mutual Support of Perspectives. Well-established norms are continuously augmented and reaffirmed through widespread conformity. Precisely because most of us live up to group expectations, social life takes on the appearance of being orderly and predictable. Each time we handle an object correctly or approach other people in appropriate ways we unintentionally lend further support to a behavior pattern that has come to be taken for granted. With each act we reinforce the expectations of others. Each time we give a smile of approval or reassurance to an act of conformity or a frown of disapproval to noncompliance we are bolstering the perspectives of others. Thus, as Sumner (1906) writes, each person is an agent of the folkways. We are continually watching other people's reactions; if they respond to our acts in the expected manner, we continue what we are doing with assurance that it is not out of place. Nor is such mutual support confined to cooperative transactions. We bolster one another's perspectives even in quarreling. If someone we insult does not become angry, we are at a loss as to what to do. To the extent that human beings live up to one another's expectations, they are augmenting one another's perspectives and are thereby maintaining the existing social structure.

When group expectations are not met, the situation becomes problematic. Transactions are often truncated, and the participants face disconcerting experiences. If clear violations of norms occur frequently enough, they lead to questions about the world we take for granted. We feel insecure, for we do not know just what to anticipate. The process of mutual support stands out in sharp relief when we find ourselves in such strange situations. At first we stand about awkwardly, wondering what to do. Then we proceed cautiously, constantly watching for the reactions of others. Sometimes we just imitate whatever the others are doing, without understanding what is happening. In the absence of support from others, people sometimes develop doubts about what they perceive; some may even question their own sanity. In a well-known study Asch (1951) subjected participants in an experiment to a test that consisted of comparing the lengths of various lines. Each subject was assigned to a group, all of whose other members were confederates of the experimenter. In the first two trials the confederates gave true responses, and the group easily agreed on the correct answer. But in succeeding trials all the confederates agreed that two lines of dissimilar length were the same, leaving the subject the lone dissenter. Although two-thirds of the subjects insisted that the others were mistaken, the rest changed their judgments to conform with that of the majority. As in Hans Christian Andersen's tale of the emperor's new clothes, people often pretend to see what others insist they see. Sometimes this is deliberate pretense; in other instances people are uncertain or actually persuade themselves that they are mistaken.

Since norms vary so much from one community to another, we might conclude that they are arbitrary. They are arbitrary in the sense that there is rarely a single way of doing anything. But norms are not arbitrary for those who live in the community. Those who have learned to perceive and think in terms of the categories of a given symbolic environment actually have little choice. It is for this reason that severe social sanctions are so seldom used. They are unnecessary in most contexts, for most people rarely consider the possibility of committing inappropriate acts. But the sanctions are there, and, when infractions are regarded as serious enough, they are invoked. Norms do provide a framework within which social life goes on.

SUMMARY AND DISCUSSION

In each community complex networks of social norms provide frameworks within which countless transactions are carried out. All newcomers learn these norms, largely by participating in the transactions, at first with difficulty and later with more confidence. As they partake repeatedly in similar transactions, they come to conceive of themselves as human beings of a particular sort. Although coercion plays an important part in society, much of the regularity in human life arises from self-regulation. Self-regulation is a cybernetic process in which a person adjusts in advance to expectations imputed to other participants in transactions. Most people do what they consider fair and decent. When transactions are recurrent, such expectations become fixed. Then people reinforce one another's perspectives, each by continuing to act within the range of acceptable conduct as defined by norms. Each person, by living up to his or her own standards, thereby contributes toward maintaining the fabric of society. Thus, even though life conditions are constantly changing, the established patterns of concerted action are reinforced largely by the continued self-regulation of socialized participants.

Both in the social sciences and in daily discourse we run the risk of reification — that is, of treating abstract concepts as if they were concrete objects. Thus, we sometimes think of society as a thing that somehow molds and restricts our behavior. Some even regard society as some kind of monster; they write of a "sick society" that "causes" crime, neurosis, and unhappiness. They write as if the various patterns of concerted action existed independently of the human beings involved. But social structure is only an abstraction; the fact that human beings act in expected ways makes the patterns discernible. As Edward Sapir (1949:104) writes, "While we often speak of society as though it were a static structure defined by tradition, it is, in the more intimate sense, nothing of the kind, but a highly intricate network of partial or complete understandings between members of organizational units of every degree of size and complexity, ranging from a pair of lovers or a family to a league of nations or that ever increasing portion of humanity which can be reached by the press through all its transnational ramifications. It is only apparently a static sum of social institutions; actually it is being reanimated or creatively reaffirmed from day to day by particular acts of a communicative nature which obtain among individuals participating in it."

SUGGESTED READINGS

Becker, Howard S., et al. 1961. *Boys in White: Student Culture in Medical School.* Chicago: University of Chicago Press.
   An empirical study of how medical students acquire the technical skills and ideology of the profession.
Garfinkel, Harold. 1967. *Studies in Ethnomethodology.* Englewood Cliffs, N.J.: Prentice-Hall.
   A pioneering discussion of the manner in which presuppositions are formed and reaffirmed in social interaction.
Goffman, Erving. 1963. *Behavior in Public Places.* New York: Free Press.
   An insightful description of the various norms that facilitate the encounters of strangers in public places.
Lott, Bernice. 1981. *Becoming a Woman: The Socialization of Gender.* Springfield, Ill.: Charles C Thomas.
   An account of the continuing socialization of women in American society based on data drawn from diverse sources—clinical, experimental, and descriptive.
Strauss, Anselm L. 1959. *Mirrors and Masks: The Search for Identity.* Glencoe, Ill.: Free Press.
   A treatise on the formation and transformation of the individual's sense of personal identity while participating in social transactions.
Wylie, Ruth C., et al. 1979. *The Self-Concept.* Vol. 2. Lincoln: University of Nebraska Press.
   A critical appraisal of hundreds of empirical investigations relating self-concepts to a broad range of variables.

VII

SOCIAL STRATIFICATION

Soon after World War II an American anthropologist asked a drum beater in Ceylon (now Sri Lanka) how he felt about being in a low caste. The man responded: "From the Puranic ages we have been classified as tom-tom beaters; that is the way it was and that is the way we like it. We would like to be of higher position, but what is the use of wishing for what is impossible? If we were, who would then beat the drums? If the Henaya were not a Henaya, then who would wash? Everything would be upset and it would not be good for the people" (Ryan, 1953:259–60). Such fatalistic acceptance of an unenviable position is difficult for most Americans to comprehend. We live in a society in which upward mobility is possible and a high value is placed on achievement through individual effort. Yet, where a system of social stratification is well established, most of the people—including those at the bottom—accept their lot as if it were natural. Some may become apprehensive at the prospect of changes, even those changes that might be to their advantage. Such reactions are not uncommon in stable societies.

These observations lead us to the problem of social inequality. Everywhere human beings seek certain objects—among them, useful resources, suitable mates, deference, security. In all communities some people manage to enjoy a greater share of what is desired than others. Some go through life without doing a single day of strenuous work; others spend virtually their entire lives in drudgery. In most communities human beings are classified and ranked in some manner, and in this chapter we examine some of the more common systems of ranking.

Although numerous patterns of social stratification have developed, sociologists for the most part have focused their attention on only a few of them. The work of Karl Marx has strongly influenced the study of social stratification, and as a result disproportionate stress has been placed on social class. Some sociologists have even tried to squeeze historical data on several different types of ranking into this scheme of analysis. Class distinctions play an undeniably important part in many societies, but human beings have been ranked on the basis of other criteria as well, among them religion and ethnic identity. In this chapter we focus on the ranking of people in communities; status distinctions in social worlds and organized groups will be taken up in chapter 8.

Everyone other than those in the most privileged positions receives less than a fair share of valued objects. How are such systems of inequality maintained? The usual answer is that inequities are perpetuated by force. Although this is sometimes the case, such explanations can be misleading. Systems of social stratification vary considerably in the extent to which they are institutionalized; when they are well established, coercion is actually minimal. The popular notion that the underprivileged live in perpetual terror is simply not true. Ghastly occurrences happen from time to time, but they are not the rule. In this chapter our attention centers on ranking systems that are well established. Later, we shall see what happens when such systems undergo change and when they are challenged and on occasion overthrown.

BASES OF SOCIAL STRATIFICATION

Social Status in the Community. People who live together and participate repeatedly in common transactions develop some kind of organization, and *social status* is the position that a person occupies within such networks of social relationships. Since each position is part of a larger pattern, each status is related to each of the other positions in understood ways. Each status may be identified in terms of rights, privileges, and immunities for the incumbents. Persons of high rank who are arrested, for example, are often released on their own recognizance, when others are required to post bail. Each status is also defined in terms of duties and responsibilities. Those who enjoy high rank are often expected to take the lead in emergencies, even though they may not have any special qualifications for handling them. The roles one is permitted to enact depend largely on one's status, be it privileged or underprivileged. A wealthy child who announces his desire to become a happy-go-lucky beachcomber is told that he must develop the self-discipline necessary to meet the requirements of his station in life. Thus, a person's status in a community is important, for his or her life chances depend on it. Our chances in marriage, what possessions we may acquire, the work we are likely to do, the places where we live, the people with whom we associate, the deference with which we are addressed, and the opportunities open to our children all depend on our station in the community. A person's status—landowner, government official, manual laborer, bootlegger, or slave—constitutes the basis of his or her ties to the rest of the community. Without it one is an outsider who has no particular claims on anyone else. In rapidly changing contexts some individuals are cast into ambiguous positions on the margins of two or more social worlds and may experience severe difficulties defining their relationships to others. Persons defined as criminal or insane are condemned to a special status and for all practical purposes are excluded from the community.

Inequality of some sort is apparently found everywhere. Human beings in all communities are distinguished from one another in terms of age, sex, and natural ability. Children, unless they happen to be aristocrats, are not as important as their elders and do not have the same prerogatives. In most communities women have been relegated to subordinate positions. Exceptionally talented or retarded persons are usually treated differently from others. In speaking of *social stratification*, however, we are concerned with the ranking of broad *categories* of people, not the ranking of individuals. Social stratification consists of a complex network of norms. There are common understandings as to how human beings are to be classified and how those in each category are to be treated. The various categories are ranked, and the members of each category are accorded similar rights and duties, regardless of age, sex, or other personal attributes. Other norms regulate the relationships between people in different categories. Thus, one's fate rests upon being placed in a category. Each level in a stratification system tends to become a subcommunity, a place in which the members are able to live out their entire lives. Furthermore, these patterns of differential treatment tend to persist from generation to generation (Mayer and Buckley, 1970:3–9). Although we each occupy several statuses—one in the community and one in each of the social worlds and groups in which we participate—our station in our community supersedes all others.

The popular concept of "one's place" refers to one's standing in the community. Those who hold the same rank conceive of themselves as located in comparable positions in some kind of hierarchy, and they are able to locate themselves in relation to people of higher or lower rank.

Popular beliefs develop about the characteristics of the members of each category. Except in small communities, where everyone knows about everyone else, these conceptions become stereotyped. Each category is defined in terms of certain traits, even though it is known that some individuals do not possess them. That ethnic categories are stereotyped is well known, but the characteristics slum dwellers assign to the wealthy are just as simplistic and rigid as those the rich assign to the poor. Thus, incumbents of each rank approach one another with well-defined expectations. What a person actually is, then, is less important that what people generally believe the members of each position to be. One's status includes an understanding of how one is evaluated by others. We develop self-concepts that place us in a category, and for most people living up to the duties that make up their stations in life becomes an important basis for self-respect.

Criteria for Ranking. Systems of social stratification vary in several ways, and one of them is the basis for classifying and ranking people. The criteria differ from one region to another. Although cross-cultural comparisons reveal how much these criteria vary, once a procedure is established, people come to regard the categories they use as representing natural divisions of humanity. Ethnic identity is one of the most common bases for ranking. Where a color line has been established, as in the various European colonies before World War II, the lowest-ranking European had certain rights denied the most esteemed native. Religion is another frequently used basis for ranking. In many Middle Eastern communities whether one is a Christian, a Jew, or a Moslem is the most important consideration. Social class is a third basis for ranking. A person's class position depends on how he or she contributes to the economic system; thus, in an industrial society we can distinguish among managerial personnel, manual workers, and farmers. In some communities various combinations of these criteria are used.

Even though diverse criteria are used to classify people, in most communities the different levels are readily discernible, for each category tends to develop a distinctive life-style. Members of each stratum tend to congregate in common areas of residence, to enter characteristic occupations, and to marry among themselves. Those in the most privileged rank are usually easy to locate. They occupy the most desirable land and have the greatest political power. They usually have higher incomes, more comfort, and more time for diversions. The privileged often cultivate skills for gracious living, observe traditions, and point with pride to their genealogies. They also enjoy the most prestige and conceive of themselves as superior to the others. Those on the bottom of the social scale are also easy to locate. They are denied access to various occupations and are usually segregated into the least desirable areas. In some communities those at the bottom are poverty-stricken and preoccupied with daily problems of survival. They are held in low esteem and often conceive of themselves as unimportant and undeserving. Their low status does not mean, however, that they have no rights; even those of low status have claims that are respected by people who outrank them. Where the differences between the top and bottom levels are noticeable, intermediate ranks generally develop between them. Those in the middle also develop characteristic life-styles. Among the orientations often found in the middle ranks is a tendency to admire and emulate those above and to keep a safe distance from those below. Hence, much concern develops over maintaining appearances.

Differences Between Ranks. The actual differences between categories vary considerably from one community to another and are likely to be most noticeable immediately after military conquest and subjugation. Thus, soon after the European colonization of various parts of Africa and Asia the contrasts between the colonists and the natives, both physical and cultural, were so great that both sides remained convinced that they constituted different species and that the chasm between them could never be crossed. As the natives who came into contact with the colonists became acculturated to European ways, however, the diversity became less and less apparent. Since people who communicate develop similar perspectives, the extent to which differences between ranks develop and persist depends on the patterns of differential contact and association that become customary. Where there are barriers to social interaction between incumbents of different ranks, those in each category develop their own communication channels and a distinct culture. In most instances the contacts between members of unequal rank tend to be categorical, while personal contacts are usually limited to people within each level.

Subtle differences arise that in turn reinforce the barriers. Even when persons of different ranks use the same language dialectal differences may develop. Although most Americans have little difficulty understanding one another, there are class differences in sophistication and refinement of speech (Schatzman and Strauss, 1955). Although class differences in England have been reduced since World War II, the linguistic differences there are more obvious; Cockney is the language of the working class. In village India, where the members of different castes are in daily contact, dialectal differences have been detected (Gumperz, 1958). Where such diversity develops, members of each rank develop somewhat different symbolic environments. Since everyone is ethnocentric, role-taking across ranks becomes more difficult.

The extent to which the members of each category identify with one another varies. If several categories are assigned low rank—as in communities with several ethnic minorities—the differences among them tend to be emphasized as each group takes care not to be identified too closely with others whom they despise. Those who enjoy high rank, especially if they are outnumbered, tend to develop considerable group solidarity. If the people in each category become culturally homogeneous, they tend to develop consciousness of kind. The perception of resemblances among themselves and differences from outsiders leads to a strong sense of mutual identification. As the members of each category are treated as if they were all alike, such differential treatment in itself reinforces their sense of being alike. Thus, people develop self-concepts in terms of the rank they occupy. They identify with a stratum and assume for themselves its rights and duties. Once we form such self-concepts, the category with which we identify usually becomes our most important reference group. We are most responsive to the expectations of those with whom we identify. Thus, each stratum becomes a social world.

In any stratified community strangers must be able to identify one another in terms of rank so that they can avoid awkwardness and approach each other with appropriate deference. Where the differences are obvious, this is easy. Members of each category are readily identified in terms of dress, language, manners, or physical appearance. These external marks serve as *status symbols,* readily visible indicators of rank. When long periods of contact reduce cultural differences, status symbols assume even greater importance. In his discussion of American society in the late nineteenth century, where social mobility was common and where people were often uncertain of where they stood, Veblen (1934) notes that possessions often became significant indicators of position. He coined the term "conspicuous consumption" to refer to purchasing something simply to show others that one can afford it. Acute sensitivity to skin color or religious rituals also arises when other differences between categories are not readily apparent.

Social Mobility. Systems of social stratification vary considerably in the extent to which they become institutionalized. When each category is clearly defined, the boundaries between the ranks become firmly established. Each person then knows just where he or she stands in relation to everyone else. The privileged try to retain their advantages for their children. Therefore, pressures arise to perpetuate the system of inequality and to make it hereditary. The cultural differences are transmitted to succeeding generations, and stratification systems can persist for centuries. But if communication takes place across boundaries, class, religious, and ethnic lines tend to become blurred. As the members of different categories become more and more alike culturally, the system tends to break down.

Social mobility refers to a person's moving from one rank to another, and communities differ in the extent to which such movement is possible. When a stratification system is institutionalized, social mobility is regulated. In some instances, as in the caste system in India, one can only be born into a position; in others one can achieve higher rank only through clearly defined sequences of training and achievement. Where ranking is based on ethnic identity, mobility is usually more difficult than where it depends on class or religion. In some cases a third ethnic group is located between the rulers and the ruled. For example, in many European colonies Chinese, Indians, and Arabs have occupied ranks between the colonists and the natives, making it almost impossible for talented and ambitious natives to move into privileged circles. Such intervening ethnic groups often become the object of intense hostility. But social mobility of any kind is difficult. The greater the cultural differences between ranks, the more difficult it becomes to cross the boundary. The language and customs of another level are difficult to acquire in a single lifetime, and even those who succeed feel awkward and out of place. In transition, their status is often not clearly defined, and this uncertainty frequently leads to anxiety in the upwardly mobile.

Since each person's life chances depend so much on rank, ambitious people strive to improve their status—for their progeny, if not for themselves. If social mobility through individual effort is possible, attempts at upward mobility usually consist largely of parallel striving, competition for the limited possibilities for advancement. If such individual mobility is extremely difficult or impossible, those who are dissatisfied are more likely to engage in a concerted effort to overthrow the stratification system. As Marx pointed out, only if people in a given class position identify with one another and become conscious of their common interests can they be mobilized for political action. After the Protestant Reformation, various religious groups in Europe contended for control over their respective governments, and in the twentieth century many ethnic minorities have pressed for the right to determine their own destiny in wars of national liberation.

PATTERNS OF SOCIAL INEQUALITY

Complex Stratification Systems. In small communities the system of ranking people is relatively simple. In many tribal communities everyone other than a few specialists, such as the chief and the shaman, occupies the same rank. In some systems people are ordered into a hierarchy of horizontal layers. Thus, in the South before the Civil War all Afro-Americans — even those who were free, had acquired some wealth, and were respected in their community — were ranked below the lowest white person. In actual practice this was not always the case. The word of a trusted slave was sometimes taken over that of a white person widely reputed to be unreliable. But the ideology was clear. Although the term "stratification" suggests that people are ordered into layers, in fact most ranking systems are far more complicated (Fallers, 1973; Berreman, 1981).

The oldest and certainly one of the most complex forms of social stratification is the caste system of India. Although different types of units are called "castes," there are four major categories (*varna*) that are recognized throughout the subcontinent. They are the Brahmans (priests), the Kshatriyas (warrior-rulers), the Vaisyas (merchants and farmers), and the Sudras (servants, peasants, and laborers). Membership in a *varna* enables people from distant parts of India to assess one another's local status. In each locality the *varna* are further divided into castes, sometimes called *jatis*. No one knows just how many *jatis* there are; in 1901, when the last attempt was made in the Indian census to count them, they numbered over 2,300. Some had only a few members; others had millions.

Although there are some exceptions, each caste has a traditional vocation — barber, potter, weaver — a calling that is regarded as its sacred duty. In many communities each caste is further divided into subcastes, endogamous units within each occupational unit; each subcaste is an extensive kinship group. At the bottom of the social scale — even below the Sudras — are the outcastes, the "untouchables." They are by tradition the sweepers, scavengers, tanners, and latrine cleaners. During the period of British rule Europeans were superimposed above the entire system.

Everyone belongs to a caste; membership is hereditary and for life. Since each caste is supposed to be strictly endogamous—that is, the members must marry among themselves—there is no possibility of altering one's inherited rank. Each caste has norms governing its relationship with other castes, rules concerning physical contact, dining together, and eating food prepared by outsiders. Any transaction that jeopardizes the hierarchy is taboo. Each local subcaste is like a brotherhood; each has a name by which the members identify themselves, and each has a distinctive way of life. Each local unit enforces its own regulations.

Since social mobility is impossible, the ambitious can improve their lot only by raising the standing of the entire caste. Brahmans periodically reevaluate the various units, and the prestige of a caste in any community is closely guarded. Emphasis is placed on purity—avoiding pollution by contacting those of a lower caste or by touching dirty objects, such as the dead or bodily emissions. The entire system is supported by custom and law and reinforced through religious ideology. Each person is believed to have all eternity to work out his or her salvation, and those who perform their duties satisfactorily in this life are assured a more favorable position upon reincarnation. Since India became independent in 1947, there have been numerous attempts to modify this rigid system. The new constitution gives political rights even to the lowly outcastes; their lot is improving, for their votes are now eagerly sought. With increasing industrialization and urbanization the caste system is gradually breaking down in metropolitan areas, where people are too busy to continue making such distinctions. In cities Hindus of all castes now eat in the same restaurants, go to the same movies, and rub shoulders on buses. But in the villages of rural India the old patterns persist (Ghurye, 1950; Mayer, 1960).

The estate system that developed in Europe after the breakdown of feudalism in the twelfth century is another stratification system in which people were not located in horizontal layers. Everyone belonged to one of three estates, and each estate had a considerable range of ranks. The first estate consisted of clergymen, all members of the Catholic church. They ranged in status from poor parish priests to archbishops. Although they varied considerably in power and prestige, all clergymen enjoyed certain rights and had certain responsibilities, such as administering the sacraments. The second estate consisted of the nobility—public officials, military commanders, and judges. They also had varying amounts of wealth and power, but they were all addressed with some measure of deference. They developed consciousness of kind and had special claims on one another. Thus, noblemen waging war against one another sometimes suspended their fighting to go to the aid of a fellow aristocrat threatened by a peasant revolt. They were horrified at the thought of a woman of noble birth in the clutch of rabble. Imprisoned aristocrats were addressed with respect by their jailers, who in turn were answerable to their own rulers. The third estate included everyone else: the common people, the bourgeoisie — the merchants, professionals, and entrepreneurs — craftsmen, peasants, and laborers. Some financiers (third estate) were far more wealthy than magistrates (second estate) in small communities, but this did not alter their position relative to the crown or to the clergy.

Modern Lebanon, a nation carved out of five provinces of the Ottoman Empire after World War I, exemplifies just how complicated classifying and ranking systems can become. The population is approximately half Christian and half Moslem, with each side further subdivided into several well-established denominations. The Christians include Maronites, Greek Orthodox, Greek Catholics, and Armenians; the two large denominations of Moslems are the Sunni and the Shiite. Other groups include the Druze, the Jews, and, since the founding of the state of Israel, an estimated quarter million Palestinians. In Lebanon religion is not a voluntary matter, as it is in Europe and the United States. Atheists are placed in the category of their parents. Since religious conversions and intermarriage are rare, membership in a religious group is for all practical purposes hereditary.

Before Lebanon became independent in 1945, leaders of the various groups agreed that public offices would be distributed among the major denominations in proportion to their numbers in the 1932 census. The president was to be a Maronite Christian; the prime minister, a Sunni Moslem; the speaker of the parliament, a Shiite Moslem. Positions in the parliament, government offices, the military, and public schools were allocated to the various denominations at a ratio of six Christians to every five Moslems. Although some villages and urban neighborhoods have mixed populations, most of the populace is segregated into areas traditionally occupied by members of their group. In Beirut the two most heterogeneous areas are at the extremes of the economic ladder; the very poor — other than Christians — are congregated in a slum area, and the very wealthy of all denominations live in the most modernized part of the city. There are no formal norms restricting occupations to any religious group. In fact, however, most plumbers, photographers, jewelers, musicians, and tentmakers are Armenians; hotels, tourism, banking, and import-export enterprises are largely owned and staffed by Christians; and Moslems are concentrated in agriculture, meat and produce marketing, and light industry (Starr, 1978). Among the several issues involved in the civil war that broke out in 1975 was the demand by discontented Moslems for changes that would improve their lot.

Class Stratification. Much of the literature on social stratification centers on the study of class, without doubt one of the most common and important forms of ranking. The interest stems largely from the writings of Marx, and even those who disagree with him have worked within his conceptual scheme. Marx contends that class position is where one is situated in the organization of production; thus, a *social class* consists of persons who share a common situation in the economy.

In his analysis of nineteenth-century Europe Marx distinguished three main classes: landowners who receive rent, capitalists who receive profits, and workers who receive wages. What people do to earn a livelihood provides certain characteristic experiences, which sooner or later influence their beliefs. Thus, industrial workers are not only preoccupied with better wages and protection against unemployment but also may become alienated from work that becomes a meaningless routine in which they contribute so little to the collective product. Similarly, entrepreneurs become so concerned with profits, corporate mergers, and stockholders' demands that they have no comprehension of what the workers want. If people with such similar interests share their experiences through communication, they are likely to develop a common outlook and mutual identification. Class consciousness is even more likely to develop if those occupying the same class become involved in conflict with another class.

Although Marx was describing European society during the early phases of industrialization, class stratification is found elsewhere as well. In ancient China, the economy was largely agricultural, and the vast majority of the people were peasants. Although some acquired enough wealth to hire help, many were barely able to eke out an existence. Above them was the gentry, a small leisure class that lived on rent collected from peasants. The gentry controlled local governments. Since literacy was a prerequisite for official positions, most officials were drawn from the gentry, and they protected the rights of their class to continue collecting rent (Fei, 1946). In ancient Rome the highest rank was held by the patricians, most of them landowners; below them were the equestrians, whose income came from constructing public works, collecting taxes, and lending money; next in rank were the plebeians, the common people; on the bottom of the scale were the slaves, drawn from peoples conquered by the Roman legions.

Most Americans have difficulty grasping what is involved in class stratification, for we live in a society with relatively little class consciousness. However, novels and motion pictures provide some familiarity with the relatively stable class system in Victorian England. Although the system has changed considerably since the end of World War II, even today English class lines are more readily discernible than those in the United States. The privileged classes — the titled aristocracy, the *rentiers,* and others of great wealth — developed a distinctive life-style. They lived on country estates, acquired titles, cultivated a refined style of speech, and developed a complex set of customs enjoyed in closed circles in London's West End or in the elegance of the French Riviera. The boys attended "public schools" like Eton or Harrow and matriculated to Oxford or Cambridge, where they studied the classics, rather than more modern subjects, and where great emphasis was placed on proper "breeding." Although not all these university students had been born into privileged families, the aristocratic way of life was one that could not easily be cultivated in a short time. At the bottom of the scale were the working classes, those engaged in manual labor or routine unskilled work. They are often depicted in stereotyped form, with their Cockney accent, informal modes of dress, and coarse manners. Between these strata came the middle classes — the public servants, the managers, the professionals, the independent farmers, the shopkeepers, and the traders. These people also developed a characteristic life-style, which stressed respectability and directed a large proportion of their limited income to their children's education and domestic help. The English people at that time were class-conscious; most of them recognized and acknowledged superiority and inferiority, associated largely with others of their station in life, and took pride in knowing their place and conforming to the expectations of their peers as well as those above and below (Lewis and Maude, 1949).

Since American society has been shaped largely by immigrants from Europe, remnants of the European class system are still discernible. The patterns have undergone considerable modification, however, not only because of changes in the economic base but also because of the media of mass communication. There are vast differences in wealth, income, and political power and considerable diversity in life-styles. The wealthy and the privileged have developed a culture resembling that of the European aristocracy with its emphasis on breeding, genealogies, heirlooms, and philanthropic public service (Warner and Lunt, 1941; Baltzell, 1962). Most Americans, when questioned, describe themselves as middle class. But those who are better off tend to view the aristocratic way as their ideal and seek that way of life for their children, if not for themselves. They stress respectability and value education and achievement through individual effort. Students of the labor movement note that unionization has been difficult; some suggest that the ethnic heterogeneity arising from successive waves of immigration has impeded the formation of class consciousness and worker solidarity (Perlman, 1928). Countless studies of class differences in the United States disclose a number of general tendencies: Those with higher incomes are more likely to have stable marriages, to have fewer children, to send their offspring to college, to be more conservative politically, to vote regularly, and to read a newspaper daily and are less likely to be victims of robberies. But Americans are not ranked into classes with clearly defined boundaries.

Ethnic Stratification. Another common form of ranking human beings is ethnic stratification, in which one's status in a community depends on "race." The color line is a stratification system in which the primary criterion of rank is common ancestry, real or fictitious. One of the clearest instances of a color line has developed in the Republic of South Africa, where the population is divided into categories defined exclusively in biological terms. The highest rank is held by the so-called Europeans — descendents of Dutch settlers of three centuries ago and of the more recent English colonists. Persons of African ancestry are called "Natives," whether they be Basuto, Bechuana, Zulu, Xhosa, or of many other ethnic groups. Most of the Asians are from India, although some Chinese and Malayans still remain. The Coloured consist of people of acknowledged mixed ancestry, mostly offspring of European and Native unions.

Even before the Nationalist party came into power in 1948, a rigid pattern of segregation had been instituted. Most of the Natives lived in reserves, areas set aside for them to continue their tribal life. The rest tried to improve their lot by working for Europeans. A large number were farm laborers; others lived in compounds operated by gold and diamond companies. Some lived in *locations,* segregated areas in cities, or were confined to servants' quarters in the rear of European homes. They were not free to come and go as they pleased but were required to carry passes; anyone caught without a pass was subject to prosecution as a vagrant. Natives were limited to the most menial occupations and were not permitted to vote. Coloureds held a somewhat more favorable position; they could own property. In Cape Province, if they were able to meet certain qualifications, they were allowed to exercise the right of franchise. The rules concerning residence were not so rigid for them, and they could aspire to more respectable occupations. While the property rights of

Asians were restricted, they also enjoyed a more favorable position than the Natives.

In 1948 *apartheid* became the official policy; this represented an effort to define ethnic differences more clearly and to establish institutions to preserve the "racial purity" and way of life of the Afrikaners (persons of Dutch ancestry). The policy not only reinforced previous governments' restrictions but called for even more segregation and ultimately the separate development of each ethnic group. Asians and Coloureds were deprived of some of the advantages they once had, and there was a tightening of registration and pass laws. Since membership in ethnic categories is hereditary, under these laws there is no possibility of altering one's status (Dvorin, 1952). Considerable resistance has developed among some of the minorities, but this has only made most Afrikaners more rigid and determined. One reason for their intransigence is their absolute conviction that the members of each category constitute different species.

An ethnic group consists of people who conceive of themselves as being alike by virtue of common ancestry and are so regarded by others. In most cases the common ancestry is fictitious. Nonetheless, ethnic stratification is a common form of ranking; such distinctions have been made throughout history and in most parts of the world. The ancient Greeks referred to all other groups as "barbarians" and did not hesitate to subjugate them as slaves. In Burundi the population is divided into three categories. The Bahutu are of medium height and much like other Bantu-speaking people in central Africa; most of them are farmers. The Watusi, who are primarily herders, were at one time believed to be a superior "race"; they enjoyed a position of privilege until an uprising in 1959. At the bottom of the social scale are the Twa Pygmies, who are primarily potters and hunters—a pariah group. Members of all three categories speak the same Bantu language. Although some intermixing has been going on for centuries, certain genetic differences are still evident, for the most conspicuous criterion for classification is height. The average Watusi stands about sixty-nine inches; the Bahutu, about sixty-five inches; the Pygmies, about sixty-one inches (Albert, 1960).

Since ethnic groups are often segregated, usually by choice, those who identify in this manner partake in common communication channels and thereby develop distinctive cultures. Hence, the characteristics that make up the stereotyped conception of each group—such as cleanliness, aggressiveness, reliability, walking gait, sense of rhythm, food preferences—are all cultural traits. Even though ethnic identity rests on inaccurate premises, its importance should not be underestimated. People act in terms of their definitions. If they develop consciousness of kind, loyalty to one's "race" may supersede all other bases of classification in uniting people for some common endeavor.

To the extent that the members of each ethnic group share a common culture they are in fact different from nonmembers, and such differences enter into encounters involving outsiders. When participating in common transactions, therefore, members must be able to identify others by their appropriate categories. Since people who share such cultural traits are erroneously believed to have inherited them, ethnic groups are often distinguished in terms of characteristics that are in fact inherited — such as skin color, hair texture, and facial features. Where such features are not sufficiently distinctive — as in the case of Jews — family name, language, and religion may also be used. By custom names are usually inherited, and some mistakenly think that children inherit a natural proclivity to speak the language of their parents. This misconception, however, is absurd; the child of a French missionary brought up in China could certainly grow up with a fluent command of Chinese. Even though such beliefs have all been demonstrated to be false, inherited features continue to serve as status symbols, readily visible indicators of how people are to be classified.

Once classified in terms of such physical uniforms, people in each category are addressed as if they had certain traits. To the extent that ethnic groups develop distinctive cultures, such marks become accurate indicators of what outsiders can expect in dealing with them. Once acculturation begins, however, these status symbols become less reliable. Confusion about this matter frequently impedes social change. Although cultural traits can generally be attained in a single generation, hereditary marks cannot be changed so easily. Thus, where differences between ethnic groups are believed to be inherited, social mobility becomes very difficult.

Status in Mass Societies. Although one can readily distinguish between those at the top and those on the bottom, the ranking of people in modern mass societies is becoming more difficult. Production is increasingly carried out in huge corporate units. Hence, the wealthy and privileged, once consisting largely of landed aristocrats, now includes corporation executives, specialists in some professions, and large shareholders. As Mills (1951) shows, the old middle classes — independent farmers, businessmen, and professionals — are being displaced by new categories — managers, technicians, salaried professionals, sales personnel, office workers — all employees of corporations. Readily accessible education and the media of mass communication are making information about various life-styles available to anyone who cares to pay attention. Thus, as the cultural differences among various categories are reduced, lines of demarcation between ranks that were once clearly drawn are becoming more and more difficult to locate. Furthermore, with increasing urbanization people are spending more time with strangers. In large cities many transactions are carried out by participants who are unaware of one another's rank. Although some urban dwellers appear affluent and others appear poverty-stricken, in most urban transactions citizens-at-large share the same rank. Thus, for most people in mass societies status in the community matters only where one is known and recognized.

In American society today status is measured in terms of several criteria, remnants of different stratification systems — occupation, income, education, ethnic identity, and sex. Furthermore, the standard that is emphasized differs from one reference group to another. Such diversity of criteria leads to all kinds of inconsistencies (Lenski, 1954, 1956). It is commonly believed, for example, that members of ethnic minorities are less educated, do menial work, and therefore have less income. Yet Afro-American technicians and Chinese scientists are becoming as commonplace as Caucasian laborers. It is not unusual to see a mixed military unit commanded by an Afro-American sergeant. Gardeners may have much higher incomes than bank employees, and college graduates are often fortunate to find work as stock clerks or supermarket checkers.

Sometimes embarrassing dilemmas arise. Hughes (1958:102–15) describes the difficulties that confronted a woman engineer in the 1950s. By custom a plane's designer was expected to go up on its maiden flight and then give a stag party for the engineers and workers who built it. Although her co-workers urged her to forgo this practice, she insisted on going ahead. She took her flight and paid for the dinner — as an engineer. After one round of toasts she left the party — as a lady. (Such circumspection may not be seen as necessary today.) When such inconsistencies occur, confusion arises, for the reciprocal claims and obligations are not clear. The people who attain status not expected of them may develop new self-concepts, but others do not always recognize their claims. Perhaps because ranking is so ambiguous, Americans often suffer from status anxieties, not knowing just where they stand in relation to their neighbors and to others with whom they come into contact. Perhaps this anxiety accounts for our concern with status symbols and our susceptibility to fashion movements.

Although communist nations have been established with the avowed objective of abolishing inequalities, this has not yet been accomplished.

They have eliminated the extremes of wealth and poverty, but considerable differences have developed between the income and privileges of high echelon executives, scientists, and technicians and those of workers performing routine tasks. Increasing industrialization has reduced differences between capitalist and socialist economies; those who enact key roles in production and have heavy responsibilities are rewarded, and the advantages they enjoy tend to be passed on to their children. Conditions in the Soviet Union and in Eastern Europe since World War II demonstrate that a privileged class can emerge and perpetuate itself even after the abolition of immense personal wealth (Lane, 1971; Connor, 1979).

REAFFIRMATION OF STATUS DIFFERENCES

The Persistence of Inequalities. Systems of social stratification, once they become institutionalized, tend to persist in spite of the tensions that arise from countless inequities and frustrations on the part of the underprivileged. Those historical contexts in which stratification systems have been perpetuated for long periods disclose some of the conditions under which patterns of inequality can persist. In well-established systems all inhabitants can locate themselves in terms of their status in the community, and most of them try to fulfill the obligations of their position. Those who know their place understand their rights and duties and try to live up to them. It is not only the underprivileged who meet their obligations; everyone in the system, from the apex to the bottom, assumes the responsibilities of his or her category.

Stratification systems of all kinds rest on stereotyped beliefs about the various categories of people who occupy the different strata. As members of each category develop a distinctive culture, outsiders pick out some conspicuous traits, exaggerate them, and construct a shorthand depiction of them. Thus, Brahmans have long believed that the lower castes are made up of innately inferior people who not only pass on their tainted heredity but can contaminate those of purer breed by contact. They have inherited irremovable forms of ugliness, uncleanliness, disease, intellectual inferiority, or moral depravity. Nazis had similar beliefs about Jews. For a long time the low status of Afro-Americans was based on the ridiculous belief that they were ignorant, irresponsible, superstitious, lazy, happy-go-lucky, ostentatious, and musical; they were also believed to have a special liking for chicken and watermelon (Klineberg, 1944). Many feudal lords regarded their peasants as pack animals who were inherently incapable of refinement.

Those who occupy low statuses also have stereotyped conceptions of the people above, although the characterizations are not so negative. Even though people in direct contact often realize that the individuals with whom they associate do not have such traits, these inaccurate characterizations persist through selective perception. For example, if an Afro-American entertainer happens to have an exceptionally good sense of rhythm, his performance confirms the belief; the ineptness of clumsy Afro-Americans passes unnoticed. Such beliefs are also reinforced by intentional conformity. Sometimes people in lower ranks deliberately imitate the model of what is expected of them; some Afro-Americans have used contrived humility, portraying the antics of an "Uncle Tom" to get what they want. Similarly, some manual laborers refuse to assume responsibilities for tasks that they could perform easily; by acting as if they are incapable of making decisions, they avoid unwanted burdens. Although such stratagems enable them to avoid irksome situations, they also reaffirm beliefs that manual laborers cannot be counted on to do responsible work. Thus, whether or not there are real physical or cultural differences between categories is not as important as what people *believe* about one another. Any noticeable difference tends to confirm the alleged existence of many other differences.

The Responsibilities of Status. As one examines the perspectives of those who have enjoyed high rank for several generations — Brahmans, feudal lords in medieval Europe, plantation owners of the antebellum South, European clergymen — one finds remarkably similar orientations. On the whole, they conceive of themselves as decent human beings who by virtue of their superior intelligence and refinement are fit to rule. They often stress breeding, as if they have inherited rather than learned their treasured attributes. The elite are conscious of their rights, privileges, and immunities; since they regard them as natural, they react sharply if these are questioned. Contrary to popular belief, the most common orientation of such privileged people toward those of lower ranks is not hatred but condescension. Fear and hatred develop only in situations in which their status is being challenged. They view those of lower status as inferior human beings, much like children, and explain their conduct in terms of widely accepted stereotypes, often using a somewhat different vocabulary of motives than they apply to their own kind. The privileged often believe that if such people are provided with basic needs and given facilities for some amusement, they will be happy, keep out of mischief, and somehow manage to get along.

Those who enjoy high rank often develop a code of honor. Personal integrity is taken for granted, and any questioning of their honesty is regarded as a serious affront. They are also conscious of the obligations of their position. They regard it as their duty to keep the community going, to make key decisions, and to rule for the benefit of everyone living there. They teach their children the proper way to approach those of lower status, often emphasizing the concept of *noblesse oblige,* the obligation to be kind to those less fortunate than themselves. Those of high rank frequently assume responsibility for looking after the welfare of their subordinates. Just as wealthy Americans once distributed bread baskets for the poor, many plantation owners took a personal interest in their slaves and looked after their families. Acts of kindness are not uncommon. The English ruling classes have at times been extraordinarily willing and eager to ameliorate the lot of the masses, both at home and in their colonies. For many, philanthropy was a sacred duty, a trusteeship that attended their wealth. As with other norms, of course, deviations do occur. There are individuals who are callous toward others, but they tend to be the exceptions. Those who abuse their privileges and exploit their advantages, as was the case with some plantation overseers and slave traders, are looked down upon and condemned. Acts regarded as especially vicious or unfair may even be punished. Although such paternalism is often resented as patronizing by people who are upwardly mobile, since it presupposes the inferiority of the beneficiary, it is accepted by those who acknowledge their position.

Most people occupying the lower ranks of well-established stratification systems — be they serfs, slaves, members of the working class, a religious or ethnic minority, or of a lower caste — accept their station in life and do their best to meet their obligations. They acknowledge the manner in which their category is defined in the community and conceive of themselves in these terms. They realize that many of the characteristics attributed to them are inaccurate, but they accept the evaluation. That persons of low status form unfavorable self-concepts and develop a deep sense of inferiority is well documented. Rath and Sircar (1960) describe the unfavorable stereotypes that low-caste Hindus form of themselves; Banks and Grambs (1972) describe similar self-concepts among Afro-Americans.

People in subordinate positions tend to overestimate those above them, often regarding members of the elite as basically different kinds of people — more refined, more intelligent, and more capable than is actually the case. Hence, the elite deserve their privileges. Since low-status persons do not believe they themselves deserve such privileges, they do not feel badly about not having them. Those who know their place live up to the duties they have incurred by virtue of their classification; they accept their fate and make the best of it. They also develop no aspirations beyond those conventionally allowed for people like themselves. When people become reconciled to their low status and accept it as inevitable, they submit patiently and make it a sacred obligation to live up to the expectations of the community. Once people accept a station, they can develop self-respect by being competent in their category. They can take pride in doing their work well — being a trusted servant, working their way to supervisor of a labor gang, or becoming a master artisan who does fine leather work. Peasants take great pride in their ability to extract maximum yield even under adverse weather conditions. Since they conceive of themselves as unimportant, they can live with inequities that outside observers would regard as outrageous.

Where systems of social stratification are stable, children of all ranks are socialized to live up to the obligations of their station in life. They are not instructed with malice, but in the spirit of teaching them correct manners to be used in dealing with various categories of people. Just as wealthy children are taught not to act snobbishly, poor children are taught to address others respectfully. Most of all, children are taught to identify themselves with their own category, to appreciate what they contribute to the community, and to take pride in doing their own part well. Children born into lower ranks are warned of the differential treatment they must expect. They are also warned about overstepping the bounds, that they may be permitted to play with more privileged children when they are young but that they must expect to revert to lower status when they grow up. They are taught the limitations of their station and are encouraged not to aspire for the impossible. If the son of a poor peasant announces that he wishes to become a physician, others discourage him, at first good-naturedly and later with scorn and ridicule. Many studies of ethnic minorities, even in communities in which social mobility is possible, show that the aspirations of the children tend to be modest and realistic (Goodman and Beman, 1968). Thus, children of all ranks learn that there are different kinds of human beings and that some of them are entitled to a different fate — because of what they are alleged to be (Della Fave, 1980).

That people in lower ranks accept the community's estimate of them is revealed in their ambivalence toward the few unusual individuals who are upwardly mobile. A person of exceptional ability who is granted some special privileges is viewed with both pride and hatred. A prominent member of an ethnic minority whom outsiders honor as a "credit to his race" is often hated within the group as someone who "thinks he is too good for us." The pride arises from the demonstration that someone within the lowly category has actually excelled—a living example of what can be done. But jealousy arises toward a person who dared to do the unexpected and succeeded. Where members of different strata speak somewhat different languages, mastery of the tongue of a higher rank often leads to condemnation; it is often viewed as snobbery. Similarly, members of ethnic minorities or of lower classes who aspire to marry upward are condemned. Many define intermarriage as unnatural, claiming that it involves mixing different species. Within pariah groups many rumors develop of the frightful experiences of those who intermarried. Among the Eta in Japan, who are physically indistinguishable from other Japanese, there are many tales of the misfortunes of those who tried to "pass" and were exposed (DeVos and Wagatsuma, 1966). Some of the opposition to upward mobility comes from fear. Members of despised categories are afraid that a serious violation of community norms by one person can lead to reprisals against all of them.

The Management of Tensions.   Where access to desired objects is unequal, frustrations are inevitable, especially among those who receive the smaller portions. Resentments arise but are often suppressed or channeled in ways that do not challenge the existing social order—festivals and dances, massive sports programs, parades and circuses. Considerable tension is drained in all low-status categories by the telling of jokes. Tales of the skillful exploitation of the foibles of the privileged spread quickly, as do countless anecdotes about how someone has taken advantage of an outsider's stereotyped conception. For a long time the best jokes among Afro-Americans were those in which Jim Crow practices had backfired on a Southerner (Powdermaker, 1943). Art also provides numerous opportunities for the symbolic expression of indignation. The decorative arts of the various ethnic groups subjugated by European colonists disclose their conception of the white man; the figures often appear ridiculous with their cigars, hats, and firearms. The conquerors are often reproduced in obvious mockery (Lips, 1937). The *kalela* dance was long a popular pastime in the Copperbelt in Zambia (formerly Northern Rhodesia). The central figure was the "governor," who stood in the middle of the courtyard in resplendent attire, decorated with medals; the other dancers circled slowly around him, led by a drummer—in military formation, officers and enlisted men each with badges of rank. These dances appear to be a pantomime of Europeans (Mitchell, 1956).

In Timbuctoo, where different ethnic groups had long been segregated into separate quarters, opportunities for expressing hostility were afforded by the *alkura,* a game resembling hockey, between teams from different quarters. During the rough-and-tumble of the contest a slave could strike a nobleman with impunity; it was understood that blows received in the game were to be taken without ill will (Miner, 1953:240–42). Esoteric cults of all kinds also provide opportunities for discharging tensions. In England in the early nineteenth century, when industrialization produced considerable discontent among urban workers, evangelical religions, especially Methodism, provided outlets for catharsis. A hypothesis has been proposed that such practices constitute a form of expressive symbolism; the ritual enables the underprivileged to act out in dramatic form hostilities that are deeply felt but cannot be asserted directly. By providing outlets for aggressions, these activities divert energy away from protests; by relieving tensions, they reinforce the existing social order (Gluckman, 1963).

Even in the most underprivileged categories exceptional individuals emerge who quickly learn the ways of their rulers. Unless avenues are provided for them to gain some kind of self-respect, they may turn out to be dangerous. Should they have the qualities of "natural leaders," they could become bitter rebels who mobilize their fellows for insurrections. In many communities special arrangements are made for accommodating such individuals; they are granted special privileges that are denied to others. Many conquerors have found it easier to rule their subjects indirectly through traditional chieftains. Parts of India and Malaya were ruled by the British through native princes, and immediately after World War II there were still over three hundred sultans and regents in the Dutch East Indies. *Co-optation* is the procedure whereby the more competent members of low status are elevated to a higher rank. As such persons are accepted and given the responsibilities that accompany higher positions, they often develop strong allegiances to their new associates. Co-optation has recently been condemned by those advocating rebellions, for it deprives the lower ranks of leaders and reinforces the rulers with additional talent. Others view the practice merely as a way of rewarding outstanding ability — not as a deliberate political stratagem. In either case such limited and closely regulated upward mobility of exceptional persons tends to perpetuate the existing system.

If noticeable discontent develops in the lower ranks, demands to eliminate or minimize costly inequities usually come from members of more privileged strata, especially from intellectuals. Although some officials may favor repression, others argue for piecemeal reforms. Well-established stratification systems are not likely to encounter serious challenges, for those in the lower ranks fully appreciate the disparity of political power. The outraged few who are foolhardy enough to rebel have difficulty recruiting others to join them. Those who have attempted uprisings — such as Nat Turner, John Chilembwe, and Che Guevara — have encountered opposition among the very people whose lot they were trying to improve. Insurrections that lack popular support are crushed ruthlessly, and the leaders are often subjected to exemplary punishment. Public executions are symbolic acts, a message that tampering with the stratification system will not be tolerated.

PRESERVATION OF SOCIAL DISTANCE

One condition for the persistence of systems of social stratification is the preservation of social distance between members of different ranks. As long as social contacts between people of different strata remain categorical, they know one another largely in terms of their respective abilities to enact conventional roles. When social distance is reduced, however, they get to know too much about one another's individual idiosyncrasies. Human beings are at bottom very much alike. As they come to appreciate one another's inner experiences, they begin to identify with one another as human beings. Once another person is defined as being much like oneself, each realizes how inaccurate the stereotyped beliefs are. Members of different categories who get to know each other on a personal basis at first regard their friend as an exception; as they meet others through their friend, however, they begin to appreciate more fully how erroneous and ridiculous the stereotypes are. They develop serious misgivings and questions about what they previously took for granted; then they have increasing difficulty enforcing the invidious distinctions that are customary. Thus, as long as social distance is maintained, stratification systems are perpetuated in spite of close and frequent contacts between members of different ranks.

Etiquette and Social Distance. Numerous transactions in which persons of different ranks are brought together in sustained association occur in any community. One way in which such people maintain social distance is through etiquette, the formalization of interpersonal contacts. Etiquette prevents people from learning too much about one another's personal characteristics. Those who are polite do not disclose their individuality; they say and do the correct things, and one does not know whether they are pleased or are merely complying with customs. After spending an evening with a polite stranger at a formal dinner party, one comes away knowing only that he or she is pleasant and well mannered. It is possible for people to work together amicably for years and still not get to know one another as human beings. There is no ill will. They may even get to like one another; but they never relax their personal reserve. Servants of long standing often get to know their employers quite well, but all parties maintain considerable pretense to keep their respective places. Many employers who were genuinely fond of their servants have been astonished to discover later how much the servants disliked them. Thus, in stratified communities in which an etiquette develops, people of different ranks meet one another in an unambiguous, consistent, and hierarchical manner. Whatever they do together, they do it correctly. This enables them to maintain differences in spite of their daily contacts.

One of the most elaborate etiquettes governing contacts between strata developed in the American South during slavery, and remnants of these practices persist to this day. Masters were in daily contact with some of their slaves, but social distance was maintained through a complex set of rituals. Black people, even those who were free, were required to remove their hats when addressing those who were white. When a sidewalk was narrow, they were expected to get off to allow the others to pass. Bowing and scraping was expected; black people never entered a house through the front door; they could not eat with their masters at the same table. Black people were expected to address white people respectfully as "sah," "boss," or "mistah." In turn they were addressed as "you," "boy," "mammy," or "uncle." Those who were known personally were addressed by their first names; titles such as "mister" or "miss" with the surname were never used. Many Southerners were relieved when Booker T. Washington was awarded an LL.D., for it had become embarrassing to address a person of his stature as "Booker."

Although outside observers sometimes regarded these practices as degrading, most of the participants viewed them simply as a matter of having good manners. Doyle (1937) notes that a visiting Yankee who addressed a black man as "mister" was not necessarily regarded as a fine person who refused to discriminate. The slaves were embarrassed, for they did not know how to respond. They sometimes ridiculed such outsiders as ignorant and uncouth. These practices were not based on the belief that black people were dirty or repulsive. Many white children were reared by black nurses, with whom they were in close physical contact. The rituals were symbolic; they were indicators of status differences. Many features of this etiquette persisted into the 1960s, when the civil rights movement made a concerted effort to eliminate them.

Sometimes forbidden contacts occur inadvertently, in spite of the efforts of all parties to maintain appropriate distance. If so, the person of higher status often feels polluted. In the caste system in rural India, for example, pollution may occur in several ways. One may accidentally touch the corpse at a funeral or touch menstrual blood. One may eat food prepared by members of the wrong caste or unknowingly sit on a chair that had been used by an outcaste. In an emergency one may have to use a latrine reserved for another caste. After a passionate sexual encounter one may discover that the partner is of a lowly caste. Upon realizing the offense, the polluted person experiences the disgust aroused by having touched something dirty. In many stratification systems purification rituals have developed for the nullification of pollution. Until offenders have finished the appropriate rites, they are expected to stay away from other members of their own caste. If the pollution occurred in an unusual way, a caste council may determine the type of purification required. Those who persist in forbidden contacts may be excommunicated from the caste. Purification rituals are a form of expressive symbolism, a means of neutralizing the revulsion occasioned by defilement (DeVos, 1967). They reinforce beliefs in differences among castes and the prohibition of certain forms of closeness. They also reaffirm the self-concepts of persons of high status.

Patterns of Differential Association. When stratification systems are well established, the division of labor in the economy tends to coincide with status differences. Although incumbents of various ranks may work together in common transactions, they perform different tasks. Those belonging to privileged strata are often prohibited from doing menial work, and members of lower ranks are expected to do work that is in keeping with their station. The distinctions found in stratified communities are exemplified by the relationship between officers and enlisted personnel in military organizations. They work together toward common goals, but they rarely forget that they hold different ranks. A lieutenant may be very popular with his men, and an easy camaraderie may develop, but neither side relaxes completely. Officers may joke about other matters with their men, but most of them consider it beneath their dignity to air their personal problems, as they might with another officer. Just as enlisted personnel do not squeal on each other for minor rule infractions, workers of lower rank keep their differences to themselves. Thus, even when members of different categories work together, they see one another primarily as role-players rather than as human beings.

Furthermore, job ceilings are maintained in many stratified communities, and workers of lower ranks are not likely to be advanced beyond a certain point. The limitations long imposed on Afro-Americans are notorious (Johnson, 1943). Natives of European colonies who became acculturated to European ways, some even graduating from European universities, were hired only at the lower echelons of government or business bureaucracies. Although they were granted privileges not extended to other natives, they were seldom advanced to senior executive positions. Even in England, where neither conventional nor formal norms prohibited it, for brilliant persons from a working-class background to move into executive positions was extremely difficult. They had to learn a new dialect and a different set of manners and to familiarize themselves with a life-style that could not be acquired in a few years. When Dalton (1959:148–93) checked the background of executives in four firms in the American midwest that claimed to promote personnel on the basis of ability alone, he found a disproportionately large number of top-level officials who were Masons, Republicans, members of a yacht club, and of northern European descent. These findings suggest that talent alone may not have been enough. Such job ceilings tend to perpetuate stratification by limiting income. Except for the few who are unusually frugal or lucky, incumbents of lower ranks seldom earn enough to afford more esteemed life-styles.

Various forms of segregation also minimize the chances of lowering social distance. Social contacts in financial transactions tend to be impersonal and occur within clearly defined institutional contexts. The joking and conviviality are often superficial. Even when the people involved genuinely like one another, they do not relax their personal reserve. Much of the goodwill displayed masks all kinds of doubts and suspicions. Residential segregation plays an important part in perpetuating differences. Even when members of various categories work together, each night they go home to different quarters. Working together does not mean that recreational activities are also shared. In her study of a New England town before World War II, Anderson (1938) notes that men who greeted one another in such a jovial manner during the day exchanged only nods or weak smiles when they happened to meet in a theater lobby in the evening in the company of their wives. Unpleasantness was avoided; everyone was polite; but the distinctions were preserved. Furthermore, membership in voluntary associations, such as social clubs in which people "let their hair down," is generally limited by rank. People at each level have their own clubs, and outsiders may enter only as servants or as honored guests. Simmel (1950:40–57) points out that pure sociability occurs only when participants can approach one another as equals. Thus, members of each category are able to participate in easy, secure, personal contacts only with one another. Only the ambitious who are upwardly mobile object to such arrangements; others feel more comfortable among people with whom they share a common culture and whom they know as individuals. They feel at home only when they are among their own kind; such segregation, however, inadvertently reinforces social distance.

Limitations placed on educational opportunities also prevent members of lower ranks from attaining competitive advantages. In much of Europe before World War II it was extremely difficult for children from working-class families to obtain a college education. Most of them simply could not afford it. In England even middle-class boys were seldom accepted at preparatory schools such as Eton and Harrow, where they could acquire the language, manners, and tastes expected of gentlemen. A small number with exceptional ability were awarded scholarships or were sponsored by some wealthy patron. Once they were transformed into gentlemen, most of them joined the elite, for they had become culturally different from the people among whom they had spent their childhood. In European colonies missionaries provided educational opportunities for natives who showed unusual aptitude, but most could not acquire the technical skills necessary to compete for desirable jobs. This situation has been changing. Most industrial nations now have public school systems, and the media of mass communication provide avenues for learning about the life-styles of the privileged. Nonetheless, opportunities for children from low-income homes still remain limited.

Virtually all stratified communities regulate mate selection. All castes are endogamous, and, where there is ethnic stratification, intermarriage is usually regarded as unnatural. Since ethnic traits are believed to be inherited, people in all ranks feel uneasy about "mongrelization"—the contamination of their lineage. The thought of having grandchildren with "defects" is horrifying, and even members of lower ranks oppose miscegenation. Even in communities stratified by class young people are encouraged to marry within their station. Although Americans have the legal right to marry just about anyone they please, many special arrangements are made to minimize the chances of involvement between inappropriate partners. Scott (1965) shows how active participation in college sororities before the 1960s tended to narrow the range of mate selection; sorority activities were arranged to maximize members' chances of meeting the right kind of people. Sometimes laws are passed prohibiting intermarriage; the Nuremberg laws of Nazi Germany provide an extreme example. Actually, such laws are unnecessary when a stratification system is well established, for young people of different ranks seldom have opportunities to know one another well enough to consider marriage. The reinforcement of conventional norms by formal norms occurs when consensus concerning the desirability of maintaining social distance is breaking down.

Norms enforcing endogamy are widespread, for intermarriage does effectively reduce social distance. The intimacy of marriage partners usually results in mutual identification as human beings. Furthermore, intermarriage often brings the couple's families and friends into close personal contacts with incumbents of different rank. Such exposure discloses the ridiculous nature of most stereotyped beliefs.

The Regulation of Competition. The complex network of norms that makes up any system of social stratification actually prevents or minimizes direct competition between persons of different ranks — competition for jobs, for mates, for land, or for whatever else that is desired. When direct competition does not occur, there is less likelihood that rivalry and conflict will develop. Those in positions of privilege most strongly support the norms governing social distance. If incumbents of high rank become demoralized and fail to observe such procedures, the entire system is likely to collapse. This is especially true when those in elite positions no longer live up to their responsibilities. Then, others find it more difficult to continue to respect them. In such contexts serious questions about inequities arise.

Since persons of high rank enjoy so many advantages, it often appears that the procedures for maintaining social distance were instituted deliberately to ensure their position. At times this has been the case. But few leaders understand human society sufficiently to establish such complex practices intentionally. Wherever such arrangements develop, a stratification system is more likely to persist. Like so many other patterns of concerted action, these arrangements probably emerged through natural selection and subsequently became institutionalized.

SUMMARY AND DISCUSSION

In most communities of any size people are classified and ranked in some manner. Once such patterns of social stratification are institutionalized, a high degree of consensus develops concerning the boundaries of each category, the characteristics of the people in each category, how the categories are to be ranked, and the appropriate relationships between incumbents of the different strata. The complex network of norms that makes up a stratification system is constantly reaffirmed by the conformity of all parties, including the underprivileged. People at each level develop appropriate self-concepts, and most of them maintain their self-respect by conducting themselves in ways that are consistent with these beliefs. All members of the community are socialized into the system. But differential rewards make inequities noticeable, and such inequality can last only if the people remain convinced that members of the categories are indeed different. Once they identify across boundaries as human beings, the system is likely to collapse. Thus, as long as social distance is regulated, neither the norms nor the stereotypes underlying the system are likely to be questioned, and it will persist.

Idealists who oppose inequality frequently charge that those who benefit from them have deliberately established stratification systems. In fact systems of social inequality, though they perpetuate numerous injustices, are seldom the products of malicious design. Even colonists who live in luxury at the expense of their subjects justify their activities in terms of noble motives. Stratification systems develop through collective adaptations; they are not made by scheming politicians. As these developmental processes continue, drastic transformations appear to be in store for the near future. Status differences will not disappear, but human beings may be ranked by different criteria. Just as the media of mass communication have transformed the world into a global village, the rapid development of automation may create a world of two classes — those whose technical knowledge will be in short supply and those for whom there will be little work. Technological unemployment is already here. As the pressure of population on available resources becomes intense, it seems likely that serious contentions will arise over the distribution of what is left.

SUGGESTED READINGS

Bendix, Reinhard, and Seymour M. Lipset (eds.). 1966. *Class, Status and Power: A Reader in Social Stratification.* New York: Free Press.
  An anthology of articles and excerpts from standard references on class stratification.
Doyle, Bertram. 1937. *The Etiquette of Race Relations in the South.* Chicago: University of Chicago Press.
  A detailed account of the norms of interpersonal contacts between black people and all others during the period of slavery in the American South.
Mannoni, Dominique O. 1956. *Prospero and Caliban: The Psychology of Colonization.* Pamela Powesland (trans.). New York: Praeger.

Psychological analysis of the dependency relationships that develop between the privileged and members of minority groups.

Mayer, Adrian C. 1960. *Caste and Kinship in Central India.* Berkeley and Los Angeles: University of California Press.
An ethnographic study of the complexities of the caste system in a village in central India.

Mills, C. Wright. 1951. *White Collar: The American Middle Classes.* New York: Oxford University Press.
A classic study of the evolving middle classes in the United States during the mid-twentieth century.

Shibutani, Tamotsu, and Kian M. Kwan. 1965. *Ethnic Stratification.* New York: Macmillan.
A comparative analysis of the formation, maintenance, and dissolution of systems of ethnic stratification.

VIII

SUSTAINED ASSOCIATIONS

Within the memory of many people who are still living, most injuries and illnesses were treated by family physicians — sometimes fondly remembered as "horse-and-buggy doctors." Once established in a community, many such doctors remained there, serving the same clientele throughout their careers. They knew most of their patients by name, sometimes two or three generations of the same family, and were familiar with their quirks as well as their physical conditions. They knew many of their younger patients literally from the moment of their birth. With the explosion of medical knowledge and the development of highly technical specialties, it has become impossible for any doctor to keep abreast of the latest developments in medical research. Increasing specialization and greater sophistication in each field have transformed medical care. Doctors are still doctors, and they still dispense medical care, but their relationship to patients and colleagues has changed. More and more patients are treated in clinics and hospitals staffed by specialists. Those with multiple disorders or with complications are shunted from one specialist to another. Such teams are able to provide superior medical care to more people, but many — physicians and patients alike — have complained that the transactions are becoming too impersonal. Thus, medical students are again being encouraged to become general practitioners — for a time an object of scorn within the profession. As this example suggests, the manner in which various tasks are carried out in a community depends on the way in which people are organized into groups to accomplish them. Thus, we must have some understanding of

204

different kinds of groups, the conditions under which people become associated in these ways, and the manner in which each type of group operates.

In all communities people in sustained association repeatedly carry out similar transactions. As such groups persist, their boundaries tend to become more clearly defined, and they develop readily discernible patterns of concerted action. Since a group's members are in continued contact, they often develop a sense of belonging together in a distinct unit. Their relationships to one another also become more clearly defined. Human interests and the circumstances under which they are pursued vary extensively, and many kinds of collectivities are formed. Groups vary along several dimensions, including size and spatial distribution of their members. They also differ in the clarity of their boundaries. Some are open to anyone who is interested; others admit only those of high rank in the community or persons who have passed stringent qualification tests. Groups also vary in the type of activities that occupy them and in complexity as well as in the extent to which the patterns of joint endeavor are institutionalized. Social scientists have studied all kinds of groups — peasant families, teams of co-workers, inmates of brothels, military units, business corporations, departments in bureaucracies, service clubs, motorcycle gangs. One central problem in sociology is to ascertain how various types of groups work. How do the members contribute toward carrying out joint transactions? How is the coordination of their efforts accomplished? What part does leadership play in directing such activities? Since it is impossible to cover all types of groups, the emphasis in this chapter falls on two of them: the large, complex organizations with bureaucracies, which are playing an increasingly important part in mass societies, and primary groups, the small coteries that can be found everywhere.

Although the boundaries of some groups are unclear, each is a separate entity that develops in its own way. Some groups — such as universities, some religious denominations, or the medical profession — persist for centuries, but most associations are more transitory. While some groups give the impression of stability, even those that persist are ongoing entities that are shaped, maintained, transformed, and dissolved as their members pursue their interests and cope with changing conditions. Throughout a group's lifetime, however, its boundaries remain relatively stable, and the members find their activities shaped to some extent by the organization's requirements. Once a group has come into being, we may ask how it maintains its patterns of concerted action in the face of constantly changing circumstances. How does it perpetuate its characteristic patterns of activity? Groups vary in their cohesiveness. Some groups persist even in the face of adversity; others collapse as soon as the members find participation a bit costly. What are some of the conditions under which groups persist?

CONSTELLATIONS WITHIN COMMUNITIES

Human beings are brought together in many ways; they may be related by kinship, perceive some common interest, or happen to live, work, or be imprisoned together. Whenever the same people meet repeatedly to carry out similar transactions, they come to identify with one another as part of a distinguishable entity — a group. Each group develops its own goals, patterns of concerted action, procedures for inducting newcomers, ways of making decisions, and measures for discipline and control over its members. Most of us spend considerable time pursuing careers in the various groups to which we belong — sometimes units within larger associations. When a group is well organized, its members find themselves involved in typical career lines; careers of ministers, teachers, political bosses, or corporation executives demonstrate the extent to which human lives are circumscribed by group membership. A waiter in a European gourmet restaurant has to serve many years of apprenticeship, starting as a busboy and gradually acquiring the multitude of skills essential for his calling. Prostitutes, gamblers, and thieves usually develop their careers as active members of various groups. Group membership also shapes important elements of our sense of personal identity. As we acquire the customs of a particular group, we incorporate the accepted ways of thinking and doing things into our behavioral repertoires. When a transaction takes place within a group, the other members usually constitute our reference group — the audience for whom we perform.

Kinship Groups. With the exception of foundlings everyone belongs to some kinship group, but anthropologists have shown how widely the organization of kinship groups varies. Most inhabitants of industrial societies tend to think of a family as consisting of a married couple and their socially acknowledged children, a unit that usually lives apart from other relatives. This is often called the "nuclear family," whose members are bound by biotic descent and exclusive sexual contacts. But in many communities families are much more extended; each family is a large clan. Where polygamy prevails, the children live together and regard all adults in the household as their parents. In some sectarian communities, such as the Hutterites, the husband is recognized as the head of each household, but each family is but an auxiliary unit of the religious colony; the family does not exercise independent control over work, authority, or the training and discipline of children (Lee and Brattrud, 1967).

Kinship units may also develop somewhat independently of genetic links and sexual relations. Malinowski (1927) shows how in matrilineal families the roles of the mother's brother include responsibilities that are elsewhere assigned to the father. There are also fabricated kinships. In cases of adoption, for example, the legally recognized father is not the biotic parent. Likewise the nurturing role of mothering need not be performed by the woman who gave birth to the child. The mother's sister, the child's grandmother, paid nurses, teachers, or governesses may be mother surrogates. Institutionalized procedures have developed everywhere to regulate mating, rearing children, and inheriting property, but the customs and laws vary enormously. No matter how the family is defined or organized, however, it is an arena in which a limited number of people live in close and sustained association.

Kinship groups are vital in shaping one's life chances, personality, and self-concept. All children require a long period of care by a limited number of individuals with whom they usually develop relationships of intimacy and from whom they initially learn community norms and values. Families, however they may be organized, prepare children for life. Kinship groups often determine one's status in the community. Where rank is hereditary, as in caste and in ethnic stratification, much interest develops over one's family tree; certain abilities, susceptibility to some diseases, and other features are believed to be inherited. In class stratification income and place of residence often limit one's life chances. Many personality traits are shaped early in life in the course of coming to terms with the demands of elders upon whom a child is dependent. Furthermore, the various traits that children develop are evaluated within the family, and conspicuous features — clumsiness, physical attractiveness, special talents — may come to be defined as an integral part of the individual. Thus, in most cases, a person develops his or her initial beliefs about the kind of human being he or she is while participating in kinship groups. One learns to identify oneself in terms of a family name and adopts the obligations charged to the group.

Occupational Groups. In virtually all communities people are organized into groups to earn their livelihoods. Where the technology is relatively simple, inhabitants get together in different combinations to accomplish various tasks — one grouping to construct boats, another to plant crops, and still another to wage war. The same individuals are involved, but they enact different roles. As the economy becomes more complex, however, the division of labor becomes more specialized. In medieval Europe traders formed mercantile guilds. Established at first as protective associations, the guilds developed into powerful organizations that virtually dictated many features of economic life. Each guild determined its own membership, controlled the prices and quality of the goods, protected its merchants from outside competition, and became a social club where the members could meet informally to consider common problems.

At the same time European artisans joined together to form craft guilds. The members were divided into three ranks. The highest status consisted of the masters, who knew their craft and met guild requirements. To become a master one had to serve an apprenticeship for two to seven years. Aspirants lived with a master while learning the craft, receiving other training and lessons in etiquette as well. When apprentices could meet guild standards, they were advanced to the status of journeyman, which entitled them to work by the day for wages. If journeymen amassed sufficient capital and had perhaps completed a masterpiece, they could become masters and set up their own businesses. This procedure ensured quality craftsmanship and maintained the reputation of the group. Like a fraternity, each guild protected its members' interests. In modern industrial communities work is organized around corporate units of several kinds — producers, distributors, retail outlets, service organizations. Those employed in such groups often form unions, enabling the workers to protect their interests.

In modern mass societies a person's occupation is probably the most important single index of his or her standing in a community. Beyond their name and ethnic affiliation, people tend to identify themselves in terms of what they do for a living. Those who do not work cite the family breadwinner's calling. Occupation has much to do with where people live; sometimes this is a matter of income, but people frequently go out of their way to live in areas where they feel people like themselves should live. Occupation also has much to do with the kind of people with whom one associates. Each well-established occupation tends to become a social world. People working in the occupation get to know many others involved in the same line of work. Many beliefs and assumptions about the kind of human being one is depend on one's job. Thus, membership in an occupational group is important, for a person's self-concept is shaped while pursuing a career in this group.

Of particular interest in modern societies are the professions. The various tasks performed in industrial societies are becoming so complicated that there is an increasing tendency toward greater specialization. Each profession—such as medicine, law, engineering, or teaching—is based on a body of highly technical knowledge that is used to perform essential services. What distinguishes the professions from other occupations is their monopoly on knowledge and skills, much like the medieval guilds. Both patients and the rest of the community acknowledge a surgeon's special competence, which is attained over a long period of training. Once qualified, surgeons do work that is so technical that only others who have been similarly trained can judge its quality. Thus, the judgments of professional workers can be questioned only by other experts in the same field.

Professional work often entails making decisions that seriously affect other people's lives; because of this weighty responsibility, professionals are generally granted high esteem and considerable autonomy. The term "professional" has been used to refer to occupations enjoying high prestige; as work in other areas becomes more specialized, however, other occupations are beginning to assume similar characteristics. For example, can clients actually judge the competence of plumbers or auto mechanics? Can anyone without a detailed knowledge of what is involved in police work judge fairly an officer's performance in a difficult situation? Thus, many lines of work are becoming too technical for nonspecialists to evaluate, and many occupational groups are taking on some features of the established professions.

Most professions have clearly drawn boundaries. A sense of group consciousness develops, and clear distinctions are made between members and outsiders. Each professional group establishes and enforces its own standards of performance, which are generally higher than the minimum level of competence required by law. Members of esteemed professions—doctors, lawyers, military officers—are also expected to live up to a code of ethics established by their peers. Each profession develops its own prestige ladder. Most of the members are interested in one another's work and are constantly judging it. One's status within a profession depends on the manner in which other experts evaluate one's performance. Thus, other members of the profession become the most significant reference group for whom one performs. Professional workers conceive of themselves as experts endowed with knowledge not possessed by others; they recognize the special responsibilities they assume from being able to do what others cannot do. Being able to meet professional standards becomes a matter of personal pride. Each profession has its own communication channels, and each develops its own values. Since special competence forms the basis of their sense of identity, those who join a profession seldom leave (Goode, 1957).

To ensure meeting high standards most professional groups insist on controlling the training of recruits to their ranks, and considerable formal training is usually required. Some institutionalized mode of validating competence is also controlled by the professions; the state grants licenses, but only after recruits have satisfied the requirements set by the relevant profession. Since no one else is able to judge the newcomers' qualifications, the professional association itself decides who may or may not join its group. But technical skills are not the only qualifications to be met. Practitioners are expected to adopt appropriate attitudes and values, and some indoctrination usually takes place (Becker et al., 1961). Newcomers must also learn all kinds of informal norms to get along with their colleagues. Career lines do not necessarily follow the announced ideology; in medicine, for example, considerable political maneuvering is involved in arranging internships and residencies as well as in becoming established to practice in a community (Hall, 1948; Freidson, 1970).

Disciplinary problems arise in all groups. Some members refuse to comply; others are irresponsible. Competition among members may get out of hand, becoming transformed into ugly rivalries. Where so much responsibility is involved, the misconduct of a few may damage the reputation of the entire group. Since professional groups claim that outsiders are unable to judge their work, they must police their own members. Thus, most professional groups claim the right to regulate themselves. Doctors and lawyers long maintained a code of ethics that discouraged them from advertising their services, from derogating openly the competence of fellow practitioners, and from stealing one another's clients (Hall, 1946). Most American doctors are careful to observe a referral system, refusing to accept the patients of other doctors unless it is clear that the clients have rejected them. When mistakes are made, doctors try to cover for one another—at least before outsiders.

Within the profession itself chronic and flagrant violators are punished by the imposition of various sanctions. Sometimes the punishment is informal; other doctors simply refuse to refer patients, and in time the violator becomes isolated. In some serious instances a doctor may be suspended or even expelled from the profession; state licensing bureaus usually cooperate. Some groups have formal procedures for terminating membership, such as degradation ceremonies; once epaulets are torn off an officer's shoulders, he is permanently barred from the profession of arms. Should any professional association fail to live up to such responsibilities, even a vaunted calling may lose its mystique and be unable to maintain its prestige. Many Americans are now raising embarrassing questions about the medical profession, and some kind of federal regulation may be instituted (Mechanic, 1967).

Voluntary Associations. When a community becomes too large for the inhabitants to know one another on a personal basis, voluntary associations of all kinds tend to develop, unless they are proscribed by law. The diversity of interests brings together those who share common concerns. Americans have gotten together to pursue all kinds of interests — to demand political changes, to worship as they choose, or to pursue various forms of recreation. An amazing variety of associations has emerged as more leisure time becomes available — for coin collectors, auto racing fans, serious bridge players, surfers, parachutists, music lovers, museum supporters. Such groups cultivate special skills, facilitate the acquisition of supplies, set standards of performance, and provide fellowship. Social clubs and fraternal associations provide local services as well as opportunities for business contacts and camaraderie. Such groups may at times become actively involved in politics. If some regulation contemplated by the government is likely to infringe on the benefits of war veterans, for example, patriotic associations are likely to mobilize public support to oppose it. Such groups may become the key reference group to those who become deeply involved. Advancing one's career in some voluntary association may become more important than what one does to earn a living.

Most associations have avowed goals — establishing a symphony orchestra, cultivating tastes for fine wines, securing their members' political rights. They usually develop an ideology to justify and explain what they do. Although such groups often appear to have been instituted to fulfill some purpose, an examination of their history reveals that this is usually not the case. The goals often undergo change in the course of their realization. Although such groups can often be described teleologically, most are in fact trial-and-error experiments that have developed their structure through groping and only gradually attain clarity and coherence (Ginsberg, 1930). Avowed goals usually crystallize after the people have gotten together. As an organization persists, its purposes are increasingly clarified. Once they are established, various tasks are articulated for their accomplishment. Sociological studies disclose how goals are displaced as life conditions change. For example, when polio was effectively controlled by the Salk vaccine, the National Foundation for Infantile Paralysis shifted from exclusive concern with polio to an attack on a variety of diseases (Sills, 1957:253–65). Thus, the structure of voluntary associations develops in a succession of collective adaptations.

Since access and egress are relatively easy in voluntary associations, they clearly manifest some general principles that apply to most other groups as well. A group tends to develop patterns of concerted action that enable its members to pursue most effectively what they define to be their interests. As life conditions change, procedures are often transformed to become more effective. Once such action patterns become institutionalized, they provide a normative framework within which the members can carry on. Once a normative framework is established, there tends to be a self-selection of personnel. Those who share the interest being pursued are attracted and become more committed; others become dissatisfied and leave.

NETWORKS OF PERSONAL CONTACTS

The Reduction of Social Distance. One of the most important forms of human association is what sociologists call a primary group. A *primary group* consists of a constellation of individuals who know one another on a personal basis, who see and treat one another as unique individuals. Such groups are found everywhere. We are born into some primary groups, such as our family. Others form among people who happen to be in sustained contact for a long period—as in a neighborhood gang, a squad in a military organization, a work unit in a factory, patients in a chronic ward of a hospital, prisoners who share a cell, or roommates in a dormitory. Members of outlaw groups such as bandits and smugglers, who must depend heavily on one another, also tend to form very close personal ties.

The mark of a primary group is the reduction of social distance through sustained and unspecialized contact. The members develop highly individualized knowledge of one another; they know something of one another's idiosyncrasies, aspirations, and personal problems. Hence, their role-taking is personalized; they take into account the distinctive interests and traits of specific individuals. Thus, if a woman knows that her brother dislikes whining but has a weakness for beauty, she takes this into account in her dealings with him. If groups are small enough, each member has numerous opportunities to learn about the others. As contacts continue over a considerable period of time, further occasions keep arising for the individuals to get to know one another intimately. Furthermore, the interaction of people who are together a great deal tends to become unspecialized. Members of primary groups observe one another doing many different things in a variety of contexts; thus, they are able to learn about many facets of one another's personalities. Precisely because the members know so much about one another, most of them are able to relax their personal reserve. As a sense of mutual identification develops, the members are able to let down their guard, although individuals differ in the extent to which they are able to relax their defensive stance. They act more spontaneously in one another's presence. This enables each member to reveal and detect individuality — the unique features that make each person a distinct object. Secrets and special meanings are often shared. When together, they are backstage, and they can engage in candid discussions of staging problems and even rehearse for difficult transactions involving outsiders. The members become interdependent. They count on one another for support of a sort they do not expect elsewhere — such as advice on private matters, warning that one has halitosis, or scratching one another's backs. Primary groups are thus characterized by a sense of intimacy, a sense of belonging together. It should be emphasized, however, that although members of primary groups get to know one another quite well, they do not necessarily like one another. Indeed, some of the most intense hatreds arise among people who are intimately involved.

The boundaries of most primary groups are difficult to define, for each member has a different combination of friends who drift in and out. Each member's personal friends are usually accepted and in many transactions treated as part of the circle. Although we often do not think of it, a pet dog or a child's imaginary companion may also be included, for the feelings attributed to them are often taken into account in planning joint activities. Furthermore, mere physical proximity does not necessarily result in the formation of primary groups. Members of the same work crew will not become a primary group unless they do other things together as well — eat lunch, go bowling, double-date, visit one another's homes. Unless they do many different things together their relationships, though friendly, remain categorical. Some prisoners, soldiers, and patients refuse to participate in common activities, preferring to remain marginal, maintaining friendly contacts as a matter of expediency but otherwise remaining aloof. It should also be noted that most of the small groups studied experimentally in laboratories are *not* primary groups, for most of the subjects are strangers. Some ritualized relationships between individuals — such as blood brotherhoods, compadre and godparent relations — are quite formal and should be excluded. However, strangers who come together in encounter groups often develop very intimate ties through self-disclosures of secrets and the intensity of their contacts. Such ties, however, are usually transitory.

The Culture of Primary Groups. Since its members are in close and frequent contact, each primary group develops its own communication channels. Hence, the members of each primary group develop a distinctive outlook and culture. Although it may not differ too much from adjacent primary groups, each coterie develops its own language, special symbols, and informal norms of conduct—each a product of its unique history. Thus, within each family informal norms arise that are known to all its members but not to outsiders, such as a family's use of "wa-wa" for water, adopted after one of the children's pet terms. If the parents regard their status in the community as higher than that of their neighbors, they may instruct their children to live up to their own standards, being courteous to others but remaining aloof.

Since the classic study by Roethlisberger and Dickson (1938:379–548) on the Hawthorne plant of the Western Electric Company, students of industrial organizations have recognized that informal norms that differ considerably from company regulations develop in each factory unit. A number of common understandings had developed among the workers who were studied—don't be a "rate buster" by working too efficiently; don't be a "chiseler" by working too slowly; if one is a straw boss, be a "regular guy" who does not enforce regulations too stringently; don't be a "squealer." The workers had developed their own conception of what constituted a "fair day's work," a production standard that fell below the level that management regarded as desirable and below what several of the workers were capable of doing. The faster workers simply stopped working earlier than the others; those who were slower were taunted to keep up. Thus, in most work crews the members form their own norms concerning the manner in which various tasks are to be accomplished, the length of coffee breaks, the frequency with which the bathroom should be used, the appropriate modes of dress, and the manner in which management personnel are to be addressed (Homans, 1962:75–90).

Although the conventional and formal norms of the community provide a broad framework within which primary groups operate, members of each primary group view the customs and regulations somewhat differently. This disparity is the most apparent in the family, where parental authority is defined in custom and sometimes by law. Even when everyone acknowledges that parents are supposed to be addressed with respect and obeyed, what one mother can get her children to do another mother cannot. Even though the children may appear obedient in the presence of outsiders, there is considerable variation in the kind of authority different parents are actually able to exercise at home. Another widely accepted norm is that members of primary groups are supposed to like one another. While appearances may be maintained before outsiders, actual sentiments often clash with norms concerning affection. Spouses, siblings, and relatives sometimes dislike one another intensely, and some of them may develop deep guilt feelings about their inability to feel affection. The same is true of norms concerning friendship. Friends are supposed to be close, to approach one another without ulterior intentions, reciprocate favors, and perhaps overlook status differences as irrelevant; whether such norms apply varies from one primary group to another. Adolescent boys, especially in working-class neighborhoods, are expected to stress values such as achievement, popularity, or virility in sports; some gangs do, and others do not. An infantry squad that has sustained a succession of severe casualties may develop a taboo against the formation of close friendships; replacements are indoctrinated to be professional soldiers who simply have a job to do.

Most informal norms are consistent with the standards of the larger organization or community. When they are incompatible, difficulties may arise. In areas marked by interethnic tension, for example, even when derogatory statements about other ethnic groups are seldom made before outsiders, intensely negative estimates are made within the privacy of primary groups. Thus, many stereotypes that are disavowed among strangers are reaffirmed in private. Some factory managers may reject the quotas set by various work units and attempt to increase output through piece rates and other incentives. Some resentful groups may respond to such measures by engaging in deliberate slowdown tactics. Since inmates of psychiatric wards are at the mercy of the staff, most of the informal norms that develop among patients support the formal objectives of the hospital. But the patients do coach one another on how to hide symptoms that could get them into trouble and how to enact behavior patterns that will facilitate their getting out. If some attendant is regarded as unbearable, the patients may teach each other how to fake disturbances so that they may be transferred elsewhere. Thus, what is done in each primary group depends on the definition of the situation that develops among its members. If this definition does not coincide with what is acceptable in the community, outward compliance may occur when someone else is watching. In private, however, people who know one another usually maintain their own counsel and act in terms of what they actually feel and believe. When conventional norms provide options, the choice made by an individual is likely to correspond with the primary group's informal norms. Much of what we do depends on the expectations we impute to close companions.

Interpersonal Relations. Each primary group develops a distinctive network of interpersonal relations. How the networks are shaped depends on the personalities of those involved and how they react to one another. A primary group may be split into cliques. Internal distinctions develop through personal preferences. Some individuals like each other; some are liked by others but do not reciprocate. Some members are popular; others are respected but not especially liked. A few individuals are disliked by everyone and tend to become isolated, even though they remain in the group (Moreno, 1953). Some members may become dependent on others. Each member's status within a primary group, his or her personal standing, depends on the manner in which he or she is evaluated by the others. Certain individuals stand out as "natural leaders," and they exercise disproportionate influence over the others. A leader is a person who has followers, and in primary groups leadership depends largely on personal qualities. In adolescent gangs, for example, there is a spontaneous gravitation toward certain individuals, usually those who embody most conspicuously the accepted values of the group —such as virility, intelligence, and special skills in athletics (Whyte, 1955). Some studies show that leaders are generally more considerate than the others, that they are usually more adept at role-taking. Jennings (1943) shows that popular leaders not only uphold group standards but also apply them more severely to themselves than to the others.

Since the members of primary groups participate together in so many transactions, they tend to develop many personal claims and obligations. The sentiments that various members form toward one another are important in that they facilitate acts that are consistent with these feelings and inhibit acts that seem contradictory. Thus, impulses that are consistent with sentiments are reinforced and carried out with ease. We rush to the aid of people we like; if someone we dislike is in trouble, our inclination is to ignore the matter. When we are in a position to punish someone who has been the source of many frustrations, we must be careful not to be carried away. Conversely, impulses that are inconsistent with sentiments tend to be inhibited. It is very difficult to do anything that might hurt a close friend or relative; we can imagine readily how hurt the person would be, and we feel guilty. Similarly, just as we find it difficult to address with respect people we disdain, we are reluctant to do favors for those we detest.

Problems frequently arise, however, because of the network of obligations that tie together the members of a coterie. A person one resents, perhaps from jealousy, may get along quite well with everyone else. The claims and obligations that arise in primary groups are personal; they may or may not coincide with those that make up the conventional roles that the same individuals enact. In a Japanese family, for example, the husband by custom occupies the highest status; whether he actually exercises the prerogatives of his rank varies from one family to the next. When outsiders are present, his wife enacts subservient roles. If she is dominant, however, she makes most of the decisions; conventional forms are then followed as she permits her husband to announce what she has decided to do.

How are transactions organized and executed in primary groups? Both role-playing and role-taking are highly personalized. Individual idiosyncrasies are taken into account in working out a division of labor. A person who is sickly is excused from heavy work, and an aggressive individual is delegated tasks that require assertiveness. Decisions are usually made by those who are regarded as most competent; since the skills of various individuals are well known, different persons may assume leadership in different transactions — playing games, fighting outsiders, petitioning to correct grievances, negotiating a trade. But decision makers seldom act in isolation; they usually consult the others. Leadership plays an important part in determining what to do, for the line of action is often shaped through deliberation. Thus, transactions in primary groups are usually worked out on a person-to-person basis. If disagreements arise, informal arrangements are negotiated. Agreed-upon arrangements are informal and are changed to meet contingencies. If some patients in a psychiatric ward decide to play tricks on the staff, for example, they proceed until one of the patients becomes anxiety-ridden and immobilized; then they adjust and redirect their activity. Similarly, rules to be observed in a gang fight are modified when the best fighter is injured or cannot appear.

Enforcement of Informal Norms. When the informal norms that develop in primary groups contradict formal or conventional norms, the sanctions of the community cannot be used to punish violations. Racketeers cannot go to the police when they are cheated; hence, gangland violence flares in efforts to collect gambling debts, to protect or discipline prostitutes, or to enforce agreements in transactions involving illicit drugs. Juvenile gangs fight in the streets for the same reason; if someone poaches on their territory to roll drunks, they have no recourse to the law.

Even in more prosaic settings each primary group must enforce its own norms, and a variety of informal sanctions are used to bring transgressors back into line. Frequently the penalty consists of verbal expressions of displeasure; even a glance of annoyance on the face of a friend is often enough to inhibit deviant acts or to arouse feelings of guilt or shame. Physical violence is also used. Children are punished with spankings. Rate busters in factories discover that their tools have been "misplaced," and some may suffer "accidents." Particularly revealing is a study by Speroff and Kerr (1952) of eighteen work crews doing dangerous work in a Chicago steel mill. In sociometric tests the men were asked how they felt about one another, and their preferences were checked against medical records. If industrial accidents are unintentional, their distribution among workers should be random. However, the figures revealed that the most popular workers were accident-free; those who were disliked had the highest accident rates. Probably the most effective negative sanction is the regulation of social distance. Gossip is very effective as a deterrent among people whose lives are intertwined. Those in disfavor may be snubbed or even ostracized. The refusal to honor personal claims is also a powerful sanction.

The influence of other members of primary groups is widely recognized, and it shows up in studies made in countless contexts. In a study of voting, for example, Berelson and his colleagues (1954:99) divided a sample of voters into four categories: people who knew that three, two, one, or none of their best friends planned to vote for the Republican candidate. They found that 61 percent, 37 percent, 23 percent, and 2 percent respectively showed their intention of voting the same way. Informal sanctions are usually effective because most human beings strive to maintain their personal status among those with whom they identify most closely. Most people make costly sacrifices, sometimes even giving up things they desire most in life, to comply with the wishes of their friends or family. Personal esteem in the eyes of close friends is far more important to most people than their status in the community. However lowly their rank elsewhere, people make an effort to maintain their personal reputation among those who know them. Even prostitutes and beggars, who are so often regarded with disdain, make an effort to preserve their standing among their peers. Without the respect of those we know personally we are largely isolated. Just as soldiers outside their own companies are not much more than serial numbers, most people in mass societies feel like replaceable cogs in huge machines. They count for very little except to the handful of people who know them as individuals.

Some people are not responsive to primary group pressures — the rate busters, the rebels, the loners—and students of small groups have been studying the problem. Although the first two studies do not deal with primary groups, the findings are suggestive. Festinger and his associates (1952) investigated people's tendency to change their opinions when they learn that others disagree with them. They found that members of esteemed groups are more likely to change their views in order to comply than those in less attractive groups. Dittes (1956) gave the subjects in twenty experimental groups false ratings of themselves; some believed themselves to be highly regarded, and others felt rejected. Conformity to group norms was more noticeable among those with a low level of self-esteem. Menzel (1957) asked some doctors for their estimate of a new drug (public expression) and compared this with pharmacy records (actual use). He also did a sociometric test. Physicians who were less popular and less sure of themselves tended to avow conformity, even when they did not actually prescribe the drug as they claimed. In their study of delinquent gangs Short and Strodtbeck (1965) concluded that compliance with primary group demands, especially when it may be costly, depends on the extent to which a member is psychologically dependent on the group. Human beings are generally responsive to the expectations of those who control resources that are important to them. Hence, such dependency may arise in many ways. In many cases it is a matter of sentiments. Those who have strong ties with others in a primary group find it almost impossible to oppose it. Those who dislike or even hate some of the other members, however, may violate the norms just to spite their enemies.

OPERATION OF FORMAL ORGANIZATIONS

An increasing number of transactions in modern mass societies are being carried out in large, formal organizations directed by bureaucrats. Whenever large numbers of people are confronted with complex undertakings, their efforts are likely to become organized in this manner. In considering such large groups we tend to think of corporations such as General Motors and IBM or of government agencies such as the Department of Defense. But voluntary associations tend to develop this type of structure if they succeed, grow, and become well established. Hospitals in urban communities are organized in this manner, as are universities. Even professional football teams are now run by executives, who are advised by staffs of specialists. Organized crime has also grown and become entrenched to the point that its operations require administrative personnel. Bureaucracies are not limited to industrial societies; gigantic enterprises were mounted in ancient Egypt, China, and Rome. But this type of social structure is becoming more commonplace in modern societies. Indeed, it is not possible to understand what happens nowadays without some comprehension of how bureaucracies work. How are social transactions carried out in these huge, complex enterprises? How are the component parts organized? And how are the contributions of thousands of participants coordinated?

Bureaucratic Management. Formal organizations are characterized by a clear statement of purpose and explicit designs for carrying out specified activities. An extensive division of labor develops among the members, and trained experts carry out highly technical tasks. Each participant, say, a worker in a General Motors assembly line, performs a specialized task, sometimes with little understanding of how his or her contribution fits into the final product. The pronounced division of labor creates problems of coordination; therefore, an administrative staff is needed to maintain communication channels and to exercise the authority necessary to ensure cooperation. The term *bureaucracy* refers to a clearly defined organization of administrative officials and supervisory personnel. Those who do the actual labor are frequently excluded, although it is difficult to distinguish between staff and line personnel in many organizations. Thus, the mere size and complexity of many undertakings requires an administrative staff to coordinate the work of others and to maintain the organization itself.

Explicit procedures are established to regulate the contributions of various subgroups to achieve clearly specified objectives — to build refrigerators, to treat diseases, to educate young people, or to wage war. Control is by formal norms, and the operations are standardized. Written regulations provide the normative framework within which the entire organization operates. Thus, formal organizations are highly institutionalized, and for most of the personnel there is little room for spontaneity or personal autonomy. In theory, the whole organization is designed by rational principles to attain maximum efficiency; the aim is to avoid arbitrary and unnecessary action by imposing discipline. The outcome is a collective product to which each has contributed in some small way (Weber, 1968:956–1005).

Where the division of labor is highly specialized, tasks tend to be defined explicitly. Each participant is a specialist who develops expertise in a particular task. Each member's status within the organization is clearly defined. The rights and duties of the incumbents of each position

—accountant, department head, public relations officer—are specified in written regulations. No matter who occupies the position, the duties and standards of performance do not change; the various roles to be enacted are the same. Thus, incumbents of each office have a working conception of what is expected of them; they need only compare themselves with previous incumbents. To the extent that employees identify themselves with an office, they accept the duties as personal responsibilities. They feel that they should dress and act the part and hold themselves accountable for the proper performance of their roles. Work is expected to be done in an impersonal manner; sentiments are not supposed to interfere with the performance of duties.

Indeed, many transactions can be executed most efficiently if the participants act with cold detachment. To take an extreme example, infantry officers sometimes face difficult decisions in critical situations —whether to send on a very dangerous mission a close friend who is known to be competent or a new replacement who will not be missed but is less likely to get the job done. In such contexts decisions presumably are made to implement most effectively the goal of the entire organization (to win the war), and sometimes individuals have to be sacrificed. Just as military officers are judged in terms of their ability to accomplish such difficult tasks, regardless of their personal feelings, others in formal organizations are expected to perform in the same manner. Teachers are expected to evaluate their students' work impartially; how they feel about each student should be irrelevant. This is, of course, an ideal that many bureaucrats are unable to meet. Nonetheless, in complex organizations persons tend to become personnel—replaceable cogs in large machines.

Offices are usually organized into a hierarchy, and formal norms define the relations among the positions. Thus, the status ladder is defined by regulations. Many bureaucrats become preoccupied with advancing their careers by moving up the hierarchy. They welcome opportunities to push policies that benefit the organization, for attracting favorable notice and getting credit means a greater likelihood of promotions. They also want to avoid mistakes, especially those that might embarrass the entire organization. A costly error could result in being passed over for promotion or even being dismissed. Those who have been with an organization long enough to qualify for pensions and other benefits are likely to become very cautious. Thus, workers in bureaucracies frequently become task-oriented rather than people-oriented; they are primarily concerned with fulfilling role requirements. Many become more concerned with making their own work easier and avoiding trouble than with serving their clients. Rather than risk being disciplined, they prefer to play safe by remaining within the rules. College students sometimes complain of being treated like IBM cards, and we read periodically of grotesque miscarriages of justice because of government red tape. Some destitute widow or senior citizen is cut off from essential services because of a technicality or unfavorable interpretation of a rule. Much of the criticism of bureaucracies on grounds that the workers are callous arises from the fact that employees cling to their hard-earned status; they feel that their hands are tied by regulations, and they are afraid to act on their own.

Bureaucratic Decision Making. All groups, including formal organizations, must come to terms with the demands of the changing context in which they operate. Unexpected events occur; uncertainties are uncovered; and problems keep arising. Thus, administrative decision making is a continuous process. Just how it is done varies from one organization to another, but there are some common features. Ideally, the objective is the continued mobilization of resources to accomplish the goals of the organization, while protecting its integrity and the morale of its personnel. But bureaucrats, even those at the top levels of management, are not free to do whatever they wish. Formal norms define the scope of their authority; in addition a heritage of precedents may have been established by previous officeholders. Furthermore, administrators must take several categories of people into account—their immediate staff, other personnel in the organization, the organization's clientele, relevant interest groups, and the general public.

How the executives involved define the situation determines what decisions they make, and their views depend on their comprehension of the facts and on their estimates of the possible consequences of the various alternatives. Although key decisions are made by the chief administrator and carried out in his or her name, in fact most bureaucratic decisions are collective products. Most modern executives work with teams, and they depend heavily on their professional staffs. Few individuals know enough to make on rational grounds the kinds of policy decisions that bureaucrats are often called upon to make. Each administrator has advisors and consultants. All of them depend on staff reports and the usual communication channels. When the necessary information is highly specialized, they must depend on the summaries and recommendations of experts. Those who make the actual decisions and bear responsibility for them are often at the mercy of their subordinates; in many cases administrators do not actually know what is happening in the lower echelons of their own organizations. Decision-making procedures are so institutionalized in well-established groups that the continued operation of the organization does not depend on any single person. Even the sudden death of the chief executive does not alter the day-to-day performance of the group. To the extent that decision making is institutionalized any individual's capacity to alter the course of events is limited.

Once it becomes known that some policy decision is pending, parties that are likely to be affected engage in various political tactics to influence it. Different departments within an organization often develop incongruous interests. Practices that would be convenient for one department could create all kinds of difficulties in another. Each innovation affects various parts of the organization differently, and some changes are bound to disturb vested interests. Once policies are formed, the regulations of the organization are used to enforce them. Hence, political tactics also center around influencing or controlling the hierarchy. Rivalries arise among ambitious bureaucrats, who use occasions for change as devices for personal advancement. Politics, often skillfully camouflaged to give the appearance of service to the organization, goes on constantly as various bureaucrats compete for status and influence. The leaders of formal organizations are often political jugglers, astute at working out compromises and placating the losers (Mouzelis, 1968). After all, subordinates who are overruled remain part of the group, and their support may become essential in some future emergency.

Authority and Coordination. Since offices are organized into a hierarchy, each section is controlled by the level above. Supervisors are accountable to a superior officer, not only for their own decisions but also for the work of their subordinates. The hierarchical organization of responsibility defines each official's task and restricts decisions to choices among already specified alternatives. The decisions on one level in the hierarchy define the responsibilities for the next level below, so that all officials have goals set for them by their superiors. Through this distribution of responsibility it becomes possible to get maximum effort from people whose relationship is impersonal. Orders go down through regular communication channels, and only the details of local implementation are left to those of lower status. Policy decisions are made at the top, but officers of lower rank make many procedural decisions. In this manner responsibility is fixed; accountability is pinpointed; and control is facilitated. Thus, each office becomes a cog in a large machine.

Hierarchies often create severe personal problems, for injustices and unfair advantages frequently arise — in most cases quite unintentionally.

Impersonal criteria for evaluating performances tend to promote impartiality; bureaucrats often become so concerned with achieving specific results that they set aside their personal feelings about their subordinates and clients. A common complaint is that they are afraid to take chances, but those who have invested their entire lives in an organization have much to lose by making a costly mistake. All groups face disciplinary problems, but such problems sometimes become especially acute in formal organizations. Impersonal discipline is hard to take. Thus, to ensure loyalty to the organization, efforts are often made to reward executives handsomely and to make them feel that their careers are secure.

Regulations provide a broad normative framework, and they are usually followed. When formal norms are not effective in meeting the needs of a particular situation, however, they are likely to be bypassed and replaced by informal arrangements. Formal procedures sometimes inadvertently create problems. Emphasis on strict discipline and adherence to rules, intended to assure consistency and impartiality, leads some officials to think of regulations as ends in themselves rather than as means of accomplishing objectives. The rigid conformity that results may prevent adaptation to unexpected situations and may interfere with effective operation. In such instances adjustments are often made through the adoption of informal norms. If problems arise that cannot be handled by established procedures, new ones are worked out by those who are on the scene. Rules on a hospital ward are subject to constant negotiation; they are argued, stretched, or ignored to meet the requirements of the situation. Doctors make their own arrangements with the nursing staff; such negotiated agreements allow the day-to-day work to be done, sometimes in ways that are in clear violation of formal norms. Similarly, in his study of executives and supervisors in industrial plants Dalton (1959) reveals that much of what actually happens in a factory is organized in unplanned transactions involving key workers. Power struggles between staff and line personnel as well as between ambitious officials also affect what occurs; those with common foes sometimes form alliances and make informal arrangements among themselves to do the work in their own way. Top executives of large organizations seldom know what is actually happening; they depend on their subordinates for reports, and the latter often do not disclose rule violations.

Recruitment of Personnel. Any group's effectiveness depends on its personnel. Formal procedures have been established to recruit, train, advance, and retain competent workers. In most formal organizations technical training and experience are a condition of employment. Since offices are impersonal, they are supposed to be filled by those who have the technical qualifications. The objective is to prevent the intrusion of kinship ties, property interests, or political partisanship into personnel decisions. The rationale is simple: Any organization decreases its proficiency by nepotism. As people in nations that are now becoming industrialized are learning, the appointment and advancement of personnel on grounds other than ability leads to costly incompetence in high places. To the extent that tasks become professionalized the need for expertise reduces the importance of other considerations, such as family connections or high status in the community. Although advancement in a hierarchy is seldom based on ability alone, in the long run this criterion is more likely to prevail in formal organizations than in other types of groups. Thus, affirmative action programs have met less resistance in formal organizations, where the appointment of persons from unpopular or unconventional categories can be justified on grounds of competence.

CONDITIONS OF GROUP SOLIDARITY

The Problem of Perseverance.   Among the perennial interests of sociologists is the problem of group solidarity. Under what conditions do groups persist or collapse? On encountering economic adversity members of some families are drawn closer together. Both parents go to work, the breadwinner perhaps even moonlighting. The older children drop out of school to earn what they can; the others share various household chores. Under similar circumstances other families fall apart, and each member goes a different way. Some political parties are at their best when they come under fire; others disintegrate at the slightest trace of popular opposition. Of particular interest is the performance of formal organizations. Some corporations consistently outproduce others. Some armies are known to be dependable; others are so unreliable that even their allies mock them. Units of a large organization also differ considerably among themselves in the quality of their performance.

Any group, large or small, can be identified in terms of its recurrent patterns of concerted action. As long as the members continue to comply with one another's expectations, the patterns will persist. Since each person is capable of some measure of autonomy, however, group structures are perpetuated only as long as the individual participants are willing to honor their obligations. When a sufficient proportion of the participants defect, the pattern will disintegrate. The defection of those who enact key roles often results in immediate collapse. Even social sanctions become ineffective when consensus breaks down. In the last analysis, then, our interest is narrowed to a single question: Under what conditions will members of a group continue to comply with its norms, even when such conformity involves considerable sacrifice and pain? This question brings us to the consideration of group morale.

Morale refers to the degree of effectiveness with which social transactions are carried out — whether this involves fighting an enemy or caring for patients in a hospital. Variations in morale are usually manifested in style of performance, the manner in which tasks are performed. When morale is high, participants not only get along and help one another, but the emotional climate is one of enthusiasm. When morale is low, the group is characterized by chronically poor performance, carelessness, high accident rates, high turnover, high absenteeism, and an emotional climate of futility. When demoralization goes beyond a certain point, factionalism becomes rampant, and concerted action breaks down altogether. Morale becomes especially important when groups encounter adversity. Those with high morale will rise to the challenge, but the others are likely to collapse. Such variations in morale cannot be explained in terms of social norms; groups that persist and those that do not are often similarly organized. Morale also varies independently of material resources. Some of the richest organizations are ridden with strife and are among the first to collapse under pressure. We must look elsewhere for an explanation of the persistence of effective teamwork.

Efficient coordination results from the willingness of the individual participants to subordinate purely personal interests to a common purpose. It is the product of selfless giving — the readiness of most participants to continue to do their share even when it involves considerable personal sacrifice. Petty rivalries and grudges are temporarily forgotten, and the members do whatever they feel is necessary to bring their tasks to successful completion. Efficiency arises from intelligent teamwork and frictionless acceptance of a division of labor. Group members do not so much surrender personal autonomy as freely adopt group goals and identify their interests with those of the team. Quality of performance cannot be prescribed or coerced (Hocking, 1941). When soldiers are ordered to march smartly, one can distinguish readily between simulated enthusiasm and spontaneous commitment. Whether individuals are willing to make sacrifices in behalf of their group depends on whether they believe the effort to be worthwhile. These are complex decisions, and sociologists must avoid dangers of oversimplification. But numerous studies suggest that decisions to devote maximum effort to tasks are made among people who know one another on a personal basis; high morale rests on the kinds of beliefs that arise in primary groups (Mandelbaum, 1952).

Reactions in Primary Groups. Even the largest organization is made up of adjacent and overlapping primary groups. Most participants in large organizations or communities define situations from a viewpoint that they share with those with whom they are in direct contact. Each primary group has its own communication channels, and the perspective that develops in each local unit serves as a filter through which a succession of situations are viewed and defined. Each primary group is in this respect autonomous; its members think for themselves and compare their views. Whatever they may say in the presence of outsiders, among themselves the members candidly evaluate various objects and situations and decide for themselves whether the required effort is worthwhile. Thus, local definitions may differ considerably from official pronouncements. Participants are likely to commit themselves to maximum effort only when most of them honestly believe that the successful completion of transactions will benefit themselves or those with whom they identify. Once a task is defined as desirable or necessary, the tension level rises; the emotional climate becomes one of enthusiasm, and this gives direction to the attitudes of everyone present. Thus, high morale depends on the contributions of individual participants, and these in turn depend largely on the expectations imputed to other members of the primary group.

All organizations are held together by personal attachments that have developed among their members. People who are in daily contact tend to form all kinds of moral obligations. We have seen how members of work units in industrial organizations develop their own culture. Thus, the enthusiasm with which the formal goals of an organization are pursued depends on the extent to which they are supported by the informal norms that arise in its component primary groups. Such support does not necessarily rest on a genuine commitment to the formal goals; in some instances it is simply a matter of self-interest. For example, if a well-liked man has encountered serious financial difficulties, others in his work group may decide to suspend their standard of a "fair day's work" and allow him to work as fast as he can. Workers may decide to put in extra effort just before Christmas, perhaps hoping to be rewarded with a bonus. After interviewing demoralized American troops in Vietnam, Moskos (1970:134–56) concluded that the soldiers were willing to fight only when something was at stake that they themselves believed to be worth the effort. Conversely, if the members of a primary group oppose a policy, they may deliberately sabotage it. In his study of a state mental hospital Scheff (1961) discovered that reforms administrators introduced with the best of intentions were subverted by the hospital attendants. By controlling communication channels and maintaining a united front, they were able to nullify changes that they found irksome and threatening.

Members of professional and technical staffs also come to know one another on a personal basis. Such persons often perform for two reference groups — their organization and their field of specialization. If they become so disgusted with their organization that they see it merely as a place to pick up their paychecks, their performances may leave much to be desired. But specialists also identify with their profession; indeed, their calling may become the center of their lives. For some living up to professional standards, regardless of their feelings, becomes a matter of personal pride. Since specialists often make key decisions, their attitudes toward various transactions may turn out to be decisively important. Disgruntled technicians can subvert organizational goals even more easily than other workers.

High-level executives also form primary groups and spend much time with others of similar rank both in their own organization and in others. They tend to define situations from a standpoint shared only by those who enjoy very high status. The astuteness of executives in forming and implementing policies becomes very important. Top administrators can exercise considerable discretion; the directives they receive from above are often stated as abstract principles, and they are expected to create the specific procedures to implement them. Contradictions among various policies enable administrators to find suitable justifications for just about any policy they choose to adopt. If they encounter opposition, they often retreat into labyrinths of regulations to defend themselves. They may even create crises to make their point. They can falsify records or "accidentally" lose crucial memorandums. Most important, they may act vigorously or plod along sluggishly. Since top administrators have so much power, their subordinates watch them carefully for any hint of their personal preferences. If an executive pushes a program vigorously, subordinates conclude that they had better take the matter seriously. Thus, the private views of executives do make a difference, especially in the style of performance of those in lower ranks. The manner in which a policy is carried out may well depend on the predilections of certain key executives.

Evaluation of Key Objects. Whether or not maximum effort is forthcoming depends on what the participants actually believe to be worthwhile. Their conviction, in turn, often hinges on their evaluation of key objects, an estimate that takes shape in the spontaneous interchanges that go on within each primary group. Among the most important objects is the organization's announced goal. Is victory in an athletic contest really important? Is it worth the painful conditioning and other sacrifices that must be made? Is the war really worth winning? Is anything at stake that is worth dying for? Are production quotas really worth meeting? Is meeting the announced goal really essential, or is it just a way of getting a local bureaucrat promoted? People who know one another discuss such questions candidly. They recognize ideologies and party lines for what they are, and, although they do not necessarily reject them, they evaluate them in terms of their personal interests. If people feel that they are just being used to advance someone else's career, they are not likely to extend themselves. Those who work too hard under such circumstances are dismissed as stupid, and the evasion of exhortations to comply becomes commonplace.

Numerous studies of variations in morale among different segments of large organizations have focused on unit supervisors. Although attention has centered on different styles of leadership, what is apparently more important is the manner in which supervisors are evaluated by their subordinates. In some military organizations, for example, officers who are "unmilitary" seem to elicit more effective performances from enlisted men. An officer who demonstrates personal concern for the welfare of his men — bending regulations, countermanding orders, and sometimes even participating in passive resistance against higher authorities — often gets better results than a stern disciplinarian. An officer who understands the outlook of enlisted men and tempers enforcement of regulations to provide the most considerate care that the circumstances permit is more likely to evoke peak performances from soldiers, who develop personal loyalty to him (Bassan, 1947; Homans, 1962:50–60). Studies of supervisors in industrial organizations have produced similar results. Kahn and Katz (1953) also found productivity higher among clerical workers in units with permissive and supportive supervisors who are more people-oriented than task-oriented. Authoritarian leadership often results in poor performances.

Studies suggest that morale is likely to be higher in units in which the supervisor is *not* an ideal bureaucrat, but a person who is concerned with workers as human beings. If the members of primary groups define their supervisor as a decent person, they may on occasion work very hard just to please and reward their leader. But merely being concerned with people is not enough. Soldiers and workers expect their leaders to be competent as well. But Fiedler (1967) suggests that observations such as these may hold only under limited circumstances. In an ambiguous situation, such as infantry combat, a permissive leader who uses persuasion may well be more effective, but in a clearly structured transaction an authoritarian leader may elicit a more consistent and reliable performance. Such hypotheses require further investigation.

How the organization itself is evaluated by its members is also important. If a group develops a record of consistently effective performance, its members often come to place a high estimate on the unit. Efficiency then tends to become self-perpetuating, for upholding the unit's reputation becomes an additional objective within its component primary groups. The development of high morale, thus, is a cumulative process. If informal norms result in exceptional achievement, the members become aware of their accomplishments and of how outsiders view them. As they develop pride in their record, maintaining that level of performance becomes a worthy objective. The members then expect one another to make the necessary sacrifices so that the standing of the unit will not be tarnished. It becomes taken for granted that high standards will be maintained. Members of elite groups place enormous pressures on one another to uphold their prestige. For example, the Green Berets — a special, all-volunteer unit organized for guerrilla warfare by the U.S. Army during the Vietnam War — maintained very high standards. The men conceived of themselves as different from the draftees; they were the "best" (Cockerham, 1977). Such consistent, reliable performance is what is commonly called high morale. The term refers to a sustained orientation, not to a single efficacious performance. The importance of self-appraisals is widely recognized. Members of military units and athletic teams are constantly urged to be proud of themselves. In the last analysis, then, high morale becomes a matter of how the participants conceive of themselves. It rests on their regularly defining a succession of transactions as worth doing well, for it would be beneath their dignity to do otherwise.

Solidarity of Primary Groups. Thus, formal and conventional norms provide the general framework within which various transactions are executed, but style of performance depends on individual reactions and the meanings that are nurtured and sustained in primary groups. If the members of local units become sufficiently disenchanted, they may become involved in sullen slowdown tactics. In some instances they may launch a campaign of sabotage, carefully and skillfully camouflaged to appear to be a succession of accidents. If the leaders of communities and large organizations remain unresponsive to such protests, serious rebellions may develop.

Thus, style of performance as well as organizational solidarity may depend on the ability of primary groups to enforce their own norms, keeping recalcitrant members under control. Of course, members of primary groups do not always develop consensus or agree on what to do. Some individuals may wish to perpetuate some costly form of activity long after others have given up, or just a few may wish to withhold cooperation. Those who dislike what is happening in their primary group often try to leave, but this is sometimes not possible. Malcontents often cannot afford to quit their jobs or to separate from their families and friends. If forced to remain where their personal interests are no longer served, it is just a matter of time before they become resentful. The dissatisfied often delight in criticizing and embarrassing those with whom they disagree, as they live out lives of frustration. Primary groups differ considerably in their ability to control recalcitrant members, but the pressure they can exert is not to be underestimated. In his study of the U.S. Senate, which one member described as "just like living in a small town," Matthews (1959) discovered that senators who conform to the chamber's customs and informal norms have better records in getting the legislation they sponsor adopted. This is not the only community in which conformity pays. All primary groups can exact painful penalties from those who refuse to do their part.

SUMMARY AND DISCUSSION

Whenever the same people interact regularly over time, they come to identify themselves as members of a distinct group. Groups of all kinds emerge in all communities. Some are small, and others become huge. All kinds of activities are carried on within them. Each group develops its own patterns of concerted action; if it persists, the normative framework becomes fixed. Once group activities become institutionalized, there tends to be a self-selection of personnel. Those who find participation worthwhile are attracted to it, and others depart at the earliest opportunity. Some groups are ephemeral; others last for centuries. In modern mass societies formal organizations have assumed increasing importance, for large-scale production has been found to be the most effective way of accomplishing many tasks. Once procedures are established in such complex organizations, they become difficult to change, and they are perpetuated even in the face of disaffection on the part of many of their members. It is sometimes believed that such organizations operate as they do because everyone is compelled to follow regulations. If this were so, the groups would become machines and the members, merely robots. Since unhappy individuals often can do little about their fate, they sometimes feel that they are mere cogs in a machine. A close examination of what actually happens within formal organizations discloses, however, that their members are no less human than those in other groups. If they are dissatisfied, they discuss their difficulties candidly with their friends, even if they continue to maintain a front before higher officials. If enough people become dissatisfied, performance becomes desultory. In the face of adversity the group itself may collapse.

Since formal organizations operate most effectively when things are done in an impersonal manner, they are often criticized as being dehumanizing. Although the efficiency of large-scale production is widely acknowledged, formal organizations have been criticized for their rigidity, self-serving tendencies, and ubiquitous red tape. Conservatives who attack "creeping socialism" and "big government" fear that the increasing bureaucratization of various phases of life will result in the stifling of initiative and freedom and result in stagnation. Radicals, especially Karl Marx, have also expressed their disdain for bureaucracies. In spite of such widespread vituperation, however, complex organizations have grown larger and more numerous, and there is every indication that this trend will continue. Thus, one of the major problems confronting humanity in the twentieth century, in both capitalist and socialist economies, is how to make bureaucracies work more efficiently and how to make them more responsive to their clients' needs.

SUGGESTED READINGS

Dalton, Melville. 1959. *Men Who Manage.* New York: Wiley.
> An empirical study of the manner in which the managerial personnel in four American companies accomplish their daily tasks.

Freidson, Eliot. 1970. *Profession of Medicine.* New York: Dodd, Mead.
> A sociological analysis of the organization and operation of the medical profession in modern industrial societies.

Homans, George. 1950. *The Human Group.* New York: Harcourt, Brace.
> An attempt to construct empirically grounded hypotheses about primary groups — a model even for those who disagree with the theory.

Leinhardt, Samuel (ed.). 1977. *Social Networks: A Developing Paradigm.* New York: Academic Press.
> A collection of articles on networks of personal contacts, ranging from ethnographic studies to mathematical analyses.

Mandelbaum, David G. 1952. *Soldier Groups and Negro Soldiers.* Berkeley and Los Angeles: University of California Press.
A critical review of the literature on primary groups, followed by an account of the desegregation of the U.S. Army during the Korean War.
Merton, Robert K., et al. 1952. *Reader in Bureaucracy.* Glencoe, Ill.: Free Press.
An anthology of articles and excerpts from standard references on formal organizations.

IX

REGULATORY INSTITUTIONS

In ancient Greece the usual penalty for homicide was exile. In the early Roman republic a citizen under a death sentence was given a choice between execution and expulsion, and in the Roman Empire deportation to certain islands became a common punishment for serious offenses. Until 1776 certain categories of English convicts were transported to American colonies; after the colonies' independence and until 1853, they were sent to penal settlements in Australia. In Russia, under both czarist and communist regimes, prisoners have been sent to Siberia; recently the Soviet Union has expelled some prominent political dissidents. With the growth of nationalism and acceptance of the doctrine that ties between a state and its citizens are indissoluble the expatriation of criminals has become less frequent. Nonetheless, banishment from the community is still used as punishment for selected deviants, although in most instances it no longer involves the physical departure of the culprit. The condemned are now conferred a special status—that of being an outsider.

The organization of any community and its component parts consists of a complex network of norms—formal, conventional, and informal. What gives communal life the appearance of stability is the compliance of most people with most norms most of the time. Yet almost everyone experiences temptations to do things that run counter to clearly defined obligations, and most of us succumb from time to time. Sometimes such impulses become so pressing that they get out of hand. Every community includes some individuals who are unable to meet minimum standards of acceptable conduct. If something is not done about them, chaos would ensue. Thus, in every community procedures have developed to coerce the recalcitrant—public humiliation, physical punishment, imprisonment, execution, or expulsion. In modern mass societies these procedures have become institutionalized. They are carried out by specialists who work in formal organizations: the police, the judiciary, and the various custodial agencies.

How is a community's normative framework maintained in the face of constant pressures to violate norms? What procedures are used to handle persons whose conduct is regarded as unacceptable? What is the fate of those who persist in violating norms even in the face of anticipated punishment? Since many social scientists have studied this subject, it is not surprising that a variety of theories have been formulated. A number of controversies still rage among specialists in this field, but in this chapter we can review and organize some of the key ideas that have been entertained.

COMMUNITY REACTIONS TO DEVIANCE

Deviant behavior is usually regarded as a violation of any established social norm, and at first glance it would appear that nothing could be more obvious. A closer examination of what is involved, however, reveals that the matter is far from simple. Norms define the range of appropriate conduct, and in real life so many mitigating circumstances arise that it is sometimes difficult to ascertain whether a given act constitutes a violation. Even when norms are clearly specified violations are actually commonplace, and many instances either pass unpunished or draw only mild reprimands. Many violations of conventional norms—improper attire, poor table manners, occasional errors in grammar—are not taken seriously; offenders may be ridiculed or become the object of some gossip. Violations of formal norms are not always punished; many instances are not even reported to the authorities. Indeed, law enforcement officials actually handle but a small percentage of the illegal acts that are committed. Police statistics disclose that many crimes are never solved, and these statistics do not include cases that go unreported. Data from several sources, especially from confessions, reveal that many criminal acts are never detected or recorded (Turk, 1969:15–16). Thus, we must specify more accurately what constitutes deviance. Who are the people who get into serious trouble? How do they get there? What characteristically happens to them?

Recurrent Patterns of Deviance. What is regarded as reprehensible differs from one community to another. In each culture certain acts are singled out as serious offenses that require control; people who commit such offenses are defined as evil, demented, or otherwise unacceptable. In village India the violation of caste etiquette, especially of the rules of endogamy, can result in the offender's being banished for life. In renaissance Europe witchcraft was a most serious crime, and it is estimated that a half million suspects were executed (Currie, 1968). A few centuries later trade unions were viewed as criminal organizations. Wherever ideological purity is stressed, as in many religious and political groups, dissidence is regarded as far more dangerous an offense than homicide, for it is viewed as an attack on all the people. Thus, two eminent Russian novelists—Boris Pasternak and Aleksandr Solzhenitsyn—have been punished severely for doing what writers in other countries have been doing for centuries. The Catholic church considers the use of birth control devices or remarriage after divorce as sufficiently odious to merit excommunication. No particular act is inherently criminal, and just about everything human beings do has been defined as undesirable in some context. *Deviant behavior* consists of whatever is defined in a community, social world, or group as sufficiently reprehensible to require some kind of punishment. But the extent to which such definitions enjoy consensus varies considerably. Since modern mass societies are so diversified, defining deviance becomes especially difficult; in some instances what is condemned in one reference group is admired in another.

Despite the broad range of variation, certain types of conduct are likely to get people into serious trouble in most societies. There is probably no community in which violence against other members is not somehow regulated. Except where there are extenuating circumstances, aggravated assault is widely condemned. Although the value placed on human life varies considerably, homicide is usually permitted only under specified conditions, such as war. There are indications that even professional "hit men" do not see murder as desirable. Property rights are defined in many different ways, but they are generally protected. In some cultures well-known folktales are regarded as the private property of given families. In others land is assigned in perpetuity to various families, regardless of who happens to be using it at the moment; therefore, it cannot be sold. Even in socialist communities, where private property is less important than it is under capitalism, property can be transferred only under conditions specified in custom and law; violations are defined as theft and punished. Thus, norms on intramural violence and on property rights are taken seriously in most communities, and offenders are usually defined as criminals.

The consistent violation of cultural axioms, especially those concerning perception and cognition, generally evokes dismay. Individuals who perceive their surroundings in an idiosyncratic manner or reason in ways that others cannot follow generally encounter serious difficulties. Those who respond to voices no one else can hear, laugh when others find nothing funny, complain of being controlled from outer space, or find it necessary to burn themselves to remove filth no one else can see are usually labeled "crazy." If we recognize that reality is a social process, these people live in a symbolic environment that does not enjoy consensus. They are often a nuisance, and impatient friends and relatives, exhausted after years of pleading, reluctantly ask that something be done. Such persons often elicit fear, for what they do is incomprehensible and unpredictable. They are intolerable in any society, and they are likely to be set apart as exceptional — bewitched, mad, or not quite human. But the boundaries of this category are seldom defined clearly and vary from one culture to another. Insanity is not a crime in most communities; it is often regarded as beyond the individual's control. Such people are usually defined as ill and are sent to healers (Murphy, 1976). Since they are not regarded as morally responsible for their own conduct, they are usually treated differently from criminals. In most instances they are segregated, and steps are taken to see that they are cared for and prevented from injuring themselves or others.

In every community there are persons who are deemed incapable of meeting adult responsibilities: those who are viewed as retarded, those who suffer some serious impairment, or those suffering from some incapacitating disease. In some instances alcoholics and drug addicts are also included among the incapacitated. Although such persons are sometimes mocked and teased by children, in general they are not held accountable for their condition. They are usually set apart as different, and special arrangements are made to care for them. Sometimes such arrangements, even though they are made with the best of intentions, actually make things even more difficult for the persons involved. Mercer (1973) shows how youngsters of considerable ability are sometimes mistakenly labeled as incompetent by faulty testing, sent to special schools, and inculcated with behavior patterns believed appropriate for the mentally retarded. People who are blind are sometimes treated as if they are totally helpless, even when they are capable of enacting most adult roles. Although the physically disabled are neither condemned nor banished in most communities, they too are in effect outsiders, for their special needs are largely ignored.

Popular Reactions to Deviance. When some act defined as unacceptable disrupts the routine of a community, public attention becomes focused on it. Reports of reprehensible acts generally arouse emotional reactions and are followed by demands that something be done. Acts of violence, such as armed robbery or murder, usually arouse fear and resentment. The rape of young children or elderly women is often defined as unnatural and arouses disgust and revulsion. Where a stratification system is well established, fornication between persons of different ranks may also be condemned as unnatural. Such illicit affairs may be tolerated as long as the principals are discreet; once the affair is exposed, however, even friends may be forced to express their disapproval. The most violent emotional reactions are aroused by acts that cannot be explained in terms of the vocabulary of motives accepted in the community. A "senseless" murder arouses intense fear. It is incomprehensible, and one cannot predict what the perpetrator will do. Those who are accused are defined as dangerous objects, and popular demands arise to bring them under control.

In small communities such problems are usually handled in a traditional manner. In modern mass societies transgressors are turned over to special agents of the community, such as the police and the courts. Such custodians of public order are charged with the task of detecting, apprehending, and punishing offenders. As several students of deviance have pointed out, apprehension by the authorities is a decisive step in the process of a person's being labeled as unacceptable (Tannenbaum, 1938). Emphasis shifts from the act to the person. An individual accused of violating a norm is placed into a special category of human beings — those who are beyond the pale. The person comes to be labeled because of some offense, sometimes only a single act. Once labeled, however, the entire person is defined as evil or incompetent.

Deviant Status. An offender who has been apprehended by authorities and goes through the formal procedure of being judged and condemned is conferred a special status — as an outsider. Thus, a person defined as a deviant occupies a special position in the community, one who is no longer an accepted member (Becker, 1963). In the United States prisoners are not only segregated but also are deprived of many other rights enjoyed by other citizens. Convicted felons can neither vote nor hold certain government jobs, and other aspects of all inmates' lives are subject to stringent control. Similarly, a juvenile delinquent is a ward of the court and subject to its discretion. The degradation ceremony often makes it clear to onlookers and to the principal that what was allegedly done is utterly reprehensible. The person then revises his or her self-concept, accepting the label of addict, criminal, or psychopath.

However, only a fraction of all the people who violate norms are stigmatized in this manner, and most of the activities of individuals who are so labeled are similar to the activities of those who are not banished. Thus, even habitual criminals who spend most of their lives in prison accept many of the values of the larger community; child molesters and others convicted of "perversions" not only occupy the lowest status in prisons but also are frequently tormented by other prisoners. Deviant status is ascribed to people because of the type of object they are believed to be rather than because of what they have done (Turk, 1969:8–18). Thus, it is not the violation of norms per se but the status ascribed to alleged offenders that determines how others react to them. A community cannot deal with a person it cannot define, and a deviant is a person who is defined as wicked or incompetent.

Those who have been convicted of engaging in a reprehensible act are placed into a category—insane, witch, thief, murderer, traitor, addict. Each category is defined in stereotyped terms, and one false assumption underlying this procedure is that everyone in each category is alike. We can see the absurdity of this assumption simply by looking more closely. Homicide may be organized and executed in many ways. One man may kill another in a moment of passion, when he catches his best friend making love with his wife. Another murderer may be a professional killer who is fulfilling a contract. Still another may be a compulsive killer who can find relief from painful anxieties only by enacting a ritual that includes homicide. Although law enforcement officials usually make distinctions among murderers, many people simply regard them as culpable and demand that they be punished. Psychiatrists have long noted that persons labeled as insane differ from one another as much as those who are regarded as normal; each person is insane in his or her own way. Yet they are all confined to institutions and often treated as if they were alike. The same is true for other forms of deviance. People steal for many reasons, just as they become addicted to alcohol or other drugs under a variety of circumstances. Once labeled, however, they are usually treated as if they were all alike.

Another key assumption underlying the segregation of deviants is that they are pathological, that they are fundamentally different from the rest of humanity. Normal people presumably would not act as they do.

Thus, criminals are often regarded as inherently evil. Some early students of criminology viewed the "criminal type" as an inferior human being who had inherited certain mental aberrations. No evidence has ever sustained such a belief. Drug addicts and homosexuals have sometimes been regarded as outcasts, and others kept their distance. Those who presume a category of people to be abnormal do not expect its members to be like others. In 1975, when Sergeant Leonard Matlovich disclosed his sexual preferences to contest the legality of the ban on homosexuality in the U.S. Air Force, some officers found it difficult to believe that a gay soldier could have compiled such a distinguished combat record. Even those who insist that sexual preferences are a private matter sometimes feel uncomfortable in the presence of avowed homosexuals. They sense something "different" about such persons, even though they act in a manner as civilized and competent as anyone else. Thus, human beings feel apprehensive upon coming into contact with those who are presumed to be different from themselves. A moral bifurcation develops in each community—a separation of upright citizens who meet their responsibilities and of outcasts who are regarded as being of a different breed.

A third assumption, equally false, is that members of each of the deviant categories become unacceptable in the same manner. This assumption follows logically from the belief that each category is homogeneous. In fact those who become labeled deviant achieve that status through several different routes. For some the forbidden deed is a practiced trade; for others it is a compulsion; for still others it may consist of complying with the expectations of an unpopular reference group. Thus, offenders in each category consist of many different kinds of people. The third assumption arises in part from the search for "causes." A very common but simplistic way of explaining anything is to cite some antecedent event or condition that is regarded as responsible for it. Questions arise concerning the "cause" of rape, murder, theft, or insanity. The kinds of antecedent conditions frequently cited include congenital defects, poor environment, lack of education, broken family, overprotective mother, improper toilet training, the curse of evil spirits, a covenant with the devil, wicked companions, combat fatigue, intense pressures. But no class of deviant acts can be explained so simply. A broad range of deeds enacted under diverse circumstances are classified into a limited set of categories. There is no single antecedent event or condition that can account for all of them. Each human being develops a unique career line; some spend part of their lives in a deviant status, but each deviant arrives at that position in his or her own way. To explain how a particular person became a criminal or landed in an asylum requires a detailed examination of his or her biography. A number of regularities are discernible, but these are not the equivalent of any simple "cause."

Thus, we must distinguish between those who violate social norms and those who are conferred the status of deviants. Although persons who persist in violating norms that are regarded as important are more likely to find themselves stigmatized, many violators do escape undetected. The number of people who have violated tax laws but have not yet been apprehended is impossible to estimate. Both men and women have worked as prostitutes to raise money for some capital investment. Many homosexuals do not divulge their sexual preferences to outsiders since they know that some would condemn them. Some homosexuals have incorporated their community's disapproval of homosexuality into their own value systems and look upon themselves disparagingly. Performing for conflicting reference groups, they are likely to feel the pressures of contradictory expectations, developing feelings of guilt or inferiority. This internal conflict is the lot of any outsider who feels strong allegiance to mainstream norms.

DEVELOPMENT OF DEVIANT CAREERS

Some people get into serious trouble only once. They become involved in a single infraction, perhaps in a moment of desperation, or under intense and sustained stress they suffer what is frequently called a nervous breakdown. Although they are incarcerated, they return to the conventional world upon their release. We are now concerned, however, with those who persist in deviant conduct, who adapt to their surroundings by making deviance a way of life. There are many ways to earn a living; a number of them are illegal, but some prefer to take the risk. They may spend much of their lives in jail or struggling with law enforcement officials. Others become so incapacitated that they are permanently labeled mentally ill and wander in and out of hospitals and halfway houses for most of their lives. What regularities are there in the formation of such deviant careers? In raising this question we are not asking how people come to violate norms; our interest centers on how people attain deviant status and maintain it. Explaining stigmatization is not the same as explaining norm violation. Although the following discussion is confined to crime and mental illness, many of the generalizations apply to other forms of deviance as well.

Labeling as a Social Process. The notion that slums "cause" delinquency and crime is nonsense; millions of children grow up in such areas, and most become law-abiding citizens. As Miller (1958) points out, however, the kinds of values stressed in such neighborhoods — such as being virile and street wise and seeking excitement — tend to encourage behavior that is defined as delinquent. Certainly all kinds of models of illegal activity are readily available (Cloward and Ohlin, 1960). Activities that often begin as play — breaking windows, annoying people, climbing over roofs, stealing from grocery stores — become part of the adventure and excitement of young life. But adults take the nuisance more seriously and demand suppression. If so many youngsters engage in such activities, why do some persist when others grow up and go to work? Several scholars note that whether or not a boy moves toward the status of a criminal depends largely on his being caught and convicted (Tannenbaum, 1938; Becker, 1963), which is often a matter of accident. Those who violate norms more often are more likely to be caught. Some seek prestige among their fellows by being more daring; in some circles being "bad" becomes a claim to recognition. They may even want to be caught so that the police validate their status in the neighborhood as a "tough kid." Serving time in a reformatory or jail becomes for them a badge of honor.

The same kind of developmental pattern has been observed in cases of mental illness. Many people encounter severe personal problems. Disturbances in interpersonal relations, sustained frustration, or domination by unreasonable parents can all result in the formation of traits that others find obnoxious. Whether such persons are labeled insane and segregated depends largely on the reactions of close associates and the authorities — in this case psychiatrists and judges. When a man is defined as an "oddball" and avoided, he is treated as abnormal and may come to conceive of himself as different. When his family and colleagues can no longer tolerate him, they may insist on his seeking medical treatment and have him committed to an asylum. Scheff (1966) shows that this is a crucial part of the labeling process. Thus, what begins as a personal problem leads to a change of status, and the misbehaver may spend the rest of his life incapacitated, frightened, and unable to meet the ordinary problems of life.

But many other people whom psychiatrists would diagnose as neurotic or psychotic are never stigmatized. They somehow manage to get through their daily routines. Indeed, some neurotic traits may enable people to excel. A gifted person with idealistic aspirations may become a compulsive worker who makes significant contributions to the community as a composer, an executive, a scientist, an exceptional baker, or an orchid grower. Rosenhan (1973) shows how difficult it is to differentiate between the sane and insane, even within an asylum. This is not to suggest that the syndromes described by psychiatrists do not exist; as with the popular concept of "race," however, the real differences among people do not coincide with the boundaries of each category.

Since the status of outcast is conferred by authorities, those who are able to protect themselves are less likely to be banished. Thus, the likelihood of becoming an outsider is greater for those who occupy the lower ranks of the stratification system of the community. Indeed, statistics show that a disproportionate number of deviants of all categories are drawn from the poor and from ethnic minorities. A poor youngster who is arrested for stealing is quickly labeled as incorrigible. A thief from a well-to-do home is likely to be defended by an attorney; the parents pay for the stolen objects; and the charges are often dropped. Hollingshead and Redlich (1958) show that the recorded incidence of mental illness is higher in the lower classes. An obnoxious person from the lower classes is more likely to be diagnosed as psychotic, receive less individual treatment, and be confined in a state hospital. Wealthy individuals with similar traits are often treated privately by psychiatrists. If they require special surveillance, companions or tutors may be hired. If intensive care is required, they can go to expensive hospitals where they not only receive treatment but are less likely to be stigmatized. Perhaps the classic example is that of Howard Hughes, who was described as an "eccentric recluse." From all published accounts he was apparently suffering from a severe contamination phobia, one that would have hospitalized most people, but his great wealth enabled him to establish and maintain an environment that was ritually clean.

Even when persons of high rank are caught in illegal activity, they are less likely to be stigmatized. In some communities the wealthy are immune from prosecution in all but the most heinous offenses. Sutherland (1949) refers to the violation of laws by "respectable" people as "white-collar crime." Such offenses are commonplace—violations of price and rationing laws by merchants, unfair labor practices by corporations, violations of pure food and drug laws, embezzlement by executives, criminal negligence by doctors, illegal handling of bankruptcies, illegal rebates and bribery, restraint of trade in violation of antimonopoly laws, infringement of patents and copyrights, underpayment of income taxes, misappropriation of public funds.

The enforcement of such laws is often handled by special agencies in hearings that often resemble juvenile court procedures. Such lawbreakers are usually not defined as *real* criminals; they do not conceive of themselves as criminals; and they are seldom imprisoned. A negligent doctor's license may be revoked; impure food may be seized and destroyed. Most white-collar offenders are fined and placed on probation. When such convictions are reported in the mass media, they are often presented in ways that do not arouse intense emotional reactions. Since such persons enact many useful conventional roles, they seldom lose status in their community, even if they are convicted. An interesting exception is the prosecution of witches in continental Europe. Since the inquisition courts elicited confessions through torture, it was virtually impossible for the accused to escape conviction. The property of the guilty was confiscated and used to finance further prosecution; therefore, wealth could not protect the accused from torture. A substantial proportion of the convicted consisted of men of considerable means. In England, however, where confession through torture was prohibited and where property was not confiscated, most convicted witches were poor women (Currie, 1968). Thus, not all persons believed to have violated formal norms are accorded criminal status. As Victor Hugo pointed out in *Les Misérables,* some people are incarcerated and stigmatized simply because they cannot afford to defend themselves.

Differential Association. An adolescent boy who is constantly involved in activities disapproved of by those around him is bound to be defined as dissolute or vicious. Especially if he is caught and formally conferred the status of delinquent, he is treated differently from other boys. Adults address him with apprehension or hostility. His teachers characterize him as incorrigible and try to avoid him. His neighbors call him a bad boy and caution their children to stay away from him. Even members of his own family often join in the denunciation. When punishment turns out to be ineffective against his stubbornness, his parents give up their efforts to socialize him. He finds it difficult to get a job or to establish a relationship with a "good girl." Thus, he is excluded from many circles and activities. Although girls are often defined as delinquent on quite different grounds, such as alleged sexual promiscuity, those who are so labeled are set apart in much the same manner.

Such differential treatment draws outcasts into the company of others who are similarly rejected. They get to know one another; many of these associates are people who are already committed to a life of deviant conduct. If they remain in sustained contact, they develop their own communication channels; they become participants in their own social world, one with values that differ markedly from those of the rest of the community. In the underworld, for example, interest centers on acquiring goods by illegal means, marketing them, and avoiding the police. A person is respected for acquiring specialized skills, whether it be in handling firearms or blowing safes. They also learn to redefine common objects in ways that are rejected elsewhere. They learn to hate the police and to see "straight" people as hypocrites and suckers, if not as potential victims. They also learn the various justifications used by people engaged in illegal activities; since police officers do things that are illegal, they are often regarded as the most hypocritical of all. Inevitably they acquire a somewhat different vocabulary of motives. Punishment, though it is expected when one is caught, is defined as unjust, and much attention is devoted to tactics to avoid detection and prosecution. As they grow older and more sophisticated, they learn other values. Among professional thieves, for example, the most highly respected are the "right guys." They do not betray fellow violators to the police; they are coolheaded and do not take unnecessary risks or act in anger; they are reliable. Among thieves a "solid crook" is not only technically skillful but also trustworthy (Sutherland, 1937). Actually, these are values that can be found in primary groups everywhere. Thus, it is through differential association with people who live by violating the law that a person acquires roles and meanings that are condemned elsewhere as criminal (Sutherland and Cressey, 1960).

Consistency in the manner in which criminals are treated by others affects the crystallization of their self-concepts. Since their parents and siblings, the judge, the probation officer, and others in the straight world all treat them as lost causes, they label themselves as deviant and acknowledge the rejection of the conventional world. They realize that they are set apart as a different kind of human being. The only people who respect them are those who occupy a similar status. To pursue a successful career in the underworld, they must excel in activities that are likely to get them into further trouble with the police; thus, they will probably be caught and imprisoned again. Each time they go to jail their self-concept and perspective are further reinforced. Once they have been stigmatized, the outcasts turn to one another for moral support, technical assistance, and rationalizations for their way of life. Role-taking is easier for those who share the same fate; they feel they are being treated unfairly, something that only those in the same position can appreciate fully. The longer they participate in a deviant social world, the more they become accustomed to seeing life from this standpoint. Most of their friends are among the rejected, and most of the personal obligations they wish to honor are to people like themselves. Their associates' reactions constantly justify behavior patterns that others regard as clearly unacceptable. Thus, confirmed criminals do what they regard as appropriate and intelligent, and receive the support of others in their social world. Any person who has group support for his or her life-style is likely to be much more stubborn about changing it than someone who is acting alone.

Once the banished have cast their lot with a deviant social world, they act in ways that are likely to bring them acceptance and respect within their own reference group. Each social world is organized, and most of the participants follow familiar career lines. Once people conceive of themselves as criminals, they act in ways that are consistent with this definition. Younger members of the underworld develop their "rep" by vandalizing, defying the police, and showing courage in gang fights (Short and Strodtbeck, 1965). In some circles one can win admiration by being a "stand-up cat"—a person who consumes drugs to demonstrate toughness and street skills. The known dangers of heroin and the risks involved are seen as ways of demonstrating one's daring (Finestone, 1957; Feldman, 1968). The prestige ladder of the underworld is different from that of the rest of the community. In both worlds, highest on the ladder and most respected are those who have acquired sophisticated technical knowledge and have been successful. But upward mobility, advancement up the prestige ladder, in the underworld is reserved for heroes who are admired and emulated for their success in crime. If their exploits are covered in the mass media, they gain even more respect. Some compete with others to see who can execute the most daring caper and get away with it. Thus, striving for status goes on within this social world as it does elsewhere. Since a high value is placed on deviance, a person must learn to do what the mainstream community condemns and learn to do it well. Once committed to a deviant career, individual criminals try to develop self-respect from the standpoint of an audience consisting of people like themselves.

Coping with Stigma. Outcasts are not unaware of the disapproval of the rest of the community (Sykes and Matza, 1957). They are sufficiently exposed to formal communication channels to realize that most people condemn them. Most outsiders feel stigmatized. When people who are completely convinced that they are in the right are punished, they react as martyrs, as do those who are persecuted for their religious beliefs. Although delinquents and criminals resent punishment, they do not respond as martyrs. The kinds of rationalization criminals often use presuppose a recognition of wrongdoing. Some even show a sense of guilt; this implies acceptance of some of the values of the larger community. Sometimes they take care to protect straight friends from becoming involved in illegal activities; and very few criminals, even the very successful, urge their children to follow in their footsteps. Indeed, it appears that most criminals have a very low level of self-esteem. Nonetheless, there is a sense of injustice. Outsiders often feel that they have been mistreated. Continued rejection and constant clashes with the police harden and reinforce antagonism against the conventional world.

Even after offenders have paid their penalty and are discharged from correctional facilities, it is very difficult for them to change their status. Psychiatrists generally agree that the border between insanity and normality is impossible to define; once one has been confined in an asylum, however, it is very difficult to overcome the mark of disgrace. Even when some convicts decide that prison life is ridiculously wasteful and that they would prefer to go straight when they are released, it is difficult for them to find satisfactory employment. Job applicants are asked for references. In many instances they are asked under oath whether they have ever been a psychiatric patient or a convict. Many positions, such as government service, are not open to anyone with a record. Even when laws do not proscribe hiring stigmatized persons, many employers are afraid to do so. Fellow workers, upon learning where the new colleague has been, are often not sympathetic. Fear is a frequent reaction, and if such persons are not rejected outright, they are kept at a polite distance. Some people may even be cruel, going out of their way to torment "jailbirds" or "crazies." Former psychiatric patients not only find most desirable jobs closed to them but encounter many difficulties in coping with other aspects of the conventional world. It is not surprising, then, that they are often drawn together. Former patients often form their own social world; they meet in halfway houses, various encounter groups, outpatient clinics, and welfare offices and instruct one another on obtaining adequate financial support and meeting other challenges.

Once a person forms a self-concept as someone who is different from other people, it is very difficult to alter his or her way of life. The recidivism rate for convicts and psychiatric patients is quite high. This is so precisely because they continue to define situations from a standpoint they share with others of deviant status, even after they have been released from custody. Given underworld values, for example, many of the things a released prisoner is asked to do appear meaningless, if not stupid. Why should a specialist in armed robbery work at a service station for a few dollars an hour? His week's pay comes to an amount he could steal easily in a single transaction that would require but a few moments. Thus, confirmed criminals are not likely to reform unless some kind of conversion occurs—a displacement of perspectives. Unless there is some other group, such as a religious cult, that is willing to accept them, the pressure to continue their deviant ways is too great. To terminate their criminal careers they must break off all personal contacts with underworld friends, and this loss of primary group support leaves them isolated just when they must struggle to overcome the barriers of stereotyped beliefs.

ENFORCEMENT OF FORMAL NORMS

Violations of formal norms that are taken seriously lead to the invocation of organized sanctions. Offenders are confronted by agents of the community. In modern mass societies police work has become highly specialized, and especially in urban areas the officers are employed by large, formal organizations. After being arrested, the accused are confronted by a complicated judicial system. In criminal cases the proceedings are organized to ascertain only whether the party is guilty, not to establish how some deviant act took place. Thus, the objective is confined to ascribing status: normal or outcast. Those adjudged unfit to continue participating in the community are remanded to a variety of custodial organizations—prisons, asylums, detention homes. To understand how the custodians of public order perform, we must remember that they too are human beings and that they work as members of complex organizations directed by bureaucrats. They are expected to operate within clearly defined procedures, to submit to hierarchical control, and to perform their duties in an impersonal manner.

Law Enforcement as Conflict. Although police officers provide many services—rescuing lost children, helping doctors in emergencies, settling family quarrels, directing traffic—they are also locked in continual conflict with those who are labeled as criminals. This is what makes police work so dangerous. Unlike the military, however, police officers cannot engage in all-out war, for their foes are not clearly segregated from other people. They must exercise considerable care, especially when they are forced to use lethal weapons. Thus, police officers and habitual offenders define each other as enemies, develop stereotyped conceptions of one another, and form the kind of values that arise frequently among people involved in combat. Each side closes ranks against its opponent. Like other combatants, the members feel that they must protect one another as they carry out dangerous assignments.

Since conflicts between the police and the underworld have been going on for centuries, numerous formal and conventional norms have developed concerning the manner in which the struggle is to be conducted. Procedural laws provide the framework within which the various transactions occur. Many of these norms restrict what law enforcement officials may do. In the United States, for example, officers are required to inform the accused of their rights even before they begin to question them. They may place wiretaps on telephones only under conditions specified by law. They are not allowed to torture prisoners into divulging information, a practice still used in many countries. All offenders have a right to counsel, and there are definite rules on admissible evidence. At times the police must release a person they know to be guilty because their evidence is inadmissible in court. Experienced criminals are well aware of these norms; they are also aware of the kinds of penalties imposed for various illegal acts. Many thieves do not carry weapons even though they would feel safer with them. They try to avoid killing a police officer. Any homicide is likely to elicit trouble, but killing an officer sometimes brings massive retaliation that may affect many of the murderer's friends. Sophisticated offenders are able to assess fairly accurately the strengths and weaknesses of their own position relative to that of the police. Thus, law enforcement involving habitual offenders sometimes takes on the character of a game — a contest between rivals in which both parties know the rules.

Effective police work is sometimes hampered by such regulations; hence, all kinds of informal arrangements develop, many of them illegal. To carry on their conflict with the underworld police officers must have some knowledge of what is going on among their enemies. Intelligence work of this kind cannot be done without establishing contacts in the underworld, and this creates possibilities for corruption. Many opportunities arise for bribes. Since officers are poorly paid for dangerous work, some succumb to temptations. The frustrations conscientious officers face sometimes lead them to illegal acts, such as unauthorized wiretaps and overzealous prisoner interrogations. Sometimes plea-bargaining deals are made with those willing to "squeal" on someone who has committed a more serious offense, and informers are sometimes paid with heroin confiscated in a drug raid. However, police officers do not indiscriminately sanction illegal actions by their cohorts. Most police officers disapprove of "crooked cops."

The very nature of police work requires each officer to exercise discretion, and this leads to other problems. No effort is made to enforce all laws at all times; all-out enforcement would keep the police too busy and would fill jails too quickly. Upon detecting an offense, individual officers must judge whether it is serious enough to warrant arrest, whether a warning would suffice, or whether to ignore it (Skolnick, 1975). Police often do not enforce unpopular laws; they tend to ignore marijuana smoking, for example, unless the offense is so flagrant that they must take action. The fact that each officer must make such personal judgments often leads to preferential treatment. In slum areas police officers can order the denizens about with relative impunity; in wealthy suburbs, however, where they must deal with people who can afford to hire an attorney, they must proceed with more caution. It is not surprising, therefore, that charges of police brutality usually emanate from persons of low status.

The Social World of the Police. Since every police department has its own communication channels, formal and informal, the members become part of a common social world. They often develop stereotyped conceptions of their foes, referring to them as "creeps," "hoods," "bums." Some work on the assumption that recidivists in particular are basically evil and unworthy of being treated like normal human beings. They account for criminal offenses in terms of a vocabulary of motives that imputes wicked, selfish intentions; sometimes they find it difficult to comprehend the mitigating circumstances cited by defense attorneys.

Although the police are sometimes condemned for their stance, outsiders often forget the kinds of experiences that most officers have. They see their comrades being killed or injured in the line of duty. Furthermore, almost daily they see the victims—an old woman who has just been robbed of her life savings, a child who has been left mangled by a drunk driver, a terrified woman who has been raped. They also feel the impact of the grief and anger of the victims' friends and relatives, for it is their unpleasant duty to inform them of what has happened. Most officers readily admit that their work is dirty, unpleasant, and dangerous. They also realize that they sometimes break the very laws they are supposed to enforce. Yet most of them remain convinced that the work has to be done by someone. Thus, many officers conceive of themselves as participants in a crusade against evil. Even when they are denounced as "pigs," they still regard themselves as the maligned custodians of public order.

Police officers are well aware of the hatred with which they are viewed by outcasts, but they often become resentful when they are condemned by other segments of the community. Laws are usually formulated by intellectuals who are concerned with abstract principles, and those who must enforce them often find them difficult to understand. Enforcement officials sometimes see themselves as involved in constant conflict with a dangerous foe who appears to have unlimited reserve strength, and they feel that their hands are tied by rules that favor their enemies. As is true of many combat organizations, the police force tends to become isolated from the rest of the community. Police officers develop their own culture. Among themselves, common understandings develop about which offenses are to be taken seriously. When a rapist killer is loose in the community, they often go all out to detect and apprehend him, but they enforce many other laws reluctantly, only when evidence is thrust on them by someone who demands prosecution. Even officers who accept bribes regularly risk their lives in pursuing serious offenders. Some who have acquired considerable wealth "shaking down" small-time criminals have also won commendations for solving baffling murders. They decide among themselves how much violence is to be used in various contexts (Westley, 1953).

The police also develop group solidarity, protecting one another on assignments and refusing to "squeal" on colleagues who violate what they consider minor regulations (Westley, 1956). They oppose civilian review boards, for they are convinced that outsiders cannot understand the risks they run or the split-second decisions they must make. Furthermore, they are members of organizations within which they are pursuing careers, and commitment to the organization and its values is rewarded. As a general rule a "policeman's policeman" is an unusual person who has built an enviable record of law enforcement while respecting the informal norms of colleagues. Such a person becomes the model for the young officer who wishes to acquire higher status within the group. Most officers perform for a reference group that consists largely of their comrades, their families, and their friends.

Any organized body of armed personnel is a potential threat to the community. The police must remain politically neutral, retain overall respect for the law, and maintain discipline. Because of the unusual nature of police work, however, such requirements present many difficulties. Since officers often work alone or in small units with friends, efficient law enforcement requires self-discipline on the part of each individual. No one can be kept under constant surveillance. Before armed persons can consistently place their duty before their private interests, they must be committed to professional standards and develop pride in their organization. Thus, urban police departments emphasize care in recruitment and training, the development of pride in the calling, and the importance of impersonal performance of duties. If officers develop enough pride in themselves, they will watch one another. Personal pride is then reinforced by their expectations of each other. Once officers accept professional standards, the primary group will enforce them. Thus, effective performance depends on high morale in the organization.

Custodial Organizations. Those who are adjudged guilty or incompetent are formally conferred the status of outsider. Unless they are executed, they are segregated; imprisonment is a form of exile from the community. Historically, all kinds of justifications have been given for prisons: protecting society by isolating offenders, deterring future crimes, rehabilitating those who need guidance. In fact, however, criminals are defined as people who have intentionally committed a reprehensible act; hence, they are being punished. Those who are classified as insane are not regarded as morally responsible for their deeds; they too are banished, but the rationale is that they must be protected from injuring themselves or others. We cannot understand what happens in prisons or asylums unless we recognize that they are formal organizations, controlled by a bureaucracy and staffed by personnel who are pursuing careers within them. Promotion up the hierarchy depends on the employee's ability to meet organizational requirements — to maintain order and to remain within the budget. Thus, problems are usually resolved in terms of staff needs rather than inmate interests. Prison guards are not primarily concerned with rehabilitation; they are preoccupied with keeping the premises clean and avoiding trouble. Attendants in asylums often feel that they have to protect themselves from both the patients and the professional staff; their aim is to maintain control. Patients who do inconvenient things are labeled "disturbed" and punished, sometimes brutally. Many staff members tend to look down on their charges as inferior human beings, and they realize that most people in the outside community do not really care about them.

Prisoners must find ways to survive in such contexts. The inmates have their own communication channels, and several studies reveal that they develop their own culture (Clemmer, 1940; Sykes, 1958). One common understanding is that a prisoner should be a "right guy" — not to cooperate with the guards and certainly not to "squeal" on fellow inmates. Although it is often assumed that prison authorities have complete control, they do not. Most prisoners do not feel any duty to obey them; there are limits to further punishment that can be inflicted; and rewards such as mail, visiting, and recreational privileges are not important enough to provide a basis for coercion. Hence, violence, fraud, theft, sexual assaults, and drug use are commonplace. Another key informal norm is not to interfere with the activities of fellow prisoners. Those who are already denizens of the underworld find themselves in a familiar setting, well organized and with contacts extending outside the prison. Those whose past behavior best exemplifies what the outside community rejects—experienced and sophisticated career criminals—enjoy prestige. Younger prisoners learn the lore of the underworld as well as many technical skills from them.

Guards who are in daily contact with the prisoners work out a modus vivendi. The cooperation of prisoners is necessary to keep the place clean and free of disturbances, and guards who are "good Joes" can win this cooperation by overlooking various offenses and avoiding situations in which they are likely to discover them. By making such deals guards can maintain a semblance of order, and the prisoners are able to pursue their interests surreptitiously. Prisoners who enjoy high status in the underworld, who often have contacts and money outside, are in a better position to maintain order; they sometimes help the authorities in return for special privileges. Even "square Johns"—those convicted of crimes of passion or white-collar criminals who are not committed to a life in the underworld—also comply with these norms (Irwin and Cressey, 1962).

Inmates of asylums are more helpless than prisoners; they are at the mercy of the staff and must learn to cope with its demands. Despite all the difficulties in communication that precipitated their incarceration, they also develop informal norms that enable them to survive more comfortably (Dunham and Weinberg, 1960). Considerable pressure is placed on each patient to acknowledge his or her impaired condition as an illness. Many find this difficult to accept, insisting that they are only temporarily incapacitated by a nervous breakdown. But neither staff members nor fellow patients will accept this explanation for their presence in a psychiatric ward. They are urged to relax their defenses. Emphasis is also placed on getting along with others, even those who are obnoxious. They learn to tolerate one another's eccentricities; permissiveness is stressed, and each patient is urged to suspend judgment toward the others. A high value is placed on being discharged, and patients often rank one another in terms of who is closest to being released. Many realize that too candid disclosures of their difficulties may delay discharge; hence, they learn to conceal symptoms such as hallucinations. Those who violate such informal norms are condemned as deviants and isolated; those who conform often receive considerable support in coping with their personal difficulties (Caudill et al., 1952). Thus, the informal norms that develop do ease adjustments to hospital demands, protect patients against abuse, and teach them how to effect an early release.

It is widely recognized that the system of law enforcement that has developed in industrial societies does not deter deviant behavior, fails to rehabilitate most offenders, and actually facilitates the perpetuation of outcast groups and their values. It merely provides a temporary exile of offenders who are caught. Imprisonment fosters a hatred of society and especially of the police. As newcomers are socialized to the requirements of prison life, they become more committed to underworld values. Thus, the inmate culture affects the careers of outcasts not only while they are in custody but also after their release. Sometimes minor offenders become so estranged that they become lifelong criminals. Similarly, any lengthy confinement in an asylum tends to reinforce a patient's self-concept of being fundamentally different from other people. Those labeled as insane are sometimes rewarded for enacting stereotyped roles; when they do what the staff expects of them, they may be credited with having insight into their illness. The informal norms that facilitate accommodation in correctional facilities are reaffirmed by both the inmates and their keepers. By approaching each other with stereotyped beliefs, they support one another's perspectives. Thus, the contradiction is inherent in the organization of communities; both custodians and outcasts are trapped within it. More enlightened policies, aiming toward rehabilitation rather than punishment, have misfired. Some prison guards, asylum attendants, and probation officers have good intentions, but their hands are tied by regulations. Nonetheless, violations of key norms cannot be ignored.

LEGITIMATION AND THE MORAL ORDER

Legitimation as a Social Process. In all communities certain persons and groups have the responsibility for maintaining order. Some officials, especially the police, have considerable *power*—the capacity to get things done even in the face of opposition. In modern mass societies the right to use force to coerce the recalcitrant rests with the government. Although most of us take the existence of governments for granted, this type of regulatory institution is relatively new. By the fifteenth century, governments had developed only in Europe and Asia, scattered areas in Africa, and a few places in Latin American—among the Maya, the Aztec, and the Inca. Thus, most societies in the history of humanity have not had governments but have been small communities in which most of the inhabitants knew one another. In such communities all members are participants in a number of overlapping and intersecting groups— kinship units, age and sex groups, religious bodies. Each group regularly takes charge of specific transactions; each has its own norms and enforces them (Colson, 1974). As communities grow, however, special procedures become necessary for making decisions, settling disputes, and regulating serious deviance. Communities without governments are becoming more and more rare; with increasing industrialization they will probably become obsolete. Today the territorial boundaries of all nations are clearly defined; within each unit a government claims exclusive sovereignty — that is, officials claim a monopoly on the legitimate use of coercion to enforce order.

Authority is the recognized right to rule, using force if necessary. Authority is clearest when there is an established hierarchy in an institutionalized context — parent over child, teacher over pupil, employer over employee, guard over prisoner, coach over athlete. Authority rests on the legitimate use of power, and *legitimation* is the acceptance of control by all the parties involved. Where authority is well established, the rulers assume that they have the right to give orders, and the subjects acknowledge their duty to obey. Rousseau once wrote, "The strongest is never strong enough to be master always, unless he transforms his strength into right, and obedience into duty." No one is strong enough to rule by force alone; thus, the objective is to govern by trust rather than by coercion. For example, drivers obey traffic officers' directions not because they wear pistols but because drivers accept their right to regulate traffic. Most people recognize the difficulties that would arise if some drivers did not cooperate; hence, they concur that it is their duty to contribute their part.

Legitimation is the foundation of government. Authority rests on the beliefs of the ruled, beliefs that enjoy a high degree of consensus. Many principles have been cited as sources of the right to rule — divine will, democratic election, private property, hereditary succession, seniority, special competence. Unless the use of power is justified by linking it to widely accepted values, the governed are less willing to obey; they may even challenge the right of those who are trying to rule. Whenever justifications fall into question, authority is weakened and control can be maintained only by force. When a group has disproportionate power, it may be able to preserve an unpopular government for a while, but there are limits to this. Many complex transactions require cooperation on the part of many that force alone cannot secure. For example, armies of occupation often find that they cannot maintain control without taking hostages. In the last analysis authority rests on the consent or at least the acquiescence of most of the people (MacIver, 1947). Subjects need not necessarily be pleased with their rulers, but they must accept the right of those in authority to rule.

Law enforcement depends largely on public opinion. What constitutes deviance is a matter of consensus. If concerned people feel that duly constituted authorities are derelict in their duty, they may take the law into their own hands. Popular justice is more commonly found in frontier communities, but vigilance committees are formed periodically elsewhere when the police are unwilling or unable to act. Precisely because of this potential, most officials are responsive to outraged public opinion. Something must be done, and sometimes they resort to expressive symbolism to alleviate the anxieties of those who are upset (Edelman, 1964). If some spectacular offense focuses attention on vice, for example, the police sometimes make well-publicized raids on brothels and gambling establishments, creating the impression that they are doing something. Once public attention has shifted elsewhere, charges against those arrested in the sweeps are sometimes dropped. Even dictators cannot afford to ignore public opinion. If they do, their authority may be questioned. When laws become unpopular, they become difficult to enforce. Without public support governments face constant difficulties and occasional rebellions.

Human Society as a Moral Order. In *Nineteen Eighty-four* George Orwell describes a totalitarian state in which the police keep every citizen under continuous surveillance. At present this is not feasible technologically; even in prisons monitored through closed-circuit television it is not possible to watch everyone. But even if some madman wanted to regulate the lives of the populace in such a manner, it is doubtful that any society based on fear of punishment alone could survive for long. Except in problematic situations life goes on fairly smoothly precisely because most people engage in moral conduct and continue to support one another's expectations. Those who conceive of themselves as law-abiding citizens do what they consider appropriate and decent. Most people comply habitually with well-established norms, rarely realizing they could do things differently. Even when they notice a possibility of cheating, most people do what they regard to be the right thing. Those who do violate an important norm usually experience guilt or shame. Most people act consistently in ways that enable them to maintain self-respect in their own eyes. There are many occupations in which one works alone — plumbers, doctors, mechanics, teachers, gardeners. Those who take pride in their work live up to their responsibilities, doing the best they can under the circumstances, whether or not anyone else is watching. Most citizens make a reasonable effort to earn their way in life; they have modest ambitions, are willing to work or fight for what they consider worthwhile, and act in ways that are consistent with their self-concepts.

Whenever we are tempted to cheat, obligations to people we know on a personal basis tend to reinforce our sense of right and wrong. With the exception of a small minority who become isolated—sometimes called sociopaths—just about everyone is bound in an intricate network of personal ties in overlapping primary groups. It is very difficult for us to do things that we know will hurt or disappoint people with whom we identify, especially those whom we like and respect. Facing friends after a serious offense is very painful, and most people fight off temptations in order to avoid having to do so. Those who have made such sacrifices for others are usually held in high esteem; sometimes they are even honored as heroes or saints. Since such persons embody their primary groups' values, they serve as ideal models. Thus, our sense of justice and fair play is constantly reinforced in primary groups. Park (1950:87, 180) contends that the boundaries of a moral order extend as far as people are able to identify with one another as human beings. Thus, the boundaries of moral order differ somewhat from one person to another. Some identify with all human beings; others identify only with some categories—their class, ethnic group, community, or extended family—and show little concern for outsiders. We must be careful not to confuse the moral order with Judeo-Christian morality. Individuals perform for different reference groups, and Judeo-Christian values constitute but one of many standards of conduct.

When a community becomes too large for everyone to know one another on a personal basis, formal sanctions must be used to institutionalize the moral order (Redfield, 1953; Wirth, 1956:110–32). Even when social contacts are largely categorical, most people continue to engage in moral conduct; however, one can no longer count on voluntary conformity. Since strangers feel no particular personal obligation to one another, their sense of decency sometimes needs to be bolstered by formal norms. Thus, as communities grow, law enforcement officials become more essential.

Occasionally a crisis occurs in which regulatory institutions are neutralized, and what happens in such contexts is revealing. Records of what occurs when a police force goes on strike, when people are trapped on an isolated island, when metropolitan areas are shut down by a blackout, or when civilians are trapped in areas contested by rival armies—all reveal that most people continue to act as they always had in the past. If anything, they band together to help one another. When the police went on strike in Montreal in 1969, some disturbances occurred, but only persons who had been held back by fear of punishment—criminals, political extremists, people with special grievances, and some thrill seekers— acted differently (Clark, 1969). The looting that takes place in blackouts is limited largely to the impoverished, and even among the poor the vast majority do not participate. Such observations disclose that most people comply with norms for reasons other than the fear of punishment.

The Segregation of Offenders. Émile Durkheim (1933) raises the question of why regulatory institutions persist, since they neither deter criminals nor rehabilitate them. He argues that enforcement procedures provide a ceremonial reaffirmation of the values of the community. The various agents involved—the police, the judicial system, the prisons— symbolize the community as a whole. The solemnity of the courts, the majesty of the law, and the supposedly impartial enforcement of justice are ritualistic expressions of the common will of the people. For example, the punishment of a murderer may not instill fear in potential killers, but it does reaffirm the community's belief in the sanctity of human life. Similarly, punishing a thief reaffirms the belief in the sanctity of property. When violators are punished, the norms are reinforced.

The solidarity of any community is enhanced when the populace is united to defend it against a common foe. Offenders are defined as enemies of society. There is little sympathetic identification with enemies; they are viewed as a different breed of animal. A reprehensible offense evokes fear, and the people unite to defend themselves. The aggrieved party finds a champion in the agents of government, although in many cases demand for punishment comes more from an outraged public than it does from the indignant victim. Hence, the conviction and punishment of criminals is viewed as being for the good of the whole community. The enforcement system reinforces the responsibility of decent citizens to obey laws and comply with conventional norms. Thus, the belief that crime does not pay, whether or not it is correct, does contribute to perpetuating the existing social order.

Durkheim's position is difficult to test. Certainly regulatory institutions are not deliberately created or maintained for ceremonial purposes. But his contention is worth considering. If flagrant violators of norms are banished from society as pathological, those within the moral order find it easier to comply even when it is costly. Numerous situations may tempt any citizen to violate some norm; but if individuals are able to conceive of themselves as normal and responsible citizens, they are more likely to conform. "I will not behave like a depraved criminal," insists the citizen tempted to violate a norm. As long as outcasts are segregated and their alleged deeds are defined as abnormal, the normative framework is more likely to persist. Furthermore, seeing what kinds of deviation elicit the greatest outrage helps define the range of acceptable conduct, indicating just where the line is drawn. Sending the unacceptable into exile helps to define the boundaries within which normal people are expected to perform (Erikson, 1966).

SUMMARY AND DISCUSSION

Since each person participates in so many transactions each day, deviations from social norms are commonplace. In most instances minor violations pass unnoticed, are deliberately overlooked, or elicit only mild reproach. When someone does something that is defined as reprehensible, however, the deed evokes deep emotional reactions. Those who are caught are defined as a menace to the community; if they are not executed, they are banished by being ascribed a special status — that of an outsider. Those so segregated often establish their own communication channels and develop their own cultures. If they become committed to a deviant life-style, they continue to be condemned and remain separated from others. Special agents of the community, such as the police, are charged with controlling outcasts; they too become isolated from the rest of the community, for law enforcement requires them to function as a combat organization. Regulatory institutions are ways in which the hostility of a community is directed against its foes. Thus, the normative framework of each community is constantly reaffirmed both by the conformity of most of the people with moral codes and by the expulsion of those regarded as incapable or unwilling to engage in moral conduct. But effective law enforcement requires public support; the legitimacy of government rests on its acceptance by most of the people. Thus, the conditions that enable any community to maintain the appearance of stability are consensus and self-regulation. At bottom each community is a moral order.

Some people who are labeled incompetent do not exercise sufficient personal autonomy to be held accountable for their deeds, and they are usually more pitied than condemned. But those who are defined as unwilling to comply with key norms become the targets of communal wrath. Most outsiders, however, even during their banishment, do not cease to be human; they form moral orders of their own. They form meaningful contacts with other outcasts and among themselves live by primary group values. Although thieves who are strangers feel no particular obligations to one another, anyone involved in a common network of personal contacts is likely to face ostracism or even violence for not being a "right guy." The very fact that so many outcasts form their own societies is an indication that they are indeed capable of self-regulation and moral conduct.

Thus, social structures of all kinds persist to the extent that the participants in transactions continue to engage in moral conduct. A high incidence of deviant behavior, whether or not the culprits are caught and stigmatized, indicates that a moral order is undergoing transformation, that perspectives are beginning to change significantly. When consensus breaks down, people begin to question the appropriateness of previously established norms, especially in contexts in which conformity is costly. Many begin to wonder what constitutes the right and decent thing to do, perhaps even sympathizing with some outcasts or challenging government authority. Thus, when consensus breaks down, life become less predictable. Life conditions keep changing, but in many instances conventional and formal norms cannot be reconstructed rapidly enough to keep pace. All kinds of difficulties and misunderstandings arise. Most of us are familiar with such problems, for we live in a rapidly changing society. The remainder of this book deals with the manner in which collective adaptations are made in such contexts.

SUGGESTED READINGS

Cressey, Donald R., and David A. Ward (eds.). 1969. *Delinquency, Crime, and Social Process.* New York: Harper & Row.
   A comprehensive anthology on deviant behavior, the formation of deviant careers, and some consequences of attempts at regulation.
Erikson, Kai T. 1966. *Wayward Puritans: A Study in the Sociology of Deviance.* New York: Wiley.
   A sociological analysis of deviant behavior and its management, using the early Puritans in New England as a case study.
Goffman, Erving. 1961. *Asylums.* New York: Doubleday.
   Perceptive observations on the characteristic experiences of persons incarcerated in mental hospitals.
MacIver, Robert M. 1947. *The Web of Government.* New York: Macmillan.
   A sociological analysis of government, with particular attention to the kinds of beliefs that provide legitimation.
Scheff, Thomas J. 1984. *Being Mentally Ill: A Sociological Theory.* Chicago: Aldine.

A study of the processes through which individuals are labeled as mentally incompetent and the manner in which that status is perpetuated.

Skolnick, Jerome H. 1975. *Justice Without Trial: Law Enforcement in Democratic Society*. New York: Wiley.

A sociological study of police work, with particular emphasis on the informal norms that enable officers to accomplish their tasks.

X

PROBLEMATIC SITUATIONS

One of John Dewey's many contributions to twentieth-century thought is his contention that human beings engage in reflective thinking only when confronted by a problem. We are creatures of habit who act in familiar ways until some difficulty interrupts our routine. When driving an automobile, for example, we execute a number of complex movements without much awareness, while talking to other passengers; only when something unusual happens do we focus our attention on the task of driving. Thinking consists for the most part of an imaginative rehearsal of alternative ways of meeting the problem. For example, suppose that we need some essential ingredient to finish cooking dinner. A severe rainstorm has just ended, and en route to the grocery store we encounter a flooded gutter. We consider several possibilities. We could just wade through, but our shoes may leak and our slacks would get soaked. We may consider broad jumping about ten feet, but landing on a wet pavement could be dangerous. We glance up and down the street for a narrow crossing, but the nearest one is at least a half block away. We search for a plank or a large rock to use for a bridge but cannot find one. We may become enraged and decide to go home but realize that we still need something to eat.

Each alternative considered is a plan of action. Tentative solutions are pretested in the imagination prior to commitment in overt conduct. The ability to make imaginary trial-and-error efforts gives human beings an advantage over most other animals; overt trial-and-error can be costly, sometimes even fatal. Dewey goes on to say that the effectiveness with which people are able to think depends on past experiences in similar contexts and on their emotional reactions. We have seen that mild excitement facilitates thought by focusing attention, sharpening perception, and enhancing critical ability. But intense emotion tends to be disorganizing and makes problem solving more difficult (Dewey, 1910). Although problematic situations may arise anywhere, even in the most stable settings, they are more likely to be encountered in contexts that are changing.

Successful patterns of collective adaptation, once established, persist for a time and provide a framework within which subsequent transactions may be channeled. But life conditions are continuously changing. No matter how stable some societies may appear, difficulties keep arising. The classification and ranking of people in a community as well as their spatial distribution are periodically revised. Groups are constantly being formed, modified, reconstituted, and dissolved. Changes are sometimes confined to specific norms, but on some occasions they are so pervasive that a person who has been away from the community for a decade would have difficulty recognizing his or her former home. Some changes occur suddenly; others take considerable time, perhaps centuries. Although one sometimes gets the impression that life in a rapidly changing society is utterly chaotic, most of the transformations happen in recurrent ways. Over and again normative frameworks are modified or displaced in much the same manner, and our concern in studying transitional processes is to describe some of the regularities in transformation. Under what conditions do once-established patterns of concerted action break down? What are the characteristic experiences and reactions of people when confronted with situations in which social norms prove inadequate? How do they cope with situations marked by confusion and frustration? How are transactions undertaken in the absence of an adequate normative framework? How do new patterns of concerted action develop? How do they become established to serve as the framework for subsequent activities?

People caught in situations in which previously established patterns of concerted action have become outmoded are not quite sure what to expect of one another. They are often surprised at what others do and may even be disappointed and hurt by their friends' actions. Two or more people confronted by a problematic situation react much as lone individuals do: They think about the situation and summon their intellectual resources. But there is one crucial difference between individual and collective problem solving: communication. Whenever more than one person is involved, some kind of communication is essential to work out a collaborative response. Thus, in studying the manner in which people jointly cope with problematic situations, we must focus on communicative processes. How people communicate varies with the intensity of their emotional reactions; therefore, the degree of collective tension that develops becomes a critical variable. Attention in this chapter thus focuses on two questions. What are the characteristic ways in which people try to cope jointly with problematic situations? How does the degree of collective excitement generated affect the manner in which they come to terms with the situation?

CRISIS AND COLLECTIVE ADAPTATION

Emergence of Problematic Situations. A *problematic situation* is one that cannot be met with an already existing normative framework. Thus, any situation becomes problematic to the extent that previously established norms no longer provide an adequate guide for concerted action. An obvious example is an emergency. Although most communities have procedures for coping with disasters, some catastrophes are so severe that such measures are clearly inadequate — a huge fire, a gigantic earthquake, a devastating flood, a relentless epidemic, or an extended famine. Although most communities have regulatory institutions, from time to time infractions occur that cannot be handled through these procedures — a compulsive killer on the loose, indiscriminate bombings by terrorists, or an offense so outrageous that the people demand immediate retribution. Or a barrier may interrupt a transaction. A group of pioneers trekking toward a new homeland may encounter a mountain they cannot cross with the equipment and personnel at hand, or they may be attacked by hostile natives who resent their intrusion. Barriers are often social; staff members in a bureaucracy working on a new program may find its implementation blocked by an intransigent executive who refuses to take them seriously. A situation may also become problematic from attrition; exhausted firefighters after battling a holocaust for several days may be confronted by a sudden and unexpected shift in the wind. Sometimes well-established institutions break down from being overloaded, from the inefficiency of a complacent staff, or from corruption. In all such contexts the persons involved cannot proceed on the basis of previously established expectations, and the line of action comes to a temporary standstill. A problematic situation is one in which people are forced to reflect, to reevaluate, and to plan. Something out of the ordinary clearly has to be done.

A situation may also become problematic because it poses a dilemma, a set of equally unattractive alternatives. Each possibility offers some advantages and some drawbacks, and there is no easy way of deciding which is better. Thus, pioneers may come to a fork in the trail; one route is direct but passes over rough terrain and across dangerous rivers, the other route is easier but ten times the distance. Young people often find that the expectations of their peers conflict sharply with those of their parents, especially over questions involving drugs or sex. Delegates at a convention to nominate a presidential candidate may be called upon to choose between two well-qualified candidates; one can provide more patronage but is less likely to win the election, but the stronger candidate is less inclined to dispense political favors. The decision must be made quickly so that the opposition party does not gain too great an advantage. Many other political issues are of this character. In the 1970s many Americans became tortured over affirmative action programs. Employment opportunities in some occupations became limited for white male applicants because of the preferential hiring of women and members of ethnic minorities. The rationale for the practice was well understood, but was it fair to place the burden on men who themselves had never engaged in discriminatory activities? What was the decent thing to do? The fact that a choice is possible makes the situation problematic.

Situations may also become problematic because of ambiguity. If a context is inadequately defined, people simply do not know what to do. Innovations of all kinds frequently lead to puzzlement. If something has never happened before, there are no precedents to follow. Orson Welles's famous broadcast on Halloween of 1938 touched off mass panic among people who thought this country was actually being invaded by Martians (Cantril, 1940). Since we had never before encountered Martians and had no conception of what they wanted, what was there to do? When the flamethrower was first used in World War I, opposing troops broke and fled, just as the Aztecs were terrorized by Cortez's cannon. Of course, what is strange to some people may be familiar to others. A family that has never encountered a house fire may be paralyzed in a situation that would be quite routine for a fireman. Especially instructive are records of what happens among people who become isolated and must fend for themselves, such as the survivors of the mutiny on the HMS *Bounty* who settled on Pitcairn Island (Silverman, 1967) or the thirty Japanese who spent seven years together on the island of Anatahan, not knowing that World War II was over (Fukami and Cross, 1969). Their circumstances were so extraordinary that they had to improvise all kinds of arrangements in order to survive.

Although problems arise everywhere, even in the most stable communities, they are more likely to emerge in rapidly changing contexts. Problematic situations vary along several dimensions. The number of people involved and their geographical distribution vary considerably. Some difficulties are confined to members of a single primary group; others are of concern only to members of a community or of a social world; some are of concern only to members of a specific organized group; still other problems, such as those involving pollution following a nuclear accident, would upset people throughout the world. Problems also vary in severity. Some are trivial: Should a group of students spend the evening bowling, watching movies, or studying? Others are of critical importance: Should a nation with limited resources develop nuclear weapons? Problems also vary in their suddenness and persistence. Some, such as a tidal wave, arise without warning, and emergency measures must be organized quickly. Others, such as the search of the discontented for a more meaningful way of life, are prolonged and may even become chronic.

In spite of these variations, however, problematic situations have several features in common. People are temporarily immobilized; most participants do not have a clear notion of what to do, and they do not know just what to expect of one another. What makes such situations so trying is that something of value to the participants is at stake. Those who are involved feel that they should take some kind of action; in many instances they experience a sense of urgency, for time seems to be limited. If the normative framework does not provide an adequate guide for concerted action, the people involved in the situation must work together to improvise some way of coping with it. Thus, a crisis is a turning point. Previously established norms break down, and the people realize that something unusual must be done. A crisis is a crucible out of which new patterns of concerted action may emerge.

Formation of the Public. In each problematic situation people who share a common concern are brought together to form a *public*. Events have consequences, and Dewey (1927) defined a public as consisting of those who perceive the possibility of being affected by the consequences of an event, who are sufficiently interested to pay attention to what is happening, and who may intervene, if necessary, to ensure desirable consequences and avoid obnoxious ones. Thus, each problematic situation generates its own public. Publics may be large or small. Who constitutes a given public depends on the manner in which people are oriented toward the difficulty that has disrupted their routine of life. A public seldom includes everyone in a community. Those concerned with governmental policy on highway construction, the arrest of a popular hero, or busing to achieve school desegregation are seldom more than a small minority of the inhabitants of any community. A severe earthquake would create a public that includes almost everyone in the area, but many are not affected even by national emergencies. Thus, each public's boundaries are set by interest in some event that has attracted attention and by the limits of effective communication. In mass societies it is not uncommon for people who share a common concern to be dispersed geographically.

A public is *not* an established group. It does not have a fixed membership; it consists only of those who regard themselves as being affected by the possible consequences of an event. Some publics may include organized groups; if an issue arises over price and wage controls, both unions and corporations would become active participants in the public. In many problematic situations, however, old groupings prove inadequate to handle the emergency, and people who had previously had little contact may be brought together for the first time. Sometimes previously opposed parties find they have a common cause; in time of war, for example, many past differences are temporarily forgotten. Furthermore, the composition of most publics undergoes constant change. In the early 1960s the public in the United States concerned about our intervention in Vietnam included only those who were anxious about foreign policy, families with members in the armed forces, pacifists, and those with business interests. As the fighting went on, young people in particular began to mount protest demonstrations; each incident brought in additional participants. At the same time some of the earlier participants lost interest and departed. By the late 1960s continuation of the war became a national issue; so much opposition had developed that President Johnson decided against seeking reelection. Thus, with each new development a public undergoes some changes in membership. In addition, as the situation develops, the manner in which the participants are aligned may also change (Bogart, 1972:89–96).

The extent to which participants become involved in a public varies considerably. As Lippman (1925:40–74) points out, each public is made up of people with two kinds of orientations — activists who are deeply involved and a larger body of concerned observers. *Partisans* consist of those who regard themselves as deeply implicated in the crisis; they follow closely the latest developments and do whatever they can to ensure the results they seek. Thus, the core of each public consists of people so concerned that they feel they themselves must do something.

They often organize into partisan groups or join already existing ones, for they realize they can pursue their objectives more effectively by joining forces with others with similar interests. The partisans propose specific solutions, attack those who disagree with them, and strive to do something about the problematic situation, although what they do differs from one context to another. Since partisan activity is time-consuming, most people can be enthusiastic advocates in only a few publics at a time.

Other members of the public, in most instances the majority, are interested enough only to pay attention and to keep themselves informed. Those who make up the *spectator* component of the public do not participate actively in trying to meet the problem, but the reactions of this audience are vitally important. In many problematic situations partisans propose alternative ways of meeting the difficulty, and the issue is settled when most of the spectators align themselves with one of the proposed solutions. In such contexts *public opinion*, the response of the public, assumes decisive importance. In many situations public opinion is not readily discernible. If the reactions of a substantial proportion of the concerned converge, however, the trend becomes more conspicuous. Whenever public opinion is recognizable, it places limitations on what can be done in a problematic situation. In a democratic nation elected officials who fail to take heed are voted out of office. Even dictators cannot afford to ignore public opinion; to do so could lead to serious protests and disruptions.

The spectator component of the public is also important in that its presence tends to neutralize arbitrary coercion and unfair tactics on the part of the partisans. The spectators are arbiters before whom the activists perform. The audience is like a referee. It sees to it that certain minimum standards of decency and fair play are maintained. If a problem is to be solved intelligently, underhanded tactics cannot be tolerated. Just as elders intervene in quarrels between children when one party does something deceitful, concerned spectators in a public debate over a communitywide problem may intervene if either side does something arbitrary or unfair. If a partisan group is detected using unscrupulous tactics or if fraud or corruption is disclosed, outraged spectators may align themselves with the opposing side. Some of the spectators may become so indignant that they join the activists on the other side. In numerous instances, such as the Watergate scandal, outraged public opinion altered the course of history.

Decision Making and Leadership. Since problems of all kinds arise constantly, all communities and groups have some established procedures for decision making. Government is a social institution for making decisions on problems that affect the entire community and for implementing and enforcing the policies. Town hall meetings in small communities allow maximum public participation in policy formation. Jury deliberation is a widely accepted means of solving a dilemma. In formal organizations standard procedures have developed for coping with problems — appointing investigative committees, consulting experts, calling conferences of executives. Primary groups — gangs, families, cliques of co-workers — also have characteristic ways of meeting emergencies. In most problematic situations, then, the public turns initially to those in positions of authority, whose responsibility it is to make decisions. If established decision-making procedures provide solutions that are acceptable to the public, the problem is resolved. The necessary adjustments are then made in an orderly manner.

However, in many problematic situations the difficulties cannot be resolved through established procedures. In some emergencies the authorities cannot act quickly enough, and members of the public must make decisions on their own. In other situations the boundaries of the public do not coincide with those of a community or a group, and no one is in a position to make a binding decision. In many other instances the verdict of the authorities is unacceptable to the public. In all such circumstances the crisis is compounded, and the public continues to demand some kind of action. In this chapter we focus on situations in which established decision-making procedures are inadequate and collective adaptation requires some special effort on the part of those who make up the public. Leadership assumes importance in such contexts. The transactions that are attempted are not institutionalized, and participating individuals have an opportunity to affect the outcome. In routine contexts the presence of extraordinary individuals may not even be noticed, for they are not permitted to deviate too far from the roles they enact. In a crisis, however, the ingenuity and special skills of those who happen to be on the scene often spell the difference between success and failure.

DECISIONS BY COLLECTIVE DELIBERATION

The most common way of meeting problematic situations is through *collective deliberation*. Those who are involved talk things over, pool their intellectual resources, and decide on the best thing to do. Town hall meetings, family councils, committee meetings of bureaucrats, conferences, group therapy sessions, and parliamentary debates are all attempts to cope with problematic situations through discussion. Deliberation is most likely to succeed if the best available information is given to those who are most competent to judge; then they present their decision to other members of the public for approval. Hundreds of experimental studies have been conducted on joint problem solving, and Collins and Guetzkow (1964) and Kelley and Thibaut (1969) summarize the findings.

For our purposes, however, it will be more helpful to examine a specific case to see what happens in an actual crisis. In October 1972 a plane carrying the Uruguayan rugby team to a match in Chile crashlanded in the Andes during its flight from Montevideo to Santiago. After units of the air forces of three nations had searched the area for eight days, the rescue mission was terminated; because of the subzero temperature and lack of food, there seemed to be no possibility that the fifteen athletes, twenty-five friends and relatives, and five crew members could still be alive, even if they had somehow survived the crash. Ten weeks later, two members of the team staggered into a farm in Chile, seeking aid. Miraculously, sixteen of the victims were still alive. Since the manner in which they had survived, by eating the bodies of the dead, aroused so much controversy and notoriety, a detailed narrative was prepared from retrospective accounts. It provides an excellent description of how people caught in a problematic situation coped with their difficulties (Read, 1974).

Collective Exploration. Before taking any kind of action, members of a public must develop consensus, a common definition of the situation. People must have some conception of what has happened, where they stand, and what they might reasonably expect. Thus, problematic situations create an immediate demand for news. *News* is not mere information; it gets its distinctive features from being a phase of interrupted activity. Action has been suspended, and news is urgent information that is needed to make completion of the transaction possible. When a situation is ambiguous, where there are alternatives, where some decision is to be made, information that might affect the outcome becomes "live matter." News is news only for its public, only for those whose activity has been interrupted. Once a decision has been made the information is no longer news; it becomes history (Park, 1955:71–142). Since intelligent decisions require reasonably accurate information, news is sought initially from sources that are defined as reliable. We turn first to formal communication channels — radio, television, newspapers. Except where censorship is suspected, these channels are generally accepted as reliable sources of news. If information from such established sources is plausible, we accept it, and it becomes the basis for further discussion.

If adequate news is not available through formal communication channels, members of the public are forced to turn to rumors. When immediate action appears necessary, the people have to work on the basis of the best information they can get, even if some of it is unconfirmed. Rumors develop in any problematic situation in which the formal channels have been discredited or if the relevant information is of a sort that does not usually appear there. In disasters, when events are moving very rapidly, one cannot reasonably expect to get all the necessary details quickly enough through formal channels, and informal channels emerge spontaneously. Since victims of disaster are struck indiscriminately, status distinctions become irrelevant; social distance is reduced immediately; and people on the scene exchange whatever information they have. A lively interchange ensues. Diverse interpretations of what has happened are presented, along with apprehensions and conjectures. These are combined with partial information that happens to be available. Participants provide whatever information they possess. Some express their opinions, and others give suggestions. Some agree, and others disagree. Some keep asking questions, and others demand evidence for everything that is said. Some vent their feelings, expressing their wishes and fears (Bales, 1950). From this welter of exchanges members of the public try to develop coorientation. When such definitions are subsequently discovered to have been mistaken, they are dismissed as rumors. When adaptive efforts turn out to be successful, however, consensus constructed in this manner is not so condemned. Thus, contrary to popular belief, rumors are not necessarily false.

Nor are people caught in such emergencies necessarily gullible, especially if tensions can be kept under reasonable control. The few individuals whose emotional reactions get out of hand must be restrained, and their hysterical outbursts must be neutralized. Leadership is especially important, for the critical ability of those who assume key roles in decision making becomes decisive. Although participants in experimental studies of problem solving may not be overly concerned with accuracy, people caught in real crises cannot afford to be careless; their lives may depend on accurate information. Thus, if the tension level has not become too high, constant efforts are made to check the accuracy of each report. Those presumed to be better informed are sought out and questioned. It is not unusual for some rumors to become more accurate as they develop, for errors are eliminated through denials or the presentation of negative evidence (Caplow, 1947; Danzig et al., 1958). Rumors take shape through natural selection. Alternative possibilities are presented and considered. When collective excitement is moderate, the basis for selecting items from which consensus is constructed is plausibility — consistency with what is already taken for granted. Since implausible or erroneous items are rejected, the definition that is constructed through discussion is likely to be a reasonable one, one that makes sense to most members of the public. Rumors are shared definitions of problematic situations that are improvised as those who are involved carefully assemble and evaluate the most reliable information they can gather (Shibutani, 1966:63–94).

Discussions in collective problem solving tend to follow identifiable phases of development (Bales and Strodtbeck, 1951; Foote and Hart, 1953). Initial efforts are directed toward forming a general orientation to the situation. Thus, after the Andes crash the survivors first tried to find out where they were. They turned to the crew and tried the radio. After taking care of immediate needs, they sent out teams to explore the area. Once coorientation has been established, attention turns to a second problem: What should be done? Decisions on what to do with the injured were based on recommendations made by the two medical students aboard. They agreed on rationing the remaining food, arranged to keep the wounded as comfortable as possible, set up their shelter to minimize the cold, and then considered various ways of sending for help. Once a program of action has been agreed upon, something that does not always happen in deliberation, attention turns to a third question: How is the plan to be implemented? After studying numerous conferences, Bales (1955) discovered that the exchanging of information occurs most frequently in the initial third of the meetings; the exchanging of opinions occurs most frequently during the middle third; and the exchanging of suggestions occurs most frequently in the final third. Such ordering is easy to understand. If activities are not taken up in this order, considerable confusion could arise. Parties making diverse proposals for action would be talking past one another, for their remarks would rest on different assumptions. Thus, collective problem solving is much like individual thinking; alternative ways of defining the situation and the consequences of each plan of action are examined carefully before a decision is made. In sum, if emotional reactions can be kept under control, members of a public cope with problematic situations through deliberation, constructing consensus through a critical examination of the best available information.

The Emergence of Issues. When a public is heterogeneous, consensus is more difficult to achieve. How people become aligned into factions differs somewhat from one issue to the next; even in small communities in which most people know one another on a personal basis those who are allied on one question may become bitter rivals on another (Beals and Siegel, 1966). If members of the public are drawn from somewhat different cultural backgrounds, their knowledge of relevant features of the situation may differ, and reaching a common definition may require considerable argument. In most instances, however, issues over orientation can be resolved by the available facts (Guetzkow, 1953). Thus, after listening to radio broadcasts and the reports of the teams that had surveyed the area, the twenty-seven survivors of the Andes crash agreed that the search for their wrecked plane had ended, that there was no food in the vicinity, and that most of them did not have the strength to hike out of the wilderness.

Most issues arise over the question of what to do, over competing plans of action. The public is then split into two or more factions, each trying to persuade the others that its proposal is most likely to succeed. As the discussion proceeds, temporary alliances may form and then dissolve as the views of the various factions coincide or diverge. Several of the people huddled in the frigid plane wreck realized that the only way for them to survive was to begin eating the bodies of the dead, but they hesitated to speak up. Only on the tenth day did the group begin an open discussion of the subject. Although the proponents volunteered to allow others to eat their own bodies when they died, most of the others held back, clinging to the hope of being rescued. At first only a few tried eating small bits of frozen flesh; as the days went on, others joined them. In the end the program was accepted reluctantly, for there seemed to be no alternative.

If disagreements arise, self-consciousness is enhanced, and the discussion tends to become more critical. In strategic interaction a premium is placed on facts. Each position is subjected to its opponents' critical analysis; implausible statements, weak arguments, and unsupported contentions are readily refuted. Facts become important because they can stand up under critical examination. Participants in arguments become self-conscious; they are careful and deliberate about what they say. Each party is responsible for its utterances, and ridiculous statements elicit unpleasant reactions. Each person must retain his or her critical ability; those who lose their tempers are likely to lose the argument. Regulating one's emotional reactions is often difficult in such contexts, but each must make the effort. Thus, deliberations involving important issues tend to be rational. The Andes survivors all found the thought of eating the flesh of their dead friends repulsive, but as their hunger intensified, even the opponents listened carefully to the proposal and its justifications: The taboo against cannibalism was only a social convention; it was God's will that they do their utmost to live; the souls of the dead were gone, and all that was left was meat. It was a fearful decision, but the alternative was to starve and freeze to death.

Forming a Plan of Action. In many deliberations consensus is never achieved, and each disgruntled party goes its own way — sometimes to disaster. Even when a measure of coorientation is achieved, some are not convinced and only acquiesce reluctantly. The ideal resolution of a problematic situation involves integrating the various interests represented, thus giving all parties a stake in the plan of action. The integration of diverse viewpoints, described in a classic statement by Follett (1923:24 – 59), is sought in many discussion groups, but it is very difficult to attain. An ideal program of action is a collective product; it is not the mere addition of individual proposals but a new formulation in which each of the different interests has a place. Thus, agreement is achieved by harmonizing differences. Each person, through role-taking while participating in the discussion, learns something that he or she had not understood before. Thus, all participants in some way redefine themselves and one another.

If the different concerns are integrated in this manner, effective action is most likely to result, for the program will enjoy wholehearted support. Everyone can identify with the collective product, for each participant has a personal stake in it. The participants then develop a sense of mutual identification, and morale is likely to be high. This is precisely what happened among the Andes survivors. Since there was no possibility of moving the severely injured, everyone agreed that the two strongest athletes should go out to seek help. To prepare them for their ordeal, everyone agreed that the two should receive the best food, get the most rest, and exercise daily to build their stamina. Everyone contributed whatever he or she could, and miraculously the plan worked! Quakers seek this type of agreement in what is called the "sense of the meeting," but even they have difficulty attaining it.

Although such ideal resolutions are seldom achieved, comparing actual and ideal discussions enables us to specify some of the conditions of effective deliberation. Probably the most common barrier to such solutions is the presence in the public of inflexible individuals. If even a single obstinate party refuses to budge, successful deliberation becomes almost impossible. If a clique attempts to dominate the discussion, intimidating others into silence so that only one viewpoint can be considered, the ideal cannot be achieved. Guetzkow and Gyr (1954) show that agreement is more likely to be attained when discussion focuses on task-oriented needs rather than on self-oriented needs. They also found that differences are more likely to be resolved if the participants happen to like one another, and this contention is certainly borne out by the experiences of the Andes survivors. If some party tries to dominate a discussion, the best that can be expected is a compromise. Those who make concessions are horse-trading; their interests remain opposed. Voting is a form of compromise; although the losers may go along with the decision, they cannot be expected to be enthusiastic. Although a compromise may be better than nothing, subsequent cooperation is not likely to be enthusiastic. Some individuals are so rigid that even a compromise is impossible. As all these observations suggest, one essential condition for successful deliberation is that all parties be willing to be guided by the product that emerges from it.

A problematic situation is most likely to be resolved successfully if the best available information and sound judgments are brought to those most competent to carry out the action. In some instances minority opinions turn out to be correct, even though they are not popular. Thus, all parties must be given a hearing. A person of low status may be exceptionally well informed on a particular topic, and an unpopular view may provide the wisest course of action. But people holding unpopular views often suppress them; a few may push their position for a time but then acquiesce in the face of opposition. Guetzkow (1953) found that when many disagreements arise, especially on a personal basis, participants tend to withdraw. Sometimes people who can contribute something important hold back from shyness. Everyone is more likely to participate in small groups in which most members know one another well enough to speak candidly; inequality of participation increases with the size of the public (Bales et al., 1951). When a public is large, the most aggressive and assertive, but not necessarily the most competent, are likely to exercise disproportionate influence. Unless each faction continues participating in the discussion until its interests are somehow represented in the final product, the members will be dissatisfied with the solution and less than enthusiastic about implementing it. Thus, unless the most competent persons in the public are willing to participate actively in deliberation until the issue is settled, the ideal is not likely to be attained.

Some believe that effective communication will solve all problems, and this may be the case when those who make up a public share similar values. However, in many publics different factions pursue diametrically opposed interests, and the more effective the communication, the less likely it is that any consensus or agreement will be reached. Indeed, as each side appreciates more fully what its opponent's position actually is, it becomes more apprehensive. Where there is a genuine conflict of interest, therefore, agreement is not likely to be achieved through deliberation.

Outcomes of Joint Discussion. Collective deliberation has many possible outcomes. Where consensus is achieved and a program of action is agreed upon, a common effort is made to implement the plan. But often no agreement can be achieved. In many instances different factions within a public arrive at separate decisions, and each segment goes its own way. Studies reveal that this is what frequently happens after severe disasters. The victims get together with their families, close friends, and others who happen to be in the vicinity; the people in each group then make their own arrangements to escape, rescue others they happen to encounter, and do whatever they feel is necessary to protect themselves. Personal differences are temporarily forgotten. The major difficulty relief agencies face is not panic but the reluctance of such groups to accept aid or directions from outsiders. They reserve the right to make their own decisions and often refuse to obey orders that would actually coordinate rescue efforts. Thus, disorganization arises from the separate and independent actions of many small units, each coping in its own way (Fritz and Marks, 1954). In general, if emotional reactions can be kept under control, people caught in problematic situations tend to act rationally. They define the situation on the basis of critically evaluated evidence and act in a manner that makes sense to them. In some instances new patterns of concerted action develop from such deliberations.

RECURRENT PATTERNS OF CROWD BEHAVIOR

The tension level rises in many problematic situations, especially where important values are at stake. If an adequate solution is not found quickly through discussion, people who make up the public may explode in some form of crowd behavior, brushing aside those who call for careful deliberation. The direction such transactions take depends on the emotional climate that develops, and *crowd behavior* may rest on any emotion that can be communicated — anger, fear, revulsion, joy, grief, or even embarrassment (Lofland, 1981). Angry mobs are commonplace, and collective grief can be observed at funerals of popular heroes. However, once social distance among the participants has been reduced, the prevailing mood may change suddenly, for the participants are highly sensitized to one another's reactions. The untimely appearance of an unpopular figure at a funeral for a martyr may transform collective grief into violent aggression, or the sudden show of force by the police may send an infuriated mob into pell-mell flight. Thus, when intensely excited people converge on a scene, decisions are reached in a manner that contrasts sharply with critical deliberation.

Collective Aggression. Probably the most common form of crowd behavior is collective aggression against what is evaluated as a frustrating object. Chapter 5 covers the basic principles of crowd behavior, and the example of a lynch mob serves well to review them. Although lynchings have played a conspicuous part in American history, especially during the Reconstruction in the South and during the expansion of our western frontier, they are by no means limited to this country. Such mob violence has occurred throughout the world. Lynchers are initially brought together by a report of some heinous offense — murder, rape, horse stealing, kidnapping, treason. Where law enforcement procedures are absent or deemed inadequate, what to do with the criminal becomes a problem. At the center of such gatherings is the activist component of the public. Although outsiders desiring to exploit the situation sometimes succeed in directing mob action, the partisans usually consist of local people who are most concerned over what has happened, such as the victim's friends and relatives. In the milling that takes place a succession of agitators harangue those who have assembled. Those who are able to express accurately the feelings shared in the audience succeed in getting a hearing; others are ignored, or their remarks are drowned in jeers. Demand for news is urgent, but relevant information is not likely to become available quickly enough through formal communication channels. As the people become impatient, they grasp at any item that seems relevant, and rumors abound. Reports that are inconsistent with the developing mood, such as positive character references for the accused, are rejected. Rumors that are consistent with the mood develop quickly. Thus, the emotional climate facilitates some reports and squelches others, eliminating from consideration several possible ways of defining the situation. When emotional reactions can no longer be controlled, consistency with the prevailing mood rather than evidence or plausibility becomes the basis for selecting and assembling information to define the problematic situation. The accused becomes characterized as a rapacious monster whose continued existence is a threat to the community. In most instances the depiction is not accurate. The definition is constructed in one-sided communication; it is more a product of the lynchers' reactions to one another than a reflection of the facts.

As emotional reactions intensify through mutual reinforcement, the composition of the public is altered by the self-selection of personnel. Many who are not in sympathy with the developing mood depart voluntarily; others who disagree are expelled, sometimes violently. The key to an understanding of crowd behavior is the narrowing of attention. Through selective perception and communication attention focuses increasingly on a single object; this attentiveness often resembles an obsession. Preoccupation with the object leads to a temporary loss of self-consciousness. To the extent that one loses awareness of oneself as an object, one receives no negative feedback, and self-regulation becomes minimal. Critical judgments become more difficult. Thus, as similarly excited people converge, consensus is formed from a perspective that is constricted by emotional reactions. Emergent norms develop, and in the absence of dissidence the judgment appears unanimous.

The participants become suggestible, responsive to proposals they would reject under other circumstances. An enraged person is already mobilized to assault the hated object; a loud demand that an attack be made or the sight of others launching an offensive is often enough to touch off already organized dispositions to act. Behavior does not cease to be moral; people still do what they believe to be appropriate, but they now define the situation from a perspective that is temporarily constricted. Once action gets under way, the division of labor arises spontaneously. Every participant is anxious to contribute whatever needs to be done; the transaction is carried out efficiently, for morale is high. Aggressive crowds remain charged until tension is dissipated. If lynching the offender is enough, the participants disband. If it is not, they may attack other objects until they are exhausted, as in the hockey riot in Montreal. Once tension has been dissipated, the perspectives of the participants revert to their usual state, and some members of the crowd are astonished to see what they have done.

Collective Lust: Speculative Bubbles. A fascinating phenomenon that periodically shocks capitalistic systems is the speculative bubble, an explosive outpouring of economic activity involving the buying and selling of securities, land, or other commodities at prices that bear no relation to their potential income yield. Bubbles differ from routine economic activities in the speed with which the transactions occur. There is a period of feverish exchanges, as people buy at the current rate and sell a bit later at a profit. Because of the sudden, artificial increase in demand, the prices spiral upward to ridiculous extremes. Once the demand is punctured, the enterprise collapses, leaving many speculators in ruin.

Among the famous bubbles are the tulip mania in Holland in the seventeenth century, the South Sea bubble in England not long thereafter, and the Florida land boom of the 1920s. The prevailing mood is one of greed, an orientation toward an object evaluated as precious—a source of pleasure, power, or pride. The typical stance of a person obsessed with a valuable object is to covet it; to protect and nourish it, when he or she possesses it; to dispose of it only in return for exorbitant compensation. No common goal ever develops in a speculative bubble. The participants are greedy, coveting profits for themselves and using others as instruments to obtain them. However, each person acts under the influence of a shared mood developed through communication. How are otherwise cautious people drawn into such risky adventures? How are experienced financiers induced to overlook their realization of the dangers?

Speculative bubbles begin with the announcement of some startling event, such as the discovery of gold or the formation of a financial enterprise of extraordinary promise. As attention focuses on the desired object, its value is magnified in communication. Rumors lead to the formation of romantic visions of untold wealth. Constant talk of the enormous profits made by acquaintances as well as plans of what to do with the riches create an emotional climate that is expansive and enthusiastic. Visions of wealth and glory override commonsense considerations, and skeptics are brushed aside; they are scorned as people too stupid or cowardly to join the venture. The Mississippi bubble began in 1719, when the French government granted John Law, an entrepreneur, the exclusive right to trade in the Louisiana territory, the East Indies, China, and the South Seas (Mackay, 1932:1–45). When stocks of the Mississippi company were offered for sale in Paris, the demand was so great the price rose more than 20 percent in a few hours.

What makes such situations problematic is that those who lust for profit are faced with a continuing dilemma. Those who have the good fortune to acquire a precious object must choose between selling at once for a neat profit or holding on a bit longer in hopes of even greater gains. As people whose financial judgment is respected continue to buy even at ridiculous prices, even the skeptics start wondering if they might be mistaken. Will they be left behind? At the peak of a bubble great optimism prevails; many feel there is no limit to the profits that can be made. Even experienced financiers, who realize that there are limits to spiraling prices and intend to get out in time, are caught in the fever. Though they realize that a danger point is approaching, they are tempted to squeeze in a few more transactions. At the height of the Mississippi bubble special booths had to be set up in a public park to accommodate the speculators. Many were injured in the crush. Since Mr. Law had no time to see all the applicants, even the most privileged people in Paris, including aristocrats, had to use various stratagems to get his attention.

The final phase of a speculative bubble is the "bust" — what is sometimes called a financial panic. Since demand is based on faith that prices will continue to rise, once confidence is shaken, a wave of selling follows. Once selling gets under way, prices drop rapidly, for everyone wants to unload. When the Mississippi bubble collapsed, several investors were crushed to death as they rushed to banks to dispose of their stocks for whatever they could salvage. Those left with the worthless securities were impoverished. One conspicuous feature of the "bust" is the vindictiveness with which enraged speculators seek out those they hold responsible for the debacle. Law's carriage was attacked by mobs, and he was almost lynched. Caricatures of him appeared in Paris newspapers, and he became the butt of lewd jokes and songs. Before long he was forced to leave the country.

The vengefulness with which the promoters are pursued suggests that the participants are embarrassed. Experienced brokers feel foolish, and the others are convinced they have been cheated. They demand a scapegoat. Such reactions indicate the extent to which their perspectives had been constricted during the heat of excitement. Since the great Wall Street crash of 1929 and the worldwide depression that followed, government regulations prohibit such extensive speculative schemes. Financiers continue to manipulate markets within the limits permitted by law, however, and similar phenomena arise periodically on a smaller scale. In what is called panic buying, rumors of a shortage of some essential product lead to a stampede to purchase it, thereby creating a real shortage.

Collective Fear: Panic. When people are confronted by great danger, they respond in several characteristic ways. They may cooperate to bring the danger under control; they may engage in an organized withdrawal; in some instances they become involved in wild flight. Excellent accounts of the manner in which human beings react to extreme peril can be found in descriptions of the bubonic plague that swept through Europe in the fourteenth century, killing at least a quarter of the population on the continent. Accounts are available in the writings of Boccaccio, Daniel Defoe, and Samuel Pepys, as well as in numerous historical sources.

Since it was not yet known that the plague was transmitted by fleas from infected rodents, doctors were helpless to prevent or combat it. Whenever an object is evaluated as dangerous, the instinctive reaction is fear. If possible, one tries to avoid it. Thus, attempts were made to segregate plague-ridden towns; areas known to contain infected people were cordoned off with troops; the sick were quarantined in their houses, and those who tried to leave were executed. As the dangerous object approaches, one may attempt to placate it or attack it from defensive anger. Many interpreted the disaster as retribution for their sins, and flagellants in processions whipped one another in efforts to atone for them. Jews, even though they too were among the victims, were accused of poisoning the wells and were persecuted for it. Witches, agents of the devil, were also hounded. If the dangerous object cannot be avoided, one tries to escape. There were hasty departures—mass migrations from urban centers. Aristocrats, officials, teachers, priests, and doctors all fled, leaving the poor to fend for themselves. Some husbands and wives deserted each other; some parents abandoned their children. Some committed suicide (Hecker, 1859:1–74; Nohl, 1960). The relative ease with which frightened people panic depends largely on how well they know one another and the manner in which they are organized. Thus, groups that are trained to face danger—firefighters, police officers, soldiers— seldom break in panic, unless they have reached an advanced stage of demoralization.

Although collective panic is a rare phenomenon, it is so spectacular that most people have heard of instances in which hundreds have died needlessly because of it. A particularly costly case is the fire that broke out on 28 November 1942 at the Cocoanut Grove, a popular Boston night club. Although firefighters responded immediately and had the flames under control in about twenty minutes, almost five hundred people were killed, most of them at the main entrance, which had become jammed when too many tried to get out at the same time. Two other exits were open, and about half the people were able to escape through them (Veltfort and Lee, 1943).

The typical experiences of those caught in collective panic indicate that they feel a sense of impotence in the face of physical annihilation. The threat is overwhelming and imminent. Some become psychologically isolated from other people, feeling that they must make it out on their own. Smelser (1963:136–39) suggests that flight is more likely to occur when an escape route appears to be open but may close quickly.

Collective panic has been described as a group "in dissolution" in contrast to a group "in being." Frightened individuals each try to save themselves; they forget their obligations to others, and the group disintegrates. Such desperate measures result from intense fear. Although each person experiences the fear separately, its intensity is the product of social facilitation — seeing the aversive reactions of others reinforces one's own fear. Furthermore, the definition of the situation is constructed in communication, which in some cases is almost instantaneous. In such contexts approaching peril may touch off a stampede. One person's bolting for safety can set off a chain reaction among the suggestible. People may trample one another, oblivious to what they are doing. Panic is usually terminated when the participants reach safety or when they drop from physical exhaustion.

The typical reactions of those who have survived panic flight reveal how much intense fear temporarily alters people's perspectives. Fear constricts attention and foresight, and the victims become obsessed with the dangerous object. Since attention is so focused, available alternatives are not noticed. Although all people find it difficult to maintain their poise in such contexts, there are vast differences among individuals in their capacity for self-regulation. Some persons manage to remain detached from the excitement. Much looting has been reported during the bubonic plague and other disasters — although they may be frightened, looters still take time to pick up valuable objects. Many believed the plague to be heavenly retribution for widespread immorality; since even those who had not sinned were victimized by the pestilence, however, some became hedonistic and spent their time in drinking and debauchery. Those who succeed in escaping danger through precipitous flight often go into hiding. Those who emerge unscathed spend considerable time and effort explaining and justifying their conduct. Such actions suggest that they might have acted differently, had their usual perspective not been altered.

Collective Joy: Communal Catharsis. Participants in joyous occasions sometimes become so excited that their celebrations get out of hand. The successful completion of some important enterprise — such as victory in a long, hard-fought war — touches off a noisy carnival. Such outbursts also occur when a local athletic team wins a national championship. People who had been under severe strain for a long time suddenly feel a sense of release. As the happy celebrants come together in a climate of conviviality, they relax their personal reserve. As they converge, they excite one another further by their yelling, singing, dancing, hugging, and kissing. Rhythm is often a unifying agent. When people are listening to music or dancing together, the recurring, pulsating beats enable large numbers to act in unison. Singing together, clapping hands in rhythm, or yelling in cadence not only raises the general tension level but also dissolves social distance and creates a sense of closeness. Sometimes the excitement gets out of control, and some participants engage in acts that appear to contradict the prevailing emotional climate. Destructive acts sometimes occur, although the vandalism, fistic brawls, and looting often take place in a devil-may-care atmosphere. Festivals have sometimes ended in sexual orgies. What makes such situations problematic is that the people are so happy that they do not know what to do; there is much pent-up tension and no particular way to release it.

Although there is no necessary connection between collective excitement and religion, some of the most intense forms of emotional expression are found in religious cults. Their festivities, which provide such a stark contrast to the staid comportment usually expected in traditional churches, have been observed in many contexts. In medieval Europe the epidemic of bubonic plague was followed by the rapid spread of a dancing mania among the grateful survivors. During the early days of the industrial revolution in England, John Wesley's preaching to the urban proletariat periodically resulted in intense excitement. In the United States numerous camp meetings were held during the expansion of the western frontier; especially famous is the Kentucky revival at the turn of the nineteenth century.

Throughout the world there are religious groups whose services include moments of mass frenzy and ecstasy. The participants become so excited that they break out in all kinds of involuntary movements and convulsions. Many of the behavior patterns observed resemble what psychiatrists label hysterical reactions. A forceful preacher can sometimes get worshipers at revival meetings deeply upset over their sins and the possibility of severe retributions; someone who can no longer stand the excitement explodes in some unusual reaction that initially shocks the others, such as gutteral sounds that resemble the bark of a dog. Because of the intense suggestibility of excited people, others soon find themselves doing the same thing. Such activities thus appear to be contagious. Other forms of behavior often found in such contexts include uncontrolled laughter—sometimes called the "holy laugh." Dancing may include rhythmic leaping, spasmodic jerking, and groveling on the ground. Some individuals have hallucinations. Others may claim that God is speaking to them, and celebrants crowd around to listen to the message. It may consist of glossolalia—ecstatic utterances that the audience claims to understand. Accounts of the revivals on the western frontier indicate that curious bystanders who had gathered to scoff and mock the proceedings sometimes found themselves inexplicably drawn into the dancing and other activities (Cleveland, 1916:89 – 92).

Such unrestrained expression is cathartic; there is a sudden release from pent-up tension, and the resulting experience is euphoric. The participants enjoy the sense of intimacy, and their awareness that others are doing the same thing and sharing the same experience provides mutual reinforcement. In addition there is sometimes a sense of direct communion with some supernatural object—a deity, a totem, a heroic figure, or a charismatic leader. Thus, it is not surprising that those who have enjoyed such experiences are anxious to repeat them. During the Kentucky revival people traveled long distances to attend camp meetings, seeking out in particular preachers who were reputed to be lively. Durkheim (1915) contends that religion originated in such expressive crowd behavior. Participants in such activities sometimes become depersonalized. Much like someone who has been hypnotized, they become aware of their own movements, as observers viewing themselves, and realize that they have no control over what they are doing. This feeling of being controlled by some external force constitutes the sense of obligation in its extreme form. When such experiences are combined with euphoria, celebrants may feel that they are in direct contact with God. With repetition the movements become more exact and may eventually crystallize into rituals (Langer, 1942). Various objects that come to be identified with the joyous experience, such as totem animals, may become the group's sacred symbols. Whether or not Durkheim's hypothesis concerning the origin of religion is correct, such crowd behavior has been observed in the early phases of religious movements throughout the world.

Crowd Behavior and Problem Solving. Although the various forms of crowd behavior seldom resolve difficulties, they do constitute joint efforts to cope with problematic situations. If the level of collective excitement becomes too intense, self-regulation is impaired, and attempts are made to cope with problematic situations in terms of definitions formed from a constricted perspective. Sometimes acute tension is necessary to accomplish some difficult transaction, as in a suicidal infantry charge or the rescue of a drowning child by bystanders. Sometimes catharsis not only enables participants to feel better but also leads to conversions to a more effective life-style. In most instances, however, the consequences of crowd behavior are negative, often disastrous. Attention becomes too focused when people are excited, and they forfeit part of their capacity to cope efficiently with problematic situations through a critical examination of alternatives. After some spectacular instances of crowd behavior — resulting in the overthrow of a government or the massacre of some unpopular group — victims have accused those who benefited from such incidents of deliberately planning the affair. Although attempts of this kind have been made, in most cases the beneficiaries have been as surprised by what happened as the victims. Crowd behavior seldom develops according to plan. Goals emerge after the mob has gathered. The kinds of proposals made depend on the agitators who happen to be there, and the appeals to which the others respond are those that express their feelings in that context. Since the participants are unaware of other solutions that are readily available or reject those that are inconsistent with the prevailing mood, such transactions are often self-defeating. Thus, the folk wisdom of many peoples includes warnings against letting emotions get out of control in crisis situations. People are urged to remain calm, to stay clear-headed. Excitement can be very costly. Perhaps the high value placed on rationality arises from a recognition of the dangers involved in losing it.

POLICY FORMATION IN MASS SOCIETIES

Decision Making in Mass Societies. Problematic situations arise constantly in mass societies, many of them of communitywide significance. Attempts are often made to resolve them through collective deliberation, but, because of the enormous numbers of people involved, these transactions take on a somewhat different character. When critical issues are involved — such as war or peace, economic changes, pollution control, or constitutional amendments — the public that forms often involves millions of people. Most of the public consists of spectators, who do little more than follow the news, exchange views with their friends, and occasionally donate money or vote in support of an option they favor. Most policy decisions that affect large communities are made by a relatively small number of officials, usually bureaucrats who hold key positions in government, corporations, unions, or other organizations that become involved. Although most bureaucratic decisions are collective products, the number of persons involved in the decision-making process is small when compared to the multitudes that may be affected by the outcome. Decision makers usually realize that their decisions may affect the lives of millions, and most of them try to take public opinion into account.

As in other publics, those who feel most strongly about the matter get together, formally or informally, to do whatever they can to pursue the results they seek. How partisans organize and the political tactics they use depend on the political structure of the community; thus, just how large a proportion of a community is able to participate in decision making, directly or indirectly, depends on the form of government. Some governments do not tolerate the formation of groups that are not officially sanctioned. In an absolute monarchy partisans may petition for a favor from the monarch or bribe his or her advisors. If a religious group has strong influence over the government — as in medieval Europe or in some Islamic states — supporters of a cause try to reach and win the support of religious leaders.

Where the government is centralized, as in the Soviet Union, those who share similar views on a given issue communicate informally and then approach those who hold strategic positions in the army, major political parties, the government bureaucracy, relevant industrial units, or intellectual circles (Griffiths, 1971). Where freedom of association is permitted, activists join or support existing organizations; if no adequate group exists, they may develop new ones through social movements. Since mass societies are marked by cultural diversity, such groups reflect the range of interests and values pursued in each segment. Where there is popular participation in government, public discussion occurs on a large scale; arguments on various sides of an issue are presented over the mass media, touching off thousands of local discussions. When the public is very large, collective deliberation consists of partisans competing with one another to influence decision makers before an audience of concerned spectators.

In the United States laws are used to promote social change: the abolition of slavery and child labor, the arbitration of labor-management disputes, the prohibition of practices deemed dangerous. Hence, serious efforts are made to influence legislators and executives. Each issue generates a different public. Each issue activates a different combination of partisan groups. The membership of these groups, the manner in which they are organized, and the tactics they use vary from one issue to the next. Some are just collections of outraged citizens; others are well organized, consisting of representatives of corporations, unions, professions, branches of the government, churches, farmers, ethnic groups, and various other voluntary associations. Many have well-filled treasuries, hire staffs of highly paid specialists, and distribute regular publications. Furthermore, their alignment keeps changing; groups opposed to each other on one issue may join forces on another. Thus, environmentalists and developers who are constantly embroiled in disputes over land use may join forces to oppose mandatory busing as a way of desegregating schools, and corporations and unions may become allied in fighting price and wage controls as unwarranted government interference. In a real sense "politics makes strange bedfellows."

Nor are partisan groups static entities. They are active, striving organizations that operate in an ever-changing arena. Each advances its own interests and defends itself against encroachments. Success depends on the tactical skills of the leadership, for each group operates in a precarious setting. Partisan groups in this country use a wide range of tactics. Many operate as pressure groups, sending lobbyists to legislative bodies. They may attempt to participate in the drafting of laws by working with staff members and by manipulating committee hearings. They may mount a campaign to have an intransigent official removed from office. They may attempt to persuade the chief executive to veto legislation they cannot block at lower levels. They may engage in litigation in the courts (Gross, 1953). They may also employ extralegal tactics: spying, planting rumors at cocktail parties attended by decision makers, blackmailing, or even employing prostitutes.

Where decision makers are subject to sanctions from spectators, considerable effort is made to influence public opinion through propaganda. The issues are then likely to be stated in simplistic terms, and spectators are often forced to choose between two stereotyped alternatives — sometimes stated in slogans. In the 1970s, for example, the problem of school desegregation was reduced to a choice between busing and anti-busing. Such gross oversimplification made a careful examination of the complex problem almost impossible. The same was true of such issues as the death penalty, gun control, and public funding for abortions.

Assessments of Public Opinion. The importance of public opinion has long been recognized. In ancient Rome politicians were concerned with *vox populi,* the voice of the people. Since the French Revolution, numerous political theories have taken it into account, and after World War I it has become fashionable for all governments to call themselves "democratic" — implying that they exist for the benefit of most of the people. In spite of widespread acknowledgment of the importance of public opinion, however, there is no agreement on how it might be assessed. This is not surprising, for in a mass society it is almost impossible to ascertain the composition of most publics. Not only are problematic situations numerous and sometimes interrelated, but the composition of each public and the alignment of its members keeps changing as deliberation proceeds. Furthermore, the views of the people in each public keep changing; even if one could ascertain public opinion on some issue at a given time, it may change in a few months, when a policy based on such opinion is implemented.

Why should anyone be concerned with anything so nebulous and difficult to ascertain? Both decision makers and experienced partisans are preoccupied with public opinion, for a mistaken assessment of it can be very costly. Although the extent of their responsiveness to popular views varies, most decision makers realize they can avoid difficulties by not alienating people unnecessarily. In representative governments a politician who is blamed for a serious mistake may lose the next election; if people become upset enough, they may even institute a recall.

There are numerous instances of miscalculations. Immediately after World War II, for example, the failure of the British government to announce plans for immediate independence led to widespread discontent in India. Although many issues were involved, attention centered on the fate of the Indian National Army (INA), made up largely of soldiers who had surrendered to the Japanese at Singapore in 1942 and were subsequently accused of collaborating with the enemy. When the government announced its intention of trying some members of the INA for treason, public opinion became inflamed. What was significant in India was not that the INA had worked with the enemy but that it had dared to stand up against the British. When police fired on INA supporters, dissatisfactions swelled, and strikes and demonstrations swept the nation. In February 1946 the British government announced that negotiations would begin at once for the independence of India (Thorner and Thorner, 1949:640–42). Similarly, public opinion in France forced the government to grant independence to Algeria, just as widespread objections at home forced the United States to withdraw from Vietnam. Even where popular participation in government is more limited, miscalculations by officials can lead to serious uprisings, as in East Germany in 1953 and in Hungary in 1956.

During the initial decade of the civil rights movement to secure more equitable treatment for Afro-Americans nonviolent tactics were emphasized. Thousands of partisans from various ethnic groups went to the South to participate in mass demonstrations, sit-ins in violation of local ordinances, and willingly accepted punishment to call public attention to various injustices. The protesters were met by mob violence, bombings, and shootings by night-riders; several of them were murdered. The police set upon demonstrators with fire hoses, cattle prods, and vicious dogs; they attacked unarmed and defenseless protesters with tear gas and nightsticks—all in full view of an international television audience. Americans throughout the nation were so shocked and disgusted that considerable sympathy developed for the civil rights cause (Garrow, 1978). Many who had previously only looked on became outraged activists; thousands wrote angry letters to their senators and representatives demanding remedial action. Many white Southerners were so embarrassed that they withdrew support from the White Citizens Councils and the Ku Klux Klan. What had been intended as a warning to dissenters boomeranged into mass demands for the cessation of police brutality. Such actions and reactions certainly facilitated passage of the Civil Rights Act of 1964 and the Voting Rights Act of 1965.

However, when rioting became identified with the movement, beginning with the burning and looting in Watts in 1965, and when widespread publicity was given to acrimonious statements by a handful of extremists, the goodwill began to erode (Campbell, 1971). The growing opposition coincided with widespread reactions against the rebellion of college students. Although the Free Speech movement, which started in Berkeley in 1964, attracted favorable attention on college campuses throughout the world, the excesses of some of the partisans—especially their flaunting of obscenity and sex—elicited serious opposition elsewhere. Working-class people in particular were outraged by student takeovers of buildings and demands for more control over educational policy. Minority groups' demands for reparations and preferential hiring led many to object that the demonstrators were pushing too hard. Studies reveal that those with less education tended to be more hostile toward both movements (Ransford, 1972). The backlash contributed to the election of Ronald Reagan, whose major campaign pledge was to bring the state university under control, as governor of California. As the inflation of the 1970s squeezed those with modest incomes, widespread demands arose for fiscal austerity in government, which meant among other things less money for busing to desegregate schools, welfare programs for the poor, and enforcement of affirmative action. Thus, when a substantial proportion of the spectator component of the public aligns itself with a partisan position, the opposition is faced with inordinate, perhaps insurmountable, disadvantages.

Public opinion affects the formation of public policy only to the extent that decision makers take it into account. Public opinion is a composite opinion, and in a mass society it is seldom unanimous. It may not even represent the views of the majority of those concerned, for some partisan groups through skillful tactics may create the impression of extensive support for their program. The responsiveness of decision makers to public opinion depends on their assessment of it. But public opinion is not easy to appraise; several procedures have been used, and none of them has proved satisfactory. One obvious source of information lies in conspicuously expressed views, but there is no assurance that the individuals who make themselves heard represent the public. Furthermore, there are differences between privately held and publicly expressed views. Advocates of partisan groups get special attention, although they are listened to with a deference that is proportional to the numbers they are believed to represent. Eloquent statements and press comment must be evaluated carefully, for they may enjoy little popular support. Public opinion polls are being used with increasing frequency throughout the world, especially since sample survey techniques have been improved. In the past pollsters sampled the population of a community, even though many of the respondents were not members of the public, but now they can distinguish among an "attentive" public (those who are aware of the issue), an "informed" public (those who participate in deliberation), and the unconcerned (Almond, 1960:138).

Most politicians supplement the results of polls with information from other sources; some political parties have developed intelligence networks to monitor the views of rank-and-file members. Protest demonstrations are taken into account, especially if they appear to be spontaneous. Outbreaks of violence indicate indignation on the part of some members of the public, but there is always the possibility that a demonstration was staged by a small but wealthy partisan group. Politicians sometimes float trial balloons, just to see what public reaction will be. Since many people acquiesce on matters that they define as not affecting them directly, however, trial balloons can be misleading. Once people realize that their vital interests are actually involved, their reactions can be explosive. Voting patterns in democratic societies are studied with great care, but it is widely recognized that a victory at the polls does not necessarily indicate broad support for the winner's program. In modern China public opinion is monitored through party workers' assessments of the mood of the people and careful examination of underground literature, letters to editors of newspapers, and grievances that appear on wall posters.

Popular Despotism in Mass Societies. When critical issues are at stake, the tension level invariably rises. If collective excitement intensifies in the large publics formed in mass societies, efforts to cope with the problem may take on many of the characteristics of crowd behavior. Especially noticeable is intolerance of dissidence, and this creates the appearance of unanimity. An expansive feeling and a sense of invincibility may also develop. As the issue is given widespread coverage in the media of mass communication, a common object of attention arises among people who are widely dispersed geographically. People become obsessed with the object—a psychotic killer on the loose, corruption in high places in government, an unconventional religious cult, invasion by a fanatic enemy. Evaluations of the object and common emotional reactions are conveyed in newspapers, radio, and television; through positive feedback the feelings are intensified. The mass media also propagate plans of action. Thus, in the 1960s angry ghetto dwellers in various American cities were able to see on television what protesters elsewhere were doing; this provided a model for infuriated people who could find no other way of expressing their views. As the mass media cover such activities, participants may even develop exhilaration from being part of something "big," from realizing they are in the spotlight. The boundaries of any crowd are set by the limits of effective communication, and the media of mass communication facilitate the rapid dissemination of timely patterns of concerted action.

In what is sometimes called mass hysteria popular demands arise to bring dangerous objects under control. This phenomenon is particularly noticeable when some spectacular crime catches the public fancy. In 1888, when "Jack the Ripper" was taunting the police in London, terrified people not only made informal arrangements to protect themselves but also placed intense pressure on officials to do something at once. In desperation, skeptical but helpless officers were even forced to consult spiritualists in their quest for the killer (Barnard, 1953). Similar reactions were touched off by the "Boston strangler" in the early 1960s (Frank, 1966). In 1932 the kidnapping of the son of Charles Lindbergh, when the flier was still a national hero, touched off a rash of similar abductions in the country. People became so preoccupied with the crime that any stranger who struck up a conversation with a child did so at the risk of being lynched. So much outrage developed that kidnapping was made a federal offense (Waller, 1961). Intense fear of communism developed in the United States soon after World War I and again in the 1950s, resulting in the hounding and persecution of anyone suspected of being part of the international conspiracy (Murray, 1955). Subscription to magazines regarded as dangerous, past membership in disapproved organizations, or even being seen in the company of someone suspected of treason was enough to lead to serious accusations of subversive activity. People whose integrity had never before been questioned were forced to undergo lie detector tests to hold their jobs. Sometimes, when international relations deteriorate, patriotic factions in each country become so enraged that they demand action, touching off a war fever. Indeed, most wars enjoy widespread popular support during the initial phases.

Although unanimity about anything rarely develops in a mass society, because of selective communication one gets the impression that everyone is in agreement. As an emotional climate of fear or anger develops in a community, only those remarks and proposals that are consistent with the prevailing mood are taken seriously. Fear and hatred may be expressed openly, but any opposition is quickly silenced. Neutrality is thus almost impossible. Anyone who is not clearly sympathetic with the developing mood is identified with the dangerous object. Epithets such as "nigger lover" or "revisionist" become commonplace. The few who have the courage to speak their convictions face taunts and threats; they are sometimes subjected to violence and must be protected by the police. Since such dissenters are defined as dangerous, they become targets of obscene telephone calls; their homes may be bombed or fired upon by night-riders; their children are tormented in school. Thus, the emergence of popular despotism cuts off free and open deliberation. Arguments are not considered on the basis of evidence; a number of alternative solutions that might have been considered are suppressed. Those who are able to control their own emotional reactions are immobilized and are forced to watch in silence.

In such instances public officials may be pushed into decisions that they personally regard as inadequate or unwise. A particularly notorious case is the outbreak of the Spanish-American War in 1898. Cuban revolutionaries had been struggling to free themselves from Spanish colonial rule for more than three decades, and considerable sympathy for the insurgents had developed, especially after the Spaniards instituted repressive measures in 1896. When the battleship USS *Maine* sank in Havana with a loss of 260 men, many Americans were outraged, even though there was no evidence of Spanish complicity. Partisan accounts in several prominent newspapers inflamed public opinion. Those who sympathized with the Cubans were joined by expansionists, and "Remember the Maine!" became a popular battle cry. American officials then went ahead with plans to intervene, even after the Spanish government had taken steps to meet their demands (Wilkerson, 1967).

Another illustration is provided by the rigid and unenforceable laws on sexual psychopaths that were common before World War II. A study by Sutherland (1950) discloses that most of these laws had been passed in great haste soon after some spectacular crime had aroused public demands for protection. Legislators were stampeded into passing overly stringent laws that tied the hands of the police and the judiciary. Similarly, just as special court procedures were instituted for persons accused of witchcraft in earlier periods, those suspected of complicity with communism in the 1950s were not given fair trials. Indeed, officials were forced to institute loyalty oaths and to pass other restrictive legislation, even though most of them realized that such measures would be ineffective. Of course, some of the decision makers are themselves caught up in the excitement, but many know better. Yet they are often powerless to resist, for an unpopular decision could be their last official act. John F. Kennedy's book *Profiles in Courage* is about the few who had the fortitude to stand up against such widely and intensely supported demands. Thus, when the level of collective excitement is intensified, problem solving in mass societies may take on the characteristics of crowd behavior.

SUMMARY AND DISCUSSION

When the previously established normative framework no longer provides an adequate guide for concerted action, people are confronted by a problematic situation. As long as the level of collective tension remains moderate, those who are involved in such crises attempt to cope with them through collective deliberation — through the pooling of critically examined intellectual resources. Many new patterns of concerted action arise in this manner; solutions that develop in such emergencies are repeated, and those that continue to be satisfactory crystallize into new norms. Thus, many social changes are enacted through deliberation and planning, and leadership and astute decision making play an essential part. However, the vital needs experienced in emergencies often create severe emotional reactions. As collective excitement intensifies, critical interaction is replaced by crowd behavior, in which situations are defined from a constricted perspective. People who are excited also become suggestible, doing things they would suppress under other circumstances. Crowd behavior seldom resolves problems satisfactorily, although it may at times play an important part in destroying social institutions.

When problematic situations arise in mass societies, efforts are made to resolve them through deliberation. But decision makers must take public opinion into account, and here again intense excitement may affect the outcome. The costliness of decisions made under great stress often becomes obvious only in retrospect, long after much damage has been done. Therefore, many people struggle to maintain self-discipline in crisis situations. They appear to appreciate intuitively the dangers of letting emotions get out of hand. Disaster victims remind one another constantly of the dangers of panic.

Given the importance of finding satisfactory solutions to problems, within communities and societies of all types procedures have become established to maximize the chances of success. Dewey (1938) contends that scientific method is a formalization of problem-solving procedures that have been found most effective in the past. The aim is to define problems precisely, to formulate tentatively each alternative way of resolving them as hypotheses, and to evaluate them critically in terms of evidence. Similarly, democratic government is a formalization of efforts to form public policy through careful collective deliberation. For example, in the New England town hall meeting an effort is made to cope with problems in a manner that benefits the majority with minimum cost to minorities. Why are freedom of speech and the protection of minority rights so important? Problem solving is most likely to succeed if the most accurate information available is placed in the hands of the most competent persons, and those whose views are unpopular may be the most competent. In the long run, then, rigid commitment to any ideology — political or religious — is likely to be costly, for it reduces the alternatives that may be considered. Similarly, controlling emotional reactions is decisive. Scientists who act professionally on the basis of personal desires are not likely to succeed. Thus, political theorists from Plato on have warned of the dangers of mob rule. Once the matter is seen in this light, we can understand readily why such high value is placed on rationality in problem solving.

SUGGESTED READINGS

Coleman, James S. 1957. *Community Conflict.* Glencoe, Ill.: Free Press.
>   A comparative analysis of the manner in which public policy is formed as American communities cope with problematic situations.
Gross, Bertram M. 1953. *The Legislative Struggle: A Study in Social Combat.* New York: McGraw Hill.
>   An account of the political maneuvering and infighting involved in the formulation of federal laws in the United States.
Lindzey, Gardner, and Elliot Aronson (eds.). 1969. *The Handbook of Social Psychology.* Vol. 4. Reading, Mass.: Addison-Wesley.
>   A review of the literature on group problem solving in chapter 29 (H. H. Kelley and J. W. Thibaut) and on crowd phenomena in chapter 35 (S. Milgram and H. Toch).

Park, Robert E. 1955. *Society*. E. C. Hughes et al. (eds.). Glencoe, Ill.: Free Press.
An anthology of Park's writings on crowd behavior, on public opinion and the news, and on problems facing mass societies.
Shibutani, Tamotsu. 1966. *Improvised News: A Sociological Study of Rumor*. Indianapolis: Bobbs-Merrill.
A study of the different ways in which problematic situations are defined by the participants involved in them.
Smelser, Neil J. 1963. *Theory of Collective Behavior*. New York: Free Press.
A value-added analysis of the step-by-step development of various forms of crowd behavior.

XI

SOCIAL DISLOCATIONS

In 1950 an interviewer from a team of social scientists studying the industrialization of the Middle East entered Balgat, a hamlet about eight kilometers from Ankara. Despite its proximity to the city, Balgat was isolated, for there were no roads in this mountainous area. The unquestioned ruler of the community was the *Muhtar*, the chief. The interviewer had to receive his consent before talking to anyone else; the inhabitants went to him for advice on various questions; and he made decisions in their behalf on the basis of the classic values of the Ottoman Empire — obedience, courage, and loyalty. Owner of the only radio in the community, he invited selected villagers to hear the newscast each evening; when it was over, he interpreted the news for them. No one questioned his word. In contrast, the person held in lowest esteem was the grocer, the only man in the area who was not a farmer. Although born in Balgat, he had seen the city and longed for a better life. He was disgusted with his neighbors for their lack of interest in the outside world; in turn he was condemned for his unconventional views and even suspected of being an infidel.

When some members of the research team returned to Balgat four years later, they were astonished at what had happened. A road had been built, and regular bus service was available to the center of Ankara. The community had become incorporated into the metropolis as one of its districts, and its population had grown tenfold. Electricity had been supplied, water had been piped in, and there were more than one hundred radios, a school, and a police station. Except for a handful who

299

worked their own holdings, the men had forsaken farming; most of them were employed in factories in the city. The chief, who was about to be replaced in an upcoming municipal election, accepted the changes and acknowledged that the villagers had gained many material advantages. Although he was disappointed by the conduct of some of the youth, he felt that their excesses would pass as they became more accustomed to the new ways. The grocer had died, but he was no longer despised. Indeed, the others contended that he had been the wisest of them all, although they had not realized it. One even referred to him as a prophet (Lerner, 1958:19–42). Such sudden and drastic transformations in status and life-style are unusual, but this is certainly not an isolated case. Throughout the world today similar changes are taking place, often leaving the elders bewildered and the young hopeful but anxiety ridden.

There is no such thing as an unchanging community, for nothing ever happens twice in the same manner. Anthropologists who have sought old cultures in pure form, uncontaminated by any outside ideas, have had great difficulty in locating them. In the mass societies in which we live changes are continuous. New social worlds come and go; new patterns of concerted action are improvised; and once well-established patterns undergo modifications. Even rituals acquire new meanings. At any given time and place, however, many features of the normative framework remain intact, providing a base of operations. Even where innovations occur so frequently that they are expected, people would not be able to cope effectively without a backdrop of familiar norms. Different segments of normative frameworks are displaced at varying rates. In this chapter we look at communities in which changes are so drastic and extensive that disruptions arise. In such contexts we are able to observe various transitional processes in exaggerated form, in clear relief. This will facilitate our understanding of transformations that are less drastic, not so obvious, and extended over longer periods. What characteristically happens to people who are caught in such sudden transitions?

In their classic study of the incorporation of Polish immigrants into American life, Thomas and Znaniecki (1927) contend that social disorganization—crime, delinquency, broken families, and dependency —is the incidental by-product of rapid social change. This is not necessarily true, for deviance may be found in stable communities (Malinowski, 1926), and extensive changes may occur with a minimum of disruptions (M. Mead, 1956). But many sociologists have failed to distinguish between deviations from established norms and dislocations that arise when some patterns of concerted action are displaced while others persist. Disruptions of the latter type are commonly found in rapidly changing communities; indeed, there are remarkable similarities in diverse historical contexts — the decline of the Roman Empire, the waning of the Middle Ages, or the industrialization of various nations from the eighteenth century to the present. In the third world an effort is being made to achieve in a few decades through planning what industrialized societies have attained over centuries of unplanned development. Serious disruptions and conflicts are commonplace. Until we have more adequate knowledge of how societies change, it seems unlikely we will develop a rational guide for this unprecedented effort. The interval between the breakdown of one normative framework and the establishment of a new one constitutes a period of transition, and such periods are usually marked by uncertainty, confusion, error, and fanaticism. This chapter focuses on some of these features of transitional periods.

EMERGENCE OF INCONGRUITIES

What are some of the conditions under which drastic social changes take place? Certain types of circumstances serve as turning points in the history of any community, pivotal junctures at which a succession of collective adaptations results in the formation of new patterns of concerted action and renders many previously established norms obsolete. Communities that appear unchanging are usually isolated, rest on relatively stable ecosystems, and manage to handle difficulties through institutionalized procedures for problem solving. Thus, changes in the ecosystem, the breakdown of isolation, or the inability to resolve problematic situations in an orderly manner frequently touches off recurrent sequences of events — often leading to transformations that no one had anticipated. In many instances the changes are cumulative.

Ecological Transitions. The social structure of any community rests on a given ecological base, and any change in the web of life requires readjustments on the part of all organisms in that habitat, including human beings. Any change in the relationship between a population and its natural environment requires adaptations — for survival. If the pressure of a growing population on available resources becomes too great, a catastrophe will occur. Such imbalance may result from a rapid growth in population, the exhaustion of necessary resources, or a change in technology that leads to different demands on available materials.

The great famine in Ireland in the 1840s led to the departure of over a million people, most of them to the United States (Woodham-Smith,

1963). A few decades later the Plains Indians were driven out of their settlements not only by the encroachment of settlers but also by their introduction of the rifle, which led to the rapid extermination of the buffalo. The buffalo had been an essential part of the Indian culture, the means by which young people gained status in their society. The Indians were subsequently segregated into reservations and displaced by the advancing pioneers, whose birth rate was higher (MacLeod, 1928). The Cumberlands area in eastern Kentucky has become a vast slum, largely because of the pollution from coal mining that had once brought great prosperity to these communities (Caudill, 1963).

Pressures may also arise from a sudden decrease in population. The bubonic plague that decimated Europe in the fourteenth century — the temporary dominance of a bacillus — was followed by a century of economic stagnation. Since there were fewer people to feed in the cities, markets collapsed, and grain prices fell. Impoverished farmers had to move to cities, and many rural areas became deserted; it is estimated that 70 percent of the farms in central Germany were abandoned. An apocalyptic mood developed, and many people expected an imminent cosmic cataclysm in which the wicked would be destroyed (Huizinga, 1954). The guilt-ridden became preoccupied with religion, perhaps providing one basis for the Protestant Reformation. When the population of Polynesia was decimated by the coming of Europeans, most of the deaths resulting from diseases against which the natives had not developed immunities, many old norms collapsed (Oliver, 1951). Thus, changes in the balance between population and resources make the previously established normative framework unworkable, and new patterns of concerted action must be developed. In some cases the only alternative is emigration. Such transformations result eventually in the formation of different arrangements better suited to the new web of life.

Technological innovations, new ways of utilizing energy for human purposes, are often welcomed, especially when their utility in the pursuit of accepted values is readily demonstrated. But their effective implementation often requires other changes that are not foreseen in the beginning. As Marx insisted, any community's normative framework rests on a particular mode of production. Any revision of the manner in which energy is utilized creates new needs. New categories of people rise to prominence and acquire political power. Some traditional patterns of cooperation appear inefficient, perhaps even ridiculous, and they are rejected as old-fashioned. As continuing to do things in conventional ways becomes more costly, pressures arise to do things differently. The widespread adoption of automation, for example, has rendered much unskilled labor obsolete and has increased the demand for professional and technical workers (Wallace and Kallenberg, 1982). Such changes will no doubt alter previously established patterns of social stratification.

Since industrialization raises the general standard of living, it has been welcomed throughout the world. Greater output results from more efficient production, but industrialization also requires the adoption of many new patterns of concerted action. Thus, its early phases are always marked by many dislocations. There is rapid population growth, greater concentration of people in urban centers, and the spawning of slums. The proportion of farmers and unskilled workers in manufacturing decreases, and the proportion of semiskilled workers increases rapidly. There is a dramatic rise in the number of office workers, clerks, and technical, professional, managerial, and administrative personnel. Many others enter service occupations that were previously unknown. At the same time the techniques of many artisans and craftsmen become outdated; except for the outstanding few there is no more demand for their specialized skills. As social life is reorganized for more effective production, class differences tend to supplant ethnic and religious affiliations as the basis for the classification and ranking of people.

The adoption of a money economy leads farmers who had previously worked for subsistence to produce as much as they can and to barter or sell the surplus. Many farmers discover that they can earn more by working in factories than they can by tilling the soil. There are many changes in the perception and evaluation of objects; human beings, for example, come to be viewed as labor—something to be hired out for money (Boeke, 1942). As a high value is placed on money, people become sensitized to possibilities of acquiring wealth, and with accelerated social mobility emphasis is placed on achievement through personal effort. The decreasing importance of inherited status leads to further changes in family structure and in the socialization of the young. Thus, adoption of a different mode of production leads to the reshaping of perspectives, interpersonal relations, and community structure.

The Breakdown of Isolation. Historians have noted that periods of rapid social change follow extensive migrations (Teggart, 1939). Migrations of all kinds lead to the formation of cultural frontiers, where people from different cultural backgrounds participate in common transactions, exchange goods and services, and become acquainted with different ways of doing things. Even though the groups may remain segregated for a time, they learn from one another. Many of the cultural frontiers of the past three centuries have been the product of the movement of Europeans to various parts of the world; their conquest and subjugation of the peoples they encountered and their imposition of an industrial economy have resulted in drastic transformations in the cultures of the subject peoples. Although many colonies have become independent since World War II, none are reverting to their precolonial ways. The population of the United States consists largely of descendents of a succession of ethnic groups that have migrated from various parts of the world—most of them from isolated peasant communities. Each immigrant group started at the bottom of the social scale and gradually assimilated into the larger population. As they did so, the culture of their ancestors has undergone modification and only traces of it remain. Both natives in European colonies and immigrants to the United States started by working for those who dominated their communities and eventually adopted their culture. Thus, the migration and contact of peoples lead to the formation of new communication channels. People on both sides have new experiences, and there is a gradual reduction of social distance. Even the caste system is beginning to break down in the large cities of modern India.

The establishment of new communication channels can terminate isolation in several ways. Education has played an important part in surmounting traditional detachment. In European colonies missionaries, with their unbounded faith in education, provided opportunities for a limited number of natives to acquire European language and culture. Although their intent was to create a means of transmitting a religious faith, there was no way to keep the literate from reading secular literature. In the United States education has been compulsory, and the immigrants welcomed the opportunity afforded their children to learn at government expense. Military service also opens new communication channels. Africans who had served in the foreign legions of European armies not only learned to use modern weapons but also learned enough about other matters to become leaders of revolutionary movements against their rulers. Their demands for justice were based on European concepts. Political propaganda also opens new channels. In rural China in the 1940s, for example, Communist agitators told peasants of a different way of life in other parts of the world, especially in the Soviet Union. Downtrodden women in particular were persuaded that their dismal fate was not dictated by nature and that there were many other possible ways for them to live (Belden, 1949).

Mere exposure to new communication channels leads to questions about previously established norms, especially among those who have found them painful or costly. New channels introduce ideas that challenge and undermine what previously had been taken for granted. New technology, such as television and motion pictures, is now challenging many local superstitions, even among the illiterate. As in Balgat, the mere building of a highway to a previously isolated community leads to dramatic transformations. In modern times isolation is breaking down everywhere, and all communities are becoming less stable. Redfield (1941) compares several communities in Yucatán and finds that greater contact with the outside world is related to increasing secularization, individualism, and disorganization of the indigenous cultures of Mexico. Modern mass societies are undergoing continuous change.

Failures of Government. Many well-established social institutions, including governments and economic systems, are questioned when it becomes apparent that they are incapable of dealing with recurrent difficulties. In rapidly changing contexts many problematic situations arise that involve a large proportion of the population and are difficult to resolve to everyone's satisfaction. In most instances attempts are initially made to cope with predicaments through already established decision-making procedures. If they prove adequate, transformations can be made with relatively few disruptions. The history of England, for example, is a remarkable record of a succession of orderly collective adaptations to drastic changes in life conditions.

In many instances, however, rulers fail to recognize the extent of the changes in circumstances and the inadequacy of standard procedures. Their attempts at reform tend to be episodic, often confusing, and wasteful. Repeated failures lead not only to greater discontent among those who suffer but also to queries even by those who have not fared so badly. A ruler's inability to handle satisfactorily the problems that people regard as important often leads to challenges to the legitimacy of the government itself. Efforts are made to develop political organizations that can deal more effectively with recurring crises. Totalitarian regimes of all kinds represent attempts to cope with a multitude of complex problems in an integrated manner, although they too have difficulties with their "hooligans," "revisionists," and "counterrevolutionaries."

The inability of governments to deal adequately with serious problematic situations often results in large-scale conflicts — civil and international wars. In his monumental study of war, Wright (1942:381–83) concludes that such struggles arise when societies change too quickly for an orderly adjudication of differences. Wars, however, lead to other dislocations. Losers in particular must come to terms with drastically altered conditions. One need only glance at the dramatic changes that have taken place in Japan since World War II. Japan had not lost a war in twenty-six hundred years, and the nation's invincibility was a corner-stone of its sense of identity. Defeat thus provoked deep soul searching and the questioning of many basic values that had been taken for granted (Tsurumi, 1970). But even victors face a multitude of new problems. The development of nuclear weapons has affected almost every facet of modern life.

Inconsistencies and Misunderstandings. In each community, social world, and organized group new norms emerge and old ones become extinct, as one problematic situation after another is resolved. Since people living in the same community partake in many common transactions, however, considerable confusion arises as innovations in one sector contradict those in another. Segments within each community are changing, often simultaneously but in different ways. Thus, the successful solution of a problem in one sector may create aggravating difficulties in another. Social dislocations arise when different social units in a given community adapt independently to problematic situations. When this happens, misunderstandings arise; people work at cross-purposes, even when they are acting with the best of intentions. Accusations of fraud and indecency are made, and as incongruities and frustrations mount, many new dilemmas develop. People cannot act together without consensus, but coorientation becomes difficult to establish and maintain when there are many alternative definitions of the same situation. Small isolated communities achieve the appearance of stability by integrating major patterns of joint activity into a consistent social fabric and segregating people who pursue vastly different life-styles. But in modern mass societies this type of stability is unattainable.

Even after changes have occurred many have difficulty appreciating the fact for some time. They find it difficult to believe what they see, for their assumptions about the world are contradicted. Some refuse to believe what they see or try to ignore it, but they cannot do so indefinitely. Faced with repeated incongruities and frustrations, increasing numbers begin to raise questions about what they had previously taken for granted. Such questioning is not easy, for it involves the breakdown of an orderly symbolic environment. If cultural axioms that had never before been challenged turn out to be false, where else could one have been mistaken? The questioning of cultural axioms tends to be cumulative. In time even sacred beliefs are questioned. Is parental authority really paramount? Must all laws be obeyed? How important is virginity? Does the use of drugs inevitably lead to degradation? Is there really a God? Such confusion makes planning for the future difficult. Habitual ways of doing things are shaken, and the "cake of custom" is broken. Just as immigrants to the United States and their children have shed much of their ancestral cultures, many natives in the developing nations who have moved to urban centers are becoming detribalized, the first step toward forming another normative framework that will eventually enable them to cope more effectively with their new circumstances.

As people who are involved in such transitions talk things over, they often discover that they had been supporting norms that are no longer taken seriously. Each person had been complying with previously established norms, concerning sexual relations, for example, on the assumption that everyone else actually believed what they were supposed to believe. In fact, however, many had privately changed their views; not knowing that many others had also changed their minds, they had continued to enact their conventional roles. They had all been victims of pluralistic ignorance, maintained by impression management. Then someone, like the youngster in Andersen's fairy tale who insisted that the emperor was wearing no clothing, raises an embarrassing question. This leads to a realization that most people had altered their perspective; they simply had not disclosed their beliefs. Norms once regarded as essential had become rituals, hollow formalities followed simply because people were afraid to violate them. Thus, people are often astonished to discover that they had been supporting one another on patterns of concerted action that only a few of them really took seriously.

Further strains arise that make continuation of the old ways difficult, if not impossible. Repeated failures lead to disillusionment. As they become disillusioned, many openly reject the old norms, sometimes scoffing at them and calling those who comply old-fashioned or stupid. Under such circumstances individuals turn to their own resources, and members of various primary groups develop new informal norms. New patterns of concerted action are improvised, although at first they may not be used among strangers. During transitional periods several different lines of action are attempted, and coordination often breaks down. Once people begin to question cultural axioms, they become sensitized to new possibilities. Once disenchanted, many are willing to try innovations, including alternatives they would never before have considered. Once they realize that the established procedures are not matters of necessity and that deviations will not result in catastrophe, resistance to change is weakened. They accept in principle the notion that new ways are not necessarily evil. In such contexts a new normative framework emerges, one that is better suited to extant life conditions.

FACTIONALISM AND MARGINAL STATUS

The Formation of Diverse Perspectives. Innovations affect various segments of a community differently, thus generating diverse interests. A community is then split into factions, some favoring the new and others defending the old. Factionalism may occur along several lines. People may become divided in terms of class interests. Labor unions oppose technological innovations that will render many of their members' jobs obsolete. The wealthy are not so concerned with inflation; although they may be inconvenienced, inflation does not constitute as severe a crisis for them as it does for those already living on the margin of their incomes. An innovation that favors one ethnic group at another's expense, such as affirmative action programs, is likely to create a split along ethnic lines. Or a religious group may be outraged by violations of its basic tenets. In modern Islamic nations changes favored by Western-educated technicians, professional workers, and intellectuals—many of whom have become atheists—are opposed by those who still take their creed seriously. With each innovation some segment of the community develops new interests. Since the perspectives of people in a changing community are not altered simultaneously, each faction lives in a somewhat different symbolic environment. Furthermore, since members of opposing factions approach one another with different assumptions, they cannot communicate effectively, and this exacerbates an already difficult situation. The clarity with which such factions are defined varies from one historical context to another; at times the animosity becomes so intense that it erupts in civil war.

Where changes occur continuously, as in modern mass societies, it is not unusual for the split to occur along generational lines, with youth favoring the new and elders defending the old. Although it is not possible to identify a generation as clearly as demographers can specify age cohorts, perceptible contrasts in outlook can often be found between those in different age groups. Such disagreements are especially apparent between immigrants and their offspring; since the two generations have grown up in different cultural contexts and may even speak different languages, their respective orientations are dissimilar in spite of close personal ties. Soon after a revolution children trained in schools of the new regime may clash with their parents, some of whom appear to be traitors. Children reared in cities often cannot understand the views of parents who had migrated from rural areas. Thus, in numerous contexts members of different generations may develop incongruous orientations toward a variety of objects.

Students of the sociology of knowledge have contended that in a changing society members of each generation tend to develop a somewhat different perspective, for they are subject to dissimilar influences during their most impressionable years. Thus, many Americans who were adolescents in the 1960s, amid the turmoil of the Vietnam War and the various liberation movements, have difficulty communicating with both those who are older and those who are younger. However, each generation does not speak with a single voice. Mannheim (1952:276–320) points to the differences among Germans who were children and adolescents during World War I. Some never recovered from the war and retreated from politics; others became politically active, determined to prevent the recurrence of war; others never left the battlefield, continuing their struggle by other means. These factions were in constant opposition, but they shared similar presuppositions and understood one another. Thus, each community has survivors of a previous epoch who are still in control; they face opposition from an active generation that is still struggling to establish itself as well as the young who look forward to the downfall of the status quo. In each case an outlook that once was regarded as aberrant eventually takes over (Marias, 1968). Although severe factionalism does not arise in all instances of social change, when it does, it is worth examining, for it reveals in sharp relief the processes that occur even in less volatile contexts.

When innovations are introduced, factions favoring the old square off against those favoring the new. Such struggles occur in many contexts: radicals against conservatives in politics, advocates of revitalization against fundamentalists in religion, assimilationists against separatists in ethnic minorities, as well as the young against the old. Regardless of the innovation under debate, there are discernible patterns in both the progressive and the conservative intellectual stances. Those favoring change often believe that rationality should be used to construct a better world, that injustices should be eliminated through planning and reform. Those opposing change often regard society as the product of organic growth; since social institutions incorporate the wisdom of the ages, tampering with them may lead to disaster. Proponents of change often believe that evil is rooted in society; many reformers today believe that crime and mental illness are products of a sick society. Conservatives often argue, however, that evil is rooted in human nature and that social institutions are designed to keep it under control. Advocates of change often consider individual rights paramount, placing a high priority on the happiness and well-being of as many individuals as possible. Their opponents often argue that the group is more important than its individual members; if people would only meet their responsibilities to others, everyone would be better off. Those favoring change often assume that all human beings are equal and that social institutions should be based on this principle; conservatives believe that people are in fact unequal and that failure to recognize this could result in stupid blunders. Defenders of the status quo often believe that any settled scheme is better than an untried project. Innovators argue, however, that people must be willing to experiment; otherwise, everyone will remain mired in the limitations of the present (Mannheim, 1953:74–164; Huntington, 1957). Although it seems unlikely that this bipolarization occurs in all historical contexts, it has been found frequently in European cultures in recent centuries.

Struggles Within Primary Groups. The clash between factions becomes especially painful when it occurs between two generations within the same family. The closeness, interdependence, and affection that bind those involved lead to internal conflicts and intense guilt feelings. The generation gap that concerned so many Americans in the 1960s is certainly not new; members of different generations have in various contexts found it impossible to communicate effectively. Throughout American history almost every immigrant group has encountered similar difficulties, when children educated in American schools clashed with parents from European or other backgrounds over such matters as parental authority, choice of mates, and property distribution. Such intergenerational strife is commonplace during the early phases of industrialization, when many farmers are forced to move to cities to work in factories. In the developing nations migrants come into close contact with members of other tribes whose cultural backgrounds are very different; many of the young adopt behavior patterns that are well suited to city life but condemned in their tribal community.

Industrialization tends to break up the multigenerational kinship groups found in so many small communities. The struggle is between preserving traditions and preserving individual freedom. The intensity of such clashes varies from family to family, for it depends on the inflexibility of the persons involved. It is especially acute when the parents regard the old patterns as sacred and refuse to budge. Young people who have found satisfaction from the new practices are much like converts to a cult; they are intolerant of those who are unwilling to try new things and dismiss them as hopelessly out-of-date. Where there are linguistic differences, the problems are even more aggravated. Even if the children are bilingual, they usually know just enough of the parental language to partake in daily transactions but not enough for extended discussions of moral issues.

The generation gap persists in spite of close and frequent contacts because the two factions begin with different assumptions. Their respective orientations rest on dissimilar cultural axioms. Those who argue often cannot understand one another, no matter how hard they try. Precisely because their differences stem from unstated premises, they cannot even clarify their respective positions. Hence, misunderstandings become more aggravated with each exchange. Many disagreements stem from each side's taking different values for granted. Questions arise, for example, over what makes life worthwhile. Those on one side assume that individual happiness is of paramount importance; hence, their orientation is individualistic and hedonistic. Those on the other side assume that the preservation of the family and its status is decisive, for this provides everyone with a secure base of operations.

Many disagreements arise over the definition and evaluation of key objects. Some people believe that communism is wicked and atheistic; others see it simply as another political ideology. Differences arise in the vocabulary of motives used. Especially in cities, where individualistic motives tend to prevail, it is taken for granted that each person should look after his or her own interests; those who profess altruistic concerns or try to act in terms of moral precepts are often viewed as hypocrites. Serious misunderstandings also arise over what is to be condemned as deviant behavior. Americans no longer agree whether certain sexual acts constitute perversions, whether cohabitation outside of marriage is immoral, whether the smoking of marijuana is the first step to degradation or merely a way of relaxing, or whether refusal to serve in the armed forces is an act of treason (Chilman, 1979). In many slum areas prostitution is recognized as illegal but not necessarily as immoral. Some view it as a practical way of getting by, but others see it as the ultimate form of depravity. Thus, seeing their children calmly practicing or condoning deviant acts horrifies the parents.

When people who have been in sustained, intimate contact disagree over such matters, both sides feel severe inner strains. Much ambivalence develops, and in some families the rivals come to view one another with contempt, sometimes even hatred. One major barrier to communication is their inability to understand one another's emotional reactions. Basic differences in values and in conceptions of deviance lead to what appears to be inappropriate affect—laughing at something another person finds horrifying or expressing outrage over something another regards as trivial. If the emotional reactions of another person seem totally out of place and groundless, it becomes difficult to identify with him or her as a human being. Effective role-taking becomes impossible, and social distance increases at once. The other person appears grotesque, a monster devoid of human feelings and not part of one's moral order.

The young may try hard to explain what they consider a rational position. But if their parents react with revulsion, the children become disgusted and wonder how people who are otherwise intelligent can be so unreasonable. Sometimes their anger becomes so intense that they go out of their way to spite their elders. They may flout old norms unnecessarily, just to provoke their parents. Attacking conventional norms may become a point of honor for those who favor innovations. The parents in turn conclude that their children have become immoral. They see themselves as failures; they have tried their best to rear their children properly and wonder where they have failed. They are hurt and bewildered; they wait apprehensively for some catastrophe to befall their offspring. Thus, people who had once been bound by ties of affection now find themselves confronting strangers. Those who are rejected by significant others often develop severe guilt feelings; they feel inferior and inadequate. The young who are not expelled by irate elders leave home as soon as they can, seeing this as the only way to pursue a reasonable life.

Coping with Cross-Pressures. If the polarization between the new and the old is extensive, a third faction is likely to develop, one that straddles the center with a dual orientation toward change. Members of this faction have been referred to as *bicultural* (Polgar, 1960). They are familiar with both cultures and see something of merit in both perspectives. Many children of immigrants, for example, become truly bilingual, proficient in both languages. They recognize that some of their elders' ways are prudent, but they also feel that some of the procedures of the new community should be adopted. In rapidly changing communities it is not unusual for diverse, sometimes contrasting, norms to exist side by side. In many instances the contradictions are hardly noticed; indeed, in mass societies most people are in a sense multicultural in that they participate regularly in several social worlds. Those who have different perspectives manage to get along by making allowances for divergent views and keep difficulties to a minimum by complying overtly with norms they do not take seriously. Thus, people who develop dual orientations have incorporated into their personal outlook the perspectives of two reference groups whose norms are inconsistent. They participate in two social worlds; they live in terms of two sets of norms and enact roles for two different audiences. Both factions usually accept such persons, even though they realize these people are not totally committed to their respective standpoints.

From time to time, however, bicultural persons find themselves involved in transactions in which contradictory norms converge. They face inconsistent and sometimes contrasting expectations from the opposing reference groups. Thus, youngsters in the 1960s who found sexual freedom and drugs attractive were also concerned with their parents' objections, which they understood even if they could not fully accept them. We all do our best to act in a moral manner. We perform for an audience to which we impute expectations and try to live up to these expectations. But when the two audiences make contradictory demands, one cannot possibly satisfy them both. No matter what one does someone will be disappointed. Those who realize that whatever they do will be wrong in the eyes of one of the reference groups are plagued with feelings of guilt—a way of punishing oneself for failing to live up to one's own moral standards. Furthermore, such persons often find it difficult to define themselves as decent human beings; they suffer what is sometimes called a "crisis of identity." If a self-concept is indeed a reflection of the manner in which one believes one is regarded by others, what happens to a person who looks simultaneously into two mirrors and sees sharply contrasting images? The self-concept of such a person includes contradictory assumptions and evaluations of him or herself as an object; what is approved in one reference group is condemned in the other. Thus, bicultural people often develop divided loyalties and ambivalent attitudes, become hypersensitive about matters involving self-esteem, and become preoccupied with status symbols. Such persons often develop a deep sense of inferiority, even when they have been successful and are generally respected in their community. The feelings of inadequacy do not arise from low status but from their inability to live up to their own moral standards.

As those who are trapped in such cross-pressures try to cope with their difficulties, many of them contribute to the community's eventual acceptance of innovations. If there are enough people with dual orientations in any community, they often form a social world of their own and develop their own distinctive culture. Thus, in the United States children of immigrants have formed their own hybrid cultures. Eurasians in various cities in Southeast Asia as well as the Cape Coloured in South Africa have similarly formed their own social worlds. To the extent that they develop group solidarity they become tricultural. They are familiar with the norms of all three reference groups and learn to employ them in different combinations as they move from one transaction to the next.

The easiest way for bicultural people to get along is by compartmentalizing their lives. They divide their activities into segments and become somewhat different personalities in each social world. As they move from one transaction to the next, they switch perspectives and enact different roles. When they are with their parents, they assume one orientation and act in accordance with it; when they are with their peers, they use another outlook and act differently. From time to time embarrassing situations arise when they are confronted simultaneously by representatives of different reference groups, but they can get through most situations by keeping their audiences segregated. In mass societies most people learn to shift gears in this manner as they go along, although not everyone faces such severe contradictions. Having always to be careful and deliberate makes life difficult; impression management requires constant self-consciousness. One cannot really relax and act spontaneously, and some people even become habitually hesitant and cautious. Studies reveal that people who feel trapped in cross-pressures tend to put off making decisions. Voters who are caught in such cross-pressures, for example, tend to put off making up their minds until late in the campaign or vote a split ticket; in many cases they simply do not vote (Berelson et al., 1954).

Another way to resolve the difficulties of competing cultural demands is to find work in which one's familiarity with both cultures can be used to advantage — as an interpreter, a go-between in negotiations, or a restauranteur serving the cuisine of one group for clientele of the other. By helping to bridge the gap between factions, bicultural people may become important agents of social change. By virtue of their exposure to more than one culture, they have wider horizons and can understand more things. They may also be more detached and rational in situations in which others become overly emotional (Simmel, 1950:402–8).

The Marginality of Pacesetters. Such inner conflicts are exaggerated for those on the forefront of social change. Those who become involved in any type of social mobility before it has become customary feel the cross-pressures most intensely, and they sometimes suffer severe personality disorders. A woman who enters a profession that is overwhelmingly male may not be fully accepted by all her male colleagues, even if they do not question her competence; at the same time she may be condemned by some women for her arrogance in entering the profession. Similarly, members of an ethnic or religious minority who are among the first to get out of "place" also face condemnation from both sides. Afro-Americans who became intellectuals when others had few opportunities for a formal education (DuBois, 1911), Africans in European colonies who were among the first to be converted by missionaries (Turnbull, 1963), native chiefs who were incorporated into European colonial administrations (Fallers, 1955), successful racketeers who outgrew their origins, and children of intermarriages in communities in which such liaisons were still forbidden — all have faced rejection from both sides. During the urban turmoil of the 1960s black police officers were sometimes condemned both by their white colleagues and by other Afro-Americans (Alex, 1969).

Pacesetters are not only rejected by both sides but face the additional difficulty of not being able to form their own society, for there are seldom enough of them in a given community. At first those on the vanguard of social change try to identify with the group that has higher status. When they are not accepted there, they cannot retreat to the group of lower rank, for they no longer share its culture. People occupy a *marginal status,* then, when they are rejected by both the group to which they aspire and the group from which they came. They are marginal in that they are on the border between two social worlds without really belonging to either. Although not all pacesetters become marginal, many people who are ahead of their time find themselves isolated in this manner. Most bicultural people avoid becoming marginal, but those who do usually suffer intense personal conflicts. Park (1950:345 – 92) declares that studying the lives of such marginal people can reveal in exaggerated form the processes of social change.

Many who find themselves in marginal positions settle for one of the shelters available to other bicultural persons, but some remain isolated and suffer severely. When they can no longer cope with the difficulties confronting them, some withdraw from society, becoming recluses and finding occupations that require little contact with other people. Others abandon everything and submerge themselves in a pariah group. Still others retreat into chronic intoxication with alcohol or other drugs. For some withdrawal may take the form of psychosis or suicide (Stonequist, 1937). The hippie movement of the 1960s placed a high value on certain forms of withdrawal from mainstream society; but whereas most marginal people are isolated, there were enough hippies to enable them to form their own social world and support one another.

Others who occupy marginal status may react aggressively. Some rebel and become active in militant political groups. Some become leaders of social movements in behalf of the minority group from which they emerged, sublimating their intense anger into demands for social justice. Revolutionary movements of all kinds have been led by an uncommonly large number of persons in marginal positions—educated natives rejected by European colonists, déclassé aristocrats, intellectuals unable to pursue conventional careers, women who entered professions ahead of their times, ambitious members of the working classes who were barred from advancement. Such persons identify completely with their cause and work tirelessly for it, even though they actually have difficulty getting along with the rank-and-file members of the categories in behalf of whom they toil. In his study of fanaticism in social movements Hoffer (1951) contends that participants who show fanatic dedication are people with a low level of self-esteem who can come to terms with themselves only by identifying with a worthy cause. He labeled such persons "true believers," and there is no doubt that such members make major contributions to all kinds of collective enterprises.

Some marginal persons seek positions in which they can be judged primarily in terms of their unique ability rather than in terms of status—such as scholarship, the fine arts, athletics, or entertainment. Even when these people manage to get into more conventional occupations, they often advance to the top of their field, for they have the drive and dedication to excel. Such individuals often lead miserable lives and are despised by those who are close to them, but they sometimes produce great works of art, industrial empires, and new governments. Thus, being caught between factions may enable incumbents who are rejected to compensate with fanaticism that enables them to make significant contributions to a changing society. Outstanding work is not done *only* by persons trapped in marginal status, but it does require uncommon dedication. Lasswell (1948) and Horney (1950) both suggest that intense devotion to any cause is one way of compensating for a low level of self-esteem, but a person may learn to despise him or herself in many different contexts. The efforts of marginal persons to win self-respect constitute only one source of innovations.

DEMORALIZATION AS A SOCIAL PROCESS

Under some circumstances social units cease to operate efficiently. This can happen to communities of all kinds—in the slum areas of large cities, in a nation that has been embroiled in a long and unsuccessful war, or in periods preceding a revolution, as in China in 1945. It can happen to organized groups of all kinds—in the breakdown of morale among American troops during their final years in Vietnam, in the disorders in urban schools in the United States in the 1970s, or in the collapse of an athletic team made up of gifted athletes who are no longer able to play together. Thomas and Znaniecki (1927:1128) define social disorganization as the "decrease of the influence of existing social rules of behavior upon individual members of the group." Social norms consist of the expectations with which human beings approach one another. They do not collapse when some individual fails to comply; this is deviant behavior and is punished. Norms collapse when an increasing proportion of the people involved in transactions no longer take them seriously, when their mutual expectations break down.

Difficulties arise as increasing numbers in a community or group refuse to comply with formal and conventional norms or do so only reluctantly. Demoralization is usually a time-consuming process. How much time it takes varies from one context to another—months, years, decades. Changes in overt behavior may occur abruptly, as in a community that has just been subjugated by a conqueror, but the transformation of perspectives takes more time. Before normative frameworks can change, there must be some detachment from the old moral order, a transitional period during which previously established transactions become progressively more difficult to execute. It is a period of misunderstandings and hurt feelings, but eventually new patterns of concerted action emerge and crystallize. Although the drama appears confusing, the process of disintegration is regular and occurs repeatedly in the same manner.

The Growth of Individualism. Sustained periods of unfulfilled expectations lead to disillusionment. With increasing disenchantment individualism tends to become widespread. Faced with many contradictions, increasing numbers conclude that they must look after themselves. Since they cannot possibly please everyone anyway, why should they try? Demands arise more frequently that each individual be recognized as a unique object. Fewer and fewer continue to perceive themselves as parts of larger units who must sacrifice their personal needs in behalf of the unit. They see themselves as unique individuals entitled to the fulfillment of their distinct desires. In evaluating various proposals they begin to ask: What is in this for me? Those who are bicultural or marginal are among the first to develop such orientations, for being able to see things from more than one perspective makes it easier to see flaws in basic assumptions. But such questions are not confined to people with dual orientations. Others also begin to wonder why they have to comply with norms when it is painful or costly to do so. When artisans who had devoted much of their lives to cultivating their craft find that their work is not appreciated, that cheap, machine-made products are preferred, they stop making costly sacrifices to achieve perfection. Thus, as philosophers of history have long observed, individualism becomes commonplace in periods of rapid and extensive change (Toynbee, 1946).

As old and encrusted procedures become increasingly cumbersome, more and more people begin to improvise. Thus, periods of transition are marked by creativity and innovation. While some cling rigidly to the old patterns, many others become receptive to new possibilities. The disenchanted are especially sensitized to hedonistic pursuits. Feeling balked and frustrated, they become alert to new possibilities of consummation. They seek self-expression, new ways of overcoming their ennui. As hedonistic values become more widely accepted, objects come to be evaluated largely in terms of the pleasures they can provide. Emphasis is often placed on sexual pleasures, on the consumption of food, beverages, and drugs, and on just having fun. At first only the more daring try innovative practices; when others see them doing with impunity what had previously been forbidden, they follow suit. Those who invent new modes of pleasure are admired and often win a following. Even those who hang back from adopting the new practices do not object to what the others are doing; indeed, they look on with curiosity and interest. Thus, in the 1960s many American parents who had not dreamed of allowing their children to experiment with drugs relaxed their objections, and some even joined them in such exploratory adventures. In this manner increasing numbers begin doing things that had previously been condemned as deviant.

Low morale, the inefficient performance of transactions, results from the unwillingness of participating individuals to subordinate their personal interests to group goals. As increasing numbers begin to question the wisdom of complying with established norms, the moral order is undermined. Most people are not willing to make sacrifices for nothing; they will continue to conform when it is necessary or when noncompliance would be unwise, but they otherwise feel no desire or obligation to perform conscientiously. Individuals no longer feel it is their duty to do what they had once regarded as the correct and decent thing. While not everyone becomes indifferent to his or her responsibilities, an increasing proportion of the participants cannot be counted on except when their private interests happen to coincide with group objectives.

Thus, demoralization results from the unwillingness of increasing numbers to make their own desires subservient to collective aims. Once this happens there is usually a period during which a facade is maintained. When some outsider is watching, people go through the motions of complying with regulations and conventional norms, but in private they do as they wish without remorse. Thus, formalities continue to be observed, but they become empty and meaningless. Such periods are marked by cynicism. People speak contemptuously of those who persist in working hard. Those who lack the courage to deviate begin to feel that they are "suckers"; they feel stupid, and they sometimes find it necessary to justify their persistence. It is also a period of tolerance. All kinds of unconventional practices are permitted, and any remaining conformity often arises more from fear of punishment than from a sense of duty.

Reorientation of Primary Groups. Just as the high morale of any social unit depends on the extent to which the informal norms of its component primary groups support its objectives, demoralization occurs when members of primary groups define transactions as ridiculous and conformity as stupid. Since conversations among persons in intimate contact cannot be controlled from above, the various problems that arise are discussed candidly. Among close friends one expresses doubts about the wisdom of continued compliance. Thus, during the latter phases of the Vietnam War, especially during the prolonged period of disengagement, it became apparent that most American enlisted men no longer believed they were involved in a worthwhile enterprise. Many openly flaunted peace symbols. Observers agreed that Americans fought well, but only when they were attacked. In isolated operations many merely went through the motions of patrolling, going out of their way to avoid contact with the enemy. Further fighting seemed pointless, for the men were convinced that nothing would change when they departed. They were not willing to risk their lives uselessly. Enlisted men questioned orders; if the explanations were not satisfactory, some flatly refused to obey. Career officers, commissioned and noncommissioned—scorned as "lifers"—and young draftees did little to hide their mutual disdain. The use of drugs that obviously would impair combat effectiveness became widespread (Moskos, 1970:144–52; Heinl, 1971).

Similarly, many of the youngsters forced to attend inner-city schools fail to see the relevance of the curriculum to their daily lives, and the rationale provided by teachers and many of their elders of the importance of education for their future fails to make sense to them; hence, what they are required to do feels like an exercise in futility. Why should they exert themselves to learn things that are meaningless?

When close friends agree that continued conformity is senseless, persistence becomes more and more difficult, even in cases where one personally prefers to do so. Disagreements arise within primary groups if some individuals persist in complying, placing their duty above their personal preferences. Cliques are formed, the divisions resting on the extent to which members support the old ways. Where the members had been bound by strong ties of affection and mutual respect, primary groups manage to remain intact even under very difficult circumstances (Angell, 1936). Where some of the members already dislike one another, however, arguments become more strident, and those in opposing cliques begin to question one another's sincerity. Considerable time is devoted to monitoring one another's activities, and suspicions are often confirmed through selective perception. As mutual distrust develops, some erstwhile companions are astonished to discover that they have become virtual strangers. As the individual members go their separate ways, some primary groups are dissolved, and many others are reconstituted as those of like mind get together. Once such schisms occur, former comrades no longer try to maintain their self-respect before one another; they may even go out of their way to spite each other. Of course, the members of each extant primary group—established or renovated— remain responsive to one another's expectations.

If rules can be enforced only when authority figures are present, the old moral order has broken down. As the previously established normative framework progressively becomes a hollow formality, each primary group decides which of the formal and conventional norms it will take seriously, which it will follow only when compliance is inescapable, and which it will disregard altogether. Although a few primary groups may continue to support the old ways, most develop various maneuvers for circumventing the rules. They devise various stratagems for protecting violators, thus making transgressions even easier. Large-scale noncompliance requires the collaboration of the disgruntled. When sullen factory workers launch a slowdown campaign, for example, they can succeed only with the concurrence and support of a substantial portion of their fellows.

Thus, demoralization does not arise from the deterioration or depravity of individuals—lone malcontents tend to become isolated—but is the product of new expectations of how things are to be done. Demoralization develops when an increasing proportion of the people on the scene improvise informal norms that are not consistent with the goals of the larger unit. It is initially manifested in style of performance. The emotional climate becomes tense and gloomy; participants become sluggish in contributing to transactions; bickering develops as each clique looks after itself. Although demoralized units may continue to operate for some time at a low level of efficiency, if they are confronted by some crisis requiring extraordinary effort, they are likely to collapse. The members of various factions are more concerned with saving themselves and their friends than they are with saving the larger organization. Thus, demoralization refers to the breakdown of collective enterprises, not from external pressure but from the unwillingness of most of the personnel to perform duties they do not regard as worthwhile.

The Defiance of Authority. Although it is understood that in some circumstances compliance is necessary, common understandings develop in several primary groups to be as uncooperative as possible. Apathy becomes widespread; many pretend they do not care and make an ostentatious display of being uninvolved. Failure is not so painful or humiliating for those who refuse to make a commitment. Widespread insubordination becomes commonplace; noncompliance becomes the thing to do. Extremists compete with one another to see who can go the farthest in violating norms while escaping punishment. The most imaginative violators gain prestige and are admired in some circles as heroes. Thus, since the late 1960s, American inner-city schools have reported open defiance of regulations, attacks on teachers, arson, assaults on fellow students, theft, intimidation and extortion, and rampant truancy. In 1978 there were 1,856 assaults, 1,097 robberies, 310 suspicious fires, 1,243 cases of disorderly conduct, 68 cases of sex abuse, and 317 incidents involving weapons in the New York City school system (Kleiman, 1979; Baker and Rubel, 1980). Under such circumstances absenteeism also becomes commonplace. In 1970 the U.S. Army reported more than 65,000 deserters from its four infantry divisions in Vietnam (Heinl, 1971).

If those in positions of authority do not recognize the extent of the disaffection and institute effective reforms, they are likely to face further breakdowns. If they try to reimpose order, they may be confronted by organized campaigns of passive resistance and disruption. Thus, personnel who have become incapable of working together to accomplish formal objectives manage to cooperate informally to undermine authorities, who become symbols of an unpopular organization. Some primary groups become actively engaged in guerrilla warfare against the organization. Even fear of punishment is brushed aside, and constituted authorities face many acts of defiance. Most of these are symbolic acts, deeds that enable the disenchanted to express their resentment and hostility. In many American schools in the 1970s sabotage and vandalism became widespread. Since police officers could not be placed every-where, the students and teachers had to fend for themselves. Many on both sides became unconcerned with instruction; their problem was sur-vival. Thus, demoralization is a cumulative process; once it begins, au-thorities become largely impotent to deal with it.

Although violence is not a necessary part of demoralization, it occurs frequently. Malcontents take advantage of the disorganization, and small bands may terrorize the organization or community. Juvenile gangs are ubiquitous in slum areas, and bandits are commonplace in frontier zones and situations marked by anarchy. Competition develops among toughs to show off their daring and virility. Taking remedial action in such contexts becomes very difficult; authorities are often unable to persuade the victims of terror to testify against their tormentors, and they cannot always count on their colleagues to do their part. Those who persist in trying to reinstitute order become defined as enemies and become targets for retaliation. In Vietnam, for example, bounties were raised by common subscription for the heads of various officers who were singled out as particularly odious. After the costly assault on Hamburger Hill in 1969, *GI Says,* an underground newspaper, openly offered a bounty of $10,000 for the death of the colonel who had ordered and led the attack (Heinl, 1971:31). Many rumors developed over the "fragging" of unpopular officers, and the Department of Defense subsequently disclosed that 551 such incidents occurred between 1968 and 1972, leaving 86 dead and over 750 injured (Cortright, 1975:43–44). Teachers in urban schools have been similarly powerless. In 1972 alone, 541 teachers were as-saulted in the schools of New York City. Without legitimation, authority collapses.

The Collapse of Formal Controls. When the people who enjoy high status in any system of social stratification become demoralized, many use their advantages primarily to pursue personal interests. They forget about noblesse oblige and spend much of their time cultivating their pleasures, even resorting to illegal means to satisfy their greed. Many of the more intelligent members of the privileged strata openly acknowl-edge that things are changing; some even mock themselves as anachro-nisms. As they begin to alter their self-concepts, they voice doubts about their right to the benefits and prerogatives they enjoy. They find it diffi-cult to maintain pride in their position. When persons of high status fail to meet the responsibilities of their rank, their subordinates also begin to question their right to the special privileges they enjoy. Those of lower rank had deferred to them on the assumption that the latter were superior human beings—because of their breeding or education. Once they realize that such people are no better than themselves, they lose respect and wonder why they should continue to accept their ascendancy (Della Fave, 1980). Thus, when increasing numbers of people of high status—members of "good families"—begin violating formal and conventional norms, the old moral order is about to collapse. Such conditions often prevail just before the outbreak of revolutions.

In some instances high officials become demoralized. They talk things over in their own primary groups, and many of them conclude that the situation is hopeless. They continue to enforce formal norms only when they are being watched and cannot escape responsibility. As they too begin to look after their personal interests, many become corrupt. The disclosure that high officials in government or in a ruling political party are involved in graft and corruption undermines the confidence the people once had in their ability to govern. Once it becomes clear that most authorities no longer care what happens, political control may break down and a condition approaching anarchy may develop. Bands of outlaws may roam through the countryside terrorizing the people, as in "bloody Kansas" during the Civil War era, in Colombia in the early 1950s, or in Uganda after the fall of Idi Amin. When the government cannot be counted on even for protection, people often establish mutual aid groups, such as the vigilantes, to defend themselves. Although the disintegration of society seldom reaches this point, it does happen from time to time.

DEVELOPMENT OF COLLECTIVE ANXIETY

Anxiety as an Emotional Reaction. The breakdown of a clear picture of the world makes the future unpredictable. Unlike the inhabitants of stable village communities, who have a clear conception of the kind of careers they are likely to lead, people caught in rapidly changing contexts face many uncertainties. They are not sure what to expect, and planning becomes difficult. Observers in diverse historical settings have noted that such sustained insecurity elicits anxiety among those who are affected. This common reaction has been described in many ways—uprootedness, alienation, estrangement, social unrest. How large a sector of a community becomes involved depends on the nature of the disruption. The impact may be concentrated on some occupational group, such as coal miners who have been put out of work by a technological innovation. Being unemployed, they can no longer maintain their self-respect before their children. Or some ethnic minority may be upset when members of the younger generation find the life-style of affluent neighbors more attractive than the traditional ways. In some instances, as in the United States in the 1960s, a substantial portion of the youth may become involved in collective anxiety.

Kierkegaard (1957) is widely credited with defining *anxiety* as an avoidance reaction, much like fear, except that no specific object can be pinpointed as the source of danger. Those who face sustained uncertainty develop apprehensions but are unable to locate the menacing object. Anxiety has also been characterized as the fear of the unknown (Riezler, 1944). An anxiety-ridden person's stance is one of expectant attention — hypersensitive, constantly searching for something without knowing what. The imagination is likely to become disordered; since one cannot focus attention on anything in particular, it becomes difficult to concentrate. The person experiences strong impulses to do something — to move, to attack, to escape — but in the absence of an object there is nothing to do. The person feels threatened but unable to cope with the situation. The experience is one of uncertainty and helplessness. Coping reactions vary considerably from person to person; behavior often becomes random and vacillating, or one may become immobilized. Thus, anxiety is an avoidance reaction without a specific object. It is an emotional response to danger, and it strikes those who anticipate unmanageable demands. It has all the characteristics of autonomic nervous system arousal — accelerated heartbeat, breathing difficulties, sweating, and trembling.

Like other emotional reactions anxiety varies in intensity. Mild anxiety makes a person more alert and better prepared to cope with the challenging situation. Kierkegaard insists that some degree of anxiety is unavoidable; anxiety develops whenever decisions must be made. In any situation involving choice one may commit an error; hence, anxiety is a necessary component of freedom. Maturity, he contends, is the ability to experience and tolerate anxiety. But intense anxiety, often described as a sense of impending doom, may result in the paralysis of thought and action. We experience the threat as overwhelming and may be immobilized. Freud (1936) and many other psychiatrists contend that many of the symptoms of various mental disorders constitute attempts of an organism to defend itself against chronic reactions of this kind. However, maladjusted individuals may develop acute anxiety states independently of social change; severe difficulties in interpersonal relations, which can occur in the most stable of social contexts, can provoke such reactions. Although it is commonly believed that personality disorders of all kinds are found more often in rapidly changing societies than in stable ones, evidence on this matter is not clear (Eaton and Weil, 1955). Nonetheless, such reactions have been observed frequently in transitional periods.

Reactions to Sustained Uncertainty. Sustained frustration, whatever the source, leads to certain characteristic experiences (May, 1953). One common reaction is disillusionment with the world. Everyone is taught many ideals. When many things happen that contradict them, however, they are exposed as fatuous shibboleths. Ideals appear perverted when we see others, including those we had been taught to respect, circumventing them. If such persons, including one's parents, deny they are cheating, they appear to be hypocrites. Then, one begins to wonder if anything is sacred. People become bewildered, for they no longer know what to believe. As old values are called into question, they wonder why they should work hard or make sacrifices. As increasing numbers come to feel that their legitimate aspirations are being thwarted, individualistic and hedonistic tendencies are reinforced. Disappointment and discouragement become widespread; work becomes unsatisfactory and monotonous; life seems pointless.

Another common reaction to sustained frustration is a sense of helplessness, a feeling that one is an impotent victim of circumstances. People try repeatedly to meet problematic situations sensibly, but somehow they do not seem to be able to find satisfactory solutions. The inability to cope effectively leads to a sense of not knowing what to do. Some develop serious doubts of the possibility of controlling their own destiny. Of course, in mass societies everyone becomes involved in gigantic transactions in which individual participants can in fact do little to alter the course of events, but anxiety amplifies this sense of impotence. If one feels that one's life is controlled from without, then there is little reason to make commitments or serious efforts to achieve anything. What will happen will happen. Why make sacrifices when there is no assurance that they will matter?

A common product of such reactions is confusion concerning one's personal identity, what in the 1960s was called the crisis of identity. Since values form the basis of many assumptions about oneself, serious questions about their validity lead to self-estrangement. In a stable society most career lines are well defined; in a rapidly changing context, however, one cannot be so certain of what to anticipate. As one becomes detached from customary moorings, defining one's status becomes increasingly difficult. A person with self-respect can act with pride and confidence. When one's self-concept becomes unclear, however, one is less certain about what to do, for specifying moral conduct becomes difficult. In many cases delayed gratification appears pointless, but a life devoted to hedonism soon becomes empty and lonely.

Those who have difficulty finding genuine satisfaction begin to have other doubts about themselves—wondering what they are doing on earth and what kind of human being they are. Young people in particular begin to wonder what kinds of activities and experiences will bring them a genuine sense of fulfillment and peace of mind. Thus, questions arise over how one is to define oneself as an object. Which of the many beliefs and assumptions about oneself are sound, and which are false? Unless a person can feel that his or her existence is of some importance, life itself becomes pointless. As increasing numbers search for their particular places in their world, they become involved in a quest for some kind of meaning in life.

The Communication of Anxiety. If many people in a community are upset simultaneously, they soon become aware of one another's condition, communicate, and thereby develop an emotional climate. Dissatisfied individuals are often sensitized to others who are similarly distressed, for they are all looking for solutions to their difficulties. They watch one another to see what is happening, searching for hints of possible routes to gratification. Discussions arise in many contexts—within families, among friends, at work, at school, in public forums. Those who are anxiety-ridden usually find it easy to communicate, for they have so much in common. They are often astonished to find that others feel as they do, that so many others are on the same "wavelength." Since their sensitivities are reciprocated, anxiety-ridden people often stimulate one another in a circular manner, thus reinforcing one another's feelings. Through such interstimulation and response the general tension level rises, and the individuals become even more responsive to each other. Positive feedback intensifies emotional reactions. Thus, anxiety is communicable; indeed, at times those involved are so sensitized to one another that it may appear infectious. Collective anxiety consists of much more than the mere aggregation of anxiety-ridden individuals, just as collective panic differs from individual fear. The anxieties of individuals come and go, but an emotional climate is sustained over a longer period because of the reciprocal reinforcement of perspectives. This situation makes possible all kinds of transactions that require a division of labor. To the extent that the participants contribute to an emotional climate and are affected by it, they are prepared to act together.

One common result of the communication among anxiety-ridden

persons is the emergence of an object that is held accountable for the malaise, such as "alienation." Thus, vague and inchoate discomforts come to be labeled, defined, and explained. Each person's anxiety probably developed in a particular biographical context—sexual inadequacy, awkwardness in social contacts, inability to cope with authority figures. Sustained frustration, however, leaves a common core of experience. An effort is made to locate the general "cause" of the disquietude, and one of the simplest ways to explain anything is to blame someone or some condition. A wide variety of phenomena have been blamed: overprotective mothers, sexual repression, stringent toilet training, the baseness of human nature, encroachment of inferior "races," class conflict, dehumanization, Communist conspiracies, fundamentalist religion, the "establishment." Such labels and explanations are stereotypes; even though some may contain an element of truth, they are simplistic explanations of complex phenomena. Nonetheless, they enable people to make sense of themselves and their world and give them something specific to fear and avoid, an object against which to vent hostility.

The objects targeted in such contexts are not mirrorlike images of real objects; these targets are constructed and formed in social interaction. Of the many objects proposed, only a few prevail. Explanations that are the most plausible and expressive of what most of the people feel gradually become dominant through a process of natural selection. Once an object is identified and aroused feelings can be directed toward something specific, anxiety is transformed into discontent.

Manifestations of Collective Anxiety. One common occurrence in situations marked by collective anxiety is the exploration of new possibilities. With widespread questioning of old values, especially those that had been regarded as sacred, a search is made for alternative ways of doing things. Previously forbidden practices often attract special attention. For example, in the 1960s many Americans became preoccupied with various drugs and unconventional forms of sexual activity. There is much random behavior. People appear to be seeking something without knowing just what. Movement is therefore erratic and aimless. As people become sensitized to new possibilities, suggestibility is enhanced, and fashion movements sweep through various social worlds, especially among the young. People also experience an urge to move about, and some wander from one community to another, seemingly without purpose. At first only the reckless few migrate, but many others who lack the courage are equally restless and curious about the experiences of those who try. The itinerants find a ready audience wherever they stop, and information is exchanged eagerly. As they learn of fascinating new possibilities, increasing numbers join the vagabonds. Students of revolutionary movements have suggested that such wandering may play an important part in directing discontent (Edwards, 1927:23–36).

Another manifestation of collective anxiety is aggression against the object blamed for the malaise. It is defined as the enemy, and hostile outbursts are directed against it. As the anxiety-ridden project their apprehensions toward the world, it is not unusual for them to perceive their surroundings as dangerous. They impute foul motives to others, express fears of repression, and seriously entertain rumors of diabolical plots against them—such as the establishment of detention and labor camps for dissenters. Civil disturbances of all kinds become commonplace; protest demonstrators sometimes get out of hand and become ugly mobs; strikes and boycotts are called. As authorities try to restore order, they are identified with the enemy, and many challenge their right to enforce outmoded customs and laws.

In such periods various underground groups are organized, including social bandits who devote most of their efforts to attacking unpopular objects—the rich, the powerful, the privileged. Even though their terrorism occasionally injures innocent people, they often win popular support, for their attacks are selective and aimed at widely condemned objects. The discontented regard the bandits as their champions and protect them, idealize them, and develop legends about them, such as those of Robin Hood (Hobsbawn, 1965:13–29). Many terrorist organizations of the 1970s apparently viewed themselves in a similar manner; their weapons were far more destructive than those of their predecessors, but their outlook and tactics were the same (Laqueur, 1977; Schreiber, 1978). Although authorities often fear that a revolutionary movement is under way, such uprisings are in fact episodic and scattered. There is no overall planning or coordination; people in separate communities just become so angry that they partake in spontaneous outbursts of violence.

Another manifestation of collective anxiety is withdrawal from the community. In increasing numbers the discontented reject the society in which they had been reared and search for alternative life-styles. They are especially attracted to the unconventional, the unusual, the forbidden. Some experimenters seek increasingly drastic innovations—the strongest hallucinogens, the most unconventional forms of sexuality, or satanic religious practices. Many of these activities may be regarded as a form of expressive symbolism; they provide ways for people to vent frustrated inclinations and dispositions. None of the practices remains in fashion for too long; as increasing numbers become familiar with them, the restless go on to still newer things. Such periods are also marked by the flocking of the discontented to communes and other esoteric cults — early Christianity, the Ghost Dance religion, the cargo cults, Father Divine's Mission, the Black Muslims, the Unification Church. The philosophies and religions that attract the dissatisfied are usually alien to their native culture; thus, many Americans in the 1960s turned to Eastern religions. Such cults permit people to withdraw from circumstances they find unbearable and enable them to pursue a more meaningful life (Lofland, 1966; Stoner and Parke, 1979). Such activities often arouse great enthusiasm; many of the hippies of the 1960s saw themselves as the wave of the future, the vanguard of a superior way of life.

When all efforts to cope with the sources of discontent fail, an emotional climate of despair and resignation may develop. People come to feel that continuation of any effort to resolve or escape difficulties is futile. They define the situation as utterly hopeless and lapse into apathy. Unlike anxiety-ridden people, they no longer expect anything. As self-deprecation becomes commonplace and people define themselves as worthless objects, mobilizing them for any kind of effort, even to help themselves, becomes difficult (Banfield, 1958). Residents of American Indian reservations during the early twentieth century and some groups of unemployed inner-city youth in the 1970s succumbed to such despair. Unskilled and semiliterate people find themselves unemployable in an industrial society and feel condemned to a poverty-stricken life in disintegrating housing, broken families, and dependence on public welfare or crime. The classic study of the unemployed in Marienthal, Austria, in the midst of the depression of the 1930s describes the kind of despondency that makes understandable the appeal of any alternative — even participation in the Nazi movement (Jahoda et al., 1971).

SUMMARY AND DISCUSSION

Drastic changes in life conditions make it difficult to continue executing social transactions in the conventional manner. As difficulties mount, people faced with incongruent expectations begin to raise questions about matters they had previously taken for granted. Those who are thus upset from the previously established routines of life become increasingly sensitized to new possibilities. As different patterns of concerted action begin to take shape, persons conspicuously involved in the vanguard of social change often find themselves occupying marginal status. They may suffer severe guilt feelings, but the manner in which some of them resolve their personal difficulties often contributes to the establishment of innovations better adapted to the new circumstances. As pressures mount, increasing numbers stop complying with the old norms. Demoralization is a gradual process in which the disenchanted in ever greater proportions become detached from various features of the old moral order. As increasing numbers become estranged from the old order, there is much confusion, and collective anxiety develops. This elicits characteristic disturbances—including widespread discontent, angry protests, utter despondency, and a desperate search for alternative life-styles. Such contexts provide the crucibles from which new social institutions emerge.

Loss and pain for some people is an inevitable part of social change. Thus, those who live in transitional periods often feel sorry for themselves and point to the many frustrations they encounter. They complain of living in a world in which events are unpredictable and cite the numerous confrontations, disorders, and violence. Some critics condemn any change as evil. They mock the awkwardness and pretensions of those involved in class mobility, condemn the assimilation of ethnic minorities as genocide, and fear socialism as if it were a dread disease. However, these critics overlook what has been emphasized by some sociologists—among them Georg Simmel and Robert E. Park—that a changing society is also an open society, one that offers freedom and possibilities for improvement. Isolated and stable societies are inflexible; they provide opportunities only for those who enjoy high status. Those born into the bottom ranks of a stable society, such as the Chinese peasants before the Communist revolution or the outcastes in village India, lead predestined lives lacking any way other than sheer accident to escape their fate.

SUGGESTED READINGS

Feuer, Lewis S. 1969. *The Conflict of Generations.* New York: Basic Books.
  A sociological study of the formation of student protest movements based on case materials drawn from the past two centuries.

Hostetler, John A. 1980. *Amish Society.* Baltimore: Johns Hopkins University Press.
  The efforts of a religious community to preserve its culture while coping with the demands of living in a mass society.

Shibutani, Tamotsu. 1978. *The Derelicts of Company K: A Sociological Study of Demoralization.* Berkeley and Los Angeles: University of California Press.
  An analysis of demoralization as a social process, using a company of Japanese-American troops in World War II as a case study.

Stein, Maurice R., et al. (eds.). 1960. *Identity and Anxiety.* Glencoe, Ill.: Free Press.
   A collection of articles concerning the characteristic personal problems faced by people living in rapidly changing social contexts.
Stonequist, Everett V. 1937. *The Marginal Man.* New York: Scribner's.
   A pioneering study of marginal status and the various strategies used to cope with incompatible demands.
Wallerstein, Immanuel (ed.). 1966. *Social Change: The Colonial Situation.* New York: Wiley.
   The ecological and social problems confronting the people caught in the rapid transformations occurring in the developing nations.

XII

SOCIAL MOVEMENTS

Most changes in human society are unplanned. When the ecosystem is upset, as when natural resources are exhausted, people just do the best they can to cope with shortages. People often welcome technological innovations because of their obvious advantages; only later do they realize that effective implementation will force many revisions in social relationships. In time the cost is accepted fatalistically. Government agencies often introduce new procedures, and only a small proportion of the people to be affected are even aware of the new policies until they have become well established. Many changes occur in small increments, and their accretion often passes unnoticed. Human beings rarely look very far into the future; instead they focus on the immediate task of dealing with one problematic situation after another. Thus, in many cases we simply back into new ways of doing things. However, some changes are brought about through the concerted effort of people who are discontented with their lot in life. Those who are dissatisfied get together, mobilize their resources, seek public support, and mount a collective effort to alter their way of life. Such enterprises are called *social movements.* Since some of the participants are often drawn from the least privileged strata in the community, many social movements are bootstrap operations.

History records a wide variety of social movements. Some have swept over vast areas—such as the Crusades in medieval Europe in which Christians from all walks of life were mobilized to recapture sacred territory from the infidels, the Protestant Reformation that followed a

332

few centuries later, the Ghost Dance among American Indians from the Mississippi River to California in the nineteenth century, or the cargo cults that developed in various islands in the South Pacific a few decades later. Socialism began as a loose confederation of disenchanted intellectuals and has now succeeded in transforming half the world. Other social movements have affected large communities, such as the secessionist movements in the Balkans in the early twentieth century and in the European colonies after World War II. Still others have been limited to specific categories of people within a community — peasant movements, labor movements, feminist movements, or the civil rights movement of the 1960s. Some movements are confined to specific social worlds, such as French impressionism, which revolutionized modern painting, or jazz music in New Orleans and Chicago. We are concerned thus with a broad range of phenomena that arise in diverse historical contexts. How such enterprises develop is limited by what the government will tolerate. Where free speech and the formation of voluntary associations are severely circumscribed, for example, the disgruntled are forced to form secret, underground organizations. Yet social movements have many features in common, and the purpose of this chapter is to identify some of these regularities. How do discontented people mobilize their resources to alter their way of life?

FOCUS OF COLLECTIVE DISCONTENT

Sources of Direction. Social movements are most likely to arise in communities shaken by numerous dislocations and the ensuing collective anxiety. They emerge in rapidly changing contexts, and to the extent that they succeed they give direction to the transformations. In most instances the earliest protests come from outraged intellectuals (Brinton, 1952:42–53). Journalists, scholars, novelists, artists, frustrated officials, and crusading politicians are among the first to call attention to various injustices. In most instances the early critics are much like voices in the wilderness and are not taken seriously. In time, however, their indictments identify and label inequities, provide explanations of what is wrong, pinpoint blame, and suggest courses of remedial action. Thus, the Protestant Reformation received a firm impetus when Martin Luther, already recognized as a brilliant theologian, posted the Ninety-five Theses in 1517. Before the French Revolution works of the philosophers of the Enlightenment were discussed avidly, and a leading part in the agitation was played by Freemasons — at that time an organization of ambitious aristocrats, bankers, and intellectuals. Socialism arose amid the chaos that marked the early phases of industrialization in Europe. Writings such as Proudhon's *What Is Property?* and the *Communist Manifesto* by Marx and Engels evoked widespread interest among those sympathetic to the plight of the working classes. The Abolitionist movement was given considerable momentum by the novel *Uncle Tom's Cabin;* many Americans who had opposed slavery as a matter of principle were shocked into protest by this fictional depiction, which enabled them to identify with slaves as human beings.

Indeed, books have played an important part in the early phases of many social movements, among them the Book of Mormon and Hitler's *Mein Kampf.* Among the illiterate the word of prophets provides the initial direction. After the Plains Indians had been pacified by the U.S. Cavalry, for example, the prophet Wovoka preached that the world was coming to a catastrophic end and that a regeneration of Indian life, in which dead ancestors would return to partake in an idyllic existence, would follow. Therefore, Indians should make peace with white men, return to their own culture, and engage in the Ghost Dance (Mooney, 1965).

Discontent may also become focused as an incidental by-product of activities unrelated to social movements. During World War II, for example, Japanese propagandists tried to tighten their grip over areas conquered in Southeast Asia by popularizing the slogan "Asia for the Asiatics." Although the people there were not impressed with the sincerity of Japanese militarists, increasing numbers came to feel that they should indeed control their own destiny. Hence, after the Japanese were driven out, European colonists who had expected to return to their lives of privilege were shocked to find that they were no longer welcome. At times spectacular events transform perspectives. The disclosure that the Nazi government had massacred six million Jews sent shock waves throughout the world. One result was that Zionism, a movement that had languished from lack of support among Jews, was suddenly embraced as the solution to an age-old problem.

Popular music has played an important part in many political movements, but nowhere is its impact more apparent than in the sudden change in the lyrics of songs in vogue among the youth of the 1960s. Romantic ballads and novelty tunes were replaced by songs of social criticism that raised penetrating questions about long-accepted values and institutions (Denisoff and Peterson, 1972; Glazer, 1972). Many who had been attracted to the songs of Bob Dylan or the Beatles just to be in vogue came away discontented with their daily routines. Those who had not been dissatisfied with anything in particular became incensed at the "establishment" and began participating actively in various protest movements. Thus, popular songs gave a definite direction to the anxieties and idealism commonly found among young people everywhere; in some ways rock music became a battering ram to assault the life-style and politics of mainstream America, although there is no evidence of a conspiracy in the music industry to overturn the status quo.

As collective discontent begins to swell, agitators emerge in each local community, giving speeches and circulating pamphlets. If an effort is made to suppress such dissidents, informal communication channels are formed, and an underground press may develop. Although defenders of the status quo often blame agitators for all difficulties, in fact agitators are usually unable to get a hearing. Malcontents and prophets of doom are ubiquitous, and they are usually dismissed as "kooks." Sooner or later most of them are imprisoned, become alcoholics, or give up their efforts, convinced that others are either hopelessly insensitive or stupid. The aroused sensitivities of the listeners make them responsive to such appeals; those who have started to raise questions about what they had previously taken for granted are especially susceptible to new ideas. Being dissatisfied with things as they are, they become receptive to new possibilities. Thus, it is the responsiveness of the discontented that enables agitators and prophets who would otherwise be ignored to win large followings.

The Emergence of Ideologies. As collective discontent continues to mount, intellectuals step up their efforts to clarify the situation. Since people who face sustained uncertainty tend to become suggestible, many of them become responsive to views they would otherwise reject as implausible. Competing ideologies emerge to define what is wrong, provide an explanation of it, and propose a remedial program. Thus, in nineteenth-century Europe Marx and Engels accounted for the poverty-stricken condition of the urban proletariat in terms of class conflict. They argued that owners of the means of production pursued their class interests, even when this required the exploitation of those who worked for them. They proposed, therefore, that ownership and control of the means of production should be vested in the community and administered in the interests of all inhabitants. This would reduce inequities at once, and class differences could eventually be eliminated altogether.

After World War II natives who had become acculturated to European ways blamed their plight on the continued domination of colonists, who had placed a ceiling on their upward social mobility. Their proposed solution was national liberation: Once ethnic minorities had won the right to govern themselves, such injustices would disappear. Religious ideologies — early Christianity, the Ghost Dance of the Sioux Indians, the Black Muslims — often develop among the impoverished and powerless, among people who are convinced that nothing can be done to alter the abysmal conditions under which they live. Their programs stress the moral regeneration of the downtrodden people. Acceptance of such perspectives enables the discontented to reinterpret their experiences, give meaning to their lives, and develop self-respect.

Although there are many kinds of ideologies, most are characterized by internal logical consistency, a simplistic explanation of complex problems, and a utopian view of the product of their program. Both the explanations and the programs advocated are gross oversimplifications. Although Marxist thinking on various phases of human life has been elaborated into an extensive, technical literature, only scholars specializing in it are familiar with its details; the party line presented to potential converts remains simple. In most instances some group, some institution, or some condition is blamed as the "cause" of all the difficulties. The objects blamed are stereotyped: the establishment, white power structure, Yankee imperialism, revisionists, hooligans, male chauvinist pigs, Jews, Communists. Acceptance of such ideologies focuses attention on a limited number of objects and enables the discontented to make sense of their plight.

Many ideologies also include a *utopian vision,* a faith that the successful execution of the program will lead to the formation of a perfect society. Many social movements have been characterized as millenarian in that their supporters believe that success will usher in a thousand years of idyllic existence (Talmon, 1968). Christians look forward to living in paradise after the Second Coming of the Savior; Marxists dream of total communism in which even government bureaucracies will wither away; Nazis dreamed of the magnificent civilization Aryans would create. Although their opponents dismiss such beliefs as myths, partisans base their activities on these premises. Whether or not such ideas are accurate, their acceptance enables diverse people to cooperate in moving toward a common goal. Thus, if some readily identifiable object can be singled out as the "cause" of all the difficulties, the feelings and resources of the discontented can be mobilized into a joint effort to eliminate it or bring it under control. The hated object becomes the symbol against which all efforts can be organized, and it provides a clearly defined goal and evokes the spirit of cooperation and sacrifice necessary to get the task accomplished.

Acceptance of such explanations leads many of the discontented to redefine themselves. Adoption of a different perspective leads people to perceive themselves in a different light. Those who occupy low status regard their lot in life as inevitable because of their inherent inferiority. Before World War II many Afro-Americans accepted their subordinate position as something that could not be helped, just as many natives assumed that their European colonial masters were superior and invincible. Until recently many women assumed that they were inferior to men. A self-concept consists of a set of beliefs and assumptions about oneself as an object. Some key assumptions are challenged by new ideologies. The redefinition occurs neither suddenly nor easily. Even when an innovative suggestion strikes a responsive chord, the people affected at first only entertain doubts about what they had long taken for granted. A transitional period of vacillation usually follows. After they are convinced intellectually they must keep reminding themselves that they had been acting on the basis of false premises; before the change crystallizes they need constant reassurances in words and deeds from many others.

Once people have redefined themselves, once they become convinced that they have the same rights as other human beings, they resent any kind of differential treatment. Thus, if the discontented alter their self-concept, they come to feel that they are being deprived of something that is rightfully theirs. They feel they are being cheated. Then, what had previously been accepted as natural becomes unbearable. Noticing the discrepancy between their conception of their legitimate rights and the actual situation elicits anger; they are no longer willing to accept it. Even if their circumstances have actually improved, those whose expectations have risen still feel outraged (Williams, 1975). Thus, one key to an understanding of social movements is the transformation of the self-concepts of the discontented.

The Process of Group Formation. The effective implementation of an ideology requires some kind of organization, and a variety of groups emerge among those who make up the most concerned segments of the growing public. Some social movements are guided by a single partisan group; others are pushed along by several, each with a somewhat different ideology but all moving in the same general direction. Where freedom of association is permitted, voluntary associations of all kinds spring up; where political protest is illegal, secret societies are formed. Just who gets involved in which group depends on how the discontented are located in various networks of personal contact (Snow et al., 1980). In the beginning the disgruntled meet informally in various local communities to decide how they should proceed. In some instances already existing groups concerned with the same matter enter the political arena. Thus, during the civil rights movement of the 1960s organizations such as the Congress of Racial Equality (CORE), the Student Nonviolent Coordinating Committee (SNCC), the Black Panthers, and the Southern Christian Leadership Conference (SCLC) were joined by well-established groups such as the National Association for the Advancement of Colored People (NAACP), the American Civil Liberties Union (ACLU), and a number of religious denominations. New communication channels are formed, making it easier for the concerned to keep up with the latest developments. The activities of such partisans affect even those who do not become members. The spectator component of the public is bombarded with new objects and proposals. As the civil rights movement developed, for example, millions of uninvolved Americans followed the key events and eventually took a stand.

Partisan groups vary in size and structure, ranging from small outlaw bands to huge mass organizations. The leadership of some groups is elected; other groups are founded by a single person who remains the acknowledged leader to the end. Some groups are directed by unusual individuals who are believed by their followers to possess extraordinary qualities, perhaps divine gifts, that set them apart from ordinary human beings. Such *charismatic* leaders become majestic objects, symbols that unite the members. Major protest movements among Afro-Americans have been led by such exceptional persons — Marcus Garvey, Father Divine, and Elijah Muhammad. Similarly, revolutionary movements have been galvanized by leaders such as Fidel Castro, Mahatma Gandhi, and Jomo Kenyatta. Their organizations, sometimes called messianic movements, have some decided advantages over others. Decision making is simplified; since the members are in awe of their leader, they accept without question whatever he or she says. Furthermore, since intense and total commitment is summoned by the leader, problems of maintaining discipline are kept to a minimum (Weber, 1968:241–45).

Each partisan group is committed to an ideology and a program of action. Many participants accept their ideology literally and take it for granted that the successful execution of their announced program will resolve the problem. But some leaders distinguish between their actual objectives, which are known only to those within trusted circles, and the political rhetoric they address to the public. In the early 1940s the Chinese Communists realized that a candid statement of their ultimate goals would not attract support even among poor peasants; hence, they joined other political parties in agitating for "double reduction" — reduction of rents and reduction of interest rates (Hinton, 1968:86). Many observers therefore regarded them as agrarian reformers. Not until they assumed control did their commitment to Marxism become apparent. This strategy of withholding key aspects of a new ideology is a common practice that has at times led to crushing tragedies. After World War II most Germans expressed astonishment at disclosures of what had happened in their concentration camps. In *Mein Kampf* Hitler had written openly of the desirability of exterminating Jews, but most Germans had not taken it seriously. The proposal had struck them as so implausible that they assumed it was nothing more than political propaganda that would enable the Nazi party to attract anti-Semitic people who were otherwise not interested in its program. Upon learning of the massive extermination, many Germans were shocked to discover that the Nazi leaders had actually carried out their inconceivable plan.

Of the many partisan groups that emerge in periods of collective discontent only a few survive. Some are suppressed by the government; they collapse when their leader is imprisoned or killed. Others that are agitating for change must compete with one another for public support. Social movements develop in a period of flux. Each partisan group develops in its own way, and new associations keep forming. Groups that were initially prominent are dissolved when the situation changes and their appeal becomes irrelevant. Strong coalitions arise; the consolidation of several local units produces regional organizations. Acceptance depends not only on the leaders' organizational skills but also on the relevance of the ideology. When Carroll (1975) examined the adoption of the Ghost Dance among thirty-seven tribes of Plains Indians, for example, he found acceptance high not among those who were closer to the point of origin but among tribes that had only recently been deprived of buffalo. Thus, many ideas are presented, but only those explanations of the malaise that are plausible to the discontented are taken seriously. The ideology that most eloquently expresses the feelings of those who are restless attracts and holds attention. Only agitators who are able to strike a responsive chord in the audience are able to win a following. Thus, in the competition among partisan groups for public support only those with an ideology that appeals to a substantial portion of the discontented survive to become the leading organizations in the social movement. The number of active groups is thereby reduced through a process of competition and natural selection.

Social movements are led by the partisan groups that survive the competition of ideologies. Active participation in such groups, even in those that do not survive, provides the context in which new ideas and new self-concepts are reaffirmed. Talking to others who have had similar experiences and making discoveries together enable unhappy people to see more clearly the possibilities of a better life. Changes in self-concept are tenuous, and they will disappear unless they are reiterated and reinforced. Discussions with others of like mind reaffirm one's new sense of personal worth. Merely attending meetings provides a sense of doing something worthwhile, and just reciting the slogans of the movement can make one feel better. All this not only makes the past unbearable but dedicates each participant to a program to change it. Being with others who feel the same way provides a sense of support, sometimes even of invincibility. In such contexts collective enthusiasm develops, and high morale is generated. The participants become determined to do their part in the collective effort to change the old order.

Convergence of Social Movements. In communities marked by severe dislocations a number of parallel social movements commonly develop. Nineteenth-century America saw movements against slavery, child labor, and alcohol (which was presumed to degrade the working classes) —all demands for reform on humanitarian grounds. West of the Mississippi the Plains Indians developed not only the Ghost Dance but also several similar movements, including the Peyote cult and the Great Message. These religious movements all facilitated accommodation to life in reservations. During the rapid industrialization of Japan following the Meiji revolution, radical college students and militarists became rivals for public support; both were objecting to materialism and the loss of traditional values (H. D. Smith, 1972). In the 1960s the United States was swept by several liberation movements—for ethnic minorities, college students, women, homosexuals, and the elderly. Although these movements had different objectives, their rhetoric and political strategies had much in common. Such mass movements are not planned; there is no central leadership to guide and coordinate the activities. Nonetheless, the net product of the convergence of such disparate efforts is the channeling of discontent in a particular direction. Since large numbers of people have been upset by the same conditions, it is not strange that a variety of similar social movements should arise. Whether the proposed solutions of such social movements are alike or diametrically opposed, all of them address the same problems.

Social movements propose many programs of action. When such efforts turn out to be unproductive, some advocates become sufficiently desperate to pursue what may be regarded as the penultimate solution —to leave their homes to seek opportunities elsewhere. The discontented become involved in mass emigration, as the Garvey movement proposed for Afro-Americans early in the twentieth century. Large-scale migrations that develop in such contexts have many of the characteristics of social movements. The developmental pattern is cumulative (Mac-Donald and MacDonald, 1964). At first only the adventurous few leave, for the most part young men. If they are well received and find conditions preferable to those at home, they communicate with their friends and relatives, urging them to join them. Persons with such direct contacts are usually the next to leave. As glowing rumors of the new land spread among the discontented, the trickle becomes a broad stream; those who had gone ahead help resettle the others, as in the mass migration of Europeans to the United States. Indeed, in Sweden emigration became the thing to do; it became so popular that it was labeled "Amerika fever" (Lindberg, 1930). The same kind of movement occurred among Afro-Americans in the South who saw greater opportunities in northern cities (Frazier, 1939:271–324). Such migrations sometimes do solve problems. The most dissatisfied find new lives elsewhere; those who remain behind find that the pressure of population on available resources has been reduced.

RECURRENT PATTERNS OF DEVELOPMENT

The boundaries of most social movements are difficult to define. Since they address key issues, the concerned public is often large. Although the partisan groups are easy to identify, there are many spectators whose attention is focused on common objects and who are oriented toward similar goals. From time to time some of the spectators participate actively, and their reactions have much to do with the fate of any movement. Each social movement is unique. Each has a distinct history; each develops step by step as the various types of participants come to terms with a succession of changing circumstances. Even branches of what is avowedly a common movement differ drastically—compare the development of communism in the Soviet Union, Yugoslavia, China, Italy, and Cambodia. Thus, social movements vary along several dimensions. They pursue dissimilar objectives. Each movement is organized differently. Some are dominated by a single partisan group; others are spearheaded by several prominent associations; still others, such as the Chicano movement in the American Southwest, are made up of hundreds of organizations concerned with similar problems but each going its own way. The type of leadership involved varies considerably. Each partisan group has its own ideology; some differ so much from the symbolic environment of the community that outsiders cannot understand them. Furthermore, the ideologies and even the goals of some movements keep changing. As a movement develops, different kinds of political tactics are adopted. Yet social movements have enough in common that we can recognize them as constituting a single class of phenomena. We may begin our effort to formulate generalizations about them by classifying them in terms of some broad patterns of development. The typology is a rough one; there are numerous exceptions, but it provides a useful point of departure.

Mobilizing Public Support for a Cause. Where free association is permitted, reformers attempt to mobilize people of goodwill in behalf of a worthy cause. Especially where public policy is formed through popular participation this is an effective way of changing practices defined as objectionable. Americans in particular seem to have a passion for social reform. As de Tocqueville points out, whenever anything is found wanting, Americans organize to do something about it. The goal of a reform movement is usually limited in scope; it is to change a specific feature of the existing society that is viewed as unjust. Examples include movements to provide better care for orphans, to provide medical care for the indigent, to legalize the use of marijuana, to conserve natural resources for future generations, or to eliminate discrimination against women and ethnic minorities.

The beneficiaries of most reform movements are the politically weak or those otherwise unable to protect their own interests. Thus, during the early stages of the industrialization of Europe, factory workers were not only exploited but had little recourse to redress. During this period intellectuals developed a number of movements—among them socialism, anarchism, and syndicalism—to improve the conditions under which the urban proletariat had to live. In nineteenth-century America slaves were helpless, and the abolitionists tried to mobilize outside support in their behalf. The Anti-Slavery Society was organized in 1835, and in three years it had 1,350 chapters with a quarter million members. Although a handful of fugitive slaves and freedmen participated, most members were from the privileged strata (Filler, 1960). After the Civil War many Americans of high rank became convinced that the poverty and other difficulties faced by recently arrived European immigrants arose from their drinking habits. Success required moral character, and temperance was seen as the solution to their problems. The Woman's Christian Temperance Union (WCTU) was organized in 1874. Its members' stance was paternalistic; they wanted to help the underprivileged earn their way to higher status (Gusfield, 1963). The civil rights movement was initiated by black and white intellectuals in behalf of Afro-Americans who were not yet aware of the political power they could generate simply by getting together. Although the Congress of Racial Equality (CORE) was organized in 1942, it did not attract attention until the 1960s, when it led a nonviolent campaign to open public accommodations to Afro-Americans. About half the members at that time were black, mostly middle-class adults and college students (Bell, 1968). The various movements for the conservation of natural resources are carried out in behalf of all humanity on the assumption that most people are too shortsighted to fight for the interests of their progeny.

Although reformers are sometimes accused by their opponents of being dangerous radicals, their stance is actually conservative. Their aims are limited. From their standpoint the established order is basically healthy, and they believe that modifying a few practices would make the status quo even better. Thus, reform movements reaffirm values already accepted in the community. Reformers begin with unquestioned values — such as personal freedom or equality of opportunity — and then point to the discrepancies between such ideals and actual conditions. They demand changes that would make social institutions comply more closely with already accepted standards. The leaders and most of the participants in reform movements are drawn from the more privileged strata of a community. As a matter of principle they work in behalf of people whom they regard as less fortunate than themselves. Precisely because so many reformers are drawn from the more affluent segments of a community, the police cannot harass them without risking serious repercussions. Thus, reform movements operate from a position of strength; precisely because they do not challenge the status quo, their position is unassailable on moral grounds (Delaisi, 1927:57–59; Blumer, 1951:211–13).

Since reform movements push for the implementation of already accepted ideals, they generally operate in the open. In the United States the partisans form voluntary associations, open to anyone who is interested. Most reformers cooperate with others who profess similar views, and at times various groups form loose confederations and pool their resources. They may even band together to form a political party. Thus, if the goal of a movement is to bring some practice into line with already accepted values, its basic strategy is to make a public issue of the changes it demands. Reformers call the public's attention to their grievances, seek their support, and try to shame their opponents into submission. In their efforts to persuade the government to adopt their program, they often operate as lobbyists. Sometimes they file suits in courts in behalf of the dispossessed or call for a referendum. Sometimes a few who are deeply committed may resort to direct action. Extremists in the WCTU occasionally broke into saloons, destroyed furniture, and preached sermons. Most members, however, were content to fight for a constitutional amendment to make the sale of alcohol illegal.

If sustained efforts to bring about such changes turn out to be unproductive, many partisan groups divide into factions. Some members want to continue the struggle; frustrating as it may be, they feel that the cause is worth pursuing. Others despair of ever accomplishing anything and drop out of the movement. Still others conclude reluctantly that they cannot achieve their objectives within the existing political order and become more belligerent. As their demands become more strident, they become isolated from the others; in time they break off to form their own partisan group. For those who become committed to overthrowing constituted authority—be it an intractable tradition, a powerful church, or a government—there is a displacement of goals.

Many revolutionaries begin their careers as moderate reformers. Long before Martin Luther challenged the authority of the Catholic church, for example, he struggled within the church hierarchy for reasonable changes. Only after being defeated in a succession of confrontations did he take the decisive step (Grimm, 1973:75–116). Harsh suppression tends to galvanize disillusioned reformers into dedicated revolutionaries. Many leaders of insurrections—differing in their ideologies as much as Mahatma Gandhi, Adolf Hitler, and Ho Chi Minh—have spent considerable time in jail, where they became firmly committed. Many terrorist organizations—such as the Sinn Fein, the Mau Mau, or the Viet Cong—have been staffed by fighters who began as reformers. Once a partisan group becomes subversive, it is forced to operate underground. Few nations permit parties dedicated to overthrowing the government to operate within their borders; even when such groups are not outlawed, they are kept under constant surveillance. Revolutionaries are labeled as extremists, and most reformers turn away from them in fear. Their radical proposals are rejected as too farfetched and dangerous. But if collective discontent is not assuaged in some manner, such movements may acquire increasing support.

Mobilizing Beneficiaries for Action. In a second type of social movement attempts are made to organize the beneficiaries themselves to fight for their own interests. Partisan groups recruit members from among the discontented. Since human beings can be classified on the basis of diverse criteria, several categories of people have been designated as beneficiaries. Youth movements have played an important part in history (Feuer, 1969). Many social movements have been based on class differences: the middle classes against the nobility, peasants against their landlords, workers against their employers, farmers against business interests. Within the labor movement syndicalists in particular have attempted to mobilize workers for direct action—boycotts, demonstrations, sabotage, strikes. They have eschewed forming wealthy unions directed by powerful officials and have concentrated on developing solidarity among the workers themselves. Sometimes the aged have been brought together, as in Dr. Francis Everett Townsend's "Ham and Eggs" movement of the 1930s. Feminist movements have developed in various parts of the world during the past century. Religious groups have fought for their rights, and sometimes people who share a common language have fought for official recognition of their tongue. In recent times numerous ethnic movements, which have sometimes developed nationalistic aspirations as well, have flourished. When repressive laws and pogroms in Eastern Europe convinced some Jewish leaders that they could not count on benevolent Gentiles, Zionism, a movement to establish an independent Jewish state, came into existence. Several nationalistic movements developed in the Balkans in the early twentieth century, just as many national liberation movements formed in European colonies soon after World War II.

Such movements are usually organized by intellectuals and by the more privileged and articulate members of the subordinate and discontented categories. Thus, nineteenth-century Polish nationalism was essentially an upper-class movement; the peasants did not participate, for they distrusted both the landowners and the urban intellectuals. Pan-Slavism developed when the more affluent Czechs, Slovaks, Serbs, Croats, and Bulgarians concluded that they could not fare well under the Ottoman or Hapsburg empires (Kann, 1950). The independence of India appealed most to Indian professional workers, who had an English education but were blocked from advancement on ethnic grounds. Similarly, most national liberation movements since World War II have been led by persons of marginal status, acculturated to European ways but not accepted as equal by the colonists. Most of the active participants in the ethnic movements in the United States in the 1960s were college students; although the leaders professed to speak for the entire minority group, their programs have proved most beneficial for those in the middle classes. The same is true of the women's liberation movement. The more articulate and affluent members of low-ranking categories feel the pangs of discrimination most acutely, often finding their careers blocked by job ceilings. Even if they are better off than other members of their category, they feel the grievances more intensely.

The basic problem faced by most movements of this type is the development of consciousness of kind, for most categories of people are actually heterogeneous. Since the activists are so devoted to their cause, they are hurt and puzzled when so many others fail to develop enthusiasm for an enterprise that is avowedly in their interests. The problem can be seen most clearly in former European colonies. Most of the new nations in Africa and Southeast Asia are territorial units created by European colonial offices for administrative convenience; hence, the subjects brought together in them were not necessarily members of the same ethnic group. Nigeria, for example, was a political unit created by the British; it includes the Yoruba, the Fulani, the Hausa, the Ibo, and many other ethnic groups. It is not easy to persuade people who differ so much in language, culture, and religion that they are all Nigerians. Furthermore, each ethnic group is made up of people of different classes. Zionists once believed that all Jews were alike; the founding of the state of Israel shocked them into realizing just how many different kinds of people conceive of themselves as Jewish (Patai, 1953). Thus, during the initial phases of many ethnic movements a "cultural renaissance" is promoted, glorifying the group's language, art, and literature. In a deliberate effort to bolster ethnic pride, history is rewritten to stress the contributions made by members of the group.

Organizers of labor movements have encountered similar difficulties. Until the 1930s some American workers regarded unions as criminal organizations, and they feared retaliation from the government. Some felt personal loyalty to employers, whom they knew and trusted; and others were suspicious of intellectuals, whom they could not understand. Class consciousness has not developed among American workers partly because of the ethnic animosities among them and partly because of their conviction that the prospects for upward social mobility are favorable (Perlman, 1928). More recently, the women's liberation movement has encountered serious problems arising from class differences; consciousness-raising sessions have been conducted in various local communities to persuade women of diverse backgrounds that they indeed share many interests. Social movements have had varying degrees of success in mobilizing the discontented. Some have won large followings; others have failed, and the leaders of partisan groups have become self-appointed representatives for categories of people who are in fact largely indifferent to them.

Once the key issues have been identified, social movements evolve in various ways. Some develop into political parties, as did the Labour party in England. Others form loose federations of voluntary associations, as in women's liberation. Still others become elite organizations, such as the Bolshevik party, to guide the masses to their salvation. These movements usually begin by asking for reforms — the elimination of a few practices they find especially obnoxious. If requests for such limited changes are turned down, however, demands may be escalated. For example, in the beginning many ethnic movements asked merely for formal recognition of their language and culture and some legal guarantees of their status. When these were denied, demands arose for political self-determination. Similarly, many labor movements began by asking only for laws to protect workers from blatant exploitation. Refusal led to the spawning of more radical organizations.

Moral Regeneration of Beneficiaries. The goal of a third type of social movement is not to change social institutions but to renovate the lives of the discontented by remolding them, by persuading them to perceive their world differently and to live by a new set of values. Such enterprises are often called religious movements, even though some of them are unconcerned with deities or the supernatural. Examples include the Ghost Dance, the Jehovah's Witnesses, the Black Muslims, and the early phases of many of the world's religious denominations. After the traditional ways of the South Sea islanders had been disrupted by the coming of Europeans, cargo cults developed on several of the islands. Believers looked forward to a catastrophic occasion on which the Europeans would be expelled, their own ancestors would be resurrected, and all of them would be able to enjoy boatloads of manufactured goods (Worsley, 1957).

The ideologies of such movements are more radical than those of revolutionaries; they diverge far more drastically from the commonsense view of the world accepted in the communities in which they arise. Their aim is the adoption of a new symbolic environment — a different way of looking at the universe and the place of human beings in it. Such groups repudiate the prevailing social order and propose a better life either in another world or in one that has been drastically transformed. The participants seldom concern themselves with social reforms; they expect the changes to occur miraculously. Since the new perspective is so different, all situations come to be defined in dramatically contrasting ways. Most important, those who become converted redefine themselves. Those of low status, who had felt inferior to others, revise their self-concepts and consider themselves among the few who know the truth and who will be saved. Although there are some exceptions, such as the cargo cults, the good life is defined in terms of self-respect rather than in terms of material gains.

Social movements of this type emerge among those who are totally disillusioned. They usually develop among people who acknowledge their lack of political power, among the poverty-stricken and among members of the most despised categories. They arise among those who realize that any fight against the established order would be suicidal. They may develop in several different contexts. Religious movements are often founded by a charismatic leader—Muhammad, John Wesley, Wovoka, Father Divine—a prophet who promises salvation to those who follow his or her instructions, counsel that is often believed to have originated from some more powerful source, such as God. Sometimes they develop in camp meetings of the discontented. The Kentucky revival at the turn of the nineteenth century consisted of a succession of such gatherings of frontier settlers who were concerned with their salvation. They were gala occasions that enabled people from remote areas to get together. News of unusual happenings attracted increasing numbers, and several new groups emerged, including the Baptist church (Cleveland, 1916; Weisberger, 1958). Revival meetings are still taking place; the "born-again" movement is flourishing amid our mass society.

Religious movements may also begin as schisms within already established churches. When the "disinherited," as Niebuhr (1929) calls them, find that the staid denominations are not meeting their needs, they break off to worship in their own way. Groups called "holy rollers" are usually products of such schisms. Their meetings are often marked by intense emotional expression. As collective tension mounts, participants often engage in wild, frenzied movements—jerking, barking, convulsive dancing. Participants often experience such communal catharsis as total ecstasy.

The partisan groups that develop in such contexts become associations of strict believers. Their characteristic stance is one of rejection of the established social order. If the goal of a social movement is the adoption of a different symbolic environment, its basic strategy is to seek converts and otherwise maintain distance from the outside community. If such groups are persecuted, they become secret societies. Even if they face no opposition, they are likely to keep others at a polite distance. To the extent that such groups are concerned with outsiders at all, it is to seek converts. The members are convinced that they know the true road to salvation, and they wish to share their good fortune with as many others as possible. They look with pity at those who are still lost, and they engage in proselyting. Otherwise they wish to be left alone to practice their rituals and to reaffirm their beliefs. They derive solace from being in the company of fellow believers; in their camaraderie they enjoy each other's support. Whenever expressive behavior occurs, the participants reexperience ecstasy, and each occasion reinforces their faith that they will be saved.

OPPOSITION AND GROUP SOLIDARITY

Opposition to Social Movements. If the program of any social movement is to be carried out, one or more partisan groups must mobilize material and human resources and coordinate the efforts of the members. Concerning the manner in which such enterprises are organized, one key consideration is the fact that all social movements are to some extent at odds with the status quo. Even if the change advocated is minor, it affects someone. Any change is made at someone's expense; if nothing else, people will have to change some of their habits. Therefore, all social movements encounter some kind of resistance. Each group involved in a social movement develops its structure in a succession of collective adaptations to the circumstances it faces. Although some groups appear to have been set up for some purpose, many internal arrangements are the product of efforts to cope with external pressures. Thus, virtually all partisan groups appear to be goal-oriented. In many instances, however, the goal takes shape *after* the group has been in existence for some time; it is hammered out and clarified as the members cope with various problematic situations. Many characteristic features of such groups are reactions to opposition.

Social movements face varying degrees of opposition — debate, ridicule, sporadic violence, sustained persecution. The extent of the hostility faced by any group depends on the manner in which it is defined in the larger community, not on its ideology or even the actual threat it poses to the status quo. Any group evaluated as a dangerous or frustrating object is likely to elicit antagonism. Where participation in unions is regarded as deviant behavior, the labor movement has to operate in secrecy. Religious movements that have made no demands on the outside community have faced severe oppression. Most religious movements ask only to be left alone. Yet the Amish and the Hutterites were forced to flee Europe because of persecution; although neither group has altered its ideology or life-style, in the United States and Canada they have faced only ridicule. The Jehovah's Witnesses were almost exterminated in Nazi Germany, even though the members of this religion did not actively fight against any government program.

In general, of all social movements the reform movements face the least opposition. Since reformers are reaffirming already accepted values, those who succeed in attracting public attention are difficult to attack on ethical grounds. A common stance of their foes is one of amusement and exasperation. Reformers are often caricatured as persons of goodwill who are impractical and visionary. Questions are raised about the practicability, rather than the desirability, of their program. For example, the WCTU was told that it was impossible to prevent people from drinking alcoholic beverages. An effort may be made to identify a movement with some unpopular object. Abolitionists were warned of the danger of being overrun by diseased and mentally deficient black people, just as CORE was attacked as an organization that sanctioned promiscuous sexual contacts among members of different ethnic groups. Proponents of the use of fluoride to reduce tooth decay have been attacked as being part of a communist plot. At times reformers' own actions — excessive displays of zeal, for example — leave them especially vulnerable to ridicule.

Any social movement that makes serious and costly demands on a community will face severe opposition. Any successful revolutionary movement will alter the social stratification system, reducing or eliminating the privileges of those of high rank. Subversive movements are clearly recognized as dangerous, and they usually elicit violent reactions. During the struggle for national liberation in Kenya, for example, the rebels — labeled by their opponents as the Mau Mau — were crushed ruthlessly. The colonists became obsessed with the organization, which was characterized as a band of primitive savages bent on massacring all Europeans. They were thought to derive special pleasure from splitting open the stomachs of pregnant women. The members were believed to take blood oaths, accompanied by the swallowing of a foul concoction — menstrual fluid, putrefying flesh from graves, or still-warm brains of women and children who had just been murdered (Majdalany, 1963; Kariuki, 1964). There could be no compromise with such uncivilized brutes. Faced with such harsh persecution, partisans must go underground. Then, changes become necessary in the group's internal structure. Subversive organizations become organized for war. Since centralized leadership is necessary for combat efficiency, a hierarchical authority structure tends to develop. Strict discipline also becomes essential (Simmel, 1955:88 – 89). Emphasis is placed on cohesion; without it such groups are not likely to survive.

Withdrawal from the Community.   The extent to which social distance is maintained from the larger community varies considerably from one social movement to another and among partisan groups within the same movement. The manner in which a group retreats from outside contacts does not depend on the actual hostility it encounters; it depends on the degree to which the members feel threatened by such associations. Reformers are usually the least isolated, for they have little reason to feel intimidated. Although some organizations are driven underground, others leave of their own initiative. Bittner (1963) suggests that the more a movement's ideology differs from the commonsense view of the world accepted outside of it, the more it is likely to emphasize internal solidarity. Where there are stark contrasts, outsiders appear ominous; they are perceived as frightening even when they are not antagonistic. Thus, even when they have no reason to fear persecution, some religious movements—the Amish and the Jehovah's Witnesses, for example—withdraw from fear of contamination. The members feel that unregulated contacts between themselves and outsiders are undesirable and potentially dangerous. Some groups virtually secede, forming communities of their own in isolated areas; all communication with the outside is left to designated representatives. Even when external contacts are not prohibited, dedicated members tend to cut themselves off from old ties. They may continue to see their families and old friends for a while, but in time they find that they have little in common. Although they may retain mutual goodwill with others, most of their meaningful associations become limited to other participants in the movement.

Some political and religious movements totally repudiate the existing social order. A *sect* is a voluntary association of believers. They deny the legitimacy of the outside world and wish to live apart from it. The sense of being in opposition to outsiders is important, for it helps to clarify the identity of the group and to secure its boundaries. Either one is a believer or one is not. To the extent that a group withdraws from the larger community, its internal structure is likely to assume certain characteristic features (Simmel, 1950:345 – 76). To maintain a clear distinction between believers and infidels recruitment and training procedures become clearly established. A conversion experience may be required for entry. Other measures may develop to maintain isolation. Endogamy may be enforced; anyone who marries an outsider is excommunicated. Members may also be prohibited from participating in outside activities, such as attending public schools or entering military service. Special norms of eating, dressing, or hairstyling may be strictly enforced. The members tend to develop a characteristic stance, often called the "sectarian attitude." Thus, members of social movements who feel threatened become preoccupied with group solidarity, and such organizations often show fierce tenacity in the face of grave adversity.

As members of a social movement become isolated, the distinction between in-group and out-group becomes exaggerated, and the sectarians are drawn together to form their own social world. Outsiders are viewed with increasing apprehension. In contrast, camaraderie develops within the group. Past status differences among the members are forgotten. Differences in rank are often kept to a minimum; everyone is addressed as a brother, sister, or comrade. As social distance among members is reduced, they feel at home together. Some persons, who had previously been isolated and lonely, develop a sense of closeness and of belonging for the first time. Through differential association each sect develops its own universe of discourse and its distinct culture. Each develops its own vocabulary — often conventional symbols used to designate special meanings. If a group is ridiculed for some of its peculiarities, as the Hutterites were mocked for their beards and austere dress, such items become badges of honor, an official uniform that serves as a symbol of group membership. Such practices often persist long after the circumstances of their origin have been forgotten. The group's distinctive values are stressed, and each movement develops its own heroes and saints — people who best exemplify in their conduct its key values. Each sect develops its own status ladder, and the members perceive their careers in terms of it. The members are expected to live up to high standards; moral purity is emphasized even in movements that are not primarily religious. The members evaluate themselves and one another in terms of these standards and form and maintain self-concepts in terms of sectarian criteria. The other members constitute the most important audience — reference group — for whom each person performs. Thus, loyalty to the movement is reinforced by close and satisfying personal ties (Lofland and Stark, 1965).

As a social movement withdraws from the community, its ideology tends to become more explicitly formulated. As various difficulties are encountered, the ideology is elaborated to account for them. Failures must also be explained. Movements that make predictions — such as the coming of judgment day — face the problem of disconfirmation. If sincerity and hard work are not rewarded, the failures are explained in terms of unfair tactics by rivals, the stupidity of outsiders, bad luck, or slight errors in judgment. If a key point is not confirmed, the explanation is incorporated into the ideology (Sears, 1924; Festinger et al., 1956). Once an ideology is established, it becomes a sacred object to be defended against all infidels. The ideology is absolute; there can be no compromise; and total commitment is demanded. Deviation from dogma is regarded as treason. Some movements become so rigid that they appear devoid of practical wisdom. Sensitivity to unusual opportunities, capacity to learn from experience, and flexibility of interest are dismissed as indications of decadence. Precisely because dissidence is not allowed, schisms are likely to occur whenever serious differences of opinion arise. Those who disagree are labeled heretics and expelled, and dissidents often go off to form their own partisan group. Heretics are frequently hated more venomously than disbelievers; after all, they have had the advantage of knowing the truth (Coser, 1956:60–72, 95–104). Thus, all external sanctions are nullified, and the movement develops a monopoly over its members' commitment. Accomplishing the goals of the movement becomes a sacred mission.

As a social movement becomes isolated, its members begin to view themselves as a select group. They conceive of themselves as a different kind of human being. The world is divided into the saved and the lost, believers and disbelievers, saints and devils. The faithful will enjoy salvation. Others may repent, be converted, and qualify; but their time is running short. Since the members look on the outside world as decadent and hopelessly lost, they want no part of it, and they consider their life-style the only correct way to live. Those who must suffer are viewed as martyrs to a great cause. Sectarians often regard themselves as the "elect"—an elite group. After all, they know the truth, when others are too stupid to see the obvious. Revolutionaries who pursue egalitarian goals are often contemptuous of the common people in whose behalf they profess to toil. In *What Is To Be Done?* Lenin declares that the working classes cannot be trusted to discover their own true interests; if left alone, they would follow the path of forming unions rather than making a commitment to socialism. Therefore, the masses must be guided by an insurgent vanguard possessing superior knowledge of the laws of history. He also insists that this vanguard should consist of a small, carefully selected group of professional revolutionaries operating under centralized authority with strict discipline.

In time, sectarians become increasingly detached from the moral order of the larger community from which they were recruited. Detachment from outsiders makes the rejection of their values easier. When members of a subversive movement must resort to violence or terrorism, for example, such detachment makes their work easier. Outsiders are not part of their own moral order. Hence, if some innocent people are killed, it is a small price to pay in an effort to create paradise. People who are fighting for a noble cause sometimes become merciless. Since they are merciless in making demands on themselves, they often have no compassion for others (Simmel, 1955:39).

Relations to Rival Organizations. Partisan groups within the same social movement are avowedly striving for the same objectives. Although their goals are more likely to be achieved through cooperation, this seldom occurs. Although temporary alliances are formed from time to time, sustained collaboration is usually found only in reform movements. Most reformers do not feel threatened, and they generally welcome support from any source. Each partisan group develops in its own way. If one is severely weakened, it may merge with a larger organization. In most political movements, however, the various partisans, to the extent that they deal with others at all, try to exploit them. Religious sects tend to ignore similar organizations. Although Jehovah's Witnesses do not attack other religious movements, neither do they participate in interdenominational activities.

Most subversive movements are made up of secret societies. Each tends to remain isolated, turning against its rivals as well as its avowed enemies. Reformers who believe that their aims are similar to those of revolutionary movements sometimes make overtures for cooperation. If help is badly needed, it may be accepted. In general, however, revolutionaries view reformers with contempt and include them among the enemies. After all, should reformers succeed in pushing through their program, popular discontent will be reduced, and the people will be less responsive to more radical appeals. Thus, in *What Is To Be Done?* Lenin makes it clear that no other organizations should be permitted to compete with a revolutionary party in obtaining access to the masses. Intense hostility is directed against rival organizations. Although all subversive groups are opposed to the same regime and seem to share many interests, they often devote considerable time and effort to monitoring and attacking one another. Various Marxist groups have been carping at one another for over a century; Malcolm X was assassinated purportedly by Black Muslims with a slightly different ideology; the factions within the Palestine Liberation Organization have been unable to stand united even in severe emergencies. Two factors account for such infighting. First, rival partisans operating in the same community are competing for the support of the discontented. Personnel and resources are limited, and groups with the more radical programs are at a disadvantage. Second, although the ideological differences may seem minuscule to outsiders, the members of each group are convinced that their program is the only correct one. In their competition for the limited support available, the rivals may come to fear one another more than they fear their avowed enemies.

When difficulties arise among groups that have withdrawn from the community, appeals for adjudication usually cannot be addressed to established authorities. If the differences cannot be resolved in negotiations among the leaders, each group must take steps to protect its own interests. Just as smugglers and racketeers must enforce their own demands, revolutionaries find that they too must on occasion resort to violence. Since they cannot attack one another openly without risking loss of popular support, conflicts between such organizations often become vicious and underhanded. Some groups have special units to handle such operations. The Fruits of Islam, for example, is a branch of the Black Muslims whose duty is to maintain order within the organization, to protect it, and to deal with other difficulties (Lincoln, 1961). Some revolutionaries have even resorted to delivering their rivals to the secret police, thereby eliminating them without having to resort to violence. Such infighting among partisans is common. Sometimes the fighting is instigated by outsiders: the FBI infiltrated various underground groups in the 1960s and deliberately initiated feuds to encourage them to eliminate each other. Often the disputes arise after a period of factional cooperation. When successful insurrections are accomplished by a temporary coalition of subversive groups that have been rivals for decades, factional rivalry usually returns soon after the victory.

Many social movements that might otherwise have succeeded collapse from the inability of rival partisans to pool their resources. The frequency of such suicidal factionalism has prompted attempts to account for it. Many leaders and dedicated core members of partisan groups have been characterized as fanatics who seem to feel a personal responsibility to save the world. The movement becomes their sole aim in life; thus, they seem rather inflexible and often impractical. It has been suggested that such persons are often the product of opposition; many social movements have been led by people who have been hurt badly, especially in their interpersonal relations — such as those who have occupied marginal status. They tend to be power-oriented, and their stance makes them enraged at anyone who disagrees with them — be they dissidents, rivals, or enemies. Often they are intellectuals who have learned more about human beings from books than from direct associations; hence, they work with stereotyped conceptions of both their enemies and the very people they profess to serve. They live in terms of principles derived from a philosophical position; their commitment is total, and they see any compromise as surrender.

Many attainable reforms have been lost because of a leader's refusal to settle for anything short of his or her utopian vision. Such persons are so self-righteous that it never occurs to them that they might be mistaken. Since they have difficulty relating to others on an equal basis, they cannot get along with leaders of rival organizations. Many enterprises are led by persons whose level of self-esteem is so low that they must compensate for it by identifying completely with a grand cause (Hoffer, 1951). This hypothesis helps account for stamina and tenacity in the face of adversity; without these a social movement cannot succeed. It also helps explain rigidity of convictions and difficulties in working with others. However, this hypothesis has yet to be demonstrated to be correct.

PROBLEMS FACING SUCCESSFUL MOVEMENTS

Accomplishments of Social Movements. Ascertaining what constitutes success for a social movement is often difficult, especially if the rhetoric is taken seriously. If success is defined as acceptance of the central part of the program and its incorporation into the established normative framework, most social movements fail. Some come to be viewed as dangerous and are exterminated by their enemies. Sometimes the leaders' excessive zeal and strident rhetoric evoke a backlash that makes the situation even worse than it was. Most attempts to mobilize public support for a cause wither away from lack of sustained interest. In the heat of excitement after some spectacular event a large public forms and several movements may get under way; as other exciting events develop, however, attention turns elsewhere, and many of the newly formed groups are deserted.

But some social movements do alter the normative framework of communities. Christianity, once feared in the Roman Empire as subversive, is now so widely accepted that most people have forgotten that it began as a social movement. In many parts of the world the labor movement may be regarded as having succeeded. Unions are recognized, and collective bargaining is an accepted procedure for settling disputes with management. Many ethnic movements that pushed for nationalistic secession after World War II have succeeded in forming independent nations, free of colonialism. In many instances this has led to some land reform, welfare programs, better educational systems, and drastic changes in social stratification. Of course, success does not necessarily mean that a movement's program will be adopted and maintained. The WCTU and other temperance workers won adoption of the Eighteenth Amendment; but Prohibition, which proved to be unenforceable and facilitated the rise of organized crime, was repealed in 1933. Similarly, the Nazi party and the Japanese militarists won control of their respective nations, but the result was a disastrous war that destroyed them.

Even when social movements succeed, their accomplishments fall short of the dreams of the leaders and core activists. This failure is inevitable. Since complex problems had been defined in simplistic terms, even the achievement of the avowed aims—elimination of the alleged "cause" of discontent—does not rectify the situation. Displacing the colonial administration has not resolved most of the problems facing developing nations. Communists have not eliminated class conflicts; although the classes they opposed may have been neutralized, new class differences are emerging. Furthermore, the rhetoric of most social movements is excessive. To attract and hold public support they must make large promises, such as the utopian vision that victory will usher in a perfect society. If successful leaders fail to develop more realistic analyses of the conditions they face, their efforts will flounder. In most instances the majority of the supporters, who are drawn from the spectator component of the public, are willing to settle for much less than what they had been promised. They are satisfied when the more conspicuous problems have been resolved and conditions improve. Thus, even when all objectives are not achieved, significant parts of a program may become incorporated into the established order.

Since a social movement seldom attains all its goals, some of the more committed members may try to keep the organization intact to continue the struggle. But this effort often leads to serious problems. Ironically, many of the difficulties arise from the disappearance of opposition. Solidarity arises from the challenge and dangers of having to struggle against great odds; once the fight is over, most members see no need to continue to make sacrifices. Coalitions of groups that are united by a common foe fall apart. When a social movement is made up of several groups, some may be satisfied when others are not. Serious conflicts may arise among the victors. In some instances factional quarrels continue until one organization is able to suppress all its rivals.

Problems of Leadership and Control. When a social movement is no longer at odds with the larger community, a different type of leadership is needed — administrators. If a religious movement succeeds, it is likely to grow, often becoming a large denomination directed by a bureaucracy. The same is true of successful reform movements. When a revolutionary movement is victorious, as in the Soviet Union and China, its program becomes official national policy, and its leaders become the new rulers. Thus, the most active partisans of successful social movements often become officials in large, formal organizations. As social movements develop, they need different types of leaders. Initially direction comes from intellectuals who raise embarrassing questions. As people become angry, agitators and organizers assume command. As a group takes shape and fights its way through the political arena, it needs tacticians.

In formal organizations, however, executive tasks must be performed. Decisions have to be made in a regularized manner, and enough discipline is needed to implement policies. Skillful fighters and tacticians are not necessarily good administrators. From time to time an unusual individual, Fidel Castro, for example, is able to perform all these tasks. In most instances, however, there is a successive displacement of leaders. Unless a social movement can develop leaders with the necessary skills at various phases of its formation, it is not likely to survive.

As organizations become larger and more complex, authority tends to become centralized. In his classic study of socialist parties and labor unions Michels (1949) contends that even in associations avowing a democratic ideology decision making tends to fall into the hands of a small number of officials. When a group is small, decision making tends to be more democratic; leaders can still hear and take into account the views of many individuals. As the group grows, however, popular participation in management becomes more and more awkward, time-consuming, and costly. Especially in periods of crisis, decisions must be made quickly, and there is no time to consult everyone. Furthermore, many of the problems facing formal organizations are dull or incomprehensible to most rank-and-file members. Most members actually do not want to participate actively in the political process; they have many other interests and prefer to be led by those whom they regard as better qualified to make decisions. Thus, most union members are content to pay their dues as long as their interests are protected. A small circle of officials, with the aid of an administrative staff, makes more and more decisions. This trend tends to perpetuate the leadership and separate the rank-and-file members from policy formation in the organization. This tendency Michels calls the "iron law of oligarchy."

As the tasks performed in an organization become more complicated, implementation of its program requires coordinating the activities of an ever larger number of people. In turn, coordination requires more and more specialized knowledge. In time numerous specialists — ministers, military experts, enforcers, lawyers, accountants — perform the essential executive tasks. As an organization grows, it tends to develop a large staff of paid full-time workers. Once the specialists have been in office for a time, the experience gained by the administrative staff becomes indispensable for the organization.

During the early phases of a social movement the status of most of the members tends to be equal. As tasks become more specialized, visible differences in rank tend to develop, and the distinction between leaders and followers becomes accentuated. Officials often find that they face distinct problems that are not understood by those who are not in executive positions. Since the officials soon develop their own communication channels, they form a perspective that differs from that of rank-and-file members. Although they remain loyal to the movement, they see things from a different standpoint. When they encounter difficulty in getting things done in the face of resistance from the ranks, they sometimes become disgusted with the "stupidity" of their followers. Thus, as a bureaucracy develops and its work becomes more technical, a gap forms between the officers of an organization and the rank-and-file members.

In addition, the privileges associated with leadership further separate the leaders from the others. Since many of the tasks are so technical, officials tend to be drawn from those with better educational backgrounds. Preexisting cultural differences are reinforced, and by rising to power the leaders become part of the more privileged segments of the community. They soon develop class interests. Once the leaders become accustomed to their new style of life, they are reluctant to give it up. They become concerned with retaining their advantages and passing them on to their children. The leaders of American labor unions are paid high salaries and live more like corporate executives than like most members of their organizations. The same is true of high officials of the Communist party in the Soviet Union or of the Catholic church. Such oligarchic tendencies have been observed in many different contexts. When Lipset and his associates (1962) discovered one exception to this rule, social scientists the world over began looking for others, but thus far their search has been in vain.

Once a bureaucracy has been established, the officials often develop a vested interest in perpetuating the organization itself. Nor is it just the top executives who develop such concerns. Professional and technical workers and even members of the clerical staff form similar interests. To the extent that such officials develop their own perspectives through differential association, they may act for their own interests rather than for those of the group as a whole. As they become increasingly preoccupied with fortifying the organization and their positions within it, they sometimes forget some of the ideals for which the movement was launched. In some cases they may even adopt policies inconsistent with the original goals of the movement. Leaders may also perpetuate a movement that has been so successful that it is no longer needed. The movements to eradicate poliomyelitis and tuberculosis succeeded; rather than disbanding, both organizations began raising funds for other medical causes (Sills, 1957).

As offices in an organization become sources of influence as well as affluence, a power struggle frequently develops among the leaders. Some of them alter their self-concept; they come to believe in their own greatness. Some even develop a lust for more power. As they become preoccupied with moving up the bureaucratic hierarchy, they often exploit the special information at their command in efforts to outmaneuver their rivals. Some may use organizational channels to turn themselves into popular heroes and to manipulate support for their policies. Such rivalries become especially pronounced when a charismatic leader must be replaced. The leader is often deified to continue as a symbol of unity, but others must take over the tasks of administration. In his discussion of the routinization of charisma, Weber (1968:1111–57) notes that the central problem is replacing charismatic authority with a rational procedure — the formalization of decision making and of succession. The founder's spontaneity and creativity must be replaced by a set of formal norms. As a charismatic leader approaches retirement, authority is often distributed to a nucleus of disciples who can rule in his or her name. The leader sometimes designates an heir. If not, a committee of lieutenants generally takes over on an interim basis, and in time a procedure is established for selecting executives and specifying the extent of their authority.

Problems of Group Solidarity. Most successful social movements come to terms with the established order long before reaching their original objectives. Purists are disillusioned, and their alienation leads to factionalism. Splits between fundamentalists and revisionists are commonplace in both political and religious movements. Those who are satisfied contend that utopian visions are impracticable, but the deeply committed object to giving up the struggle. Furthermore, oligarchic tendencies disturb those who feel left out. They charge that the leaders have deserted their ideals, that they have sold out to the opposition, that they have been co-opted.

When a religious movement succeeds, it becomes an accepted denomination. The commitment and diligence of the members make them prosperous and respectable, and outside opposition to the group disappears. It establishes friendly relations with other churches, and coexistence becomes the policy. Practical problems, such as getting authorization to perform marriage ceremonies for its members, forces the group to seek formal recognition by the government. Most members are no longer upset about the conditions that had originally brought them into the movement; they no longer feel discontented or lost. As the church becomes respectable, the intensely emotional meetings are replaced by more sedate rituals. Schisms arise as dissidents break off to form new religious movements they believe to be more consistent with the original goals (Niebuhr, 1929; Johnson, 1961). Thus, Baptists today no longer resemble the sectarian movement that arose in the Kentucky revival, and the Black Muslims have become a wealthy and powerful organization. Similar tendencies are found in successful political movements.

When a social movement succeeds, members of the next generation often fail to understand the zeal of the founders or the need to maintain discipline. As those who had fought the early battles die out, younger people born into the movement who have not suffered the difficulties faced by their elders form a different perspective. Once a movement is accepted, the members no longer have to maintain a defensive stance. Many in the younger generation find it difficult to understand their elders' views. Is austerity really necessary? Fear of contamination seems ridiculous. Thus, the sectarian attitude seldom lasts beyond the founding generation. In the Soviet Union there are many indications — the refusal of college graduates to appear at jobs to which they have been assigned, the cynicism of intellectuals about what appears in the mass media, as well as political dissidence — that many young Russians no longer have the revolutionary zeal of their predecessors. They never lived under the czars; they have never gone hungry or seen the poor die from lack of medical care. Many wonder if a dictatorship of the proletariat is still necessary. If there is no longer any danger of being overthrown by class enemies, why is it necessary to curtail free discussion and association? Thus, many of the problems of maintaining group solidarity arise from accommodation to the outside world.

Unless it adopts special procedures to maintain its isolation, a successful social movement merges into the established institutional order. The abolitionists and many other movements have simply disbanded when their program was accepted. Successful political movements often become wealthy political parties. A few groups, such as the Amish and the Hutterites, have maintained their isolation. They continue to live in segregated communities, and some have adopted special procedures to regulate acculturation so that their way of life will not be disrupted too severely (Eaton, 1952). The Jehovah's Witnesses have more contacts with outsiders, but they also retain their separation. Cohesion is easy to maintain as long as the members continue to feel threatened. As the actual danger subsides, leaders may find it necessary to exaggerate or to manufacture perils, perhaps even creating an enemy, to maintain the unity of the group. Thus, as life conditions keep changing, what was a social movement becomes part of the moral order. It is then challenged from below by others who are discontented. Then people who had once been militant protesters beome involved in efforts to suppress opposition from new social movements. When this happens, the enterprise has run its course.

SUMMARY AND DISCUSSION

Social movements arise among people who are discontented with their lot in life, but misery alone does not lead to the development of such collective enterprises. Unless people are convinced that they deserve a better fate and that it is possible to affect their circumstances, they are not responsive to appeals that they consider new possibilities. As more and more conclude that their condition is unacceptable, agitators begin to get a hearing. For a time a number of competing proposals are entertained; then ideologies that strike a responsive chord in a substantial part of the public win followings. As attention focuses on a limited number of objects, collective discontent takes on a definite direction. Various groups are formed in attempts to implement these ideologies, and as their efforts converge a social movement is launched. There are many kinds of social movements. Virtually all of them encounter some kind of opposition, and many of the characteristics frequently found in such undertakings — dogmatic conviction that the members know the truth, fanatic dedication to the cause, hatred of dissidents within the group, inability to make reasonable compromises — emerge as reactions to such resistance. If a social movement is successful enough to win some measure of acceptance, both the sectarian attitude and group solidarity become attenuated. Then some of the idealists become disillusioned, break ranks, and organize other social movements. Leaders of successful movements often become involved in suppressing protests against the new moral order.

Although social movements seldom accomplish everything they set out to do, the impact of those that have been even partly successful has altered the course of human history. Most social movements have humble origins, but their cumulative impact has been enormous. Many familiar social institutions are products of such undertakings. The world today would certainly be different had various groups of Christians, abolitionists, feminists, and socialists failed in their struggles. As long as substantial numbers in a community feel they are being cheated of what is rightfully theirs, such collective enterprises are likely to develop. Governments may succeed in suppressing them for a time, driving the discontented underground. If so, the explosion is likely to be greater when it finally comes. The joint efforts of discontented people to improve their lot in life have played an important part in shaping society thus far, and it seems likely that human beings will continue to strive toward the realization of various utopian visions.

SUGGESTED READINGS

Cannon, James P. 1944. *The History of American Trotskyism.* New York: Pioneer.
  The schisms and factional infighting during the development of an underground political movement.
Cohn, Norman. 1970. *The Pursuit of the Millennium.* New York: Oxford University Press.
  An account of the manner in which the impoverished in medieval Europe were drawn into radical millenarian movements.
Lincoln, C. Eric. 1961. *The Black Muslims in America.* Boston: Beacon Press.
  The formation of the inner structure of the Black Muslim movement during the mid-twentieth century.
Michels, Robert. 1949. *Political Parties.* Glencoe, Ill.: Free Press.
  An analysis of the growth and consolidation of oligarchical tendencies in successful political movements.
Niebuhr, H. Richard. 1929. *The Social Sources of Denominationalism.* New York: Henry Holt.
  Classic study of how the poor and discontented in established churches break off to form their own sects, only to succeed and attain respectability.
Zald, Mayer N., and John D. McCarthy (eds.). 1979. *The Dynamics of Social Movements.* Cambridge, Mass.: Winthrop.
  The resource mobilization approach to social movements, placing emphasis on the component organizations and their efforts to cope with authorities and one another.

XIII

SOCIAL RECONSTRUCTION

Talent scouts for professional baseball teams in the 1930s and early 1940s knew of the vast reservoir of talent in the Negro leagues, but they could do nothing more than observe wistfully. Soon after World War II, however, Branch Rickey, president of the Brooklyn Dodgers, decided that this had gone on long enough. He arranged to bring Jackie Robinson into his organization and thereby stirred a national controversy. Many predicted that the experiment, though noble in intent, would never work. After all, many of the great stars were from the South, and they would refuse to play. What would happen in the locker rooms, where the players would have to shower together? Who would be his roommate when the team was on the road? Would angry fans not boycott the team? The venture was fraught with difficulties.

Since ugly incidents had to be avoided, the man to break the color line had to be not only exceptionally talented but also able to put up with the humiliations that would be inflicted by prejudiced players, hostile umpires, and impetuous fans. Rickey had to find a gifted athlete "with guts enough *not* to fight back"—at least not until his status was well established. Through his spectacular performances and gentlemanly conduct Robinson soon won over his teammates and Brooklyn fans, and before long other clubs were looking for Afro-American players (Robinson and Duckett, 1965).

Four decades later, baseball teams throughout the nation now draw players from various ethnic groups. Black athletes are an integral part of American sports, even on the campuses of southern universities. Afro-

American stars are among the heroes of numerous teams, and fans no longer even think about the skin color of the player who gets the decisive hit in a championship game. Young Americans are often astonished to learn that desegregation occurred so recently, and they find it difficult to conceive of a time when professional athletes were not judged solely on the basis of their performance on the field. Although few innovations stir as much controversy as this one, many have not been welcomed. Once a new practice has been established, however, people wonder in retrospect why anyone had gotten so excited.

We tend to think of innovations largely in material terms — jet planes, computers, rockets, detergents, plastic wares — but our concern here is with the establishment of new patterns of concerted action. We are interested in the disappearance of patterns that had once been accepted, the modification of old procedures, or the formation of new ways of executing social transactions. Thus, the introduction of a new concept of management may have a much larger impact than a new technology. Since the manner in which people coordinate their efforts or oppose one another rests on their definition of objects, any alteration of custom or law involves some change in outlook. What is actually displaced are the expectations with which people address themselves and one another as well as what they take for granted as natural. Thus, social change is basically a mental process; it involves the transformation of the perspectives of the people involved. The study of social change, therefore, requires us to again turn our attention to the manner in which human beings divide their experiences into objects, the manner in which objects are defined and evaluated, and the manner in which they are symbolized.

Society is in constant flux; transformations of some kind are going on continuously — in primary groups, in social worlds, in organized groups, and in communities. Most changes occur in small increments over a long period of time and pass unnoticed. Years later the elderly recall longingly that things were different in the "good old days." *Innovations* — the displacement of one pattern of concerted action by another — are discernible only when the patterns are sufficiently different and the transition sufficiently abrupt. Precisely because changes are so pervasive, we must look at situations in which they are easy to identify. In periods of rapid transformation we are able to see in clear relief processes that are more difficult to observe in less dramatic contexts. Our concern in this chapter is with how noticeably different patterns of concerted action, whatever their origin, become accepted to serve as the basis for subsequent activities; how innovations become incorporated into the existing normative framework; and what happens during the time that this transition is taking place.

SELECTIVE ACCEPTANCE OF INNOVATIONS

Innovations as a Social Process. Innovations may be introduced in several ways. The most unambiguous and usually the quickest form of change is the promulgation of new formal norms. For all practical purposes they are imposed on the populace involved; formal norms often constitute external conditions to which adjustments must be made. New laws in communities and new regulations in organizations are usually articulated as clearly as possible, announced ahead of time along with the date on which they are to take effect, and accompanied by some indication of the penalties to be imposed for noncompliance. After victory at the polls or in a war or revolution, a new government simply announces what the people are expected to do. Administrators who are trying to deal with a current or anticipated problem institute many smaller changes in formal regulations. A successful reform movement may force the adoption of a different policy.

Models of different ways of doing things may come from several sources. Contacts with people from different cultural backgrounds provide exposure to previously unknown behavior patterns. These arouse curiosity. After the adventurous few have tried them successfully, they are adopted by increasing numbers of others. The media of mass communication now make diverse models readily available and often popularize and speed their adoption. Practices introduced as fashion movements may be taken lightly in the beginning, but when some item demonstrates its utility, such as low-cut shoes or wristwatches, it survives. Missionaries, teachers, political agitators, traders, prophets, corporation agents, and government publicists — all propose new ways of doing things that may strike a responsive chord in those who are looking for better things.

The adoption of new patterns of concerted action is a complex process. Participants in new social transactions are called upon to enact different roles and to modify some of the claims and obligations that made up their old roles. Increasing acceptance of the social equality of the sexes, for example, is transforming many traditional patterns of family life. As more women enter the job market, more husbands are taking over some of the tasks once regarded as women's work. Thus, as the status of some of the participants changes, people become related to one another in different and unfamiliar ways. These new patterns lead eventually to the redefinition and reevaluation of various objects; of particular interest are the changes in the participants' self-concepts. Such transformations usually occur in small increments, but their cumulative impact may be considerable.

The perspectives of people in a community seldom change simultaneously. Adopting innovations usually involves a transitional period during which misunderstandings abound, when people tolerate what they regard as deviance, when improvisation and negotiations are necessary. The transition period may be brief, or it may persist for a long time. Changes of formal norms are largely a matter of people finding out what is expected of them. But the legitimation of a new government policy often involves setting aside facilities and resources that are needed for implementation. If resources must be taken away from other activities, resistance may develop. Thus, adoption requires at least verbal acquiescence to the new practice, if not its full acceptance; overcoming resistance may take some time. In the transformation of conventional norms the period of transition may span several generations. Customs usually persist long after the conditions under which they had originated have passed. We are creatures of habit. We go through most of each day doing things in familiar ways without even considering other possibilities. Even when we realize that a practice has become a hollow ritual, we often continue to comply as long as others are also going through the motions. Most customs rest on cultural axioms, which are questioned only after some unusual events have shaken people out of their complacency. Even after overt behavior patterns have been displaced, the underlying assumptions may remain unchallenged. Thus, superstitions about the natural roles for women are likely to persist long after discriminatory practices have been eradicated. The problem is that of reestablishing consensus so that people can approach one another with shared expectations. Until they share new meanings people find it necessary to negotiate on a personal basis as they adjust together to the new circumstances.

The Diffusion of Innovations. Most innovations are introduced into a community through already established communication channels. However, the receptivity of individuals varies considerably; they have differential sensitivity to change, and each innovation is perceived somewhat differently in each reference group. Some people embrace a proposed change with enthusiasm. Those in business, for example, are usually enthusiastic about any technological innovation that offers possibilities for more profits. Others adopt a wait-and-see attitude. Still others are adamantly opposed; they see the proposal as dangerous, something that could destroy the moral fabric of their community. In the beginning, then, an innovation is usually adopted only by a small segment of a community, some organization or social world for which it is most relevant. As it becomes more familiar to the others, they too may adopt it.

Although people usually learn about innovations through formal communication channels, they are not likely to adopt them on that basis alone. Even in societies like ours, in which the mass media are well developed, networks of personal contacts play a crucial part in the diffusion of innovations. Before adopting changes people consult their close associates, especially those whom they respect for their specialized knowledge. Studies of the introduction of new drugs in the medical profession show that the process is not one in which each doctor makes a decision on the basis of the merits of the medication. When the discovery of a new drug is announced, specialists who are deeply involved in the professional community consult one another to share their appraisals of its therapeutic effectiveness. Physicians with close personal ties to the specialists tend to be among the early adopters. Doctors who are not so involved in the professional community tend to become isolated; they learn about the new drugs later from medical journals, sales representatives of pharmaceutical firms, and the mass media (Coleman et al., 1957).

Studies of the adoption of new farm equipment reveal a similar pattern. Farmers go out of their way, often into distant areas, to consult those whom they regard as most competent to judge; some even cross state boundaries to benefit from the expertise of those reputed to have sound judgments (Lionberger, 1961). Katz and Lazarsfeld (1955) found that housewives tend to follow the recommendations of women whom they most respect as homemakers in adopting new consumer products. When faced with uncertainty, then, people turn to trusted sources. They consult a trusted friend or colleague who transmits technical information, relates his or her personal experiences with the innovation, and supports those willing to take a chance (Rogers, 1971).

Resistance to Innovations. Because Americans place such a high value on creativity, we often fail to recognize that any innovation constitutes a deviation from established usage. We are often surprised, therefore, when most innovations encounter opposition, even when their potential value is acknowledged. Thus, many practices that are widely accepted today — government pensions for the aged, abolition of child labor, enfranchisement of women, free medical care for the indigent — all faced vigorous opposition. Such resistance becomes more understandable when we realize that such changes in some way threaten those who have a vested interest in the status quo. Thus, it is not strange that landowners will oppose any move that may lower their rents; corporations will oppose any innovation that will cut into their profits; and unions will oppose labor-saving inventions that will render some of their members obsolete.

When we view such opposition by others, it is easy to suggest that they are being selfish, that they should be willing to give up some of their advantages so that more people can benefit from the change. But selfishness is more difficult to detect when it involves our own interests. For example, how would most young Americans react to a proposal, such as the policy adopted in China during the Proletarian Cultural Revolution, requiring all young people to work for a few years in agriculture, in industry, or in the armed forces before they become eligible for a college education? Even anticommunists can see merit in Marx's slogan: From each according to his abilities, to each according to his needs. But would educated people in an automated society accept it graciously if it meant that those with technical training would be overworked while others would be able to spend much of their time in leisure?

Resistance arises even among specialists who are committed to seeking the most efficient innovations. Morison (1966) provides an account of the unwillingness of naval officers to adopt a new aiming device, even after repeated demonstrations that it would make naval gunnery more accurate. Its use would have required considerable reorganization, and this was discomforting. New ideas are especially prized in science. Investigators are constantly hoping for breakthroughs and honor those who make innovations that reshape scientific thought. But an examination of the record is discouraging. Charles Darwin's theory of organic evolution, which forms the cornerstone of modern biology, was first greeted with ridicule. Opponents caricatured Darwin's position and lampooned it. Nor were religious zealots the only ones who accused Darwin of contending that human beings had evolved from monkeys — a statement he never made. Similarly, psychoanalysis now forms the basis of much of modern psychiatry, but Sigmund Freud was called a sex maniac and a charlatan by members of the medical profession. Many eminent scientists — including Hermann von Helmholtz, Max Planck, and James Cannon — have commented on the vicious and unreasonable opposition innovators face (Barber, 1961).

Worthwhile scientific contributions survive despite such resistance, for all hypotheses are subject to reality testing. In the long run accurate hypotheses become accepted, even when they have uncomfortable implications. In many areas, however, accuracy cannot be tested or is not necessarily a key criterion. For example, art critics necessarily rely on personal judgments, and controversies can persist for a long time. One need only consider the fate of the French impressionists. Although their paintings are now revered throughout the world, in their lifetimes most of the artists were subjected to derision. It is easy to forget that specialists too live in their own social worlds. They seek status in the eyes of their reference groups, and the prevailing values of their social worlds serve as a filter for the appraisal of innovations. Any change that threatens to date their own work arouses severe emotional reactions that make it difficult for them to be fair and impartial.

Resistance to innovations is not necessarily calculated opposition. In many instances the critics simply feel uncomfortable about the changes. We feel uneasy when established procedures are not followed, for we do not quite know what to expect. Innovations disturb our sense of order and fill us with anxiety, even when we can see that the change has excellent potential. For example, many students complain that memorizing small and insignificant details just to pass a course examination is a waste of time; in a few weeks they will have forgotten them. Should a professor take such complaints seriously and devise an open-book, problem-solving examination that tests comprehension rather than memory, however, many students become so upset that they drop the course. They acknowledge that they are more likely to acquire useful knowledge in this manner, but many do not know how to prepare for examinations except by memorizing details. On the basis of numerous observations of this sort, Marris (1975) proposes the hypothesis that any object that disrupts one's orderly view of the world arouses anxiety, for it makes one's life unpredictable. Thus, our instinctive reaction to many innovations is discomfort and annoyance.

Many innovations are first adopted by people who occupy marginal status. Barnett (1941) points out that in many instances those most receptive to innovations are the disinherited, the discontented, and the deviant. Dissatisfaction of any kind sensitizes people to the possibility of doing things differently. Furthermore, such persons do not have a vested interest in the existing order and are more likely to examine various proposals more dispassionately (Rogers, 1971).

Utility as the Basis for Selection. Many innovations are proposed, but few are accepted. Many are suppressed, and others are just forgotten from lack of interest. Experience thus suggests that some kind of selective process is operating. In the long run innovations that facilitate the pursuit of already established values are most likely to be adopted. Changes that make possible the more effective pursuit of generally accepted goals are welcomed. In Gambell, Alaska, for example, where contacts with outsiders were first made in 1894, the Eskimos accepted first the tools that were useful for their own way of life. Outboard motors were placed on native boats; rifles replaced spears and bows and arrows for hunting; metal pots and pans were adopted for cooking; and kerosene pressure lamps supplanted seal-oil lamps (C. Hughes, 1960:17). Similarly, Menzel and Katz (1955–56) found that in the adoption of drugs used for treating acute conditions, where the results are soon visible, only 7 percent of the doctors got their information from colleagues; for drugs used to treat chronic ailments, however, where the results are not so readily visible, 22 percent relied on information from their associates. Reassurances are not necessary where the benefit is obvious. Thus, demonstrated utility is a key selective factor. Technological innovations are usually accepted with little resistance, for their advantages are apparent.

Where demonstration of utility is inconclusive, an innovation may be rejected or its adoption delayed, even when it is consistent with established values. The study by Erasmus (1961) of the acceptance of modern medicine by Indians in Ecuador is instructive. In their culture all diseases were attributed to uncleanliness, psychological states, or a change in temperature. Treatment in most instances consisted of bathing or an appeal to the supernatural. In Quito, illnesses diagnosed as having a supernatural etiology continued to be treated by witch doctors, but even these folk specialists recommended that patients suffering from tuberculosis, appendicitis, or diphtheria go to Western doctors. The doctors had passed a pragmatic test; they had demonstrated their ability to treat these disorders in a manner that witch doctors could not. Such proof overcomes initial resistance. Among the same Indians, however, all attempts to institute preventive medicine failed. Its results are not spectacular, and showing convincingly the relationship between success and the therapeutic measures is difficult. In the absence of definite proof acceptance often becomes a political question.

Since each new practice must be incorporated into larger patterns of concerted action, changes tend to be cumulative, and this can lead to serious problems. Implementing even a simple innovation requires some transformation in previously established norms; if nothing else, personnel and resources must be committed in different ways. Thus, an innovation that is adopted becomes the basis for future selections. Once it is accepted, people develop new interests and become sensitized to other possibilities. One change often leads to many others, and recognition of this fact sometimes results in serious political contention. In some instances resistance collapses once people realize that their fears were groundless. Before Medicare was instituted in 1965, for example, the plan was bitterly opposed by the medical profession; a survey of New York doctors showed that only 38 percent favored the proposal. Soon after passage of the legislation, however, 70 percent expressed approval, and six months later 81 percent supported the program. Although individual doctors refused to participate, no organized boycott developed (Colombotos, 1969). In many other instances, however, a succession of problematic situations arises, and a brutal political struggle may ensue.

PATTERNS OF SOCIAL MOBILITY

Although some innovations fit neatly into the established normative framework, the implementation of others disrupts old social relationships. Of particular importance are changes in relative status — the rank a person holds within a community and in each of the component organizations, social worlds, and primary groups in which he or she participates. The formation of new patterns of concerted action enhances the status of some participants and lowers that of others. Sociologists generally use the term *social mobility* to designate those movements from one level to another in the stratification system of a community, where rank depends on the manner in which one is classified. Thus, if the basis for stratification is class, social mobility consists of a person's entering an occupation that differs substantially from that of the wage earner of the family into which he or she was born; economic interests and life-style would then differ from those of the parents. If the basis for stratification is ethnic identity, social mobility consists of successful assimilation into another category. If the basis for stratification is religion, social mobility consists of a conversion, followed by confirmation in the new church. In most stable communities social mobility is very difficult, even though exceptional persons do manage to move into more desirable positions. In rapidly changing contexts, however, higher status can often be achieved through individual effort. In such societies individuals feel more pressured to make something of their lives.

Redistribution of Competitive Advantages. Systems of social stratification, the ranking of categories of people who have distinctive cultures, become attenuated as the cultural differences between class, ethnic, or religious categories are reduced. As such differences decrease, the stereotyped conceptions of each category become less convincing. The customary social distance is also relaxed, leading not only to a further reduction of cultural differences but also to a recognition of the ridiculous nature of the beliefs on which the system rests. As distinctions among the various ranks decrease, open competition develops for jobs, land, mates, and other valued objects. Such competition had previously been regulated so that members of different categories did not vie directly with one another. Whereas the more desirable occupations had been reserved for those of more privileged ranks, jobs become available for others who have acquired technical knowledge and specialized skills. Whereas members of different categories had been segregated, wealthier members of once subordinate categories find that they can afford better housing and move to more desirable places. Whereas intermarriage had not been tolerated, as those of lower ranks become more attractive in terms of prevailing standards, members of different categories find themselves becoming rivals for the same partners. In the process of natural selection success goes to the most competent. If competitive advantages are redistributed, if those who had been in lower ranks acquire the capacity to compete more effectively, the more diligent and able persons of humble origin are able to outbid those who had been born to advantages. The outcome of competition, then, is a redistribution of desired objects.

The most common way for persons born into lower ranks.to enhance their competitive advantages is through education. By opening new communication channels, education enables the underprivileged to acquire the necessary skills to compete more effectively for whatever is in short supply. It also cultivates a taste for objects that are valued among those who are well off. Schooling enabled both the natives in European colonies and the children of successive waves of immigrants to the United States to become acculturated and to improve their lot in life. In the nations now undergoing industrialization the need for trained personnel is leading to the establishment of more effective school systems; this in turn is likely to create a large population no longer content to remain on tribal reserves. What may begin as the token co-optation of a few individuals of exceptional ability may open the floodgates for increasing numbers to acquire specialized skills.

Once competitive advantages have been redistributed, the ensuing direct competition effects many status inconsistencies and produces considerable resentment on the part of the old guard. During the transitional period many people appear to be out of place. Some members of the lower categories develop attributes associated with the privileged; they acquire better jobs, have more income, and live in better housing. At the same time many who had been born to privilege encounter difficulties in holding their own and discover that they can no longer take various prerogatives for granted. The transitional period is especially difficult for those who find themselves slipping from the esteemed ranks. Since many people continue to observe customs even when compliance is no longer necessary, those formerly of high rank may still be addressed with deference. But if they become too demanding, they may encounter challenges, hostility, and even ridicule. No longer able to enforce their ascendancy, they become confused and embittered; they resent the intrusion of upstarts, but there is little they can do.

The upwardly mobile also encounter difficulties. Although they may have acquired the cultural traits necessary to participate in higher levels, they may not be fully accepted. Their claims are not always recognized, and sometimes they face humiliating incidents. As they encounter what they regard as unfair barriers to their advancement, they too become resentful. In some instances generational differences develop, and the older people perceive the new beneficiaries of change as out-of-place deviants. The younger generation often accepts the changed situation and fails to understand why their elders are so upset. The opening of competition among people who had previously not been rivals in the same arena is usually disruptive, and it often results in vicious conflicts.

Shifting Bases of Authority. Established patterns of authority may encounter serious challenges. Patriarchal family patterns, found throughout the world, especially in agricultural communities, are frequently defied during periods of transition. As children become better educated than their parents, they refuse to continue taking orders from their fathers. If the parents consult them before making important decisions, conflicts can be kept to a minimum, but fathers who insist on enforcing unquestioned authority encounter numerous difficulties. Such familial conflicts have been commonplace both among American immigrants and among detribalized natives in the various nations now undergoing industrialization. Power — the capacity to coerce — rests on one party's controlling resources essential for the other's well-being or survival. In patriarchal family systems, the father controls all the family assets, thus exercising absolute control over all members of his family. Disobedient wives and children may be banished and thereby find themselves without any means of livelihood. But innovations may alter such power relationships.

What happened in the Dutch East Indies during the nineteenth century, when money was first introduced into the economy, provides a good illustration of such transformations (Boeke, 1942). Money is impersonal; it can be used in many ways, regardless of who possesses it. It therefore alters conventional dependencies and tends to undermine patriarchal authority. Native parents continued to farm for subsistence with some bartering of their surplus, but young people discovered that they could earn more than their parents by working as laborers in plantations and factories. Many refused to work at home without some compensation. More important, the young were no longer dependent on their parents, and the more audacious rebelled against traditional authority. Conflicts were especially severe in decisions concerning mate selection, the one feature of patriarchal family patterns most disliked by the young. The elders saw marriage as a way of perpetuating the family and its standing in the community; the partners involved were but means to a more important end. But young people wanted to choose their own mates. When such conflicts became severe, young people earning money enjoyed an option their elders never had: they could leave home and set up an independent family. Thus, as the young raised their status within their primary group, family patterns were transformed. The availability of outside employment raised the younger generation's competitive advantages and broke their dependency on their parents. Patriarchal authority has been similarly diminished in many other historical contexts. Nisbet (1964) shows how in ancient Rome the unquestioned power of the father was undermined by the extensive military service required of young citizens.

Technological innovations as well as other changes may render obsolete some previously esteemed categories of people and thus undermine whatever authority they may once have commanded. A dramatic example is what happened to the knights of medieval Europe and to the samurai in medieval Japan with the introduction of firearms. These warriors had enjoyed great prestige and power, for they controlled most of the available means of might. With a lifetime of studying, training, and conditioning they developed their technical skills to the point where no one else could challenge them. Indeed, their power was so great that a code of honor developed to prevent its abuse. Heavy responsibilities accompanied their privileged way of life; they were expected to be cultivated gentlemen who protected the poor and weak. Once firearms were introduced, however, the warrior classes could no longer enforce their demands, and the privileges they had taken for granted eroded and eventually disappeared. Technological advances in weaponry have rendered cavalry officers and battleship admirals almost as obsolete as samurai, and fighter pilots may soon become equally useless.

Similarly, medieval guilds have no place in an industrial society;

indeed, artisans of all kinds and even professional workers are finding it increasingly difficult to maintain their standards in highly bureaucratized organizations, where advancement depends on many considerations other than the quality of one's work. The nationalization of industries and farms in socialist nations transforms once-important landlords and industrialists into managerial personnel, if they are fortunate enough to remain with the enterprises at all. Like witch doctors, aristocrats are becoming anachronisms in the twentieth century. Tribal units that were once powerful and respected no longer fit into modern national states; their languages are too parochial and their cultures too simple.Tribal chieftains are being replaced by government officials. The noblesse oblige that was once an important part of the gracious life-style of high-ranking persons is rapidly becoming a vestige of the past. Like Don Quixote, those who continue to follow such codes of honor appear totally out of place.

Subjective Aspects of Mobility. Social mobility is more commonplace in rapidly changing contexts than in isolated communities. Although its importance has long been recognized, sociological investigations of this phenomenon are just getting under way. An important part of American national ideology is that each individual has the opportunity to improve his or her status through conscientious effort. Immigrants often live in poverty without complaining; although only a few have lofty aspirations for themselves, they dream and struggle for a better life for their descendents. Most studies of social mobility have focused on changes in class position. Studies of intergenerational mobility usually compare the occupation of the father with that of the son. They disclose that, although there has been considerable upward and downward mobility, most children of all ranks tend to remain as adults at roughly the same level as their parents. Sons do not necessarily seek the same kinds of jobs as their fathers, but how much schooling an American boy obtains is related to his father's occupation and educational background. Children of educated parents are more likely to go to college, and this training influences their career choices (Blau and Duncan, 1967). Serious questions have been raised about what such studies actually measure (Wilensky, 1966; Strauss, 1971:1 – 14), but they do track certain external manifestations of social change. However, these inquiries largely ignore the subjective side of social mobility, the inner experiences of individuals who move from one status to another.

Upward social mobility is both desired and admired. However, it is an anxiety-provoking experience, even though most of the upwardly mobile are willing to pay the price. Those who are ambitious are acutely conscious of the lowly position from which they begin; in their drive to ascend they plan, labor, and sacrifice. Learning something of the culture of the rank they wish to enter requires anticipatory socialization. Much of the awkwardness and pretentiousness of upwardly mobile persons is the result of inadequate comprehension; especially important is their lack of familiarity with informal norms. They must learn step by step what most members of the higher rank have absorbed since childhood and take for granted, such as appropriate modes of speech and etiquette. Since they must constantly monitor their own behavior, their excessive self-consciousness interferes with effective performance. They often lack spontaneity, and failures make them even more self-conscious. If they are not accepted immediately, they may become resentful and acutely sensitive to slights.

Even if they succeed in entering esteemed occupations and are able to purchase fine homes, they continue to feel somewhat out of place and are haunted by feelings of inadequacy. The upwardly mobile often overestimate the persons they envy, relying only on outward impressions and not knowing these individuals intimately enough to realize that they too have doubts about themselves — over other matters. Even when people attain high status and are obviously respected, their problems continue. Although their self-concepts have been modified, many still suffer from a low level of self-esteem. They continue to feel that they must prove themselves, for they still lack confidence and self-respect. Much of what aristocrats and others of high status mock as the ways of the *nouveau riche* are awkward struggling attempts to compensate for feelings of inferiority. In most instances establishing a family at a higher rank requires more than one generation.

In rapidly changing contexts some people move downward, and this is a humiliating experience. Those who have been removed from positions of privilege by defeat in war or revolution as well as those who have been rendered obsolete by some innovation often lead pathetic lives. Former aristocrats who are forced to work as waiters for want of any specialized skill, refugees from civil wars, and actors who become alcoholic beachcombers — all face serious personal problems. Some try to maintain appearances, clinging to status symbols of their old life-styles. They scoff disdainfully at the poor taste of the upstarts who have surpassed them and complain of the inadequate deference with which they are addressed. They take the rejection of their claims as additional evidence of the inferiority and stupidity of the people around them. Among themselves they speak longingly of their code of honor and bemoan the fact that the genteel traditions into which they were born have no place in the new age. They dwell on the past glories of their family and tell their children repeatedly that they are better than the urchins among whom they live. Even families that have managed to retain remnants of their lofty status are often characterized by the demoralization that has been depicted in novels such as Thomas Mann's *Buddenbrooks* and in plays by Tennessee Williams about once-affluent families of the Old South.

The Reclassification of People. To the extent that there is a redistribution of competitive advantages, people are reallocated into different positions through a process of natural selection. As the occupation, income, life-style, and cultural characteristics of the members of previously established categories change through social mobility, the old distinctions gradually lose their utility. Persons once segregated by their differing statuses are drawn together to partake in new patterns of concerted action. The history of the United States provides an illustration. Each wave of immigrants was culturally distinct from the people who were already here; hence, it was important for the others to classify them so that they would know how to treat them. As the children of the newest arrivals were educated in American schools, however, they became acculturated. Furthermore, as they became more like other Americans, they were no longer concentrated in the least desirable occupations. Americans of European descent no longer emphasize their differences; even when some old cultural traits persist, these traits are irrelevant in most transactions.

In recent decades skin color is also becoming less important, for people who are culturally alike are able to enact conventional roles adequately, even if their appearance is different. Thus, despite the efforts of leaders of some ethnic minorities to mount separatist movements, ethnic differences are gradually becoming less important as the basis for status. It becomes increasingly pointless to make obsolete distinctions. As young Americans congregate today, for example—to talk politics, smoke marijuana, listen to music—it is far more important for them to know whether someone is straight than it is to know that person's class, ethnic, or religious background. If their customers demand the same goods and services, it is pointless for merchants to stress ethnic or religious distinctions. Thus, as the old categories become useless, once-important distinctions cease to be made and eventually become extinct.

As people participate regularly in new patterns of concerted action, new categories for classifying people emerge. As the new categories become established, individuals not only are reclassified in terms of different criteria but also are reevaluated and ranked in new ways. For example, in nations that once were European colonies, the Europeans have been displaced at the highest levels by the native leaders of independence movements. The educated, detribalized natives now control the destiny of these nations. European traders, teachers, and professionals are often welcome and still enjoy high rank, but they are no longer in a commanding position. At the same time, young people who have migrated to the cities are forsaking their ancestral culture. In the urban centers they are treated alike regardless of tribal origins. Hence, in the cities consciousness of kind rests increasingly on class and nationality and decreasingly on tribal affiliations. Since the new industrial communities tend to be secular in outlook, religious differences also tend to become less important.

Thus, new ways of classifying people emerge that reflect more accurately the distinctions that matter in the new patterns of concerted action. As the inhabitants are reclassified and reranked, in most instances their spatial distribution in the community also changes. With the reorganization of social transactions, people come to identify themselves and one another in terms of categories that are more effective in enabling them to carry out their various roles. There develops a system of social stratification that is more consistent with the new conditions. In time the new classifications become conventionalized and come to be taken for granted.

ESTABLISHMENT OF SOCIAL NORMS

Recurrent Problematic Situations. When problematic situations recur, sooner or later new patterns of concerted action develop to resolve the difficulties more effectively. In many instances these new patterns involve the formation of new groups or the reconstitution of old ones. When enough people are dissatisfied with the distribution of goods, for example, a black market is likely to develop, even where penalties are severe. Youngsters in slum areas who feel unsafe form juvenile gangs, just as workers who find management unresponsive to requests for reasonable changes join unions. In frontier communities those who become weary of chronic disorders form protective associations, such as vigilance committees. But old associations do not die easily. Some persist by altering some of their norms; they may adopt new membership criteria and modify some procedures. Other norms are retained long after they have outlived their usefulness. Universities, for example, still maintain some practices that are vestiges of the feudal era, anachronisms that survived the challenge of the youth movements of the 1960s. As a general rule, however, groups that are unable to make the modifications necessary to handle pressing problems do not survive, for the difficulties tend to accumulate to the point that the members become demoralized and disillusioned.

One of the most neglected theories of social change is that formulated by Sumner (1906:2–8), who was concerned with the formation of customs. He contends that conventional norms are seldom the product of deliberate design and planning; most of them arise as collective adaptations to altered life conditions. When life conditions change, many old procedures no longer work. No matter how drastic the transformation, however, life goes on and people must find other ways to meet the problem. At first blundering trial-and-error efforts are made to satisfy the new needs. Of the numerous solutions attempted, procedures that seem to work well are repeated, and others are forgotten. Thus, utility is the key selective factor; expediency and gratification are the most important considerations.

How do successful adjustments become widely accepted? Sumner stresses the importance of communication. Whenever people undergo a derangement of their way of life together, they become sensitized to one another. They watch each other and go out of their way to study solutions that others find satisfactory. Those with similar interests learn from one another as they compare experiences, give each other advice, and correct mistakes. When members of vigilance committees in the American West discovered that a man they had lynched in the heat of excitement was in fact innocent, they instituted trials to reduce the chances of such injustices. When informal trials also turned out to be inadequate, they adopted more formal arrangements. Thus, each difficulty creates a new problematic situation that calls for further changes. As the new procedures are improved and elaborated, they become more complicated. The transactions tend to become better integrated and more orderly. New patterns of concerted action thus develop through natural selection. The patterns that prevail in the end are those that work to the satisfaction of most of the people involved (Cooley, 1918:3–18).

The repetition of successful patterns of concerted action leads to their establishment as social institutions. As a transaction is repeated, the participants develop similar expectations of one another. Each is able to anticipate what the others are likely to do; hence, each knows how he or she can best contribute to the common enterprise. Each participant is then able to get ready, develop the proper attitude, and rehearse parts that may be difficult. Newcomers can even be instructed as to what to expect. The contributions made by the various participants soon become fixed, and these habitual patterns are recognized and named. As such expectations are repeatedly confirmed, they are reinforced and eventually come to be taken for granted. Once most members of a group, social world, or community accept a new pattern, all others must adjust to it, even if it does not especially please them (Berger and Luckmann, 1966:50–85). Thus, social norms of all kinds are products of joint action. Activity comes first; if it is successful enough to be repeated, a pattern develops (Park, 1955:13–21). To a greater or lesser extent, this process occurs continuously in every society.

The Crystallization of Roles. In most problematic situations the initial division of labor is negotiated on a person-to-person basis, and in this manner informal arrangements begin to take shape. Each individual contributes whatever he or she can, and soon it becomes apparent that some persons can perform certain tasks more effectively than others. Relevant skills are tapped; thus, the two Andes survivors who had some medical training were called on not only to care for the wounded but also to decide what to do with them. Those with specialized knowledge about the goods being handled often become focal points in black market operations, just as vicious fighters frequently become gang leaders.

What each person contributes to the creation of new roles depends on his or her interests, aspirations, and skills (R. Turner, 1962). In a newly formed group one person may assume responsibility for preparing the physical facilities for gatherings; another may take over security arrangements; others may volunteer to tidy up after the meetings. As the same individuals continue to execute the same tasks, expectations of the members become fixed. When others express surprise whenever an individual fails to carry out his or her duties, a set of informal norms has become established. How a transaction is initially organized, then, is often a matter of accident; it depends on the particular combination of interests among the individuals who happen to be present during the early phases of development.

As the transactions are repeated, the various tasks are elaborated and more clearly articulated, and each person's specific contributions become easier to identify. The role of each individual becomes more clearly defined. Since roles are component parts of transactions, they are always related to other roles. Each new role becomes related to the other roles in understood ways, and those who are involved become bound by a network of reciprocal claims and obligations. As an appropriate vocabulary of motives develops, those who are enacting each new role can explain their own conduct — to themselves as well as to others. Such explanations facilitate impression management. Even when participants feel no enthusiasm for their roles, the obligations are defined with sufficient clarity to make a suitable performance possible. Even when a gang leader would prefer to avoid a confrontation, he may feel honor bound to act fearlessly.

As a transaction becomes better established, the essential tasks must be accomplished, whether or not those who usually perform them are present. Common understandings develop that each component part of a transaction is to be executed in a given manner. As the various tasks become standardized — the organizer, the guard, the custodian — the roles become impersonal. What had once been done by a particular individual becomes a task that any competent person can perform. Once personnel become interchangeable, a conventional role has been established. The standards of performance also become impersonal; the same criteria are applied to anyone who enacts the role. Performers are often compared with their predecessors to see how well they meet the ideal model. Furthermore, those who enact the role regard satisfactory execution as their duty and feel ashamed if they fall short of group expectations. A union steward is expected to stand up for the rights of other workers, even at the risk of incurring the wrath of management, just as the gang leader is expected to act defiantly toward the police — otherwise members of the group feel disgraced.

If the transaction is incorporated into the routine of a formal organization, the roles become offices, and the rights and obligations that constitute the position are spelled out in job descriptions and regulations (E. C. Hughes, 1958:56–57). This pattern of development is found in many historical contexts, even in the underworld. A study of the Mafia reveals that the practice of providing protection in return for tribute began in Sicily on the basis of family ties and face-to-face contacts. As the organization grew in complexity and expanded to cover large areas, many non-Italians became involved. Mafia activities are now directed by bureaucracies in regional, national, and international organizations — with a board of directors and numerous specialists (Anderson, 1965).

Routinization and Integration. As a transaction recurs, the pattern of concerted action is reinforced with each performance. As a new practice is incorporated into the normative framework of the community, it may be necessary to make further adjustments to eliminate glaring inconsistencies. On the western frontier, for example, the procedures of vigilance committees had to be altered to comply with federal laws. Once a new practice is recognized and understood by all interested adults in a community, including those who do not participate directly, it may be regarded as legitimated. Thus, police officers working in slum areas often recognize the territorial prerogatives of various gangs. When transactions outlive the generation that first put them together, newcomers are instructed on the proper procedures. Then, the same pattern is likely to persist until another problematic situation is encountered.

Innovations are sometimes costly to some parties, and serious resistance may develop. Such exactions must be explained and justified. When the Andes survivors decided that they had to resort to cannibalism to survive, most of them were filled with revulsion. The advocates quoted Jesus, contending that no greater love can be shown for others than to give one's life so that they could live. Those who expected to die gave the others explicit permission to eat their bodies. Other justifications were given by vigilantes when they discovered that they had hanged the wrong person; they acknowledged their error but insisted that under frontier conditions a few innocent people had to be sacrificed to deter the wicked from running wild. When some painful practice cannot be justified in any other way, the devout sometimes contend that "the Lord works in mysterious ways." Although some transactions appear to have been created to accomplish some announced purpose, in many instances the justifications develop after the pattern is well on its way to acceptance. Once norms have been established to this point, deviance can be identified. Then, to assure conformity, group sanctions develop to enforce the new procedures.

As the various objects involved are evaluated, the expressive component of the transaction begins to take shape. Inappropriate emotional reactions are disruptive and must be controlled. Thus, norms emerge concerning how the participants are supposed to feel. As both the instrumental and expressive components of a transaction are established, some parts of it may become ritualized. Some behavior patterns may take on a symbolic significance unrelated to the problematic situation in which they emerged. For instance, courtroom decorum symbolizes the seriousness of what is being undertaken there. In a new religion a certain form of expressive behavior may be identified as the true route to salvation and become a sacred ritual—a form of expressive symbolism that enables believers to relieve tensions that might otherwise be difficult to discharge. In the American South the practice of lynching began before the Civil War as a convenient way of intimidating Yankee abolitionists who were agitating among the slaves. During Reconstruction it became a way of keeping former slaves in their place. As the practice was repeated, it became something of a ritual and at times was carried out without enthusiasm just to remind black people that they were not to tamper with the stratification system.

The Revision of Self-Concepts. Integral to the establishment of an innovation is the modification of participants' self-concepts. Most people periodically revise their self-concept, the beliefs and assumptions they have of themselves. In particular, these revisions accompany an individual's entrance into a new group or regular participation in a new set of transactions, such as attending a new school or beginning a new job. One's basic sense of personal identity remains much the same, but one assumes new responsibilities and makes different claims on others. In many instances neophytes do not for some time realize that their assumptions about themselves have changed somewhat.

New beliefs about oneself are initially tenuous. Beginners lack confidence in what they are doing. Questions keep arising about proper procedures, and personal difficulties may occur when some features of the new tasks turn out to be unpleasant. But the sympathetic support of colleagues serves to reinforce the new definitions. Hinton (1968:378–95) describes how young recruits to a Communist cadre developed and reaffirmed their altered self-concepts in meetings with fellow party members. After the Chinese Revolution the social order had changed so drastically that many did not know how to act. There was much introspection and self-criticism. This self-exploration led the recruits to seriously question things they had previously taken for granted about themselves; suggestions and criticisms from their peers also called attention to previously unnoticed traits. But learning of similar troubles the others were having created sympathy and added to self-understanding. Party leaders provided clear definitions of behavior patterns that were desired as well as those that should be suppressed. Through these critiques and directives, the recruits developed a determination to act in "correct" ways. They learned to see their contributions as worthwhile and appreciated, and their personal dedication to the cause was reinforced. As a result, the new recruits were led to reevaluate their personality traits and to redefine themselves. In less structured ways, most people who live and work together regularly come to share a similar conception of their world and to locate themselves in it.

The establishment of new behavior patterns generally takes time. Doing unfamiliar things is initially uncomfortable. Persons enacting new roles usually do not realize that others address them differently—

perhaps with more deference—until they have been performing in a different manner for some time. Then they notice that they are doing easily things that had once been difficult. Self-conscious effort gives way to habitual action. Once the new participants have revised their self-concepts, they need only engage in moral conduct—doing what they regard as proper for themselves. They thereby contribute properly to the transaction merely by exercising self-discipline. When all the participants involved in an innovative transaction have altered their self-concepts, the moral order has been revised.

RECONSTRUCTION OF PERSPECTIVES

The Problem of Consensus. Our conception of reality is a symbolic reconstruction of the natural environment. Although the natural environment is in constant flux, our symbolic environment is relatively stable. This stability is what enables us to view our ever-changing surroundings as if things were orderly. Any change in our habitual orientation tends to elicit anxiety. Although most transformations occur in small increments, some changes are too drastic and extensive to escape notice. Painful frustrations from the exhaustion of resources, loss in war, or a change in patterns of social inequality—all require a revision of our perspectives. Some objects must be redefined or reclassified, and new objects must be constructed. Changes in vocabulary may be needed to communicate effectively about the new circumstances. Unless those involved in common transactions change their perspectives simultaneously, however, they cannot establish coorientation. Thus, consensus is always developing through continuous communication. Each innovation alters the situation, and each person involved must redefine it. Even if we have no direct contact with an innovation, we often learn about it; indeed, most of us learn much more about our world through communication than we do through direct experience. Thus, each new pattern of concerted action requires some transformation of perspectives.

The formation of consensus in changing contexts is especially difficult in mass societies. Mass societies comprise so many social worlds, organizations, and primary groups—each of them developing somewhat independently of one another—that communication is always difficult. Innovations that are confined to a single group or social world are of no concern to outsiders as long as such activities remain segregated. But those who live in the same community sooner or later become involved in common undertakings. To avoid the misunderstandings that arise among people whose symbolic environments differ, the community members must revise their respective outlooks to arrive at the minimum coorientation necessary to carry on. This transition period can be lengthy and marked by breakdowns and frustrations.

The Construction of Objects. To facilitate the execution of new patterns of concerted action it is often necessary to construct new objects or to reconstitute old ones. Human experiences are organized into units, and new objects are simply different ways of organizing our experiences so that we can mobilize our efforts effectively. In our society new objects — laser beams, viruses, astronauts — are constantly coming into existence, and old objects are being redefined. In class societies of the past the poor had long been dismissed as inferior creatures; as social distance breaks down, however, there is increasing recognition that poverty does not make a person any less human. As the impact of the women's liberation movement becomes more extensive, women are no longer viewed merely as chattel to be used by men. Furthermore, objects that are no longer useful are passing out of existence; only a historian of science is likely to know what phylogistan is, and only a small segment of the population takes witches seriously.

The meaning of an object is the appropriate way of acting toward it, and meaning rests on common understandings concerning the characteristics of the object. Meanings are subject to continuous reality testing. People act on the assumption that an object has certain attributes. If the action is successful, the premises are confirmed and reinforced. If the action is only partly successful, questions arise over the accuracy of the characterization. If acts based on cherished beliefs fail, they are rejected and the meaning is revised. Thus, the status of witch doctors is declining throughout the world. Ethnic stereotypes break down most easily where individual performances can be tested — as in athletics or in scientific research. Similarly, the characterization of a new object is shaped through reality testing. If a new procedure's utility is obvious, it is rarely necessary to do more than call this to the attention of others. Seeing a laser beam cutting through a sheet of solid steel is enough to convince just about anyone. Beliefs that work are accepted, even when some people feel uncomfortable about them. Where reality testing is possible, erroneous beliefs tend to be eliminated. Although the symbolic environment is a reconstruction of nature, it is not a figment of the imagination. Reality has a recalcitrant character; things are what they are, and some depictions turn out to be more accurate than others. Action based on false assumptions is likely to fail, except by accident. Although reality testing is a complex social process in which some errors are perpetuated, in the long run consensus is formed more easily where the utility of an object is relatively easy to demonstrate.

As new meanings are established and symbolized, the objects are also evaluated. In diversified societies such as ours a new object may be assessed differently in various segments of a community. Doctors who see the laser beam's potential for healing welcome the innovation; others who can foresee how it might be used in warfare wish it had not been invented. Some Americans regard the variety introduced into sexual practices as disgusting and degrading; others celebrate the change as a form of liberation. Furthermore, old objects are frequently reevaluated. Before World War II many Americans viewed black people as inferior objects. Since the stereotyped conception was based on the antics of comedians like Stepin Fetchit, many assumed that black men were cowardly. But Afro-Americans eventually appeared on television in a variety of challenging situations, including infantry combat and pressure-packed championship games, and not many Americans today take the old stereotyped characterizations seriously. Although some hostility still exists against the upward mobility of Afro-Americans, condescension and contempt are disappearing. Witches are no longer feared and burned; those who take witchcraft seriously are often dismissed as eccentrics or lunatics. Emotional reactions depend on the evaluation of objects, and consensus on some meanings may not develop for several generations.

As new meanings are repeatedly reaffirmed through successful use, characterizations of objects come to be taken for granted. Once such beliefs are incorporated into a symbolic environment, it becomes difficult for people to conceive of other possibilities. Thus, most Americans today simply assume that professional baseball teams should hire the most competent players available. Any owner who refused on ethnic grounds to sign an athlete as gifted as Jackie Robinson would be not only condemned as a bigot but also dismissed as stupid. Once the meaning of an object has been established, succeeding generations are instructed and coached on the proper ways to feel and to do things.

Difficulties in Reality Testing. If the utility of a new belief can be demonstrated unambiguously, it becomes accepted even by those who find it inconvenient. However, many difficulties arise that thwart accurate testing. As Burke (1954) emphasizes, perspectives, once formed, tend to interfere with their own revision. A way of seeing things is also a way of not seeing; once a pattern of expectancy has been established, it is readily confirmed through selective perception. All societies develop blind spots, often on matters of critical importance. People in each culture develop a trained incapacity for seeing what is obvious to outsiders. In their colonies, for example, most Europeans assumed that the natives' lowly positions were inevitable because of their inferior genetic makeup. They regarded competent individuals as exceptions and granted them special privileges; any exception, however, always implies a rule. Thus, the belief that the natives were inherently incapable of acquiring technical skills was not seriously challenged until the very eve of revolutionary uprisings.

Even in the realm of scholarship, where every effort is made to examine the best available evidence, diverse findings arise from selective perception. National histories are notoriously inaccurate. For example, English historians treat the Sepoy Mutiny of 1857–58 quite differently than do Indian historians. The native troops (sepoys) had been issued new rifles that required the greasing of cartridges before they could be loaded; Hindu troops feared that loading the weapons would require their biting into beef fat, a violation of a religious taboo; Muslim troops were apprehensive that the grease was pig fat, a violation of their taboos. English historians see the consequent uprising as the result of a misunderstanding based on a superstition; they regard it as an aberration, a temporary setback, amid a solid background of British achievements. Indian historians, however, view the rebellion as the first expression of nationalism, even though it was not a mass uprising and was suppressed with the aid of loyal sepoy troops (Tinker, 1958). Similarly, the American Revolution is viewed quite differently by historians on the two sides of the Atlantic (Kallich and MacLeish, 1962). Even when serious efforts at verification are made, the testers cannot always read the results.

Reality testing may also fail when criteria of judgment are adopted that make a fair examination difficult or impossible. In the trials conducted during the Inquisition, those accused of witchcraft or of consorting with the devil had to prove their innocence by meeting impossible standards—such as remaining afloat when thrown into water while bound hand and foot (Lea, 1888:430–58). Similarly, a witch doctor may explain an illness in terms of the victim's unintentional breaking of a taboo and claim it can be cured only by ceremonial purification. If the ritual works, the patient's recovery confirms the doctor's diagnosis; if the patient dies, the taboo was just too strong. A military innovation, no matter how promising it is in theory, can be tested conclusively only in combat (Lang, 1972:60–61). If it is a complex device that requires several years to perfect, it may not be ready for use until the war is over. Those who are convinced that a scientific study of human behavior is impossible often demand that psychologists produce immediately hypotheses that can be tested by standards that hold in the physical sciences today. Since psychology is still a young discipline, such a requirement is unfair, but the detractor's belief is confirmed. In such instances the testing procedure dictates the conclusions.

Many new beliefs are accepted without adequate proof, especially when those who may be inconvenienced by them are too weak to protest. Some beliefs, of course, such as articles of religious faith, cannot be tested empirically. Many other beliefs pass unchallenged when no particular occasion arises for testing. Once legends have become widely accepted, they are difficult to dislodge. Thus, most Christians today still believe that Nero fiddled while Rome burned, even though historical research does not support the contention. Some beliefs simply cannot be tested because all available sources of relevant information are unreliable. But inaccurate views are not necessarily fatal. Americans generally refer to the Pilgrims as their "founding fathers" and see the movement of pioneers across the prairies in covered wagons as part of their cultural heritage, although most Americans are descendents of immigrants who did not arrive until long after these events. People who participate together in numerous transactions come to share a similar perspective — common memories, common attitudes, common sentiments. This shared perspective facilitates their developing group solidarity in times of national emergency. Many presuppositions that make up any symbolic environment will in time be demonstrated to be false.

Affinity of Ideas and Interests. People with different cultural backgrounds frequently disagree over beliefs. If the competition between ideas cannot be settled through a clear test, the issue may be decided politically. This process of arbitration has led to charges, widely entertained, that ideologies are constructed deliberately to justify convenient practices. Of course, such attempts have been made. Active participants in social movements will adopt a particular symbolic environment and try to persuade or even force others to accept their conception of the world. Books are rewritten and extensive educational programs are devised to gain acceptance of particular ideas. Such promotional campaigns have sometimes achieved the wide acceptance of ideas subsequently demonstrated to be false. In the long run, however, other considerations enter the picture. Scholars of folklore once entertained the theory of the etiological tale — the supposition that legends are created to explain things, such as the origin of some ethnic group (Gennep, 1910). Waterman (1914) tested this contention by examining the folktales of contiguous tribes of American Indians. He found that the same stories were diffused among them but were used to explain different things. This diversity of use suggests that folktales are not invented to explain or justify a particular practice. Stories that people find entertaining are perpetuated, and some are later found useful in justifying already established beliefs or mores.

If the utility of an idea cannot be demonstrated, interests tend to serve as the basis for acceptance. In dealing with the relationship between economic practices and religious beliefs, Weber (1946:284) writes of the elective affinity of ideas and interests. Ideas may emanate from any source, but people are more responsive to beliefs that tend to justify their interests. Such selective receptivity appears to be a factor in many well-established systems of social stratification. Behind the caste system in India stands the Hindu religion. Hindus believe in reincarnation; each individual has all eternity to work out his or her fate, and each lifetime is an opportunity to improve one's status. Those who comply faithfully with caste norms will be born into a higher rank in the next life. Although such beliefs help perpetuate the inequities of the caste system, there is no evidence that the ideology was formed deliberately in order to sustain it.

Students of folklore have noted that tales popular among oppressed peoples often express hopes they dare not proclaim openly. The conquered Saxons collected a number of legends about the exploits of Robin Hood against the hated Normans. Black slaves in the American South revived the ancient tales of Brer Rabbit, who triumphed over larger and stronger fellow creatures through ingenious hoaxing and humbug (Wolfe, 1949). Negro spirituals emerged spontaneously in the communal excitement of religious meetings, but through natural selection only those that reflect the more persistent sentiments of the downtrodden slaves have survived (Park, 1950:284–300).

All human beings have a vested interest in accuracy. Knowledge is an instrument for living; the more accurate it is, the more effective a tool it provides. Each symbolic environment is much like a map. If it is not reasonably accurate, it cannot serve as an effective guide for finding one's way about the territory. Indeed, in some instances an inaccurate map may turn out to be worse than none at all. The more accurate our characterization of the world, the more likely it is that we can use objects effectively in adaptation. When an ideology is maintained through political force, external compliance may continue for some time. When the beliefs do not work, however, people begin to express skepticism in private. Dedicated members of revolutionary movements often continue to recite the party line long after they have developed personal doubts, much as the religiously devout recite their catechisms. Among personal friends, however, they scoff at official views and ridicule those who take such beliefs literally. In time, then, faulty beliefs may be exposed for what they are, simply because they cannot pass in reality testing. Some false beliefs do last for centuries. In the long run, however, human knowledge is likely to become progressively more accurate. Although folk wisdom contains many superstitions, many of the basic beliefs have withstood the test of time. Science is gradually displacing all other forms of knowledge; since it is more accurate, it works more effectively. But no symbolic environment will ever become an absolute copy of reality. Even scientific knowledge is constantly being reformulated as errors continue to be eliminated. Our orientation toward the world develops through natural selection. As we examine competing ideas in terms of their utility, accurate beliefs are more likely to survive.

SUMMARY AND DISCUSSION

In his critique of efforts to account for social change in terms of diffusion, Malinowski (1945) shows that the organization of a community develops in a succession of collective adaptations to problematic situations. Although the case he cites is an unusually brutal one, it does illustrate his point. When diamonds were first discovered in South Africa, labor was needed to operate the mines. Although the European colonists offered to pay, the natives were not interested in working for money, for they had no use for it. The Europeans instituted a head tax, which had to be paid with money. The natives worked long enough to pay the tax for themselves and their families, then departed. Since mines could not be operated efficiently without a stable work force, contracts were introduced. But the natives would not honor them, for putting marks on a piece of paper had no significance in native law. Then the Europeans erected compounds in which they incarcerated contract laborers until their terms had expired. Malinowski stresses that none of these practices was imported from England or the Netherlands. Distinctive needs developed in the situation of contact, and the procedures established were attempts to meet them.

The structure of any community develops continuously as new problems arise; history may be regarded as the resolution of a succession of problematic situations. Procedures are formed to meet distinctive needs, and the successful ones become institutionalized. The innovation is integrated with other patterns of concerted action to become part of the community's normative framework. As other problems arise, further transformations are made. The implementation of many innovations requires some revision of established social relationships; sometimes these changes involve social mobility on the part of some segments of the population. As repetition fixes mutual expectations, the various norms become firmly established. They provide the framework within which joint endeavors are carried on — until something else happens to render them ineffective. Then further modifications occur. Inconveniences and inconsistencies tend to be explained away as the accepted procedures are justified as the correct and natural way of doing things.

Human societies, however stable they may appear, are undergoing continuous evolution. The principle of natural selection provides the key for accounting for the development of new patterns of concerted action, just as it accounts for the evolution of organic forms. This analogy was recognized soon after Darwin's formulation. Unfortunately, however, some of the early writers used the principle erroneously — in efforts to justify the status quo. Their work was soon condemned as "social Darwinism," even though it was a misapplication of Darwin's ideas (Hofstadter, 1955). For some time social scientists rejected anything connected with the theory of evolution, but they were throwing out the baby with the bath. The organization of social transactions in any community is the product of collective adaptations, efforts on the part of human beings to cope as best they can with life conditions, using the most effective cultural tools at their command. These patterns serve as temporary frameworks within which concerted action is carried on, until another change in life conditions requires further adaptations.

SUGGESTED READINGS

Barnett, Homer G. 1953. *Innovation: The Basis of Cultural Change.* New York: McGraw-Hill.
   The process of innovation, the conditions under which it occurs, and the kinds of people who are likely to become actively involved.
Burke, Kenneth. 1954. *Permanence and Change: An Anatomy of Purpose.* Los Altos, Calif.: Hermes.
   A treatise on the manner in which perspectives are reaffirmed and on the difficulties that arise when they undergo transformation.
Frazier, E. Franklin. 1957. *Black Bourgeoisie.* Glencoe, Ill.: Free Press.
   A description of the social world of affluent Afro-Americans in the mid-twentieth century — describing behavior patterns often found among the upwardly mobile in other groups.

Malinowski, Bronislaw. 1945. *The Dynamics of Culture Change.* New Haven: Yale University Press.
How new social institutions emerge following the contact of peoples from different cultural backgrounds.
Marris, Peter. 1975. *Loss and Change.* New York: Doubleday.
An analysis of the sense of loss that accompanies transformations in an individual's social context or personal career.
Rogers, Everett M. 1971. *Communication of Innovations: A Cross-Cultural Approach.* New York: Free Press.
A critical review of the findings of more than five hundred studies of the introduction, dissemination, and acceptance of innovations.

Part Four

AGONISTIC PROCESSES

XIV

POWER AND POLITICS

Although conflicts of all kinds have been the source of intense agony and widespread suffering, few actually appreciate the enormous cost that has been paid. During World War I, nine million military personnel and thirty million civilians were killed; in World War II, seventeen million military personnel and thirty-four million civilians were killed. In just two wars in the twentieth century ninety million lives were lost. No one knows just how many perished in the rioting among outraged Hindus and Muslims during the partition of India and Pakistan, but some estimates place the number at about a million. Other bloody encounters include the Taiping Rebellion of 1850–64, the La Plata War in South America of 1865–70 (Richardson, 1960), and the succession of massacres that have occurred more recently in Cambodia. The execution of six million Jews in Nazi Germany stands unparalleled in human history.

These figures cover only the dead; they do not include the maimed, the orphaned, and the psychologically scarred who never quite recovered from the shock of death and devastation. The statistics on smaller struggles may be less impressive, but the suffering of those involved is no less horrifying. Thus, it is not surprising that so many people have condemned all conflict and have longed for its extinction. Virtually all utopian visions are of a world devoid of violent confrontations. Even professional soldiers condemn war, and those who have participated in combat—be they infantrymen or members of juvenile gangs—have found it a terrifying experience. Even revolutionaries who are convinced that justice can be attained only through violence wish that they could reach their goals by some other means. The brutality and destruction are often explained in terms of the depravity of human nature; many even think of conflict as a pathological phenomenon. Since peaceful coexistence is assumed to constitute the normal state of affairs, deadly conflict is seen as a perversion. This assumption renders the subject even more difficult to comprehend.

Although widely condemned, conflict exists in every community. Communities differ considerably in the severity and extent of violence ordinarily tolerated, but hostile outbursts erupt from time to time everywhere. Rivalry and conflict of some sort are apparently endemic to human social life. Our discussion in this chapter is confined to antagonism between groups; we shall not be concerned with struggles between individuals nor with intrapersonal conflict. Intergroup conflicts vary along several dimensions—avowed purpose, duration, scale—for human beings fight for many different things. Groups band together for a range of reasons to fight one another—nation against nation, family against family, police against the underworld, or strife among class, ethnic, and religious groups. The number of people involved may be a mere handful or several million. Some fights are localized; others affect virtually everyone on the globe. The complexity of the issues varies, as does the manner in which the combatants are organized for the struggle. The duration also varies, from a quick fight to confrontations that persist for centuries. Some conflicts are latent and suppressed, breaking out periodically in sporadic outbursts of violence. Others are openly acknowledged, and the brutality is unrestrained.

As much as enemies in conflict disassociate themselves from each other, they are in fact interlocked in a set of common transactions. All adversaries are interdependent, for what each side does depends on the actual or anticipated behavior of the opponent. Each side tries to anticipate the moves of the other, and tactics often include manipulating the opponents' expectations to trick them into making mistakes. Thus, *agonistic transactions* are constructed in a succession of reciprocating adjustments made by adversaries. Each tries to maximize gains and minimize losses. Deliberately or inadvertently, each helps shape the opponent's goals, and the course of action is built up in the give-and-take between them. Thus, even though each side may believe it is acting autonomously, what happens in any contest cannot be understood merely by studying one side. Enemies must be studied in relation to one another; the behavior of the combatants becomes comprehensible only when viewed within the larger context. Although political rhetoric usually describes confrontations in clear-cut terms, a close examination reveals that most fights are not simple; they are muddled, confusing affairs punctuated by considerable blundering. Conflict is a recurrent transaction in which some people are brought together temporarily to form uneasy combinations, units that sometimes perform with remarkable efficiency.

In spite of the acknowledged importance of intergroup conflict, until recently sociologists have devoted little attention to it, leaving the study of hostile encounters to historians and political scientists. But conflicts are among the most important types of social transactions, and our objective is to identify some regularities in the manner in which they are conducted. Each dispute is unique; each altercation has a distinctive history. Yet, when conflicts are viewed comparatively, many common features become discernible. Among the characteristic patterns of development, we note that with few exceptions even the most brutal conflicts begin in arguments. Since disagreements are unavoidable, various institutional procedures have been developed for carrying on in the face of opposition. Many quarrels within communities are settled through a normative framework, just as many differences between nations are settled through diplomacy. In most instances violence erupts only when the established procedures for handling disputes turn out to be inadequate. This chapter discusses such efforts to resolve differences within a normative framework. Chapters 15, 16, and 17 consider some of the ways in which opposition becomes intensified, gets out of hand, and leads to bloody confrontation.

CONFLICT AS A SOCIAL PROCESS

Emergence of Rivalries. The objective fact of opposition — that one party to a transaction can succeed only at another's expense — does not necessarily lead to conflict. Merchants selling comparable wares compete for the patronage of a limited number of customers, but they overlook their opposing interests to join forces in various chamber of commerce programs. As many union organizers have discovered when trying to mobilize workers for collective bargaining, workers who share common class interests may be so divided on other issues that they cannot be organized into a cohesive unit in opposition to management. Similarly, revolutionaries frequently encounter difficulties in getting the downtrodden to recognize themselves as an exploited group; Marxists have long complained of "false consciousness."

Thus, rivalry and conflict are *not* reactions to objective conditions;
they arise from the definition of the situation. Specifically, conflict arises
when parties to a common transaction become polarized into two or more
rival factions because some participants come to define certain others
as opponents. Although outside observers might label conflicts as
unrealistic — since there may appear to be no real opposition of interests
— the people fight because they believe that such an opposition exists.
Members of various social units — primary groups, organizations, stratified categories, entire communities — become convinced that others are
infringing on their rightful interests.

When one party concludes that it cannot pursue what it regards as its
legitimate interests because another stands in its way, it defines the
opponent as an obstacle. The obstacle is soon evaluated as a frustrating
object and becomes the target of aggression. Various factions on each
side may define the situation somewhat differently, and the definitions
may change considerably as the transaction develops.

Under what conditions are such definitions most likely to develop?
Many rivalries arise when competitors realize that their interests are
opposed and take steps to minimize their opponents' chances. Competition arises when valued objects are in short supply. What is regarded as
sufficiently valuable to be worth fighting for differs from one culture to
another, but certain kinds of objects are sought almost everywhere —
comfortable places to live, interesting work, attractive mates, high income, deference, a sense of security. Where such objects are plentiful,
difficulties do not arise, unless someone gets too greedy. Until recent
times serious quarrels seldom developed over air or water. Where clean
air or usable water becomes scarce, however, as in a polluted area or an
arid desert, bloody fighting may occur for the limited resources. Unequal
distribution in itself does not lead to conflict. If the underprivileged
believe that persons of higher rank deserve a greater share, they are not
likely to object. Competition is transformed into rivalry when each side
develops the belief that the opponent can succeed only at its own expense
and takes steps to protect itself. Then the other side is identified as the
"cause" of one's not having enough and is evaluated as a frustrating
object. This act of redefinition alters the coping strategies used by both
sides. Parallel striving is replaced by political tactics. Each side keeps the
opponent under surveillance and responds to each threatening move. In
competition victory goes to those who happen to have the competitive
advantages in that context; in rivalry victory goes to the party with
political power.

Rivalries are also likely to develop when circumstances force people with incongruent interests to participate in common transactions that make them interdependent and force them to deal with one another. Numerous inhabitants of each community pursue incompatible interests; as long as they remain segregated they are unlikely to become embroiled in difficulties. A religious sect is normally left alone; if it launches a vigorous campaign to proselyte nonbelievers, however, resistance is likely to develop. In many instances people with different values are forced together simply because they must share the same resources. For example, hostilities may arise among the owners of a chemical plant sending waste materials into a lake, commercial fishermen who are upset over the depletion of their source of livelihood, and environmentalists who object as a matter of principle to the killing of any wildlife. Although such parties often make wild accusations against one another, each is engaging in moral conduct. The company is trying to make reliable products as cheaply as possible; the executives authorize the dumping of waste because that is the most economical way of disposing of it, not because they desire to ruin the lake. The fishermen want to support their families, and the environmentalists want to preserve resources for future generations. None of the people are malevolent, and none desire to make life difficult for the others; under different circumstances they would have little trouble getting along with one another. Since they are forced to share limited resources, however, they cannot pursue what each regards as his or her rightful goals without encroaching on the others. None can give in without making costly sacrifices. The parties come to define one another as obstacles. Although such issues sometimes explode into ugly confrontations, malice usually does not enter the picture until *after* the rivalry gets under way.

Furthermore, as the popular adage goes, "It takes two to make a fight." Difficulties develop only when the party accused of being an obstacle persists in its objectionable activities or intensifies frustration even more by fighting back. If the party that is blamed "turns the other cheek," accepts responsibility, and offers to make amends, the matter is settled. Thus, rivalries emerge only when both sides define the situation as a contest and take steps to protect their interests.

Formation of Political Publics. Political arenas develop in problematic situations in which members of the public disagree over what should be done. A political public is a divided public. We cannot understand what happens in politics without looking at the overall arena and its cast of characters — the adversaries, the spectator component of the public, and the relevant authorities. (The identity of the relevant authorities depends on the public in question—government officials, parents, employers, teachers.) The major burden in any rivalry is carried by members of partisan groups, those most concerned with the interests at stake. Where an issue is recurrent, as in struggles between management and labor, the partisan groups become well organized. But new issues keep arising in each community, and the people become realigned on each issue. The criteria in terms of which a public is divided differ from one issue to another. Former enemies may join forces for a particular struggle. As the contest unfolds, some of the issues may change, and new partisan groups may be activated. Each adversary's orientation may also change, and the alignment of various factions on each side of the struggle may undergo modification as well.

Partisan groups are not free to do whatever they wish, for they must carry on before an audience—the spectator component of the public and the authorities. They cannot afford to ignore laws against fraud and violence, informal codes of ethics in relevant social worlds, or the general sense of decency and fair play that prevails in a community. In politics adversaries make moves against one another with an eye on the potential reactions of their audience. Tactics must be tempered out of consideration for what the public will tolerate. Some extremists in partisan groups become so enraged that they demand immediate action, but their comrades often hold them back. Unreasonable demands and violence not only invite reprisals, but they also evoke widespread condemnation from the audience. In the long run impetuous action tends to help the opposition. Since the spectators limit what can be done, many political tactics are addressed more toward them than against the adversary. Edelman (1964) contends, therefore, that political analysis should include not only what the partisans do to one another but also what these events mean to the observers.

Violence is generally used only as a last resort. Most adversaries, no matter how much they may grow to hate one another, share many interests. Inhabitants of the same community are parts of a common ecosystem; they may need each other for everything other than the particular point of contention. They are also members of the same moral order, and this further limits what they can do. In most instances it is to their mutual advantage to cooperate on some matters, even when they are opposed on a specific issue. Other interests transcend the single bone of contention, and crosscutting ties inhibit open and unrestrained hostility. Labor and management cannot afford to destroy one another, for neither side can survive without the other. In most rivalries the two sides have a common stake in reaching some kind of settlement; thus opponents initially resort to politics and make serious attempts to negotiate some mutually satisfactory arrangement.

Most communities have institutionalized procedures for resolving disagreements, and these norms are usually enforced by those in positions of authority. Authorities presumably view the dispute from the standpoint of the entire community rather than from a limited partisan perspective; this stance should enable them to act as arbiters. Most differences are settled in arguments carried on according to rules. In the United States, for example, adversary proceedings in courts are well established. Each party is given an opportunity to present its case, and a judge or jury renders a judgment. Larger issues may be settled by a referendum or an election. It is generally understood that the losers will accept the judgment; if they do not, authorities may have to enforce the decision. It is only when disputes cannot be resolved through such legal procedures that opposition becomes intensified. If dissatisfaction mounts to the point where authorities and spectators are defied, rivalry is transformed into conflict.

Power as a Social Relationship. How a rivalry develops depends on the relative power of the adversaries. If the balance of power is disproportionate, a contest is less likely, for the weaker party will comprehend the situation and not press its claims. Instead the weak may turn to manipulation—being evasive, resorting to guile, but avoiding direct confrontation; members of minority groups often use such tactics (Thomas et al., 1972).

What is power? *Power* is the capacity to coerce another to do something that he or she does not want to do. The coercive element comes from the stronger party's capacity to inflict negative sanctions—some form of punishment or withdrawal of essential support—if the other does not submit. Thus, any party controlling an essential or desired object—money, promotions, sexual favors, means of violence—can use it for coercion. In capitalistic economies, for example, corporations have enormous power; they can determine the location of plants, hire and fire personnel, control investments, and set prices. An uncooperative community may be driven to bankruptcy. Power, then, is the capacity to get things done even in the face of opposition.

Power is not a static quality that inheres in some attribute of the dominant party, such as physical strength, intellectual brilliance, or special leadership abilities. The extent to which such personal qualities may become the basis of power varies inversely with the degree to which the transaction is institutionalized. Although individual skills are important in crisis situations, in well-established transactions power is a component of the various roles being enacted. Each role is related to all other roles in sets of reciprocal claims and obligations, and anyone enacting a dominant role—leader of a work crew, teacher in a classroom, parent at home, police officer in traffic—has power by virtue of position. The dominant party need not be able to mete out punishment personally, for enforcement procedures are already established. In government, for example, organizations of armed specialists enforce legitimate orders. The expectation that deprivations will be inflicted for noncompliance is part of the perspective of all concerned parties. A holdup man and his victim, an offender and a police officer, a recalcitrant child and a mother—all share a common definition of their distinct situations.

The price to be paid for defiance is taken for granted. Indeed, in institutionalized contexts compliance with legitimate requests or orders is often cheerful and without resentment. When a general asks a sergeant to follow a given route, he does not have to explain or justify; he just assumes that his order will be carried out. In most instances the possibility of disobeying does not even occur to the sergeant. Such commands are rarely questioned. If there is any reluctance, the mere threat of inflicting penalties is usually enough to gain compliance (Lasswell, 1948:7–19). Authority is a power relationship that all relevant parties accept. Thus, the authority of the coach is seldom questioned by his athletes, nor do secretaries challenge executives; subordinates usually regard obedience as their duty. Since compliance is the norm, any resort to recurrent threats suggests that a power relationship is breaking down. Only in a demoralized army do enlisted men talk back to their officers. If threats fail and actual punishment must be inflicted repeatedly, the relationship is about to collapse. The greater the consensus, the less the need for threats or force.

Since the roles enacted in various transactions depend on the participants' social status, many power relationships are parts of a system of social stratification. Thus, high-ranking persons are usually addressed with deference. But coercion may be exercised in particular transactions. Power is limited by the capacity to inflict sanctions, an ability that may vary from one transaction to the next. A professor may have considerable authority in a classroom but is just another citizen in a grocery store or in highway traffic.

In particular contexts unusual circumstances may neutralize the capacity to inflict deprivations. Some rebellious children master the technique of intimidating their parents in a supermarket by holding their breath, throwing temper tantrums, or in some other way attracting the attention of sympathetic outsiders. They can thereby force their parents to submit temporarily to their demands; once the family returns home, of course, parental authority is reinstituted. In international conflicts public opinion may serve to restrain a nation's use of its coercive power. The United States had nuclear weapons capable of annihilating all of Vietnam, but public opinion at home and abroad would not tolerate their use. Instead, the conflict was largely waged on the ground, a form of combat in which the United States was at a disadvantage. A seemingly weaker nation may also be able to defy an ostensibly more powerful one through alliances with third parties. Thus, in 1979–80 Iran was able to successfully challenge the United States, which could not use its military might to rescue the hostages without risking war with the Soviet Union. Power relations may also be transformed or terminated by a change in a participant's status. Once soldiers have been discharged, they can thumb their noses at their former officers, just as employees who have been fired can speak with impunity to their former bosses.

Power is a reciprocal relationship, remaining intact only as long as the subordinate party continues to submit. As Simmel (1950:182–83) points out, the subordinate party is never deprived of all choice; there always remains the possibility of paying the price. If a child is so enraged that he does not care about being beaten, his parents can no longer coerce him. If armed robbers confront a victim who is so depressed that she no longer cares what happens to her, their pistols and threats are not a source of power. The thieves may shoot the woman and get her money, but they have to do it themselves; they cannot force her to do their bidding. Thus, if the weaker party reaches a point of desperation and no longer cares what happens, the power relation is terminated, even when the capacity to inflict punishment remains intact. People who actually have nothing to lose are invulnerable to threats (Blau, 1964:230–31). Thus, the *Communist Manifesto* exhorts the proletariat that they "have nothing to lose but [their] chains." The impoverished are often unresponsive to radical agitation, however, for they can still lose their lives and their families.

When disagreements arise between persons of unequal rank in well-established transactions, the weaker party submits and makes the best of the situation. Rivalries are most likely to arise in contexts in which power relationships are not clearly defined. Contests of all kinds develop in problematic situations, where previously established status is no longer relevant. Struggles for power are commonplace whenever new patterns of concerted action are emerging. They also arise in contexts in which an old system of social stratification is breaking down, when it is no longer clear who actually has power. Furthermore, political scenes are marked by constant change. Those who enjoy considerable power in one situation may find themselves trapped in another. As public attention shifts, the power of partisans who had depended on watchful spectators may suddenly vanish. As issues change and new coalitions arise, the balance of power between adversaries becomes ambiguous, and contests may be waged to see just who does have the capacity to coerce in the new context. Politics is one of the world's oldest games; it consists largely of acquiring power and learning to use it effectively in pursuing various goals. The objective is to influence the course of events, and coercion is one of the major tactics. One essential skill in the art of politics is the ability to perceive the balance of power in specific situations, especially when the opponent's capacity to coerce is temporarily neutralized.

TECHNIQUES OF NEGOTIATION

Negotiation Between Partisan Groups. Whenever serious rivalries develop in a community, pressures are placed on the partisans to settle their differences short of violence. Except when the balance of power is lopsided, the most common procedure is negotiation. In chapter 5 we discussed bargaining between individuals; our concern now is with negotiations between partisan groups. All kinds of agreements are constantly being negotiated — detente between nations that provides each with a greater sense of security, labor contracts between teachers and school boards, territorial boundaries between adjacent juvenile gangs, a division of labor between bureaucratic departments, the termination of a costly war. In some cases a party may just pretend to negotiate to gain time for gathering intelligence, for disseminating propaganda, for seeking aid from third parties, or merely for learning something of the opponent's tactical skills. Once it becomes clear that the opponent can neither be tricked nor coerced, both sides settle down to negotiate in good faith, each seeking the best bargain possible under the circumstances. The aim is for contending parties to arrive at some kind of mutually acceptable arrangement that will enable each to carry on in spite of their differences. Neither gets everything it wants, but this is better than fighting, when the loser may get nothing. Negotiation occurs, then, when each party can see at least one set of conditions preferable to conflict.

Political publics differ considerably in the extent to which they become structured. The relative ease with which disputes can be settled through negotiation varies with the extent to which the partisans can be united into organized groups. Where a partisan group is well established

—a union, a corporation, a juvenile gang, an army, a clan—the leaders can engage in negotiations in its behalf. When an issue is explosive, however, concerned persons on both sides often become splintered into factions, some favoring negotiation and others demanding more aggressive action. If such factions are unable to compromise, arguments arise over who will represent the group. In such contexts traditional leaders or eloquent agitators may succeed in attracting much attention, even though they speak only for small factions. In struggles between ethnic groups, for example, those who make demands for "my people" often enjoy very little popular support among those whom they claim to represent. Negotiations involving such self-styled leaders usually turn out to be unproductive.

Negotiation is a serial process consisting of a succession of moves and countermoves that leads to some kind of settlement. When the adversaries are not sufficiently organized, however, difficulties arise throughout the process. To do their work effectively negotiators must have a clear conception of what each side wants and what terms it is willing to accept. But if the public is large and heterogeneous, there may be so much diversity on such matters that no agreement develops on either side. In many instances it is not possible to ascertain what most of the people want, and serious objections may not be articulated until after some settlement has been announced.

Information control is essential in bargaining; effective impression management increases the chances for favorable terms. If neither side can discipline its members, however, some angry agitator may inadvertently disclose facts the negotiator had hoped to keep hidden. Independent acts by unruly individuals not only embarrass negotiators but sometimes make agreement impossible. Even if the negotiators arrive at a settlement they believe to be fair, the terms cannot be implemented unless each side can persuade its members to accept them. Some negotiated peace treaties become unenforceable when dissidents go off on their own to launch campaigns of terror. Failures of this type have often led to the formation of organized groups. Many labor unions have been established after the workers learned through a succession of disasters that they could not fight effectively for their rights without the unity and discipline of an organization (Hiller, 1928).

Moves and Countermoves. A variety of tactics is used in negotiations. Public announcements interpreting events from a partisan standpoint are made; demands are presented indignantly; threats are made of sanctions to be imposed if the demands are not met; concessions are offered as if they were gifts. Some moves are only feints, but others are intended quite seriously. The bellicose posturing is inevitable; after all, the two parties are in opposition, distrust each other, and are determined to defend themselves against any unfair encroachment. Since each partisan group has its own definition of the situation, negotiators sometimes have difficulty understanding one another. Even when coorientation is established, they still disagree over what ought to be done.

One type of move made in the course of negotiations is the *commitment*. Each side offers something that it knows the other wants enough to be willing to give up something of value in return. Before any concession can serve as an inducement, however, there has to be some guarantee that the commitment will be kept after negotiations have ended. In general, a commitment is likely to be taken seriously when it would be too costly for the opponent not to honor the pledge. Once a corporation and a union sign a labor contract, neither side can violate it without inviting government intervention; furthermore, the spectator component of the public is likely to react negatively. If one nation guarantees the borders of another, it must live up to that agreement or lose its credibility in all future negotiations, even with other parties. An illegal or immoral commitment is likely to be honored; if it is broken, the aggrieved party need only disclose what its opponent had proposed.

Another common type of move is the *threat*; this consists of informing the adversary of a costly loss to be inflicted if a previously made offer is not accepted or if reasonable concessions are not made. Plausible threats are seldom taken lightly. A long strike would be very costly to a corporation, just as an effective lockout could destroy a union. Nor can threats be made lightly, for there is always the possibility that a bluff may be called. Those caught bluffing face the difficult choice of losing their credibility or paying the price of actually carrying out the threat. What is called "brinksmanship" is generally regarded as a foolish practice. In general, a threat is effective only if the opponent can be convinced that the party making it has both the capability and the determination to implement it. When a struggle of attrition is threatened, each side must assess the relative discipline and morale of the two sides. Toward the end of the fighting in Vietnam threats of further American military action fell on deaf ears, for the Viet Cong was well aware of the demoralization of American troops. Similarly, nuclear threats are ineffective as long as everyone assumes that civilized officials would have more sense than to do anything so self-defeating.

The outcome of negotiations depends not only on the skill of the negotiators but also on the relative strength of the adversaries. Each side wants to negotiate from a position of strength, but the political arena keeps changing. An alliance with a third party may bring vast resources to one side, just as an unexpected change of economic conditions may suddenly strengthen the other. Rank-and-file members of one side may become demoralized; it is for this reason that intelligence services are essential. Relative strength may also change from shifts in public opinion. Loss of public support at home forced the French government to grant independence to Algeria, just as it weakened the position of Americans negotiating a peace treaty with Vietnam. Since situations keep changing, inflexibility is a major disadvantage. When a rigid commitment has been made to some position, negotiators cannot take advantage of unexpected shifts in the balance of power. In some cases contingencies are manipulated deliberately in order to give negotiators maximum advantages. During the final phases of the fighting both in Korea and in Vietnam many soldiers died on the battlefield, not for the territory over which they fought, but to provide strategic advantages to negotiators.

Negotiators and Their Constituents. Negotiations are often carried on by specialists who are more sophisticated than the persons they represent. Adversary proceedings in courts are conducted by attorneys, and negotiations between nations are carried on by diplomats. Some people are professional negotiators. Although they work hard to get maximum benefits for their constituents, presumably they could represent a party whose beliefs differ considerably from their own. Just as some criminal attorneys despise their clients, some diplomats disagree with their government's position. Negotiators are usually well educated, have cosmopolitan perspectives, and pursue elegant life-styles. Opposing attorneys and diplomats often have more in common with each other than they do with their clients. Thus, they often understand one another and can readily reach a suitable agreement. Realizing that their clients would not accept it, however, they must continue to haggle. Much of the bargaining occurs backstage, where the negotiators are free to depart from their public roles. They may be on quite friendly terms. When they finally reach a settlement, they may even agree on the details of public statements to be made for the benefit of their respective audiences. The negotiators may even agree not to disclose certain details that would upset some of their clients.

Even if the negotiators agree, the settlement may not be acceptable to their constituents. Negotiators are well informed and tend to act rationally, but some of their constituents may react emotionally. Rank-and-file members of a union may refuse to accept an agreement and may call a wildcat strike; the board of directors of a corporation may fire its negotiators. Even if an agreement is formally ratified, one or both organizations may have trouble enforcing it. In some instances, even when the majority of the participants accepts the new arrangement, extremists who feel betrayed may form their own group and continue the struggle.

Third-Party Intervention. When quarrels become especially bitter, negotiations are facilitated by the intervention of a third party—a neutral group respected by both sides that offers its good offices to mediate the dispute. The aim of *mediation* is not to determine who is right and who is wrong, but to develop some arrangement that is acceptable to both parties. Since extremists on both sides oppose all efforts at compromise, mediation is not a pleasant task. Nonetheless, mediators can provide many useful services. In some cases all they can do is reopen communication channels, but this can be vital. Outsiders may also be able to restrain the combatants so they will listen more carefully to each other. In some instances mediators can furnish and check information, making possible a more accurate assessment of the various proposals that have been made. Impartial units may also investigate on their own and recommend actions that had not even occurred to the opponents. In general, mediators tend to strengthen the hands of the more moderate factions on each side. One reason contending groups accept mediation so readily is that neither side has to surrender its right to go on fighting. The recommendations of mediators are not binding, and the final decision still rests with the adversaries.

When rivalries threaten to get out of hand, the authorities, supported by public opinion, may insist on some kind of arbitration. *Arbitration* differs from mediation; a third party hears the arguments and renders a judgment, which is then binding on the rivals. Courts of law provide an institutionalized form of arbitration. The contenders' representatives present whatever evidence they can to support their position. Arbitration is effective only when the third party is powerful enough to enforce its decisions. If its authority is weak or if enforcement procedures do not exist, as in international relations, arbitration will work only when the rivals agree voluntarily to accept whatever award that is made. Thus, in most contests neither side wins everything it wants; each settles for the best it can get under the circumstances. As soon as relevant conditions change, the struggle is reopened; thus, the political scene is always in a state of change.

TECHNIQUES OF PERSUASION

Human beings act according to their definition of the situations in which they are involved, and the objective of propagandists is to persuade them to define situations in ways that favor the partisans who employ them. *Propaganda* consists of techniques for altering perspectives through the manipulation of symbols and events. Persuasive efforts are seldom directed at rival partisans; although adversaries can occasionally be persuaded to change their minds, it does not happen often enough to justify the effort. The primary target of most propaganda is the spectator component of the public. Since spectators often affect the outcome of contests by aligning themselves with one of the partisan positions, their approval, or at least their acquiescence, is important. With solid public support the hands of the opposition may be tied; furthermore, considerable pressure can be brought to bear on authorities to act in desired ways. Political manipulation of this sort is an ancient practice, but in modern mass societies propaganda has become a huge enterprise. Large organizations staffed with specialists of all kinds conduct extensive research and planning sessions to plot publicity campaigns for one cause or other. Many such organizations will work for almost any client able to pay their fees. The basic procedure is to manipulate the flow of relevant information. Since human beings communicate through a variety of gestures, a broad range of techniques has been developed.

Problems in Informational Strategy. Some intellectuals think that rank-and-file people are gullible and will believe anything if it is repeated often enough. Both historical experience and experimental studies reveal that this is not true; most human beings are neither gullible nor stupid. Unlike communication that facilitates coordination among parties to a cooperative undertaking, persuasive communication is intended to influence the audience to do something that will benefit the speaker. For this reason all persuasive communication is likely to encounter some measure of resistance. The expectation, however slight it may be, of being used for another's purposes tends to arouse people's suspicion. Thus, all propagandists are confronted with the problem of somehow overcoming their audience's critical stance. All publicists must concern themselves with establishing and maintaining *credibility* of the source. Unless members of an audience trust the source of information, they will be skeptical, even if the message happens to be accurate. A report is most likely to inspire confidence if it appears to come from a disinterested party, someone who has nothing to gain from disseminating the information. What is taught in schools is generally accepted, for it is assumed that educational activities are designed for the benefit of the audience. When some item of information is likely to be met with suspicion, publicists try to attribute it to some trustworthy source. Studies reveal, however, that sometimes the connection between a dramatic message and a questionable source is forgotten, thus allowing eventual acceptance of an account that was initially rejected. This behavior has been called the "sleeper effect" (Hovland et al., 1953).

Propaganda is often assumed to be false, since we habitually use the word to dismiss statements attributed to someone with whom we disagree. Precisely because falsehoods can be exposed, however, most experienced publicists do their utmost to avoid them. Astute politicians who differ in ideology as much as Winston Churchill and Che Guevara have advocated telling the truth whenever possible, even when it is embarrassing, to protect the credibility of the source. Furthermore, to be effective, information must be plausible to the target audience; messages are not likely to be taken seriously unless they are consistent with what people already take for granted. Any report that violates a cultural axiom is not likely to be heard, let alone understood. What is presented through the media of mass communication is usually discussed by people in thousands of local groups. An account that seems implausible to people is unlikely to be accepted in such deliberations; in some instances the original report may be distorted beyond recognition. During the depression, for example, Communist party agitators tried to proselyte troubled American workers with slogans and catchwords that had appealed to Europeans in similar circumstances; their effort was a total failure, for the appeals did not "make sense" to most Americans (Lasswell and Blumenstock, 1939).

The constant repetition of implausible messages is usually very costly. Just as the blatant repetition of any party line evokes cynicism, implausible items that are repeated over and again become labeled as phony propaganda. Furthermore, the audience loses respect for those who repeat them. To be effective, then, propagandists must know their target audience; they must understand its values, axioms, and assumptions. But difficulties remain. In politics what one party says is not necessarily what another hears; rivals often misunderstand one another even when they are listening carefully. Even when partisans are defining a situation as accurately as they can, their statement may appear to be a deliberate lie to outsiders.

One essential step in informational strategy is the suppression of undesirable news. Unless inconvenient knowledge can be neutralized, perspectives cannot be manipulated effectively. Censorship is seldom recognized as a component of propaganda, but it is nonetheless essential (Lippmann, 1922:43–44). All totalitarian states control formal communication channels, and even democratic governments resort to "managed news," especially in times of crisis. Censorship, however, creates serious problems. It has always been costly, for it tends to discredit the source. If one does not tell the truth, sooner or later the fraud is exposed; then the entire channel is questioned.

Wherever censorship is known to exist, as in time of war, people simply take it for granted that certain types of information will not appear in the mass media and turn elsewhere. They rely on foreign sources, rumors, and the underground press about all matters they assume are being censored. Much gossip develops about various leaders, for adverse publicity about them is not expected in formal sources. Official justifications for inconveniences often become the butt of unsavory jokes. There have been some instances, as in Italy under Mussolini, in which virtually all formal communication channels were viewed as a joke (Davis, 1941). Of course, under some circumstances censorship is accepted. In 1960, when President Kennedy was accused of "managing" the news, the Gallup poll discovered that 62 percent of a national sample believed they were not being told the whole truth on political matters, but many respondents considered this quite proper. They believed that some items of vital information should be restricted to those in high government circles.

Manipulation of Symbols. A great deal of promotional activity is carried out through formal communication channels. In modern societies the most common procedure consists of manipulating the content of the media of mass communication. In mass societies this is the only way in which people who are widely dispersed can learn about objects of common concern. One frequently used tactic is the misrepresentation of facts. Experienced publicists prefer not to lie; instead they emphasize favorable information and overlook inconvenient items so that the overall impact is likely to result in the desired definition of the situation. Expedient emotional reactions are encouraged through a careful selection of provocative words. Care is exercised to make the messages appear reasonable, for reports that do not make sense or fly in the face of widely held beliefs only evoke insurmountable resistance.

Where possible an effort may be made to allow the audience to draw its own conclusion from the alleged facts. Many propagandists contend that people who cannot be persuaded through preaching and exhortation can be won over if they are convinced that they are making up their own minds. But experts disagree on this matter. Some studies reveal that the audience sometimes misses or distorts the essential point. Since people may reach the wrong conclusion, some publicists believe that any promotional piece should explicitly state its message (Hovland et al., 1953; Klapper, 1960).

Although many fear that the public can be persuaded to believe anything if the mass media are tightly regulated, this is clearly not the case. The contents of the mass media are accepted at face value only in communities in which the people evaluate them as reliable sources of information. Such faith has to be earned through performance; where the media over many years have provided information that has proved an adequate guide for daily judgments, people are likely to accept their content without question. Where a channel is suspected of serving the interests of certain corporations, political factions, or government officials, however, people will accept only the routine news, such as weather forecasts and the results of athletic contests. Most Americans appear to have considerable faith in the mass media, even though they realize that some of the news is slanted.

Another condition for effective persuasion through the mass media is the absence of competing sources of information — such as the religious press, union newspapers, political tracts, or well-established networks of informal contacts. Furthermore, when too many people are familiar with the facts, misinformation will only tarnish the reputation of the source. In time of war, for example, officials may wish to hide battlefront catastrophes or blunders from the civilian population. Sooner or later, however, thousands of soldiers who were involved will return home, and their accounts will spread quickly in the form of rumors. Where an underground press is active, such deceptions will be widely publicized. Similarly, if the mass media contradict facts that are known to specialists, reports of errors are likely to leak out. Thus, the manufacturing of false information is likely to succeed only when there is no possibility of anyone's checking. Even then, embarrassing details may be disclosed many years later. Some publicists have gotten away with bald lies. Whenever falsehoods are exposed, however, the reputation for integrity of those responsible is diminished. Such disclosures often lead to widespread cynicism.

Where the target population is largely illiterate, the print media are obviously of limited utility. Motion pictures and television may still be used; indeed, these channels have proved very effective for both education and political propaganda. The Chinese Communists have made very effective use of the stage. Dramatic teams have toured the nation, staging performances in one village after another. For busy peasants the plays provide a pleasant respite from their harsh life. The dramas are usually about people like those in the audience, facilitating sympathetic identification with the characters. The plots are easy to understand; the travails and injustices long endured by the people are eliminated by triumphant Communist heroes (Belden, 1949; Hinton, 1968). People who wish to become literate are given educational aids — flash cards showing ideograms or comic books with simple messages — that they can learn to read during lunch breaks. Once they have learned to read, people can study more advanced texts, which consist of propaganda.

Since there are definite limitations to persuasion through the mass media, attempts have been made to exploit informal communication channels. The aim is to introduce desired information into primary groups, where people feel at home and have no particular fear of exploitation. Numerous efforts have been made to plant rumors that would favor one political cause or other. In local elections, for example, rumors that some candidate has the secret backing of an unpopular group have shifted support to the opposition (Smith and Sarasohn, 1946). Although such campaigns have sometimes worked, this tactic is unreliable, for it is impossible to control spontaneous conversations among friends. People discuss reports that are plausible to them, but standards of plausibility vary considerably in a diversified society. Thus, some messages become so twisted in the course of transmission that they may actually boomerang on the initiator (Shibutani, 1966:185–213). In an effort to exercise better control over content, some publicists have devised slogans, catchwords, jingles, and popular songs whose point depends on the exact wording. Popular songs in particular have helped crystallize sentiments and united large numbers in support of a cause (Rogers, 1949).

Other attempts to exercise some measure of control over the flow of conversations in primary groups include the efforts of political parties to use members of their local units to disseminate messages. In the Soviet Union, for example, Communist party members and those who aspire to membership — people distributed throughout all segments of the population — have been instructed to provide "correct" interpretations in various informal settings in which they are involved. They do not deliver lectures; that would be self-defeating. In natural settings, such as over lunch with co-workers, they merely explain the party's position in their own words and in terms that make sense to their associates (Inkeles, 1958:67–131). In China an even more effective setting exists. People in all walks of life are organized into small groups — at their place of residence, in their work units, and even within the Communist party itself. Whenever a problematic situation arises, deliberation occurs in these groups, where participants are expected to express themselves candidly. This provides a convenient channel for the dissemination of any message of critical importance. There are indications, however, that such efforts have not always been successful (M. Whyte, 1974).

Linguistic communication is not the only way symbols are used for promotional purposes. Efforts can be directed to create desired emotional climates by manipulating status symbols. Politicians often aim for the "bandwagon effect"—gaining the votes of people without political commitments by forming the impression that one side is so strong that it is certain to win. In the United States the practice of displaying symbols in support of one contender or the other is not taken seriously; people use bumper stickers and lapel buttons to promote all kinds of causes, often in jest. In certain elections abroad, however, such tactics have assumed greater significance. In Germany in the early 1930s the major contenders were the Nazi party and the Iron Front, a socialist workers' organization. The socialist leaders followed the conventional practice of discussing issues in speeches containing historical facts, statistics, and familiar arguments. The Nazis staged spectacular demonstrations, wore colorful uniforms, strategically displayed swastikas, and greeted one another on the streets with a salute of "Heil Hitler!" In one election after another they scored spectacular gains. In 1932, in the face of considerable opposition, the director of propaganda for the Iron Front was given permission to depart from the consideration of issues and to fight back in kind, but only in the state of Hesse. There the Iron Front used its own symbols— three arrows to compete with the ubiquitous swastikas and a clenched-fist salute with the shout "Freedom!" to counteract the Nazi salutations. The partisans soon became embroiled in guerrilla fighting over symbols, destroying and defacing each other's emblems. The efforts apparently weakened the impression of Nazi dominance, and the Iron Front won in Hesse, although the Nazis succeeded throughout the rest of Germany (Chakotin, 1940). This contest involved the use of both expressive and referential symbolism.

Manipulation of Events. Words are not the only means by which human beings communicate. Any act can be communicative, and several procedures have been developed for manipulating perspectives through the deliberate enactment of symbolic acts. The staging of politically significant events is an ancient stratagem; an act is performed not for its ostensible purpose, but for the impact it is likely to have on an audience. One example is the public torture and execution of criminals. Although drawing and quartering an offender fulfills the professed goal of punishing the criminal, the rationale for the spectacular display is to deter observers who might be tempted to commit the same offense. Similarly, anarchists have resorted to terrorist acts for their psychological effect on the general public. They are not so naive as to think they can destroy a government by violence alone. The objective of what has been called "propaganda by deed" is publicity: to call attention to injustices in the hopes of getting a hearing, to provoke retaliation and thus win sympathy for themselves and their allies, and to warn their foes that the government does not have the capacity to protect them. Civil disobedience is yet another example of a staged symbolic act. During the early phases of the civil rights movement the "sit-in" demonstrators called attention to laws they regarded as unjust by refusing to obey them; the violent reactions of Southern officials brought the protestors the desired national publicity and widespread support for their cause.

The success of propaganda by deed depends on publicity. For this reason such tactics seldom work in totalitarian states, where censorship makes the necessary public notice difficult to attain (Laqueur, 1977). There are other limitations to the effectiveness of such techniques. Spectators can tolerate a nuisance, but they become enraged if the inconveniences become too great or if too many innocent bystanders are injured. Once enough people are angered, authorities can institute severe repression that may crush the protestors.

In modern mass societies many political transactions are so gigantic that no single person can do much to alter the course of events. In a world that is so difficult to understand and influence, people gain some measure of reassurance from leaders whom they regard as capable and effectual. Thus, any person who can create the impression of being able to affect the course of events is likely to gain widespread support for public office. Officials in mass societies are symbolic leaders. Their followers know little of them as actual human beings; they know only the public image, a concept that leaders often have to struggle to maintain (Klapp, 1964). Those who dramatize their competence through symbolic acts are eagerly accepted, and conspicuous strong performances can propel a person into candidacy for high office (Edelman, 1964:73–94). It appears that President Nixon's spectacular trips to Russia and China contributed substantially to his landslide reelection in 1972. Conversely, any indication of indecision, weakness, or loss of control can be disastrous; it throws serious doubt on the individual's ability to cope with heavy responsibilities. Senator Kennedy's accident at Chappaquiddick—a single episode in a long, distinguished career as a public servant—has seriously hampered his quest for higher office (Hall, 1972:63–64).

Efforts have also been made to manipulate emotional climates by staging events. The pervasive tension aroused by disconcerting events, such as the urban riots of the 1960s, may be defused by symbolic acts—in this case the appointment of a commission of inquiry to provide assurances that the government was taking action. Even if no reforms are made, public concern is settled. Numerous attempts have been made to mobilize support for a cause by staging huge demonstrations. The massive Nazi rallies in Nuremberg, recorded by Leni Riefenstahl in *Triumph of the Will*, were apparently effective. Such gatherings promote crowd behavior and provide opportunities for the symbolic expression of deeply felt grievances and hopes. Nothing expresses group solidarity as much as massing face-to-face in large numbers in some kind of unified action; those who yell, sing, and applaud together often develop a strong sense of communion, sometimes even of invincibility. Participation in such demonstrations is often cathartic. Inhibitions are loosened, as people are able to relax their personal reserve and feel the potent support and exhilaration of a crowd. As conventional social distance is reduced, the participants become less critical and more suggestible. Thus, symbols and messages presented during this state of euphoria magnify their commitment to the cause. Such excited people have often been stampeded into support for a program about which they had known little at the beginning of the meeting.

Deeds speak more loudly than words. The manipulation of events is often an effective form of propaganda precisely because questions do not arise about the credibility of the source. Such tactics do not even have the appearance of propaganda. The events are actually executed, and news about them is reported by eyewitnesses or others who have nothing to gain from disseminating the information. Since the reports come from disinterested sources, the audience is not suspicious and has no sense of being manipulated.

No technique of persuasion always works. Each audience is receptive to different objects, and what succeeds in one historical context will fail miserably in another. Publicists sometimes do not understand why some successful campaign worked as well as it did. In some instances adversaries have accused one another of using clever propaganda when neither side had conducted a premeditated campaign. Hitting on the precise thing to say or do is often a matter of luck.

TECHNIQUES OF COERCION

Coercion is effected by manipulating sanctions, inflicting punishment on those who refuse to comply, or offering bribes to those who will. Some partisans, especially those inexperienced in politics, become so accustomed to using coercion that they may resort to it even when it is not necessary. In most instances, however, coercive tactics are used as a last resort, for measures that are regarded as excessive or unfair are often self-defeating. Violence is usually costly; it frequently provokes counterviolence as well as demands for suppression. In this section we focus on coercive tactics in which an effort is made to avoid or minimize the use of violence. Most of them fall within the limits accepted by public opinion and law.

Manipulation of Resources. One commonly used technique of coercion is the manipulation of resources. Whenever one party controls materials or funds essential for the survival or well-being of another, threats of withholding them may be used as a weapon. Blockades and boycotts are used in conflicts between communities. Thus, in the civil war in Nigeria in 1967–70 Biafra was starved into submission, and in 1967 Great Britain asked the United Nations to impose economic sanctions against Rhodesia for its refusal to allow more African representation in the government. In 1960 five of the world's largest oil-producing nations established the Organization of Petroleum Exporting Countries (OPEC); since then, the OPEC nations have exacted numerous concessions from various industrial nations by manipulating both the supply and price of crude oil and sometimes by trade embargo. American corporations have been able to obtain favorable arrangements in various communities by disclosing plans to relocate factories elsewhere, by refusing to contribute to the campaigns of local politicians, or by threatening to make investments that would favor a politician's rivals. Consumer boycotts may also provide an effective means of coercion. During the early phases of the civil rights movement firms accused of discriminating against Afro-Americans were threatened with boycotts. Since even giant corporations could not afford to risk losing 15 percent of their market, most of them agreed to comply with nondiscrimination agreements.

If one party actually does control resources essential for another's survival, as in the case of OPEC, the dependent party must either submit or face costly consequences. The industrial nations are desperately seeking alternative sources of energy; until they succeed, the oil-producing nations will exercise considerable power. Such tactics are effective, however, only when those making the demands are able to implement their threats. Blockades and boycotts require sacrifices on the part of the suppliers; they must give up their profits. Unless the suppliers can exercise sufficient self-discipline, the program will break down. Economic sanctions in international relations have created inconveniences but have rarely been effective, for suppliers not directly involved in the contest are reluctant to participate. They cooperate with blockade runners and surreptitiously supply the needed goods through indirect channels. Some flatly refuse to cooperate. Thus, in the 1930s the League of Nations embargo against the Axis powers failed, as did the British call for action against Rhodesia in 1967.

Consumer boycotts also require self-discipline, for the people must do without goods they really desire. Attempts to organize such campaigns among Afro-Americans were largely ineffective until the civil rights movement heightened ethnic consciousness so that considerable community pressure could be placed on those who did not comply. Public opinion also plays an important part. Measures that inconvenience too many people uninvolved in the contest arouse widespread resentment. Thus, the effectiveness of the manipulation of resources as a political tactic is contingent on the degree of dependency between target and supplier, on self-discipline, and on what the spectator component of the public will tolerate.

Withholding Essential Cooperation. If rival parties are interdependent, those whose services or facilities are essential may bring pressure on the opponent by refusing to do their part. In a strike, for example, workers temporarily withhold their services; by abstaining from work they bring production to a standstill. Even if they do not walk off their jobs altogether, well-organized slowdown tactics can force management to make concessions. In the same manner management may decide on a lockout; by closing down the plant it deprives workers of their means of livelihood. To fight effectively each side must be united and organized, and the line between them must be clearly drawn. Unless strikers are conscious of their common interests and identify with one another, a work stoppage cannot become a coercive weapon. Even among dissatisfied workers are those who believe that a strike would be morally wrong or foolish, and such persons must be brought into line. Sometimes hostile reaction by management unites the workers. When strikebreakers are brought in or when goon squads assault shop leaders, even dissidents may become sufficiently enraged to participate with determination. Intransigence on the part of management may also lead to sabotage of valuable equipment.

Coercion through the suspension of cooperation may also be found in other contexts. Civil disobedience — political noncooperation — is a tactic used by a large but weak population against a strong government. The power of government is legitimated only when most of the people recognize the ruler's right to give orders and regard obedience as their duty. Passive resistance, what Mahatma Gandhi called *satyagraha*, challenges the authority of the government. When a substantial part of the population refuses to appear for work, the community is paralyzed. Since the authorities cannot incarcerate everyone, social life grinds to a halt. Civil disobedience may consist of refusal to obey what are singled out as unjust laws, refusal to pay taxes, or refusal to perform essential duties. Public defiance of the law is usually premeditated; it must be made clear to the authorities that the defiance is not a mere convergence of private acts of rebellion but an organized protest. Such tactics have been strongly influenced by pacifists such as Tolstoy and Gandhi. Most campaigns in the twentieth century — the protests against British rule in India in the 1930s, the Danish refusal during World War II to enforce Nazi regulations against Jews, the native protests against apartheid in South Africa, and the early phases of the American civil rights movement — have been largely nonviolent. Such passive resistance creates numerous inconveniences for the government and is difficult to counter without arousing public sympathy for the weaker party (Kuper, 1957).

If both sides withhold essential cooperation, sooner or later the struggle becomes one of attrition. Each side suffers costly losses, and victory goes to the party that is able to outlast its foe. Thus, group solidarity and self-discipline are absolutely essential for carrying on such a struggle. Mere anger is not enough, for the enthusiasm of crowd behavior fades as soon as the emotional reactions subside. There must be an agreed-upon justification for making the sacrifices; otherwise with increasing numbers of defections the campaign will fail. Executing a successful strike requires organization. Many new transactions must be performed — maintaining communication among various task forces, picketing, distributing food to the needy. In a long strike maintaining high morale becomes a serious problem. On Sundays, when the participants are not together picketing, it may be necessary to organize picnics and other social events in order to reaffirm necessary convictions and reinforce determination (Hiller, 1928:79–99). Similar morale problems have been known to arise in civil disobedience campaigns.

Such tactics can be effective only when the two parties are actually interdependent. A strike can be a potent weapon only if no alternative sources of labor are available, just as a lockout will work only if there are no comparable new jobs for the affected employees. When enough scab labor can be brought in, strikes are broken. Much of the violence in the history of the labor movement has resulted from the use of such strike-breaking tactics. When college students in various countries staged strikes in the 1960s, they were successful only when the administration, often nudged by factions within the faculty, decided to make concessions. Where the administrators refused to budge, as in some Japanese universities, the strikes went on for years. As long as schools are supported through public funds, research and other activities can be carried on without students. Hence, demands regarded as unreasonable may be ignored with impunity.

Furthermore, strikes and campaigns of civil disobedience can succeed only if the rest of the public is willing to tolerate the inconvenience. The spectators tend to be indifferent or sympathetic until the dislocations begin to interfere seriously with their normal activities. For example, a strike in the winter by coal miners may turn out to be disastrous. After some innocent people have frozen to death, public reaction becomes so intense that the government forces both parties to reach an agreement. Angry mobs may attack the protesters. Thus, withholding essential cooperation can be an effective political tactic only when the rivals are actually interdependent and when the public will tolerate the ensuing inconvenience.

Patterns of Extortion. Extortion is another common coercive technique. By seizing some object that is valuable to their adversary, partisans are able to make demands of even a very powerful opponent. The principle is simple: to coerce by threatening to destroy the precious object in the event of noncompliance. Since the 1960s, various guerrilla bands have resorted to hijacking airliners and threatening to kill hostages unless imprisoned comrades were released from prison. Some groups have also demanded huge sums of money to carry on their operations. This practice reached an unprecedented point in 1979, when the government of Iran permitted some outraged partisans to seize the U.S. Embassy in Teheran and then participated in holding the captured Americans hostage while making a succession of demands. The practice of taking hostages to intimidate a population is an old one. Numerous armies of occupation have used it. During World War II the Nazis shot hostages — often the most popular and prominent citizens of a community — whenever resistance fighters did something they found unacceptable. Such calculated bloodshed was part of the Nazis' strategy for maintaining control over a large population with a relatively small number of soldiers.

Another type of extortion depends on information control. Those who possess information that could discredit an adversary's reputation in the eyes of a relevant public may force compliance with various demands — paying blackmail or making political concessions. This type of extortion was widely used in various parts of Asia as a means for a weaker party to seek redress. In India a man who had been victimized by some injustice could sit in front of the malefactor's home and simply starve to death. Since everyone in the community understood the man's purpose, his death exposed the wrongdoer to shame and public censure (Brailsford, 1934). In medieval Japan unemployed samurai sometimes pressured feudal lords for jobs by threatening to commit hara-kiri before their mansions. In more recent times various officials, corporation executives, and others enjoying high status have been forced to make payments as well as other concessions in return for the suppression of damaging information. Such tactics work for the simple reason that the fate of any person, even the rich and powerful, depends on his or her reputation. Even when embarrassing disclosures do not lead to total disgrace, they diminish one's effectiveness.

In societies in which humanitarian values prevail, where officials would be condemned and feel guilt-stricken over the death of hostages, such tactics can be effective — for a time. Should the precious object become forfeit, however, the tactic falls flat. The effectiveness of extortion depends on how high a cost the victim is willing to bear. How important is the reputation of a person who enjoys high status? As long as the cost is not excessive, the victim continues to pay the blackmailer. Beyond a certain point of desperation, however, the victim stops caring about anything.

Government authorities face difficult decisions when pressured by terrorists who seize hostages. To yield to terrorist demands or to sacrifice human lives: either action has enormous costs. Except in a few instances in which the hostages were children, the government of Israel has flatly refused to negotiate with extortionists. Similarly, when guards are taken hostage in prison riots, any demand that prisoners be released in exchange for them is met with flat refusal. For the same reason the hijacking of airliners in the Soviet Union simply has not succeeded. Thus, as in all power relationships, the capacity to coerce holds only as long as the disadvantaged party is willing to reciprocate. Once the victim refuses, there is little the extortionist can do. Indeed, such defiance places the extortionist in a very difficult position. The terrorist knows that killing hostages will evoke public outrage, just as the blackmailer knows that the disclosure of embarrassing information will discredit himself as well as his victim. Should the extortionist follow through on a threat, the reaction of the spectator component of the public will be negative. When partisans go too far, even their supporters may disavow them. In the face of extremists' intimidation the public often demands a repressive government response; disgusted citizens may even welcome a military dictator who vows to end such practices.

SUMMARY AND DISCUSSION

Agonistic transactions develop whenever two or more parties define one another as opponents and become conscious that they can pursue their rightful interests only at the expense of the other. Since each party believes it is pursuing its legitimate interests, it defines the other as an obstacle. Seen in this light, rivalry and conflict appear to be an unavoidable part of social life. Except in rare instances, as when the very survival of our species is at stake, it is unlikely that all human beings will share the same interests. It seems unlikely that all valued objects will ever be available in abundance, and it is difficult to imagine a diversified society in which incongruent interests of some kind would not develop.

Whenever disagreements arise, the outcome depends largely on the balance of power between the opponents. If power relationships are well established, the stronger party usually gets its way. When the balance of power is in doubt, however, contests of all kinds arise. Whenever possible, rivalries are pursued within a normative framework — in courts of law, through diplomacy, or by other forms of negotiation. Since the spectator component of the public often plays an important part in settling quarrels, considerable effort is expended to persuade the concerned audience that one position is more meritorious than another. Various techniques of coercion short of violence may also be used, but these are effective only under limited conditions. Partisans must be especially careful not to alienate the spectators, for in the long run that is self-defeating.

Since politics is a way of pursuing what the partisans regard as their legitimate interests, it is not surprising that in every era human beings have attempted to utilize the best available knowledge to develop strategies that maximize their chances of victory while minimizing costs. Machiavelli is not alone in urging that this be done; generals, chess masters, lawyers, and politicians have devoted their lives to such study. Many have attempted to create a science of politics. In the twentieth century a mathematical theory of games has been used in efforts to identify optimal strategies under various conditions; large research institutes equipped with the latest computers have been organized to pursue such inquiries (McDonald, 1950). As impressive as game theory appears, it rests on two questionable assumptions: (1) that decision makers have access to all the relevant information and evaluate it effectively and (2) that decision makers always act rationally. Most leaders do try to collect all the relevant facts, but it is often difficult to tell just which facts are relevant until after the contest is over. Most leaders do try to act as expediently as possible, but even the steeliest yields to human emotions. Indeed, the more dedicated people are to a cause, the more difficult it becomes for them to act dispassionately. Thus, although scientific knowledge has proved extremely useful, in the last analysis success in politics depends on the strategist's ability to appraise specific situations realistically, to develop tactics that are likely to work in particular contexts, and to mobilize available resources to implement specific plans of action. This suggests that politics will always remain an art.

SUGGESTED READINGS

Edelman, Murray. 1964. *The Symbolic Uses of Politics.* Urbana: University of Illinois Press.
>An analysis of the symbolic significance of political acts, an innovative approach to the study of political processes.

Hiller, E. T. 1928. *The Strike: A Study in Collective Action.* Chicago: University of Chicago Press.
>A pioneering study of how unions mobilize their members for a prolonged strike.

Lasswell, Harold D. 1927. *Propaganda Technique in the World War.* New York: Knopf.
>An analysis of the basic themes developed by both sides in their propaganda campaigns during World War I.

Lasswell, Harold D., and Abraham Kaplan. 1950. *Power and Society.* New Haven: Yale University Press.
>An attempt by a political scientist and a philosopher to specify some basic concepts and hypotheses for the analysis of political processes.

Schelling, Thomas C. 1960. *The Strategy of Conflict.* Cambridge, Mass.: Harvard University Press.

A game theory approach to the study of conflict, stressing the reciprocating nature of political strategy.

Simmel, Georg. 1955. *Conflict and the Web of Group-Affiliations.* Kurt Wolff and Reinhard Bendix (trans.). Glencoe, Ill.: Free Press.

An early formulation of a sociological theory of conflict, still worthy of serious study.

XV

BIPOLARIZATION

Theologians have long been troubled by the apparent contradictions between the existence of evil and the power and goodness of God. If God is all powerful, he can prevent evil. If God is all good, he must want to prevent evil. Yet pain, anguish, and suffering undeniably exist. Making sense of this inconsistency was a lifelong preoccupation of Saint Augustine. What is evil, and whence does it come? One of his answers was that what seems to be evil, when viewed in isolation or in a limited context, is an essential element of a universe that in its totality is good. The universe is made up of an immense number of objects, each moving toward the realization of its own potentiality. Each entity in its proper place in the scheme of things is good and glorifies its maker; each contributes in a different way to the perfection of the universe. Nothing God created is inherently evil. Within a circumscribed context, however, some things may take on the *appearance* of evil. For example, what is good for hunters enjoying their quarry is obviously not good from the standpoint of their prey. In addition Augustine noted that what is seen as evil provides a contrast against which the good shines more brightly.

It is difficult to find anything so widely condemned as evil as the way human beings treat their opponents when they become embroiled in conflict. Some sadists and bullies enjoy violence and confrontation, but most combatants are people who are reasonable and decent in other contexts. They get along with their friends and neighbors, and many are loved and respected by those who are close to them. But something seems to happen to them when they become involved in a fight; they are transformed into brutes. They plot maliciously against the enemy, and those who ordinarily do not take sadistic delight in the suffering of others enjoy contemplating the pain their foe will experience. Furthermore, combatants often assume a stance that strikes neutral observers as unreasonable. They become inflexible, rigidly dedicated to principles they might question under other circumstances. They willingly make enormous sacrifices, sometimes their own lives, to pursue their goals. Fighters perform many courageous and dangerous acts in behalf of their cause, but after the conflict is over some of them wonder about what they have done. Bemedaled war heroes sometimes confess to their friends, "I don't know why I did it."

World history offers countless instances of combatants committing vicious acts out of hatred and vindictiveness. What turns decent citizens into such ferocious fighters? Is human nature inherently evil? Some scholars have concluded sadly that human beings are basically atavistic, that violent animal instincts lie just below the veneer of civilization. Some have even sought the sources of human barbarism in animal behavior. Taking a cue from Saint Augustine, however, we might consider another approach to understanding brutality. The actions of people embroiled in conflict depend on their definitions of the situation, specifically, on their definitions of the contest in which they are involved, their enemy, and themselves. This is the approach we will take to provide an alternative explanation of barbarism and brutality.

INTENSIFICATION OF RIVALRIES

If rivalries are not settled satisfactorily through politics, consciousness of incompatible interests is enhanced. The tension level tends to rise, and the public becomes increasingly polarized into enemy camps. Such polarization can be seen in the formation of a strike mentality among disgruntled workers, in the growth of interethnic tension in a contested area, or in the coming of war. As collective excitement mounts, those who feel a deep sense of frustration band together formally and informally, and thereby reinforce their anger. Activists on each side, who are sometimes labeled hotheads even by their own comrades, take it upon themselves to harass or attack their opponents. They continue to emphasize what they regard as inequities and seize every opportunity to make negative remarks or to take hostile action. They conduct themselves in ways that make their stance unmistakable. Thus, emotional reactions are intensified through selective communication and become increasingly difficult to check.

Alignment of Personnel. How do people become aligned with one another to engage in conflict? How do they choose up sides, so to speak? In struggles between communities the lines usually predate the strife. In fights that break out within communities, however, a clear-cut split is not likely to develop until one issue becomes paramount and supersedes all others. As long as people are concerned simultaneously with several issues, many remain aware of what community members have in common and make an effort to keep their emotional reactions in check. In many intracommunal conflicts the lines of demarcation follow already recognized divisions: landlords versus tenants, radicals versus conservatives, labor versus management, farmers versus city people. But this is not always the case. Human beings can be mobilized to fight on the basis of any recognizable criterion, and their alignment depends on the issue. When one issue supersedes all others, the public is polarized into two opposing camps. Attention then becomes focused on a limited number of objects, and other concerns become secondary. Thus, the alignment of people differs somewhat in each political public.

Since battle lines vary from one issue to the next, most opposing camps are made up of a temporary coalition of factions. Each camp consists of people who happen to share a common interest in one key issue; they may disagree on many other matters less important for the moment. The leaders of the various factions may dislike and distrust one another; in some instances they may have more respect for the enemy than they do for some of their allies. They are united primarily by considerations of expediency; in some struggles each side is held together only by a common enemy. That both camps are temporary coalitions is a matter of crucial importance; indeed, it is difficult to understand the course of many conflicts unless we keep this in mind.

After the initial enthusiasm of the fight has passed, some strains within each camp are inevitable. The factions may disagree on the major target for aggression, how to wage the struggle most effectively, each faction's contribution to the total effort, or how to divide up the spoils after victory. If too many decisions appear to be slanted against them, some factions may come to feel they have become entangled in someone else's quarrel. As the conflict develops, the issues may change somewhat. Then the degree of commitment by each faction may also change, and this may lead to some realignment of personnel. Especially if the fighting does not go well, old enmities may reemerge. In many cases the difference between victory and defeat may depend on the ability of the leaders to prevent their coalitions from falling apart.

Even though both camps are coalitions of people who disagree on many matters, as the struggle takes shape, each side develops a consciousness of kind. Attention focuses on the single criterion that binds them, be it nationality, class, ethnic identity, language, or religion. The position taken on the single issue becomes all important—to win the war, the strike, the revolution. Differences from the enemy are emphasized, the contrast facilitated by selective perception and cognition. Those values that are *not* shared with the enemy are stressed, while the differences within each group are minimized or glossed over. The more emotionally involved people become, the more reluctant they are to admit to issues of contention among allies. This is most apparent in time of war. After the Japanese attack on Pearl Harbor in 1941, for example, most Americans forgot their many disagreements and closed ranks. National defense was the paramount consideration, and everything else became secondary.

Clarification of Boundaries. As a rivalry is intensified, the boundary between the in-group and the out-group is drawn with increasing clarity (Coser, 1956:33–38, 87–104). As the opponents become more sharply distinguished, they adopt names for themselves and for their enemy. The labels each side assumes for itself are laudatory—patriots, crusaders, freedom fighters—and those used for the foe are insulting—finks, pigs, gooks. Identification symbols—uniforms, emblems, marks of ethnic identity, religious rituals—are displayed with pride. Once opponents are identified by such symbols, it becomes easier for them to think and talk about each other.

As the enemies become more clearly differentiated, consciousness of kind on each side is further reinforced through differential association. As those who are allied become involved in many common transactions, social distance among them is lowered. In many cases people who previously had little contact are pleasantly surprised to discover that their new partners are human beings and not at all like the stereotyped conceptions they had held of them. Repeated personal contact further reduces social distance and leads to the formation of many new communication channels. As communication is facilitated among the members of each camp, each side develops a distinctive outlook. Thus, those who have joined forces actually do become more alike. As the differences between "us" and "them" become exaggerated, the people on each side find it easy to identify with their comrades. In spite of their numerous differences they become convinced that they share a common fate: "We are all in this together."

Boundaries between the opposing sides and identification among allied factions then solidify further as differential treatment and hostile acts by the enemy help define the position of each party. Once members of allied factions realize that the distinctions they make among themselves do not affect their status, they learn to forget the pointless differences. Since they are all treated as alike by their enemy, they sooner or later come to recognize the commonality of their interests. Upon realizing that they share a common fate, they are likely to close ranks and mobilize to protect their common interests. As they struggle together in pursuit of common goals, they come to conceive of themselves as being alike. Thus, each side's hostile acts help solidify the enemy and define its aims.

As the boundaries of each group are clarified, it becomes increasingly more difficult for anyone to remain neutral, and ever larger proportions of the spectator component of the public are drawn into the partisan groups. In the beginning many of the spectators are not fully committed to fight. As friend and foe are identified with increasing clarity, the issues become less ambiguous, and fence sitters are pressured to make up their minds. Those who suggest further negotiations are condemned. Those who are not obviously enthusiastic supporters of the cause may be suspected of being in sympathy with the enemy. Thus, many people are drawn into the conflict more through social pressure than through personal convictions.

Transformation of Goals. Each adversary's position is stated in simplistic, stereotyped terms that can be understood easily. Such oversimplification serves several purposes. First, most people usually do not understand complex political issues, and they become impatient with detailed analyses. Second, a careful diagnosis may disclose weaknesses in one's own position as well as call attention to inconsistent interests within each camp. Especially in coalitions composed of suspicious factions, the positions must be stated in very general terms, for they must be acceptable to everyone. Grievances are usually expressed by finding fault, since the easiest way to explain any discomfort or inconvenience is to blame someone. Hence, the enemy is accused of being the "cause" of everything that has gone wrong. Third, as the tension level rises, people tend to become less critical and more suggestible; they can be mobilized more easily around slogans and battle cries. Serious discussions of issues become extremely difficult; most people are too angry and eager to get on with the task of doing something. Persons who are able to articulate such feelings most effectively emerge as leaders of efforts to seek redress. Although some leaders and intellectuals may view such rhetoric cynically, rank-and-file members of the public usually take it seriously.

Much of what happens in any conflict is the result of intense anger, and any understanding of adversarial behavior must rest on an appreciation of how human beings characteristically perceive, think, and act when they are enraged. Since the enemy is defined as responsible for all grievances, it is evaluated as an obstacle — a frustrating object. The most common explanation of hostile behavior is the frustration-aggression hypothesis: If an organism is blocked or impeded as it moves toward a goal, it tends to turn aggressively against the source of frustration (Dollard et al., 1939). If the obstacle is too formidable to attack, aggression may be directed against a substitute object that happens to be available. Thus, an infuriated employee who cannot retaliate against his domineering boss may lash out against a fellow subway passenger or yell at his wife when he gets home. Such displaced aggression — a form of expressive symbolism — plays an important part in all conflicts. Aggression may also be directed inward, with the frustrated individual blaming him or herself for being inadequate. Efforts to compensate for such guilt also contribute to the viciousness found in conflicts.

Although the frustration-aggression hypothesis is just a formal statement of what is widely recognized in daily life, its formulation has resulted in extensive research that has thrown considerable light on these phenomena. Several qualifications have been added since its original formulation (Newcomb and Hartley, 1947:257–96; Berkowitz, 1962). When confronted by frustration, people turn against whatever they define as the instigator. Even if violence does not erupt immediately, those who feel thwarted are poised to move aggressively. As frustration intensifies, they become impatient with talk and demand action. At that point keeping hotheads in line becomes increasingly difficult.

As their anger intensifies, partisans increasingly see the contest in what students of game theory call "zero-sum" terms — one side's gains come only at the expense of its opponent's losses. Victory can be attained only with the total defeat of the enemy. Once a contest is so defined, complementary interests with the opponent are brushed aside and temporarily forgotten. The goals of those mobilized for action are thereby transformed. The people on each side had originally gotten together to pursue or defend their vital interests; once a contest is defined in zero-sum terms, however, destruction or neutralization of the enemy becomes the key objective. The enemy must be defeated or brought under control at all costs; this objective supersedes all other considerations. That this all-out effort will require the mobilization of personnel and resources becomes widely recognized, and people prepare to make the necessary sacrifices. Once conflict reaches this stage, the various norms against violence are cast aside — at least until the essential objective is achieved. In many conflicts anger becomes so intense that the original issue is forgotten; winning becomes a matter of self-respect and honor. In time of war, for example, many officials realize that annihilation of the enemy is unnecessary and unwise, but they may advocate such total destruction to facilitate mobilization. Enraged people take such appeals seriously, and the leaders subsequently have considerable difficulty restraining those who are fighting from engaging in unnecessary slaughter.

Conflicts develop over time in a succession of hostile interchanges. By the time many agonistic transactions are terminated, the situation has changed so much that the original issues have become totally irrelevant. How fights begin is often unclear; in many instances people simply blunder into them. After a vicious conflict is over historians may select some spectacular event, such as the storming of the Bastille, as the starting point. Most conflicts, however, have been under way for a long time before the initial blow is struck. When issues are not resolved politically, the dissatisfied split into hostile groups, convinced that their interests are incompatible. As the struggle takes shape, each side helps the other define its own position and purpose until both conclude that the only way out is to fight. Once the two sides are clearly identified, each side tends to blame all frustrations on its opponent. This trading of recriminations suggests that much of the ensuing brutality consists of displaced aggression. Once the fighting is under way, it becomes a point of honor to stay with it to the bitter end. Thus, once hostility is launched, events get out of hand. Sober leaders, who had certain political objectives in mind, are no longer able to restrain their infuriated followers.

FORMATION OF CONTRAST CONCEPTIONS

To better understand the viciousness found in human conflict we must examine the manner in which the combatants define key objects in the situations in which they are involved. How do enemies characterize themselves and their foes? Except in fights within primary groups the opponent — class enemies, foreigners, idolators, members of a savage "race," polluters — is always an abstract object. People construct objects through selective perception and communication. Some astute observers

(G. H. Mead, 1929; Sullivan, 1950) note that those who become involved in conflicts construct typical personifications of one another.

The Enemy as a Frustrating Object. Combatants characteristically see their adversary as an obstacle to the pursuit of their legitimate interests. This perception, like any other, is not the result of a mechanical recording and decoding of sensory clues. What one perceives depends on what one is doing; perception is always selective. Furthermore, emotional reactions constrict perspectives. Whenever people become upset, their attention becomes focused; they become hypersensitive to some sensory cues and blind to others. Thus, anger produces a form of tunnel vision that makes us acutely sensitive to the alleged source of our frustration.

An infuriated man mobilized to attack is especially alert to any of his opponent's weaknesses that he might exploit. His imagination fills with alternative ways of inflicting pain and humiliation. He is also sensitized to what is dangerous about his opponent but is likely to overlook any act of kindness or other favorable attributes. His attention also centers on various negative traits that justify his hostile inclinations and hatred. Once he is convinced that his enemy is determined to harm him, he anticipates hostile moves from his opponent. Thus, his expectations further reinforce his conception of his foe as a frustrating and dangerous object.

Combatants' perceptions also reflect their interpretations of their opponents' actions. To understand another's conduct, an observer necessarily imputes motives (intentions) to the actor, whose actual thoughts and intentions remain hidden. When one woman strikes another, for example, we can see the blow, but whether she acted from anger, to defend herself, to help a friend, or by accident is a question we can answer only by making inferences about her inner experiences. We try to explain what we have seen by imputing a motive, a "cause" for her conduct. The imputation of motives is thus a cognitive activity that enables us to make sense of what we perceive. If we know the woman, we seek an explanation that is consonant with our general opinion of her. If we like her, we will tend to explain her behavior by imputing benevolent motives. If we dislike her, we will tend to attribute foul motives to her conduct. Her action will therefore be perceived differently by her friends and her rivals.

Similarly, combatants tend to see malice and malevolence in everything their adversaries do. If the enemies fight tenaciously in the face of formidable opposition, they are dismissed as fanatics; if allies cling obstinately to a difficult position, this is proof of their courage. When allies decide to retreat from a hopeless situation, they are making a strategic withdrawal; if adversaries pull back under similar circumstances, they are obviously cowards.

Once conflicts become severe, partisans construct an object of their enemy by imputing to it all the traits and values most despised in their own culture. The enemy is thus construed as an abstract object that symbolizes the antithesis of all the values most cherished in one's own community (Voegelin, 1933:181–208). The enemy is greedy, dishonest, and vicious. Enemy soldiers rape and torture children and would kill their own mothers on command. They are godless, perverted, and pathological despots.

Moral Bifurcation in Conflict. The self-concepts of combatants develop during the course of conflict. Partisans tend to define themselves in idealized terms. People seldom acknowledge fighting for greed or lust. Especially in major conflicts in which large numbers are mobilized for combat, people view themselves as decent human beings striving to protect their rightful interests by fighting for the values most cherished in their culture—freedom, honor, justice. Thus, all partisans assume the stance of self-righteous indignation and elevate themselves to a position of moral superiority. They perceive themselves as activated only by noble motives; their intentions are always good.

As conflict is intensified, the objects the partisans construct of each other constitute a direct contrast. Persons moved only by ideal virtues are struggling against the most despicable creatures imaginable (Copeland, 1939). Especially in war the two sides are viewed as a direct antithesis of each other (Wright, 1942:1079–1117). Should those on one side happen to learn that people in the enemy camp are making similar claims about themselves, it seems comical and absurd. Combatants are not cynical, however; most of them actually believe they are fighting for the most noble values of their own community.

As the struggle is prolonged and intensified, the opposing sides are increasingly isolated from each other. The social distance between the embattled camps varies somewhat from one conflict to another. The distance between foes in an international war is usually greater than in a civil war, and various factions on each side may have somewhat different conceptions of their adversary. As social distance increases, the contrast between friend and foe becomes greater. As social distance is maximized, the enemy tends to become dehumanized. Perceiving the opponent as a human being becomes more and more difficult. The enemy is lacking in such human sentiments as love, loyalty, and a sense of decency. Enemy soldiers can bomb and machine-gun hospitals, strafe helpless women and children in the streets, abandon their wounded comrades to die or be captured, and even sacrifice their own families in the fanatic dedication to their foul cause. They are so horrible that they can scarcely be recognized as belonging to the human species. Hatred increases social distance to the point where identification and role-taking assume a different character. Once such dehumanization occurs, role-taking of the enemy becomes purely impersonal, much like that of a confidence man who feels no sympathy for his victim. Since a combatant must be able to anticipate the enemy's moves, role-taking is essential for effective fighting; it is done in a purely rational manner, however, and sentiments are excluded. Furthermore, since a partisan's own position is unqualifiedly correct, the enemy's refusal to support it constitutes further proof of the opponent's sinister, subhuman nature.

Thus, a moral bifurcation tends to develop in all conflicts. All prolonged fights are transformed into a struggle between good and evil—often between absolute good and absolute evil. The conflict becomes defined in moral terms because the enemy is personified as unrelieved evil; the fight was "caused" by wicked people who enjoy wreaking misery upon others. "They" are God's enemies, despoilers of all virtues. "We" engage them because of our love of humanity and our hatred of injustice and oppression. Each camp sees itself as the champion of a righteous cause. The struggle against the enemy thus becomes a moral crusade in which any decent person would gladly participate. Since one's own position is so righteous, anyone who does not agree becomes suspect. In the middle of the cold war of the 1950s, for example, anyone who questioned the wisdom of combating Communist ideology with arms was suspected of being part of the conspiracy. Similarly, the police see themselves as being in perpetual conflict with criminals who are constantly exploiting innocent victims. They are flabbergasted when such monsters are given "breaks" by "do-gooders" and unenlightened judges. In the same manner members of the underworld cite the brutal and unfair tactics used by "pigs."

Neutrality thus becomes impossible in any intense conflict. Chances for conciliation are cut off; anyone who suggests mediation by a third party is suspected of collusion with the foe. That combatants define themselves as participants in a moral crusade explains their sanctimonious stance. They resent anyone who questions their motives, and they often assume that those who disagree with them are immoral. Being involved in such a noble enterprise reinforces commitments to goals, justifies hatred, and overcomes resistance to brutality and killing. Many political observers have noted that perceiving the enemy as evil facilitates maintaining group solidarity (Coser, 1956:104–10). In many instances there is little concern over the outcome of the struggle; it is taken for granted that the right side will prevail in the end.

Escalation as a Reciprocal Process. Once contrasting conceptions of good and bad objects are established, a double standard of morality is implemented (Sumner, 1911:10–13). Different criteria are used in judging contributions to transactions involving allies and those directed at the adversary. While involved in combat, warriors may engage in treachery, bribery, and murder and take unfair advantage of chance opportunities that arise—all acts that are reprehensible by their community's peacetime standards. Instead of being condemned, however, they are acclaimed as heroes and rewarded. Thus, conflict leads to a displacement of norms. Fighters are honored for treating enemies in ways that would be otherwise judged criminal and immoral, and persons with sadistic tendencies are freed of the customary restraints of civil law and mores. The ethical dualism that makes brutality possible is based on the premise that since enemies are not human, they are *outside* the moral order. Enemy combatants are just "things," not human beings, and therefore killing one is much like swatting a fly or mosquito. Thus, the community grants the soldier its moral dispensation and sanctions murder without remorse or guilt. Dehumanization of the enemy is what makes viciousness commonplace in conflict.

As the fighting goes on, viciousness escalates, for contrast conceptions tend to become self-fulfilling prophecies (Merton, 1957:421–36). Since combatants on each side perceive their enemy as evil, they commit brutal acts. The victims' friends are outraged; such atrocities prove that the opposition is indeed remorseless and inhuman. Those who had entertained doubts about the viciousness of their foe are reassured; then they can perpetrate atrocities of their own. But such retaliation has the same effect on the other camp. The opponent is in turn infuriated. Such positive feedback provides mutual confirmation of the contrast conceptions. The suffering induces further loyalty to the cause and strengthens the determination to exterminate evil. Thus, in college students' protests in the 1960s the more severe the control measures the authorities instituted, the more the protest tended to escalate into violence (Morgan, 1970).

Both in the Soviet Union and in the United States hawks have become convinced that their opponents are developing laser beams capable of neutralizing missiles in flight. Each side is therefore working desperately to be the first to develop such a weapon. Both may well succeed; if they do, the race toward bankruptcy will advance to its next phase. Once the boundaries of the moral order are crossed, customary constraints give way to unlimited license on the part of the committed partisans. Seeking vengeance becomes a matter of honor, and runaway escalation often occurs. As combatants act in terms of contrast conceptions, brutality on each side reaffirms the beliefs of the other. Those involved in the fighting often become brutes who actually resemble the objects their enemies have constructed of them.

As both sides become more aggressive, moderate leaders tend to be replaced by more militant ones. The leaders on both sides find themselves under increasing pressure. Since the followers become so infuriated and make increasingly strident demands for vengeance, reasonable officials find it difficult to retain control. As various factions compete for a following, extremists enjoy an advantage. They have a long record of hating the adversary, and they often point to their moderate rivals' "softness." During the 1960s leaders in the civil rights movement faced such pressures to become more militant (McWorter and Crain, 1967). If moderate leaders do not harden their position, they are likely to be displaced by extremists who demand immediate and violent action. Those who counsel patience and reasonableness are often accused of collaboration with the enemy. Enraged people accept centralized authority, censorship, even despotism—anything to facilitate more effective combat. If moderate leaders somehow manage to maintain control, dissident factions may go off on their own to commit acts the organization has not sanctioned. Since their acts are often vicious, they may even embarrass the official leadership. Extremists are essentially prisoners of their own beliefs; they are involved in a relentless battle against unrelieved evil.

Participation in Moral Crusades. Throughout history—in war after war, in revolution after revolution, in one intracommunal fight after another—partisans have characterized themselves and their enemies in much the same manner. Since values differ from one culture to another, one would expect contrast conceptions to vary somewhat from one context to the next. Apparently, however, many key values are transcultural, for the characterization of the enemy is remarkably similar in diverse historical contexts. Fights are always between good and evil (God and devil), decent and immoral, normal and pathological, democratic and despotic. The enemy is always sinister, irrational, intractable to reason. Several observers note that enemies often develop mirror images of one another. In the cold war between the United States and the Soviet Union opposing leaders have described one another in almost identical terms. Each side views the other's goal as world domination; each believes that ordinary citizens in the other country are friendly but have been deceived and manipulated by villainous leaders (Barghoorn, 1950; Brofenbrenner, 1961).

Foes in other contexts have worked with similar contrast conceptions. Marxists hate their class enemies as passionately as they in turn are hated; members of rival ethnic groups make the same charges against each other. The mutual hatred of criminals and law enforcement officials persists even within prisons, and in the campus turmoil of the 1960s students and administrators accused one another of being deceitful monsters. Similar charges are exchanged by rival juvenile gangs, and even the witches in children's fairy tales have the same familiar attributes. Religious groups have been especially intolerant of disbelievers. Perhaps religious wars have been so brutal because there is no doubt among the participants that they are on the right side; they can fight without fear, for they cannot lose. The Islamic tradition of *jihad* (holy war) is not unique. All serious conflicts evoke similar sentiments.

Because of the ferocity and destructiveness of conflict, we are inclined to explain what happens in terms of atavistic instincts and foul motives. Especially from the standpoint of neutral observers most fights appear wasteful, pointless, and self-defeating. Of course, there are sadists who enjoy inflicting pain on others, mercenaries who enlist in quest for booty, and pirates who are under no illusions about their lust for plunder. There are those who seek power at any cost, but they constitute a small minority. In large-scale conflicts, especially in modern mass societies, most participants conceive of themselves as being involved in a moral crusade. They abhor violence and engage in it reluctantly as a duty. This attitude suggests that much of the viciousness found in conflict is only the natural reaction of decent human beings who are struggling desperately to overcome a wicked object, one that has been constructed in their imagination through selective perception, cognition, and communication. Although we seldom see it in this light, fighting for most people constitutes moral conduct. In a crusade against evil their sense of honor makes them take aggressive action. Their self-respect forces them to contribute their share to the enterprise. They fight gallantly and make enormous sacrifices in behalf of those with whom they identify — the community threatened by evil. Most combatants are meeting what they regard to be their moral obligations.

HOSTILE OUTBURSTS WITHIN COMMUNITIES

Intergroup rivalries are bound to develop in any community. Families and clans become involved in feuds; members of juvenile gangs glare at one another across their territorial boundaries; police officers and the underworld are locked in perpetual struggle; and members of class, ethnic, and religious groups periodically find one another intolerable. When such groups are organized and segregated from each other, difficulties are usually resolved through negotiations among the leaders. Intramural violence on a large scale erupts only when the established political procedures are inadequate. Most outbursts of violence within communities are expressions of pent-up hostilities; much of such violence consists of aggressive crowd behavior directed against people who have been defined as frustrating or dangerous. Three types of disorders are often confused. In the United States, for example, the term "race riot" refers to any outbreak of violence involving ethnic groups. It is necessary, however, to distinguish among (1) conflicts in which members of two ethnic groups attack each other (as in Detroit in 1943), (2) massacres in which enraged partisans assault a helpless minority group that does not retaliate (as in Atlanta in 1906), and (3) violent protest demonstrations by desperate members of minority groups (as in Watts in 1965). The same distinctions may be made in examining disorders involving other types of groupings.

Struggles over Relative Status. Tensions are likely to develop during transitional periods, when a previously established system of social stratification is breaking down but a new system has not yet evolved to replace it. When the rights and obligations of various categories of people are no longer clearly defined, misunderstandings are bound to arise. In such contexts opportunities that had previously been reserved for the privileged are gradually opened to others. At first a limited number of gifted individuals of lower rank are permitted special privileges, but in time others begin to qualify in increasing numbers. As those who had previously been confined to lower ranks are able to get better jobs, they earn more income and can compete more effectively for other desired objects. They see to it that their children are educated and in an even better position to compete.

Most intramural conflicts erupt during such periods of uncertainty. The vicious fighting that followed the Protestant Reformation arose where it was unclear which religious group would have greater influence over the government. Before the Civil War in the United States, when the status of black people was fixed in custom and law, black and white people lived together in a clearly defined and somewhat stable situation. During Reconstruction, however, when many of these norms broke down, considerable tension arose. The first Ku Klux Klan was organized, and lynching and other forms of intimidation became commonplace at this time (Doyle, 1937). During the personnel shortage in the two world wars the status of Afro-Americans rose once again, and this period of change saw more rioting. Similarly, the fighting in India between Hindus and Moslems flared when the British were leaving and the new nation's fate was in doubt. Thus, bitter animosity develops within communities when the relative ranks of two or more categories of people are changing and direct competition for desirable objects, which had previously been regulated, is thrown open. Those who had previously enjoyed a privileged position see such changes as encroachments on their private domain; some view them as a personal affront. They are convinced that inferior people have no right to desirable jobs, land, mates, and political influence that had been reserved for their own kind. They complain that their subordinates are getting uppity and out of place.

Although such transformations cannot occur without the acquiescence of the more secure members of high rank, those who do not fare well in direct competition become enraged. They feel that their rights are being trampled. Many businessmen resent their employees' joining unions. Having toiled long and diligently to build up their firms, they ask by what right can upstart workers tell them what to do. Those who are unable to keep pace in economic competition often complain that the newcomers are unfair; they work too hard, use family members as unpaid labor, and pool their financial resources in unconventional ways. The movement of working-class people or ethnic minorities into neighborhoods once reserved for the privileged may be perceived as an intrusion, and intermarriage arouses a deep sense of revulsion in some who view such liaisons as unnatural or perverted. Thus, persons of high rank often perceive the upward mobility of a lower-class person both as a threat to their way of life and as an insult. They define the upstarts as dangerous objects who threaten everything they hold dear or sacred.

Those who are struggling to improve their lot perceive such resistance as obstacles to their legitimate aspirations. In the United States blue-collar workers and members of ethnic minorities believe that they have a perfect right to press for a better life and resent what they regard as discriminatory practices. Workers see management attempts to discourage the formation of unions as a threat to their livelihood. Members of ethnic minorities who desire better homes resent keenly the tactics used to maintain segregation — housing covenants, differential interest rates, and gang violence. Since they can afford the housing, they feel they have a right to it. Although there may be little enthusiasm for intermarriage in any group, many persons of lower rank argue as a matter of principle that people have the right to marry whomever they choose. They resent in particular the implication that one of their number is not good enough to marry someone in another category. During periods of upward mobility expectations keep rising. Those who succeed take their gains for granted and see no reason not to strive for more. Upwardly mobile people are hypersensitive to slights, and they often perceive discrimination in situations where none has actually occurred. Although they have altered their self-concepts somewhat, they are not sufficiently secure in their new status to take their advantages for granted. Thus, those who are upwardly mobile evaluate people in higher ranks as unfair, as frustrating objects. The privileged are trying to deprive them of something that is rightfully theirs, something they have earned. Many develop a burning hatred for those who stand in their way.

With one camp fearing the other as dangerous and being viewed in turn as a source of frustration, tensions mount and political contention begins. One frequent charge is that the rival is seeking unfair advantage by increasing relative numbers through immigration and excessive reproduction. Minorities and the poor have often been accused of "breeding like rabbits." Even though most transactions involving people from the two sides are carried on without difficulty, misunderstandings arise with increasing frequency. Disagreeable incidents occur, and those in the two camps perceive them differently. Rumors develop that express and reinforce the already prevalent ill will. Contrast conceptions are formed on both sides through selective communication. The opponent is blamed as the "cause" of all difficulties. Attention focuses increasingly on the differences between the two groups, and in time the unlikeness becomes the key issue that overshadows everything else.

In such contexts violence erupts when some spectacular incident unites the partisans in each camp to fight. Thus, vicious rioting erupted in Chicago in 1919 after a rumor that a black youngster had been killed while swimming and that a white policeman had refused to arrest the murderer (Chicago Commission on Race Relations, 1922). The 1943 riot in Detroit occurred under similar circumstances (Lee and Humphreys, 1943). In most instances only a small proportion of the people on the two sides actually participate in the violence, but the clashes receive widespread publicity. As reports spread, tension increases and the fighting usually continues until the authorities are able to restore order. If order is not restored quickly, extensive massacres may occur, as in the Hindu-Moslem riots in India (Collins and LaPierre, 1975).

Persecution of Unpopular Minorities. Intramural violence is not confined to fights between contending groups; in many instances the assaults are more one-sided. Especially when an unpopular group is evaluated as dangerous, its members are harassed and periodically subjected to mob violence. Massacres have occurred throughout the world. Beginning in 1895 the Armenians in the Ottoman Empire became the targets of a succession of massacres. Many Turks viewed them as a threat to Islam and as potential allies of powerful Christian nations, especially Russia. The Armenians had previously accepted their subordinate position in the empire, but a nationalistic movement had inspired some of them to demand greater political and economic rights. Many Turks viewed this growing dissatisfaction as a threat to their dominance and feared that one of the great powers might use the "Armenian question" as a pretext for attacking them. Armenian settlements were sealed off; soldiers started the slaughter, and popular participation followed. Many of the men were killed; women and children were sometimes offered the choice of accepting Islam as the price for being spared. Many women were held captive and raped; looting was widespread; the dead and wounded were stripped of their clothing; and even doors and windows were taken. What could not be carried away was destroyed. Estimates of the number killed range from 50,000 to 300,000 (Nalbandian, 1963; Nansen, 1976). Similarly, Eastern European Jews were subjected to repeated pogroms in which mobs surrounded the ghettos and then went in to rape, murder, and plunder. Beginning with an especially vicious massacre in Kishinev, some 690 pogroms took place in Russia alone from 1903 to 1906.

What singles out a group for persecution is not necessarily its members' behavior but the manner in which they are defined and evaluated. Even in small communities, where persons from various categories are in frequent contact, social distance may be maintained through etiquette and other conventional practices. Through differential association cultural differences may persist for centuries, and stereotyped concepts are maintained in spite of the contacts. Persecution often develops when people who have been set apart as different become the object of fear (Brailsford, 1933). Thus, Mormons were hounded in various parts of the Midwest until they were finally forced to migrate to Utah; especially in Missouri they were the targets of considerable violence from 1833 to 1846. They were labeled as "peculiar people." Their industry and thrift had enabled them to purchase much land, and this created some resentment. What aroused suspicion, however, was that they were friendly with Indians and practiced polygamy. They were also accused of being abolitionists, a charge the Mormons repeatedly denied (O'Dea, 1957:45–75).

Eastern European Jews were also regarded as a people apart—accused of being responsible for the crucifixion of Christ. Since they were not permitted to farm in many areas, they had to compete for the limited industrial, service, and trade opportunities in the towns. Conditions were harsh, and some resorted to illegal tactics to eke out a living. Some were known to be socialists, and this aroused further suspicion. Just before the carnage in Kishinev rumors emerged of ritual murder—the alleged killing of Christian children, supposedly as part of Jewish religious rites. The only newspaper in the community accused the Jews of being swindlers, liars, parasites, and exploiters of Christians. The editors organized a Christian Welfare Society to purchase weapons and distributed a handbill of an alleged imperial decree granting permission to inflict "bloody punishment" on Jews during the days of Passover. Thus, popular passions were aroused and intensified through selective communication.

Although there is evidence of official encouragement in some massacres, most are the spontaneous reactions of frightened and outraged people. Once contrast conceptions have been formed and tensions intensified, violence is touched off by some spectacular incident, some trivial event that ignites an already explosive situation. Sometimes the rash act of a partisan faction touches off a conflagration. Before the massacres in Turkey terroristic acts by some Armenian nationalists received widespread publicity. Then a procession of Armenian protesters in Constantinople touched off a riot; this was labeled a rising against which honorable Turks had to defend themselves (Nansen, 1976:286–94; Laqueur, 1977). Early in 1903 the mutilated body of a peasant boy had been found near Kishinev, and immediately before the massacre the community was inflamed by a rumor that Jews had murdered a Christian servant girl. As in all crowds, there was a self-selection of personnel. Many remained at home and did not participate, and a few even assisted their persecuted friends. But those indebted to usurers took special delight in extinguishing their liability. Many of the local officials, police officers, and soldiers, drawn from the same population as the rioters, were in sympathy with the crowd. They refused to intervene or did so only halfheartedly. In Kishinev the police did not interfere and troops did not arrive for two days. By then the rioters were so exhausted that order was easily restored. The result was 44 killed, 583 wounded, 700 homes wrecked, 600 shops looted, and 10,000 in need of relief (Dahlke, 1952).

Rebellions of the Oppressed. When degradation is so severe that life appears hopeless, some partisans from the bottom rung of the stratification system rise in rebellion. Their despondency over their plight leads them to conclude that anything would be better than continuing as they have; even when they realize that the chances of success are remote, they prefer to fight. Although authorities are defied in such uprisings, in most instances there is no serious thought of overthrowing the government. In many cases there is no particular objective. Collective protests are usually passionate and spontaneous explosions rather than cool and calculated efforts to bring about changes. Many participants do not even consider the consequences. Most slave revolts are of this nature, and they are rare. In ancient Rome only three outbreaks involved one hundred thousand slaves or more. Although several slave uprisings occurred in the Caribbean islands, there were only three serious challenges in the American South (Aptheker, 1943).

Long before European colonialism was defied by national liberation movements, rebellions broke out from time to time; John Chilembwe's insurgence in Nyasaland (now Malawi) in 1915 is a notable example (Rotberg, 1971). Peasant revolts are also desperation measures, and most have been local and expressive. Civil disturbances among the impoverished have occurred in cities throughout the world—in ancient Rome, China, and India. Protest demonstrations have been commonplace, especially during the early phases of industrialization; and, since the French Revolution, urban mobs have played an important part in politics. Mutinies in the armed forces are also desperation measures; the penalty for mutiny is severe and well known, and soldiers will not join unless they see themselves in a hopeless situation. Prison riots are also of this genre. The prisoners are under no illusions of winning their release; they are merely protesting unbearable conditions. Such outbursts have also occurred in some Communist states—in East Germany in 1953, in Hungary in 1956, and in Czechoslovakia in 1968.

Although exceptionally gifted persons occasionally rise from the rank-and-file members of oppressed categories, most leaders of such uprisings are in marginal positions or are outsiders. Who organized the three major slave revolts in the American South? Gabriel was an accomplished blacksmith who lived outside of Richmond; Denmark Vesey was a free artisan who had once worked on a slave ship; Nat Turner was a literate preacher. All were familiar with life-styles that contrasted sharply with the fate of most slaves. Such partisans usually have great difficulty winning the support of those in whose behalf they risk their lives. People of low status are fully aware of the odds against them, and fear of punishment keeps them from participating. What can an impoverished peasant lose? He can lose his life; his wife and daughters may be forced into prostitution; and his other children may be sold into slavery or killed. Peasants not only may refuse to take part but also may warn their friends against joining the revolt, pointing out that violence will invite a backlash that may affect even those who do not become involved. Nor are such fears unfounded. Official reaction is usually immediate; martial law is imposed, and troops are sent at once to restore order. The conditions being protested are seldom corrected. At times uprisings involving only a handful of rebels have resulted in massive retaliation that has been costly to the entire category for several generations.

Although most rebellions are expressive, some protesters begin with a vague hope that someone will respond to their demands. Hobsbawm (1965: 108–16) suggests that mobs in pre-industrial cities expected to achieve something and attacked selected targets. The burning of Watts in 1965 and the razings that followed indicated the depth of the desperation felt by Afro-Americans condemned to urban ghettos, and there are indications that some of the protesters thought their action might attract enough attention to alter official policies (Feagin and Sheatsley, 1968). There have been occasions, however, when such spontaneous outbursts of grief and anger have developed into serious insurrections. Goals sometimes emerge *after* an incident is under way (Lammers, 1969). Sometimes a charismatic leader emerges to unite the disconsolate, or other groups with grievances against the government may join them. Thus, the peasant revolt Pugachev led in 1773 spread so quickly that it almost toppled the Russian government. The Mexican Revolution of 1910 began in a succession of peasant uprisings; when the various rebel groups joined forces, they found themselves in control of the country. The mutiny in 1905 on the Russian battleship *Potemkin* began when some sailors became enraged upon being fed maggot-infested meat. When the ship's doctor declared the food edible, a scuffle ensued in which an officer was shot. Realizing that they faced execution, the sailors seized the ship to protect themselves. When they learned that a revolution had broken out in Odessa, they decided to join it and tried to persuade comrades elsewhere to take over the fleet. Revolution was not the initial objective, but the goals kept changing as the mutiny developed (Hough, 1963). Similarly, the initial complaint in the 1953 East German uprising was against intolerable work conditions. As protests spread throughout the country, however, some began demanding the replacement of Communist officials. The outbreak was then labeled a counterrevolution rather than a strike and was quickly suppressed (Brant, 1957).

Rebellions seldom succeed, even when they win some initial gains. Once anger begins to cool, the leaders face difficulties in mobilizing personnel into effective fighting units. The few risings that have succeeded have encountered serious problems; since the leaders have no definite plans for reform, the winners do not know what to do. Just as strikes are likely to fail until unions are organized, popular protests without organization soon dissipate.

INTERVENTION IN CIVIL DISORDERS

Control of Internal Violence. No government can tolerate intramural violence for long without risking a serious challenge to its legitimacy. We need only witness what happened in Colombia in the 1950s and in Lebanon in the 1970s. Law enforcement agencies are expected to maintain order, and failure to do so elicits demands that officials take remedial action. Although sympathetic observers may tolerate disorders for a time, when food and other necessities become difficult to obtain and when innocent bystanders are killed, calls mount for the cessation of violence. Continued failure can lead to demands for a new government, and military dictatorships have been welcomed by peoples weary of the inability of civilian governments to maintain order.

The manner in which authorities intervene depends on their definition of the situation. Most governments are responsive to the claims of the more privileged strata, but some officials may have sympathetic ties with other segments of the community. If the officials themselves feel threatened, they react decisively; slave revolts, prison riots, and military mutinies are suppressed immediately — often ruthlessly. In totalitarian regimes a challenge from any autonomous group is seen as a threat to the government itself and is likely to be put down at once. In most instances, however, local police are able to restore order, for government authority is seldom challenged in intramural outbursts. The participants realize that violence is illegal and fully expect officials to make some effort to intervene. If the police are unable to control the situation, martial law is instituted, and troops are called in to ensure public safety. The objective is to restore order until tempers have cooled; then the civilian government can resume power. If necessary, civil courts are superseded by military tribunals; curfews are imposed, and violators may be shot. In severe crises the constitution may be suspended temporarily, and certain rights may be nullified for the duration of the emergency. As long as troops remain loyal to the government, not many rioters can persist for long.

Thus, in most contexts violence is limited by what the government is willing to tolerate.

Governments are expected to remain neutral in intramural quarrels. Even when officials sympathize with one side or the other, they usually try to be as impartial as the circumstances permit. Any intervention on behalf of one side is done surreptitiously, and the outward appearance of neutrality is maintained. The major problem facing officials in intramural conflicts is to prevent partisan groups from attacking each other; law enforcement personnel find themselves trapped between two hostile mobs. They urge those in both camps to exercise restraint; they offer their services to mediate quarrels; and in some instances they may even insist on arbitration. When a detested group is being persecuted, governments have sometimes risked their popularity by insisting that the violence be terminated. In some pogroms, for example, feudal lords rushed to rescue the Jews. Such acts were not necessarily altruistic; in many cases the lords sought to protect their sources of credit and loans.

But a policy of neutrality is sometimes difficult to enforce, for local officials may be aligned with one side. Even when they are under strict orders to be fair, it is difficult for them to do so in emotionally charged situations. The police may favor one side by passivity; they overlook violent acts committed by one side, while being excessively harsh when arresting offenders on the other side. In many riots in the United States police have looked on while Afro-Americans were being beaten but have intervened decisively when others were in danger (Grimshaw, 1969; Marx, 1970).

Difficulties in Crowd Control. Most instances of intramural violence consist of crowd behavior, in which the self-regulation of the participants is impaired by intense excitement. Thus, officials must deal with enraged and unreasonable citizens. Maintaining control over crowds always presents difficulties. In many instances a massive show of force is enough to disperse crowds. When the people are angry enough, however, they may even defy military units, and local commanders have felt compelled to order their troops to fire directly into mobs. When the authorities themselves are frightened, they may even order massacres to intimidate the opposition into submission. In Petrograd in 1905, for example, when some three hundred thousand demonstrators formed a procession outside the Winter Palace to present the czar a petition objecting to various injustices, troops fired into the crowd to make an example and thus to discourage further protests. In European colonies, where a small elite ruled large numbers of natives, serious demonstrations have been handled in a similar manner. In Amritsar in 1919, when thousands of Indians were protesting the British government's business-as-usual attitude after their contributions to World War I had demonstrated their capacity for self-rule, troops fired into the crowd. The protesters were holding a mass meeting in an enclosure with only one exit, and the killing of 400 of them outraged public opinion both in India and in England (Brailsford, 1933). Although the commanding officer was dismissed, the massacre became a symbol of British oppression and served as a rallying cry for Indian nationalism. Troops can bring unruly mobs under control by force, but firing at unarmed citizens often elicits widespread public reactions. In some instances the reactions have proved very costly to the government.

The kind of tactics local officials use in their efforts to control crowds depends on the extent to which the rioters have the support of the spectator component of the public. Where there is widespread sympathy for the rioters, the police must be especially careful to exercise restraint. Since they cannot use their weapons, they must rely on other tactics to disperse crowds. One common procedure is the elimination of agitators, but here the police are at a disadvantage. If they permit agitators to speak unhindered, the tension level may rise to the point that a suggestion from a single person might trigger violence. If they remove agitators unobtrusively, others will immediately replace them. If they remove agitators conspicuously, their intervention only intensifies the crowd's resentment, and the officers themselves become targets of hostility. Another common procedure is the wedge; troops divide the crowd into progressively smaller segments until various groups of individuals find themselves isolated. When the reciprocating support of others disappears, the participants become self-conscious. The psychological unity of the mob is broken, and each frightened individual runs to save himself (Turner and Killian, 1972:159–77).

When the authorities are bound by humanitarian values and by concerned public opinion, crowd control becomes especially difficult. In the various protest demonstrations in the United States in the 1960s, for example, the rioters were mostly college students from affluent homes, youngsters whose parents could afford to hire attorneys to take legal action against officials. Many intellectuals sided openly with the protesters; they were critical of any police action and demanded that authorities correct some of the sources of the discontent instead. The participants were often conscious of the restraints imposed on the police. Many were ignorant of the decisive manner in which mobs throughout history had been suppressed, and they made charges of police brutality at the slightest use of force. In many instances, even when the police tried to remain impartial, their very presence was so resented that it escalated the violence. Police officers were seen as symbols of the hated "establishment" and became the targets of hostility (Marx, 1970).

Even when the police or army is authorized to use force to quell disturbances, mobs that are angry enough will fight back. In 1978 and 1979 Iranian troops fired into crowds rioting against the shah. But the protesters were not deterred; they became so enraged that increasing numbers took to the streets each day, and in the end the shah was forced to abdicate. In some instances, as in the uprising in Hungary in 1956, irate protesters have hurled rocks at tanks.

One recurrent problem is to maintain discipline and high morale among law enforcement personnel. Soldiers and police officers are placed in a difficult position. They are insulted and spat on; they are showered with debris; on occasion they may be shot at or have firebombs thrown at them. They see their comrades being beaten or even killed. Unlike soldiers on a battlefield, however, they are not free to defend themselves with their weapons. Many rioters and observers find role-taking impossible, and they do not realize what a frightening experience a riot can be for the officials. Since soldiers and police officers are human, they themselves become enraged and are sometimes transformed into a hostile mob. A notorious case occurred during the Democratic convention in Chicago in 1968. After considerable provocation many officers lost their self-discipline and went on the offensive in what has been described as a "police riot." They seized, beat, or arrested anyone in the vicinity who resembled a Yippie, as well as many Afro-Americans—including a large number of bystanders (Walker, 1968). Thus, one problem that officials must consider in any civil disturbance is the reliability of law enforcement personnel. If the sympathies of the policing squads are in doubt, it may be unwise to commit them to action. In the disorders of the 1970s, for example, the government of Lebanon was reluctant to commit its army, even though it was regarded as one of the best in the Middle East.

Persecution as Public Policy. When officials find it convenient to support popular prejudices, they may encourage and even participate in the violence. Victims of massacres and riots often charge such complicity. Since governments are supposed to maintain order, such charges are usually denied; but after some time has passed embarrassing details are disclosed. Although the massacre on Saint Bartholomew's Day in 1572 was a popular slaughter, there is evidence that both the French government and the Catholic church were involved in arranging it (Noguères,

1962). The Ottoman government was involved in the massacre of the Armenians. Once the settlements had been sealed off, many of the assaults were launched and terminated by the sound of a bugle; some of the attacks were initiated by frontier regiments of Kurds or by Turkish soldiers, and popular participation followed. Once the people had been exhorted to retaliate against Armenian nationalists, the army intervened only when Armenian defenses became too effective. Care was also taken to protect foreigners (Nansen, 1976). In the pogroms that began in Kishinev Russian officials, who suspected many Jews of being socialists, did little to discourage the growing frenzy of anti-Semitism. The rioters included soldiers, policemen, civil servants, and priests. The assaults were planned and organized, and communication was maintained among the attacking units by students riding on bicycles. Although some wealthy Jews were able to secure protection for themselves by bribing the police, they could not persuade local authorities to intervene in any other way (Dahlke, 1952).

On some occasions the full power of the government has been used to eliminate an unwanted group. One notorious case is the expulsion of the Moors from Spain in 1609 (Lea, 1901), and the incorporation of anti-Semitism into public policy in Nazi Germany is another. One of the largest massacres in history took place in Indonesia in 1965 after the army put down an attempted insurrection. When it became clear that the plotters were Communists, infuriated Indonesians ran amok. They had endured centuries of Dutch colonial rule, enslavement by the Japanese during World World II, and the long struggle for freedom against both Dutch and British troops. Now they saw their hard-won republic threatened by a revolutionary takeover. The army was immediately purged of Communists, and gangs of Moslem youth burned down the party headquarters in Djakarta. Just how many died in the ensuing turmoil is not known, but an estimated 750,000 Communists, Chinese, and other unpopular people were massacred. Entire villages were wiped out, and corpses packed some rivers like logjams. In some areas the killing was done by mobs backed by military units; in others it was done by the army itself. Thus, in just a few months one of the largest Communist parties in Asia—second in number only to China—was annihilated (Neill, 1973:354–57).

SUMMARY AND DISCUSSION

When rivalries are not settled satisfactorily through politics, opposition is intensified until the participants become polarized into enemy camps. As partisans become increasingly militant, boundaries between the opponents become more clearly defined. As each side becomes convinced it cannot pursue its legitimate interests as long as the opposition remains active, destruction or immobilization of the enemy becomes the overriding objective. People the world over act much alike in conflicts, and a key determinant of their behavior is the manner in which the combatants define themselves and their enemy. Each side interprets its own deeds generously, avowing idealistic values and motives. The enemy is perceived as a diametrically opposed group. Acts performed by the enemy are attributed to meanness, lack of compassion, greed, or cowardice. Since opponents in an intramural conflict are part of a common moral and ecological order, such struggles create special problems of interdependence. They also present serious problems for the government; if it cannot control the violence, its legitimacy may be challenged.

Participants in all conflicts use selective perception and communication to construct monsters in their imagination and then fight gallantly to overcome them. Although sadists have their day, most of the brutality consists of the natural reactions of decent, outraged people united in a crusade to protect their most sacred values against evil. Most people do not fight because they enjoy death and destruction; they fight from moral conviction and from a sense of decency and self-respect.

How human beings behave when they are involved in conflict escapes adequate comprehension because it is so difficult, for the general public and social scientists alike, to avoid taking sides in the discussion of a conflict. Once we identify with one side, even only vicariously, we adopt a partisan perspective and see things in terms of contrast conceptions. One of the most difficult accomplishments for any individual is to stand back and remain dispassionate when personal interests are involved. Dispassionate analysis seems so cold and inhuman; indeed, we tend to condemn people who try to avoid forming contrast conceptions. Jesus called for an appreciation of the position of one's enemy. He was much admired for it, but in the end he was lynched; after all, the people of Judea could have called for the execution of Barabbas.

Yet our value judgments interfere with our comprehension of conflict, for they keep us from distinguishing between political rhetoric and analysis. Sociologists often form contrast conceptions of phenomena of which they personally disapprove: dictatorships, prejudice, crime and delinquency, mental disorders. Our disapproval makes even the formulation of problems difficult; we become preoccupied with ascertaining what is *wrong* with such people and how they became that way instead of simply asking how things happen as they do. Comprehension and effective control require being as dispassionate and realistic as possible, though total objectivity is impossible. To understand what happens in any conflict one must be able to take the roles of all major participants; conflict is a drama in which the cast of characters includes key personnel on both sides. Thus, the comprehension of conflict is rendered difficult by the emotional reactions of social scientists themselves. Calculating politicians and successful generals have succeeded in developing such detachment; perhaps one day sociologists will also learn to stand back, at least temporarily. We need not agree with Saint Augustine that the universe is perfect; nor do we have to refrain from condemning as evil those deeds of which we disapprove. But we need to recognize that what is defined as evil depends on one's perspective.

SUGGESTED READINGS

Chicago Commission on Race Relations. 1922. *The Negro in Chicago.* Chicago: University of Chicago Press.
  An account of the interethnic clash in Chicago in 1919, with an analysis of the social context in which it erupted.
Coser, Lewis A. 1956. *The Functions of Social Conflict.* Glencoe, Ill.: Free Press.
  A restatement of some of Simmel's hypotheses on how the structure of groups is affected by participation in conflict.
Heirich, Max. 1971. *The Spiral of Conflict: Berkeley 1964.* New York: Columbia University Press.
  An analysis of how the confrontation between students and administrators developed in the Free Speech movement in Berkeley in 1964.
Kriesberg, Louis. 1973. *The Sociology of Social Conflicts.* Englewood Cliffs, N.J.: Prentice-Hall.
  A sociological analysis of the manner in which conflicts emerge, develop, escalate to violence, and are terminated.
Pope, Liston. 1942. *Millhands and Preachers: A Study of Gastonia.* New Haven: Yale University Press.
  A description of how various segments of the community became involved in the cotton mill strike in Gastonia, North Carolina, in 1929.
White, Ralph K. 1968. *Nobody Wanted War: Misperception in Vietnam and Other Wars.* New York: Doubleday.
  A study of the sharply contrasting ways in which the struggle in Vietnam was defined by the various parties involved.

XVI

ORGANIZED WARFARE

Warfare is probably as old as humanity. As it has developed over the centuries from tribal confrontations to global conflagrations, the art and technical means of mass homicide have also grown in both potency and complexity. There is now serious talk of bacteriological warfare, of manipulating weather conditions, and even of laser weapons to be used in outer space. Yet with all these transformations the human side of war does not seem to have changed. Whether we read Homer's chronicle of the struggles on the plains of Troy, Tolstoy's novel on the Napoleonic invasion of Russia in 1812, or journalistic accounts of what is happening in the world today, we find the same extremes of nobility and baseness, heroic strength and cringing cowardice, compassionate self-sacrifice and bestial cruelty, obedience unto death and panic flight. We find soldiers struggling to reconcile their sense of honor with their instinct of self-preservation and those at home stoically accepting enormous sacrifices while dreading news of death or injury to their warriors at the front. Over and over the elation of victory is followed by disillusionment. Although modern warfare appears quite different from past struggles, people square off to fight one another in much the same spirit and for much the same stated reasons. Nor can anyone doubt the importance of war in human history; we need only reflect on what the world would be like today had Adolf Hitler won World War II.

War refers to conflicts between communities. Since human beings have identified with one another on the basis of diverse criteria, have lived in a variety of communities, and have fought with so many different kinds of weapons, warfare covers a wide range of phenomena. People have mobilized for combat in many different ways. Given this range of variation, are there regularities in struggles that are mounted between rival communities? How are people and resources organized to fight outsiders? What characteristically happens to the social relationships among people who are mobilized for war? What kinds of tactics are used to enhance or to wear down group solidarity in struggles of attrition? We are concerned neither with the technology of war nor with military strategy, but with the manner in which human beings organize and execute these gigantic enterprises. Our interest centers on modern mass societies, and most of our illustrations are drawn from recent conflicts.

WAR AS A SOCIAL INSTITUTION

Institutionalization of Conflict. Warfare is an old and recurrent practice, and the procedures followed have become established in custom and even formalized into law. Any kind of concerted action can be executed more effectively with organization, and even the struggles between tribal communities are carried on in terms of a complex network of norms (Turney-High, 1971). Furthermore, war enjoys legitimation. The prerogative of each community to remove obstacles to its rightful goals or to protect itself against the encroachment of others is widely recognized and accepted. Preparations for war are made well in advance. In modern times all nations, even those seldom involved in war, maintain expensive establishments of professional soldiers, specialists whose responsibility it is to bear the brunt of the fighting. In time of peace they devote themselves to preparations for combat. Key positions in military organizations are held by the officer corps, who provide the backbone of the bureaucracies, determine their policies, and decide who else is to be recruited during an emergency. In spite of the costliness governments the world over continue to prepare for war, although they recognize that weaponry has become so destructive that perhaps no one will survive a global war.

In modern societies war is a transaction that is defined by a set of conventional and formal norms; the rules of war consist of international agreements that are taken seriously and followed with remarkable consistency. Once the leaders of a community become convinced they cannot attain their goals in other ways, they launch an attack; this is usually accompanied by a formal declaration of war. Once war gets under way, there is a displacement of norms; a different set of rules is activated, and many others are suspended for the duration:

1. Belligerent parties are legally regarded as having juristic equality, even though they may differ markedly in size and strength. In spite of the vast differences between the United States and Vietnam, neutral nations were expected to treat them as equals, and in the peace negotiations the two parties addressed each other as peers. If a civil war is recognized as a war rather than an internal dispute, the two sides also expect outsiders to treat them as equals.
2. Once war is declared, the belligerents may use their armed forces to inflict violence against one another in a manner that would never be tolerated in peacetime.
3. Within each camp contracts with enemies are suspended; resident enemy aliens are placed in a special status; and trading with the enemy is prohibited.
4. All communities not directly involved in the fighting are defined legally as neutral. Even when some of them are more sympathetic to one camp than the other, they are expected at least to maintain the appearance of being impartial. Overt assistance to one side is defined as an unfriendly act and may constitute grounds for attack by the offended camp.

Thus, modern war is defined in law, and this displacement of peacetime norms is terminated only by a formal peace treaty. Although violations occur from time to time, these common understandings provide the framework within which warfare is carried on (Wright, 1942:694–95).

Even when a community is fighting for its very existence, its members try to live up to these expectations. Indirect diplomatic relations are maintained through third parties, even while the slaughter continues on the battlefields. Embassies of neutral nations look after the interests of enemy aliens, facilitate the repatriation of diplomats who were trapped on enemy soil, make possible an exchange of prisoners, and take care of other problems that arise. They may also help to end the conflict when both parties have decided that they have had enough. The legal rights of prisoners of war have been detailed in the Geneva Convention of 1929, and most combatants go to considerable trouble and expense to honor them. Much-needed doctors, nurses, and medicines are withdrawn from the civilian population to treat wounded prisoners. Captured soldiers can sometimes receive mail and gift packages from home through agencies such as the International Red Cross.

Most combatants also abide by restrictions on the use of outlawed weapons — such as poison gas and germ warfare. Amid carnage in which thousands are being massacred, many have wondered what difference there is between humane and inhumane slaughter. Since such arrangements are incongruent with the rhetoric of all-out commitments to destroy the enemy, the whole affair sometimes takes on the appearance of a game. Adherence to these rules is especially noticeable among professional soldiers, and at times confrontations between two well-organized armies resemble a boxing match more than they do a fight to the finish between two infuriated people. This observation led Jonathan Swift to refer to war as "that mad game the world so loves to play."

Once the displacement of norms is terminated by a peace treaty, each side is responsible for living up to its terms and for policing its own forces. Some of the terms may be unpopular, especially among the vanquished; dissidents who are convinced that the fighting should continue are brought under control by their own police and army. An unusual example of the legal responsibilities of modern governments in enforcing peace treaties came immediately after World War II, when the Dutch tried to reimpose colonial rule over Indonesia. When resistance was encountered, the defeated Japanese government was ordered to use its troops to help quell the uprising. Although the new struggle was of no concern to them, Japanese soldiers actually went through the motions of fighting the revolutionaries (Wertheim, 1959:79–81).

Thus, modern warfare consists of concerted action carried on within a normative framework. Much like adversary proceedings in a courtroom, fighting between communities takes place according to well-established rules, even when the participants are in a state of desperation. Just how well these norms are established is revealed by the outrage expressed at deviance. When Japan attacked Pearl Harbor in 1941 while its peace envoys were in Washington, D.C., the assault was seen as a flagrant violation of international law; it provoked so much anger that it united an otherwise divided nation. Whenever charges are made that an illegal weapon has been used, considerable effort is made to have inspections conducted by neutral parties — even in the middle of the fighting.

Rule breaking in international relations is viewed much like deviance within a community. Even if the deviant nation cannot be punished, its reputation is damaged; it is defined as a cynical party that can no longer be trusted. Most professional soldiers, who are more familiar with these rules than others, attempt to enforce them even under difficult circumstances. Even when they cannot, they try to make an outward appearance of compliance. Guerrilla fighters are sometimes unfamiliar with these norms, and their tactics are frequently characterized as uncivilized. Most officials apparently find it expedient to conform, even in situations in which it is costly or humiliating. In the long run compliance is advantageous to all parties, for it does make fighting more predictable and the aftermath more orderly.

Transition from Peace to War. The transition from peace to war is usually gradual; contests between communities with incompatible interests begin long before there is any fighting. The Prussian military strategist and theoretician Karl von Clausewitz writes that "war is nothing but the continuation of politics by other means." Although a declaration of war or an opening attack can be pinpointed in time, the actual starting point of a conflict is difficult to ascertain. When disagreements arise, in most instances the initial step consists of negotiations through diplomatic channels. If diplomacy does not produce the desired results, most nations resort to various tactics of nonviolent coercion and persuasion. Economic sanctions — which may include discrimination against the adversary through exchange controls, multiple rates, tariffs, and quotas — are frequently used. An embargo may be instituted to reduce the rival's war-making capacity, although embargoes are often self-defeating in the long run because they make the opponent more self-sufficient or force it into arrangements with other sources. Trade may be used as a weapon to disrupt markets; purchases may be stopped, and supplies may be refused. A nation may refuse to pay its debts or make loans to a traditional enemy of the foe. Propaganda offensives may also be mounted — usually directed at neutral communities in an effort to gain their sympathy and support. Subversive activities may also be organized in efforts to weaken unfriendly officials and to replace them with others who are likely to be more cooperative.

As tension mounts between rival communities, threats may be exchanged — such as the mobilization of troops, ostentatious maneuvers close to border areas, or belligerent statements by high officials. Sometimes, when war fever develops among the soldiers, border incidents may occur that are not sanctioned by either government. What was intended only as a symbolic threat may result in overt hostilities. In most cases the final move before a formal declaration of war is the severance of diplomatic relations. Thus, the recalling of an ambassador has become a symbolic act to indicate intense displeasure with what another government has done. An ultimatum may be issued. Only when such tactics prove unproductive, however, is serious consideration given to war.

The Decision to Wage War. Most of the participants in a war are swept into it; they rarely have anything to say about whether they wish to become involved. A war does not begin unless some government starts or blunders into it, and the decision to wage war is made by a small number of people in executive positions. Responsibility for such decisions is dictated by the political structure of the community. A monarch may consult a small body of advisors, while in republics a collective decision is reached by a controlling unit of the national bureaucracy. An effort is made to evaluate relative resources. Material resources are usually easy to assess, but the morale of the populace and of the armed forces is more difficult to estimate. Some observers believe that if relative strength could be measured accurately, many conflicts would probably be settled short of physical contests; it is unlikely that responsible leaders would declare war unless they believed they had a good chance of winning.

Although every effort is made at rational calculation, emotional reactions frequently interfere with the judgments of even the most experienced politicians. A study by Janis (1972) of six major foreign policy decisions — two of them effective and four of them fiascos, including the Bay of Pigs invasion — reveals that when the level of collective excitement rises among a closely knit group of decision makers, their deliberations take on some of the characteristics of crowd behavior. The participants avoid challenging weak arguments; they fail to consider alternative courses of action; and they work with stereotyped conceptions of an immoral foe. With the appearance of unanimity critical thinking subsides.

When viewed in retrospect, many decisions to wage war appear foolhardy, sometimes just stupid. Other studies of the policy-making process are disheartening, for they too show that many crucial decisions are made in an atmosphere of confusion and misunderstanding (Stoessinger, 1978). To understand how wars begin one must discern how the decision makers define the situation in which they are involved. They act on the basis of their personal convictions, and the political theories they take seriously play a decisive part. Many wars have been launched by the devout to advance religious interests. Nationalistic ideologies have led to attempts to establish ethnic hegemony, to redress threats to national honor, and to act on the basis of unsound population theories. During the past two centuries many leaders have been convinced that maintaining a balance of power is essential for the survival of their community and have acted on this basis, but historical evidence shows no justification for such a belief (Wright, 1942:743–66). Some Marxist leaders feel honor-bound to do whatever they can to facilitate what they regard as the inevitable transformation of the world into a socialist paradise, just as many who oppose them believe in the domino theory and are prepared to fight anywhere in their own defense. Many wars are waged on the basis of total misconceptions. In the American Civil War, for example, Southern leaders had a caricatured picture of the North; they overreacted to what they saw as the election of a "Black Republican" and overlooked what many of them recognized as their own inferior fighting capacity (Farrell and Smith, 1967). Once leaders become convinced they cannot attain their just interests through political means, they conclude that they must fight to save what is worth living for or to survive.

We must also take into account the position of the decision makers in the internal politics of their own community. Partisan groups, which sometimes place special interests above national concerns, are constantly making demands on them. Personal ties to the munitions industry or to military cliques may enter the picture, although such bonds often consist of shared ideological commitments rather than allegiance to specific lines of action. In some cases the security of their own authority may be at stake; they are concerned with retaining control over the government. When opposition between classes, parties, regions, or ethnic groups becomes intensified, officials may encourage hostility toward an external foe in an effort to unite the community. Some may even start a war to draw attention away from domestic problems. Leaders are sometimes pushed into wars they personally do not favor; when war fever becomes intense, public demands force them to take more militant stands. However, in other cases, ambitious politicians have been restrained by opposition from pacifists and other powerful segments of the public.

Scholars have long sought to ascertain the "causes" of war — objective conditions that always precede such conflicts. Most frequently cited are population pressures, nationalism, changes in the balance of power, economic interests, and chauvinistic ideologies. All such explanations have been examined critically in the light of historical evidence, and Wright (1942) finds countless exceptions to each of them. Even the anticipated exhaustion of natural resources does not necessarily lead to war; some people simply accept their fate. Objective conditions become important considerations in initiating wars only if the decision makers define them as sufficient grounds for fighting. Therefore, we must distinguish among (1) the considerations that enter into a decision to wage war, (2) the rhetoric used to justify the decision to the public, (3) the rationalizations the decision makers use, and (4) the explanations scholars develop afterwards when they try to make some sense of what happened.

MOBILIZATION OF POPULAR SUPPORT

Affirmations of Group Solidarity. Until the development of national states most wars were fought by volunteers and professional soldiers, and the main concern of civilians was to stay out of the paths of the contending armies. Napoleon was among the first to demonstrate the capacity of nations to generate military power by developing popular enthusiasm, which could then be used to reorganize the economy for war and to create large armies by mass conscription. Modern warfare requires the total mobilization of personnel and resources; it has been estimated that if 10 percent of the population is under arms, the remainder is needed to provide the necessary material support (Wright, 1942:305). Thus, modern warfare requires enormous sacrifices by all the people. Civilians are part of the war machines; they supply much of the labor and are essential to maintain the economy. Hence, they may be subjected to bombardment and may suffer many casualties. Since the entire population must be mobilized, government control over communication channels and the economy becomes essential. Mass support for the war effort is mobilized through propaganda and assured through legal and social constraints. Although organizing people may pose logistical problems, in the beginning morale is high. The popular reaction to the outbreak of war is usually one of collective enthusiasm and determination. But maintaining public support and cooperation becomes more difficult when the fighting has continued for some time.

The perception of an external threat tends to unite the people within a community, especially in time of war. With the outbreak of hostilities each camp's boundaries are sharply defined, and the distinctions between the opposing groups are magnified. Each community is unified by its common ideals; its customs, institutions, and values are reaffirmed repeatedly. If the country is old enough to have a history, its military heritage is cited, and heroes of past wars are recalled and venerated. Thus, the first theme of domestic war propaganda is the glorification of the community, which reinforces the idealized self-concepts that have emerged. Group solidarity is augmented by mass meetings and patriotic ceremonies. Families with sons in the armed forces display emblems, and posters appear proclaiming that "we do our part" (Wright, 1942:1012–42). Just as unions are created through strikes, new nations may emerge in struggles against "oppressors"—as in the various wars of national liberation. In such instances a history stressing the achievements of warriors of the ancient past or even legendary characters may have to be invented. As the distinctiveness of the community becomes more clearly defined, consciousness of kind is intensified.

Effective mobilization for war requires a reorganization of the economy and of many other features of the social structure. Many new transactions have to be enacted, and the conventional division of labor must be revised. Furthermore, morale becomes a critical consideration. High morale requires the widespread subordination of personal interests to a common purpose, and everyone is called on to make sacrifices for victory. Internal antagonisms must be suppressed, at least for the time being. In mass societies, characterized by such diverse interests, people must be persuaded that defeat would be catastrophic for everyone. National interests are overriding, and internal quarrels are defined as unpatriotic. Mobilization for war often brings together people who have little in common, and their effective cooperation requires both organization and persuasion. Thus, another theme of domestic propaganda is unity: We are all in this together. Persons of low status are persuaded that their lot would deteriorate even further should the enemy win the war. During World War I European socialists tried to convince the working classes in their respective countries that they had no stake in the conflict, but their calls for worker solidarity fell on deaf ears. During World War II many Afro-Americans wondered whether they had anything to gain through participation. The government instituted some desegregation in the name of national unity and reminded them of the racist policies of Nazi Germany and militarist Japan. Since the enemy posed a threat to all Americans, most Afro-Americans participated willingly, some with great distinction.

Reinforcement of Contrast Conceptions.   Contrast conceptions are reinforced through propaganda. One's own war aims are lofty; this is a war to end all wars or a war to defend human civilization. The enemy blocks the way to a permanent and honorable peace. Thus, a standard theme in domestic propaganda is that the adversary is the antithesis of all community ideals. The foe's brutality is easily established; atrocities are committed, and they are reported with considerable exaggeration. The opponent is the cruel and destructive perpetrator of dark deeds. The enemy mistreats the helpless; special emphasis is placed on injuries to women, children, the elderly, and members of the clergy. The enemy enjoys mutilation. During World War I, when the German army was surprised by Belgian resistance, it was charged that the Belgian *francs-tireurs* were carrying about bucketfuls of eyeballs gouged out of dead German soldiers (Langenhove, 1916). The war is thus a defense against a menacing aggressor. There is no ambiguity about whom the public is to hate; the enemy has a long record of lawlessness, and all the blame is on the other side (Lasswell, 1927:47–101). Those who had been uncertain now find a cause that gives meaning to their lives.

The enemy is an abstract concept, not an object formed through direct experience. It is a stereotyped object constructed through selective communication. With the outbreak of war both sides close ranks, and all enemy communication channels are cut off. The normal processes by which most objects are subject to reality testing are halted; contrast conceptions cannot be tested during a war. All information attributed to enemy sources is dismissed as inaccurate, and there is no possibility of correcting false beliefs. Indeed, another common theme of wartime publicity is that the enemy has an ingenious propaganda machine. Once people can be convinced that the adversary is an efficient propagandist, a powerful barrier is interposed between dangerous news and the concerned public. Difficulties are likely to arise on both sides. Leaders are bound to make mistakes; there will be reverses at the front; some graft and corruption are likely to be exposed; actions taken by allies may leave much to be desired. Such inconvenient news is likely to leak through despite censorship. Once the enemy's prowess in propaganda has been established, however, any inconvenient news can be neutralized by attributing it to the adversary. Unfavorable news is a specimen of cunning enemy propaganda, and everyone must be on the alert against such tricks. It is unpatriotic to repeat such negative items; one is inadvertently serving as an enemy agent (Lasswell, 1927:79–80). Furthermore, even spontaneous interchanges among the people become one-sided. Like any other form of behavior, conversations are subject to group sanctions, and making impartial statements becomes difficult. Those who doubt that the foe is so diabolical must remain silent or choose their company carefully, but those who hate the enemy are free to express themselves as viciously as they please. As all enemy sources are discredited and candid discussions are restricted, correcting contrast conceptions becomes impossible.

The people on both sides therefore become convinced that they are involved in a mass crusade against evil. Since the enemy is the source of all grievances, any sacrifice is worth making in an all-out struggle against a wicked monster. Then the goal of the enterprise is transformed—what had once been a struggle to defend freedom or to attain some more limited objective becomes a crusade for the destruction of unrelieved evil. People often forget what they are fighting for and remember only what they are against. Some may even find themselves enjoying massacres; they define acts of cruelty simply as ways of meting out just punishment to malevolent villains, who are only getting what they deserve. Recruiting people to participate in such a noble undertaking is not difficult; indeed, remaining aloof is difficult for anyone with self-respect. Those who fail to show enthusiasm for the cause are suspected of being unpatriotic. The zealous compete with one another to see who can make the most damaging contribution. Many feel they are not contributing enough; their own sacrifices seem so puny when compared to those of others. Struck by pangs of guilt, some construe themselves as crusaders in a sacred mission dedicating their lives to exterminating the enemy.

Participants in modern wars frequently develop a characteristic orientation. They are convinced of the rectitude of their cause. Since the enemy is unqualifiedly immoral, there is no question of which side is right. It is not uncommon for combatants to claim that God stands with them. They are also convinced of the inevitability of victory. Since they have mobilized to fight against evil, how can they possibly lose? Any defeat is seen as a temporary setback that will in time be avenged (Blumer, 1943). Furthermore, the participants usually work with a utopian vision, a belief that victory will usher in a millennium of peace and happiness. The lyrics of popular songs during the two world wars expressed these hopes. From an analysis of such behavior, Wright (1942:1099–1103) declares that wars are about ideas rather than things, potentialities and hopes rather than actual conditions. Those who hate death and destruction participate willingly in the hope of creating a better world. Wars are waged by people who dream of peace. The utopian vision is also a common theme of wartime propaganda (Lasswell, 1927:102–13). Beliefs such as these provide the basis for group solidarity. A group held together only by custom or fear will fall apart upon encountering serious adversity, but those who conceive of themselves as part of a crusade for sacred values will show tenacity even in disaster. If they are beaten in battle, they will regroup and rededicate themselves to forge ahead with even greater determination.

Emergence of Popular Heroes. Those who are credited with making significant contributions to the war effort become heroes. Klapp (1948) indicates that heroes emerge in dramatic encounters—in situations on which public concern is focused and that are marked by human interest. Heroes emerge in situations filled with uncertainty, when an important issue is unresolved and the outcome is still in doubt. Anyone who contributes conspicuously to a favorable solution in such a suspenseful encounter becomes a delivering hero. Such situations are commonplace in war. A person is recognized for making a decisive contribution to an important cause; a hero is one who actually accomplishes what thousands of others wanted to do. Heroes therefore become the object of people's gratitude and admiration. They are eulogized in songs and showered with gifts; mass meetings and parades are held in their honor. In time of war such individuals are honored over and above traditional leaders, who are simply expected to do their jobs. Thus, the most capable members of each community strive to perform in ways that will bring them such acclaim, and such efforts do in fact contribute substantially to winning a war.

In a mass society most people cannot meet their generals, presidents, or exemplary fighters; hence, they respond not to the actual individuals but to their conceptions of them. Popular heroes in mass societies are necessarily abstract objects constructed through selective perception and communication. Wartime heroes are the embodiment of the values for which the people are fighting; in many cases they are characterized as the type of persons who are needed in that context. Many of these beliefs may be false: heroes' exploits tend to be exaggerated, and all kinds of legends develop about their virtues. Selfish acts pass unnoticed or are explained away, and the most noble motives are attributed to them. Heroes thus become symbols with whom people can identify, an inspiration for others. In some instances special pains are taken to cultivate a certain type of conception; publicists may be hired to release information likely to create the desired impression. Heroes sometimes encounter difficulties in living up to their image; some regard the sacrifices required to maintain their front as part of their contribution to the war effort. At times such persons protest that they do not have the traits attributed to them (Edelman, 1964; Klapp, 1964). Once such personifications are formed, however, they tend to be self-sustaining—at least for the duration of the war.

Sometimes popular heroes become charismatic leaders, and their importance in time of war is widely acknowledged. Charismatic leaders rule by virtue of the extraordinary attributes they are believed to possess. Their influence rests on mass appeal, for people follow them uncritically. At times they have inspired thousands to make an effort that exceeds anything the people themselves thought possible (Weber, 1968:1134–43). Nearly prostrate communities have been rallied by the call for discipline and selfless sacrifice by someone who had caught the public eye—such as Joan of Arc. Winston Churchill's doggedness inspired millions during World War II. All Allied armies needed to confirm the death of Adolf Hitler; they wanted to make certain he would not rise again to lead another campaign against them.

Growth of Popular Despotism. As the tension level rises, transactions in each community assume many of the characteristics of crowd behavior. Critical discussions of war-related issues become increasingly more difficult. Popular fury turns against anyone who dissents, and neutrality becomes impossible. Anyone who is not enthusiastically contributing to the war effort is suspected of harboring sympathies for the enemy. As friends and relatives are killed, hatred of the enemy intensifies. One must not fail to avenge the dead. Hunting for heretics becomes a popular pastime, and citizen groups take it upon themselves to expose those suspected of treason. Anyone not caught up in the war spirit—profiteers, black marketeers, draft dodgers—is uncovered and denounced. Those who do not feel enthusiasm must pretend that they do; the appearance of unanimity arises; and conformity is enforced by popular despotism (Wright, 1942:103–17).

The harassment of dissidents sometimes becomes so insistent that government intervention becomes necessary to prevent disruptions that would impede the war effort. Conscientious objectors frequently become targets of criticism. Even when their religious principles are clearly established, others still become angry at the "slackers" who refuse to carry their share of the load. Enemy aliens are placed in an especially difficult position and often must make ostentatious contributions to avoid persecution. The mass hysteria that developed on the Pacific Coast during the spring of 1942 had much to do with the internment of all persons of Japanese ancestry in relocation centers. Although very little violence took place, some authorities feared that serious uprisings might develop (ten Broek et. al., 1954). In similar situations in other wars massacres have occurred.

Thus, during the early phases of war collective enthusiasm develops, and most participants are swept along to contribute whatever they can toward victory. No one wants to be left out, and ablebodied young people volunteer for military duty without much prodding. Men not qualified for military service often become apologetic; they feel ashamed of their civilian status and sometimes petition the government for special tasks. Those who cannot fight are recruited for civil defense work—even in situations in which there is actually little for them to do. Women are urged to work in factories, to help in hospitals, to volunteer for work in canteens, and to write letters to lonely soldiers. Such symbolic acts give them a sense of being part of the noble enterprise. Some opponents of war have expressed shock that the greatest minds in history—such as Leonardo da Vinci and Albert Einstein—have contributed willingly. Corporation executives, engineers, composers, playwrights, artists, scientists—almost everyone contributes; most people regret that they cannot do more. Those making the greatest sacrifices are praised and given preferential treatment; mothers who have several offspring in the military are honored, and widows are decorated with their spouses' posthumous awards. All these activities reinforce self-concepts. Combatants believe that, if they must die, they will be remembered for the sacrifice they made in a moment of communal need. All self-respecting citizens do what they can to partake in the moral crusade.

MILITARY ORGANIZATIONS AND CAREERS

Changing technology creates new patterns of combat, which in turn alter the categories of people involved in the fighting as well as the manner in which they are organized. Tribal warfare entailed little specialization; all ablebodied young men were expected to participate, and gifted fighters were given special responsibilities. As combat techniques became more complicated, specialization developed and the profession of arms evolved. During the days of the republic, Roman legions were composed of citizen soldiers; in the Roman Empire, however, the armies consisted largely of mercenaries. Toward the end they were more like foreign legions, for few Romans could be recruited to do such dangerous work. During the Renaissance, European wars were fought by armies of mercenaries led by aristocrats, but in the seventeenth century military units began to be nationalized.

Since the French Revolution, military organizations have become larger, and mass armies once again consist of citizen soldiers—civilians serving their community temporarily in a different capacity. Most officers, however, are professional soldiers—part of a permanent establishment. Modern military technology has become so intricate that large numbers of engineers and scientists are also needed. As the scale of combat grows, logistic problems are compounded, and more support troops are needed for each front-line fighter. Thus, a large bureaucracy is needed to move combat troops to where they are needed and to maintain their fighting effectiveness. Weber (1968:980–82) observes that the bureaucratization of the armed forces has grown as the burden of fighting has shifted from members of the propertied classes to impecunious strangers. The core of the armed forces of all nations today consists of specialists, and career officers must develop the same kinds of administrative skills as civilian bureaucrats.

Autocratic Control and Discipline. Weapons are tools, and more lethal weapons are constantly being developed. However, the art of managing the people who deploy the weapons has remained much the same. Military bureaucracies are much like those in any formal organization. Since the goal of military organizations is victory in battle, however, they have one distinctive feature: despotic authority. Hierarchy of command and absolute discipline are found in virtually all combat organizations. Orders are passed down through an unambiguous line of command, and unquestioning obedience is expected. Only the details of local implementation are left to the discretion of those receiving the orders. After the Russian Revolution the Communists introduced political advisors into military units, but such division of authority has been found to be cumbersome.

As military units become more bureaucratized, the individual entrepreneurship that played such an important part in earlier wars has been largely replaced by staff work and group decisions. The principle of autocratic control, however, has been retained. Since this is the source of so much frustration, many have wondered if unquestioning compliance is necessary. The rationale is simple: Efficient coordination maximizes the chances of victory. Unless each soldier's contribution dovetails into those of his comrades, the transaction flounders. Effort must be concentrated; waste, duplication, and contradiction must be kept to a minimum. Emergencies arise constantly in battle, for the enemy moves in unexpected ways. Decisions must be made and implemented immediately. There is no time for discussions or arguments. Those who are assigned to diversionary or decoy maneuvers must do their part—without lengthy explanations of how their moves fit into a larger strategy. No formal arrangement can guarantee effective coordination in combat, but autocratic control has been found to be the most effective way of integrating the contributions of diverse units. The key is efficiency. A pragmatic criterion prevails, for the losers frequently do not survive.

Some of the requirements of modern warfare clash with the need for autocratic control. Recent technology—especially the development of missiles with nuclear warheads—requires that the weapons deployment team includes scientists, who are often difficult to integrate into military organizations. Highly trained civilians must often be inducted and given high rank; but despite their new uniforms, many of them do not think as soldiers. Thus, the isolation of military organizations is being undermined, and professional soldiers are in some danger of losing control. In modern wars many situations arise in which success depends on the initiative of individuals operating in small units. Thus, entrepreneurship on the part of individual fighters is once again becoming essential in some contexts. Highly technical work often requires the willing cooperation of educated personnel, and especially in the United States persuasion and explanation are replacing blind obedience (Janowitz, 1959). Here again, maintaining high morale is increasingly important.

Professionalization of the Military. As weapons become so complicated that recruits cannot be trained quickly to use them, skilled personnel must be retained in permanent organizations. In medieval Europe the nobility became crystallized into a warrior estate, a privileged status transmitted to descendents. The ideal of the profession of arms was the knight, who lived by a code of chivalry — to protect women, the weak, and the poor and to defend religion. A man could not be "dubbed" until he had met stringent qualifications. Knights conceived of themselves as belonging to an esteemed category, and most of them apparently took their responsibilities seriously. The samurai in feudal Japan also constituted an honored category; they too cultivated a life-style that included a strict code of honor. Nineteenth-century Prussia took the lead in developing an officers corps by establishing a special war college. Officers had to meet high educational standards and were advanced primarily on the basis of ability and achievement rather than their civilian status. In recent times the prestige of the profession of arms has markedly declined; in some circles professional soldiers are mocked as an anachronism. Nonetheless, the core of modern armies still consists of career officers — commissioned and noncommissioned — who are augmented by citizen soldiers in time of war. As complex technology lengthens the period of training required, however, the vocation of arms may regain an enhanced status.

Career soldiers devote most of their adult lives to cultivating technical expertise in the practice of violence. Contacts with civilians are limited, and their most significant associations are with their comrades. Like the police, military organizations tend to become isolated from the rest of the community. To the extent that professional soldiers partake in their own communication channels, they develop a distinct culture through differential association. Officers learn the rules of warfare, the traditions of their calling, the standard strategies and tactics, and the latest procedures for combat. They set and maintain professional standards of performance. Soldiers are trained to fight in the proper and honorable way. To the uninitiated, some of the rules may seem more appropriate to polite strategic games than to life-and-death combat. In medieval Europe, for example, a knight was honor-bound not to kill another knight except under circumstances in which the foe had a fair chance to defend himself. Sometimes combat was halted to enable civilians to gather the harvest, since they were regarded as independent of the fighting. Similarly, during the bloody feud between the Uesugi and Takeda clans in feudal Japan, fighting was interrupted annually by a truce to enable one camp to replenish its salt supply from the other. That such exemplary tales are repeated discloses something of the aristocratic origins of the profession; fighting was once viewed as an honorable way of life for cultivated gentlemen. To many victory with dishonor was worse than defeat. Professional soldiers have long performed for a reference group of their peers and have judged themselves and one another in terms of their own standards and ideals. Kornhauser (1959) argues that in mass societies values once cultivated by elite groups tend to become attentuated as personnel are recruited from lower strata; this has certainly been true of the military.

Professional soldiers, far more than civilian recruits, are conscious of the rules of warfare. Soldiers in different countries have similar perspectives. The generals are familiar with one another's theories, just as physicists the world over are part of a common universe of discourse. A body of scholarly literature has developed on strategy and tactics. Professional soldiers the world over can understand one another, for they face similar problems in dealing with politicians and public opinion as well as adapting constantly to the changing technology of combat. They often have more in common with one another than they do with the civilians in their respective communities. Since they perform in terms of similar norms, they prefer to fight one another than to deal with guerrillas. Guerrilla fighters are less predictable, for many irregulars do not know the conventional expectations. They violate the basic canons of military tactics, sometimes doing things that professional soldiers would regard as suicidal. Thus, they sometimes catch well-trained troops completely off guard. Since 512 B.C.., when the Scythian guerrillas surprised Darius's army, generals have faced difficulties in adapting to guerrilla tactics. British soldiers complained in 1776 that the American minutemen did not fight fairly—the same complaint American troops made against the Viet Cong. Furthermore, guerrilla troops do not follow the conventions for surrender. When a professional army is defeated, it executes a ceremony of surrender; the officers on both sides then assume responsibility for enforcing the terms of the peace treaty. But guerrillas fight and disappear, leaving it unclear whether they have been defeated or have just retired to fight again under more favorable circumstances.

The perspective of professional soldiers differs from that of the civilians whom they serve, and such differences lead to misunderstandings. Those committed to the vocation, officers in particular, pursue careers within their own social world; they devote their lives to moving up the hierarchy of command, and their interests do not always coincide with the policies laid down by civilian authorities. Since promotions come faster in time of war, career officers view warfare as an opportunity to enhance their status within their own reference group. Clashes also arise concerning the basis for advancement. Like other professionals, military personnel want promotions based on ability and accomplishment; they insist that competent performance be judged by professional standards established and applied by persons with military expertise. When civilian governments impose ethnic or religious quotas or insist on the advancement of those with appropriate ideological commitments or family connections, career military personnel view such demands as intrusions that undermine the organization. Since careers are sometimes truncated by technological innovations that undercut specialized modes of combat, powerful cliques of officers at various times have opposed the introduction of tanks, airplanes, aircraft carriers, missiles, and atomic submarines. These officers' professional devotion to their areas of specialization interfered with their ability to perceive the advantages of the innovation.

Another critical difference between military professionals and civilians is that in time of war career officers are less likely to share the contrast conceptions held by the general public. Many officers have traveled abroad, and some may even be acquainted with the officers against whom they are fighting. They have also performed under stress and realize how hatred distorts perception. They not only scorn mob psychology but also recognize the dangers of belittling and underestimating the enemy. Thus, when civilian leaders make gross errors in estimating the foe's intentions and integrity, career officers may feel they are being exposed to unnecessary risks. Arguments also arise concerning what actions are essential for national defense. Officers must define for the civilian authorities the requirements of military security, explain the implications of various policies, and implement military decisions. Soldiers often want more autonomy; they want more equipment and funds and more control over necessary resources — something civilians are bound to resist. Soldiers often have difficulty understanding the reasoning of the civilian leadership, which sometimes ignores what they regard as essential. Sometimes military leaders conclude that the civilian authorities are unpatriotic or irresponsible. In turn they may be condemned for their military mentality.

Military Intervention in Politics. Since an organized group of trained fighters is an instrument of coercion, relations between military organizations and the rest of the community must be regulated. In modern times the principle of civilian control over military units has received at least lip service among professional soldiers. The armed forces are supposed to serve faithfully any lawful regime, regardless of its political ideology. Some consider this as part of the military code of honor, but commitment to this principle has varied considerably. Several kinds of relationships have developed between military leaders and civilian officials. Some have worked together in pursuit of national objectives; others have operated largely in isolation; more often, individual politicians and generals of like mind have formed separate cliques, each pursuing somewhat different policies. Since military organizations are an integral part of the established political order, they usually support it. The relationship of the armed forces to the civilian community becomes especially sensitive when intervention in domestic affairs becomes necessary. When civilian officials are unable to maintain order, martial law is declared. Thus, in 1957 President Eisenhower ordered paratroopers into Little Rock, Arkansas, to quell a riot and enforce federal orders to desegregate the schools. In many other crises the support of the armed forces has been decisive in settling domestic quarrels.

Military leaders who have cultivated personal followings have sometimes seized control of the government and have ruled as dictators. During the second century B.C., popular discontent arose in Rome when a war in North Africa was prolonged. When it became known that Roman generals were being bribed by the enemy, outrage over such corruption led to the election of Marius as consul. He won several quick victories and became a popular hero. His army was not the product of traditional conscription; he had recruited and trained the men himself. Despite a rule that no consul could succeed himself, Marius held six successive consulships, and the Roman senate became impotent. After that, other popular generals recruited armies of discontented men and won their loyalty with promises of booty and land; a succession of them—Sulla, Caesar, Pompey—fought over the control of Rome.

Similar patterns of military participation in domestic affairs have persisted into modern times. Military leaders—viewing themselves as servants of the community rather than of a particular government—have sometimes seized power when they regarded civilian officials as corrupt. On some occasions military leaders have thought their country was facing acute danger and have seized control to defend it. Sometimes military control has been a temporary arrangement until a civilian government more acceptable to the generals has been instituted. On other occasions the military has operated behind the scene, with a junta ruling behind civilian puppets. In such instances the army has been used to manipulate or delay elections, to intimidate dissidents, or to arrest or assassinate opponents.

At times a populace has demanded military leadership. Widespread

popular calls for military rule have been initiated in response to prolonged periods of anarchy or oligarchy, when political factions have
become bogged down in endless squabbles in the face of a major crisis, or
when the competence or decisiveness of the civil government has been in
question (Finer, 1962). In the twentieth century military dictatorships
have become commonplace, especially in the developing nations, where
the armed forces have been the most ardent supporters of modernization.
Although many coups d'etat have consisted simply of one clique of rulers
replacing another, in recent times some military leaders have shown
more concern for the plight of the underprivileged than the civilians they
have displaced. Colonel Nasser's revolt in Egypt in 1952 was followed by
sincere efforts at social reform. In 1968 the generals who seized control of
Peru nationalized the holdings of Standard Oil; they also seized the large
sugar cane plantations and announced plans to have them run as cooper-
atives by the workers. Although their program failed and they were soon
overthrown by other generals, one of their objectives was reform. The
coup d'etat in Portugal in 1974 was also led by military leaders who
subsequently turned over the government to civilians intent on social
transformation. Although military governments can enforce regulations
more effectively, they face the same problems as civilian governments.
Unless they can meet the needs of the populace, they are likely to be
challenged.

Some military organizations have succeeded in promulgating their
values as a national ideology. The glorification of war is a recurrent theme
in world history. Even philosophers who disapprove of militarism have
conceded that war serves as a purgative. In ancient Rome idleness was
viewed as a source of corruption, and war was justified as a way of
keeping young men active. Sustained peace leads to an emphasis on
self-interest; men seek riches, forget honor, and tend to become cowardly
and weak. Militarism extols warfare as an ennobling experience in which
courage, honor, unity, and discipline are reaffirmed. The armed forces
gain primacy in such states, and warriors enjoy a privileged status. Recent
examples of militarism include Germany from the latter part of World
War I and Japan from about 1930; both were crushed in 1945.

In most instances the composition of the professional military reflects
the social stratification of the community. In a class society officers are
drawn from the upper classes; indeed, military careers may provide one
of the respectable vocations for more active members of privileged categories. But in communities where social mobility is possible, the successful may seek careers elsewhere, and members of less privileged ranks
may become officers. In Communist countries the armed forces are per-

vaded by party members; in some instances there is even an independent hierarchy of political officers. Nations that are ethnically divided sometimes exclude some groups from military service. In the Republic of South Africa, for example, the armed forces consist largely of people of European ancestry. In the United States, in contrast, a disproportionate share of the enlisted personnel is drawn from ethnic minorities, who find in military service a route to upward mobility. Minority soldiers, in particular, may face personal conflicts should they be called upon to intervene in domestic ethnic disorders.

THE STRUGGLE FOR COLLECTIVE MORALE

Morale and Psychological Warfare. When the balance of power between adversaries is about even, wars become drawn-out struggles of attrition, and the outcome often depends on communal morale. Morale —the degree of effectiveness with which the agreed-on objectives of an enterprise are pursued—plays an important part in any social transaction, but it is critical in any contest and often decisive in war. Steadfastness of intention is the essence of high morale. In most contexts it is manifested in style of execution, in the efficient and enthusiastic manner in which things are done. In times of intense stress, however, it is also manifested in the determination to persist, even in the face of death. After a war has continued for some time, the initial enthusiasm wanes, and civilians must face the grim realities of making costly sacrifices. Each individual knows of people who have been killed, maimed, and orphaned; so much property is destroyed. Those not subjected to direct bombardment must put up with inconveniences and shortages. High morale is also essential to the effectiveness of military units. During World War II the Chinese nationalist army was trained and equipped largely by the United States; although it was among the largest and best-armed military organizations in Asia, it could withstand neither the Japanese nor the Chinese Communists. The same was true of the South Vietnamese army. Since morale cannot be explained in terms of personnel or material resources, attention must turn to the expressive component of agonistic transactions.

In the last analysis high morale rests on the loyalty on the individual participants and their willingness to make selfless sacrifices for the common good. It depends on their definition of the situation. To the extent that the participants retain their conviction of being involved in a noble undertaking, morale remains high. Therefore, various techniques of psychological warfare have been developed to manipulate relevant beliefs. Modern psychological warfare has been directed at several targets: neutral communities, enemy civilians, enemy troops in specific operations, and sometimes even at enemy decision makers. The objective is to gain military advantages without committing troops, although in some operations force has been used in conjunction with propaganda offensives. Many of the tactics employed are old. In recent wars, however, more sophisticated and complicated procedures have been developed. As their utility receives increasing recognition, specialists in propaganda are becoming an integral part of military organizations (Daugherty and Janowitz, 1960).

Operations Against Civilian Targets. Civilian morale is of critical importance in modern warfare. In 1918, for example, the German armies were still intact, but the collapse of the home front hastened defeat. Civilians are subjected to bombardment, starvation, terror, and propaganda. The major obstacle faced by specialists in psychological warfare is that any information attributed to enemy sources is immediately discredited; the task is to disseminate messages that will be taken seriously. Formal communication channels may be used, but with the knowledge that they will be regarded as vehicles of propaganda. During World War II, for example, radio broadcasts were transmitted regularly to enemy territories. The Lord Haw Haw programs that the Germans beamed into England as well as the Tokyo Rose programs for American troops in the Pacific became quite popular, but they were clearly labeled as enemy propaganda. Popular commentators often build up a following of listeners who enjoy arguing back against them.

Similarly, propaganda leaflets dropped from planes are usually treated with disdain and suspicion. But children are assumed to have few such suspicions, and novelty items are dropped for them in hopes that they will show the items to their parents, an activity intended to demoralize — rather than persuade — the adults. Gifts such as soap, salt, needles, matches, and chocolates have also been dropped as reminders of the propagandist's affluence and strength. Other items include handbooks for malingerers — containing instructions on how to avoid conscription by faking tuberculosis, heart trouble, and other illnesses. Flooding an area with counterfeit money, ration cards, and blank identity cards may also create inconveniences. There is no evidence, however, that such tactics have been effective — except among people who are already disenchanted with the war.

Special techniques have been developed to overcome the automatic rejection of all enemy channels. The objective of what is called black propaganda is to create the impression that the messages are emanating from within the target community itself. Several radio programs aired during World War II were of this nature. "Gustav Siegfried Eins," a British news program beamed into Germany, claimed to speak for a German military faction opposed to the Nazi regime; it was both anti-British and anti-Hitler. The American Office of Strategic Services (OSS) developed a similar program, which pretended to be produced by dissidents broadcasting from a mobile station within Germany. After some time, when allied spies reported that many Germans were becoming skeptical of the possibility of anyone broadcasting for so long without being caught, a final program was staged in which the announcer was killed in a Gestapo raid — to lend credibility to what had been presented. The OSS also produced its own newspapers. The writers imitated the style of German journalists, included items ordinarily found in German newspapers, and added only a few embarrassing articles. The papers were then taken to a city disposal area and burned to create the impression that they had been confiscated by the Gestapo. The OSS hoped that anyone who found the remnants would believe that the newspapers had been published in Germany (H. Becker, 1949). Since acceptance of any message depends on its plausibility to the perceiver, such tactics are difficult to execute. They require accurate intelligence, and propagandists must be able to assess accurately the concerns and suspicions of those in the target audience. Efforts to evaluate the effectiveness of such operations have been inconclusive.

Since each camp is a coalition of factions, propagandists make a deliberate effort to exploit old enmities. Those who have a long history of mutual antagonism are reminded constantly of their old suspicions. To counter such tactics, one common theme in domestic propaganda is to warn the populace against enemy efforts to divide and conquer. Like other propaganda, efforts to instigate factional strife are not likely to be effective unless the target group is becoming demoralized. Those fostering internal hostilities are condemned as unpatriotic.

The calculated application of terror to manipulate perspectives is an old stratagem still in use. One common technique is the deliberate intimidation of civilians in an effort to facilitate military operations. When Genghis Khan swept through central Asia and part of Europe during the early thirteenth century, he did not have enough manpower to conquer by force alone; he relied on accurate intelligence, strategy, and propaganda. To frighten his enemies he sent ahead agents to spread rumors exaggerating the huge numbers, stupidity, and ferocity of his horsemen. Whenever enemy spies appeared, they were fed similar reports. His "numberless hordes" actually consisted of small, mobile cavalry units (Linebarger, 1948:14–16).

During the religious wars in seventeenth-century England, Oliver Cromwell was confronted by a difficult problem. Ireland was still not pacified, and a large army was advancing against him from the south. Since he did not have enough manpower to fight two enemies simultaneously, he deliberately slaughtered the people in two Irish villages, taking care to allow substantial numbers to escape. As he had anticipated, the refugees gave such exaggerated accounts of the massacres that the rest of Ireland became immobilized with fear. This enabled him to concentrate on the threat from the south (Edwards, 1927:177–79).

During World War II incendiary bombs were dropped on civilian centers in an effort to destroy morale. In 1945, leaflets were dropped on Japanese cities that had not yet been bombed warning the people that at least four of the twelve areas named would be destroyed. Then six of the cities were actually bombed. Many Japanese did leave their homes, which disrupted the economy and interfered with the movement of troops and supplies. A postwar study by the U.S. Strategic Bombing Survey (1946) discloses that about 60 percent of those interviewed had either seen the leaflets or had heard of the warnings. There was no evidence, however, that these tactics lowered morale.

Operations Against Military Targets. Reducing the combat effectiveness of troops is far more difficult than undermining civilian morale. As long as the fighting is going reasonably well, maintaining high morale among soldiers is not a serious problem. Although civilians and publicists glorify combat, the prevailing mood among those on the battlefield is intense fear. The men are preoccupied with survival and realize that efficient performance and coordination maximize their personal safety. The orientation of combat troops is pragmatic; anything that does not take into account the harsh realities of the situation is dismissed as hypocrisy. In any primary group high morale rests on informal norms, and studies conducted during World War II indicate that this is true of military organizations. Shils and Janowitz (1948) discovered that high morale in the German army did not rest on commitment to Nazi ideology but on the soldiers' personal ties to one another. As long as their primary groups remained intact, the men fought well, even in the face of great adversity. When the Germans broke through Allied lines during the Battle of the Bulge, many Americans were separated from their units. Since every available infantryman was needed to stem the tide, stragglers were reassembled and committed to battle. Marshall (1947:150–53) found that these combat veterans could be counted on to fight effectively only when in the company of others whom they knew personally; in such dangerous contexts the men did not trust strangers.

All armies are made up of overlapping primary groups, and what counts is how soldiers in sustained association define the situations in which they are involved. As long as they retain their conviction that the fighting is worthwhile, they continue to live up to the expectations they impute to their comrades. As Ardant du Picq (1921:110) writes: "Four brave men who do not know each other well will not dare to attack a lion. Four less brave men, but knowing each other well, sure of their reliability and consequently of mutual aid, will attack resolutely. There is the science of the organization of armies in a nutshell." A soldier's primary group is the only setting in which he or she can be identified as a specific individual. In such contexts most soldiers prefer risking death to being regarded as cowards. Even in the face of intense fear most soldiers fight to maintain their self-respect among those whom they view with affection and respect.

When troops are demoralized, however, many begin to question what they had previously taken for granted. If continued reverses lead soldiers to recognize that their situation is hopeless, faith in the inevitability of victory is shaken. Even then they will continue fighting as long as they feel that their cause is just. Revelations of their own shortcomings, however, may lead to reappraisals. Disclosures of corruption among their leaders, for example, raise doubts over whether the unit is actually fighting for its announced objectives or merely being used to further someone else's interests.

As demoralization sets in, utopian visions come to be regarded as myths. Soldiers begin to question whether the sacrifices asked of them are worthwhile. In such contexts factionalism is commonplace, and each clique begins to question the motives and sincerity of the others. Mutual trust dissolves, and considerable effort is devoted to watching one another to see that each segment is contributing its full share. Wholehearted concentration on the fighting itself becomes more difficult. With dissension comes individualism, and personal interests gradually displace collective aims as the basis for making decisions. Prewar intramural conflicts — between class, ethnic, or religious categories — may be rekindled. Suspicions against other factions may even supersede hatred of the enemy; the enemy is an abstract object, but rivals within the unit are real. Thus, primary group definitions no longer support the organizational goals (Moskos, 1975; Lang, 1980). Contrast conceptions then become attenuated. The soldiers question their idealized self-concepts and begin to doubt that they are as noble as they had been led to believe. When morale is high, enemy propaganda is treated as a joke, but as troops become demoralized, they become more susceptible to appeals from enemy sources.

Psychological warfare operations directed against soldiers who are confused, battle weary, and demoralized may be effective — especially when leaflets providing explicit instructions on how to surrender are distributed among those who are seriously contemplating surrender. During the latter phases of the liberation of France in 1945, studies show that about 90 percent of the Germans taken prisoner had either seen such leaflets or were familiar with their contents. In the Pacific theater similar messages were provided to Japanese soldiers who had been surrounded. Specialists in such operations have urged that care be exercised not to encourage desertion and to emphasize capture rather than surrender. An effort is made to show the hopelessness of the situation in terms enemy soldiers can comprehend, to guarantee decent treatment, and to provide instructions that minimize the chances of their being killed through some misunderstanding (Herz, 1958). Messages addressed to enemy soldiers, who once conceived of themselves as participating in a moral crusade, are worded so as not to threaten their pride or self-respect.

Psychological warfare operations have also been directed at enemy decision makers, usually in coordination with other tactics. One such campaign was launched in 1944, when Allied armies stationed in England were preparing for the invasion of Europe. It was known that the Germans still had about five thousand fighter planes, half of them stationed in the west. Since the invasion could not be attempted without control of the air, the Allies wanted first to destroy as many German fighters as possible. The German high command, however, was reluctant to commit the few remaining planes to aerial combat with Allied bombers. Hence, a propaganda offensive was directed at German civilians and soldiers. A simple question was repeated over and over through many channels: Where is the Luftwaffe? Before long, Germans began asking the same question. Civilians subjected to daily bombings were angry that so many enemy planes could fly over Germany without being challenged. When they wrote to soldiers at the front, serious morale problems developed; the men became upset that their families were not being protected against daylight bombing raids. Finally, the Luftwaffe was ordered out. Although the fighter planes shot down many Allied bombers, they were vastly outnumbered. In April alone about thirteen hundred German fighters were destroyed. By D-Day — June 6, 1944 — control over the air had been secured (Carroll, 1958). When the Allied armies landed in Normandy, they encountered fierce resistance and were barely able to secure the beachhead. Had the Germans been able to put two thousand fighter planes into the air, the outcome might have been different. But the actual results of any such propaganda offensive are generally difficult to assess.

Transition from War to Peace. As Simmel (1955:109–23) points out, the transition from war to peace is more difficult to pinpoint than the outbreak of hostilities. The final phases of a war are often drawn out and costly to both sides. In most instances there is a period of deescalation with considerable demoralization, even on the victorious side. The participants become acutely conscious of their losses and wonder if anything is worth the enormous devastation. The coalitions that had made up each camp begin to fall apart, and some begin to wonder if they had been used by some of their domestic rivals. Especially on the losing side increasing numbers begin to pay more attention to enemy sources; they raise serious questions about their war aims and about the integrity of their leaders. Absenteeism, insubordination, black market activities, and civil disorders become more commonplace. Such dislocations make both the prosecution of the war and a clear-cut termination more difficult.

Peace is a reciprocal arrangement; it can occur only when the vanquished agree to submit. Losers will admit defeat only when they agree among themselves that their situation has so deteriorated that continuation is worse than the enemy peace terms. In most cases some kind of truce in the fighting is negotiated, and in time a peace treaty is signed — symbolic acts that make it clear to all parties that overt hostilities have been terminated. If both armies remain intact and disciplined, a clear-cut termination of the war can be accomplished. But sometimes there is no consensus or discipline on the losing side. The losing government may not be able to control its own populace, and some of its military units may refuse to surrender. Some factions may refuse to accept the peace terms, accusing their leaders of having betrayed them. Although most wars stop short of annihilation of the enemy, as long as irregulars continue to resist, the victorious army may have no alternative to pursuing total destruction. The difficulties that sometimes arise in terminating hostilities suggest why war remains a well-established social institution; the common understandings concerning the displacement of norms do facilitate adaptation to the new situation (Coser, 1961).

Once the war is over, the losers are naturally dejected. They have worked so hard and sacrificed so much, but they are worse off than they had been before the fighting started. But the victors are also disillusioned, for they had struggled in the hopes of attaining a utopian vision. Not long after the victory celebration, many begin to realize that their situation is not going to change as they had anticipated. Furthermore, unity breaks down; a community that had been held together by a common foe tends to fall apart once the enemy has been defeated. Many of the prewar problems reemerge, and even the victors begin to question all the costly sacrifices. It is not strange, therefore, that wars are widely condemned as a pathological aberration.

SUMMARY AND DISCUSSION

War may be regarded as the type of collective adaptation that develops when members of one community become convinced that another community is blocking their legitimate interests. When the leaders believe they can no longer attain communal goals through political means, they institute highly organized procedures for fighting. Their definition of the situation is decisive. As the preamble to the constitution of UNESCO states, "Since wars begin in the minds of men, it is in the minds of men that the defenses of peace must be constructed." Since contrast conceptions are well established by the time quarrels reach the brink of war, personnel and resources are mobilized with relative ease. Through selective communication definitions that support the war prevail, and the fighting usually begins with great enthusiasm. Most people on each side believe they are participating in a moral crusade against evil. Modern wars are fought by specialists in arms, reinforced by citizens recruited for the duration of the emergency. Career soldiers perform for a reference group of fellow professionals, and civilians frequently misunderstand their efforts. Only after considerable bloodletting do serious doubts arise concerning the convictions underlying the conflict. After the fighting is over, in most instances the survivors on both sides are disillusioned.

People of goodwill have long condemned warfare and sought ways to abolish it. Many have concluded with regret that wars are inevitable — like disease and tragedy an unavoidable part of the human condition. Many have been especially puzzled by the fact that some of the most selfless and courageous human acts take place in time of war. Furthermore, some of the most efficient coordination in transactions is achieved in war. In his famous essay "The Moral Equivalent of War," William James suggests that the same spirit be applied in efforts to resolve other problems facing humanity. But the noble sacrifices become less puzzling when we engage in role-taking—of the participants on *both* sides. As long as people define participation in war as a moral crusade, their sense of honor and self-respect requires them to contribute their share. Civilians and soldiers alike contribute whatever they can for the good of the community. Although partisans define war as a struggle between right and wrong, once we stand back to examine the transaction as a whole, we can see that it is essentially a contest between right and right. This is what makes war such a tragedy. As long as nations—or any other type of community—retain their sovereignty, the state of anarchy in international relations will persist. Human beings are unlikely to surrender easily their right to protect their most cherished values.

SUGGESTED READINGS

Bramson, Leon, and George W. Goethals (eds.). *War: Studies from Psychology, Sociology, Anthropology.* New York: Basic Books.
An anthology of the writings of various behavioral scientists on war, including several classic pieces.
Janowitz, Morris. 1960. *The Professional Soldier.* New York: Free Press.
The social organization of the profession of arms, typical problems that arise, and the development of various career lines in this context.
Lang, Kurt. 1972. *Military Institutions and the Sociology of War.* Beverly Hills, Calif.: Sage.
An extensive annotated bibliography of references relevant to the development of a sociological analysis of war.
Marshall, S. L. A. 1947. *Men Against Fire.* New York: William Morrow.
An insightful account by a military historian of the behavior of American combat troops in World War II.
Moskos, Charles C. 1970. *The American Enlisted Man.* New York: Russell Sage.
The social organization and culture of enlisted men in the U.S. armed forces, including an account of combat troops in Vietnam.
Wright, Quincy. 1964. *A Study of War.* Chicago: University of Chicago Press.
An abridgment of the 1942 classic, one of the most comprehensive investigations of war ever conducted.

XVII

INSURRECTIONS

In modern times discontented people throughout the world have looked upon revolution as an effective way of resolving the numerous problems besetting their communities. Many, however, have a highly romanticized conception of such uprisings, drawn from selective accounts of a handful of successful insurrections—notably France in 1789, Russia in 1917, and China in 1949. They regard revolutions as popular uprisings in which the oppressed overthrow their oppressors. Displacement of the decadent rulers then leads to the formation of a new society in which everyone lives thereafter with security, justice, and perhaps freedom. Since the privileged are not likely to give up their advantages without a struggle, violence is seen as a necessary but small price to pay for such grand achievements. The "people" are seen as led by dedicated partisans, many of whom must renounce their class interests to fight for the welfare of everyone.

This idealized view of revolution has hindered many social scientists in their study of the phenomenon, for it has restricted their investigations to a limited number of cases. Some have used concepts and generalizations drawn from the political rhetoric of particular movements, and their interpretations have sometimes become quite strained. Embarrassing questions have arisen. Was the Meiji uprising in Japan in 1868 really a revolution if so few ordinary people participated? Why did the successful revolt in Mexico in 1910 result in so little reform? Was the Nazi movement in Germany a revolution? The romanticized conception of revolution has buttressed the hopes of the forlorn, but it has interfered with a realistic analysis of insurrections (Hermassi, 1975; Eisenstadt, 1978).

An *insurrection* is a concerted effort to overthrow the government, made by its people, who are convinced that their rightful interests cannot be attained under existing conditions. When such uprisings succeed and result in drastic transformations in community structure, they are called revolutions. History is replete with attempts by the discontented to overthrow constituted authority. Since authority has been organized in so many different ways, however, rebellions have taken numerous forms. Unpopular monarchs of all kinds have been overthrown. The Protestant Reformation challenged the authority of the Catholic church to control access to heaven through the sale of indulgences. But today we generally use "revolution" to refer to domestic challenges to a national state. So much authority is centralized in a national government that partisans have sought to take over the state as a means to institute change.

Insurrections, even when we focus on rebellions against the state in the past three centuries, vary in their scope, accomplishments, and tenor. Although insurrections are usually regarded as popular uprisings, the extent of popular participation varies considerably. In some countries vast numbers have taken to the streets; but other governments have been overthrown by small coalitions of disgruntled officials — often with the aid or connivance of the military. Some rebellions lead to the reorganization of the government; others retain the same authority structure but use it to pursue different policies. Sometimes the economy is reorganized; at other times there is only a redistribution of certain assets. Although some insurrections are followed by a drastic recasting of the social order, in others one category of people simply replaces another in positions of privilege. Sometimes social reconstruction is carried out over a brief period; in other instances, however, the changes do not become apparent for many generations. Some uprisings are marked by spectacular violence; in others violence is kept to a minimum.

Thousands of insurrections have been attempted, and most of them have failed. Each rebellion is unique. To the extent that there are similarities among them, however, it is possible to formulate generalizations. The central concern in this chapter is to ascertain regularities in the efforts of people who find their lives so intolerable that they try to overthrow their government in the hopes of improving their lot. Under what conditions do people challenge the legitimacy of their government? How do people become convinced that their rightful interests cannot be attained without displacing the government? An insurrection involves casting out constituted authority by illegal means. How are personnel and resources mobilized for such undertakings? Who takes the lead in such movements, and how do the leaders gain popular support? What happens *after* an unpopular regime has been ousted? How do the new leaders go about instituting the changes they advocated as rebels? How do the changes introduced by the new governments become institutionalized? Historical records are available on hundreds of insurrections, and the systematic study of this complex phenomenon is just getting under way. We shall consider some tentative generalizations, confining our attention primarily to major uprisings of the recent past.

CONDITIONS OF INSURRECTION

Insurrections often appear to erupt suddenly, and the change of government sometimes occurs overnight. Nonetheless, most are the culmination of a long, drawn-out struggle. They are not sudden reactions to some immediate crisis—such as military defeat, famine, widespread unemployment, or an unpopular law. Government authority is well established, and it takes some time before citizens in substantial numbers begin to raise questions about duties they had taken for granted. Thus, any attempt to explain rebellions in terms of simple "causes" is unrealistic. Uprisings occur only after a long succession of unresolved problematic situations, after serious issues have arisen among powerful segments of the community. In most instances intense discontent has developed among a substantial portion of the political public, and those most concerned have become organized into a number of partisan groups. The manner in which participants become aligned depends largely on how the population is classified and ranked; conflicts usually develop between those who occupy different levels in the extant system of social stratification.

Just how revolutionaries proceed depends on the form of government, in particular on the extent to which free association and free speech are permitted. If dissidence is prohibited, news is disseminated through the underground press and political grapevines—networks of people of similar persuasion. Where dissidence is not tolerated, subversive movements become secret societies. Even when popular participation is possible, in the beginning there is usually considerable disagreement within the public as to what ought to be done. Although almost everyone will be affected by the outcome of a successful revolution, in most instances the vast majority of the people in the community do not participate actively. They do not even become part of the public until some spectacular events capture their attention. When it is over, most people acquiesce and accept the consequences.

Patterns of Revolutionary Change. One common type of revolution involves a drastic transformation of the system of social stratification, in which one category of people displaces another in positions of privilege. Such insurrections are confined to the boundaries of already established communities, and they do not result in the formation of new nations. They occur most frequently in communities that are stratified in terms of class differences, and examples include the notable uprisings in France, Russia, and China as well as the Cuban Revolution in 1959. The people become aligned in terms of class interests, and the struggle is between an ascending class and defenders of the status quo. Where members of different classes pursue markedly different life-styles, adversaries are easy to identify. When the system is already undergoing change, however, other considerations—such as ethnic identity, religion, or ideological commitments—may constitute supplementary criteria. The leadership in such uprisings is not necessarily drawn from the stratum most likely to benefit from the changes advocated. The leaders of working-class uprisings, for example, often consist of young lawyers, intellectuals, and young army officers—discontented persons of middle-class background who identify with the poor.

Another common type of revolution is the nationalistic secession, recently labeled wars of national liberation. Members of an ethnic minority form separatist movements; if the dominant group refuses to make enough concessions, they launch a drive to establish their own government and to control their own destiny. When such civil wars are successful, they result in the formation of new nations. Examples include the American Revolution of 1776, the numerous revolutions in Latin America in the century that followed, the Greek war of independence in 1821, the founding of Israel in 1948, and the numerous uprisings against European colonial rule after World War II. Secessionist movements are led by members of the more privileged classes in the ethnic minority—successful businessmen, professionals, intellectuals, and military officers. Many of the leaders had occupied marginal positions. Thus, when able members of ethnic minorities are not incorporated into positions of privilege, they sometimes band together to overthrow the entire system. In the twentieth century such insurrections have been followed by attempts at rapid industrialization, where an effort has been made to use the machinery of government to change the economy and to raise the general standard of living. The sense of ethnic pride that develops during the fighting leads to aspirations of creating a great nation.

Civil wars also break out on ideological grounds, as parties committed to different values become involved in struggles to control the government. To the extent that religious beliefs form the basis of social stratification, struggles for dominance arise between religious groups. In seventeenth-century Europe numerous conflicts arose between Protestants and Catholics, and religious strife still occurs in various parts of India and Pakistan, the British Isles, and the Middle East. During its early history Islam was forced on the conquered. In recent times the Islamic literati's unhappiness over the attenuation of religious commitment in nations undergoing industrialization has led to uprisings that have established theocracies in Pakistan and Iran. Since Marxists assume that class is the only basis for stratification, they have been puzzled by such insurrections. Since they also assume that revolutions become unnecessary once the working class wins control of the government, Marxists have also been shocked by uprisings such as those in East Germany in 1953 and Hungary in 1956. The revolt in Czechoslovakia in 1968 as well as the overthrow of the "gang of four" in China in 1976 appear to be struggles over ideological differences. Although most revolutions have rested on class, ethnic, or religious differences, these are not the only criteria in terms of which people may become divided.

Challenges to the Old Regime. What are the conditions under which the legitimacy of a government is likely to be challenged? After a careful study of the history of three successful revolutions, Skocpol (1979:47–111) concludes that a government becomes vulnerable when it loses the confidence and support of important segments of the privileged strata. This makes possible the uprising of the underprivileged. Thus, in France a succession of costly wars depleted the royal treasury; tax reforms were attempted in good faith, but the changes were made in a manner that offended the rich and displeased the poor. Leaders of the privileged then encouraged popular discontent by appealing for support in their struggles against the monarchy. In Russia the magnitude of the military defeats in World War I led to a steady loss of confidence in the czarist government so that by 1917 almost everyone repudiated the autocratic regime. In China the increasing encroachment of foreign powers led to deep concern among the politically conscious members of the gentry, and in 1911 the Manchu dynasty was overthrown. But the Kuomintang government was unable to resolve the difficulties; decades of turmoil and factionalism followed and culminated in the Communist uprising after World War II. Thus, a government's legitimacy is likely to be challenged when even the privileged strata view it as incapable of dealing with crucial problematic situations.

In such contexts partisan groups advocating all kinds of reform as well as revolution intensify their activities. Intellectuals call attention to a broad range of problems, especially to the various inequities imposed on persons of lower status. As discontent becomes more widespread, many thoughtful members of privileged ranks acknowledge that the existing conditions are unjust and should be changed. In most uprisings the insurgents have received support from alienated persons of high rank. A few, who question their own right to rule, openly join the ranks of the critics. For a whole generation before 1917 there was constant talk among Russian aristocrats about revolution, and some of them even participated in subversive movements. As increasing numbers of the privileged lose faith in themselves, some scoff at the absurdities of their own institutions. Many become demoralized and hedonistic and quarrel among themselves. A united elite is seldom overthrown. When those who benefit most from the existing government lack cohesion, however, defense of the status quo becomes halfhearted.

In most cases members of the police and the armed forces — unless they are all professional soldiers or a foreign legion — become infected with the growing discontent. As enlisted personnel become sullen, their officers lose faith in their ability to fight. Even when troops are not ready to mutiny, widespread discontent makes them unreliable. They may refuse to fire on civilian demonstators, or they may even join the protesters in attacking the police and their own officers. Trotsky (1936, 1:248 – 69) describes how resentful troops in Petrograd in 1917 were held in line only by fear; once they realized that they could not be punished, they joined the revolution or went home. Thus, in many successful uprisings the balance of power has changed even before the fighting begins, and the old regime collapses at the first serious challenge. This was apparent during the final showdown in Vietnam, when the Saigon government simply turned and ran (Terzani, 1976; Dawson, 1977).

The Changing Balance of Power. Insurrections seldom develop among those who are crushed by oppression; they are more likely to occur among people who feel cramped and restrained. Thus, the French Revolution erupted in a relatively prosperous society with an impoverished government (Brinton, 1952:32; Tocqueville, 1955). Although the Russian government was breaking under the strain of a long war, by 1917 the productive capacity of the nation had risen considerably. The Communist revolution in China came after victory in World War II, when China stood as the most powerful nation in east Asia. Similarly, wars of national liberation arose in the European colonies when the standard of living had improved and a new educated elite had developed. The Hungarian uprising of 1956 followed on the heels of Khrushchev's denunciation of Stalinism, a general relaxation of political controls, and the release of many political prisoners.

Most insurrections occur after people who once occupied the lower ranks of a stratification system have developed competitive advantages and political power. Thus, prior to many insurrections the actual power of persons of low status — their capacity to coerce or to resist coercion — has already increased. But the facade of the established order remains intact; persons of higher rank continue to be addressed with deference, even though they are no longer capable of enforcing their ascendancy. Such observations led Davies (1962, 1971) to propose a widely entertained hypothesis: An insurrection is most likely when a prolonged period of rising expectations is followed by a short period of reversal, during which the gap between expectations and gratifications widens and becomes intolerable. Although the reversal is not apparent in many uprisings, most of them do follow a period of rising expectations. In such contexts many problematic situations arise, for the old arrangements have become strained. Although the balance of power has already changed, many privileged persons fail to realize it. Thus, a contest becomes necessary to ascertain who is in control.

Most insurrections are led by discontented individuals in ascending categories who find their upward mobility blocked by existing social institutions. Intense resentment develops among people who attain educational skills, wealth, or other assets but are still excluded from social distinction. The leadership of most insurrections includes frustrated intellectuals, who feel that they are not sufficiently appreciated and have not been accorded adequate status. Frustrated businessmen have also played an important part. Even after acquiring great wealth, merchants in both Europe and Asia were long despised as money handlers and not admitted into the aristocracy. Those who chafe under what they regard as unreasonable regulations have also joined insurgents. Many acculturated natives in European colonies who were excluded from privileged ranks became leaders of revolutionary movements. Those who served as junior officers in foreign legions and found their ascendancy blocked by the color line have also played an active role. Thus, when upwardly mobile people encounter socially sanctioned norms that limit their mobility, they define such norms as instances of rank injustice against everyone (Brinton, 1952:36). When the discontented become involved in subversive movements, their feelings are reinforced and given specific direction. Intellectuals formulate ideologies that explain what is wrong and propose programs for change. Once subversive movements have been organized, they may receive considerable aid—including money, military equipment, propagandists, advisors, and volunteer freedom fighters—from sympathetic outsiders. As disaffection against the government takes shape, other groups—factions in the military, unions, clans, and merchant associations—may join the insurgency.

What is of decisive importance is that the active participants in an uprising—partisans and their supporters—have altered their self-concepts. When people who had once occupied low status redefine themselves, they come to feel that they are being deprived of something that is rightfully theirs. Since they have attained competitive advantages and power, they feel that they deserve status that corresponds to their contribution to the community. When they encounter barriers to upward mobility, they feel that their legitimate aspirations are being blocked. Thus, what they had previously tolerated becomes intolerable; they feel cheated and perceive once-cherished institutions as oppressive. The rhetoric of social movements intensifies such discontent. Once people become convinced of their worthiness as human beings, they demand justice. Then, instead of accepting their fate as inevitable, they begin to question current arrangements. Whereas people who accept the social order consider it their duty to obey laws, those who believe that they are being cheated consider it their right to rebel.

Polarization Against Authority. Although governments are sometimes overthrown without widespread popular participation, public opinion plays an important part in most insurrections. Even a government formed through a coup d'etat must win acceptance by the political public for legitimation. One common misconception about revolutions is that they are reactions to severe economic deprivation and widespread misery. Misery in itself rarely leads to insurrections; people have lived in abject poverty for centuries without mounting serious protests. But misery that can be blamed on the government and its supporters can play an important part in mobilizing the discontented. If agitators can provide a plausible explanation of what is wrong and specifically place the blame for all the difficulties on the government, discontent takes on a definite direction. During the French Revolution, for example, widespread fear of brigands allegedly employed by aristocrats touched off mass panic among the peasants throughout the country and mobilized their sentiments against the monarchy (Lefebvre, 1973). Once blame is affixed to a specific party, considerable agreement emerges in the political public that something drastic must be done. People become more candid in voicing their dissatisfactions and complaints, and partisan groups become bolder in their activities.

The period preceding most insurrections is marked by considerable disorder — protest meetings, mass demonstrations, strikes, and sporadic violence. As the people become more responsive, agitation becomes easier; and both reformers and revolutionaries step up their activities. Pamphleteering becomes more open. The government may make some desperate attempts at reform; but unless they are immediately effective, such efforts are likely to reinforce the developing anger. Ineffectual reforms are viewed as insulting. Should the government overreact to protests, efforts at suppression may provoke epidemic demands for change. The massacres in Petrograd in 1905 and at Amritsar in 1919 became unifying symbols for revolutionaries, and similar blunders have resulted in crystallizing sentiment against other governments. In 1945, when Algerians celebrating the Allied victory in Europe demanded equal treatment of Moslems and Christians, the French government attacked the demonstrators with both air and ground forces, resulting in an estimated fifteen thousand casualties. This incident united the various factions opposed to French colonial rule (Wolf, 1969:235–36). In 1947, when Chinese intellectuals complained that bandits, famine, and exploitation by landlords had been tolerated for too long, Chiang Kai-shek retaliated with a campaign of harassment, imprisonment, and assassination. This solidified resistance to the nationalist regime (Belden, 1949:397–412). Such spectacular incidents not only crystallize sentiments against the rulers but also increase disaffection and create contempt for the government. Incompetent repression also makes revolutionaries more adept as conspirators, cements their organizations, and enhances popular support. Many of the previously uncommitted become so outraged that they join the insurgents.

As discontent intensifies, a crescendo of talk about revolution develops. The opposing sides become polarized, and the line between the insurgents and the defenders of the status quo becomes more clearly drawn. Both sides form contrast conceptions, the contours of which are fairly predictable and familiar to any reader of novels like Charles Dickens's *A Tale of Two Cities*. The defenders of the status quo view revolution as a disorganized affair in which insane agitators spur uncouth masses to violence; the revolutionaries represent the negation of everything of value in human civilization, and all civilized people cannot but oppose the vicious mobs of rabble. In turn, the insurgents see themselves as oppressed citizens whose only ray of hope lies in revolution against wicked authorities who have been fattened by debauchery, greed, and excess. The revolution is to be a glorious uprising of the poor and innocent, led by their Robin Hood.

As discontent and anger become focused on the government and its supporters, those who demand changes sometimes develop what has been called an "oppression psychosis." They become preoccupied with oppression and see it everywhere; hypersensitive to difficulties, they blame anything they can on their enemy. Passive discontent is thus transformed into hatred of the oppressor, and hatred of a common foe tends to produce unity among the insurgents. Under such circumstances it is not uncommon for a utopian vision to develop among opponents of the government, a belief that overthrowing it will solve all problems and usher in a millennium of harmony. This vision greatly resembles the millenarian beliefs promulgated by some religious movements or by patriots in time of war. When collective excitement is intense, people will accept ideas that are consistent with the prevailing mood—especially where reality testing is not possible. Such utopian visions provide a stark contrast to reality. Although outsiders may be skeptical and even scoff at such utopian beliefs, the vision provides insurgents with hope and strength to overcome their despair. As increasing numbers agree that overthrowing the government is the only way to secure justice, a substantial portion of the political public is prepared to welcome change. Some join partisan groups, and others are ready to welcome whatever the activists achieve.

DISPLACEMENT OF THE GOVERNMENT

We tend to think of revolutions as popular uprisings that result in drastic social change. But even when the political public includes a substantial part of the population, most citizens remain in the spectator component until the issues have been settled. Radical social changes have been instituted by governments that have come into power by displacing established regimes, but there is no necessary relationship between the magnitude of social reconstruction and the extent of popular participation.

Ascension Through Party Politics. Violence is not necessarily involved in the displacement of governments, especially in communities that permit free elections. Sweeping transformations have been instituted by social movements that have operated as political parties and have won control in elections or through negotiations. The Nazi party, which once in power drastically altered the structure of German society, achieved its mandate at the polls. As the Nazis won an increasing proportion of the votes in a succession of elections, Adolf Hitler was offered the chancellory in 1932; he refused to accept the position unless the constitution was suspended. In the next election the Nazis were chosen by 44 percent of the electorate. Only the Social Democrats opposed them in the Reichstag; all other parties agreed to grant Hitler the dictatorial power he demanded. On March 23, 1933, parliament approved his program, and the German constitution was suspended. The Communist parties of France and Italy have both disavowed any effort to seize power through violence; they intend to win at the polls and to legislate their reforms. The dissolution of the British Empire took place largely through diplomacy. Although the independencies of India, Malaysia, Pakistan, and Zimbabwe were preceded by considerable violence, in each case the transition was arranged in negotiations between the leading political party and the British government.

New governments that are established legally usually enjoy great advantages. Those who win in elections can claim a mandate from the public; hence, they begin their work with the support of a substantial constituency. Even when less than half the population supports them, as was the case in Germany, no one else can rule the country. Hence, they have the opportunity to institute the reforms they have been advocating with a minimum of opposition. Once such governments have become established, they may abrogate the constitution, abolish the existing parliament, change the judicial system, and if necessary declare martial law. By the time they begin making changes that are not popular, it is virtually impossible for their opponents to get a hearing.

Displacement of Ruling Coalitions. Drastic social changes have also been instituted by governments that have seized control in a coup d'etat. When a coalition of disgruntled civilian and military officials overthrows an inefficient and unpopular government there is usually little or no popular participation. In many instances the public is not even informed until after the transition has occurred. Few coups d'etat have resulted in significant changes in policy; they have usually constituted little more than a change of the palace guards. But there have been exceptions, especially in the twentieth century. Military leaders in Egypt, Peru, and Portugal have attempted social reforms. Several military dictators in the developing nations have committed themselves to rapid industrialization, which in turn is likely to result in many other transformations.

In both the Meiji revolution in Japan in 1868 and the Atatürk revolution in Turkey in 1920 the old regime was overthrown by a coalition of civil and military bureaucrats who feared European domination. They felt that they had to seize control from their vacillating rulers in order to head off foreign conquest. Although both transitions occurred in violent civil wars, there was little popular participation; the fight was between opposing factions of high rank. In both cases the insurgents made drastic reforms, emphasizing nationalism and rapid industrialization (Trimberger, 1978). These programs required other changes, such as mass education. Although these leaders could not have anticipated all the other transformations that followed, they destroyed the old feudal systems. Another sudden transition occurred in Czechoslovakia in 1948. In the first postwar election in 1946, the Communists turned out to be the largest party; they polled only one-third of the votes, however, and Eduard Beneš, who opposed them, was elected president. The Communists seized control in February 1948; Jan Masaryk, the foreign minister, died under mysterious circumstances. A new constitution was drawn up, but Beneš resigned rather than sign it. The newly elected legislature then suspended the old constitution and nationalized the economy (Skilling, 1976).

Military Victory by Insurgents. Governments have also been overthrown through the persistent efforts of subversive movements. Popular discontent alone is not likely to overthrow a government; mob violence and civil disorders lack direction. Insurrections require planning and coordination, and sustained effort requires organization. Each subversive movement develops an ideology and a program that provide specific direction for the discontent. At the core of such partisan groups are dedicated revolutionaries, many of whom are willing to give their lives for their cause. Some of them infiltrate key positions in order to spy on the government or to arrange for acts of sabotage. Others engage in propaganda both to call attention to various injustices and to proselyte additional members. They circulate pamphlets, give speeches, and operate clandestine radio stations. They may also incite riots, support strikes, and assist in other incidents that may embarrass the government. Some subversive movements begin as voluntary associations, but they learn quickly that they must exercise care in their proselyting, for they must protect themselves against infiltration by the secret police. Unless they develop tight organizations with definite aims, they are not likely to survive. Their aim is to reduce the political and military strength of the government, and to do this they must be able to outlast their enemy.

Most governments are too strong to challenge openly. Since a direct assault would be suicidal, subversive movements usually resort to guerrilla warfare. The main targets of guerrilla fighters are isolated police and military posts, communication lines, transportation and supply routes, and the major revenue sources of the government and of those who stand behind it. The tactics include raids, ambush, and sabotage. Guerrilla strength comes from flexibility, mobility, and knowledge of the local terrain. They attack only when they have the advantage; then they disappear. Since they present no clear target to attack, they enjoy an advantage over their adversaries.

However, guerrilla units are able to operate effectively only when they have enough popular backing to provide logistic support and cover. Only a small number do the fighting, but they need the enthusiastic cooperation of a minority and the acquiescence of the rest of the people. Lawrence of Arabia, who organized Arab guerrillas against the Ottoman Empire during World War I, stressed that such irregulars need the assistance of people sympathetic enough not to betray their activities to government troops and the police. Mao Zedong once wrote that "the populace is for revolutionaries what water is for fish." Thus, the very ability of guerrillas to operate for any length of time indicates that the government is very unpopular.

Guerrilla units also resort to assassination, bombing, kidnapping, torture, and execution. The aim of such violence is propaganda rather than destruction. They want to instill fear in the opposition, for fear sometimes temporarily paralyzes resistance and may result in some concessions. In some operations guerrillas attack simultaneously in several distant places — to create the impression that their forces are more numerous than they are. They also resort to selective terror for the psychological impact. They assassinate one person to frighten others like him or her. They burn down one village as a warning to others of the price of informing the police of their whereabouts. Such moves are political rather than military. When they succeed, they also demonstrate the government's inability to protect its supporters.

In many cases the overreaction of the government to such tactics helps solidify the partisans and strengthens the determination of those who support them. Frustrated in their efforts to halt the civil war, government troops and police often pressure the people who are supporting the irregulars. They attempt to control their movements by requiring passes and setting up checkpoints; they also resort to terror of their own. Such actions infuriate the people, for the government reaction is often arbitrary, and many who are killed or injured are innocent and uninvolved. Those who had been lukewarm in their aid to the rebels become enraged and join them; others cooperate more readily than they had in the past. Such repression also makes the guerrillas more adept. But sometimes the guerrillas overplay their hand. The usual public reaction to violence, especially if it is widespread and chronic, is to demand reinstitution of law and order. Most guerrilla fighters are young; youthful rebels have relatively little to lose, feel invulnerable, and often do not appreciate how strongly violence is resented. Hence, their leaders often caution them against doing anything to alienate the people. Their aim is to maneuver government forces into committing atrocities; then they can become the champions of the people. Guerrilla units are therefore difficult to defeat through military operations alone. Unless reforms are made to rob them of their base of operations, they may continue their activities for a long time.

Sometimes a very unpopular government is able to hang on, especially if it is buttressed by foreign support. If the struggle lasts long enough, the insurgents may become strong enough to challenge the government openly in a civil war. In such instances new governments have come into existence through a military victory by revolutionaries. When the Communists first challenged the Chinese government in 1946, government forces outnumbered them by four to one. As the fighting progressed, however, Communist strength increased. Large units of the demoralized Kuomintang army deserted and went over to the insurgents, bringing their arms with them. In the end the remaining nationalists were driven off to the island of Taiwan. In 1959 Fidel Castro's guerrillas overthrew the Batista government of Cuba. Although it was a working-class insurrection, the only support Castro received from the urban proletariat was a general strike in January 1959, when victory was virtually assured. Vietnamese guerrilla forces expelled the French colonial government, the Saigon regime, and the Americans.

Popular Uprisings Against Authority. Trotsky (1936) claims that the direct intervention of the masses in historical events is the true mark of a revolution; by this definition, there have been very few successful revolutions in history. In some instances, however, popular rebellions have led to the overthrow of the government — as in Russia in 1917. Thousands of enraged people take to the streets to demand an end to intolerable conditions. Such spontaneous uprisings are usually touched off by some spectacular incident — an assassination, a bombing, the burning of a building, a demonstration that gets out of hand, the arrest of a popular hero. The event is like a flint that ignites the flame in a volatile situation. The people are already livid with rage, and the incident merely touches off the explosion. The event becomes important for two reasons. First, the government's incompetence and inability to defend itself are dramatically exposed. Once it becomes obvious that the rulers are no longer able to punish those who disobey, those who had been holding back from fear rebel and give vent to their long-smoldering anger. Second, the event marks an open and avowed split between the defenders of the status quo and their opponents. Once the dividing line is publicly acknowledged, people must commit themselves one way or the other (Edwards, 1927:98–108).

Aggressive crowd behavior, however numerous the protesters may be, seldom overthrows a government, unless the leaders of subversive movements are able to provide direction. Most violence is of short duration and lacks organization. The authorities may be embarrassed by such disorders, but they are usually able to restore order. If the various subversive movements are able to form a temporary coalition under a united leadership, however, they can take advantage of the disorder to seize the government. By acting together in conjunction with the popular uprising, revolutionaries can use the mass protest for their own purposes. If they isolate the seat of government, seize communication and transportation centers, and neutralize the armed forces and the police, they paralyze the government. They may also kidnap or assassinate key political figures. Once the insurgents have established a foothold in the major cities, they can urge the rest of the country to follow them. If discontent is sufficiently intense and widespread, the revolt is likely to spread. Even when the government is toppled, however, unless revolutionaries are able to coordinate their efforts, a political vacuum is created. The unpopular rulers flee, but no one else is able to govern. Thus, the Mexican Revolution of 1910 began with such a conflagration that deposed the hated dictator; while the successful insurgents were quarrelling among themselves, those who had been in positions of privilege were able to recapture the government. Thus, without a definite program a revolt is likely to fail, even when it enjoys widespread popular support.

Such failures occur frequently. Revolutionaries are often unable to assess public opinion correctly. They spend so much time with people who agree with them that they form the mistaken impression that everyone else is as enraged as they are. Thus, they often make premature moves. In some instances the people mobilize in support of the government and help imprison the insurgents; in other instances they refuse to follow their lead. In the Russian Revolution the insurgents erred in the opposite direction. When the popular turmoil broke out in Petrograd in February 1917, many revolutionaries felt that the time was not yet ripe and refused to take action. Only after the uprising was well under way did they realize what was happening and join the fray (Trotsky, 1936, 1:142–52). In some cases several local uprisings occur simultaneously and in the confusion people receive only garbled news of what is happening elsewhere. While they hesitate, authorities are able to restore order. In other cases infighting prevents revolutionaries from taking advantage of the imminent collapse of the government. Leaders of subversive movements who have been rivals for a long time dislike and distrust one another. Reformers who hate the government are often more frightened by radicals, and they refuse to cooperate with them. Such disunity gives government forces time to regroup and to fight back. Thus, many armed uprisings have been put down, sometimes with huge death tolls.

STRUGGLES AMONG REVOLUTIONARY FACTIONS

Many students of revolution have concentrated on the "causes" of uprisings and have tended to neglect what happens after the victory. But political processes continue, and the kinds of social reforms made and the manner in which they are instituted depend on what happens after the old regime has been deposed. Soon after the triumph defenders of the old order are disarmed; the leaders are arrested; and a new government is organized. In most military victories and coups d'etat one partisan group prevails, and it sets up its own government, as in China in 1949. When the overthrow is accomplished by a coalition, however, a provisional government is established that includes representatives of the major factions. Even when one partisan group dominates, as in Cuba in 1959, the leaders often install a provisional government that includes several shades of opinion. In many cases an announcement is made that the new government is only a caretaker regime and that general elections will be held to decide on a constitution and more permanent rulers. The emotional climate is one of great joy, and initially the various parties work together enthusiastically. Since most people realize that the new policies will affect them, the size of the political public grows. Even those who had not been overly concerned with the preceding turmoil now pay attention, and public opinion assumes greater importance.

Problems Facing Provisional Governments. In most cases the new government includes representatives of all the major partisan groups that had opposed the old regime. Thus, provisional governments are motley affairs, containing revolutionaries of all stripes, many of whom had been rivals for decades, disillusioned reformers who had joined the insurrection as a desperation measure, and grass-roots leaders who control private armies, such as Pancho Villa and Emiliano Zapata. Also present are ambitious and frustrated politicians without ideological commitments as well as some bureaucrats from the old government who are needed to keep essential services running. As members of diverse groups come together, political activity intensifies. Idealistic insurgents clash with politicians concerned primarily with expediency. New coalitions are formed and reformed, as one program after another is debated. Compromises are demanded; and tempers flare (Reed, 1935).

The provisional government's initial tasks include restoring order and instituting urgent reforms. The police power of the state must be reestablished, for murderers, thieves, and bullies do not curtail their proclivities during insurrections, and their endeavors reflect adversely on the new government. Members of the police and the armed forces are screened for political reliability, and those who pass muster are put back to work under the insurgents' supervision. Many revolutionary regimes resort to harsh measures; their limited personnel are kept so busy that the new officials do not have time to concern themselves with due process of law. Since time and facilities for lengthy trials are lacking, criminals are sometimes summarily executed. The economy must also be restored, and emergency relief must be provided. Unless the material needs of the people are met, more discontent will soon develop.

In the beginning people are encouraged to continue business as usual, even in those sectors of the economy marked for elimination, for the goods and services are needed. Political prisoners are released from jail, and prominent members of the old regime take their places. Public executions of hated figures may be staged — symbolic acts designed to reassure the people that the past is gone forever. Much-needed reforms, especially those that had been the rallying points of the uprising, are carried out. Practices that had long been condemned — slavery, the exploitation of women, food hoarding, prostitution for foreigners — are abolished. More drastic transformations, such as the large-scale redistribution of land, may be postponed, but a promise is made that they will be forthcoming. Immediate implementation of such programs could disrupt the economy, and there are too many immediate problems. Despite the turmoil the period immediately following a successful revolution is marked by widespread optimism. People feel that they are at last in control of events, and they look forward to a rosy future.

But the new government faces many difficulties. The insurgents' inexperience in office and the need to rely on some old bureaucrats pose problems. When essential services break down, many people become impatient; some begin to wonder aloud whether they were not better off under the old regime. It may also become necessary to curb the excesses of some of the new officials. Some insurgents had spent many years in prison, had endured torture, and had seen their comrades and relatives killed. As they seek revenge, their violence shocks and alienates others. Furthermore, the differences among the various leaders become more apparent as they clash over one issue after another. Those unfamiliar with the ideological disagreements among the partisan groups become impatient at their quibbling about seemingly minor details when so many essential tasks still remain to be done. Thus, in a short while the initial optimism fades. Many had participated in the uprising believing in a utopian vision, and they are disillusioned to find that victory has not ushered in the millennium. Instead they see many new problems. As discontent grows, some demand further changes; others call attention to some features of the old regime that might be preferable. As problematic situations mount, opposition to the new government develops.

Internal Struggles for Control. Many observers have been astonished and puzzled by the turmoil and infighting that follow most successful revolutions. Many insurrections are accomplished by a temporary coalition of partisans united only by their opposition to the old regime; once the enemy has been overthrown, the coalition tends to fall apart. Even when a revolution is won by a single partisan group, factions within it often become embroiled in quarrels over policy. Although factionalism may develop along several different lines, the most frequent split is between those who have contrasting orientations toward the utopian vision. *Radical* revolutionaries demand the immediate and total implementation of their ideology, regardless of the cost. They want to press on until their ideals are realized and view any compromise as a betrayal of their principles. *Moderate* revolutionaries often share similar ideals but are more practical. They argue that trying to carry out drastic transformations too suddenly is unrealistic and would alienate too many people.

They are convinced that they are more likely to attain lofty goals if they first consolidate their position. Although radicals reject outright most values of the old regime, many moderates feel that selected features of the old order are useful and should be retained. Radical insurgents are not content with mere reform; they demand a clean sweep, in some cases including extermination of all defenders of the old regime.

Who is radical and who is moderate depends on the revolution. In the Russian Revolution the Bolsheviks were the radicals, but in the 1956 Hungarian uprising those aligned with the Bolsheviks were the defenders of the status quo. Furthermore, the split varies with the type of insurrection. Among insurgents trying to establish an Islamic republic the radicals are those who demand strict adherence to Moslem codes — such as cutting off the hands of thieves, stoning adulterers, and banning the consumption of alcohol. In some secessionist movements radicals demand ethnic purity and the expulsion of those who do not qualify.

The moderate faction consists of people who feel that they have won much of what they wanted and are satisfied; they now want to establish a solid base of operations before pressing on for more changes. They acknowledge that they have not accomplished all their objectives, but they feel confident that the problems will be resolved in time. Moderates generally begin with an advantage, for they appear more reasonable; their position is usually a compromise that is acceptable to diverse factions. The radicals accuse them of breaking faith with those who had died for the revolution, and they demand further changes. The leaders of such factions struggle not only for key government positions but also for public support. Before long the two factions form contrast conceptions of each other, and at times the fighting between them becomes vicious. The radicals may organize strikes and other disruptions that worsen the weak economy. During the Russian Revolution the moderate Mensheviks spread rumors that Lenin, the leader of the Bolsheviks, was a German agent (Trotsky, 1936, 2:85 – 112). Such struggles occur in most revolutions, and victory can go to either side. Much depends on the tactical skills of the leaders and their ability to keep their respective factions united. In the French Revolution Robespierre and the Jacobins sent many of their moderate rivals to the guillotine, but one faction replaced another in a succession of coups until Napoleon took over the country. In the American Revolution the moderates prevailed. In the Russian Revolution the radicals ousted the Kerensky regime in October 1917 and have retained control ever since.

When a serious effort is made to implement the ideology of a subversive movement, many difficulties arise. Ideologies are facile, stereotyped explanations of what is wrong, and much of the party line is political rhetoric to appeal for public support. Simplistic solutions are proposed for complex problems, and the procedures just do not work. Such failures also tend to favor the moderates, for they make the radicals' position appear unrealistic and visionary. If the moderates win the struggle for power, order is restored. Since nationalistic secessions are led by the more affluent members of ethnic or religious minorities, the moderates generally win. But the moderate faction may also prevail in class uprisings, as in Portugal in 1975. But the radicals do not disappear; they continue to press for more changes. If the new government cracks down on them, they go underground and resume their guerrilla tactics. Thus, some subversive movements are hounded by the police even after their initial triumph.

Should popular discontent continue, the radical faction may win increasing public support. The utopian vision has not yet been attained, and many keep hoping and struggling. Should the radicals prevail in the struggle for power, many other factions may desert the revolution. What so many people find frightening is that the radicals oppose many of the basic values that had previously been taken for granted. Furthermore, some of the radical programs are harsh. To cite an extreme instance, the radicals in Cambodia tried to exterminate everyone born into the wrong classes. Severe measures of this sort terrify others, and the various factions—survivors of the old regime, disillusioned reformers, as well as rival revolutionaries who had been ousted—sometimes join forces to overthrow the new government. Opposition to the revolutionary regime is often organized in remote areas; thus, the major uprising against the French Revolution in 1793 was mounted in the western provinces (Tilly, 1976). All attempts to overthrow the new government are labeled as counterrevolutionary, a word that has become a term of disapprobation. However, such movements seldom advocate reinstating the old regime. Most accept the major reforms, and their assent enables them to broaden their base of popular support. If the counterrevolutionary movement is strong enough, civil war follows. In some cases the fighting continues for many years. At times the clashes become so brutal that the participants forget the ideals for which they are fighting; personal vendettas replace political issues. Most of the casualties in the Russian Revolution came during the civil war between 1918 and 1920. Either side may win such a civil war.

Foreign Intervention in Civil Wars. Since outsiders are supposed to be neutral in civil wars, foreign intervention is often surreptitious. In the twentieth century, however, it has become more open and commonplace. Even before an unpopular government is overthrown, beleaguered insurgents often appeal for help from like-minded parties outside the community. Marxist revolutionaries in Africa have asked for the aid of Russian advisors and Cuban troops. In nationalistic secessions partisans appeal to their ethnic "brothers" abroad. The Sudeten Germans in Czechoslovakia appealed for Nazi support, just as the Palestinians have asked other Arabs for aid against Israel. In the Greek war of independence in 1821 Christians throughout Europe were asked to help cast out the infidels of the Ottoman Empire. Counterrevolutionary movements also seek foreign assistance, for the losers in a revolution have difficulty getting enough support at home. Thus, after the French Revolution deposed aristocrats appealed to the nobility in other European countries, just as Russian émigrés after 1917 sought aid from others of their class. In the 1960s many Americans were puzzled by the worldwide condemnation of our intervention in Vietnam; most Americans did not realize that others viewed our troops as supporters of a counterrevolution against the Vietnamese revolution.

In some instances the intervention of foreign armies has strengthened the hand of the revolutionary government, for the mere presence of outsiders is widely resented. Even those who are unenthusiastic about the insurrection can often be rallied to defend their country. This happened after the French Revolution, when the new government was able to recruit an army to fight off all the invaders. After the Russian Revolution armies from several nations—including England, France, Japan, and the United States—entered Russia in an effort to help counterrevolutionary units overthrow the Bolshevik regime. The Communists reorganized a Russian army that had been mauled in three years of war against Germany and repelled all the invaders. Similarly, the American intervention in Vietnam only reinforced the people's resolve to continue their long fight for independence. However, on many occasions foreign intervention has been overwhelming enough to overthrow the insurgents. Russian troops terminated the uprisings in Hungary in 1956 and in Czechoslovakia in 1968; Cuban soldiers have played a decisive role in Angola. In some instances the invaders not only have overcome the revolutionaries but also have set up their own puppet regimes.

Implementation of an Ideology. A common misconception holds that the most radical transformations occur after revolutions involving widespread popular participation, especially of people of low status. In truth, however, the radicalness of the new program does not depend on the severity of the deprivation, the manner in which the insurgents are organized, or how the transfer of power occurs. Rather, the extensiveness of the changes that follow a successful insurrection depends on the ideology of the partisan group that eventually wins the struggle for power in the provisional government, the ability of the new government to win the support of the people and the armed forces, and the astuteness of its administrators. Overthrowing the old regime is only the first step in a revolution and assures nothing in the way of social change.

The winning partisan group also writes the history of the uprising from its own perspective. The key events emphasized are those that enabled the victors to rise to power. The heroes and martyrs of the revolution are the persons who made decisive contributions to the efforts of that particular partisan group. Good examples are provided by Russia and China, where the revered are those who played prominent roles in the Communists' long struggle in their insurgency. Had the Communists failed, they would now be known only to historians. Furthermore, the explanations and justifications the victorious faction uses become the new government's official ideology. In many instances national history is rewritten from the victors' standpoint. The new histories are not necessarily fabrications; the historians select and emphasize different events of the past and interpret them from another standpoint. Thus, when a subversive movement finally prevails, its leadership and ideology leave a huge imprint on the entire community. Its leaders become the national heroes, and its ideology becomes the official position of the state.

REESTABLISHMENT OF AUTHORITY

Enactment of Social Changes. Revolutions are both feared and hoped for because of the drastic transformations that are sometimes instituted in the structure of the community. Especially if the radical faction wins the struggle for power in the new government, far-reaching reforms may be ordered. Among the changes most commonly made is the redistribution of valued objects. Socialist revolutions are followed by nationalization of the means of production. Where peasants are actively involved, land reform receives high priority. The redistribution of land and agricultural implements was one of the first accomplishments of the Chinese Revolution; the estates of the wealthy gentry were broken up into smaller plots and given to the poor peasants (Hinton, 1968:128–46). Tax reforms are also common, especially where the wealthy had previously escaped taxation or had paid only a small share. Since many twentieth-century insurrections have been guided by humanitarian ideologies, many welfare programs have been established—including slum clearance, free medical care, and free education. Various categories of people who had been exploited in the past — women, the elderly, ethnic minorities — are liberated. In China women were granted the right to vote, to hold office, and to sue for divorce; wife beating by husbands was prohibited.

Thus, new social institutions are enacted, old practices are reassessed and renamed, and new symbols develop to validate and justify a different way of life. Such drastic changes are easier to institute quickly during periods of crisis, when people are confused and do not understand what is happening. Even when they do not approve of some of the innovations, they accept them, for the spirit of change is in the air. Social planning is a form of collective problem solving, and how well it is done depends on the political skills of the leadership.

In some revolutions the system of social stratification undergoes sudden and drastic change. As the population is reclassified and placed in different ranks, many awkward adjustments must be made. Various categories of people who had previously occupied lowly positions are suddenly elevated. In the French Revolution the third estate was granted the same legal rights as the nobility and clergy; in the Russian Revolution workers and peasants were elevated to first-class citizenship. After the Chinese Revolution categories such as the gentry and landlord were eliminated, and the peasants were reclassified. In some villages peasants who had not lived in poverty complained that they had been ranked too high and stood to lose too much, but they were granted the right to appeal (Hinton, 1968:434–41, 535–47). In nationalistic secessions natives who had been the subjects of colonial rule became the rulers. In the new nations of Africa the dominant group consists largely of persons whose education is European; they had been trained for the civil service, teaching, medicine, and law but had been denied access to privileged ranks. Many had held marginal status. European administrators, traders, and teachers have been replaced by leaders of independence movements.

Military units are reorganized. After the Russian Revolution soldiers were still expected to be disciplined when on duty; when they were off duty, however, they had the same rights as other citizens and were no longer required to salute officers (Trotsky, 1936, 1:276). After nationalistic secessions young officers — commissioned and noncommissioned — may promote themselves to colonels and generals and assume key offices in government. Intellectuals who had been harassed and sometimes imprisoned become high officials. At the same time those who had previously enjoyed high status and had been addressed with deference are downgraded. Wealthy merchants, professional practitioners, and generals are all addressed as comrade or citizen and are stripped of many of their former prerogatives. Of course, not all the underprivileged benefit from the changes. In Africa and Southeast Asia the new regimes have discriminated against some of the ethnic groups that had occupied the middle ranks — Arabs, Chinese, and Indians. There is no evidence that the various nineteenth-century revolutions in Latin America against Spanish colonial rule improved the lot of the Indians, and many Africans living on tribal reserves may be no better off than they had been under European rule. Although egalitarianism is a prominent part of many revolutionary ideologies, a successful uprising does not lead to a leveling of status. One system of social stratification is replaced by another.

The implementation of some ideologies requires considerable time, and some of the most drastic transformations do not become apparent for several generations. In the twentieth century many new regimes have adopted a policy of rapid industrialization that is resulting in many un-anticipated consequences. Industrialization redistributes the populace into a different division of labor; the people become involved in large production units. Urbanization also results in various dislocations. Kin-ship ties weaken; individualistic values become more prominent, and demands arise for more personal autonomy. A national language is needed to facilitate communication among people who had previously spoken different tongues or dialects. Mass education, necessary in any industrial society, raises the literacy rate, and the development of the media of mass communication helps standardize the language. As a sense of patriotism develops, a new category of people — those who share a common nationality — comes into being. But the mass media also introduce knowledge of life in other parts of the world, which often leads to the development of new tastes. Thus, new values form, and numerous demands, which the insurgents could not have foreseen, arise. Had the revolutionary leaders known what would happen, they might well have opposed some of the reforms.

Despotism in the Transitional Period. Although many insurrections are mounted to overthrow despotism, the new government may resort to similar tyrannical measures to maintain control. If the recently estab-lished institutions are to endure, they must be backed by a government capable of enforcing the new norms, but doing so is not easy for a regime that is not yet fully legitimated. Although a revolution is carried out in the name of all the people, the ruling clique that prevails often consists of a small partisan group that does not enjoy the broad popular support of the earlier coalitions.

All new regimes face many dangers — mistakes from their own inex-

perience, overzealous vengeance that alienates people, counterrevolutionary movements, and foreign intervention. One key problem is to
restore and maintain order after a long period of violence during which
large numbers of people acquired weapons. In most instances the new
government seizes control of the formal communication channels and
discourages or prohibits dissidence. There is not enough time to consider
all sides of key issues. A unified state police system is often established.
The secret police become concerned primarily with political crimes; "enemies of the state" are regarded as far more dangerous than mere murderers or thieves. If opposition to the new policies develops, outspoken
people who are potentially dangerous are incarcerated. In many cases it
becomes necessary to build a number of new detention centers, and the
prisons of most revolutionary governments are filled with political prisoners. The aim is to restore harmony and to establish legitimacy. The
tyranny in the transitional period is intended initially as a temporary
measure, but in some instances it lasts for many decades, sometimes until
the government is overthrown in another revolution.

Some revolutionary regimes adopt a policy of terrorism. The number
of victims is usually exaggerated by opponents, and the purpose of the
terror is frequently misunderstood. The objective is not death and destruction, but the establishment of political control by creating an emotional climate of fear. The aim is to create the impression that the new
regime is omniscient, with eyes and ears everywhere, ready to deal with
any situation in a firm and forthright manner (Kohn-Bramstedt, 1945).
Thus, public executions may be staged in the hope that killing a small
number of dissidents will immobilize others who might object. Many
bureaucrats are holdovers from the old regime who serve the new government from fear of losing their pensions or of being demoted; a few
exemplary punishments are usually enough to keep them in line.

Rumors of massacres often frighten other rivals. During the French
Revolution, for example, when the city of Lyons opposed some measures
of the convention in Paris, an army was sent to pacify it. A proclamation
was issued that the city would be destroyed, all the inhabitants killed,
and its name would be blotted out forever. When Lyons was captured,
some seventeen hundred of its defenders were killed, but care was taken
to let enough escape with news of what had happened. A total of about
400,000 francs a day was then paid to laborers to tear down the buildings
that were still standing. Observers from cities suspected of discontent
were then brought in to inspect the destruction of Lyons, and during the
autumn of 1793 it was widely believed in France that the city had been
annihilated. Several other cities were seething with unrest during the

most critical months of the revolution, but opposition to the new government faded (Edwards, 1927:181–82). Sometimes massacres are permitted just to dissipate tension. Discontented people are sometimes permitted to assault beneficiaries of the old regime who are still about; this renders them too tired to complain of the new government's inefficiency (Edwards, 1927:174–77).

Terrorism has been widely condemned, especially by intellectuals who support the rest of the program. Revolutionaries have argued heatedly among themselves over its moral justification. Some, Trotsky for example, contend that selective terrorism is a way to avoid large-scale bloodshed; others, such as Lukacs and Marcuse, argue that the killing of innocent people cannot be condoned under any circumstances.

Legitimation of the New Regime. Although terrorism may keep people in line for a while, no government can stand for long on the basis of force alone. Legitimation of the new government requires winning the support or at least the acquiescence of a substantial portion of the population. Especially important is the spectator component of the public. Thus, all formal communication channels are used to conduct an extensive educational campaign. The ideology is presented and explained repeatedly, and the "correct" interpretation of various events is provided. The new classifications of people are reaffirmed, and those who disagree are denounced as traitors or counterrevolutionaries. The messages are often simplistic. Sophisticated people may even find them amusing, but they are hardly in a position to protest openly.

One tactic commonly used to garner popular support is the formation of mass organizations. Those who had been underprivileged are brought together in new groups. Illiterate peasants may be brought together to learn to read and write; the subject matter used in the instruction is drawn from the ideology. In China the women in each village were convened in small groups to compare the harsh experiences they had suffered in the past, to denounce such injustices, and to support one another in their new status. Since many of the older people can never be won over, special emphasis is placed on the young. The youth are encouraged to join mass organizations in which they participate in festivals, dances, sports programs, and gymnastics. Such programs not only provide opportunities for indoctrination but also serve as diversionary outlets for discontent. Justifications for various innovations and new symbols are repeated over and over until they come to be taken for granted.

The loyalty of intellectuals is important, for they enact decisive roles in the formation of public opinion. They plan and execute all propaganda and education, supplying and editing information and thus playing a major part in creating a new symbolic environment. Most insurgents recognize their importance. But intellectuals tend to think for themselves and cannot be counted on to support all reforms, especially those that tend to reduce their own autonomy. Thus, they are subjected to special scrutiny and control. Most revolutionary regimes have devoted considerable effort to persuading or coercing their intellectuals to assume an acceptable stance. The Nazis deported, jailed, or killed those regarded as dangerous. In Russia several embarrassing incidents have occurred, and the government has resorted to expelling intellectuals and even having them committed to hospitals for the insane.

Soon after the victory in China, intellectuals were urged to attend moral reeducation schools. The participants were organized into cells of about ten members each and were to confess their past errors. At times former students were called in to remind professors of their sins. Internationally famous scholars were forced to denounce work that had brought them recognition. The listeners criticized, made suggestions, and condemned those who held back. Marxist texts were studied, and cell leaders clarified points in dispute. The final examination consisted of preparing a confession acceptable to the party. Those whose minds were "cleansed" were permitted to return to work with their corrected perspective; those who failed were sent to labor battalions, and some were never heard of again (Chen, 1960). In spite of this extensive effort, many Chinese intellectuals apparently remained unconvinced. In the "hundred flowers" campaign of 1956–57 intellectuals were encouraged to express themselves freely. The government was shocked by the outrage and bitterness expressed; some even had the temerity to suggest that the Communists step down. The campaign was abruptly halted.

Once the new regime has been in control long enough so that it becomes obvious that it will not be overthrown, most people accept its authority. With the passing of time people become accustomed to the new patterns of concerted action and their new status; the various roles they perform become fixed in habit. For those who had never been part of the political public these changes do not constitute a serious problem. They had been unconcerned about political matters; they do not care who governs the country as long as they are reasonably satisfied with their daily routines. However, some remarkable changes in loyalty occur among those who had been active politically. The old regime's former supporters insist that its propaganda had deceived them; at bottom they have always been sympathetic to the ideals of the revolution. They recant and insist that they have forgotten the past.

By this time several foreign governments have recognized the new regime. Diplomatic relations are reestablished, and trade is resumed. Agreements such as the international postal union are signed, and relations with outsiders become normalized. Once the leaders of the new government no longer feel threatened, a period of convalescence usually begins. Some political prisoners are granted amnesty and selected practices that had been outlawed as frivolous are permitted again. Women are encouraged to wear makeup, and there is a general emphasis on relaxation and pleasure. Following the terminology of the French Revolution, such periods of convalescence have been called the *Thermidor* reaction. By this time the new moral order is well on its way to becoming established, and the revolutionaries assume that they have won their battle.

Further Challenges to the Regime. Many insurgents initially assume that a successful revolution will bring the resolution of all their problems. But life conditions continue to change, and problematic situations continue to arise. The new regime cannot rest on its laurels; it is expected to respond day after day to new situations. If problems linger, discontent develops once again. In many instances serious quarrels persist among the successful insurgents over the extent to which their ideology is being faithfully implemented, especially in regimes guided by well-defined ideologies, such as Marxism or some religious creed. A schism develops between purists who regard the ideology as the absolute truth and pragmatists who use the ideology only as a guide to meeting the problems of life. The latter tend to regard the ideology as a statement of ultimate goals. They make all kinds of compromises to avoid unnecessary difficulties in accomplishing essential tasks, and they are willing to entertain a variety of ideas in their deliberation. They argue that rigid conformity to a simplistic scheme will lead to disaster, but purists regard this position as a betrayal of everything for which they had fought. Although all challenges to the new government are denounced as counterrevolutionary, in fact some of them come from people who are more radical than the rulers. Thus, a regime that is established through one revolution may be deposed by another.

The oligarchical tendencies found in any bureaucracy pose another common source of difficulties. Once the revolutionary movement has succeeded, fighters are no longer needed; the heroes of the revolution are retired in glory, and the leadership is assumed by administrators. A bureaucracy is necessary to implement the goals of the insurrection; once established, however, the bureaucracy tends to develop its own goals (Mouzelis, 1968:7–11). Essential specialized knowledge becomes a source of power for the bureaucrats, who over time develop a vested interest in the new arrangements. Representatives of the revolution thus become defenders of the new status quo. Many insurgents find this offensive. The Cultural Revolution, launched in China in 1966, was a spectacular struggle over this issue. Chairman Mao Zedong protested that the new bureaucrats were deriving excessive personal benefit from their offices; he argued that the educated should not become a political elite, that their jobs should not be a source of individual wealth and prestige. He protested that the administration was excluding the people from full participation in decision making and was reintroducing class oppression. As opposing factions within the Communist party tried to mobilize mass support for their respective positions, they called on the discontented youth to revitalize the government. As the tension level rose, many of the youthful groups were transformed into unruly mobs. Various dignitaries were dragged from their offices, denounced and abused, and even lynched (Lee, 1978). When the economy came to a standstill, the army had to be called out to force the protesters to return to their homes.

Should the new government survive such challenges, an effort may be made to encourage and support revolutions abroad. There are indications that the example of the French Revolution facilitated other uprisings, especially in nineteenth-century Latin America. The dismantling of the British Empire after World War II placed pressure on the French, Dutch, and Portuguese to grant independence to their colonies. Castro's success has aroused restiveness in Central America, and Marxists have continued to press for revolutions throughout the world. Cuba in particular has exported large numbers of teachers, doctors, and technicians as well as troops. Such activities invite retaliation, including efforts to mobilize against all revolutions.

SUMMARY AND DISCUSSION

As in the study of war, the comprehension of revolution has been rendered unnecessarily difficult by its being romanticized by the discontented and loathed by the privileged. An examination of several cases in which an existing government has been replaced by another that serves a different constituency and institutes drastic reforms reveals that such transformations can occur in several ways. Thus, the distinction frequently made between evolution and revolution is only one of degree; what are called revolutions are spectacular turning points in the evolutionary process, a period during which changes occur more rapidly than in others. Several new regimes have been overthrown before their reforms have been institutionalized. Insurrections are usually mounted against constituted authority when large numbers of discontented people alter their self-concepts and no longer feel that it is their duty to obey existing laws. How such disgruntled people are mobilized depends on the type of political activity that is expedient under the circumstances. Although violence is not a necessary part of insurrections, whenever the regime is rigid, the uprising is likely to be bloody. After an unpopular government has been deposed, the kinds of reforms instituted depend on the ideology of those who win the political infighting that occurs within the new government. Since the new regime's legitimacy is not well established, many characteristic difficulties arise. In a few notable instances, however, ambitious programs of social change have actually been implemented despite all the difficulties.

Discontented people throughout the world, especially among the young, have viewed revolutions as a panacea for all their difficulties. Although some insurrections have eliminated unpopular social institutions, most uprisings have failed. Even when a revolutionary movement succeeds, it seldom accomplishes its announced objectives, which are usually too lofty to be readily accessible. Without such visionary goals, however, people cannot be mobilized to make the enormous sacrifices necessary to overthrow a government. Insurrections, then, are a form of collective adaptation. Once substantial segments of the population become convinced that the government is not meeting their needs, its legitimacy is likely to be challenged. This is true of revolutionary governments as well as others. As long as officials remain unresponsive to the demands of the people, they risk being overthrown.

SUGGESTED READINGS

Brinton, Crane, 1952. *The Anatomy of Revolution.* New York: Prentice-Hall.
   A pioneering effort by a historian to formulate generalizations from a comparison of four insurrections.
Coleman, James S. 1958. *Nigeria: Background to Nationalism.* Berkeley and Los Angeles: University of California Press.
   The formation of various protest movements in colonial Nigeria and the part they played in the establishment of an independent nation.
Davies, James C. (ed.). 1971. *When Men Revolt and Why.* New York: Free Press.
   An anthology of theoretical and empirical studies on some of the conditions under which people are likely to rebel.

Hinton, William. 1968. *Fanshen: A Documentary of Revolution in a Chinese Village.* New York: Random House.
   A detailed account of the manner in which a single village was transformed during the Communist revolution in China.
Skocpol, Theda. 1979. *States and Social Revolution.* London: Cambridge University Press.
   The formulation of sociological hypotheses from a comparative analysis of the revolutions in France, Russia, and China.
Trotsky, Leon. 1936. *The History of the Russian Revolution.* 3 vols. Max Eastman (trans.). New York: Simon and Schuster.
   An account of the February and October uprisings in Petrograd in 1917 by one of the leading participants.

CONCLUSION

XVIII

SOCIAL INTERVENTION

Utopian visions are repositories of the perennial longings of people throughout the world to live in a perfect society. Many European philosophers — among them Plato, Thomas More, Francis Bacon, Tommaso Campanella, Jean Jacques Rousseau, and H. G. Wells — have provided accounts of their ideal society, and their writings have struck a responsive chord in audiences everywhere. Perfection has generally been defined in terms of harmony, both within each person and in social relationships. Many have dreamed of social life without conflict. They envision a world in which human wants are fully satisfied, a world without gaps between wanting and having. Communities would therefore be without crime, and life would consist of happy labor or of rich leisure. If there must be social inequality, the distinctions would rest on some rational basis; no one would merely be born into privilege. Although most utopian thinkers have recognized the need for some kind of authority, they visualize the absence of arbitrary commands; they have viewed the preservation of order as something in which everyone can participate. From time to time members of religious cults have attempted to create such a heaven on earth — in small communal experiments that they hoped would eventually spread throughout the globe. Such a paradise never existed, and most scholars doubt it can ever be achieved. Nonetheless, most people agree that it would be desirable.

The philosophers of the Enlightenment were imbued with the idea of progress and the perfectibility of humanity. Human beings had advanced from some aboriginal condition of animal life to their current

517

dominant position in the ecosystem through rationality, and through the use of intelligence, it was assumed, they could continue to improve their material and spiritual condition until eventually arriving in utopia. The idea of progress has been a key presupposition of Western civilization (Bury, 1932; Nisbet, 1980). Americans in particular have been future-oriented, assuming that those in each generation will enjoy a better life than their forebears. Bacon's grand vision was that the development and use of scientific knowledge would create such an ideal society. Most scientists take for granted the idea of progress and work on the faith that their labors will improve the human condition. Even those who are convinced that utopian visions are unattainable hope that such ideals can be approximated through scientific research.

Can human society be reconstructed in an orderly manner to approach the utopian visions so many have found appealing? Bacon contends that to control nature one must first understand how nature works. Similarly, to improve and reform society one must have a clear understanding of how human society works. It is this knowledge that social scientists seek. Can the human mind — capable of such accomplishments as the miracles of heart surgery, of photographing Saturn's rings, of genetic engineering — develop the kind of knowledge necessary to save our species from self-destruction? Human beings have developed the capability to feed, shelter, and clothe most of the earth's population; yet millions are starving in impoverished squalor. Given the advances elsewhere, is it unreasonable to think that a more effective organization of social life is possible?

The demands on the social sciences are becoming more pressing, for there is widespread fear that human beings as a species are headed toward extinction. Unless we can keep the peace, feed the poor, and minimize the hardships that accompany rapid social change, we shall soon face disasters of enormous proportions. Our capacity for symbolic communication and thinking has enabled us to alter our environment far more than other creatures can. Thinking is a tool that facilitates adaptation, and now the development of computers has extended enormously our capacity to manipulate data and symbols. Just as the industrial revolution amplified and largely replaced human muscle power as a productive force, computers are assuming many of the tasks that have been performed by the human nervous system. Will we be able to use this technology to move closer to utopian visions, or will we use it for destruction? Many are pessimistic. As the development of automation renders many social institutions obsolete, there is danger of the permanent unemployment of a large segment of the world's population and the development of a highly polarized system of social stratification. Although most social scientists are still committed to Bacon's ideals, there has been widespread disillusionment. This disenchantment rests in large part on the realization that the best knowledge developed to date in the social sciences does not provide adequate guides for social reconstruction. Decision makers, even those who are familiar with the technical literature, still find it necessary to rely on common sense.

UTOPIAS AND PROBLEMATIC SITUATIONS

Significance of Utopias. Utopian visions — as fanciful, unrealistic, and impracticable as they may be — play an important part in the formation of any society. Such prototypes provide general goals toward which people can strive; without them human beings would be concerned only with survival. Decisions in social planning are not based on economic calculations alone; a society's utopian visions provide models to examine, to discuss, and to debate in the course of choosing among alternative paths of action. The quest for ideals overcomes the natural inertia of people, helps surmount passive acquiescence in the present, and provides the bases for reshaping the future. Many groups — Christians and Marxists are conspicuous examples — have tried to actualize their millenarian dreams. Such visions provide direction for social movements and make possible concerted effort in time of war. The design of the perfect life to come makes sustained endeavor and sacrifice seem worthwhile. The visions sometimes interfere with reasonable solutions to immediate problems, but they do provide the basis for rejecting the present and mobilizing for better things to come. Without them social change would not occur so quickly and would not take any particular direction. The demise of utopian visions and of the idea of progress may end both what we have cherished and the ways we have become accustomed to thinking about ourselves.

Visions of a perfect society also provide criteria for evaluating the present and measuring progress. Widely accepted ideals provide the standards for social criticism. Even a casual glance at history reveals the extent to which the human condition has changed in the direction of such models. If we consider the fate of the many generations of slaves who constructed the pyramids of Egypt, we can appreciate the extent to which civilizations have moved to limit drudgery and provide a more equitable distribution of the benefits of production. Many social inequalities still exist, and persons in underprivileged categories still press for a fairer share of the rewards, but the ideal of egalitarianism makes their struggle meaningful. A society's view of what constitutes injustice depends on its criteria for measuring justice; the demands of the women's movement, for example, are embedded in a tacit acceptance of ideals drawn from utopian visions.

However, utopian visions are also the source of widespread discontent. Since they describe perfection, they arouse unrealistic expectations. When victory in a revolution or war fails to usher in the expected millennium of perfect existence, those who had fought so hard and sacrificed so much are disillusioned. Many people today are disheartened that the development of science has not transformed the world into paradise. Young people in particular lose faith. They want to eliminate injustices immediately and are willing to pay a high price for such changes. When their dedicated efforts fail, they become impatient. A number of observers have noted that the idealistic young expect the impossible; then they become incapable of expecting anything because the impossible did not happen. Cynicism, apathy, and immobilization often result. Disillusionment is especially marked among those for whom perfection is compulsive, such as the "true believers."

One serious challenge to the desirability of establishing a utopia has repeatedly been leveled: All utopian visions are static. Even Karl Marx, who had a dynamic conception of history, believed that social transformations would cease once the perfect classless society had been achieved. Glaucon referred to Plato's ideal society as a "city of pigs"; others who have viewed utopias as stultifying including Nietzsche, Dostoyevski, and Aldous Huxley. Peace could become rigid fixity; material satisfaction could become bestial contentment; effortless virtue could lead to the neglect of moral conduct. Thus, arrival in utopia could bring boredom rather than lasting happiness. But human life takes place in an ever-changing universe, and human history is a record of a succession of collective adaptations to problematic situations. The structure of a society at any given time and place is simply the product of past solutions. Even if some social institution provides an excellent solution in a given context, as life conditions keep changing, it will eventually become obsolete. Even the most satisfactory pattern of accommodation is only temporary. Coping with a succession of problematic situations *is* the human condition — as well as that of all other living creatures. Thus, the task confronting humanity is not the immediate attainment of someone's utopian vision but the establishment of more effective procedures for dealing with problematic situations. The task is to establish procedures that will assure some measure of self-determination for those who are involved, maximize the chances of bringing gratifications to substantial numbers, and minimize the chances of disputes escalating into violence.

Growth of Social Planning. How can social change be accomplished in an orderly manner? Granted that it is not possible to satisfy everyone, can the quality of life be made more acceptable to more people through effective use of the best available knowledge? Social planning constitutes an effort to establish specific objectives and to design schemes to achieve them through coordinated endeavor. A popular misconception is that social structures are stable until pushed by some force—some "cause" —and thus social planning is a way to initiate or create change. But since in actuality societies are always changing, the problem in social planning is to provide some kind of *direction* to transformations.

Social planning is an ancient practice. Groups of all kinds—communities, organizations of farmers and merchants, members of street gangs, revolutionaries—have tried to design and implement plans based on the best available information. For the most part they have relied on commonsense knowledge. In mass societies, however, problems are becoming more complex, and conventional wisdom has been found to be unreliable and inadequate. There is increasing agreement that the welfare of the citizenry—problems of livelihood, medical care, and education—is too important to be left to custom and informal arrangements. Larger social units must take a hand, and national states are increasingly assuming the responsibility. The Soviet Union initiated planning on a nationwide basis in 1917, and the procedures were developed further in Nazi Germany. During World War II all combatants had to mobilize for total effort, and the use of human and other natural resources was brought under government control. Since that time, all socialist states have made extensive use of social planning, with some conspicuous successes in northern Europe. In the developing nations planning has become a necessity, for there is not enough wealth to afford too many failures; the allocation of various resources has to be organized to minimize waste. In most of the world today some measure of planning is accepted as one of the responsibilities of government. Social planning is here, and it has been institutionalized on a large scale.

The implementation of plans of action involves some loss of autonomy on the part of those involved; otherwise the efforts of large numbers of people cannot be coordinated. Irked by what they regard as unnecessary government regulation, those committed to conservative ideologies have attacked social planning as evil and undemocratic. Discussions of the subject have been obfuscated by political slogans, such as the polarization between socialism and what has been called free enterprise. In fact a comparison of the economies of the Soviet Union and the United States reveals that the differences are not so great as some would suppose. Ironically, some of the most effective planning based on the findings of the social sciences is found in various organizations in the capitalistic world—business corporations, labor unions, political parties, large voluntary associations, military organizations, and various bureaucracies within state and national governments (Lazarsfeld et al., 1967). Corporation executives cannot afford to make decisions on a trial-and-error basis, and many well-established industries apply procedures developed in the social sciences—demographic projections, polling and consumer research, standardized educational tests, programmed language instruction, behavior modification procedures. To be sure, most of this is piecemeal social engineering rather than efforts to redesign communities. Nonetheless, massive efforts have been made to reduce poverty, improve public health, provide adult education, and attenuate tensions between religious and ethnic groups. Some of the most efficient social planning to date has been accomplished by the very people who profess to oppose it.

The various issues confronting industrial societies have become so complex that expert knowledge is becoming essential. Despite complaints of the inadequacy of what has been produced by social scientists, decision makers in various communities and organizations have been turning to such specialists for whatever help they can get. Many formal organizations have established intelligence units to monitor academic research as well as to conduct their own studies. The task of these units is to gather, process, interpret, and deliver the technical information needed in decision making and in implementing policies (Wilensky, 1967). Specialists are also employed as consultants. Thus, the findings of sociology, as inadequate as they may be, are in fact being used in piecemeal and large-scale policymaking.

Popular Enlightenment. The efforts of social scientists have also affected the pursuit of utopian visions through contributions to a better-informed public. The programs of governments and other organizations are not likely to succeed without some measure of public support or acquiescence, and popularization of the findings of social research has facilitated the acceptance of new policies. The more conspicuous theories and findings of the social sciences become known to intellectuals, who play key roles in the various media of mass communication. Thus, new ideas are disseminated and become widely known. Just as the work of nineteenth-century naturalists uncovered many curious and little-known facts and made life more comprehensible, studies of the life-styles of people often regarded as deviant—criminals, homosexuals, slum dwellers, outlaw gangs, esoteric cults, unpopular ethnic minorities—have provided facts for challenging popular superstitions. One notable example is our orientation toward mental disorders. In many circles psychological disorders are viewed as illnesses—rather than moral failings—an understanding that is leading to widespread acceptance of policies that provide more humane treatment. A number of concepts developed in the social sciences have become familiar parts of our general vocabulary—acculturation, diminishing returns, marginal utility, rising expectations, relative deprivation, peer group pressure, identity crisis. As the spectator component of the public becomes better informed, partisan debates become more meaningful, and positions that rest on stereotyped beliefs can be abandoned. Popular enlightenment has led to the adoption of more reasonable public policies.

Many social scientists and intellectuals have worked with utopian visions, and their work may actually have contributed to changes in that general direction. Slavery and peonage, once commonplace, are being abolished in many parts of the world. The looting and rapine following military victories are being replaced by more restrained conduct by armies of occupation. Amenities that were once the exclusive possession of the aristocracy are falling within the reach of the middle classes and even to some who are less affluent. In many ways the industrialized world is becoming the "age of the common man," more so than other periods of history. We seem to be moving very slowly toward some of the ideals that characterize utopias.

OBSTACLES TO ORDERLY RECONSTRUCTION

Sociologists and other social scientists toil in the hopes of eventually producing more reliable knowledge, comparable to that produced in the physical and biological sciences. Would their success lead to a golden era of social reconstruction undertaken in a rational and efficient manner? It seems unlikely. Medical practitioners are able to make immediate use of the latest advances in biological research, for everyone is against disease and infirmity. But there is seldom such agreement over social problems. Even a proposal to eliminate war is likely to encounter serious opposition, especially if there appears to be some possibility of effective implementation. How can people be so intransigent when so much is at stake? Collective deliberation—the most effective procedure for problem solving devised thus far—works only under limited conditions. One reason social reconstruction does not occur in an orderly manner is that these conditions are very difficult to meet.

Planning as a Political Process. One condition under which collective deliberation can be carried out effectively is the absence of a genuine opposition of interests among those who make up the public. In modern times this condition is difficult to meet. Mass societies are made up of a bewildering array of social worlds. Each individual's perspective is limited by the distinct combination of communication channels in which he or she participates, and persons with diverse outlooks are drawn into common transactions. Most of the difficulties in mass societies arise not so much from selfishness or maliciousness as from ethnocentrism, when different parties define a common situation from incompatible standpoints. Most human beings do their best to pursue what they regard as their just interests; they engage in moral conduct. Problems arise when the participants in common transactions do not understand one another. Although people are able to pay lip service to many abstract values—such as peace, equality, or freedom—reaching agreement over what is desirable at a given time and place is much more difficult. Misunderstandings are bound to arise; we can neither expect everyone to acquire a cosmopolitan perspective nor assume that diverse parties will be able to integrate their interests. Thus, most social planning, both piecemeal and large-scale, becomes a political process (Park, 1955:38–49).

Even when all parties agree on the goals to be pursued, as in a formal organization, many arguments arise over details. Especially instructive is a study by Bergson (1964) of how large-scale planning occurs in the Soviet Union. All the major means of production are publicly owned, and decisions are made in a complex apparatus of high government and Communist party officials. But disputes arise among various factions within the party and among representatives of the military, of various industries, and of other segments of Soviet society. In setting production quotas, for example, executives of the various units involved realize that their personal success will be measured by their ability to fulfill them; they therefore seek a safety factor and object to goals they consider unreasonable. The participants struggle for arrangements that are beneficial to the units they represent. Since the demands of the various sectors are inconsistent, compromise over the allocation of personnel and resources is necessary. The same kind of infighting is commonplace in the bureaucracies of American corporations.

Another condition conducive to successful collective deliberation is the availability of the most accurate information and best knowledge to those who make and implement the decisions. All bureaucracies are organized into hierarchies, and the information given to decision makers is often manipulated. Information viewed as threatening is concealed at each level in the hierarchy, and ambitious bureaucrats concerned with their own status may even resort to deliberate misrepresentation. Subordinates sometimes remain silent about difficulties; even when they speak out, their superiors may fail to heed their warnings. Decision makers often have to depend on experts. But even in organizations with intelligence units relevant information may be translated, condensed, or even distorted before it reaches those who make the final verdict (Wilensky, 1967). Thus, even when a deliberate effort is made to maximize rationality, decisions are often the product of political maneuvering. Such maneuvering does not constitute sabotage; each executive has simply defined the situation from a limited perspective.

Breakdown of Deliberation. Another essential condition of successful deliberation is that all the participants are willing to be guided by the product of the discussion. Unless the participants are prepared to listen carefully and fairly, deliberation is likely to degenerate into a shouting match. Acrimonious opposition tends to push rivals into stereotyped positions, and effective communication becomes very difficult.

One common source of breakdowns in deliberation is rigid adherence to an ideology by one or more of the parties involved. Those who are committed to an ideology—be it Islamic fundamentalism, Marxism-Leninism, party line liberalism, or ultraconservative Republicanism—begin with the assumption that they know how to solve the problem. Intoxicated by their scheme for perfecting human life, they remain steadfast, confident that shortsighted people will eventually see the truth. Immersed in a particular symbolic environment, they do not pause to consider if they might be mistaken, and they are shocked that intelligent people disagree with them. For the committed, loyalty to the ideology becomes a matter of honor, and compromise is seen as treason. This rigidity makes open deliberation impossible, for issues can no longer be discussed on their merits. Problem solving then becomes unnecessarily difficult, since ideologues dismiss certain alternatives out of hand and may prevent other options from even being introduced. Many political activists are compulsive in their perfectionism and are unable to compromise. Thus, the very dedication to ideology that brings success to a social movement often destroys its program after it has won.

Human beings frequently do not seriously address problems until a situation deteriorates to a near disaster. The greatest resistance to any proposed change comes from those who believe that their vital interests are threatened. Corporations and military organizations are often accused of pursuing selfish interests at the expense of others, but this is true of virtually all organizations, even religious groups professing altruistic values. Although many Americans in the 1980s agree that the public education system has deteriorated seriously, any attempt at extensive reconstruction is likely to encounter massive resistance from administrators, teachers, and parents—all of whom honestly believe that their schools can be made effective with just a few changes. Serious consideration of drastic reforms arouses intense emotional reactions. Defenders of the status quo do not see themselves as selfish; they are engaging in moral conduct. When people with vested interests are powerful enough, they may perpetuate a social institution until it collapses from obsolescence.

Even when a decision has been made, difficulties often arise in its implementation. Those who carry out the new policy sometimes do not understand it; they do the best they can while protecting their own security and seniority. Workers who feel threatened by innovations sometimes sabotage the policy by making a number of illicit informal arrangements. Well-meaning reforms have been transformed in the bureaucracies charged with executing them. The aim of the progressive education movement early in the twentieth century was to teach children to think critically so that they could adapt more effectively to an ever-changing society. But many of the administrators and teachers did not have a complete understanding of the theory nor of its application. By the time the program became institutionalized, it had degenerated into mere permissiveness. Soon after World War II some psychiatrists proposed releasing borderline inmates from asylums into more productive lives in therapeutic communities. The objective was humane, but politicians bent on cutting hospital budgets forced out so many patients incapable of managing their own affairs that their exploitation became a national scandal (Estroff, 1981). Thus, many well-meaning reforms that have been adopted have been nullified by personnel who simply did not understand their intent.

Intensification of Tension. Another condition of effective deliberation is regulation of the tension level. Discussions remain reasonable and productive only as long as the participants can control their emotional reactions. In mass societies, however, people performing for different reference groups encroach on one another unintentionally. Inadvertently they work at cross-purposes. When they clash, they become enraged. Individuals on each side jump to the conclusion that their rivals are attacking them, deliberately and maliciously. Before long they begin to form contrast conceptions of one another. As the tension level rises, effective communication between the disputants breaks down. Bitter quarrels replace negotiations, and rivalry soon becomes conflict.

Implementing a new policy often requires the use of political power to coerce the recalcitrant to partake in the program. Victors who are still insecure tend to define dissidents as dangerous enemies who must be brought under control. Some of the most brutal repression has been imposed by revolutionaries trying to transform the world into a utopia. Some governments struggling for reform have become so fearful of dissidents that they have tried to suppress what they regard as treacherous ideas and have even restricted freedom of inquiry. In the long run such repression is self-defeating. Some officials have been naive enough to believe that they could convert people to their ideology merely by controlling formal communication channels. However, knowledge is a symbolic reconstruction of reality, a map; unless it is reasonably accurate, it cannot serve as an effective guide to action. Reality has a recalcitrant character; even the most powerful dictators cannot compel the truth or falsity of ideas. Sooner or later beliefs that cannot pass reality testing are rejected in informal communication channels. For a time false beliefs may be perpetuated by isolating a community from external contacts. Given the ease of communication in modern mass societies, however, it is difficult to see how the intellectuals of any community can be long isolated from outside influences. If social reconstruction is so difficult to accomplish even with accurate knowledge, insisting on false beliefs can only compound the problems.

TECHNIQUES OF CONFLICT RESOLUTION

Conflict as a Chronic Problem. Throughout the world various forms of conflict, especially war, have been condemned as a stupid way of settling disputes, and people have longed for less costly ways of reconciling differences. When problematic situations cannot be resolved through collective deliberation, however, fighting is likely to erupt. In his monumental study Wright (1942:381–82, 1284–87) concludes that wars are most likely to occur when, among groups using similar military technology, social and economic changes occur so quickly that they outstrip the capacity of institutionalized procedures for effecting adjustments. Thus, conflict is a form of collective adaptation. When rivalries intensify, people on both sides form contrast conceptions, and fighting becomes a matter of honor. Since the world is changing more rapidly than ever, many quarrels are likely to erupt. Even in a society with rational procedures for social planning incongruent interests are bound to arise. Thus, the hope of eliminating conflicts altogether seems to be a utopian dream.

People have tried to banish conflict by condemning it and preaching sermons against it. Their lack of success is predictable — the opposition of interests is endemic to human life. The task, then, is to develop ways to minimize the destructiveness of conflict. Many of our customs and laws, products of the wisdom of the ages, serve just this purpose. Many social norms minimize the chances of disputes arising and keep those that do develop within designated limits. Social organization is essential for the survival of the species, but human beings have now reached a critical stage of evolution. The winner of a nuclear war will inherit only the responsibilities of cleaning up a globe polluted with radiation and of feeding and maintaining order among the survivors. Santayana writes that "those who cannot remember the past are condemned to repeat it." Since repeating the past may prove fatal to our species, it is worthwhile to examine the attempts that have been made to resolve conflicts short of violence.

Acknowledgment of Common Interests. Certainly one of the most difficult problems facing humanity is to discourage people from acting on the basis of contrast conceptions. An ingenious study by Sherif and his associates (1961) gives some indication of what is involved and suggests an important condition under which redefinitions can occur. In the Robbers Cave experiments boys in a summer camp were divided into two rival gangs. They were housed separately and competed against one another as units in various games. Before long each group developed a sense of solidarity, and ill will against one another became pronounced. Whenever the boys were brought together in social events, they berated each other, and counselors had to intervene to stop fights. After considerable hostility had developed, the experimenters set up three superordinate objectives — three goals that all the boys earnestly worked to accomplish: repairing a pipeline to get much-needed water, starting a stalled truck so they could get food, and pooling their resources so they could rent a movie everyone wanted to see. None of these goals could be attained unless all the boys contributed. Cooperation was reluctant at first, and some disruptions occurred. As they continued to work together, however, the members of each gang were surprised to discover that their opponents were not as vicious as they had believed; by the time they broke camp many of the erstwhile foes had become friends.

This experiment highlights a social process that has been observed repeatedly throughout history. If people who are fighting recognize a common interest more important than the issue at stake, they will acknowledge their interdependence and join forces in common endeavor. This type of unity takes place within a country in time of war, when citizens who had been divided by class, ethnic, and regional differences close ranks against a common foe. Recognition of economic interdependence also leads to a break in tensions. In 1982, after decades of contention, the United Auto Workers and the automobile industry negotiated contracts involving a reduction in pay and fringe benefits in order to enable the corporations to compete more effectively against foreign producers, thus saving jobs. Other fights have been terminated by crises that affect everyone, such as the invasion of an agricultural community by a swarm of locusts. Since danger from a third party so often unites those who had been squabbling, some astute politicians have even created enemies to hold their coalitions together. The necessity for cooperation results in sustained association; this in turn leads to a redefinition of opponents.

Any hope of regulating conflict must rest on the recognition that human beings as a general rule fight not because of greed or sadism but on moral grounds. As long as we continue to perceive conflict in simplistic terms—good against evil—there is little hope of achieving or preserving peace. Rather, we must focus on reducing the formation and perpetuation of contrast conceptions. If former foes become intently involved in common endeavor, social distance between them is likely to decrease. When social distance is reduced, role-taking becomes more personalized. As the new allies realize how much they have in common, they are able to identify with one another and become more responsive to one another's inner experiences and feelings. When social distance is diminished, people identify with one another as human beings, and stereotyped beliefs—including contrast conceptions—break down. As the erstwhile foes become more reasonable, moderate leaders on both sides are able to get a hearing and negotiation becomes possible. Of course, as Sherif discovered, mere contact is not enough; animosities are only intensified and stereotyped conceptions reinforced. All perspectives interfere with their own revision, and the stance of combatants is much like that of a person who is paranoid. But joint participation in a strenuous effort to attain some important goal that supersedes all other considerations often dissolves animosities; then former enemies are willing to acknowledge their own shortcomings and to recognize the virtues of others. Such mutual knowledge reduces the sharp contrast between the opposing parties.

The objective existence of an overriding goal is not enough. The fact that all human beings have a common interest in controlling nuclear weapons has not altered the political scene. *Global 2000 Report*, issued by the U.S. government in 1980, estimates that $450 billion a year is being spent on armaments, compared with only $20 billion for economic aid. In both the Soviet Union and the United States military spending has become the major barrier to developing and maintaining a healthy economy. Yet leaders on both sides are willing to risk domestic disorders to protect their nations against ogres who are just as terrified as they are. Human beings do not respond to objective facts; they act on the basis of their definitions. As long as people cannot be persuaded to place top priority on a superordinate goal — the preservation of the species — they will continue to make preparations to defend themselves, regardless of the cost. There are many dedicated members of class, religious, ethnic, and nationalistic movements for whom the triumph of their partisan cause is more important than survival. If they cannot win, they do not care what else happens.

Mediation by Third Parties. Once conflicts are under way, they can sometimes be stopped by third-party mediation or arbitration. Since third parties do not share the combatants' contrast conceptions, they are in a better position to break the impasse. Mediation is more likely to be effective if it can be initiated before differences are so sharply drawn that considerations of prestige distort calculations of expediency. Mediation works because of the possibility of saving face. The procedure implies equality of bargaining power; neither side is admitting any weakness, and each retains the right to withdraw and to continue fighting. Since the combatants enter voluntarily, they do not give up their right to self-determination. In most conflicts there are leaders on both sides who feel no enthusiasm over the fighting, and mediation often makes it easier for such moderates to shunt aside the extremists who demand victory at any price. Both sides become especially responsive to compromises they had previously been unwilling even to consider after they have become exhausted in a protracted struggle.

Mediating disputes is an old practice, and some successful tactics have become established. Experienced mediators often strive for a truce and a cooling-off period. As the tension level is lowered, the position of extremists is weakened, and situations can be defined in a more reasonable manner. When factual matters are in dispute, one widely used procedure is the appointment of a distinguished and impartial panel to investigate and make recommendations. Although such recommendations are not binding on the disputants, they are often useful in that they disclose facts that both parties would rather have kept hidden. Fact-finding reports thus place pressure on both sides to be more reasonable. One maneuver, sometimes used in mediating labor-management disputes as well as other conflicts, is to require each side to state the opponent's position to the latter's complete satisfaction before it is allowed to state its own views. Once the combatants develop some appreciation of each other's definition of the situation, contrast conceptions tend to be somewhat attenuated, and what had previously appeared totally unreasonable begins to make some sense. As Dahrendorf (1959:225–26) points out, there can be no permanent peace unless each party recognizes justice in the cause of its opponent.

Adjudication of Disputes. Most communities have developed institutionalized procedures for settling intramural quarrels. Prolonged disputes that threaten the community's vital interests, such as transportation or medical care, are not tolerated for long. Where authority is well established, the government requires the settlement of quarrels within its jurisdiction. In courts of law each side is given an opportunity to present its case, often by attorneys who can do so without the bitterness and rancor of those more directly involved in the fight. Once a decision is made, it is binding on both parties. Where necessary, the police power of the state is used to enforce the judgment of the court.

Arbitration is a similar judicial process. A third party, presumably neutral, hears what the disputants have to say and then makes a binding decision. Many labor-management disputes are settled in this manner, although the extent to which arbitration is compulsory varies from one country to another. If public opinion supports the judgment, the two contenders often have little choice but to comply, even if they are displeased. Thus, within communities the law provides a mandatory way to settle inconvenient or dangerous disputes.

The adjudication of disputes can be effective only when the contenders are willing to abide by the judge's decision. Adjudication thus requires the two parties to surrender some autonomy. While individuals or organizations will do so in order to avoid or resolve a crisis, for national governments to cede a portion of their autonomy to an independent third party is far more problematic. In recent centuries people throughout the world have accepted the belief that sovereignty resides in national states and that all other categories of people — principalities, corporations, crime syndicates, as well as religious, ethnic, and class units — must defer to national interests. Nations are thus assumed to be the natural units to make final decisions for their respective inhabitants. National sovereignty is therefore incompatible with third-party adjudication. As long as each country reserves the right to judge its own case, it will resort to force to defend what it regards as its just interests; this is what makes international disputes so deadly and costly. Thus, many have called for setting up a world government. But even a world government would not necessarily eliminate conflict. International wars would become civil wars, although they might become somewhat easier to contain.

As long as people believe that their vital interests are threatened, it is doubtful that any procedure for resolving differences can prevent altercations. Human beings will fight whenever they are convinced that they are being deprived of something that is rightfully theirs. The one freedom that people are not likely ever to surrender is their right to rebel when they are convinced they are being treated unjustly. That people feel a moral obligation to struggle for their rights suggests that the legal regulation of violence is not likely to be legitimated until a substantial portion of the people on earth become part of a common moral order. Thus, Wright (1942:1305) stresses that the positive aspect of peace — justice — cannot be separated from the negative aspect — elimination of violence. The development of electronic communication channels, especially television, provides the technology necessary to reduce the world to a "global village." Were this to happen, it would at least become possible for human beings throughout the world to identify with one another as members of the same species. Once we recognize that human nature is much the same the world over, perhaps we will become more susceptible to appeals to reason.

VALUES AND SOCIOLOGICAL RESEARCH

Alternative Directions in Sociology. Work in the natural sciences has rested on a clear separation between statements of preference — what is good or bad, beautiful or ugly — and statements of fact. Although serious questions have been raised over whether the difference is as clear-cut as had once been supposed, it is still a useful distinction. Detachment and objectivity have always been part of the ideal of scientific research. Scientific knowledge consists for the most part of empirically grounded generalizations; hypotheses are constructed and tested in terms of the best available evidence. Scientists make judgments on the basis of facts, whether or not they approve of them or the conclusions to which they lead. Thus, science sometimes appears to be a cold, impersonal way to arrive at objective truth about natural phenomena. This does not mean that scientists as human beings are indifferent to values. Max Weber (1949) proposes that sociologists select problems to investigate in terms of their personal values; once their research is under way, however, they are to recognize facts for what they are, regardless of their preferences. This procedure has worked in the natural sciences, and it is likely to yield fruitful results in the study of society. This position, until recently widely accepted by sociologists, has come to be known as "value-free" sociology. In recent decades a number of basic presuppositions underlying sociological research have been challenged, and this is one of them. The challenge is the result of disillusionment. Despite a century of prodigious efforts to develop and test scientific generalizations about human society, the results have thus far been disappointing.

Part of the discontent stems from concern that Bacon's ideal has been eroding in the same manner as the Hippocratic oath in medicine and the code of honor in the Olympic Games. Research does not occur in a vacuum; scientists are human beings, and their activities are an integral part of the social structure of the communities in which they live. In past centuries, when research was conducted largely by independent scholars working alone or in collaboration with a handful of colleagues, Bacon's ideal was taken for granted. In the twentieth century, however, science has become a complex endeavor carried out in huge formal organizations. As participants in large bureaucracies, many scientists have been attracted to research that is most likely to enable them to advance quickly up the academic ladder. Especially in the 1960s, amid protests against the Vietnam War, many sociologists became upset over what they regarded as the misuse of their research. Just as some physicists were shocked when their work led to the development of nuclear weapons, some sociologists have objected that research in industrial relations has helped managers rather than workers, that prison research has served the interests of jailers rather than prisoners, and that studies of rebellions have helped counterinsurgency agents rather than revolutionaries.

Radical sociologists in particular have complained that only corporations and goverment agencies benefit from sociological research and have argued that sociologists should confine themselves to research that would be used for what they regard as more desirable purposes. They have called for abandonment of the posture of political neutrality and have argued that sociologists, along with other scientists, must bear moral responsibility for the consequences of their research (Syzmanski, 1970). Some have even formed a contrast conception of value-free sociology, attacking it as a nefarious tool of the establishment, and many vitriolic exchanges have followed. Others have countered that such a program could not be accomplished. Once the findings of studies have been published, there is no way for the authors to control what happens to the ideas they developed. Since scientists cannot possibly anticipate what will happen as a result of their research, there is no way in which even the best-intentioned sociologists could select studies that are guaranteed not be used for purposes of which they disapprove.

Some sociologists have become so disillusioned that they have proposed abandoning the methods of the natural sciences altogether. Social scientists had long labored on the assumption that the inadequacy of their findings was the product of the youthfulness of their disciplines and that eventually a body of knowledge comparable to that of the physical and biological sciences would develop. But some are now arguing that a scientific study of human behavior — individual or collective — is impossible. They argue that the rigorous methods of observation, measurement, and experimentation are simply not suited to the study of social life. Science is not the only form of knowledge, and they contend that the procedures used in the humanities as well as methods yet to be developed are more likely to produce the kind of understanding that would serve Bacon's ideal. Thus, various "interpretive" approaches have developed in each of the social sciences, including sociology (Rabinow and Sullivan, 1979).

Dispassionate Analysis. Knowledge is an instrument for living; it facilitates problem solving. The more accurate the knowledge, the more effective it is likely to be as an instrument of adaptation. One may find the truth inconvenient or even painful, but it still remains the most effective tool for confronting problematic situations. Science has attained the respect it commands precisely because its hypotheses are more accurate than other forms of knowledge. Reality testing is an integral part of scientific method. Its empirically grounded generalizations have proved to be the most reliable guides to human conduct. Most sociologists are not yet ready to abandon the procedures that have proved so effective in the analysis of other phenomena. The fact that something has not yet been done successfully does not make it impossible. Most sociologists still remain confident that as their discipline grows out of its infancy we shall develop more accurate hypotheses concerning regularities in the ways in which human beings think and act.

Precisely because of our concern with accuracy, maintaining ethical neutrality becomes an important consideration. Dewey (1938:494–95) points out that the uncritical injection of value judgments into research is one of the major obstacles to the development of accurate knowledge in the social sciences. When research is politicized, the investigators' emotional reactions lead them to form contrast conceptions of the objects of which they disapprove—such as crime, insanity, or war. Any such contrast conceptions interfere with adequate understanding, for they affect the manner in which an investigator formulates problems and hypotheses as well as what he or she considers to be relevant data.

Whenever difficulties are perceived in moral terms, there is a tendency to explain events by imputing vicious motives to those who are held responsible. Moral indignation also often blinds the investigator to many facts that would otherwise be obvious. All too often deeds regarded as reprehensible are assumed to be fundamentally different from those that are approved, and the moral dichotomy often prevents one from recognizing that both may be manifestations of the same basic processes. The most obvious example of value judgments interfering with understanding comes in the study of conflict. Because we condemn fighting, we attempt to explain it in negative terms. Thus, the noble and unselfish things that people do in time of war remain a mystery. When sociologists become too directly involved in a battle, they assume the stance of self-righteous indignation that characterizes all fighters, and this blinds them to many facts that are readily accessible. Thus, the attack on value-free sociology is self-defeating; politicization only hinders us from developing a more adequate understanding of the phenomena we dislike.

It is now generally agreed that absolute objectivity is impossible. All perception is selective, and what human beings perceive depends on their interests and the kinds of linguistic categories they have learned. Nonetheless, accurate knowledge is more likely to be forthcoming if inquiries are made as dispassionately as possible. Value judgments are unavoidable; one can only acknowledge them explicitly and bend over backwards to neutralize them. Otherwise sociological generalizations will only serve as justifications for political action. By maintaining some measure of detachment one is more likely to recognize evidence for what it is. By developing the most accurate generalizations possible, we are more likely to acquire a more effective instrument for the pursuit of whatever is valued.

Furthermore, the social scientist's attempt to be as dispassionate as possible does not mean that one is callous toward human concerns, as some critics of value-free sociology have contended. On the contrary, it is precisely because we do care about human needs that we want to develop instruments that are likely to reduce pain and maximize fulfillment. Since dispassionate study involves admitting things that are unpleasant, it is difficult. But it is a necessary step to developing the kind of knowledge that will enable us to transform what we dislike. Unless we strive for accuracy, we are condemned to continue acting on the basis of popular superstitions.

Continuation of the Quest. Accurate knowledge in itself is not a guarantee of a better life. The existence of a moral order maximizes the chances of the best available knowledge being used to pursue values that are shared within a community. Widely accepted values are expressed in utopian visions and other ideals, and these provide the goals toward which everyone, including intellectuals, will strive. What should sociologists do in the face of disappointments and disillusionments? We really have little choice but to continue our quest for a better understanding of how human society works. We should not be immobilized by the fact that our record leaves much to be desired. After all, knowledge does not have to be perfect to be useful. Furthermore, there are no ultimate solutions to human problems. Life conditions keep changing, and we shall have to continue our quest for relevant information.

Apart from our concern with social problems, a better understanding of how society works is helpful to each of us in pursuing our personal life. Each individual needs a realistic orientation toward the world, and the most economical form of knowledge consists of generalizations about what people do. To the extent that sociologists can provide useful guides to living, the discipline will prosper. To the extent that we fail, the discipline is likely to be replaced by more effective ways of conceptualizing and analyzing the subject matter. The proof of the pudding is in the eating. Social institutions without utility become obsolete. Unless sociologists can produce knowledge that serves some useful purpose, the discipline is not likely to survive.

SUMMARY AND DISCUSSION

A deep sense of pessimism and fatalism seems to pervade the intellectual world. Many are expressing doubts that human beings as a species can survive, let alone improve our lot. Despite the labors of thousands of scholars, sociology and the social sciences generally seem to have pitifully little to say to people struggling in a troubled world. But much of the disillusionment with these disciplines arises from unrealistic expectations. Even if social scientists actually produced more accurate knowledge, people would not necessarily attain the widely shared values depicted in utopian visions. Social reconstruction is a political process. Providing direction to the development of society is a formidable undertaking with no guarantee of success.

We are living amid the dislocations found in all rapidly changing societies. But it is in periods of social dislocation that people most often raise questions about what is important in life — what is worth living and dying for; some of the most noble expressions of human values have developed in chaotic times. Such periods of disorganization are the crucibles in which innovations develop, and perhaps a drastically different and more effective way of describing and explaining human behavior will emerge. In 1962, when the world was mourning the death of Eleanor Roosevelt, who had contributed so much toward improving the lot of disadvantaged peoples, Adlai Stevenson said with his characteristic eloquence, "She would rather light candles than curse the darkness and her glow has warmed the world." About all that sociologists can hope to do now is to light a few candles in a vast cavern, the dimensions of which are still unknown. This effort may not seem like very much, but a candle may be just enough to illuminate a ledge in time to keep us from falling off. Surely it is preferable to light candles than to complain bitterly of living in an imperfect society while plummeting headlong toward the bottom of a chasm.

SUGGESTED READINGS

Horowitz, Irving L. (ed.). 1971. *The Use and Abuse of Social Science.* New Brunswick, N.J.: Transaction Books.
> A collection of critical essays on the relationship between social research and the formation of public policy.

MacRae, Duncan. 1976. *The Social Functions of Social Science.* New Haven: Yale University Press.
> A proposal that scientific hypotheses and ethical assertions, though distinguishable, can be fruitfully combined in the social sciences.

Mannheim, Karl. 1940. *Man and Society in an Age of Reconstruction.* Edward Shils (trans.). New York: Harcourt, Brace.

A discussion of the difficulties involved in social planning, by a specialist in the sociology of knowledge.

Sherif, Muzafer, et al. 1961. *Intergroup Conflict and Cooperation: The Robbers Cave Experiment.* Norman, Okla.: University Book Exchange.

An experimental study on the development and transformation of contrast conceptions.

Wilensky, Harold L. 1967. *Organizational Intelligence.* New York: Basic Books.

A description of how relevant scientific knowledge is gathered, interpreted, and used in forming organizational policies.

Bibliography

Albert, Ethel M. 1960. Socio-Political Organization and Receptivity to Change: Some Differences Between Ruanda and Urundi. *Southwestern Journal of Anthropology* 16:46–74.

Alex, Nicholas. 1969. *Black in Blue: A Study of the Negro Policeman.* New York: Appleton-Century-Crofts.

Almond, Gabriel A. 1960. *The American People and Foreign Policy.* New York: Praeger.

Anderson, Elin. 1938. *We Americans.* Cambridge, Mass.: Harvard University Press.

Anderson, Robert T. 1965. From Mafia to Cosa Nostra. *American Journal of Sociology* 71:302–10.

Angell, Robert C. 1936. *The Family Encounters the Depression.* New York: Scribner's.

Aptheker, Herbert. 1943. *American Negro Slave Revolts.* New York: Columbia University Press.

Ardant du Picq, Charles. 1921. *Battle Studies: Ancient and Modern Battle.* J. N. Greely and R. C. Cotton (trans.). New York: Macmillan.

Arnold, Magda B. 1960. *Emotion and Personality.* Vol. 1. New York: Columbia University Press.

Asch, Solomon E. 1951. Effects of Group Pressure upon the Modification and Distortion of Judgments. Pp. 177–90 in H. S. Guetzkow (ed.), *Groups, Leadership, and Men.* Pittsburgh: Carnegie Press.

———. 1956. Studies of Independence and Submission to Group Pressure: I. A Minority of One Against a Unanimous Majority. *Psychological Monographs* 70: no. 9.

Bagehot, Walter. 1948. *Physics and Politics.* New York: Knopf.

Baker, Keith, and Robert J. Rubel (eds.). 1980. *Violence and Crime in the Schools.* Lexington, Mass.: Lexington Books.

Baldwin, Monica. 1957. *I Leap over the Wall.* New York: New American Library.

Bales, Robert F. 1950. *Interaction Process Analysis.* Cambridge, Mass.: Addison-Wesley.

———. 1955. How People Interact in Conferences. *Scientific American* 192 (March): 31–35.

———, and Fred L. Strodtbeck. 1951. Phases in Group Problem-Solving. *Journal of Abnormal and Social Psychology* 46:485–95.

———, et al. 1951. Channels of Communication in Small Groups. *American Sociological Review* 16:461–68.

Baltzell, E. Digby. 1962. *An American Business Aristocracy.* New York: Collier.

Banfield, Edward C. 1958. *The Moral Basis of a Backward Society.* Glencoe, Ill.: Free Press.

Banks, James A., and Jean D. Grambs (eds.). 1972. *Black Self-Concept.* New York: McGraw-Hill.

Barber, Bernard. 1961. Resistance by Scientists to Scientific Discovery. *Science* 134:596–602.

Barghoorn, Frederick C. 1950. *The Soviet Image of the United States.* New York: Harcourt, Brace.

Barnard, Allan (ed.). 1953. *The Harlot Killer: The Story of Jack the Ripper in Fact and Fiction.* New York: Dodd, Mead.

Barnett, Homer G. 1941. Personal Conflicts and Cultural Change. *Social Forces* 20:160–71.

Bassan, Morton E. 1947. Some Factors Found Valuable in Maintaining Morale on a Small Combatant Ship. *Bulletin of the Menninger Clinic* 11:33–42.

Bauer, Raymond A. 1952. *The New Man in Soviet Psychology.* Cambridge, Mass.: Harvard University Press.

———, and David B. Gleicher. 1953. Word-of-Mouth Communication in the Soviet Union. *Public Opinion Quarterly* 17:297–310.

Beals, Alan R., and Bernard J. Siegel. 1966. *Divisiveness and Social Conflict.* Stanford: Stanford University Press.

Becker, Howard. 1949. The Nature and Consequences of Black Propaganda. *American Sociological Review* 14:221–35.

Becker, Howard S. 1951. The Professional Dance Musician and His Audience. *American Journal of Sociology* 57:136–44.

———. 1963. *Outsiders: Studies in the Sociology of Deviance.* New York: Free Press.

———. 1967. History, Culture and Subjective Experience: An Exploration of the Social Basis of Drug-Induced Experiences. *Journal of Health and Social Behavior* 8:163–76.

———, et al. 1961. *Boys in White: Student Culture in Medical School.* Chicago: University of Chicago Press.

Belden, Jack, 1949. *China Shakes the World.* New York: Harper.

Bell, Inge P. 1968. *CORE and the Strategy of Non-Violence.* New York: Random House.

Benedict, Ruth F. 1946. *The Chrysanthemum and the Sword: Patterns of Japanese Culture.* Boston: Houghton Mifflin.

Bengis, Ingrid. 1973. *Combat in the Erogenous Zone.* New York: Knopf.

Berelson, Bernard, et al. 1954. *Voting: A Study of Opinion Formation in a Presidential Campaign.* Chicago: University of Chicago Press.

Berger, Peter L., and Thomas Luckmann. 1966. *The Social Construction of Reality.* New York: Doubleday.

Bergson, Abram. 1964. *The Economics of Soviet Planning.* New Haven: Yale University Press.

Berk, Richard A. 1974. *Collective Behavior.* Dubuque, Iowa: William C. Brown.

Berkowitz, Leonard. 1962. *Aggression: A Social Psychological Analysis.* New York: McGraw-Hill.

Berne, Eric. 1964. *Games People Play: The Psychology of Human Relationships.* New York: Grove Press.

Berreman, Gerald D. (ed.). 1981. *Social Inequality: Comparative and Developmental Approaches.* New York: Academic Press.

Birdwhistell, Ray L. 1970. *Kinesics and Context: Essays on Body Motion Communication.* Philadelphia: University of Pennsylvania Press.

Bittner, Egon. 1963. Radicalism and the Organization of Radical Movements. *American Sociological Review* 28:928–40.

Blau, Peter. 1964. *Exchange and Power in Social Life.* New York: Wiley.

———, and Otis D. Duncan. 1967. *The American Occupational Structure.* New York: Wiley.

Blumer, Herbert. 1935. Moulding of Mass Behavior Through the Motion Picture. *Publications of the American Sociological Society* 29:115–27.

———. 1943. Morale. Pp. 207–31 in W. F. Ogburn (ed.), *American Society in Wartime.* Chicago: University of Chicago Press.

———. 1951. Collective Behavior. Pp. 167–222 in A. M. Lee (ed.), *Principles of Sociology.* New York: Barnes & Noble.

———. 1969. Fashion: From Class Differentiation to Collective Selection. *Sociological Quarterly* 10:275–91.

Boeke, Julius H. 1942. *The Structure of the Netherlands Indian Economy.* New York: Institute of Pacific Relations.

Bogart, Leo. 1972. *Silent Politics: Polls and the Awareness of Public Opinion.* New York: Wiley.

Brailsford, H. N. 1933. Massacre. *Encyclopedia of the Social Sciences,* vol. 10, pp. 191–99.

———. 1934. Passive Resistance and Non-Cooperation. *Encyclopedia of the Social Sciences,* vol. 12, pp. 9–13.

Brant, Stefan. 1957. *The East German Rising.* C. Wheeler (trans.). New York: Praeger.

Breed, Warren. 1955. Social Control in the Newsroom. *Social Forces* 33:326–35.

Brinton, Crane. 1952. *The Anatomy of Revolution.* New York: Prentice-Hall.

Bronfenbrenner, Urie. 1961. The Mirror Image in Soviet-American Relations. *Journal of Social Issues* 17:45–56.

Brown, Robert. 1963. *Explanation in Social Science.* Chicago: Aldine.

Browne, Joy. 1973. *The Used Car Game: A Sociology of the Bargain.* Lexington, Mass.: D. C. Heath.

Browning, Douglas (ed.). 1965. *Philosophers of Process.* New York: Random House.

Buber, Martin. 1958. *I and Thou.* R. G. Smith (trans.). New York: Scribner's.

Buckley, Walter. 1967. *Sociology and Modern Systems Theory.* Englewood Cliffs, N.J.: Prentice-Hall.

Bulmer, Martin. 1984. *The Chicago School of Sociology: Institutionalization, Diversity, and the Rise of Sociological Research.* Chicago: University of Chicago Press.

Burgess, Ernest W. 1974. *The Basic Writings of Ernest W. Burgess.* Donald J. Bogue (ed.). Chicago: Community and Family Study Center.

Burke, Kenneth. 1954. *Permanence and Change: An Anatomy of Purpose.* Los Altos, Calif.: Hermes.

Bury, John B. 1932. *The Idea of Progress.* New York: Macmillan.

Campbell, Angus. 1971. *White Attitudes Toward Black People.* Ann Arbor, Mich.: Institute for Social Research.

Cannon, Walter B. 1929. *Bodily Changes in Pain, Hunger, Fear and Rage.* New York: Appleton-Century.

———. 1942. Voodoo Death. *American Anthropologist* 44:169–81.

Cantril, Hadley. 1940. *The Invasion from Mars: A Study in the Psychology of Panic.* Princeton: Princeton University Press.

Caplow, Theodore. 1947. Rumors in War. *Social Forces* 25:298–302.

Carroll, John B., and Joseph B. Casagrande. 1958. The Function of Language Classifications in Behavior. Pp. 18–31 in Eleanor Maccoby et al. (eds.), *Readings in Social Psychology.* New York: Henry Holt.

Carroll, Michael P. 1975. Revitalization Movements and Social Structure: Some Quantitative Tests. *American Sociological Review* 40:389–401.

Carroll, Wallace. 1958. Where Is the Luftwaffe? Pp. 373–81 in William E. Daugherty and Morris Janowitz (eds.), *A Psychological Warfare Casebook.* Baltimore: Johns Hopkins University Press.

Caudill, Harry M. 1963. *Night Comes to the Cumberlands.* Boston: Little, Brown.

Caudill, William, et al. 1952. Social Structure and Interaction Processes on a Psychiatric Ward. *American Journal of Orthopsychiatry* 22:314–34.

Cavan, Sherri. 1966. *Liquor License: An Ethnography of Bar Behavior.* Chicago: Aldine.

Chakotin, Serge. 1940. *The Rape of the Masses: The Psychology of Totalitarian Political Propaganda.* London: Routledge.

Chen, Theodore H. 1960. *Thought Reform of the Chinese Intellectuals.* New York: Oxford University Press.

Chicago Commission on Race Relations. 1922. *The Negro in Chicago.* Chicago: University of Chicago Press.

Chilman, Catherine S. 1979. *Adolescent Sexuality in a Changing American Society.* Washington, D.C.: Department of Health, Education and Welfare.

Clark, Gerald. 1969. What Happens When the Police Strike? *New York Times Magazine,* November 16:45, 76–96.

Clemmer, Donald. 1940. *The Prison Community.* Boston: Christopher.

Cleveland, Catharine C. 1916. *The Great Revival of the West: 1797–1805.* Chicago: University of Chicago Press.

Cloward, Richard A., and Lloyd E. Ohlin. 1960. *Delinquency and Opportunity: A Theory of Delinquent Gangs.* Glencoe, Ill.: Free Press.

Cockerham, William C. 1977. Green Berets: Social Cohesion in a Closed Society. Pp. 27–38 in Arthur B. Shostak (ed.), *Our Sociological Eye*. New York: Alfred.

Coleman, James S., et al. 1957. The Diffusion of Innovation Among Physicians. *Sociometry* 20:253–70.

Collins, Barry E., and Harold Guetzkow. 1964. *A Social Psychology of Group Processes for Decision-Making*. New York: Wiley.

Collins, Larry, and Dominique LaPierre. 1975. *Freedom at Midnight*. New York: Simon and Schuster.

Colombotos, John. 1969. Physicians and Medicare: A Before-After Study of the Effects of Legislation on Attitudes. *American Sociological Review* 34:318–34.

Colson, Elizabeth. 1974. *Tradition and Contract*. Chicago: Aldine.

Connor, Walter D. 1979. *Socialism, Politics, and Equality: Hierarchy and Change in Eastern Europe and the USSR*. New York: Columbia University Press.

Cooley, Charles H. 1918. *Social Process*. New York: Scribner's.

———. 1922. *Social Organization*. New York: Scribner's.

Cooper, Eunice, and Marie Jahoda. 1947. Evasion of Propaganda: How Prejudiced People Respond to Anti-Prejudice Propaganda. *Journal of Psychology* 23:15–25.

Copeland, Lewis C. 1939. The Negro as a Contrast Conception. Pp. 152–79 in Edgar T. Thompson (ed.), *Race Relations and the Race Problem*. Durham, N.C.: Duke University Press.

Cortright, David. 1975. *Soldiers in Revolt: The American Military Today*. New York: Doubleday.

Coser, Lewis A. 1956. *The Functions of Social Conflict*. Glencoe, Ill.: Free Press.

———. 1961. The Termination of Conflict. *Journal of Conflict Resolution* 5:347–53.

Cottrell, W. Fred. 1939. Of Time and the Railroader. *American Sociological Review* 4:190–98.

Currie, Elliott P. 1968. Crimes Without Criminals: Witchcraft and its Control in Renaissance Europe. *Law and Society Review* 3:7–32.

Dahlke, H. Otto. 1952. Race and Minority Riots: A Study in the Typology of Violence. *Social Forces* 30:419–25.

Dahrendorf, Ralf. 1959. *Class and Class Conflict in Industrial Society*. Stanford: Stanford University Press.

Dalton, Melville. 1959. *Men Who Manage*. New York: Wiley.

Danzig, Elliott R., et al. 1958. *The Effects of a Threatening Rumor on a Disaster-Stricken Community*. Washington, D.C.: National Research Council.

Daugherty, William E., and Morris Janowitz (eds.). 1960. *A Psychological Warfare Casebook*. Baltimore: Johns Hopkins University Press.

Davies, James C. 1962. Toward a Theory of Revolution. *American Sociological Review* 27:5–19.

———. 1971. *When Men Revolt and Why*. New York: Free Press.

Davis, Allison. 1945. Caste, Economy, and Violence. *American Journal of Sociology* 51:7–15.

Davis, Saville R. 1941. Morale in Fascist Italy in Wartime. *American Journal of Sociology* 47:434–38.

Dawson, Alan. 1977. *Fifty-five Days: The Fall of South Vietnam.* Englewood Cliffs, N.J.: Prentice-Hall.

Delaisi, Francis. 1927. *Political Myths and Economic Realities.* New York: Viking.

Della Fave, L. Richard. 1980. The Meek Shall Not Inherit the Earth: Self-Evaluation and the Legitimacy of Stratification. *American Sociological Review* 45:955–71.

Denisoff, R. Serge, and Richard A. Peterson (eds.). 1972. *The Sounds of Social Change.* Chicago: Rand McNally.

DeVos, George. 1967. Psychology of Purity and Pollution as Related to Social Self-Identity and Caste. Pp. 292–315 in A. V. S. de Reuck and Julie Knight (eds.), *Caste and Race: Comparative Approaches.* London: Churchill.

———, and Hiroshi Wagatsuma. 1966. *Japan's Invisible Race: Caste in Culture and Personality.* Berkeley and Los Angeles: University of California Press.

Dewey, John. 1898. Evolution and Ethics. *Monist* 8:321–41.

———. 1910. *How We Think.* New York: D. C. Heath.

———. 1926. *Experience and Nature.* Chicago: Open Court.

———. 1927. *The Public and Its Problems.* New York: Henry Holt.

———. 1934. *Art as Experience.* New York: Minton, Balch.

———. 1938. *Logic: The Theory of Inquiry.* New York: Henry Holt.

Dittes, James E. 1956. Attractiveness of Group as Function of Self-Esteem and Acceptance by Group. *Journal of Abnormal and Social Psychology* 53:100–107.

Dollard, John, et al. 1939. *Frustration and Aggression.* New Haven: Yale University Press.

Doyle, Bertram. 1937. *The Etiquette of Race Relations in the South.* Chicago: University of Chicago Press.

Drake, St. Clair, and Horace R. Cayton. 1945. *Black Metropolis.* New York: Harcourt, Brace.

Drucker, Peter F. 1949. *The New Society.* New York: Harper.

DuBois, W. E. Burghardt. 1911. *The Souls of Black Folk.* Chicago: A. C. McClurg.

Duffy, Elizabeth. 1941. An Explanation of "Emotional" Phenomena Without the Use of the Concept "Emotion." *Journal of General Psychology* 25:283–93.

Duncan, Otis D. 1964. Social Organization and the Ecosystem. Pp. 37–82 in Robert E. L. Faris (ed.), *Handbook of Modern Sociology.* Chicago: Rand McNally.

———, and Beverly Duncan. 1957. *The Negro Population in Chicago: A Study of Residential Succession.* Chicago: University of Chicago Press.

Dunham, H. Warren, and S. Kirson Weinberg. 1960. *The Culture of the State Mental Hospital.* Detroit: Wayne State University Press.

Durkheim, Émile. 1915. *The Elementary Forms of the Religious Life.* J. W. Swain (trans.). New York: Macmillan.

———. 1933. *The Division of Labor in Society.* G. Simpson (trans.). New York: Macmillan.

Dvorin, Eugene P. 1952. *Racial Separation in South Africa.* Chicago: University of Chicago Press.

Easterbrook, J. A. 1959. The Effect of Emotion on Cue Utilization and the Organization of Behavior. *Psychological Review* 66:183–201.

Eaton, Joseph W. 1952. Controlled Acculturation: A Survival Technique of the Hutterites. *American Sociological Review* 17:331–40.

———, and Robert J. Weil. 1955. *Culture and Mental Disorders.* Glencoe, Ill.: Free Press.

Edelman, Murray. 1964. *The Symbolic Uses of Politics.* Urbana: University of Illinois Press.

Edwards, Lyford P. 1927. *The Natural History of Revolution.* Chicago: University of Chicago Press.

Eisenstadt, Shmuel N. 1978. *Revolution and the Transformation of Societies.* New York: Free Press.

Ekman, Paul, et al. 1972. *Emotion in the Human Face.* New York: Pergamon.

Emerson, Joan. 1969. Negotiating the Serious Import of Humor. *Sociometry* 32:169–81.

Erasmus, Charles J. 1961. *Man Takes Control: Cultural Development and American Aid.* Minneapolis: University of Minnesota Press.

Erbe, Brigitte M. 1975. Race and Socioeconomic Segregation. *American Sociological Review* 40:801–18.

Erikson, Kai T. 1966. *Wayward Puritans: A Study in the Sociology of Deviance.* New York: Wiley.

Estroff, Sue E. 1981. *Making It Crazy: An Ethnography of Psychiatric Clients in an American Community.* Berkeley and Los Angeles: University of California Press.

Fallers, Lloyd. 1955. The Predicament of the Modern African Chief: An Instance from Uganda. *American Anthropologist* 57:290–305.

———. 1973. *Inequality: Social Stratification Reconsidered.* Chicago: University of Chicago Press.

Farrell, John C., and Asa P. Smith (eds.). 1967. *Image and Reality in World Politics.* New York: Columbia University Press.

Feagin, Joe R., and Paul B. Sheatsley. 1968. Ghetto Resident Appraisals of a Riot. *Public Opinion Quarterly* 32:352–62.

Fei, Hsiao-Tung. 1946. Peasantry and Gentry: An Interpretation of Chinese Social Structure and Its Changes. *American Journal of Sociology* 52:1–17.

Feldman, Harvey W. 1968. Ideological Supports to Becoming and Remaining a Heroin Addict. *Journal of Health and Social Behavior* 9:131–38.

Festinger, Leon, et al. 1952. The Influence Process in the Presence of Extreme Deviates. *Human Relations* 5:327–46.

———. 1956. *When Prophecy Fails.* Minneapolis: University of Minnesota Press.

Feuer, Lewis S. 1969. *The Conflict of Generations: The Character and Significance of Student Movements.* New York: Basic Books.

Fiedler, Fred. 1967. *A Theory of Leadership Effectiveness.* New York: McGraw-Hill.

Filler, Louis. 1960. *The Crusade Against Slavery: 1830–1860.* New York: Harper.

Finer, Samuel E. 1962. *The Man on Horseback: The Role of the Military in Politics.* New York: Praeger.

Finestone, Harold. 1957. Cats, Kicks, and Color. *Social Problems* 5:3–13.

Firey, Walter. 1945. Sentiment and Symbolism as Ecological Variables. *American Sociological Review* 10:140–48.

Fischer, Claude S. 1981. The Public and Private Worlds of City Life. *American Sociological Review* 46:306–16.

Fishman, Joshua A. 1971. *Sociolinguistics*. Rowley, Mass.: Newbury House.

Follett, Mary P. 1923. *The New State*. New York: Longmans, Green.

Foote, Nelson N., and Clyde W. Hart. 1953. Public Opinion and Collective Behavior. Pp. 308–31 in M. Sherif and M. O. Wilson (eds.), *Group Relations at the Crossroads*. New York: Harper.

Frank, Gerold. 1966. *The Boston Strangler*. New York: New American Library.

Frazier, E. Franklin. 1939. *The Negro Family in the United States*. Chicago: University of Chicago Press.

Freidson, Eliot. 1953. Adult Discount: An Aspect of Children's Changing Taste. *Child Development* 24:39–49.

———. 1970. *Profession of Medicine*. New York: Dodd, Mead.

Freud, Sigmund. 1936. *The Problem of Anxiety*. H. A. Bunker (trans.). New York: Norton.

Fritz, Charles E., and Eli S. Marks. 1954. The NORC Studies of Human Behavior in Disaster. *Journal of Social Issues* 10:26–41.

Fukami, Teiji, and Wilbur Cross. 1969. *The Lost Men of Anatahan*. New York: Coronet.

Funkenstein, Daniel H. 1955. The Physiology of Fear and Anger. *Scientific American* 192 (May):74–80.

Garfinkel, Harold. 1967. *Studies in Ethnomethodology*. Englewood Cliffs, N.J.: Prentice-Hall.

Garrow, David J. 1978. *Protest at Selma*. New Haven: Yale University Press.

Gennep, Arnold van. 1910. *La formation des légendes*. Paris: Ernest Flammarion.

Ghurye, Govind S. 1950. *Caste and Class in India*. Bombay: Popular Book Department.

Ginsberg, Morris. 1930. Association. *Encyclopedia of the Social Sciences*, vol. 2, pp. 284–86.

Glaser, Barney G., and Anselm L. Strauss. 1964. Awareness Contexts and Social Interaction. *American Sociological Review* 29:669–79.

Glazer, Tom (ed.). 1972. *Songs of Peace, Freedom, and Protest*. Greenwich, Conn.: Fawcett.

Gluckman, Max. 1963. *Order and Rebellion in Tribal Africa*. New York: Free Press.

Goffman, Erving. 1959. *The Presentation of Self in Everyday Life*. New York: Doubleday.

———. 1963. *Behavior in Public Places*. New York: Free Press.

Goode, William J. 1957. Community Within a Community: The Professions. *American Sociological Review* 22:194–200.

———. 1960. A Theory of Role Strain. *American Sociological Review* 25:483–96.

Goodman, Mary E., and Alma Beman. 1968. Child's-Eye Views of Life in an Urban Barrio. Pp. 84–103 in June Helm (ed.), *Spanish-Speaking People in the United States*. Seattle: University of Washington Press.

Gouldner, Alvin W. 1957. Cosmopolitans and Locals: Toward an Analysis of Latent Social Roles. *Administrative Science Quarterly* 2:281–306, 444–80.

———. 1960. The Norm of Reciprocity: A Preliminary Statement. *American Sociological Review* 25:161–78.

———. 1970. *The Coming Crisis of Western Sociology.* New York: Basic Books.

Griffiths, Franklyn. 1971. A Tendency Analysis of Soviet Policy-Making. Pp. 335–78 in H. G. Skilling and F. Griffiths (eds.), *Interest Groups in Soviet Politics.* Princeton: Princeton University Press.

Grimm, Harold J. 1973. *The Reformation Era: 1500–1650.* New York: Macmillan.

Grimshaw, Allen D. (ed.). 1969. *Racial Violence in the United States.* Chicago: Aldine.

Grinker, Roy R., and John P. Spiegel. 1945. *Men Under Stress.* Philadelphia: Blakiston.

Gross, Bertram M. 1953. *The Legislative Struggle: A Study in Social Combat.* New York: McGraw-Hill.

Gross, Neal, et al. 1958. *Explorations in Role Analysis: Studies of the School Superintendency Role.* New York: Wiley.

Guetzkow, Harold. 1953. An Exploratory Empirical Study of the Role of Conflict in Decision-Making Conferences. *International Social Science Bulletin* 5:286–300.

———, and John Gyr. 1954. An Analysis of Conflict in Decision-Making Groups. *Human Relations* 7:367–82.

Gumperz, John J. 1958. Dialect Difference and Social Stratification in a North Indian Village. *American Anthropologist* 60:668–82.

Gusfield, Joseph R. 1963. *Symbolic Crusade: Status Politics and the American Temperance Movement.* Urbana: University of Illinois Press.

Hall, Edward T. 1959. *The Silent Language.* Greenwich, Conn.: Fawcett.

Hall, Oswald. 1946. The Informal Organization of the Medical Profession. *Canadian Journal of Economics and Political Science* 12:30–44.

———. 1948. The Stages in a Medical Career. *American Journal of Sociology* 53:327–36.

Hall, Peter M. 1972. A Symbolic Interactionist Analysis of Politics. *Sociological Inquiry* 42:35–75.

Harvey, John H., and William P. Smith. 1977. *Social Psychology: An Attributional Approach.* St. Louis: C. V. Mosby.

Head, Henry. 1926. *Aphasia and Kindred Disorders of Speech.* Vol. 1. New York: Macmillan.

Hecker, Justus F. C. 1859. *The Epidemics of the Middle Ages.* B. G. Babington (trans.). London: Truebner.

Heinl, Robert D. 1971. The Collapse of the Armed Forces. *Armed Forces Journal* 108 (June 7): 30–38.

Hermassi, Elbaki. 1975. *Toward a Comparative Study of Revolutions.* Berkeley: Institute of International Studies.

Herz, Martin F. 1958. Mechanics of Surrender, Capture, and Desertion. Pp. 392–96 in W. E. Daugherty and M. Janowitz (eds.), *A Psychological Warfare Casebook.* Baltimore: Johns Hopkins University Press.

Hiller, E. T. 1928. *The Strike: A Study in Collective Action.* Chicago: University of Chicago Press.

Hinton, William. 1968. *Fanshen: A Documentary of Revolution in a Chinese Village.* New York: Random House.

Hobsbawm, E. J. 1965. *Primitive Rebels.* New York: Norton.

Hochschild, Arlie R. 1979. Emotion Work, Feeling Rules, and Social Structure. *American Journal of Sociology* 85:551–75.

Hocking, William E. 1941. The Nature of Morale. *American Journal of Sociology* 47:302–20.

Hoffer, Eric. 1951. *The True Believer.* New York: Harper.

Hofstadter, Richard. 1955. *Social Darwinism in American Thought.* Boston: Beacon Press.

Hollingshead, August B., and Fredrick C. Redlich. 1958. *Social Class and Mental Illness.* New York: Wiley.

Homans, George C. 1962. *Sentiments and Activities.* New York: Free Press.

Horney, Karen. 1950. *Neurosis and Human Growth.* New York: Norton.

Hough, Richard. 1963. *The Potemkin Mutiny.* Englewood Cliffs, N.J.: Prentice-Hall.

Hovland, Carl I., et al. 1953. *Communication and Persuasion.* New Haven: Yale University Press.

Hughes, Charles C. 1960. *An Eskimo Village in the Modern World.* Ithaca: Cornell University Press.

Hughes, Everett C. 1943. *French Canada in Transition.* Chicago: University of Chicago Press.

———. 1958. *Men and Their Work.* Glencoe, Ill.: Free Press.

Hughes, Helen M. 1940. *News and the Human Interest Story.* Chicago: University of Chicago Press.

Huizinga, Johan. 1954. *The Waning of the Middle Ages.* F. Hopman (trans.). New York: Doubleday.

Huntington, Samuel P. 1957. Conservatism as an Ideology. *American Political Science Review* 51:454–73.

Huxley, Aldous L. 1954. *The Doors of Perception.* New York: Harper.

Inkeles, Alex. 1958. *Public Opinion in Soviet Russia.* Cambridge, Mass.: Harvard University Press.

Irwin, John, and Donald R. Cressey. 1962. Thieves, Convicts and the Inmate Culture. *Social Problems* 10:142–55.

Jahoda, Marie, et al. 1971. *Marienthal: The Sociography of an Unemployed Community.* Chicago: Aldine.

Janis, Irving L. 1972. *Victims of Groupthink.* Boston: Houghton Mifflin.

Janowitz, Morris. 1959. *Sociology and the Military Establishment.* New York: Russell Sage.

Jennings, Helen H. 1943. *Leadership and Isolation.* New York: Longmans, Green.

Johnson, Benton. 1961. Do Holiness Sects Socialize in Dominant Values? *Social Forces* 39:309–16.

Johnson, Charles S. 1943. *Patterns of Negro Segregation.* New York: Harper.

Johnstone, John, and Elihu Katz. 1957. Youth and Popular Music: A Study in the Sociology of Taste. *American Journal of Sociology* 62:563–68.

Jones, Edward E. 1965. Conformity as a Tactic of Ingratiation. *Science* 149:144–50.

Kahn, Robert L., and Daniel Katz. 1953. Leadership Practices in Relation to Productivity and Morale. Pp. 612–28 in D. Cartwright and A. Zander (eds.), *Group Dynamics: Research and Theory*. Evanston, Ill.: Row, Peterson.

Kallich, Martin, and Andrew MacLeish (eds.). 1962. *The American Revolution Through British Eyes*. Evanston, Ill.: Row, Peterson.

Kann, Robert A. 1950. *The Multi-National Empire: Nationalism and National Reform in the Habsburg Monarchy: 1848–1919*. New York: Columbia University Press.

Kariuki, Josiah M. 1964. *Mau Mau Detainee*. Baltimore: Penguin Books.

Katz, Elihu. 1957. The Two-Step Flow of Communication: An Up-to-Date Report on an Hypothesis. *Public Opinion Quarterly* 21:61–78.

———, and Jacob J. Feldman. 1962. The Debates in the Light of Research: A Survey of Surveys. Pp. 173–223 in Sidney Kraus (ed.), *The Great Debates: Background, Perspective, Effects*. Bloomington: University of Indiana Press.

———, and Paul F. Lazarsfeld. 1955. *Personal Influence*. Glencoe, Ill.: Free Press.

Katz, Sidney. 1955. The Strange Forces Behind the Richard Hockey Riot. *Mac-Lean's: Canada's National Magazine* 48 (September 17):11–15, 97–110.

Keller, Helen. 1915. *The Story of My Life*. New York: Doubleday, Page.

Kelley, Harold H., and John W. Thibaut. 1969. Group Problem Solving. Pp. 1–101 in Gardner Lindzey and Elliot Aronson (eds.), *The Handbook of Social Psychology*. Vol. 4. Reading, Mass.: Addison-Wesley.

Kephart, William H. 1948. Is the American Negro Becoming Lighter? *American Sociological Review* 13:437–43.

Kierkegaard, Søren. 1957. *The Concept of Dread*. W. Lowrie (trans.). Princeton: Princeton University Press.

Kilpatrick, Franklin P. (ed.). 1961. *Explorations in Transactional Psychology*. New York: New York University Press.

Klapp, Orrin E. 1948. The Creation of Popular Heroes. *American Journal of Sociology* 54:135–41.

———. 1962. *Heroes, Villains, and Fools*. Englewood Cliffs, N.J.: Prentice-Hall.

———. 1964. *Symbolic Leaders: Public Dramas and Public Men*. Chicago: Aldine.

Klapper, Joseph T. 1960. *The Effects of Mass Communication*. Glencoe, Ill.: Free Press.

Kleiman, Dena. 1979. New York: Suburbs Have Trouble Too. *New York Times*, October 28:E-6.

Klineberg, Otto (ed.). 1944. *Characteristics of the American Negro*. New York: Harper.

Kluckhohn, Florence R., and Fred L. Strodtbeck. 1961. *Variations in Value Orientations*. Evanston, Ill.: Row, Peterson.

Kohn-Bramstedt, Ernst. 1945. *Dictationship and Political Police: The Technique of Control by Fear*. London: Kegan Paul, Trench, Trubner.

Kornhauser, William. 1959. *The Politics of Mass Society.* Glencoe, Ill.: Free Press.
————. 1968. Mass Society. *International Encyclopedia of the Social Sciences,* vol. 10, pp. 58–64.
Kuhn, Thomas S. 1962. *The Structure of Scientific Revolutions.* Chicago: University of Chicago Press.
Kuper, Leo. 1957. *Passive Resistance in South Africa.* New Haven: Yale University Press.
Ladas, Stephen P. 1932. *The Exchange of Minorities: Bulgaria, Greece, and Turkey.* New York: Macmillan.
Lammers, Cornelis J. 1969. Strikes and Mutinies: A Comparative Study of Organizational Conflicts Between Rulers and Ruled. *Administrative Science Quarterly* 14:558–72.
Lane, David. 1971. *The End of Inequality? Stratification Under State Socialism.* Hammondsworth, England: Penguin.
Lang, Kurt. 1972. *Military Institutions and the Sociology of War.* Beverly Hills, Calif.: Sage.
————. 1980. American Military Performance in Vietnam: Background and Analysis. *Journal of Political and Military Sociology* 8:269–86.
Langenhove, Fernand van. 1916. *The Growth of a Legend.* E. B. Sherlock (trans.). New York: Putnam's.
Langer, Susanne K. 1942. *Philosophy in a New Key.* Cambridge, Mass.: Harvard University Press.
Laqueur, Walter. 1977. *Terrorism.* Boston: Little, Brown.
Larsen, Otto N. 1964. Social Effects of Mass Communication. Pp. 349–81 in R. E. L. Faris (ed.), *Handbook of Modern Sociology.* Chicago: Rand McNally.
Lasswell, Harold D. 1927. *Propaganda Technique in the World War.* New York: Knopf.
————. 1948. *Power and Personality.* New York: Norton.
————, and Dorothy Blumenstock. 1939. *World Revolutionary Propaganda.* New York: Knopf.
Lazarsfeld, Paul F., et al. 1944. *The People's Choice.* New York: Duell, Sloan and Pearce.
———— (eds.). 1967. *The Uses of Sociology.* New York: Basic Books.
Lea, Henry C. 1888. *A History of the Inquisition of the Middle Ages.* New York: Harper.
————. 1901. *The Moriscos of Spain: Their Conversion and Expulsion.* Philadelphia: Lea Brothers.
Lee, Alfred M., and Norman D. Humphreys. 1943. *Race Riot.* New York: Dryden Press.
Lee, Hong Yung. 1978. *The Politics of the Chinese Cultural Revolution.* Berkeley and Los Angeles: University of California Press.
Lee, Shu-Ching, and Audrey Brattrud. 1967. Marriage Under a Monastic Mode of Life: A Preliminary Report on the Hutterite Family in South Dakota. *Journal of Marriage and the Family* 29:512–20.

Lefebvre, Georges. 1973. *The Great Fear of 1789.* J. White (trans.). New York: Vintage.

Lenski, Gerhard E. 1954. Status Crystallization. *American Sociological Review* 19:405–13.

———. 1956. Social Participation and Status Crystallization. *American Sociological Review* 21:458–64.

Leon-Portilla, Miguel (ed.). 1962. *The Broken Spears: The Aztec Account of the Conquest of Mexico.* L. Kemp (trans.). Boston: Beacon Press.

Lerner, Daniel. 1958. *The Passing of Traditional Society: Modernizing the Middle East.* Glencoe, Ill.: Free Press.

Lewis, Roy, and Angus Maude. 1949. *The English Middle Classes.* London: Phoenix.

Lincoln, C. Eric. 1961. *The Black Muslims in America.* Boston: Beacon Press.

Lindberg, John S. 1930. *The Background of Swedish Emigration to the United States.* Minneapolis: University of Minnesota Press.

Linebarger, Paul M. A. 1948. *Psychological Warfare.* Washington, D.C.: Infantry Journal Press.

Linton, Ralph. 1936. *The Study of Man.* New York: Appleton-Century.

Lionberger, Herbert F. 1961. *Adoption of New Ideas and Practices.* Ames: Iowa State University Press.

Lippmann, Walter. 1922. *Public Opinion.* New York: Harcourt, Brace.

———. 1925. *The Phantom Public.* New York: Harcourt, Brace.

Lips, Julius E. 1937. *The Savage Hits Back.* New Haven: Yale University Press.

Lipset, Seymour M., et al. 1962. *Union Democracy.* New York: Doubleday.

Lofland, John. 1966. *Doomsday Cult.* Englewood Cliffs, N.J.: Prentice-Hall.

———. 1981. Collective Behavior: The Elementary Forms. Pp. 411–46 in Morris Rosenberg and Ralph Turner (eds.), *Social Psychology: Sociological Perspectives.* New York: Basic Books.

———, and Rodney Stark. 1965. Conversion to a Deviant Perspective. *American Sociological Review* 30:862–75.

McClelland, David. 1961. *The Achieving Society.* Princeton: Van Nostrand.

McDonald, John. 1950. *Strategy in Poker, Business, and War.* New York: Norton.

MacDonald, John S., and Leatrice D. MacDonald. 1964. Chain Migration, Ethnic Neighborhood Formation, and Social Networks. *Milbank Memorial Fund Quarterly* 42:82–97.

MacGregor, Frances C. 1974. *Transformation and Identity: The Face and Plastic Surgery.* New York: Quadrangle Books.

MacIver, Robert M. 1942. *Social Causation.* Boston: Ginn.

———. 1947. *The Web of Government.* New York: Macmillan.

Mackay, Charles. 1932. *Extraordinary Popular Delusions and the Madness of Crowds.* Boston: L. C. Page.

MacLeod, William C. 1928. *The American Indian Frontier.* New York: Knopf.

McLuhan, Marshall. 1964. *Understanding Media: The Extensions of Man.* New York: New American Library.

McWorter, Gerald A., and Robert L. Crain. 1967. Subcommunity Gladiatorial Competition: Civil Rights Leadership as a Competitive Process. *Social Forces* 46:8–21.

Majdalany, Fred. 1963. *State of Emergency: The Full Story of the Mau Mau.* Boston: Houghton Mifflin.

Malinowski, Bronislaw. 1926. *Crime and Custom in Savage Society.* New York: Harcourt, Brace.

———. 1927. *Sex and Repression in Savage Society.* London: Routledge and Kegan Paul.

———. 1945. *The Dynamics of Culture Change.* Phyllis M. Kaberry (ed.). New Haven: Yale University Press.

Mandelbaum, David G. 1952. *Soldier Groups and Negro Soldiers.* Berkeley and Los Angeles: University of California Press.

Mannheim, Karl. 1936. *Ideology and Utopia.* L. Wirth and E. A. Shils (trans.). New York: Harcourt, Brace.

———. 1952. *Essays on the Sociology of Knowledge.* Paul Kecskemeti (ed.). New York: Oxford University Press.

———. 1953. *Essays on Sociology and Social Psychology.* Paul Kecskemeti (ed.). New York: Oxford University Press.

Marias, Julian. 1968. Generations: The Concept. *International Encyclopedia of the Social Sciences,* vol. 6, pp. 88–92.

Marris, Peter. 1975. *Loss and Change.* New York: Doubleday.

Marshall, Samuel L. A. 1947. *Men Against Fire.* New York: William Morrow.

Maruyama, Magoroh. 1963. The Second Cybernetics: Deviation-Amplifying Mutual Causal Processes. *American Scientist* 51:164–79.

Marx, Gary T. 1970. Civil Disorder and the Agents of Social Control. *Journal of Social Issues* 26:19–57.

Matthews, Donald R. 1959. The Folkways of the United States Senate: Conformity to Group Norms and Legislative Effectiveness. *American Political Science Review* 53:1063–89.

Max, Louis W. 1937. Experimental Study of the Motor Theory of Consciousness. *Journal of Comparative and Physiological Psychology* 24:301–44.

May, Rollo. 1953. *Man's Search for Himself.* New York: Norton.

Mayer, Adrian C. 1960. *Caste and Kinship in Central India: A Village and Its Region.* Berkeley and Los Angeles: University of California Press.

Mayer, Kurt, and Walter Buckley. 1970. *Class and Society.* New York: Doubleday.

Mayeroff, Milton. 1971. *On Caring.* New York: Harper & Row.

Mead, George H. 1929. National-Mindedness and International-Mindedness. *International Journal of Ethics* 39:385–407.

———. 1934. *Mind, Self and Society.* Charles W. Morris (ed.). Chicago: University of Chicago Press.

———. 1938. *The Philosophy of the Act.* Charles W. Morris et al. (eds.). Chicago: University of Chicago Press.

Mead, Margaret. 1956. *New Lives for Old: Cultural Transformation—Manus, 1928–1953.* New York: William Morrow.

Mechanic, David. 1967. The Changing Structure of Medical Practice. *Law and Contemporary Problems* 32:707–30.

Menzel, Herbert. 1957. Public and Private Conformity Under Different Conditions of Acceptance in the Group. *Journal of Abnormal and Social Psychology* 55:398–402.

———, and Elihu Katz. 1955–56. Social Relations and Innovations in the Medical Profession: The Epidemiology of a New Drug. *Public Opinion Quarterly* 19:337–52.

Mercer, Jane R. 1973. *Labelling the Mentally Retarded.* Berkeley and Los Angeles: University of California Press.

Merton, Robert K. 1957. *Social Theory and Social Structure.* Glencoe, Ill.: Free Press.

Michels, Robert. 1949. *Political Parties.* Eden and Cedar Paul (trans.). Glencoe, Ill.: Free Press.

Miller, Walter B. 1958. Lower Class Culture as a Generating Milieu of Gang Delinquency. *Journal of Social Issues* 14:5–19.

Mills, C. Wright. 1951. *White Collar: The American Middle Classes.* New York: Oxford University Press.

———. 1963. *Power, Politics, and People: The Collected Essays of C. Wright Mills.* Irving L. Horowitz (ed.). New York: Ballantine Books.

Miner, Horace. 1953. *The Primitive City of Timbuctoo.* Princeton: Princeton University Press.

Mitchell, James C. 1956. *The Kalela Dance: Aspects of Social Relationships Among Urban Africans in Northern Rhodesia.* Manchester: Manchester University Press.

Mooney, James. 1965. *The Ghost Dance Religion and the Sioux Outbreak of 1890.* Chicago: University of Chicago Press.

Moreno, Jacob L. 1953. *Who Shall Survive?* New York: Beacon House.

Morgan, William R. 1970. Faculty Mediation of Student War Protest. Pp. 365–82 in Julian Foster and Durward Long (eds.), *Protest: Student Activism in America.* New York: William Morrow.

Morison, Elting E. 1966. *Men, Machines, and Modern Times.* Cambridge, Mass.: MIT Press.

Moskos, Charles C. 1970. *The American Enlisted Man.* New York: Russell Sage.

———. 1975. The American Combat Soldier in Vietnam. *Journal of Social Issues* 31:25–37.

Mouzelis, Nicos P. 1968. *Organisation and Bureaucracy: An Analysis of Modern Theories.* Chicago: Aldine.

Murphy, Jane M. 1976. Psychiatric Labeling in Cross-Cultural Perspective. *Science* 191:1019–28.

Murray, Robert K. 1955. *Red Scare: A Study in National Hysteria.* Minneapolis: University of Minnesota Press.

Nalbandian, Louise. 1963. *The Armenian Revolutionary Movement.* Berkeley and Los Angeles: University of California Press.

Nansen, Fridtjof. 1976. *Armenia and the Near East.* New York: Da Capo Press.

Neill, Wilfred T. 1973. *Twentieth Century Indonesia.* New York: Columbia University Press.

Newcomb, Theodore, and Eugene Hartley (eds.). 1947. *Readings in Social Psychology.* New York: Henry Holt.

Niebuhr, H. Richard. 1929. *The Social Sources of Denominationalism.* New York: Henry Holt.

Nisbet, Robert A. 1964. Kinship and Political Power in First Century Rome. Pp. 257–71 in W. J. Cahnman and A. Boskoff (eds.), *Sociology and History.* New York: Free Press.

———. 1980. *History of the Idea of Progress.* New York: Basic Books.

Noguères, Henri. 1962. *The Massacre of Saint Bartholomew.* C. E. Engel (trans.). New York: Macmillan.

Nohl, Johannes. 1960. *The Black Death: A Chronicle of the Plague.* C. H. Clarke (trans.). New York: Ballantine Books.

Nystrom, Paul. 1928. *The Economics of Fashion.* New York: Ronald Press.

O'Dea, Thomas F. 1957. *The Mormons.* Chicago: University of Chicago Press.

Oliver, Douglas L. 1951. *The Pacific Islands.* Cambridge, Mass.: Harvard University Press.

O'Neill, John. 1972. *Sociology as a Skin Trade.* New York: Harper & Row.

Opie, Iona, and Peter Opie. 1959. *The Lore and Language of Schoolchildren.* London: Oxford University Press.

Osborne, John W. 1970. *The Silent Revolution: The Industrial Revolution in England as a Source of Cultural Change.* New York: Scribner's.

Park, Robert E. 1930. Collective Behavior. *Encyclopaedia of the Social Sciences,* vol. 3, pp. 631–33.

———. 1950. *Race and Culture.* Everett C. Hughes et al. (eds.). Glencoe, Ill.: Free Press.

———. 1955. *Society.* Everett C. Hughes et al. (eds.). Glencoe, Ill.: Free Press.

———, and Ernest W. Burgess. 1924. *Introduction to the Science of Sociology.* Chicago: University of Chicago Press.

Patai, Raphael. 1953. *Israel Between East and West.* Philadelphia: Jewish Publication Society of America.

Paulhan, Frederic. 1930. *The Laws of Feeling.* C. K. Ogden (trans.). New York: Harcourt, Brace.

Peck, Graham. 1950. *Two Kinds of Time.* Boston: Houghton Mifflin.

Peirce, Charles S. 1923. *Chance, Love and Logic.* Morris R. Cohen (ed.). New York: Harcourt, Brace.

Perlman, Selig. 1928. *A Theory of the Labor Movement.* New York: Augustus M. Kelley.

Petersen, William. 1955. *Planned Migration.* Berkeley and Los Angeles: University of California Press.

Piers, Gerhart, and Milton B. Singer. 1953. *Shame and Guilt: A Psychoanalytic and Cultural Study.* Springfield, Ill.: Thomas.

Polanyi, Karl. 1944. *The Great Transformation.* New York: Rinehart.

Polgar, Steven. 1960. Biculturation of Mesquakie Teenage Boys. *American Anthropologist* 62:217–35.

Postman, Leo. 1951. Toward a General Theory of Cognition. Pp. 242–72 in J. H. Rohrer and M. Sherif (eds.), *Social Psychology at the Crossroads*. New York: Harper.

———, and Jerome S. Bruner. 1948. Perception Under Stress. *Psychological Review* 55:314–23.

Powdermaker, Hortense. 1943. The Channeling of Negro Aggression by the Cultural Process. *American Journal of Sociology* 48:750–58.

Quarantelli, Enrico L., and James Cooper. 1966. Self-Conception and Others: A Further Test of the Meadian Hypothesis. *Sociological Quarterly* 7:281–97.

Rabinow, Paul, and William M. Sullivan (eds.). 1979. *Interpretive Social Science: A Reader*. Berkeley and Los Angeles: University of California Press.

Radcliffe-Brown, A. R. 1934. Social Sanctions. *Encyclopaedia of the Social Sciences*, vol. 13, pp. 531–34.

———. 1964. *The Andaman Islanders*. New York: Free Press.

Rainwater, Lee. 1966. Crucible of Identity: The Negro Lower Class Family. *Daedalus* 95:172–216.

Ransford, H. Edward. 1972. Blue Collar Anger: Reactions to Student and Black Protest. *American Sociological Review* 37:333–46.

Rath, R., and N. C. Sircar. 1960. Mental Pictures of Six Hindu Caste Groups About Each Other as Reflected in Verbal Stereotypes. *Journal of Social Psychology* 51:277–93.

Read, Piers P. 1974. *Alive: The Story of the Andes Survivors*. Philadelphia: Lippincott.

Redfield, Robert. 1941. *The Folk Culture of Yucatan*. Chicago: University of Chicago Press.

———. 1953. *The Primitive World and Its Transformations*. Ithaca: Cornell University Press.

Reed, John. 1935. *Ten Days That Shook the World*. New York: Modern Library.

Richardson, Lewis F. 1960. *Statistics of Deadly Quarrels*. Quincy Wright and C. C. Lienau (eds.). Pittsburgh: Boxwood Press.

Riezler, Kurt. 1944. The Social Psychology of Fear. *American Journal of Sociology* 49:489–98.

Robinson, Jackie, and Alfred Duckett. 1965. *Breakthrough to the Big League: The Story of Jackie Robinson*. New York: Harper & Row.

Roethlisberger, Fritz J., and William J. Dickson. 1939. *Management and the Worker*. Cambridge, Mass.: Harvard University Press.

Rogers, Cornwell B. 1949. *The Spirit of Revolution in 1789*. Princeton: Princeton University Press.

Rogers, Everett M. 1971. *Communication of Innovations: A Cross-Cultural Approach*. New York: Free Press.

Rosenhan, D. L. 1973. On Being Sane in Insane Places. *Science* 179:250–58.

Ross, H. Laurence. 1970. *Settled Out of Court: The Social Process of Insurance Claims Adjustments*. Chicago: Aldine.

Rosten, Leo C. 1937. *The Washington Correspondents*. New York: Harcourt, Brace.

Rotberg, Robert I. (ed.). 1971. *Rebellion in Black Africa*. London: Oxford University Press.

Rubin, Jeffrey Z., and Bert R. Brown. 1975. *The Social Psychology of Bargaining and Negotiation.* New York: Academic Press.

Ruesch, Jurgen, and A. Rodney Prestwood. 1949. Anxiety: Its Initiation, Communication and Interpersonal Management. *Archives of Neurology and Psychiatry* 62:527–50.

Russell, Bertrand. 1957. *Mysticism and Logic.* New York: Doubleday.

Ryan, Bryce. 1953. *Caste in Modern Ceylon: The Sinhalese System in Transition.* New Brunswick, N.J.: Rutgers University Press.

Sabagh, George, and Dorothy S. Thomas. 1945. Changing Patterns of Fertility and Survival Among the Japanese Americans on the Pacific Coast. *American Sociological Review* 10:651–58.

Sapir, Edward. 1927. Language as a Form of Human Behavior. *English Journal* 16:421–33.

———. 1949. *Selected Writings of Edward Sapir in Language, Culture and Personality.* David Mandelbaum (ed.). Berkeley and Los Angeles: University of California Press.

Saporta, Sol, and Jarvis R. Bastian (eds.). 1961. *Psycholinguistics: A Book of Readings.* New York: Holt, Rinehart and Winston.

Schachter, Stanley, and Jerome E. Singer. 1962. Cognitive, Social, and Physiological Determinants of Emotional State. *Psychological Review* 69:379–99.

Schatzman, Leonard, and Anselm Strauss. 1955. Social Class and Modes of Communication. *American Journal of Sociology* 60:329–38.

Scheff, Thomas J. 1961. Control over Policy by Attendants in a Mental Hospital. *Journal of Health and Human Behavior* 2:93–105.

———. 1966. *Being Mentally Ill: A Sociological Theory.* Chicago: Aldine.

———. 1967. Toward a Sociological Model of Consensus. *American Sociological Review* 32:32–46.

Schnore, Leo F. 1965. On the Spatial Structure of Cities in the Two Americas. Pp. 347–98 in P. M. Hauser and L. F. Schnore (eds.), *The Study of Urbanization.* New York: Wiley.

———, and Harry Sharp. 1964. The Changing Color of Our Big Cities. *Transaction* 2:12–14.

Schreiber, Jan. 1978. *The Ultimate Weapon: Terrorists and World Order.* New York: William Morrow.

Schutz, Alfred. 1962. *Collected Papers.* Vol. 1, *The Problem of Social Reality.* Maurice Natanson (ed.). The Hague: Martinus Nijhoff.

Scott, John F. 1965. Sororities and the Husband Game. *Transaction* 2:10–14.

Sears, Clara E. 1924. *Days of Delusion.* Boston: Houghton Mifflin.

Sechehaye, Marguerite (ed.). 1951. *Autobiography of a Schizophrenic Girl.* New York: Grune and Stratton.

Selye, Hans. 1956. *The Stress of Life.* New York: McGraw-Hill.

Senden, Marius von. 1960. *Space and Sight: The Perception of Space and Shape in the Congenitally Blind Before and After Operation.* Peter Heath (trans.). Glencoe, Ill.: Free Press.

Shand, Alexander. 1896. Character and the Emotions. *Mind* 5:203–26.

Sherif, Muzafer, and Carolyn W. Sherif. 1964. *Reference Groups: Explorations into Conformity and Deviation of Adolescents.* New York: Harper.

Sherif, Muzafer, et al. 1961. *Intergroup Conflict and Cooperation: The Robbers Cave Experiment.* Norman, Okla.: University Book Exchange.

Sherman, Mandel, and Thomas R. Henry. 1933. *Hollow Folk.* New York: Crowell.

Shibutani, Tamotsu. 1966. *Improvised News: A Sociological Study of Rumor.* Indianapolis: Bobbs-Merrill.

————, and Kian M. Kwan. 1965. *Ethnic Stratification.* New York: Macmillan.

Shils, Edward. 1968. Intellectuals. *International Encyclopedia of the Social Sciences,* vol. 7, pp. 399–415.

————, and Morris Janowitz. 1948. Cohesion and Disintegration in the Wehrmacht in World War II. *Public Opinion Quarterly* 12:280–315.

Short, James, and Fred L. Strodtbeck. 1965. *Group Processes and Gang Delinquency.* Chicago: University of Chicago Press.

Shrauger, J. Sidney, and Thomas J. Schoeneman. 1979. Symbolic Interactionist View of Self-Concept: Through the Looking Glass Darkly. *Psychological Bulletin* 86:549–73.

Sills, David L. 1957. *The Volunteers: Means and Ends in a National Organization.* Glencoe, Ill.: Free Press.

Silverman, David. 1967. *Pitcairn Island.* New York: World.

Simmel, Edward C., et al. (eds.). 1968. *Social Facilitation and Imitative Behavior.* Boston: Allyn & Bacon.

Simmel, Georg. 1950. *The Sociology of Georg Simmel.* Kurt H. Wolff (trans.). Glencoe, Ill.: Free Press.

————. 1955. *Conflict and the Web of Group-Affiliations.* Kurt H. Wolff and Reinhard Bendix (trans.). Glencoe, Ill.: Free Press.

————. 1957. Fashion. *American Journal of Sociology* 62:541–58.

————. 1971. *On Individuality and Social Forms.* Donald N. Levine (ed.). Chicago: University of Chicago Press.

Sjoberg, Gideon. 1960. *The Preindustrial City.* Glencoe, Ill.: Free Press.

Skilling, H. Gordon. 1976. *Czechoslovakia's Interrupted Revolution.* Princeton: Princeton University Press.

Skocpol, Theda. 1979. *States and Social Revolution.* London: Cambridge University Press.

Skolnick, Jerome H. 1975. *Justice Without Trial: Law Enforcement in Democratic Society.* New York: Wiley.

Smelser, Ncil J. 1963. *Theory of Collective Behavior.* New York: Free Press.

Smith, Carl O., and Stephen B. Sarasohn. 1946. Hate Propaganda in Detroit. *Public Opinion Quarterly* 10:24–52.

Smith, Henry D. 1972. *Japan's First Student Radicals.* Cambridge, Mass.: Harvard University Press.

Smith, Thomas V. 1937. Custom, Gossip, Legislation. *Social Forces* 16:24–34.

Snow, David A., et al. 1980. Social Networks and Social Movements: A Microstructural Approach to Differential Recruitment. *American Sociological Review* 45:787–801.

Sorokin, Pitirim A., and Robert K. Merton. 1937. Social Time: A Methodological and Functional Analysis. *American Journal of Sociology* 42:615–29.

Spaeth, Sigmund. 1934. *The Facts of Life in Popular Song.* New York: McGraw-Hill.

Speroff, Boris, and Willard Kerr. 1952. Steel Mill "Hot Strip" Accidents and Interpersonal Desirability Values. *Journal of Clinical Psychology* 8:89–91.

Spykman, Nicholas J. 1925. *The Social Theory of Georg Simmel.* Chicago: University of Chicago Press.

Starr, Paul D. 1978. Ethnic Categories and Identification in Lebanon. *Urban Life* 7:111–42.

Stoessinger, John G. 1978. *Why Nations Go to War.* New York: St. Martin's Press.

Stokes, Randall, and John P. Hewitt. 1976. Aligning Actions. *American Sociological Review* 41:838–49.

Stonequist, Everett V. 1937. *The Marginal Man.* New York: Scribner's.

Stoner, Carroll, and Jo Anne Parke. 1979. *All Gods Children.* New York: Penguin.

Stratton, George M. 1928. The Function of Emotion as Shown Particularly in Excitement. *Psychological Review* 35:351–66.

Strauss, Anselm L. 1971. *The Contexts of Social Mobility.* Chicago: Aldine.

———. 1978. *Negotiations: Varieties, Contexts, Processes, and Social Order.* San Francisco: Jossey-Bass.

———, et al. 1963. The Hospital and Its Negotiated Order. Pp. 147–69 in Eliot Freidson (ed.), *The Hospital in Modern Society.* New York: Free Press.

Sullivan, Harry S. 1950. Tensions Interpersonal and International. Pp. 79–138 in Hadley Cantril (ed.), *Tensions That Cause Wars.* Urbana: University of Illinois Press.

Sumner, William G. 1906. *Folkways.* Boston: Ginn.

———. 1911. *War and Other Essays.* New Haven: Yale University Press.

Sutherland, Edwin H. (ed.). 1937. *The Professional Thief—by a Professional Thief.* Chicago: University of Chicago Press.

———. 1949. *White Collar Crime.* New York: Dryden Press.

———. 1950. The Diffusion of Sexual Psychopath Laws. *American Journal of Sociology* 56:142–48.

———, and Donald Cressey. 1960. *Principles of Criminology.* Philadelphia: Lippincott.

Suttles, Gerald D. 1968. *The Social Order of the Slum.* Chicago: University of Chicago Press.

Sykes, Gresham M. 1958. *Society of Captives: A Study of a Maximum Security Prison.* Princeton: Princeton University Press.

———, and David Matza. 1957. Techniques of Neutralization: A Theory of Delinquency. *American Sociological Review* 22:664–70.

Syzmanski, Albert. 1970. Toward a Radical Sociology. *Sociological Quarterly* 40:3–25.

Talmon, Yonina. 1968. Millenarism. *International Encyclopedia of the Social Sciences,* vol. 10, pp. 349–62.

Tannenbaum, Frank. 1938. *Crime and the Community.* New York: Columbia University Press.

Teggart, Frederick J. 1939. *Rome and China: A Study of Correlations in Historical Events*. Berkeley and Los Angeles: University of California Press.

ten Broek, Jacobus, et al. 1954. *Prejudice, War, and the Constitution*. Berkeley and Los Angeles: University of California Press.

Terzani, Tiziano. 1976. *Giaiphong: The Fall and Liberation of Saigon*. J. Shepley (trans.). New York: St. Martin's Press.

Thomas, Darwin L., et al. 1972. Role-Taking and Power in Social Psychology. *American Sociological Review* 37:605–14.

Thomas, William I., and Florian Znaniecki. 1927. *The Polish Peasant in Europe and America*. New York: Knopf.

Thorner, Daniel, and Alice Thorner. 1949. India and Pakistan. Pp. 548–653 in Ralph Linton (ed.), *Most of the World*. New York: Columbia University Press.

Thornton, Russell, and Peter M. Nardi. 1975. The Dynamics of Role Acquisition. *American Journal of Sociology* 80:870–85.

Thrasher, Frederick M. 1936. *The Gang*. Chicago: University of Chicago Press.

Tilly, Charles. 1976. *The Vendée*. Cambridge, Mass.: Harvard University Press.

Tinker, Hugh. 1958. 1857 and 1957: The Mutiny and Modern India. *International Affairs* 34:57–76.

Tocqueville, Alexis de. 1955. *The Old Regime and the French Revolution*. Stuart Gilbert (trans.). New York: Doubleday.

Toynbee, Arnold J. 1946. *A Study of History*. D. C. Somervell (abridg.). New York: Oxford University Press.

Trimberger, Ellen K. 1978. *Revolution from Above: Military Bureaucrats and Development in Japan, Turkey, Egypt, and Peru*. New Brunswick, N.J.: Transaction Books.

Trotsky, Leon. 1936. *The History of the Russian Revolution*. 3 vols. Max Eastman (trans.). New York: Simon and Schuster.

Tsurumi, Kazuko. 1970. *Social Change and the Individual: Japan Before and After Defeat in World War II*. Princeton: Princeton University Press.

Tuchman, Gaye. 1978. *Making News: A Study in the Construction of Reality*. New York: Free Press.

Turk, Austin T. 1969. *Criminality and Legal Order*. Chicago: Rand McNally.

Turnbull, Colin M. 1963. *The Lonely African*. New York: Doubleday.

Turner, Jonathan H. 1977. *The Structure of Sociological Theory*. Homewood, Ill.: Dorsey Press.

Turner, Ralph H. 1962. Role-Taking: Process Versus Conformity. Pp. 20–40 in Arnold M. Rose (ed.), *Human Behavior and Social Processes*. Boston: Houghton Mifflin.

———. 1970. *Family Interaction*. New York: Wiley.

———, and Lewis M. Killian. 1972. *Collective Behavior*. Englewood Cliffs, N.J.: Prentice-Hall.

Turney-High, Harry H. 1971. *Primitive War: Its Practice and Concepts*. Columbia: University of South Carolina Press.

U.S. Strategic Bombing Survey. 1946. *Summary Report: Pacific War*. Washington, D.C.: Government Printing Office.

Veblen, Thorstein B. 1934. *The Theory of the Leisure Class.* New York: Modern Library.

———. 1961. *The Place of Science in Modern Civilization and Other Essays.* New York: Russell.

Veltfort, Helene R., and George E. Lee. 1943. The Cocoanut Grove Fire: A Study in Scapegoating. *Journal of Abnormal and Social Psychology* 38:138–54.

Vincent, Clark E. 1951. Trends in Infant Care Ideas. *Child Development* 22:199–209.

Voegelin, Erich. 1933. *Rasse und Staat.* Tuebingen: J. C. B. Mohr.

Walker, Daniel. 1968. *Rights in Conflict.* New York: New American Library.

Wallace, Michael, and Arne L. Kallenberg. 1982. Industrial Transformation and the Decline of Craft. *American Sociological Review* 47:307–24.

Waller, George. 1961. *Kidnap: The Story of the Lindbergh Case.* London: Hamish Hamilton.

Wallerstein, Immanuel. 1974. *The Modern World-System.* New York: Academic Press.

Warner, W. Lloyd. 1937. *A Black Civilization: A Social Study of an Australian Tribe.* New York: Harper.

———. 1959. *The Living and the Dead: A Study of the Symbolic Life of Americans.* New Haven: Yale University Press.

———, and William E. Henry. 1948. The Radio Day-Time Serial: A Symbolic Analysis. *Genetic Psychology Monographs* 37:3–71.

———, and Paul S. Lunt. 1941. *The Social Life of a Modern Community.* New Haven: Yale University Press.

Waterman, T. T. 1914. The Explanatory Element in the Folktales of the North American Indians. *Journal of American Folklore* 27:1–54.

Weber, Max. 1946. *Essays in Sociology.* Hans Gerth and C. Wright Mills (trans.). New York: Oxford University Press.

———. 1949. *Methodology of the Social Sciences.* Edward Shils (trans.). Glencoe, Ill.: Free Press.

———. 1958. *The Protestant Ethic and the Spirit of Capitalism.* Talcott Parsons (trans.). New York: Scribner's.

———. 1968. *Economy and Society.* Guenther Roth and Claus Wittich (trans.). New York: Bedminster Press.

Weisberger, Bernard A. 1958. *They Gathered at the River.* Boston: Little, Brown.

Weiss, Walter. 1969. Effects of the Mass Media of Communication. Pp. 77–195 in Gardner Lindzey and Elliot Aronson (eds.), *The Handbook of Social Psychology,* vol. 5. Reading, Mass.: Addison-Wesley.

Weitzman, Lenore J., et al. 1972. Sex-Role Socialization in Picture Books for Preschool Children. *American Journal of Sociology* 77:1125–50.

Wertheim, Willem F. 1959. *Indonesian Society in Transition.* New York: Institute of Pacific Relations.

Westley, William A. 1953. Violence and the Police. *American Journal of Sociology* 59:34–41.

———. 1956. Secrecy and the Police. *Social Forces* 34:254–57.

White, Ralph K., and Ronald Lippitt. 1960. *Autocracy and Democracy: An Experimental Inquiry.* New York: Harper.

Whitehead, Alfred N. 1929. *Process and Reality.* London: Cambridge University Press.

Whorf, Benjamin L. 1956. *Language, Thought, and Reality.* New York: Wiley.

Whyte, Martin K. 1974. *Small Groups and Political Rituals in China.* Berkeley and Los Angeles: University of California Press.

Whyte, William F. 1943. A Slum Sex Code. *American Journal of Sociology* 49:24–31.

———. 1955. *Street Corner Society.* Chicago: University of Chicago Press.

Wilensky, Harold L. 1966. Measures and Effects of Social Mobility. Pp. 98–140 in N. J. Smelser and S. M. Lipset (eds.), *Social Structure and Mobility in Economic Development.* Chicago: Aldine.

———. 1967. *Organizational Intelligence: Knowledge and Policy in Government and Industry.* New York: Basic Books.

Wilkerson, Marcus M. 1967. *Public Opinion and the Spanish-American War.* New York: Russell and Russell.

Williams, Robin M. 1968. Values: The Concept of Values. *International Encyclopedia of the Social Sciences,* vol. 16, pp. 283–87.

———. 1975. Relative Deprivation. Pp. 355–78 in L. A. Coser (ed.), *The Idea of Social Structure.* New York: Harcourt, Brace.

Wilson, Robert N. 1954. Teamwork in the Operating Room. *Human Organization* 12:9–14.

Wirth, Louis. 1956. *Community Life and Social Policy.* E. W. Marvick and A. Reiss (eds.). Chicago: University of Chicago Press.

Wolcott, Roy H. 1970. Schizophrenese: A Private Language. *Journal of Health and Social Behavior* 2:126–34.

Wolf, Eric R. 1969. *Peasant Wars of the Twentieth Century.* New York: Harper & Row.

Wolfe, Bernard. 1949. Uncle Remus and the Malevolent Rabbit. *Commentary* 8:31–41.

Wolfenstein, Martha, and Nathan Leites. 1950. *Movies: A Psychological Study.* Glencoe, Ill.: Free Press.

Woodham-Smith, Cecil. 1963. *The Great Hunger.* New York: Harper & Row.

Worsley, Peter. 1957. *The Trumpet Shall Sound: A Study of Cargo Cults in Melanesia.* London: MacGibbon and Kee.

Woytinsky, Vladimir S., and Emma S. Woytinsky. 1953. *World Population and Production: Trends and Outlook.* New York: Twentieth Century Fund.

Wright, Quincy. 1942. *A Study of War.* Chicago: University of Chicago Press.

Wylie, Ruth C., et al. 1979. *The Self-Concept.* Vol. 2. Lincoln: University of Nebraska Press.

Zborowski, Mark. 1952. Cultural Components in Responses to Pain. *Journal of Social Issues* 8:16–30.

Znaniecki, Florian. 1940. *The Social Role of the Man of Knowledge.* New York: Columbia University Press.

Name Index

Subject Index

Designer: Janet Wood
Compositor: Progressive Typographers
Text: 10/12 Palatino
Display: Palatino
Printer: Maple/Vail Book Mfg. Group
Binder: Maple/Vail Book Mfg. Group